THE TYRANNY OF MALICE

Exploring the Dark Side of
Character and Culture

Joseph H. Berke

SUMMIT BOOKS
New York · London · Toronto · Sydney · Tokyo

While the cases described in this book are based on interviews with real persons, names, professions, locations and other biographical details have been changed to preserve their privacy and anonymity.

Summit Books
Simon & Schuster Building
Rockefeller Center
1230 Avenue of the Americas
New York, New York 10020

Published by SUMMIT BOOKS

SUMMIT BOOKS and colophon are trademarks
of Simon & Schuster Inc.
Designed by: H L Granger/Levavi & Levavi
Manufactured in the United States of America

1   3   5   7   9   10   8   6   4   2

Library of Congress Cataloging in Publication Data

Berke, Joseph.
The tyranny of malice : exploring the dark side of character
and culture / Joseph H. Berke.
p.   cm.
Bibliography: p. 410
Includes indexes.
ISBN 0-671-49753-7
1. Envy.   2. Avarice   3. Jealousy.   4. Aggressiveness
(Psychology)   5. Envy—Social aspects.   6. Avarice—Social aspects.
7. Jealousy—Social aspects.   8. Aggressiveness (Psychology)—Social
aspects.   I. Title.
BF575.E65B47   1988
179′.9—dc19   88-20065
                                                            CIP

Drawing on p. 202 by Lorenz; © 1986 The New Yorker Magazine, Inc.
Cartoon on p. 56 reprinted with permission of *Punch*.
Cartoons on pp. 245 and 247 by Pete Mastin, *Black Flag*, 1985.

ISBN 0-671-49753-7

To
Dr. Norman Cohen

Contents

Acknowledgments

I would like to express my great appreciation to my friends and relatives, colleagues and patients, who have contributed to this book in many different ways. I am indebted for their incisive comments, criticisms, and suggestions, as well as for many detailed references and examples that they both directly provided and helped me to discover. Not least I am grateful for their encouragement over the many years it took to research and write this book. Many thanks to Mr. David Annesley, Mr. Sam Auspitz, Mr. Adrian Bailey, Lord Beaumont of Whitley, Dr. Eric Brenman, Ms. Jilly Cooper, Mr. Simon Callow, Mr. Simon Duberry, Mr. David Edgar, Mr. Robert Elzey, Ms. Susan Ford, Mr. William Frankel, Mr. Alex Gildzen, Rabbi Hugo Gryn, Mr. Roger Hacker, Mr. Colin Haycroft, Dr. T. T. S. Hayley, Mr. David Herrera, Mr. John Hill, Dr. Robert Hinshelwood, Dr. Alex Holder, Mr. Tony Jackson, Ms. Hazel Jacobs, Ms. Vickie Jaffee, Dr. Colin James, Mr. Martin Jenkins, Ms. Betty Joseph, Mr. Michael Kelly, Ms. Sandi Lacey, Ms. Fiona Macpherson, Mr. Olivier Marc, Mr. Peter Marsh, Dr. Donald Meltzer, Ms. Suzy Menkes, Dr. Jonathan Miller, Dr. Loren Mosher, Dr. Donald Nathanson, Mr. John Newman, Dr. Dinora Pines, Dr. Malcolm Pines, Professor J. M. Roberts, Dr. Herbert Rosenfeld, Mr. Tom Ryan, Mr. Andrea Sabbadini, Dr. Morton Schatzman, Ms. Julia Segal, Ms. Helen Silman,

Mr. David Spanier, Dr. Joan Speck, Dr. Ross Speck, Dr. Harold Stern, Dr. Alex Tarnopolsky, Mr. Alan Taylor, Dr. Thorkil Vanggaard, Mr. Peter von Schreber, Professor Peter Walcot, and Mr. Peregrine Worsthorne.

I am especially grateful to Professor Helmut Schoeck for his active support and encouragement for the project, for carefully reading and commenting on each chapter, and for generously allowing me to refer to and quote from his own pioneering study of envy. Special thanks are also due to Drs. Nina Coltart and Peter Lomas for their active support and encouragement and careful reading of and comments on each chapter.

In addition, I wish to thank the staff of the Library of the Royal Society of Medicine, the London Library, and the Regent Bookshop for helping me research the book and gather the material I needed to review. I doubt whether I could have finished the book without using the facilities of the Royal Society of Medicine, in particular.

Many thanks are due to my literary agents, Deborah Rogers of Rogers, Coleridge and White in London, and Elaine Markson and Geri Thoma of the Elaine Markson Literary Agency in New York. Aside from supporting the project in dozens of ways, they made the basic step of introducing me to my editor, Ileene Smith, to whom I am deeply grateful, not only for commissioning this book, but also for guiding its contents, structure, and style. I would also like to thank Alane Mason, assistant editor, Wendy Nicholson, associate publisher, and Sona Vogel, copy editor, for their support.

Finally, I wish to acknowledge the tremendous support that my former wife, Roberta Elzey Berke, my son, Joshua, and my daughter, Debbie, gave me during the nine years from conception to completion. Roberta read and commented on the manuscript at every stage and made many helpful suggestions. Joshua and Debbie discussed many aspects of the book with me and contributed a number of pertinent examples, especially about the resolution of malice. Not least they all allowed me the countless weekends I remained ensconced in my study thinking and writing. I deeply appreciate these essential contributions.

Introduction

Our capacity for destruction lies in the origins of malice. This is a destructiveness that takes many forms ranging from child battering to murder, from "aggro" at sporting events to terrorism and genocide. More subtly, fear of such outcomes can lead to isolation and self-sabotage, both of character and culture.

Malice has three components: perception, an awareness of something provoking an intolerable feeling; feeling, intense displeasure and vexation; and action, forceful, attacking, annihilating behavior.

An aggressive response may be essential to survival when it is self-protective and an obvious reaction to provocation. All too often this is not the case. The person who goes around with a chip on his shoulder is an unlikely example of constructive self-assertion or re-active revenge. I am concerned with another kind of malice, a passion that may not have an obvious cause yet is very intense, deep-rooted, and associated with hate, rage, chaos, and evil. Such passions accompany consciousness and are uniquely human. They are complex creatures, painfully private and publicly dangerous, fed by an inner world of fact and fantasy brought about by the interplay of perception, memory, and imagination.

Malicious hatred is all pervasive, yet it is curiously unfashionable. It is a subject relegated to fiction, while generally ignored by the social sciences. The many manifestations of this kind of hate tend to be ascribed to problems of environment or heredity. The "yob" who stabs the old lady down the block, or the man who kills his child, "must" have bad genes. Or maybe their biochemistry has gone haywire. Similarly, acts of outrageous criminality tend to be justified when done in the name of economic inequality, political oppression, or bad weather.

Man himself is the source of the malice against which he is constantly struggling. And it is only possible for him to transcend this basic malignity by knowing how, what, why, and when it arises. The alternative is to continue the blind butchery of our environment and fellow creatures that otherwise permeates our lives. R. D. Laing has succinctly described the dilemma in an essay entitled "Violence and Love" written in 1965. He points out that in the past fifty years we human beings have slaughtered over one hundred million of our own species (a figure that continues to climb). We all live under threat of total annihilation yet seem to seek death and destruction as much as life and happiness He suggests that we can only stop destroying others when we stop destroying ourselves, and that we have to begin by "admitting and even accepting our violence, rather than blindly destroying ourselves with it, and therewith we have to realize that we are as deeply afraid to live and to love as we are to die."[1]

It is possible to know, albeit harder to accept, the shadow side of ourselves, the essential darkness that breeds ill will. Envy, greed, and jealousy are the fundamental components of this malice. Their counterparts are gratitude, generosity, and compassion. Each does not exist in isolation from the other. The interplay of these forces of love and hate creates the structure of our lives, which on a personal level is called "character" and on the social level is called "culture."

Envy and gratitude, greed and generosity, jealousy and compassion, these sins and graces are the fundamental forces of human emotional life. Just as the arrangement of protons and electrons, the positive and negative forces of the physical world, defines the atom, so does the relative strength of love and hate in a person define character. Just as different combinations of atoms define the molecule, the smallest unit of matter that retains individual identity, so do different characters come together and create families, and families of families, the basic units of our society.

No one can see a proton or electron. Yet we postulate their existence and from this predict their effects. Similarly, with love and hate a person can never know for sure what another feels inside himself or herself, yet from what people say, when they can say, and from what they do, we postulate the existence of certain feelings and can predict their effects. In fact, this process is easier with people. You don't need an atom smasher to look into a stranger's eye and detect abject loathing or goodwill.

This book is a study of the negative or angry constituents of character and culture. But I shall not ignore love. On the contrary, I shall demostrate that when the negative components of our emotional life are denied or ignored (because of guilt or fear), the positive ones suffer, too. As always, love and hate are inexorably intertwined.

The overall purpose of my work is to develop a detailed understanding of our capacity for destruction as well as for making good. This is not an easy task, either for me, the writer, or you, the reader. The relative absence of comparable studies is an indication of the anxiety that envy, greed, and jealousy arouse.

The sensational press provides some of the best source material on envy, usually to condemn it. Remarkably few scientific books or papers document the emotional havoc and implacable conflicts caused by sheer hate. Some major British and American journals of anthropology and sociology have not carried a single reference to envy, jealousy, or resentment over periods of nine to fifty-two years.[2] And in the indices of two major studies of human aggression and destructiveness, one didn't mention envy at all (or greed or jealousy), and the other mentioned it only once (greed once, jealousy not at all).[3] Yet when you talk to people they are always aware of envy, usually in others. I think that envy is to modern times what sex was to the Victorians, an obsession best forgotten, denied, or avoided.

In "The Parson's Tale," Geoffrey Chaucer wrote:

> It is certain that envy is the worst sin that is; for all other sins [are] against one virtue, whereas envy is against all virtue and against all goodness.[4]

For this reason I have begun the book with a study of envy, the most malevolent of all the constituents of malice.

Historically, envy has been equated with "the evil eye," which is synonymous with the envious "I" or self. Indeed, the thirteenth-century theologian Thomas Aquinas observed: "The evil eye is affected by the strong imagination of the soul and then corrupts and poisons the atmosphere so that tender bodies coming within its range may be injuriously affected."[5] This pernicious orientation to life seems to begin at birth and, if not tempered during the course of development, may lead to a hatred of all life-giving experiences, essentially toward any source of supply.

On the other hand, greed is an insatiable desire to take for oneself what another possesses. It is damaging because of its ruthless acquisitiveness. A greedy person can admit that what he wants is good and valuable. In contrast, an envious person is not concerned with possessing, just with preventing others from possessing. For the envious or evil eye goodness must not be preserved, only attacked, spoiled, or destroyed.

Developmentally, jealousy is a later emotion concerned with relationships. Jealousy has to do with rivalry with one person for the love of another. Jealousy is always triangular, envy is dyadic. Jealousy consists both of a bitter hatred and a possessive love. Envy is pure malice.

Much of this work will be concerned with the interpersonal implications of these impulses, directed emotions felt by one person, the agent, the subject, toward another person, the target, the object. Therefore they have to be considered from the point of view of both individuals. However, the subject or object, the envier or envied, for example, need not be an individual. Envious malice can be expressed by or can be directed to a larger group of people up to and including a whole culture.

When society is the envier we can speak about institutionalized envy, malevolence and spite embodied in and expressed by the representatives of major social, economic, and political institutions toward individual citizens, the envied. Alternatively, in the case of vandalism, the envier is an individual, and it is society, or some aspect of society, that is envied. The politics of envy culminates in the effective disguise of individual enmity and its expression through the relationships between institutions, cultures, or nation-states. It is common knowledge, for example, that poor states envy richer ones, that North Korea, "a political and economic failure, hates and envies successful South Korea" or that a developed country like Britain can begrudge her partners their "economic miracles."[6]

In conclusion I will query the resolution of envy, greed, and jealousy, including the wide variety of false solutions to these feelings. Many pseudosolutions strike at the hated object in the hope that if the envied person, culture, or source of supply is eliminated, malice and spite will be vanquished as well. Similarly they strike at the desired object in the hope of deleting greed. Egalitarianism and social leveling are the contemporary expressions of this wish to eliminate envy and greed. Clearly this is an impossibility without eliminating perception and apperception, free will and imagination.

Our best hope is not to impose greater tyrannies by trying to eliminate malice or ignore it, but to try to enhance the life-sustaining elements in our lives. Most profoundly, gratitude counteracts the damage done by envy. If envy is destructive, gratitude is constructive. If the envious eye, "I," spews forth bad looks and bad thoughts, then the grateful heart mitigates the malice. As many people attest, there are glances that heal as well as hurt.

In presenting the tyranny of malice, I have divided the book into three parts. The first looks at the nature of malice, what it is, how it operates, why it exists, and what attracts it. The latter includes the essential representatives of life, the breast (the vital source), the womb (female potency), and the penis (male potency), in all their real and symbolic forms.

The second part explores the influence of malice on citizens and society. This begins with the relationship between parents and children or brothers and sisters, both as agents and victims of envy, greed, and jealousy. Eventually these interactions set the stage for more extensive and more damaging tyrannies, that of a culture or whole nation as an emissary of evil or its chosen target. In these chapters I will discuss the damage done by the state or its institutions against the individual, and conversely I will trace the effects of malicious persons against the state. All this leads to the greatest predicament, malice removed from individual intent but expressed by one nation or state against another. Part two includes the final chapter on the resolution of malice and completes the basic body of the book.

The third part is more than an extended sequence of footnotes. As well as documenting the material I have used in the text, this section provides a much more detailed discussion and elaboration of the issues raised in the individual chapters. Although the text reads well on its own, the reader should gain an even richer understanding of the nature and impact of malice by following the references and commentaries as he goes along.

Part One

THE NATURE
OF MALICE

1

So Will I Turn Her Virtue into Pitch

Envy is a state of exquisite tension, torment, and ill will provoked by an overwhelming sense of inferiority, impotence, and worthlessness. It begins in the eye of the beholder and is so painful to the mind that the envious person will go to almost any lengths to diminish, if not destroy, whatever or whoever may have aroused it.

The Russian writer Yuri Olesha has provided a superb description of the spiteful, spoiling essence of envy in his short novel *Envy*, written not long after the Russian revolution.[1] One of the central characters is Ivan Babichev, a self-hating layabout and elder brother of an ambitious people's commissar. Ivan loathes the revolution, fears the new technology, and longs for the old regime. For him life revolves around bitter obsessions, especially about his childhood when a girl upstaged him and love and attention seemed to pass him by. Consumed with self-pity, Ivan recalls a party at which he defamed and defiled "a little beauty" all dressed in pink and satin, who had the temerity to outsing, outdance, leap higher, and play better than anyone else.

> She was the queen of the ball. She had it all her way. Everyone admired her, everything radiated from her and was drawn in around her.

19

I was thirteen, a high school student. I didn't have a chance, despite the fact that I was also used to admiration, to an enthusiastic following.

I caught the girl in the corridor and gave her a going over: tore her ribbons, mussed her curls, scratched her charming features. At that moment I loved that girl more than life itself, worshipped her, and hated her with all my strength. Mussing up her pretty curls, I thought I would dishonor her, dispel her pinkness, her glow; I thought I would show everyone they were wrong.

That is how I came to know envy. The terrible heartburn of envy. It is burdensome to envy! Envy catches you by the throat, squeezes your eyes from their sockets.[2]

Ivan loved that girl, not for herself, but because he wanted to be her. This couldn't be, so he ruined her ribbons and curls (beauty), disfigured her charming features (goodness), and dispelled her pinkness and glow (life). Here is an unusual man, not in the extent of his envy but in the outspoken awareness of his ill will. Ivan shares this quality with another outstanding personification of envy, Iago, the villain in Shakespeare's tragedy *Othello*.[3]

Othello is a successful general in the service of the Venetian state. Moreover, his conquests embrace love as well as war, for he has just eloped with Desdemona, the beautiful daughter of a Venetian senator. Iago is his ensign, recently passed over for promotion by another soldier who has become Othello's lieutenant. This is the ostensible reason for Iago's anger, but it is only a rationalization. Iago's villainy is part of his nature, and as the play develops we see that his ruthless destructiveness is directed not only to Othello, but to Desdemona and others as well.

Iago is a master of cunning and deceit. To Othello, to Desdemona, to his rivals, he appears honest and helpful. But to himself and the audience his intentions are clear. After Othello has declared his joy and contentment, Iago asides that although the general may be "well-tuned now," he will not find a right note once his own plans take shape.[4] Later he adds: "Knavery's plain face is never seen till used."[5]

The ensuing knavery is far worse than physical abuse or even murder. Iago attacks his victims from within. He is a psychic sadist who wreaks vengeance on Othello by destroying his peace of mind. Iago demonstrates a central feature of envious ill will: the determination to undermine happiness and replace contentment and calm with agitation and anger, doubt and despair.

Othello confirms this mental torture. Previously he had been certain in his love for Desdemona and trusted Iago. Now confusion reigns. One moment he thinks his wife is just and honest, the other not. One moment he sees a woman who is pure and white, the other one who is "begrimed and black." Poor Othello. He doesn't know where to turn or what to think. A once tranquil mind falls prey to an agony almost beyond endurance.[6]

But Othello's pain does not satisfy Iago, whose envy also touches Desdemona. Slowly, insidiously, he ruins her reputation, as he puts it, by purveying pestilence and poisoning Othello's love.

> *I'll pour this pestilence into his ear—*
> *That she repeals him for her body's lust;*
> *And by how much she strives to do him good,*
> *She shall undo her credit with the Moor.*
> *So will I turn her virtue into pitch,*
> *And out of her own goodness make the net*
> *That shall enmesh them all.*[7]

Envy corrupts and corrodes "charming features" and love. It turns good into bad and makes life the rationale for death. To accomplish this, Iago employs a lethal mixture of slander and duplicity, a process of bad-mouthing and back-stabbing. And he makes his hatred all the more effective because he is able to convince Othello to look to him for advice and support, while turning him into a fool, *"an ass,"* who must kiss the ass of the very person who attacks his peace of mind and drives him mad.[8]

According to a compelling but incomplete legend, the eighteenth-century Viennese court composer Antonio Salieri used similar tactics to humiliate, impoverish, and ultimately murder Wolfgang Amadeus Mozart, who lived and worked in Vienna at the same time. This relationship has been dramatized by Peter Shaffer in his play *Amadeus.*[9]

Shaffer's Salieri is a cultured and immensely ambitious man who achieves considerable renown during his lifetime.[10] But in comparison with Mozart he is a musical mediocrity. And Salieri knows this. Overtly he tries to help Mozart and appears concerned about his career. But secretly Salieri plots to grind Mozart into the ground— to deter his students, to prevent his advancement, and to hinder the performance of his compositions.[11]

Fate intervenes to help Salieri in his machinations.[12] Mozart embarks on a new opera, *The Marriage of Figaro*. It is based on real people and real places instead of myths and folktales, as is the custom. The nobility becomes alarmed and raises a storm of objections, just as the court musicians vehemently oppose Mozart's use of the vernacular.[13] At Salieri's suggestion Count Rosenberg, director of the Imperial Opera, takes exception to a dance sequence and tries to have it deleted. Himself alarmed, Mozart begs Salieri to use his influence to invite the emperor to a rehearsal so he can present his case. Salieri agrees, intending to do no such thing. But entirely against the usual practice, the emperor does attend and takes Mozart's side. The dance remains. Believing that Salieri is responsible for his good luck, Mozart is grateful and decides Salieri is truly a friend. This allows Salieri to continue his dirty work and remain unsuspected.[14]

Although ill and overwhelmed by debt, Mozart continues to compose. Meawhile Salieri prospers and is regarded by the public as infinitely the superior composer, a success spoiled by his continuing obsession with Mozart's genius.

> I confess that I poisoned Mozart's reputation with the Emperor by constant slander.
> I confess that I pushed him deeper into poverty by the simplest means.[15]

Not satisfied, Salieri turns to arsenic, to destroy Mozart in body as well as in mind. Again and again he comes to Mozart in disguise and in secret, leaving bottles of poisoned wine. Finally he appears, a dark messenger of death, and demands that Mozart rush a new commission, a requiem mass. But his victim protests. He can't do it. He is sick, has just shit himself, is covered in muck. And a bitter taste in his mouth makes him think he's been poisoned. So he demands a reprieve.

Suddenly Salieri casts off his mask and reveals himself. Mozart is incredulous. How could it be? Was it a joke? Was Salieri really behind everything that happened to him? "Why?" he asks. "Why?" Yet to understand, Mozart would have had to know about a pact Salieri had made with God at an early age, when he proposed to honor God with music in exchange for fame and fortune and, more important, inspiration.

The pact seemed to bear fruit. To all Vienna, indeed to all of Europe, Salieri was a prolific and respected composer, a musical giant. But, as befits the envious man, he did not measure his worth by intrinsic accomplishments. He only considered his work in comparison with another, Mozart. By that token he and his music were nothing.[16]

Salieri sought a terrible revenge, like Ivan Babichev and like Iago. When aroused by envy, Ivan directed his ire against a pretty girl whose presence set his teeth on edge and made his lips tremble. In response he ripped her satins and bloodied her skin. He hated her beauty.

> I don't remember saying anything when I was beating her up, but I must have whispered: This is my revenge! Don't try to outdo me! Don't try to take what's mine by right.[17]

Iago directed his fury against a Venetian soldier. He hated his power. Iago's vengeance was more subtle, if not more cruel. He drove Othello to a jealous frenzy, whereby he blew fond love, and his beloved, to hell.

> *Arise, black vengeance, from the hollow cell!*
> *Yield up, O love, thy crown and hearted throne*
> *To tyrannous hate! . . .*
> *O, blood, blood, blood!*[18]

Salieri directed his rage against God and that embodiment of the divine spark, the creativity of Mozart. He could not accept "a giggling child" whose casual notes were finer than his finest efforts. He refused the privilege of perceiving the imcomparable, while remaining aware of relative mediocrity. Therefore he denied his goodness, all goodness, and became an agent of evil, God's rival, the devil. He hated himself.[19]

> I'll not accept it from you— Do you hear? . . . They say God is not mocked! . . . *Dio Ingiusto!*—You are the Enemy!— *Nemico Eterno!* What use, after all, is Man, if not to teach God his lessons?[20]

Envious revenge is fueled by arrogance and pride. It is based on imaginary hurts rather than actual injury. Although Mozart could be uncouth and derogatory, his bearing did not touch Salieri so much as his being. This was the grave offense. Similarly Iago and Ivan Babichev did not seek revenge for what had been done to them in fact. The girl was probably not even aware of Ivan's presence until he attacked her. And Othello treated Iago well, like a friend and confidant. Yet Ivan and Iago begrudged them their vitality and prowess, if not their very existence.

Begrudging is characteristic of envious people who take pleasure in depriving others of what they have or could have, without deriving any sort of advantage from this. Such people go to great lengths to inflict harm or unhappiness. In the summer of 1981 the London *Times* reported the sad story of two Greek spinster sisters, one aged eighty and the other aged eighty-five, who locked a third sister, aged seventy-five, in a stable for eight years as punishment for marrying late in life and "making us look ridiculous."[21] These ladies were no more ridiculous than Salieri, who, after all, composed music that was widely enjoyed. But in their own minds they felt humiliated, no doubt, when they thought of their own wasted lives. They gained nothing from locking up their sister, except perhaps temporary relief from their own anguish.[22]

The begrudging nature of envy helps to distinguish it from greed. Greed does not begrudge. The greedy person wants as much as he can get, and more, in order to overcome a frightening inner emptiness. He is concerned not with preventing others from having what they have, but with getting whatever is good and life-giving for himself. Security consists of a freedom from emptiness.

The envious person feels inferior rather than empty. He can't stand to see others full of life and goodness, because he is preoccupied with his own limitations and defects. So he aims to debunk and debase what others have. Security consists of an equality of emptiness.

Envy is a graspingness for self. Greed is a graspingness for life. Both are never satisfied, because the envious person can always imagine someone else has more, or is worth more than he, while the greedy person can never imagine that he can get, or will have, enough.

But greed recognizes life. The greedy person admits that there is goodness in the world. I mean that he can acknowledge and value care, tenderness, nourishment, beauty, and love. That is why greed is not as shameful as envy, which denies all these things. For the envious person, love is delusion, life is death, and God is the devil.

Greed hoards, envy abhors. The greedy person wants to get more and more, and keep more and more, and will go to any lengths to do this. Greedy destructiveness is unintended but inevitable because of the ruthless, intemperate, gnashing, voracious manner of taking things in and keeping them. Since damaged goods do not relieve hunger, the greedy person may feel compelled to seek out and acquire more of what he has damaged—a vicious, circular, self-defeating process.

Envious destructiveness is deliberate. The envious person denies goodwill or love toward the object of his ire. What he wants is to remove the bilious anger and bitter vindictiveness from within himself, to get rid of it and put it elsewhere. Since he blames what he envies for how he feels, he sets out to make it feel bad or appear bad. Any relief is temporary because the source of his torment is not in what he envies, but in himself.

This wish to force gratuitous hurt onto others is an important part of an envious, begrudging attack, typified by the case of a disgruntled Nigerian security guard who killed a visiting American banker out for a stroll in London. When caught, the man told police that he had long felt lonely and degraded, an outcast from society. One night while walking in a well-to-do area, he came across a large man who looked "rich and comfortable," someone who went to plenty of "posh places." All of a sudden he felt terribly cheated:

> I had to let off steam. I had to cut someone. . . . I stabbed him in the stomach with all the force and hatred that had been building up inside me.[23]

Crimes of theft and arson also illustrate the differences between greed and envy. The street thief and housebreaker want to empty you of what you have and get away as quickly as possible. They don't set out to do damage, which nevertheless may happen, by accident or out of frustration when they don't get what they expect. On the other hand, the arsonist who burns down a house does not wish to possess it or its contents. He wants to evacuate his own burning displeasure by discomforting the owner or by destroying the unique qualities of the house itself.[24] Thus, a man who had set fire to eight cars in Bridgeport, Connecticut, explained: "I couldn't afford to own an automobile . . . and I didn't want anyone else to have one."[25]

On the larger social scene envy and greed seem to be predominant considerations affecting the style, if not policies, of many political figures. The envy-oriented politician tends to play on people's prejudices against the rich and privileged. He argues for a lower but more equal national per capita income and is against great disparities of wealth for whatever the reason.[26]

The greed-oriented politician stresses rapid and unrestricted economic growth and development, no matter who or what gets hurt or ruined in the process. He favors high-profit policies often associated with free enterprise and capitalism. Not all capitalists are greedy, but "capitalist" has become synonymous with greed. Terms like "capitalist pig" or "imperialist running dog" convey the contempt and derision of the envious, just as "radical left" or "Trotskyite" are damnations that express the fear of people who want to hang on to their possessions.[27]

Envy and greed rarely operate separately. My colleague, Dr. Nina Coltart, has suggested the term "grenvy" to denote the fusion of these two emotional forces and the simultaneous expression of them. In 1730 Dr. Patrick Delany, a friend of the satirist Jonathan Swift, wrote a telling verse that essentially describes the way Harpyes and slugs embody grenvy:

> At highest worth dull malice reaches
> As slugs pollute the fairest peaches:
> Envy defames, as Harpyes vile
> Devour the fruit they first defile.

Devouring and defiling characterize grenvy and distinguish the grenvious act from a greedy or envious one. The grenvious impulse is more common than pure greed or envy. At least it acknowledges goodness before trying to ruin it. Envy itself admits no desire except to destroy.

The grenvious student, for example, combines stealing and spoiling. He yearns for the information and ideas his teachers possess, so much so that he will go to almost any lengths to get them. Yet as soon as this happens, he forgets what he has learned and debunks what he hasn't. Similarly, in therapy the grenvious patient is very demanding, for time, for interpretations, for help, while simultaneously mocking and distorting the therapist's thoughts. [28]

Newspaper reports of the antics of housebreakers who don't just steal but leave places a wreck also refer to grenvy. A friend of mine owned a house in London that he was planning to sell. He had left it unoccupied but locked up after moving to another house. One Saturday he received a frantic call from a former neighbor who said that there was water pouring from the house onto the street. Hurrying to see what was the matter, my friend discovered that thieves had broken in, systematically ripped out the central heating pipes, and then taken anything else of value. But the intruders had not bothered to turn off the main water, so it was cascading throughout the house. Worse than that, they left piles of their excrement all over the house and had smeared it over walls and ceilings. During the course of their investigation, the police told the owner that the damage was probably the work of a gang of teenaged vandals. Professional thieves rarely disturb anything they don't take. But it is quite common for amateurs to break into a house and defile it.[29]

This crime demonstrates two forms of spoiling. Greedy spoiling occurs when the person or place robbed is emptied, injured, or wrecked during the process of stealing. This spoiling is secondary to greed's ruthless, rapacious acquisitiveness. The plumbing damage indicated greedy spoiling, but the deliberate smearing of shit exemplified envious spoiling. By such extraneous damage, and by allowing water to flow all over the house, a pissing as well as shitting on things, the thieves expressed their contempt and hatred for the owner and for the house, too. It is this mixture of envy with greed that makes the grenvious impulse so damaging and difficult to alleviate.[30]

Envy can hide behind greed as well as fuse with it. Many people accumulate things in order to numb an overweening sense of inferiority or worthlessness. In a materialistic society these "things" might be clothes or cars. In another culture they might be titles, privileges, or work points. However, if the flow of things slows or stops, then the same unhappy people tend to feel humiliated, unworthy, and full of hate toward a world that, in their experience, has robbed and cheated them of their rights and privileges.[31] These grievances can quickly become an obsession, and their envious malice, previously held in check by the illusory fullness, may burst out against relatives, friends, neighbors, colleagues, or "the system" with annihilating accusations of selfishness, cruelty, and greed! Giving more may be palliative or not, because once envy is aroused people tend to rubbish whatever they get, while wanting more. Even good experiences may be trampled under the weight of ingratitude and discontent. Such envy surfaces in the child who "bites the hand that feeds him" and repays parental love with scorn while demanding more.

Love scorned is a central theme of jealousy. The jealous person wants to love and be loved, but he or she fears the loss of a beloved to another. If this happens, or even if there is a threat of it happening, jealous passions soon erupt. They aim to eliminate the unwelcome third party, the rival, so that the original relationship can continue. Alternatively the jealous person may be the outsider, an excluded third party full of desire who comes between two others so that a new loving relationship can begin.

Here love is the primary issue, not hate. However, jealous anger and hatred can be quite as cruel, malicious, and spiteful as envy. What differs is the focus—love lost; the direction of the anger—toward the rival; and the possibility of resolution—love regained and retained.

Jealousy is popularly associated with sexual jealousy, the subject of countless plays, films, and books. Jilly Cooper, who writes on racy topics for the London *Sunday Times,* has described her reaction when she thinks her husband is off with another woman:

> About once a year something triggers off a really bad attack of jealousy, and I turn from an insane irrational being into a raving maniac, all perspective blotted out. "He's late home from work," I reason. "He must be with another woman." Or he's early. "He must be feeling guilty about having a boozy lunch with her." And so on and on, lashing myself with misery. Once the octopus jealousy gets me in its stranglehold, it is almost impossible to wriggle free.[32]

Ms. Cooper highlights irrationality, infidelity, passion, and possessiveness. These issues arise from relationships, any relationship where two people are having fun with each other, whether sex or a "boozy lunch," to the exclusion of someone else. Jealousy is always group-oriented. It involves a threesome. In contrast, envy and greed are more primitive emotional states not concerned with relationships, as such, at all.[33]

The irrational component of jealousy stems from the tendency of the jealous person to exaggerate loss when it has occurred or to imagine loss when it hasn't, as with Ms. Cooper's husband. However, in the latter circumstance, there is usually some kernel of truth, a missed meeting, a delayed dinner, which jealous fears can play on. Envy needs no basis in fact. Therefore, while conflict over love gives rise to jealousy, envy itself gives rise to conflicts that destroy love, including jealous conflict!

Jealous possessiveness signals the wish to hold on to one's partner and never let her go. It is a further response to the threat of loss and can also serve as a warning or punishment. There is a very aggressive, as well as adoring, quality to it, as with wives who won't let their husbands out of their sight. Such aggressiveness may explain why some people are ashamed of their possessive wishes, then deny them and attribute them to their loved one. The wife who doesn't want her husband to spend a minute away from her may become a woman who constantly complains that her husband won't let her out of the flat or won't let her do anything on her own. Ms. Cooper is not like that, but she does attribute possessiveness to her own jealousy. She then experiences the jealousy as an octopus threatening to strangle her with its emotional ramifications, as opposed to her own wish to tie her husband so he can't have an affair. This possessiveness is quite different from greedy possessiveness, which treats people as if they were possessions. Ms. Cooper did not say that she had a collection of husbands or lovers. Some women do. This greedy accumulation of partners can also be a defense against anticipated infidelities.

Infidelity is the major issue for the jealous person who suspects that his loved one is having a close relationship with another. Suspicions of unfaithfulness indicate great insecurity, not only about relationships but about the individual's own attractiveness, lovability, or capacity for loving.[34] This can lead to obsessive feelings of unworthiness and inferiority and murderous attacks on anyone who arouses them—the alleged third party for interfering and the loved person, too. The direct attack on one's partner is an expression of the vindictive rage stimulated by jealousy—revenge for lost love and hurt pride. Jealous revenge is the operational link between jealousy and envy because the jilted man or woman is hitting back for disloyalty and for being cast in an excluded and inferior position. The malicious aggression that is a feature of such retribution is a form of envious spoiling of the former partner's happiness and superior charms.[35]

This link does not mean that jealousy and envy are identical. On the contrary, jealousy has a separate and distinct meaning and emotional flavoring. Unlike envy or greed, jealousy is not present at birth but only emerges after the infant is able to recognize his parents in their own right.

The distinction between the two terms can be traced back over two millennia. The ancient Greeks, who were keenly aware of envy, employed two terms, *phthonos* for envy and *zelos* for jealousy.[36] Demosthenes, the greatest of the Athenian orators, claimed that *phthonos* was the sign of a wicked nature in every way, and that the man who experienced envy was beyond pardon.[37] *Zelos*, jealousy, was considered much less bad and even connoted admiration.[38] These moral associations might be expected, as jealousy commands both love and hate, but envy is concerned only with hate.

In many countries the difference between envy and jealousy has been recognized in law. Crimes committed "with malice aforethought" are punished in full, but "crimes of passion" are treated more leniently. Obviously loss of love and infidelity are extenuating circumstances![39] Still there remains considerable confusion about the two words.[40] Jilly Cooper adds to this when she quips that people are invariably jealous of close friends or acquaintances. She herself would not mind if one of them won a Nobel Prize for chemistry or a gold medal for discus throwing. But should a chum marry a millionaire or win the pools, she would be very irritated. The worst is when people threaten her own interests:

> If one of them dyed her hair blonde and started pushing sex in a posh Sunday, I should be tempted to pop the odd bullet through her. . . . Alas, when one is in the grip of a grand passion all moral considerations go by the board. Beware, my dears, of jealousy. It is the green-eyed monster comes roaring out of the bedroom with a shotgun before you have time to leap out of bed and into the wardrobe.[41]

Although Ms. Cooper has correctly used jealousy to describe a furious response to her husband's alleged affairs, she incorrectly uses the word to convey outrage at her friends' good fortune, knowledge, or sexy characteristics. This outrage is envy. Qualities, characteristics, possessions (like a large bust, big lips, blond hair), attract envy. Jealousy would imply a state of active conflict and competition with a friend who was deploying her sexiness to entice Cooper's husband. Maybe this happened. She did not say so in the article.[42]

Whatever the usage, Jilly Cooper gives a firm warning about jealousy. It is a "green-eyed monster" liable to shoot first and ask questions after. Her allusion is to the warning that Iago gave Othello about his dangerous state of mind:

> O, beware, my lord, of jealousy;
> It is the green-ey'd monster which doth mock
> The meat it feeds on.[43]

The warning is double-edged. It refers to Othello's jealousy and to Iago's envy, which makes a mockery of Othello by driving him berserk with doubt, despair, and rage.

But could it be that Iago was not really so bad, that he was afflicted with a "grand passion" for Desdemona and only wanted to get Othello out of the way so that he could have her for himself? After all, he did accuse Othello of having slept with his wife (an indication of what he may have wanted to do). And he did scheme with Roderigo, Desdemona's former suitor, to woo her back. Perhaps Roderigo represents Iago's alter ego, and the "green-eyed monster" is not Iago's envy but his jealousy.

I'm afraid this picture does not fit the facts. The Iago Shakespeare paints is devious and scheming, a man with no redeeming virtues, a paragon of vice. His sole interest in Desdemona is to hurt Othello; in fact, he aims to begrudge both of them happiness and life. And if Roderigo represents another aspect of himself, he isn't too benevolent toward it, for he also murders Roderigo, and his wife, Emilia, too.

For Iago, jealousy, inasmuch as there is any case for it, serves simply to camouflage overweening envy. This is not an uncommon function of jealousy, to act as a defense against envy. It is especially evident in people who suffer from pathological jealousy. Sigmund Freud called this "projected jealousy" and "delusional jealousy." It is also known as "morbid jealousy."[44]

Morbid jealousy manifests itself in men and women who develop a firm belief that their partners, and various named or unnamed third parties, want to rob them of everything: want to taunt, tantalize, outrage, strip them of self-respect and self-confidence, spoil their love, and leave them feeling full of doubt and despair. Upon closer examination, these thoughts are held by people with limited self-esteem and deeply ingrained feelings of inferiority. The accusations tend to be projections of what they want to do to others.[45]

Did Othello suffer from morbid jealousy? Did he succumb to Iago's intrigues because he secretly harbored great enmity toward the woman he married? Shakespeare provides considerable evidence toward this view. Othello is a Moor, a soldier of fortune, a hustler, while Desdemona is the daughter of a Venetian senator, an aristocrat. And she is white, while he is black. I don't think these details are an accident. Shakespeare depicted the class and race conflicts of his time in order to mirror his society. Among the many reasons we continue to be fascinated by his plays is the conviction that this mirror also depicts the endless, envious, guilt-laden preoccupations of the future. Iago is no more, but no less, than another side of the modern man who cannot endure evil. Therefore he blackens others and makes them suffer instead.[46]

Nowadays envy is just as prevalent as it was in Shakespeare's time, but people are less straightforward about it. The emotional meaning and motivation of the term tends to be clouded, if not actually reversed, by idiomatic usages and theoretical justifications. Chic phrases deploy envy in order to declare admiration, interest, desire, strong feeling, frustration, resentment, indignation, and identification (or the opposite) and have become part of common parlance:

I envy you.
You'll be envied for sitting in this seat.
I so envy your new car.
What an enviable position.
I don't envy anyone with money these days.
I don't envy him trying to write.[47]

Admen advise that envy is not to be feared. On the contrary, it's a useful stimulant for "the folks back home."[48] And sociologists imply that envy, influenced by "uninhibited reference group choice," may have a salutary effect on social reform.[49] In September 1977 the Vickers Company placed a large cartoon advertisement in *The Sunday Times*. On one side of the page the reader sees a modern, open-plan office block filled with new furniture, new equipment, and smiling, cheerful people. On the other side there is an older brick building from which a multitude of clerks, secretaries, typists, and bosses peer out of rows of small, narrow windows, exclaiming, "Envy! Envy! Envy!" Some of these faces are overcome with despair, resentment, or rage, while others evince interest, admiration, and desire. The caption comments that the cartoonist wanted to convey the whole range of Vickers's products as well as the envy of those who have to make do without them.[50]

This cartoon captures the multiple meanings ascribed to envy and demonstrates how envy can be used to sell products, if not a way of life, by preying on people's latent inferiority. The central image is two adjacent buildings and two adjacent groups of office workers. Their "social proximity" provides the context for the "invidious comparisons" that follow.[51] The advert assumes the workers are unhappy about their conditions of employment. It seeks to awaken them to the relative impoverishment of their labors and implies that they should feel deprived in relation to the get-ahead employees next door (even though they may previously have been content).[52] The cartoonist seems to be aware of the theories of the sociologist W. G. Runciman, for whom envy signifies "relative deprivation." Runciman believes that "the poorest appear to be entitled to a greater magnitude of relative deprivation than the evidence shows them to feel."[53]

Feeling appropriately deprived, one man is green, sick to the stomach at the thought of what he is missing. Another is crying, and a third is in a state of near total despair. Nearby, however, his colleague can be seen gnashing his teeth in rage and resentment, while another glowers with indignation. Down a floor someone else is so frustrated at the sight of the new equipment, he can't bear to look.⁵⁴

Resentment, indignation, and frustration are often used synonymously with envy. But they are not identical phenomena, rather reactions to actual injustice or deprivation—in other words, to an actual conflict of interest. Envy is rooted in imaginary conflict, although actual events can conceal or incite it. Vickers's products may also dispel resentment or indignation, but the grievances of a truly envious person do not disappear even when the alleged source of frustration is removed.⁵⁵

The ad does try to foster positive feelings. Vickers obviously hopes and expects that all their potential customers in old brick-fronted buildings will be charmed and delighted by what they see and anticipate using. It wants everyone to emulate the new working practices of the glass-walled, fully automated get-ahead company next door. Why call this envy? Admiration is an "antidote" for envy, not the expression of it.⁵⁶ As Sören Kierkegaard has pointed out, envy embraces unhappy self-assertion, while admiration equals happy self-surrender.⁵⁷

Similarly, emulation is quite different from an envious competitiveness, which is spiteful, self-seeking, and begrudging. The wish to be like someone is based on admiration, not ill will. I presume the Vickers Company wants its new customers to equal or surpass its old ones, not disparage, damage, or grind them to the ground.⁵⁸ Yet this cartoon does incite envy, not by the overt use of the word, but by the covert message "You are not good or at least not as good as everyone else, unless you use our products."⁵⁹

Why don't people who are aroused by this message, and by the barrage of equivalent messages on TV, radio, newspapers, magazines, and billboards, immediately go on a rampage? Well, sometimes they do, collectively, as in a ghetto riot, or individually, in a seemingly unprovoked attack on a relative or friend. The government of Indonesia ended commerical television solely because the sight of unattainable goods unsettled the inhabitants of their outer islands.⁶⁰

Usually, however, envy lurks behind a facade of probable hurts or is fused with greed and jealousy, as we have seen. Most important, envy is continually opposed by gratitude, generosity, and compassion—all fundamental virtues that convey our love of life. Even Salieri was not totally motivated by malice. He admired Mozart and wanted to compose music like him so he could repay God for making him a famous man. Envy only got the upper hand when, in his view, this ambition was thwarted. Then he abandoned social duties and charitable pursuits and devoted himself to ruining Mozart's life.

Salieri, Iago, Ivan Babichev, all demonstrate the essential criteria of unrestrained envy. It is an intense, implacable, irrational, irreconcilable, spiteful passion solely concerned with spoiling, corrupting, defaming, and begrudging. No wonder it seems to operate in secret. It has always been considered one of the most deadly sins amply conveyed by the iconography of a satanic serpent and, more recently, by a bumper sticker seen on a car in Mexico: "Down with everyone going up!"[61]

2

The Evil Eye

The evil eye is the power to harm or bewitch by a malevolent look or glance. It is a gaze imbued with hostility and wickedness. According to many peoples, it is an expression infected by the devil.[1]

The belief in the evil eye is both primeval and universal and has been often associated with magic, witchcraft, and superstition. As to the threat it can pose, Rabbi Judah Low, the alleged creator of the Golem, commented, "Know and understand that the evil eye concentrates within itself the element of fire," and so flashes forth destruction.[2]

In our times people are more aware that the harm engendered by a spiteful stare has more to do with personal malicious wishes than demonic possession. Yet a penetrating gaze, a withering glance, or a dirty look can strike terror in the most sophisticated of men, comparable to the feelings aroused in the ancients by the Furies of a Greek chorus.[3] We need not be surprised. The evil eye is no less than the active expression of the envious "I."

The chill eye/"I" of envy has been acutely captured by the French painter Jean Louis Géricault in *A Mad Woman with the Mania of Envy*.[4] This painting portrays a thin, tense, nervous woman in her mid-fifties. Sharp, unbalanced eyes radiate agitation and suffering as they focus like daggers on whatever has excited her interest. A slight grimace exaggerates the comparisons she seems to register unceasingly. The woman, a servant according to her dress, is clearly obsessed by the thought of all that she doesn't have.

It is uncomfortable to look straight into her face, even in a picture, even in a copy of a picture. One soon wants to avert the eyes and shrink away.

To fully comprehend this experience, we have to consider two points of view, the mind of the maid and the reaction of the onlooker, that is, of the envier and the envied, of the subject and the object. Envy is not just an emotion. It is a profound emotional force that imposes a comprehensive alteration on the whole way that the envious person sees, feels, and acts and on the way that the envied other, the victim, responds.

Envy begins in the eye of the beholder, an eye that exaggerates, misrepresents, and selectively chooses things to hate. This eye is especially attracted to prosperity, fertility, vitality, fame, success, pride, power, and any other quality, characteristic, or accomplishment that conveys, or appears to convey, superiority or special advantage. But these things do not always stimulate envy. Much depends on the life history of the envier, his inner state, and the context, whether he is comparing himself with relatives, neighbors, friends or not.

In Géricault's picture the ominous expression of a servant's eyes hints at a background seething with frustration and deprivation. The left eye is wide open as if to emphasize a sinister, if not supernatural, transformation of whatever has caught her attention. This is an extravagant look that can turn a cloth coat into a mink and a house into a palace. As various folk sayings attest, this initial tendency toward the idealization of the object can turn toadstools into palm trees and midges into elephants.[5] Such a perception arises from a deep, gnawing sense of inferiority coupled with an instantaneous and usually unconscious comparison with the envied object. It conveys the essential idea "Whatever I am, or have, you are much bigger and better." But this evaluation cannot last long because it arouses intolerable anguish in the envier. Therefore the reverse inevitably happens. Denigration, equally extreme and unrealistic, follows idealization, in order to mitigate the effects of the original perception. Thus the elephant becomes a midge, the palm trees—toadstools, and the cloth coat—a rag.

Meanwhile the woman's other eye is narrow and squinting, as if to zero in on its target and hold it in its gaze. This eye sees selectively, focusing on enviable qualities—that is, on good ones—but ignoring the bad ones. There are many examples in Russian literature of this process:

Envy may see the bearskin, but not the moths.
Envy can see the sea, but not the leak.[6]

In other words, envious perception confirms, and adds to, envy. Again, such a perception cannot continue because of the pain it evokes. Soon the reverse will occur, and the envier will refuse to register goodness, only what's bad in people and in the world. The culmination of this process is emotional, moral, even actual blindness. It is likely that certain cases of hysterical blindness are the result of an envy so intense that the person refuses to see anything at all rather than risk seeing any goodness in anyone or anything.

The power of the evil eye, and the fear it evoked, have long been acknowledged by the special names given to the eye, to an envious look, or to a person who looks in an evil or envious way. The Greeks used the word *baskainein,* which meant to look or bewitch with the evil eye. *Baskania* meant the evil eye, or envy. The Roman counterpart was *fascinare.*[7] In contemporary usage, "fascination" means a strong, overwhelming interest in something or someone. The word has lost its malevolent undertones. But for almost two millennia fascinate and fascination connoted spells, witchcraft, and horror.[8] To get some idea of what the ancients felt when they fell under the influence of a fascinator, one only has to think of oneself held in the gaze of a rattlesnake poised to strike or of the glowing eyes of a cat in the dark. The evil eye has been commonly attributed to any animal, real or mythological, with large, protuberant, or brightly colored eyes. These have included wolves, tigers, hawks, crocodiles, snakes, and snakelike creatures such as the basilisk, which allegedly could kill at a glance.[9]

The eye with a magical power to cause harm has been called by many names. The Romans used *oculus fascinus,* the Syrians *aina-basa,* and the Jews *ayn-hara.* In modern Italy the evil eye is the *mal-occhio,* and one possessed of it is called *jettatura.*[10] People are often considered to be a *jettatura* when bad luck or damage or evil seem to follow in their wake.[11] Pope Pius IX (1792–1878) was extremely popular in Italy during much of his pontificate. Nevertheless a series of disasters that occurred during his reign led to the belief that he possessed the evil eye. The same held true for his successor, Pope

Leo XIII (1810–1903), who was held responsible for the deaths of a large number of cardinals.[12]

In English-speaking countries people tend to be aware of the evil eye but not to refer to it by name, except among ethnic minorities. This was not always the case. In Shakespeare's time the term "overlook" was widely employed to denote the act of looking at someone with the evil eye. Therefore an overlooker was an evil person who was widely feared for ill-wishing.[13] Later on, the owner of an evil eye was called a "blinker," whose victims were said to be blinked, forelooked, or eye-bitten.[14]

The English philosopher Francis Bacon observed that an envious person looks at others obliquely, and it has been said that people who squint are exceptionally envious. Perhaps this is why the English country gentleman has long feared squinting neighbors.[15]

Nowadays people are not directly preoccupied with the evil eye. But they don't like dirty looks or red, inflamed, enlarged, deformed eyes. In fact, in China envy is called "the red-eyed disease."[16] Similarly, in the cinema the most disreputable villains, and most horrific monsters, often have huge, bloodshot, shifty, squinting eyes. These caricatures of primitive fears also tend to be very sensitive about how others look at them: "Don't look at me that way, or I'll plug ya full of holes!"[17] And if this happens, or people die in any other circumstances, someone will quickly come and pull down their eyelids, not just for cosmetic reasons. It is part of a custom that can be traced back to Roman times and further.

The Romans placed coins on the eyes of the dead. This was to pay Charon, the boatman who ferried souls across the river Styx to Hades. But the coins also served as weights, to make sure that the dead could not stare at the living. Similarly, Aryan peoples closed the eyes of the dead and placed weights upon the lids. They wished to prevent the spirit of the dead person from casting a spell on those who survived.[18]

Closing the eyes of the dead remains a widespread custom. In our times it is the closest many people come to acknowledging the power of the evil eye. This is especially strong at the moment of death, for envy is most intense, vicious, and dangerous when it is directed by the dead, or those who feel dead, toward the living.[19]

What feelings fuel the envious perceptions and wishes that constitute the evil eye? When confronted by evidence of limitations and mortality, the envier feels assailed by an implacable, all-consuming anguish and despair, as exemplified by Ivan Babichev, Iago, and

Salieri. Then he or she responds with a vindictive, burning hatred toward the object of this envy. The immediate impulse is to eliminate the pain and torment by annihilating anything and everything that may have caused it. As the anguish and anger occur almost simultaneously, the two feelings tend to fuse and cause even greater suffering, evident as hostile desperation in the eyes of the envier.

An envious person will go to any lengths to reduce this intolerable inner state. He may refuse to recognize what he sees and refuse to acknowledge what he feels. Or he may dissociate himself from his feelings and attribute them to whomever or whatever he envied whether a prosperous friend, a comfortable home, or a bowl of soup. This happened with Kavalerov, Ivan Babichev's envy-ridden layabout companion who discovered that "things" stopped liking him:

> Furniture tries to trip me up. Once the sharp corner of some polished thing literally bit me. . . . Soup given to me, never cools. If some bit of junk—a coin or a collar button—falls off the table, it usually rolls under some almost unmovable piece of furniture. And when, crawling around on the floor after it, I raise my head, I catch the sideboard laughing at me.[20]

The denial of reality, by evacuating bad feelings into the external world, may afford some temporary relief, but it is no solution to the anguish and despair aroused by envy, all the more because incessant denial can turn the world into a menacing, evil place. Therefore the envier seeks to alter and destroy reality, not just deny it.[21]

Reality is everything the envier hates. His first stratagem is psychological. He acts with words and gestures to rubbish whomever and whatever he envies. His intentions are to diminish, denigrate, and debase that person or thing so completely that it will appear and be totally worthless in his eyes and in the eyes of everyone else. If the object of his envy is a person, he literally wants to fill that person with agitation and anger in order to effectively transfer his desperation to another. In this way the envier hopes that he will be released from his suffering. If not, at least he will have had a measure of revenge on his imagined tormentor.

Examples of psychically engineered envious attacks are commonplace. Who hasn't heard children respond to the accomplishments of their siblings or parents with "That's shit!" "You're all wrong!" or "That's nothing"? The businessman or scientist who attacks a colleague's reputation on spurious grounds, the housewife who spreads malicious rumors about a relative or neighbor, are familiar figures.

Put-downs allow the envier, whether child or adult, to feel superior. Boasting and bragging serve the same end. They enhance the speaker at the expense of his audience.

Kierkegaard understood this process very well, for he attributed envy to anyone who aroused envy in others, whether by self-promotion, self-flattery, or otherwise.[22] Interestingly, the Latin word for envy, *invidia,* has given rise to the English word "invidious," which is often taken to mean offensive or envious. Yet the principle definition of invidious is envy arousing. In effect, if not in intention, a braggart or show-off is an invidious person.

Excessive or undeserved compliments can lead the complimented person to feel anxious and embarrassed and easily make him a target for others' envy. The American anthropologist George Foster has described many instances where excessive praise or compliments serve or are seen as thinly disguised envious attacks. In Mali people avoid direct compliments for fear of the harm they cause. And in the Arab world well-meaning praise may be shunned because of the contrary feelings it may contain. Foster sums up by quoting from the Spanish novel *Abel Sanchez: The History of a Passion,* where a truculent character always exclaims, whenever he hears anyone praised, "Against whom is that eulogy directed?"[23]

The Greeks were particularly aware of the dangers of excessive praise, which they believed attracted the envy of the gods—*phthonos theon.* In the writings of Homer, envy of the gods seemed to represent an unnamed, indeterminate, but malevolent divine force that lay behind things when they went wrong.[24] This changed around 500 B.C. at a time when Greek society became much less rigidly hierarchical and more open—socially, politically, and economically.[25] *Phthonos theon* came to mean the specific hatred and retribution of the gods toward mortals who challenged their prerogatives or power. This concept was defined and redefined by Pindar, Aeschylus, and Herodotus in their poems, plays, and histories.[26]

In the *Agamemnon,* the chorus, "that frequent exponent of popular morality," exclaims prior to the hero's murder:

> Grievous is the burden of excessive praise, for from the eyes of Zeus is cast the thunder-bolt.[27]

Agamemnon prayed that "envy's eye" would not strike him from afar.[28] His prayers were misdirected and unanswered. He was slaughtered by Clytemnestra, his wife.

Later writers such as Euripides and Plutarch were more precise

when they declared that the "evil stings" and "poisoned arrows" of
envy originated in the eyes of envious mortals.[29] Even Aeschylus, in
his mature judgement, stated that it is impiety, the actions of men,
not the envy of immortal deities, that unleashes disaster on mankind.[30]

The Greeks realized that the envious man was charged with hostility. Moreover, they appreciated that the consequences of this hostility were not just psychological—the besmearing of a reputation or
arousal of bad feelings—but tangible, physical, and deadly. For them,
"thunder-bolts," "evil stings," and "poisoned arrows" were part of
a wide weaponry of envious anger and rage that posed a constant
threat to man, to society, to life itself.

The English classicist Peter Walcot points out that as far back as
500 B.C. the philosopher Democritus taught that the envious released
particles charged with envy ("angry atoms," "evil atoms"), particles
that "established themselves securely in those bewitched and so damaged their bodies and minds."[31] This idea was embellished by the
third-century novelist Heliodorus, who seemed to equate envy's "poisoned arrow" and "evil particles" with the very air that emanated
from an envious person. He explained that the air that surrounds us
goes deep into our body and emerges charged with emotion. Therefore the air expelled by an envious person is charged with malice. It
fills the atmosphere with a malignant quality. What we call the evil
eye is this breath of bitterness, which, when taken in by another,
penetrates deep to the marrow and can cause sickness and death.[32]
Plutarch concluded that this evil air and similar noxious "scents,"
"voices," or "any other defluxions and streams" spew forth from
the eye rather than any other conduit of the body, because "sight,
being a sense very swift, active, and nimble, doth send forth and
disperse from it a wonderful fiery puissance, together with the spirit
that carrieth and directed it."[33]

Fifteen hundred years later these views were echoed by Francis
Bacon, who called envy "an ejaculation, or irradiation of the eye."[34]
He averred that the envious gaze "emitteth some malign and poisonous spirit, which taketh hold of the spirit of another, and is
likewise of the greatest force when the cast of the eye is oblique."[35]
However, the active, destructive component of envy remained a mystery even for Bacon, a keen observer of human relationships. He
postulated poison rays rather than accept that the damage caused by
envy was the result of specific, concrete, malicious actions.

By this time few people believed in the envy of the gods as such.
The Greeks themselves didn't refer to it very much after Aeschylus.

Yet people still retained a need to distance themselves from the evil they waged on earth. So it became—indeed, had long been—the function of astrology to attribute bad fate, ill luck, divine retribution, or evil influence to the position of the planets and the stars. Bacon commented on the preoccupations of astrologers. He connected what "the Scripture calleth the evil eye" with "the evil aspects of the stars" to what he termed "envious irradiation." To this very day astrology remains the repository for popular beliefs in the evil eye, set far away, amid the heavenly bodies.[36]

Bacon, as others before him, clearly linked the evil eye with an envious anger. This is an important distinction. There are many kinds of anger, as there are many reasons for aggression. Envy is not the prime cause of all anger. Nor is all anger evil.

There are angers motivated by greed and jealousy or by frustration, indignation, rivalry, and revenge, to name but a few. There is an assertive, self-protective anger or aggression and an instrumental aggression that is part of being a member of a group, whether a youth gang or the police. Their consequences may be negative, violent, and wicked or positive and constructive. All have been seen in, and attributed to, the eye. Some eyes have been said to be devouring, possessive, and "bigger than your stomach," while others have been considered dangerous, provocative, and penetrating.

A young patient of mine spent most of one session declaiming his insatiable hunger for women. I pointed out that it seemed he wanted me to provide girls for him just as his nanny had provided sweets and that he gave me dirty looks if I didn't. He grimaced. "Ah, yes, sweets, red and round," he said, and proceeded to move both of his hands in a circular motion in front of him as if he were depicting two breasts. "You know," he added, "I sometimes feel my eyes are as big as soup plates."[37]

As for jealousy, it has long been said that "jealousy has a thousand eyes, yet none sees properly."[38]

Love, desire, and curiosity also frequent the eye. In the third century B.C.E. Pindar noted that there could be beneficent as well as destructive glances. In one ode the poet prays for "the unenvious regard of the gods" and asks Apollo "to let your eyes rain melody on every step I take."[39] And Bacon himself wrote:

There be none of the affections which have been noted to fascinate or bewitch but love and envy: they both have vehement wishes, they frame themselves readily into imaginations and suggestions, and they come easily into the eye, especially upon the presence of objects. . . . [40]

Characteristically, the evil eye is an eye without love, a savage eye holding an anger without obvious merit or cause or restraint. This eye, full of ill will, can be cunning and calculating. It can act by doing nothing, such as when an envious person deliberately fails to warn someone in danger or distress, someone he envies. The philosopher Immanuel Kant noted that in this way, by refusing to do his duty, the envier is able to give (bad) fate a helping hand.[41]

Usually the envier is too impatient to let fate take an evil course. He prefers "to consort with the hangman," as was the case with Iago and Salieri, who employed slander and swords, duplicity and poison.[42] That is what is so horrific, the sadistic quality of the envious attack, which specifically mimics the burning, consuming, spoiling, vitriolic turmoil within the envier.

On July 19, 1949, John Haigh was convicted of one of the more heinous crimes to have come before Lewes Assizes.[43] He had become friends with, robbed, and disposed of nine men and women by immersing them in a vat of concentrated sulfuric acid (oil of vitriol). At his trial he showed no remorse for the victims, but he did object to the use of the word "murder." He preferred "killings" and argued that they were necessary in order for him "to fulfill his destiny."

Haigh came from a background that was conducive to the envy of vitality and happiness—his destiny! He had been brought up in a fanatically religious atmosphere, one where newspapers and radio were forbidden and friends and neighbors were excluded from the house. The wrath and punishment of God was held over his head as a punishment for every trifling misdemeanor.

This man attacked nine members of three different families. His crime was one of greed. He managed to steal property worth thirty-thousand pounds (at 1949 prices). But the violence was typical of envy. Also typical are crimes where the victims are gratuitously debased, denigrated, or mutilated.[44]

It is somewhat more difficult to appreciate that whatever the envier does to someone or something outside himself, he also does to an image (psychic representation) of the envied person or thing inside himself. Since these internal images contribute to the contents and structure of his own mind, a very envious person can be devastatingly self-destructive.[45]

The state of affairs whereby the evil eye turns inward has been recognized by the folk sayings of many countries and cultures:

Envy cuts its own throat.
Envy devours its own master.
The envious man injures no one so much as himself.[46]

Various writers have decreed that envy is a diseased state of mind, because the envious man is his own worst enemy.[47] Certainly it causes a lot of mental "dis-ease," which the envier seeks to minimize within himself by maximizing in another. The distorted perceptions and diabolical actions I have described all serve this purpose, to defend against envy (the anguish, despair, hostility of the subject) by arousing it (in the object).

In summary, envy affects the envier in three basic ways—perception, emotion, and action. His perceptions are exaggerated and selective. This arises from, and gives rise to, feelings of great agony and anger, which in turn impel actions of extreme aggressiveness. They are a combination of psychic and direct physical attacks on whatever and whoever is envied, both externally, in actuality, and internally against oneself.

The envied person also responds according to the same three categories of perception, emotion, and action. The specific effects have to do with the state of being envied and may be similar to, or quite different from, what occurs in the envier, for the envied person is the victim, not the victimizer. Nevertheless these effects are in a dynamic relationship with the envy that precedes them. Therefore the impact of envy on awareness, feeling, and volition (in the envied person) should be considered a component of envy—that is, part of the structure of the phenomenon.

Envy, like greed or jealousy, is a directed emotion. It needs an object. Without an object to focus upon, and to influence, envy remains a possibility, but not a practical reality. Envy is not a mood. Gloom or irritation may fill the mind without reference to anyone or anything. This cannot happen with envy, which may contribute to such a mood, but only if the envier has already fastened on to something to be upset about.

It is particularly important to consider the experience and viewpoint of the envied person, because of the drastic changes that the envier can induce in him. I am not just referring to the impact of "angry atoms" or specific destructive actions. Most commonly the envier enters into and affects the inner world of the envied person by the powerful psychological mechanism known as "projective identification," which I will detail in the next chapter. Because of projective identification we can say that within the psyche of a person who feels threatened by envy, there exists an envier from whom he is trying to escape. This internalized envier may be a psychic representation of an envious friend or relative or of envy as embodied in a social institution or state.[48]

In Egypt, where the evil eye is known as "Hassad," people commonly talk about parts of the body as having been invaded by "Hassad"—that is, an internalized envier in the form of their own or others' malicious intentions. Thus one resident of a fashionable Cairo suburb believed that her husband had "Hassad" in his broken leg. Although ostensibly Westernized, she asked priests to visit her home to sprinkle special oils and intone prayers against the scourge. Still she observed, "One thing after another keeps on happening. Now it's in his foot. Perhaps we are giving Hassad to ourselves."[49]

The wish to escape from the envier, whether real or imagined, external or internal, leads the envied person to have an extreme sensitivity to the malevolent intentions of others. All his senses may be constantly attuned to detecting shafts of hatred and misfortune emanating from inanimate as well as human sources.[50]

The American playwright Tennessee Williams suffered an unbearable sensitivity to malice after the "catastrophic success" of *The Glass Menagerie* snatched him from virtual oblivion and thrust him into a sudden prominence. In his new expensive Manhattan suite, things began to break "accidentally." Cigarettes would fall onto and damage the furniture. Windows would be left open in a downpour, and his room would be flooded—events that had never happened to him before. He became very depressed.[51]

> Sincerity and kindliness seemed to have gone from my friends' voices. I suspected them of hypocrisy, I stopped calling them, stopped seeing them. [52]

Williams held the literal belief that if he stopped seeing them, they would stop seeing him, therefore he would gain protection from their enmity (the evil eye). He acted upon this belief by going to the hospital for an optional eye operation. For several weeks his eyes were covered with a gauze mask and he couldn't see. Only then did he allow his friends to visit him.

Upon leaving the hospital, with his sight restored, Williams escaped to Mexico. There he knew no one. It was a place "where you can quickly forget the false dignities and conceits imposed by success." The anonymity allowed him to write again.[53]

The hyperawareness of envy figures in many cultures as a heightened susceptibility to and inexorable obsession with the evil eye.[54] But the opposite reaction may also occur. The envied person may shut down his perceptual facilities in order to avoid awareness of envy or the evil eye. Thus, up until the last moment Mozart showed an astonishing insensitivity to the machinations of Salieri, as did Othello to Iago.

The inability to realistically perceive and respond to the dangers posed by envy occurs within an emotional framework of fear, guilt, shame, and embarrassment. Tennessee Williams was as terrified of the praise of his friends as others were of the gaze of the gods. They all anticipated that calamities would follow and could cite "hard facts" to justify their fears, although the facts (a flooded room, a sudden death) were not necessarily caused by what they feared.

The feelings that interfere with an appropriate response to malice also reflect people's preoccupations with themselves. In other words, a greedy or envious person may refuse to see in others what he refuses to see in himself. This was certainly the case with Mozart, who was often described as a vain, pompous man who delighted in cutting down colleagues with his superior talents and attendant airs.[55]

The powerful, all-encompassing fears engendered by the real or imagined envy of others can be destructive, in themselves, to the life of the envied person. Dr. Frank Gifford, a Philadelphia ophthalmologist and student of the folklore of vision, noticed that many of the physical symptoms of the patients who attended his South Philadelphia clinic occurred after they believed they had been "overlooked" by the evil eye. Their fear resulted in headache, weakness, fatigue, stomachache, and general discomfort. Many experienced an unpleasant sensation of warmth at the moment they had been overlooked.[56] In other cultures mental and physical deterioration has been described after exposure to the evil eye.[57]

Most readers would not immediately associate these symptoms with being overlooked or fear of the evil eye. However, they become quite familiar if thought of in terms of a fear of success. Marriage, the birth of a child, the purchase of a house, the publication of a book, public or professional recognition, and other forms of success are often followed by an incongruous period of retreat, turmoil, and breakdown. Some people never recover. Others restrict their achievements in the first place.[58]

The fear of success originates in the fear of the envy that success may attract. The psychologist Matina Horner and her colleagues have done systematic studies of the threats posed by success. In one test she asked 178 male and female college undergraduates to write about a girl called Anne, "who finds herself at the top of her medical school class." Three major themes emerged: a fear that Anne would lose her friends because "everyone hates and envies her"; a very negative internal state because "Anne feels guilty, unhappy, unfeminine, and abnormal"; and bizarre or exaggerated hostility due to an anticipated rejection by others. Many students did not wish to be Anne. For them the fear of envy was a predominant concern.[59]

Similar constrictions affect the Navaho Indians of the American Southwest. In recent years their life-style has elicited considerable sympathy and admiration, for they have little concept of material success or personal achievement. However, the individual Navaho is under constant social pressure not to possess what he might like or to give away what he has come to possess. If he fails, "the voice of envy will speak out in whispers of witchcraft," and he will be the object of constant attack.[60]

This reluctance to outdo others is rooted both in the fear of envy and in guilt about greed. The fear and the guilt, arising from envy and greed, are inexorably linked. Each arouses and is aroused by the other, and each may have identical, inhibiting, self-damaging consequences.

Envious guilt occurs when a person holds himself responsible for a malevolent, spoiling attack on another person or thing. It is often confused with guilt about greed.[61] Envious guilt also occurs when a person displays or uses his possessions, skills, or good fortune in a haughty, self-inflating, invidious (envy-arousing) manner. A lot depends on the intentions of the guilty party. If he deliberately sets out to make a relative or friend feel bad, then the guilt may be quite appropriate. Even when this is not the case, the person may still become the focus of ill will. He need not blame himself but often does. A state of false responsibility develops whereby the envied person feels guilty for being envied. This is a very uncomfortable, but common, situation. It leads the individual to be terrified by, and apologetic for, the envy of others. [62] This experience coincides with, and tends to be made worse by, the belief that no one can prosper or be rich (in anything, not just money) without depriving someone else of what he has or might have. Then life is like a zero-sum game where ownership equals theft and one has to be on constant guard not to possess more than the next person.[63]

· · ·

Over several millennia an intricate array of activities has evolved in order to enable people to avert the malicious interest of relatives, friends, or neighbors. Stratagems for avoiding envy range from economic camouflage to hermitlike isolation. They can be roughly divided into five categories: concealment, denial, magical self-defense, aggressive counterattack, and appeasement.

The first principle of envy avoidance is to hide whatever may attract it. This is a universal phenomenon, well illustrated by illustrious singers such as the former Beatle Paul McCartney, certain German Mercedes owners, or poor and primitive Indians (the Siriono of Bolivia, for example).

Although said to be "as rich as Croesus," McCartney has a marked reluctance to talk about or display his wealth. When asked about money in an interview in the London *Evening Standard,* he commented:

> I try not to talk about it. It's a bit like discovering a gold mine at the bottom of your garden. It's embarrassing to talk about, and there's always the fear that if you do, everyone else will want to take it off you.[64]

In Germany the very rich and powerful have taken to removing from the left corner of the rear of their Mercedes the chrome numbers that indicate they are top of the line, the most powerful and expensive models. The car has become a symbol within the country of overdoing it and its owners and occupants a target for antagonism and terrorism. Driving the more economical diesel and four-cylinder models is a form of self-protection and fits in with the old Prussian dictum *Mehr sein als schein*—"Be more, seem less."[65]

The Siriono, a tribe organized in subunits of fifteen to twenty-five people, leads a meager existence. Individual members generally eat alone and at night, because they do not wish to share food with others, even close relatives. The Indians hoard food while constantly accusing each other of stealing it. Not only do the men hide anything edible, but the women tend to conceal bits of meat in their vagina rather than allow others to have access to it.[66] These actions are not so dissimilar from those of McCartney, wealthy Mercedes owners, and others who fear the evil eye. If a Siriono does eat during the day, he tends to collect a small crowd that stares at him enviously. Celebrities like the Beatles also collect crowds that stare, both in wonder and anger.[67]

Conformity is a further way of avoiding recognition and hostility for having or doing anything outstanding. It is a capitulation to the fear of being successful, which may be fed by strong social as well as internal pressures. Sociologists have long noted, and sometimes ridiculed, the yearning for adjustment, acceptance, and popularity in America. But conformism is hardly lacking in other countries or cultures.[68]

In order to appreciate why people conform, it is useful to consider what happens when they don't. In ancient Greece the penalty for unacceptable wealth or excellence was ostracism or death.[69] The philosopher Socrates was the most notable victim of the "slander and envy of the many."[70] He was forced to drink poison.

Nowadays someone who works too hard or goes against the norm may be "sent to Coventry."[71] Yet not long ago, Dr. Lester Summerfield, a dentist in practice in Coventry, had to leave the city because he had been working too hard and making too much money. He was reprimanded and fined by the Coventry Family Practitioner Committee and the Dental Estimates Board after the board noted that his practice had grossed over one million pounds in a ten-year period.

Dr. Summerfield decided to dissolve the practice and return to his native New Zealand because he could not stand "all the hassle." While this was happening, the secretary of the local dental committee admitted that other dentists were envious of Summerfield's capacity for work, although his patients were very happy.

> He ran foul of the system on the clinical side, although there is no case where any of his patients complained, and neither was he struck off the register.
> The local branch of the committee did not like the way the dental estimates board allowed the situation to develop. The board wanted to know why he was doing so much work.[72]

Bureaucratic hassle was his punishment for hard work and success, a contemporary version of divine retribution (*phthonos theon*). To avoid this Summerfield decided to inhibit what he could do and diminish what he could earn. This is another method of secreting wealth and talent from the evil eye.[73]

The inhibition and diminution of whatever may attract envy is consistent with injunctions against ostentation one finds in the sacred writings of many peoples. The Talmud, for example, limits the number of guests and number of courses at a wedding and the quality of garments worn in public. Not all Jews are so modest, but these rules are a reminder of the dangers of arousing envy, especially among gentiles.[74]

Modesty is an excellent character trait because it not only serves to defuse envy but also evokes praise in and of itself. By being modest, the person (who may or may not be aware of being envied) seemingly adheres to egalitarian ideals and puts others at ease. In common parlance, "Oh, it was nothing at all" or "It wasn't anything, really" are typical and expected responses to praise, awards, and achievements. The words reduce hostility.[75]

To be most effective modesty must appear spontaneous and unaffected. We ascribe false modesty to vain or pompous men who linger too long on their alleged humble origins. *The Washington Post* has coined the term "humble-origins chic" to describe the posturing that characterizes American politicians who "spend the first 40 years fighting their way out of borderline poverty and hardship and into country club posh, and the second 40 years bragging about how poor they used to be."[76]

More than modesty, many people actively deny what they have or could do. Such denial ominously expands the art of secreting resources, for the envied object, whether an individual or nation, conceals things not only from others, but also from himself. One can see this process at work with people who never mention good news or, if they do, always couple it with worse news. Thus any hint of prosperity, a new house, a new job, will be accompanied by a litany of imminent disasters, an ulcer, a heart attack, and so on. In a similar vein world figures, such as the secretaries general of the United Nations, and other representatives of international agencies have an ominous tendency to diminish or deny good news (for example, the effectiveness of international aid programs) and exaggerate the bad.[77]

The consequences of such distortions of reality include a rise in international tensions and a collective helplessness and hopelessness. Thus this very defense against envy can aggravate the envy it seeks to avoid. The same cycle happens with individuals who, in order not to be envied, convince themselves that they are worse off than they are. They continue to be hated because others still see them as they are. At the same time these people may themselves be consumed with hatred (envy the enviers) because they imagine that those who envy them are really much better off.

Denial as a defense against envy proceeds from a simple self-diminishing to a deeper self-effacement and delusional sense of inferiority.[78] The English anthropologist Edmund Leach sees all these processes at work in "the contemporary British peculiarity of pretending to be poor, ill, and already in trouble." Leach observes that over and over business and government circles have moaned about the state of the economy, blaming one disaster after another on the "Gnomes of Zurich or the bankers of Wall Street," only to repeatedly discover that the country has been much more prosperous than it appeared:

> The implication . . . the English economic sickness is largely a response to fear of the envy of others: we have developed a sense of guilt about our power and affluence, and are taking it out on ourselves.[79]

If self-deprecation isn't enough to divert the envious eye, then the threatened person or nation may escalate its self-hatred by idealizing the envier. This commonly occurs when members of a victimized class or caste excessively and indiscriminately praise their persecutors. Indeed, whole countries may act in such a manner toward their regional or economic antagonists. In the end the envied "victims" may try to justify the malice of their tormentors and become like them, to others and to themselves, as when European countries ape the deprecations of Third World states at the UN.

The idealization of the envier coincides with a reversal of values whereby poverty, sickness, failure, and death are exalted and the pleasures and benefits of earthly existence are spurned. The envied person may literally isolate himself from friends and relatives and withdraw from all material pursuits. Deliberate impoverishment and asceticism complete the renunciation from anything that could give offense to others. Long ago Francis Bacon observed that such detailed attention to avoiding envy was not without its practical advantages, such as arousing pity. He averred: "Pity ever healeth envy."[80]

Pity, however, is not a satisfactory solution to envy, because in order to gain it, one has to maintain a facade of inferiority or live in an impoverished manner. Moreover, pity itself can be used for aggressive purposes, as I learned to my great discomfit while working with a man dying from cancer.[81]

Traditionally people have resorted to an array of extraordinary words, gestures, amulets, and talismans to protect themselves. These things interpose a magical, tangible barrier between the envied person and the envier. They operate by invoking a higher, greater, stronger, or better power that can divert, deflect, absorb, and thereby neutralize malicious looks and wishes.[82]

The Babylonians carved the names of gods on incantation tablets.[83] The Egyptians carried representations of the eyes of their gods. They even incised them on bodies for embalming. The eye of Horus (avenger of evil) was considered especially propitious, and in a complete or abbreviated form (the capital letter "R"), it was painted on buildings, ships, documents—anything important.[84] The popularity of this symbol persisted into modern times, when it was made part of the great seal of the United States. It appears on the back of every dollar bill.[85]

The Greeks carried replicas of the head of Medusa, basing their protection on the principle "Like cures like." This was also used by the Romans, but their most popular amulet (charm worn on the body) or talisman (similar to an amulet but displayed about the house) was a sculpture of a phallus, called a *fascinum*.[86] Roman infants received a coral phallus to use as a teething ring. As they grew older boys carried a small *fascinum* in a box around their necks. At puberty this was placed over the hearth. Large *fascina* also decorated houses and were carried in the street during festivals.[87]

These phallic figures served as lightning rods to divert the attention of the envier and deflect it away from the bearer or his home and family. Presumably the bigger and more elaborate or expensive the amulet, the greater its allure. The figurines also conveyed the message "I'm not afraid of you. I have greater strength and power than you. I defy you."[88]

With the onset of Christianity, the phallus was gradually replaced by the horns of animals or their lookalikes such as crescents, teeth, and horseshoes.[89] These amulets were supplemented by special words and gestures. In Italy the mere pronunciation of the word for horn, *corno*, has magical protective power.[90] Italians have also persevered with two gestures that are said to be highly effective against the evil eye. The first was called *manus obscenus* by the Romans and *mano fica* by their descendants. It consists of clenching the fist with the thumb thrust between the first and second fingers. The other is known as the *mano cornuta* and is achieved by enclosing the second and third fingers with the thumb and extending the first and fourth fingers of the hand. This gesture is known as "making the devil's horns." When directed against the envier the *mano fica* and the *mano cornuta* are not just defensive, but highly aggressive counterattacks.[91]

Aggressive countermeasures may be expressed magically or non-magically. They are part of a strategy of striking first and immobilizing the envier before he can hurt you. The ancients, for example, relied on the head of Medusa not merely to avert the evil eye, but to paralyze it with fear and turn it to stone. Spitting three times in the presence of a stranger is another ritual that continues to be practiced.[92] It is a defensive maneuver with offensive intentions. Many sayings are purely offensive:

> Stomachache for a long night. (Morocco)
> The curse be upon thine eye. (Ireland)
> Ill on your eye, bird shit on the back of that. (Scottish Highlands)[93]

These words aim to incapacitate the envier. I wonder whether the common toast "Here's mud in your eye" serves the same purpose.

George Foster has pointed out the dangers implicit in apparently innocuous bantering and compliments. Depending on the context, compliments may double as put-downs or as a hostile overinflation of pride in order to deny a feared rival a reason for envy (blind him to what you have) and provoke his downfall.[94] Alternatively, the envied person may flaunt his wealth and adopt a lofty superiority— a "superiority complex"—in the hope of becoming so far above everyone else that no one would dare to envy him.

If an individual, however, cannot destroy or immobilize his enviers, at least he can put them off their guard and mollify them. Aside from direct counterattacks, most of the measures I have described serve this purpose, to placate or appease those who overlook with anger. Self-diminution, self-deprecation, and self-denial are all covert means of appeasement. They seek to change the relative balance of power, pride, and possessions so that the envier can have a false sense of being bigger, stronger, and more important than he is.

Overt appeasement is equally pervasive, often taking the form of carefully controlled, culturally sanctioned expressions of hostility (by the envier) and self-abasement (by the envied). Among the Hottentot people of South-West Africa a successful hunter literally allows his fellow tribesmen to piss on him. If he has killed a lion, an elephant, or a rhinoceros, the heroic deed will be celebrated in the most dramatic fashion. The hunter has to stay in his hut until an elder invites him to come to the center of the village. Meanwhile all the men will have gathered around in order to do him honor:

> The hero now crouches down on a mat, and all the men squat down around him in a circle. The old man goes up to him and

urinates all over him from head to toe. If he is a good friend of the hero, he will deluge him with urine.[95]

Lest we titter with laughter, it is worth considering modern parents who tolerate and encourage the rebellious and delinquent acts of their children (which spoil the family honor) or international forums where small countries are permitted to hurl abuse (a verbal deluge) at bigger or more sophisticated ones. The Hottentots might find these events equally outrageous.

Sop behavior avoids the necessity of allowing the envier to vent steam. The sop is a small present, token of goodwill, or word of praise given in hope of soaking up envious resentment. It can be thought of as the loser's compensation, a symbolic sharing of good fortune. Really it is a bribe, a device to buy off envy by appealing to greed (for self-esteem or goods).[96]

The giving of sops is such a pervasive practice that one rarely thinks of it as a bribe, just as something that is done. The favors provided at the end of a child's birthday party are typical examples. Although the gifts may be a further expression of generosity on the part of the host, are they really necessary?[97] After all, the children have been fed and entertained, usually at great expense and effort. But they have not been the center of attention, nor have they received the vast array of gifts offered the birthday child. They share a position akin to Ivan Babichev when confronted by the "queen of the ball." Anyone who has seen the wretchedness and barely concealed rage in the brother or sister of the birthday child, or the distress of a young guest who did not receive a going-home present, would immediately understand this. The children need a sop to make them feel better.[98]

Perhaps the most ubiquitous sops center around death and burial beliefs designed to diminish the envy of the bereaved and of the dead themselves. Although the food given to a bereaved family by friends and relatives is an expression of sympathy and kindness, it is also a means of assuring goodwill and warding off misfortune. Similarly, the annual visits to the grave and other propitiatory rites serve to assure the dead that their descendants still think of them and wish them well (so that they won't come back and haunt them).[99] Foster believes that even these practices do not suffice. He speculates that the Judeo-Christian and Moslem concept of heaven is "basically a device invented to allay fear of the envy of the departed." Therefore "heaven" is sop behavior at its most imaginative. After all, what better means to ease the envy of the dead than to provide a celestial abode far more splendid than whatever has been left behind? Moreover, Foster muses that in societies riddled with great disparities in wealth among different social classes, the expectation of a glorious afterlife has been the best way to reduce envy between classes and make life bearable for the poor and wretched:

> And it so turns the tables that the living envy the dead, placing the latter on the defensive. Life, with its sorrows and suffering, is but a brief prelude to the true substance of existence, where all are equal before God, so that death can be anticipated with equanimity, if not with outright joy.[100]

Sops do not have to be, nor are they always, deceptive concepts or token presents. They often signify a tangible sharing of wealth, a form of generosity or charity motivated by compassion and the wish to put things right. Yet such charity is never entirely beneficent. And when things are given compulsively, anxiously, and with contempt toward the recipient, it is safe to surmise that a fear of envy is a significant factor.[101]

True sops are a temporary expedient. They reduce and delay hostility but do not eliminate it. No matter how much the envied person gives up, no matter how much good he does, the envier will still believe that the gifts won't be missed and that the very act of giving is a sign of the other's superior character. No act of self-denial or self-abasement can make an envier happy. He will always insist that whatever people do, they are increasing their happiness, while he is left with bitterness and bile. For such a person, who denies or overlooks goodness in himself, the kindness and compassion of others are cruelties intended to torment and humiliate him, stimulants for hatred and malice, and calls to the evil eye.

This attitude, and the dynamic relationship between the envier and the envied, has been eloquently portrayed by the cartoonist Handelsman in his cartoon fable "The Story of the Envious Man and of Him Who Was Envied."[102] The story begins with a picture of two neighbors, a happy dervish who always does good and an envious one, steaming with resentment. As far as the latter is concerned, the good man can do nothing right. If he says, "Good morning," his malevolent counterpart inevitably replies, "Don't 'good morning' me, you sanctimonious swine! How come my roof leaks and yours doesn't?"

Eventually the good man moves away, having had his fill of neighborly hostility. Naturally everything he does works out well. News of this reaches the envious man, who feels tortured by it and decides to follow his former neighbor and throw him down a well. This happens, but he is saved by a benevolent spirit who also teaches him how to cure the misanthropic daughter of the sultan. Everyone is delighted, and he gets to marry the girl. The fable concludes:

IN TIME, THE DERVISH SUCCEEDED TO THE THRONE. HE THEN SENT FOR HIS FORMER NEIGHBOUR.

How come you're the Sultan and I'm not? Go ahead — have me killed.

Not at all, old friend!! I am going to give you a large sum of money.

You **are** a vindictive bastard.

MORAL: One must be kind in order to be cruel.

3

Envy Loveth Not:
The Influence and Confluence
of Envy and Narcissism

Envy is an inborn, destructive motivating force, opposed to love and antagonistic to life. Writing in *The Metaphysics of Morals* in 1797, Immanuel Kant had no qualms about describing envy as "the vice of human hate," a moral incongruity that delights in misfortune (*schadenfreude*) and ingratitude. He called envy a "hate that is the complete opposite of human love" and concluded:

> The impulse for envy is thus inherent in the nature of man, and only its manifestation makes of it an abominable vice, a passion not only distressing and tormenting to the subject, but intent on the destruction of happiness of others, and one that is opposed to man's duty towards himself as towards other people.[1]

Over a hundred years later Sigmund Freud also commented on a hatred that opposes love. This is a hatred that strikes out against "any source of unpleasurable feeling," including the absence of something needed, the presence of noxious sensations, and overexcitement—an intolerable inner tension associated with the very things a person wants. Mere relief from this distress does not necessarily diminish the displeasure. On the contrary, it can remain as a pas-

57

sionate hostility toward any stimulation, even rooted in desire, that has become too painful to bear. Freud said this was a hatred "older than love."[2] His description fits a rudimentary envy that averts love and transforms intense interest and excited desire (fascination) into malevolence.

Many physical and psychic activities arouse desire and displeasure from birth. Newborn babies ingest, inhale, take in all that they need and want. Similarly they evacuate, expel, put out whatever they don't need and dislike. The psychic equivalent of taking in is introjection and of putting out is projection. Both the physical and psychic processes are means by which they interact with the world—everything going on in and around themselves.[3]

Infants tend to use these mechanisms in a straightforward way to enhance pleasure and diminish pain. But they may not. Instead they have an inherent tendency to get angry at the very existence of pain in themselves and thrust it outside themselves with a vengeance in order to spoil and devastate a world that (from their point of view) caused them to feel so bad in the first place. Vengeful evacuation and malicious projection provide an operational definition of envy.

At first Freud believed that angry attacks on the world were secondary to what he called "Eros," or the life instinct. Later he concluded that destructive forces were equal in importance and power to life-enhancing ones, and that the life instinct, Eros, was opposed by a death instinct, "Thanatos."[4] This view was strongly supported by his colleague Melanie Klein. She wrote at length about the nature of envy and argued that envy is the earliest direct manifestation or externalization of the death instinct.[5]

The concept of a death instinct is not easy to accept, not the least on ethical grounds. To many, death instinct seems ominously close to original sin. I think the duality, life–death, can best be understood as a struggle between forces aiming at growth, order, integration, and structure—an upward energy flow—and forces leading to contraction, disorder, fragmentation, and chaos—a downward spiral.[6] Conception is a psychobiological impetus to structure that draws upon all the possibilities of the genetic code and the energies that flow from the mother's body to combat a return to randomness— physical and psychic entropy. Life instinct implies the former, death instinct the latter. In fact, "impulse" is a much better term than "instinct," for it denotes an impelling force rather than an unalterable one.[7]

What Freud termed "pleasure" has to do with integration and

structure. The attendant feeling is love. "Displeasure" has to do with fragmentation and chaos. The attendant feeling is hatred. The primitive human being (fetus, neonate, infant) radiates displeasure in order to get rid of whatever opposes structure—that is, the creation of himself. This happens as a matter of course, such as when the infant evacuates urine, feces, or wind. It can also happen willfully when, during the course of development, the new being feels displeasure—gets upset and angry—and attacks—actively extends disorder at whatever has or seems to have hurt or threatened him. This rage is as likely to be directed at his own dissociated chaos and confusion—remnants of himself, in himself, as his environment—the womb, mother, father, or others.[8] The passive projection of chaos and confusion is not envy. The active, willful, vengeful evacuation of displeasure is.

There exists considerable controversy among psychoanalysts about whether envy is a primary aggressive impulse or not. Some believe that envy is a later derivative of character traits, interests, and attitudes "which only achieved their final, quasi-permanent, status towards the end of psycho-sexual development."[9] Others see it as a "secondary motivating force which may have positive and adaptive consequences in on-going development, or may lead to malignant pathology."[10] Both viewpoints treat envy purely as a reactive event. They also give it a libidinal component that envy intrinsically does not have but often appears to have, because it occurs simultaneously with love, or is fused with it, as in grenvy. Yet as early as 1915, Freud commented:

> So we see that love and hate, which present themselves to us as complete opposites in their content, do not after all stand in any simple relation to each other. They did not arise from the cleavage of any originally common entity, but sprang from different sources, and had each its own development before the influence of the pleasure-unpleasure relation made them into opposites.[11]

Regardless of this statement and Freud's later writings on the death instinct, the early analysts were reluctant to grant a central place to aggression or envy in analytic theory. One reason was that libidinal energies were assumed to originate in somatic sources (the erotogenic zones: mouth, anus, and genitals), while destructive ones did not.[12] In other words, Eros seemed to have a physiological and psychological basis, while Thanatos had only a psychological one. However, this distinction does not hold if, instead of focusing on body parts, one thinks of body processes. Then libido has to do with taking in and building up (eating, drinking, and introjection). Aggression has to do with putting out and breaking down (urinating, defecating, and projection). Clearly libidinal and aggressive impulses are rooted in the soma and psyche.[13] Using projective processes for chaotic purposes, envy is a partial expression of the delicate interplay between life-sustaining and life-ruining tendencies. The latter is obviously physical when the envier, not necessarily a child, spews forth piss and shit, spit and farts, to soil and spoil the envied object. The psychological equivalent can be found in separate, or concomitant, penetrating "poisoned rays, venomous looks, angry atoms, malign spirits, malicious defluxions and streams, irradiations and ejaculations"—the evil eye.

Still, many theorists believe that envy is too sophisticated a state of mind and pattern of behavior to exist at birth, and that the cognitive skills and sensitivity to relationships that I have described (such as in malicious comparison) only develop in the second or third year of life. From this point of view envy would have to be a later derivative because the infant does not have sufficient ego strength to be envious. Recent studies of neonates demonstrate that this is not the case. They are enormously sensitive not just to physical stimuli, but to human relationships, and can respond according to what they see and feel. Obviously these capabilities expand as the infant grows older, but sufficient evidence does exist to confirm a potentiality for envious attack from birth.[14]

While malicious aggression is the active component of envy, not all aggression is malicious. Forceful, attacking behavior may be constructively self-assertive and self-protective or destructively hostile to oneself or others. Whether aggression is constructive or destructive depends on context, motivation, and feeling. It also depends on the creature who is being aggressive. All animals act in ways that are clearly self-assertive or defensive. They want food, sex, and security.

Some zoologists and ethologists have considered territoriality or rank fighting (farmyard pecking order) to be examples of quasi-envious behavior.[15] There is not a lot of evidence that these activities fit the essential criteria of envy: despair at others' advantages; spiteful rage; and destructive attacks without procuring any advantage or material gain. Jealousy, however, is no stranger to the animal kingdom. When two male hippopotami fight over a female, the battle is not a ritual. Each is trying to destroy the other as viciously as possible, a phenomenon readily seen with other species. And jealousy aside, field-workers have noted that animals as different as orangutans and elephant seals commonly engage in gratuitous violence, often committing gang rapes and killing the females without reason.[16]

Still, envious anger is different from that aroused by frustration, revenge, rivalry, or indignation. The latter presuppose actual hurt, deprivation, or injury and are assuaged when the cause of the hostility is overcome or removed. Envy lingers on even after a frustration has been overcome, a specific hurt repaid, a rival removed, or an injustice made right. Envy may be associated with real events, but it is more than a reaction to them. *Envy is both the tension and the hostile reaction to this tension in the envier, a tension that is not dependent on, or necessarily related to, anything actually happening.* Quite the contrary, the preverbal state of unpleasure is highly sensitive to mental activity, especially perception and the power of the imagination. Aeschylus conveyed the envious state of mind through the voice of Agamemnon after he returned from Troy:

> *For not many men, the proverb saith,*
> *Can love a friend who fortune prospereth*
> *Unenvying; and about the envious brain*
> *Cold poison clings and doubles all the pain*
> *Life brings him. His own woundings he must nurse,*
> *And feels another's gladness like a curse.*[17]

Envious tension is aroused by the awareness of vitality and prosperity, indeed by life itself. Although there is no specific word in English to denote such tension, the Czech word *"litost"* comes close. According to the writer Milan Kundera, *litost* denotes a gnawing sense of inner torment when faced by another's greater skills or accomplishments, followed by the desire for revenge.[18] Kundera describes a young man out for a swim with his girlfriend. He is a beginner, she is an expert. Realizing his potential discomfort, she tries to keep to his pace but at the end gives her sporting instincts free rein and sprints ahead. He tries to keep up but can't. Quick as a flash:

> He felt humiliated, exposed for the weakling he was; he felt resentment, the special sorrow which can only be called *litost.*[19]

Like envy, *litost* is too painful to bear and too shameful to reveal. In this instance the swimmer slapped his girlfriend but couldn't admit his true motivation. Passionate hypocrisy (he claimed he was worried she might drown) protected a sudden insight into his own miserable self and the accompanying murderous response.[20] In most situations the envier aims to eliminate the torment in himself by forceful, attacking, annihilative behavior. This discharge, directed against the alleged source of the envy, constitutes a means of self-protection as well as other-destruction. Therefore envy can be seen as a mechanism of defense at the service of the death impulse. It is opposed, mitigated, but never entirely vanquished by the opposite impulse associated with love. This view is consistent with Freud's theories of the life and death impulses and the pleasure principle.[21] Life energies, or libido, promote pleasure when a person achieves growth, integration, and structure. Pain is the result of the inability to achieve life needs (that is, reduce libidinal pressures). It also results from breakdown, chaos, and disorder.[22]

The energies of the death impulse, akin to envious tension, continually resist libidinal (life) fulfillment. This is the action of entropy on the organism, whereby pleasure consists of a return to randomness. Conversely, pain lies in structure, order, and growth.[23] The two sets of tensions and tendencies are inborn. They can never be resolved, but both contribute to the richness, variety, and complexity of existence.

Although I have said that envy is an inborn force, and have been critical of those who view it as a purely reactive phenomenon, it is more accurate to conclude that envy is both inherent and reactive. The tendency toward damaging, destructive wishes and behavior is rooted in the very physical and mental makeup of a person. But what eventually transpires is a reaction to the internal tension aroused by actual or imagined events. How strong the tension will be, and how severe the response, depends on the particular envier. It also depends on the relative gradient of vitality, structure, and plain good fortune between what the envier receives and how he perceives or experiences things in himself. Envy is not just a curse, but a consequence of consciousness.

If this is so, then one would expect envy to be a universal phenomenon. As far as one can tell, it is. The German sociologist Helmut Schoeck has pointed out that almost all cultures have a word for envy or the equivalent state of mind, although they may lack such basic concepts as hope, love, and justice:

> Virtually all people, including the most primitive, have found
> it necessary to define the state of mind of a person who cannot

bear someone else's being something, having a skill, possessing something or enjoying a reputation which he himself lacks, and who will therefore rejoice should the other lose his asset, although that loss will not mean his own gain.[24]

On the other hand, not all societies are like ancient Greece or Renaissance Italy, where envy was accepted as a fact of life. People usually play down the contribution envy makes to their state of mind or social relations. They learn to keep the active expression of envy disguised and discrete, a collective practice that helps to avoid shameful guilt and retaliation.[25]

George Foster believes that it is almost impossible for the inhabitants of competitive contemporary Western societies like the United States to concede the fundamental importance of envy because of the comparative elements involved, which, when acknowledged, constantly threaten the envier with a massive loss of self-esteem:

> But in recognizing envy in himself, a person is acknowledging *inferiority with respect to another;* he measures himself against someone else, and finds himself wanting. It is, I think, this implied admission of inferiority, rather than the admission of envy, that is so difficult for us to accept.[26]

Perhaps the most dangerous aspect of envy is not envy itself, but the denial of it. Then the envious impulse cannot be modified by loving, reparative wishes. More likely the envier will use powerful projective processes—that is, the very mechanism of envy—to dissociate himself from a major part of himself, his own destructiveness. In these circumstances an individual may project a malign spirit, badness, not just to attack an envied object, but to get rid of an anguished and shameful side of himself, the side that had initiated the attack in the first place.

The consequence of such denial is a loss of self experienced as an increasing inner impoverishment. This loss stimulates murderous rage because the more impoverished the envier feels, the angrier he gets with others (with whom he compares himself) and the angrier he gets with himself (for hating and for feeling so empty). Moreover, the whole world (inner or outer reality) becomes full of dissociated destructiveness and appears to be a bad and threatening place. Hence envy gives a paranoid flavor to existence. Instead of desiring life, the envier comes to fear it.

Second, the excessive projection of envious rage leads to a disturbance in introjection. This too may become excessive, as the envier, trying desperately to compensate for his inner emptiness, savagely sucks, bites, and swallows whatever catches his eye. This explains why greed, destructive introjection, is often the companion of envy, destructive projection.[27]

Conversely, denied or unmodified envy (whether exceptionally strong from birth or aroused by hostile nurturing) can incite a harmful blockage of introjective processes. The envious child (or adult) may literally stop taking things in—food, words, ideas, stimuli. This frequently happens because the affected person believes that whatever he takes in will injure him.

An envy-induced negativity especially interferes with the capacity to receive and return love. This can have a disastrous effect on learning. Having stifled and denigrated goodness—that is, the awareness of lovable qualities in oneself or others—the individual may conclude that everything is "shit." In other words, ideas or knowledge (equal to envied food and feelings), as well as the relationships that provide them, are poisonous.[28] Many learning difficulties, whether in children or adults, follow when ridicule, rage, and fear, represented by a blank, impenetrable negativity, replace admiration and emulation. In addition, the envier may spitefully relinquish skills already learned.[29]

Psychotherapy is a learning relationship where the negative therapeutic reaction, or the inability of the patient to profit from and successfully conclude his treatment, is also connected with powerful but dissociated envious impulses.[30] In fact, these sticky bits of hostility have probably contributed to the emotional disorder in the first place. Melanie Klein emphasized that excessive envy, a hatred so strong that life-loving forces or "egoic" (rational) processes have not been able to counter it, is usually accompanied by equally excessive anxiety and guilt.[31] So not only learning may suffer. These feelings often prove the prelude to a psychotic breakdown.[32]

A paranoid orientation, a loss of self, learning difficulties, excessive greed—all follow in the footsteps of a defensive maneuver, projection, designed to evacuate envious anguish and anger elsewhere. The target may be the outer world, animate or inanimate, or it may be various aspects of one's self. Here the affected person or thing serves as a dustbin for painful, unwanted thoughts, feelings, or sensations. But the envier (the subject) allows the target (the envied object) to preserve its separate identity. Thus a son may bad-mouth his father in every way possible but still admit that "that shitty old man" is still his father. And "the old man" may still feel and behave like a father.

However, human or nonhuman "trash cans" rarely satisfy the spiteful person, who wants to do more then simply evacuate the contents of a hate-filled mind. Simultaneously and vengefully, the envier may seek to totally alter and rubbish the object, to destroy any goodness in it, and to control it so it can't fight back. In the example I have just cited, the boy can confer such an apparent power on his own words and actions, that when he looks at his father, he will literally see a piece of shit. And the father may forget who he is and be a shit.

Traditionally, the scapegoat, an animal or human figure invested with the badness of the community, involves similar intentions. In the last chapter I showed how Dr. Lester Summerfield became the scapegoat for the greed and envy of his fellow dentists. For them he was not only a greedy man, but the embodiment of greed itself. Interestingly, when the ancient Israelites did the same, they poured their sins into two goats, one to be killed and the other to be sent away or ostracized. In this way they tacitly recognized and preserved the shadier aspects of their lives.[33] Likewise the Coventry Family Practitioner Committee destroyed Summerfield's reputation but allowed him to leave. Their envy and greed remained intact, but far away, on the other side of the world.

Enviers use the psychological mechanism of projective identification to equate the scapegoat or "trash can" with its hated contents and to deny the original integrity and identity of the object. This is an offensive maneuver by which a person manipulates words, thoughts, actions, or moods to put himself, or a part of himself, into another (person, thing, mental representation) and to combine with it. Thus projective identification is both a perceptual transformation and interpersonal transaction.

From the standpoint of the subject (the envier), the envied person or thing no longer exists in its own right. The envier sees and believes that the person or thing is identical with what he has put into it or attributed to it (shit, urine, vomit, "angry particles," badness). From the standpoint of the object, the envied person may have an inexplicable sense of being or feeling different. Or he may not notice any change in himself but realize that the envier is seeing him and treating him in a peculiarly inappropriate manner. If the behavior strikes a certain chord, then slowly, involuntarily, the envied victim will begin to feel, think, and act as the envier sees him.

Projective identification is a form of analogue, as opposed to digital communication, which involves getting inside another and bringing about rather than describing experiences. It is not magic, but when done maliciously it can have a shattering effect on another's peace of mind. The quarry feels invaded and taken over by thoughts and wishes that he would normally reject. The experience is like being under attack from powerful, hostile forces that intend to drive you mad and destroy your mind, a view not far from the truth.

An unconscious appreciation of projective identification contributes to a fundamental fear of the *jettatura* and others possessed of the evil eye. The telltale glance of such an eye penetrates and fills you with malice. That is the result of projection and is bad enough. However, what strikes a note of absolute terror is the anticipation of being changed into something evil. As Francis Bacon put it:

> The ejaculation or irradiation [of the evil eye] emitteth some malign and poisonous spirit, which takes hold of the spirit of another.[34]

This process of taking hold of the spirit of another perfectly describes the action of projective identification and explains why, to the person so affected, envy is a disease, a terrible infection that can grab and subvert the soul.[35] John Aubrey, a collector of gossip and folklore who was born the same year Bacon died (1626), recorded a similar opinion in his *Miscellanies*:

> The glances of envy and malice do shoot subtilly: the eye of the malicious person does really infect and make sick the spirit of the other. [36]

Aubrey described the destructive side of projective phenomena, but I want to emphasize that projection and projective identification are normal and necessary intrapsychic and interpersonal mechanisms. Everyone employs them, for many reasons, including, for example, to form symbols and think symbolically and to establish and maintain close personal ties.[37] Envy is what gives these processes a pathological, if not deadly, significance, all the more so because they operate internally.[38] They directly affect the contents and structure of the mind and personality or, as Bacon observed, the spirit and the soul.

Up until now I have mostly emphasized external, tangible foci of hatred—fathers, therapists, successful professionals, and so forth. I have also pointed out that envious attacks do not take place just to rubbish these objects, but to evacuate and make them contain the tensions and hatreds that seem to be destroying the envier from within himself. However, all the transactions that take place between two separate people or objects can also occur within the envier himself— that is, within the boundaries of his own psychic world.

Projection and projective identification are activities that influence different parts of the self. These, of course, include phantasized or internal representations of actual relationships. Thus a person can indeed feel under attack because he is attacking the mental images of his own father or teacher or therapist.

However, a more ominous reaction occurs when, beset by envy, the envier tries to preserve himself from himself by splitting up and projectively identifying his spite and malice with and into parts of his own mind. Consequently the envier contains a multitude of envious others all threatening to attack him from within. These exist as split off and extremely hostile representations of his own envious self or of envious parents and parental substitutes.

The English psychoanalyst Hanna Segal has pointed out that envious internal figures contribute to the construction of and are comparable to what Freud called the "over-severe superego." On analysis it turns out that this superego is really an "envious superego," perhaps one of many envious bits created by internal projective processes. The ensuing (inner) attacks then center on

> not only the individual's [own] aggression [inner enviers] but also, and even predominantly, against the individual's progressive and creative capacities.[39]

In order to avoid such a psychic catastrophe, whereby a host of inner enviers assault each other, the afflicted person may utilize projective processes to deflect these enmities outward. The net effect is like picking out a pack of piranhas and throwing them into the air. Because of the action of projective identification, when these vicious little enviers land on something, and they always do, the envious person (fleeing from his own envious selves) inevitably converts elements of external reality (benign people, places, or things) into malevolent entities (witches, evil influences, bad omens). But instead of solving the problem, this maneuver compounds it, for the individual then feels threatened by malignity emanating from within himself and from without. Thus the envier becomes the envied, and the hunter becomes the hunted.

I have just been describing the creation of internal and external enviers (by splitting and by the subsequent projection of the split-up bits). Consequently one envier is usually many enviers, a bizarre configuration of malice that originates in one place but subsequently extends throughout one's internal and external perceptual worlds.

In yet another desperate attempt at self-protection, the envier, now a very envied figure as well, may try to deny and dissociate himself from whatever seems enviable and make others the envied object. This is a ruthless form of envy avoidance employed by people who shower undue praise on friends or bystanders in the secret hope that these others will be hated and they will be spared. No wonder excessive or undeserved compliments are generally unwelcome. They often denote insidious efforts to transform an ordinary person or thing into a focus of hatred.

Finally, the envious/envied person may idealize one part of himself in order to protect another. Just as his phantasy world can become full of wicked little enviers, it can also become full of hated images, ideas, or qualities. These are the equivalent of a host of envied objects. It takes a lot of work to hide these things, which, as Hanna Segal pointed out, may be aspects of one's own creative capacities, from one's own ill will. This is especially true when the malice appears in the form of an "over-severe superego" or other angry, alien figures. The ensuing game of cat and mouse with oneself can only lead to further fragmentation, confusion, and chaos. Hence the counterparts of multiple internal and external attackers (envious subjects) are multiple internal and external foci of attack (envied objects). They survive as inner nightmares or, because of projective identification, outer terrors.

The Canadian psychoanalyst W. Clifford Scott has described several patients whose lives were crippled by envious conflict with and within themselves. One was a doctor who suffered debilitating self-criticism and somatic symptoms just when his career was beginning to flourish. It transpired that one part of him felt weak and inadequate and was identified with a small, resentful child. Inwardly this child hated and was determined to sabotage the efforts of his capable side, identified with a strong adult. In fact, the attacks on himself, by himself, and in himself, were a replay of the envy he had felt, but rarely acknowledged, toward his father.[40]

Another patient was a businessman who had been thinking of embarking on a new, ambitious venture. However, after a brief period of deliberation, he decided that the project was too big and dropped it. In his therapy sessions the man mentioned that his work had taken on a dreamlike quality and that he was envious of people who could carry off big projects. During this time, Scott noticed that the person had found it very hard to dream. Those he did have were short, unproductive, and quickly forgotten. Scott interpreted that the proposed new venture was "the stuff as dreams are made on." It had become the focus of the same passionate hostilities that were otherwise directed toward his dream world. This was a man whose waking self tended to paralyze and spoil both his dreams and explicit hopes and aspirations.[41]

It is also possible to be very envious and jealous within a dream. A singer I see in therapy turned up one morning very despondent and full of self-hate. She had just woken up from a dream in which a young man, a pianist, had been talking to her about himself at a party. He came from a wealthy family, had been living in London for several years, and was in therapy. This treatment had been and continued to be very helpful. My patient immediately related the person to a pianist she had met the night before. Like her, he was just starting his career and already had had some success. He too went to a therapist and taught at a school not far from my consulting rooms. In telling me about him, she became aware of intense jealousy and envy, jealousy because she assumed that he was a patient of mine and envy because he was doing well and was better able to afford psychotherapy.[42] I related this experience to her dream and pointed out that the self-hatred she had suffered upon awakening was equivalent to the rage she harbored toward the pianist in her waking and dream life. She feared he would replace her in my affections. But this woman also identified with the dream figure who embodied her achievements and ambition. Like Scott's patient, her self-hatred represented malign anger by one part of herself, which felt small, weak, and helpless toward another, which was strong, capable, and becoming increasingly successful.

Although it is tempting to describe the singer, the businessman, and the doctor as victims of their own passions, to do so would be a gross distortion and oversimplification of their relationship with themselves and others. All three were the subject and object of envy.

The doctor's dilemma clearly illustrates this situation. In phantasy he was the aggressor who attacked his own capabilities as well as the aggressed, a victim of entrenched images of critical parents who could never be pleased. In actuality he was vaguely aware of a deep-seated enmity toward his father and feared, with some reason, reciprocal resentments toward his own growing accomplishments. So from his point of view, and ours, he was both envier and envied, the subject and object of relationships that crossed the boundaries between conscious and unconscious life.

The businessman and the singer demonstrated similar patterns, although with them it was less clear that they were actually envied. No doubt further associations would have revealed that the businessman faced real rivals, and I know that my patient is extremely sensitive to others' hostility toward her voice.

Multiple divisions between envier and envied exist in and between all people. They occur because of the pervasive use of projective and introjective mechanisms of defense and attack in intrapsychic and interpersonal relations. These splits are normal and natural and mean that we are all the subject and object of our own malice, aside from anyone else's. Although they extend across personal and social boundaries, at any given moment one pattern may predominate.

Significantly, whichever predominates, the outcome may be similar. There exist many points of confluence between the experience of the envier and the envied, each of which links the two sides and demonstrates that the perception, feelings, and action of the envied person are part of the structure of envy as a state of mind, as a feeling, as an impelling force.

Both the envious person and the envied feel aggrieved and resentful. Aggressively, if not obsessively, they wish to strike back, denigrate, and destroy the real or alleged cause of their distress, but for different reasons.

The envier is extremely sensitive to gnawing, tormenting displeasure, envious tension in himself. He tries to prevent it from happening by annihilating whatever arouses it. The impetus is a feared inferiority associated with a sense of unjust deprivation.

The envied person is equally sensitive to and tormented by envious displeasure, but he experiences it as coming from outside himself. He aims to protect himself from this displeasure and anticipated anger by attacking the attackers (evil eyes, witches, over-severe superegos) before they can get him. Aggressive countermeasures are common alternatives to defensive withdrawal, appeasement, or self-effacement. The impetus is a feared superiority associated with a sense of unjust criticism.

Certainly the envious person looks upon his envied counterpart with loathing and dread, as does the envied victim to his envier, both within the psychic domain and without. Paradoxically these dreaded objects can also exert an almost irresistible fascination for each other, a phenomenon that demonstrates the narcissistic character of the relationship between the envier and envied. They are often aspects of the same person.

Narcissism is a state of self-preoccupation. Originally applied to a consuming self-love, the concept has expanded to include any exclusive interest in and with oneself, especially as experienced in and through others. A narcissistic relationship is based on the prevailing use of primitive projective mechanisms as, for example, in envy. Hence the envious person, in defending himself against envious tension, can easily lock himself into a narrow, self-centered existence. Many enviers prefer to focus on their own image of the envied object, no matter how painful or distorted, than take the chance of discovering someone or something in its own right. After all, the object might be better than imagined, or worse, and leave them feeling foolish.

Envy and narcissism are variations of the same problem—excessive mental pain, consciously perceived as overweening inferiority and inadequacy. To begin, the envious and the narcissistic person attack this problem differently, the envier by deflating others, the narcissist by inflating himself, but their thinking, feelings, and actions run along convergent tracks.[43]

In considering narcissism, I refer to a perverted or pathological self-absorption and pride that interferes with or precludes relations with others, not a normal or healthy self-esteem that is the prelude to mutual respect and reciprocal exchange.[44] The narcissist has little or no self-esteem. On the contrary, he maintains a grandiose overestimation of his capacities and virtues, which he has built as a barrier against the underlying belief that he is unworthy and unimportant.

Like the envier, the narcissist looks upon others with an eye that puffs them up and squashes them flat as soon as he perceives qualities or features better than his own. But the extremes of idealization and denigration do not only serve malicious comparison. This person actively searches for an ideal version of himself in others in order to enhance his self-importance. As in envy, his perceptions fuel projections, little bits of charm designed to capture attention, evoke adoration, and promote identification of another man or woman with himself.[45] The "poisoned arrows" are reserved for those who don't suit this purpose or resist it. Then narcissistic interest turns into envious hatred.

For such an individual, even a hint that he or his partner is not totally admirable and desirable is a blow that wounds his pride and inflicts severe psychic pain.[46] Such blows may call forth even greater degrees of self-inflation, often in the form of arrogance and inordinate vanity.

Hanna Segal recounts a scientist who was threatened by a single critical comment.[47] One day he dreamed that he was walking in London with a dinosaur. The beast was very hungry. The man had to keep on feeding it or disaster would strike. It transpired that the dinosaur represented his vanity and the disaster a suicidal depression. The vanity maintained a fragile egotism and protected him from gnawing self-doubts. It allowed him to feel intellectually superior by making everyone else appear (and sometimes feel like) useless mental midgets. This state was both a defense against and expression of the envious hatred this man directed toward his colleagues. But there was a price to pay. The vanity had a huge appetite. If he didn't feed it, he soon saw that his colleagues were actually creative and that his own research was less than first rank. Yet when he did feed it, the ensuing insolence aroused the hostility of the very people he valued and spoiled his work.[48]

An aggressive narcissism is identical with envious self-assertion.[49] As we can see from the dilemma posed by the scientist's vanity, it can be life-threatening for the subject as well as his object. This view is found time and time again in classical mythology: vanity and hubris, indeed, any unjustified assertion of self that breaks the natural order of things calls forth retribution. The tragedy of Agamemnon illustrates this dimension of divine revenge. *Phthonos theon* meant not just envy of the gods, but the inevitable downfall that follows the arrogant overstepping of bounds, as happened to a king who believed that wounded pride (the abduction of his sister-in-law, Helen) allowed him to abandon his family, sacrifice his daughter (Iphigenia), and destroy a mighty civilization (Troy).

Throughout this century the sudden and unexpected death and humiliation of public figures who have flaunted their fame, wealth, beauty, or power has carried the same impact as a Greek legend.[50] In America Lee Harvey Oswald, Sirhan Sirhan, and Mark Chapman were drawn, like the Furies, to John Kennedy, Robert Kennedy, and John Lennon, famous men who epitomized many of the fatal contradictions of their age.[51] They preached tolerance and strength but remained aloof, haughty, and in many respects weak. They advocated humility but lived ostentatiously and had a genius for publicity and self-aggrandizement. And as politicians and superstars they championed the masses and evoked wild enthusiasms. Yet in comparison with them, and by the standards of the mass media, these men could hardly fail to leave deep wounds in the many citizens who consider themselves nonentities and try to make up for their failings by insisting that popular figures are extensions of themselves.[52]

My sketch illustrates an important aspect of the complicated relationship between famous people and their public, that of narcissistic arousal, infatuation, and betrayal.[53] On a macrosocial scale these transactions reflect and are reflections of countless small family dramas in which superficially competent but chronically cold, indifferent, or spitefully assertive parents keep their offspring in constantly devalued positions vis-à-vis themselves. From the child's point of view, their parents or parental equivalents (authority figures) are people who substitute style for substance, demand love and respect, but remain unwilling or unable to cope with real needs or feelings. The recipients of such treatment regularly reciprocate in kind but still remain frustrated and vengeful.

Narcissism begets envy. For this reason world-destroying rage can follow deprivation or gratification. A deprived child, for example, suffers not only from a lack of food, love, or warmth, but also from attendant phantasies that the depriving person has deliberately withheld these things and kept them for himself. Otherwise, he ponders, why aren't they (the tension reducers) right there when he wants them? Good care alleviates the doubts and subsequent pain and anger. However, the bad feelings may be made much worse by narcissistic parents who "see" their appetites in their children and treat them in ways that are excitingly frustrating. Inevitably the tantalized infant (or child or adult) becomes suffused with desires that cannot be contained and have to be denied in order to prevent a state of utter confusion and fragmentation.

The denial of desire or libidinal needs and feelings creates conditions akin to an upsurge of envious displeasure. In order to avoid this, the persistent but hidden hungers tend to be evacuated into the parents, an act that reinforces perceptions of them as greedy, selfish, and self-satisfying. These images combine appropriate fears and projected impulses. They lead to even more hatred because the afflicted person feels completely powerless to get what he needs or to prevent others from robbing him of the little he has.[54]

On the other hand, gratification does not necessarily lead to satisfaction. Whatever his parents give him, the infant may conclude that he will never be as good as they are or have as much as they have. It's always "You're ripe, I'm rotten." Again, this point of view can be modified by satisfying experiences. But it can also be made more poignant and bitter by relationships with people who do not give generously and altruistically. On the contrary, if they give at all, it is to prove their superiority and omnipotence. This leaves the child feeling small, helpless, unworthy, insignificant, and unimportant, while his parents or (parental) institution bask in malign, ill-deserved pride.

Attacks on the self lead to painful inner states that have been variously described as narcissistic wounds, injuries, or losses. The quality of hurt is equivalent to envious tension and seeks discharge by omnipotent self-inflation and other-denigration. This situation predominates in families where the parents or children are severely self-preoccupied and encourages a continuing narcissistic vulnerability whereby the developing child, and later adult, remains exquisitely sensitive to actual or imagined infringements of his self-esteem.

Cold, aloof, spiteful parents do not cause envy. The tendency to death and disorder precedes them. What they do is stimulate destructive impulses that might otherwise be neutralized by kindness and compassion. Therefore a relationship that should be a model for nascent psychic integration actually interferes with it and perpetuates a state of war between the forces of life and death. An aggressively narcissistic child with adequate parenting often reaches a similar impasse.[55] In either case the child may retreat into a cocoon of grandiosity and omnipotence.[56]

The omnipotence represents a false solution to a fundamental problem—how to preserve life and love from the forces of destruction, one's own and that of others. In a child or adult who is consumed with narcissistic pain, omnipotence becomes identical with goodness. Any omnipotence will do, whether creative or destructive, libidinal or antilibidinal. The person postulates that he is the source of all life and goodness. Everything beautiful and valuable is either part of him or controlled by him. Or he is Satan, the source of all evil and death, the center of the universe.

In these circumstances anything that challenges this preeminent view of reality, whether the discovery of otherness or the theories of a Galileo, comes as an intolerable deflation. It confronts the affected party (individual or institution) with an awareness of its own limitations and conjures forth a murderous rage that competes in intensity and intention with malicious anger.[57] Although often called "narcissistic rage," these destructive wishes are not an expression of narcissism. Rather, they are an expression of the failure of narcissism, the failure of a particular strategy to protect against inadequate self-esteem or excessive hate. Hence narcissistic rage represents a reversion to a primitive envious state of mind following a "flaw in narcissistically perceived reality."[58]

For Salieri this flaw, essentially an affront to his omnipotence, was the realization that the divine spark resided in Mozart and that the opera world comprised more than his own talent or conceit. With Ivan Babichev the shock came at a party when he took a backseat to a pretty twelve-year-old "Queen of the Ball." Babichev became enraged when he saw that the girl existed in her own right, not as an extension of himself.

Othello suffered a similar fate because false pride perverted his judgment and allowed Iago to play on his perceptions. He loved Desdemona as long as she appeared pure, loyal, white, and beautiful, which was how he needed to see himself. When Iago turned her "virtue into pitch," she became as black to Othello as he was to himself. Self-hatred prevailed, and he replied with self-righteous abandon toward a version of himself he couldn't condone.

Many folktales, plays, and novels celebrate the moment when narcissistic reality becomes untenable. None are more striking than the story of Snow-White.[59] It is about a princess raised in the household of a vain, self-centered stepmother. This woman, the queen, cannot bear anyone to be more beautiful. She owns a magic mirror and frequently asks it:

> Mirror, mirror on the wall,
> Who is the fairest of us all?

The mirror always asserts:

> My lady queen is the fairest of all.[60]

Meanwhile Snow-White has been growing up and has become "as lovely as the bright day and more beautiful even than the queen." One day the mirror gives a new answer to the oft repeated question:

> My lady queen is fair to see,
> But Snow-White is fairer far than she.[61]

The reply shatters a fragile preeminence. The queen is horrified. We can only presume that all her fears about being an undesirable, second-rate wife, mother, and sovereign come to the fore.

At this the queen took fright and turned yellow and green
with envy. From now on, whenever she saw Snow-White, her
heart turned over inside her, she hated the girl so. And envy
and pride took root like weeds in her heart and grew higher
and higher, giving her no peace by day or night. So she sent for
a huntsman and said: "Take that child out into the forest, I'm
sick of the sight of her. You are to kill her and bring me her
lungs and liver as proof.[62]

The Brothers Grimm vividly narrated the relationship between
narcissistic failure and envy. In this instance the awareness of another's beauty provokes a storm of malice. The queen is no longer
concerned with inflating herself. She aims to wreak revenge on a
figure who has dared disturb, however unwittingly, her lofty reveries.
She launches her attack on the actual person, any reflection of that
person, and her perception of the reflection. In the Grimm tale the
queen spares the magic mirror, representing reality. In other versions
of the story she smashes the mirror as well.[63]

Rage, fueled by an envious narcissism, does not stop at destroying
the object. It aims to eradicate any vestige of attachment in the
subject, any remnant of love, need, or longing, such as between a
mother and child or husband and wife. Any loss of pride or self-
esteem may herald the onset of a major internal battle (aside from
an external one), whereby the forces of disorder, fragmentation, and
chaos overwhelm those of order, integration, and structure. Initially
there may be a period of psychic contraction, a withdrawal from
relationships and dedifferentiation of self (regression), but the conflict
often leads to a near total cessation of feeling, thought, and perception
and can culminate in suicide. The wish is to return to an inanimate,
intrauterine existence so that all tension and excitation vanish.

Freud described this phenomenon under the rubric of the nirvana
principle.[64] It signals the point at which envy and narcissism converge,
when an adult or child who has been stripped of his illusions and is
unable to hide from an intolerable reality yields to the forces of
destruction. Then an angry state of mind reverts to an envious state
of being and pleasure in death (auto-annihilation) supersedes pleasure
in life. In gestures that are both defiant and defensive, the distraught
person demonstrates the links between ostensibly different but complementary strategies for warding off mental pain. Simultaneously
he inflates himself by assuming a posture of omnipotent destructiveness ("Envy destroys what God creates") and deflates others ("They

must be no good, otherwise why did I turn out so bad?"). Ultimately he seeks to triumph over life, experienced as painful feelings of inadequacy, inferiority, and impotency and to proclaim the primacy of death. For all too many people this convergence of envy and narcissism may be their finest achievement and serve as the final stage in a long history of unhappy self-assertion.[65]

4

On Attacking the Breast

The breast is anything and everything that sustains the body, warms the heart, and calms the mind. Far more than an anatomical entity, it is a veritable cornucopia of love, security, pleasure, and relief of pain. For these very reasons the breast lies at the center of human desire and hatred and is the most appropriate starting point for considering the myriad real and symbolic objects that attract envy, greed, and jealousy.

The earliest awareness of the breast consists of a comforting contentment and sensations such as warmth, fullness, and softness that occur in an infant after a feed. Collectively these feelings and sensations mean goodness. Therefore one's first relationship to the breast, really an abundant breast, is a relationship to a group of good experiences.[1] During the course of development, this rudimentary conception gradually acquires a more objective, independent reality. However, human nature assures that this transformation is never complete. All people long for and try to re-create the moments of sheer pleasure that suffused the early part of their lives.[2]

The positive, delightful experiences that begin at birth have three principal components. There are pleasurable, satisfying feelings, which include "all that is promising, flourishing, and nourishing."[3] Then there are calm, blissful states of the mind and body that occur after painful tensions such as hunger, colic, and anger have been alleviated. Finally there is a proper level of arousal. This is something that is constantly changing but can't be too little, too late, or too much. The infant needs both sleep and stimulation. If he is overtired, then what might otherwise catch his interest simply becomes irritating. And without an adequate flow of human contact and activity, apathy replaces repose.

The gratification of physical needs, the prompt relief of pain and appropriate stimulation, comprise the milk of human kindness to which infants, and adults, respond passionately and lovingly.[4] But this life-giving milk, as well as the giver, are constantly opposed by an equally strong mixture of noxious sensations, painful absences, and overexcitement. Collectively they mean badness and conjure forth a hatred that equals a rudimentary envy.

The noxious experiences vie for space with the pleasant ones. A late feed brings emptiness and screams. A tense mother brings rough handling and a cold touch. Basic bodily or psychic processes that the infant cannot assess or appreciate quickly become tormenting. From the infant's point of view there exists, side by side with the good breast, a bad one that takes away goodness and revels in pain.

The bad breast is a reality permeated with chaos and discontent. It can result from unrequited desire as well as direct deprivation. The tingling in the lips, the smells and sounds of mother, are intensely exciting and demand immediate gratification. Delay is unbearable and can easily transform a potential pleasure into an agonizing persecution. A fragile self cannot cope with the outpouring of stimulation and tends to repudiate what it would otherwise welcome. As Freud pointed out in "Instincts and Their Vicissitudes":

> The ego hates, abhors and pursues with intent to destroy all objects which are a source of unpleasurable feeling for it, without taking into account whether they mean frustration of sexual satisfaction or of the satisfaction of self-preservative needs.[5]

For an infant or child, the term "object" can signify an overwhelming experience, just as for an adult it can be a provocative thought. Both may protect themselves in similar ways, by denying and denigrating life wishes in order to diminish excitement. This reaction is equivalent to an envious attack and underscores the connection between envious tension and undischarged excitement. If the envy appears to have life-affirmative elements, it is because the envious attack is part of a wider drama. This begins with an eager anticipation for food, sex, or other pleasures—greedy fascination. It ends in angry, spiteful rejection once the feelings aroused have become unbearable—envious fascination. Wild swings from love to hate, from a life-loving to a life-hating posture, are especially common with children born to self-absorbed, narcissistic parents. They generally offer a breast that is excitingly frustrating, available one moment and gone the next. Or some mothers try to turn the tables and make the baby care for them. For example, a young actress who suffered from sleeplessness after the birth of her daughter developed a remedy for her nocturnal distress. Whenever she went to bed, she would pick up the baby and give her a feed. Then she would fall asleep while the baby woke up and fussed.[6]

In this instance the baby became the breast to her mother. The result was a residue of resentment and confusion that lasted late into adult life. Other women allow their babies to enjoy the breast and be nourished by it. By breast I refer to the actual bosom, a part of the body, or the baby bottle, a material object, as well as to all the care and consolation, all the good feelings, that the mother can muster.[7] Therefore, within a short time the developing child will begin to perceive that there is a source of vitality, a source of goodness, separate from himself, despite the fact that he remains dominated by his own desires and sensations. Even when the feeding experience has been essentially positive, the sense of separateness may come as a painful shock, but it also sets the stage for the child to establish its own love and allow tender passions to easily flow back into its mother.

The awareness of feeding, whether good or bad, focuses at or around the mouth, because the mouth of the infant is the specific part that seeks out and latches on to the nipple or teat.[8] The mouth makes the first tangible links with the breast as an external object. Other organs—the eyes, ears, nose, and musculature—cement the growing bonds by taking in and responding to the mother's sounds, scents, and touch. However, for months, probably years, the mouth-bosom/nipple or mouth-bottle/teat couplet remains at the center of the total nurturing experience.[9]

The mouth embodies all the infant's cravings, while the breast/nipple embodies all he or she is craving for—provisions and containment. The provisions are both obvious and elusive. They include the usual ingredients of the stuff of life, the milk, food, love, and care that come from the mother or a mothering person (father, nurse), plus an abundance of sensual delights that spring forth from the child. Each enhances the other and makes a very rich brew that imbues the breast with mythological expectations. It becomes like the horn that suckled Zeus, something that provides whatever its owner wants, a wellspring magically renewed by its own impulses.[10] But that creates a conundrum. The impulses vary from good to bad, and the child has a limited capacity to hold in and hold on to the experiences he treasures. Constantly assailed by anxieties about emptiness, he immediately tries to disgorge the bad feelings into the breast (the bosom representing his entire physical and psychic worlds) by screaming, flailing about, vomiting, urinating, and other means. So the breast has to do more than pour back indiscriminate feelings and wishes. It has to hold on to and contain the pains and hatreds, rather like a mother actually holds and comforts a crying baby. Then it has to give back something different. These superprovisions are love in place of pain, calm instead of chaos, and, in general, a strength that transcends hunger and exhaustion. They reflect an essential function of the breast, containment, and are also a product of this function.[11]

All persons lust for the life-giving and life-restoring foods that the breast provides. Adults have a slight advantage in that they can remember a good meal more easily than an infant and, hopefully, have had more good meals to remember. In other words, an adult mind has more clear-cut, developed impressions or mental representations of mothering, images that help to sustain him when hungry.[12] But greedy desires continue to buffet both infants and adults, desires even the best mother-child relationship or the fondest memories cannot eliminate.

The greedy mouth sucks, tears, scoops out, and drains dry everything of value located in or attributed to the breast, including the breast itself. The ensuing damage is not necessarily intentional; rather, it is a consequence of the ferocity of the attack. Any deprivation, but especially emotional deprivation, may provoke a ravenous onslaught. The provoker is frequently a noncontaining mother who is so preoccupied with herself that she cannot cope with the needs of her offspring. Inevitably her child tries to make up for what he or she experiences as a "rock-hard mommy" by draining the last drop of milk, energy, feelings, or interest from her parent and everyone or everything else about. This certainly happened with the daughter of the actress I just mentioned. During her childhood she was an insatiable eater, all in a hopeless attempt to get back some of the things her mother had taken, and continued to take, out of her.[13]

Greedy voraciousness tends to be fueled by an unconscious image or comparable idea of an ever-flowing, ever-present source of supply. I am describing the wish for a state of continuous, total satisfaction, the idealized internal breast. In ancient times large or multibreasted women like Diana of Ephesus represented this wish.[14] Or in Middle Eastern cultures, it can be seen in the shape of a building such as the Mosque of El Jazzar, with a courtyard surrounded by dozens of breastlike domes.[15] For modern men the same longings come packaged within the pages of such magazines as *Playboy* or *Forum*. The latter commonly carries ads that announce:

HUGE BREASTS!
Are you a lover of Colossal Boobs?
We offer you the very best in Mags, Videos, etc.
Great Value. Excellent Service. Try Us!![16]

All these pictures correspond with deep desires to possess the breast. And as we can see from those who commissioned the original sculptures or buildings or *Playboy* centerfolds, no effort is too great, for failure is almost too painful to bear. Those who don't fulfill this wish may deny it, but they never give it up. Inevitably the yearning for the ideal breast will be relocated in other people or places or things: for example, in children, thumbs or toys; or adults, an ideal mate or a fabulous holiday on a deserted beach. Yet the sequence—wish, denial, and projection—is a recipe for frustration and dissatisfaction, since the outside object rarely equals the internal expectations. This leaves the hungry person feeling even more greedy and vengeful.

Inner conflicts—that is, problems that arise primarily from within oneself rather than from without—also arouse and exaggerate the same response as inadequate or destructive mothering. Greed thrives on fear. The greedy person is terrified of a lack or loss of sustenance (such as, in an infant, milk, or in an adult, money). These provisions signify love, security, happiness, and, in general, the perpetuation of life. They oppose and are opposed by forces that threaten dissolution and death, especially envy. The greedy response is an attempt to redress the balance between life and death, goodness and badness. Many things affect this balance, including developmental traumas and deficiencies. They are not necessarily connected with an environmental failure, but they can restrict the ability of a person to take in, hold in, and utilize nourishment. Congenital handicaps include poor reflexes, breathing difficulties, metabolic disease, and a damaged sensory apparatus, while mental impediments may emerge as poor memory, wild mood swings, and an insufficient zest for life. However, even without these liabilities, everyone has to face the ebb and flow of noxious stimuli, an apparent bad internal breast that spoils calm and interferes with the wish to feed. The noxious events include wind, colic, and teething; excessive excitement; and emotional torment, in particular guilt and fear. These feelings follow angry, savage attacks on the mother for not immediately dispelling pain and, in general, for not living up to impossible expectations.

The worse fear is that the bitten breast will bite back. Young children frequently dream of being bitten or chased and devoured.[17] These fears may be phantasies projected onto the breast and nipple or acted out. Thus one little girl was referred for treatment because she would never spontaneously eat. However, in the games she played during her analysis and at home, she never stopped biting. Among many things, she pretended to be a crocodile, a lion, a pair of scissors, and a mincing machine. No wonder she wouldn't eat. She feared the terrible consequences, both to her mother and to herself.[18] However, it is not enough to state that little boys and girls tend to personify their own cruel cravings or attribute them to others. Noncontaining or oversensitive mothers can and do become very vindictive when threatened by their children's appetites.

Woody Allen demonstrated the dilemma in *Everything You Always Wanted to Know About Sex (But Were Afraid to Ask)*.[19] In one vignette he was chased through a field by a gigantic breast. One false step meant he would be engulfed and eaten. The question is: Was the trampling breast a plain projection of his own rapaciousness, or was Allen fleeing a common perception of parental intentions?

Guilt is the anguished self-reproach that follows when either child or adult hurts, or wants to hurt, the very thing he loves and treasures. The hurt can be a bite or any other hint of injury. Then guilt feeds fear. Since the guilty person believes he doesn't deserve anything, he is frightened of losing everything. Hence the fear of loss is both a cause and a consequence of greed. In addition, the guilty conscience tends to transform the good breast into a monstrous beast, often portrayed as a ferocious animal such as an alligator or shark.

The shark embraces greed, envy, and guilt-ridden retaliation. A primeval creature, it possesses an all-powerful mouth that can gnash steel chains as well as human flesh. Such an image is the perfect repository for passions that lurk in the depths of the mind just waiting to strike. It is a killer replete with appetites that know no bounds and recognize no ties. All mothers harbor shark-child-cannibals whose interests extend from their mothers' insides (mouth, brain, and belly) to their outsides (skin, hair, and clothes). Thus, the attackable breast is not just a part of the body, but the whole body, an Aladdin's cave waiting to be discovered, explored, robbed, and defiled.[20]

Such primitive notions are not restricted to primitives, although sophisticated peoples prefer to think they are. The British anthropologist Ioan Lewis relates that during his travels in the West African bush, he noticed that the natives would hide when he or other white men walked down the roads. He wondered why and managed to stop a villager before he disappeared. The man was very wary but eventually said that he was frightened of white people because they were all cannibals. Surprised, Professor Lewis asked for an explanation. The villager asserted that everyone knew whites ate black babies. For proof he obtained a tin of cooked meat. There were two pictures of healthy, smiling black babies on the label, ostensibly to demonstrate nutritious goodness. But the natives saw it as a confirmation of their worst fears, that white people like to eat black baby meat! They refused to believe otherwise.[21]

Cannibalism—or, rather, cannibalistic desires—is a universal phenomenon. As the German psychoanalyst Karl Abraham observed, it is an example of oral sadistic savagery totally devoid of concern:

> Complete and unrestricted cannibalism is only possible on the basis of unrestricted narcissism. On such a level all that the individual considers is his own desire for pleasure. He pays no attention whatever to the interests of his object, and destroys that object without the least hesitation.[22]

The narcissism Abraham described does not simply mean selfishness. It encompasses all the hurt and rage that, as I discussed in the last chapter, has to do with the realization that goodness is contained in another, and that it doesn't totally belong to the infant or adult and never can. The wish to devour—indeed, to eviscerate—the breast and body tends to incorporate the wish to spoil and destroy the contents so that no one else, including mother, can enjoy them. Hence, envy accompanies greed, because the impetus is usually hunger plus a narcissistic wound.

Greed, however, can serve in its own right to diminish envy. The idea that everyone owns or possesses more valuable things consumes and torments the envier. Endless acquisition is a way of relieving this tension. The grenvious person believes that if he owned or possessed everything (all possible pleasures, all manner of love, all people and things), then the envy would evaporate.[23] Unfortunately the emotional protection that greed provides flounders when the rate of accumulation diminishes. Then an intractable malice reappears in full fury, and the evil eye yields to the malicious mouth.

The dread aroused by creatures such as sharks or insects, snakes and old hags, has to do with envious intent located, directed, and activated from and by the mouth. The Assamese people of northeast India literally believe in the malicious mouth. Their word for envy means "mouth putting" and consists of two terrible creatures, Khoba and Khobee, who spring forth out of the mouth to burn and obliterate anything admirable.[24] Khoba and Khobee are themselves associated with biting insects and vermin that attack and ruin life-giving crops. In the Western world comparable anxieties extend to flies, mosquitoes, and gnats, little devils that swarm at picnics and not only pollute the food, but ruin the pleasure of the participants. Our Khoba-Khobees also include any reptiles that inject poison, like the viper, or carnivores that appear to mutilate gratuitously. Carping, gossiping, backbiting men and women are no less abhorrent. The English poet Edmund Spenser depicted the viperous tongue in *The Faerie Queene*:

He hated all good werkes and vertuous deeds

———————————————————————————

And eke the verse of famous Poets witt
He does backebite, and spightful poison spues
From leprous mouth and all that ever writt.[25]

Shakespeare did likewise in his characterization of Iago, a herald of evil eyes and malicious mouths. His leer diffused hatred while his words polluted a virtuous lady and crippled her husband's happiness. Contemporary Iagos—the gossip columnist, the political intriguer, and the scurrilous critic—deploy slander no less effectively and achieve similar results.[26]

Ultimately the ferocious mouth represents the guilty conscience biting and tearing away at the peace of mind of the grenvious person who has damaged his loved ones. In this respect children are particularly at risk because their reparative capacities fluctuate. It is no wonder they are prone to nightmares in which savage beasts attack them. Guilt and defenses against guilt are important elements in these bad dreams. The torment would not arise, however, unless there was concern for the breast. Melanie Klein observed that a rudimentary regard for the caring person occurs very early in the life of the infant, a fact confirmed by subsequent research in child development.[27] An unrestrained onslaught may indicate the intensity of the impulse as well as an absolute need to deny concern in order to mitigate unbearable anguish.

Denial is an elementary response to guilt. At first it centers around the damaged person or thing, but the denial soon involves the destructive impulses, too, in order to shun responsibility for them. Essentially the individual says to himself, "I don't want to know!" Therefore he tries to ensure that none of the anger, guilt, awareness of damage—in other words, any aspect of the situation—remains in himself by getting rid of it or projecting it on to others. They become the scapegoat for what he hates about himself.

When these projections focus on outer figures, the troubled adult or child may behave with self-righteous savagery toward "the evil in others"—the basis of religious and political fanaticism. However, when the projections flow the other way, they may sliver the self, that is, one's inner world. A hypochondriacal state will ensue if these dissociated fragments of envy, greed, and guilt become associated with parts of the body.[28] More frequently they coalesce into a prohibitive, punitive figure—the basis of an over-severe superego. This can take the form of a shark or parents with sharklike faces that slash and mutilate thoughts and actions.[29]

For the guilty person, the enemy is anything that engenders guilt. This includes his own desires or any object of these desires. A breast, a bottle, a toy, a caress, a feed, a good feeling, all can become pretexts for annihilating attacks when they get blamed for arousing anguish. Unless a positive, reparative exchange takes place, a vicious spiral of greed + envy → guilt → denial + projection → vengeful rage will unfold that greatly exaggerates the original damage. The entire sequence mimics envious malice. It can culminate in the extermination of love and goodness, either as felt in any by the subject or as perceived in and toward the object. This rigid, absolute defense against alleged crimes and dreaded punishments involves multiple denials and reversals of the initial desires.

Thus, "I want everything," an expression of greed, easily becomes "I want nothing," the denial of greed and avoidance of guilt.

Then, "I want nothing" reverses to "I want you to have nothing" or "I will destroy what you have," a preemptive strike expressing envy.

Finally, "You have nothing" converts to "You are nothing" or "I will destroy you," a verbal attack that encompasses anything that might rekindle remorse and reactivate guilt-ridden retaliation.

. . .

A patient of mine demonstrated all aspects of the greed-envy-guilt cycle, which reoccurred again and again in our work together. She was an intelligent woman who came to therapy desperate for insight. During the initial sessions she liked to ply me with dreams and images, while an ironic smile seemed to imbibe my interpretations. All this allowed her to leave relatively relaxed, although I would feel drained. Yet in spite of the good beginnings, her mood turned ominous, for she inevitably declaimed that I had nothing to give and rued the fact that she had decided to see me.

Subsequently the resentment and defiance spiraled. She used to shriek to my face that I was a useless human being and a lost cause, a complete shit. (On several occasions she sent me shit in the post or left it outside the consulting room door.) At the same time she carried on about knives and guns, threatening to cut me up or blow me to pieces.

Nothing helped, she hated my every word. I only began to make contact when I told her how bad I felt and conveyed my sense of desperation. Then she would calm down and grudgingly reveal she was angry (for not getting more from me), worried (that she might hurt me), and frightened (that I would get back at her).

Essentially this person hungered for my ideas and feelings. Yet she hated my knowledge and peace of mind. She wasn't unaware of the things she did, but she took pleasure in my discomfort. No doubt she anticipated I would scream at her just as her parents had done when she was a child.

In a past that intruded far into the future, she felt all cut up inside. Therefore she was determined to excise that pain and get revenge. I think she was really terrified that I would reject her (give her the chop) or, worse, make her feel guilty (drive her mad) and put her away (rubbish her).

The interplay of greed, envy, and guilt I have just described took years to work out. As with all people, these forces may oppose each other, act in tandem, or fuse (as in grenvy). There is rarely an occasion where one acts without the other. Yet the simultaneous interplay of denial, reversal, projection, and rage makes this hard to realize. With my patient there often appeared to be no immediate reason for the stasis in her life or the anxiety and confusion she contrived in mine. We had to unravel many layers of bile and bitterness in order to appreciate the tortuous strands of her destructiveness. These, in turn, were related to the different ways I represented the breast.

For her—indeed, for all people—the breast means good experiences *(peace of mind, calm, contentment, pleasure, and security)*, a part of the body *(the bosom, an exciting physical interior)*; a material object *(any container, a glass, a plate, a bottle, a jewel, a safe, the sun, the light and warmth in her life)*; a product *(food, skills, knowledge, goods, possessions and superpossessions; love, calm, and strength)*; and qualities, capacities, characteristics, and accomplishments *(patience, prosperity, vitality, creativity, fame, and, in general, "good werkes and vertuous deeds")*.[30]

This woman wanted these things. She wanted to have them or prevent me from having them. And the more her greed and envy were frustrated, the more enraged she became. However, many people take a different tack. If they can't have the breast, they prefer to become the breast.

> I am a breast. A phenomenon that has been variously described to me as "as a massive hormonal influx," "an endocrinopathic catastrophe," and/or "a hermaphroditic explosion of chromosomes" took place within my body between midnight and four A.M. on February 18, 1971, and converted me into a mammary gland disconnected from any human form.
>
> They tell me that I am now an organism with the general shape of a football, or a dirigible; I am said to be of spongy consistency, weighing in at one hundred and fifty-five pounds (formerly I was one hundred and sixty-two), and measuring, still, six feet in length.[31]

The American writer Philip Roth narrated this account of a middle-aged man who woke up one morning to discover that he had become a breast, in a novel of the same name. His newly formed body included a long pink nipple, seventeen lactiferous openings, and several seven-inch antennae.

The man had been having an affair with a beautiful younger woman. Although his initial passions had waned, he tried to maintain an affectionate but reserved relationship with her. Above all, he wanted to avoid the grinding "burden of dependence" and the "deception, placation and dominance" of marriage. He had been through a "lacerating divorce" and had just terminated a five-year psychoanalysis.

As he lay in the hospital, helpless in a bra-like hammock, he recalled his friend, "pleasure-giving Claire," his envy and strange desires to be the breast he had so often suckled. Yet for him the breast was much more than a part of the body. It was the actual practice of feeding, caring, loving, sustaining, providing, stimulating, and pleasure giving. The story of this man's metamorphosis is really the narration of his successful attack, and consequent self-punishment, on all that Claire could and did do for him. He attacked her function by taking over her function and by grotesquely parodying the relationship that existed or might have existed between them.

Roth's fiction illustrates a common fact. Many individuals hate the sense of needing or depending upon another and will do all they can to subvert or destroy dependency. By dependency I mean an appreciation of need, the taking of food and gratitude for being fed.

No one can avoid being dependent, but at some point everyone tries to begrudge the experience, because dependency involves an awareness of love-hate, guilt, loss, and grief. The dependent person attacks these painful feelings in himself by blaming others. The resultant onslaughts range from a transient grumpiness in the presence of a parent (or spouse or anyone who has, or might be trying to provide, something) to a defiant negativity.

Attacks on dependency equal attacks on the breast. They inevitably feature a contemptuous dismissal and triumphal overtaking of the functions of the envied object of desire. Melanie Klein observed these features in a patient of hers who had just had a major professional success. This woman dreamed that she was riding on a magic carpet that allowed her to peer into a room where a cow was munching on an endless strip of blanket. The dream announced her wish to triumph over her need for Klein and the psychoanalytic relationship. The carpet, and her riding high, meant that she had the magic power, the ability, to soar and outstrip a therapist whom she had derisively relegated to the role of cow.

> She associated that the endless strip of blanket represented an endless stream of words, and it occurred to her that these were all the words I had ever said in the analysis and which I now had to swallow. The strip of blanket was a hit at the wooliness and worthlessness of my interpretation. Here we see the full devaluation of the primal object, significantly represented by the cow, as well as the grievance against the mother who had not fed her satisfactorily.[32]

Klein's patient and Kepesh, Roth's protagonist, sought to deny need, get fed, and express ingratitude simultaneously. As with many children and adults, their reveries led them to believe that they had become all powerful and the source of everything. For them, "I am nothing!" reversed to "I am everything!"; "I am empty!" to "I am full!"; and "I am impotent!" to "I am omnipotent." In these circumstances dependency stops being an issue because people feel they can have whatever they want whenever they want it. They have become the breast!

The denials of ambivalence, loss, and guilt often occur together. So do the angry possession of, triumph over, and contempt for the feeding person. Melanie Klein called this combined assault on internal and external reality the "manic defense." The manic defense, really a manic attack, is a forceful means of averting hurt and asserting superiority. The triumphant feelings reek of rivalry and revenge, while the contempt serves to denigrate care and containment so there is nothing to miss or suffer guilt about. This combination of self-protection and subversion can vary in intensity from an overbearing arrogance to a manic psychosis. The difference is one of degree, not of kind.

The manic defense is probably the most common systematic way of attacking the breast, whether in the family, in psychotherapy, or elsewhere. This state of mind activates both virulent envy and devastating greed. The manic adult or child believes he has an absolute right to devour attention, emotions, devotion, activities, and assets. Even the smallest lapse is a terrible threat because it may expose the hollowness of the omnipotence and the persistence of need.[33] This state of continuous feasting over the time and energy of others has been termed the "manic feast." It is the closest most people get to unrestrained cannibalism. Manic feasting can leave its victims drained and skeletonized and confirms Abraham's description of oral sadistic savagery.

The manic state, like the phenomena that encompass the nirvana principle, signals another point at which envy and narcissism converge. Each presents a different side of the same coin. The manic individual hides his wounds by assuming a position of godlike exuberance that allows him to take and give with reckless abandon. He aims to control and caricature care.[34] Should this fail, he can burst into an even greater frenzy or flip over into a suicidal retreat. Either possibility entails an all-consuming rage with external providers.

These providers include people and places that have supplied, or might supply and replenish, feelings of inner worth, fullness, and fulfillment. Whether a relative or stranger, a home or country, they are linked with good experiences, with food, and with feeding. Therefore people and places in themselves can signify the breast and be treated as such. Yet they differ from a cornucopia or soda fountain because they are not automatically on tap and do require some care in return. Occasionally mothers do need a rest, and even a house needs a coat of paint every few years. Otherwise it stops being a good house. That is why the manic person so ruthlessly attacks his human and nonhuman environment. Even the slightest demand calls into question his own goodness and reminds him of his own limitations. So he adheres to the role of a tyrannical child. The breast must not have any life of its own. It exists solely to serve his wishes, or it will be destroyed.

Although most children do not behave this way all the time, some adults do, especially in relation to each other. The profligate lover, or Don Juan, is a well-known character with an impetuous and insatiable craving for women. Greedy for love, he seeks them out like an addict scrounging for a fix. And like an addict he is never satisfied with what he gets. He is ever on the lookout for more alluring, exciting, and self-sacrificing partners. Any hint that the woman might have her own needs, make demands, feel hurt, or have interests of her own provides a pretext for angry rejection. No one is good enough to assuage his emptiness or withstand his destructiveness. At best he turns from one to the other to avoid their harm and his guilt. Otherwise his basic attitude is drain, deceive, and discard. This kind of person, a charming Dracula, preys on the emotions of his victims and aims to insert himself inside them in order to totally possess their vitality. His actions may have a sexual motif, but they have little to do with sex. They are a vengeful vampirization of the female body and soul for what it holds and allegedly withholds. The Don Juan is not just a greedy man, but a very envious one, who believes he has the right to take what he can get and give false hopes, broken promises, and bad dreams in return. Possessiveness is his way of spitefully spoiling a woman's autonomy. He wants to make sure that she can't use and make use of her own qualities and capacities as she sees fit. The woman must remain at his beck and call. His pride depends on her subservience to him and her worthlessness to others.[35]

Basically I have been describing a man who maintains that women deceptively keep their goodies for themselves, a view not limited to Don Juans. It is typical of people with a tendency to falsely attribute greed. They take for granted that providers prefer to feed themselves and hurt those who depend on them. They also assume that if these providers are not keeping things for themselves, they must be diverting the goods to others. This assumption connects envy with jealousy and fuels the wish for revenge. It is rooted in children's ideas that if Mommy isn't available, then she must be caring for Daddy, or sister or brother, and that there are always undeserving, grasping interlopers about who are ready and able to steal her affections.

The imagined rival is a much more serious threat than a real one. He or she is a provocative self-creation. I refer to an image that feeds false beliefs about infidelity and sustains severe hostility in states of morbid, pathological, delusional, or insane jealousy. On these occasions people insist that their partners, and certain named or unnamed third parties, want to rob them of everything, taunt, tantalize, and outrage them, strip them of self-respect, spoil their lives, and leave them loveless, hopeless, and despairing. These accusations often duplicate deeply felt, overwhelmingly dangerous, guilt-ridden desires.[36] It only takes some minor event, a last straw, to precipitate the violent expulsion and relocation of the destructive impulses in a friend or relative. The effect is comparable to a Don Juan who suddenly reproaches his companion for meanness and duplicity, or an Othello who denounces his spouse for lechery and treachery. In fact, this phenomenon has been termed the Othello syndrome. It denotes a murderous obsession with the alleged infidelity of a spouse.[37]

On close examination the imagined rival is not necessarily an intruding outsider, but the original partner, the focus of envious enmity, not for being bad, but for being good. This feature helps to distinguish jealous rivalry from envious rivalry. As I have previously pointed out, jealousy involves a triangular relationship. Here the hatreds head toward the challenger and may bypass the real loved one. Hence the issues are love lost, love denied, or love called into question. On the other hand, envy is bilateral. These hatreds go directly to the primary person, often a provider seen as an adversary. Therefore, in delusional jealousy or envious rivalry the underlying issues are narcissistic rage, impotence, and dependency.[38]

Deadly rivalries can also embrace a place or setting, as happened with an acquaintance whose family owned a sheep ranch in Australia. It provided a regular income plus a treasure trove of stories about the Australian outback. Yet the man hated the place and never missed an opportunity to denigrate sheep, farms, the Wild West, or Australia. His unceasing antagonism was a barely concealed brew of greed, envy, and jealousy. The greed grew from a belief that he had never gotten his due. Although he had received substantial sums over the years, he personally felt cheated and deprived. He blamed the ranch for this and his family, too. He liked to upset his parents with bitter asides that the property was too big, too grand, too far away, and not worth a visit. But his malice boiled over whenever his father waxed nostalgic about the hardships and excitement of the old days. Such memories engaged both envious and jealous rivalry. The envy arose from a sense that the ranch was an extension of his father's strength and wealth, qualities he could never equal and which his father always held over him. The jealousy followed his conviction that the land was a literal rival for his father's affection. No matter what he did, the old man would always find lush pastures and streams more interesting. So as far as he was concerned, a sheep spread had usurped his place, and he longed to eradicate its power and prestige.

Attacks on the land and those who till it are a basic ingredient of recorded history. The Old Testament relates that Abimelech, king of the Philistines, was displeased when Isaac cultivated Gerar, the area in Israel between Gaza and Beer-sheba:

Isaac sowed in that land and reaped a hundredfold the same year. The Lord blessed him and the man grew richer and richer until he was very wealthy: he acquired flocks and herds, and a large household, so that the Philistines envied him. And the Philistines stopped up all the wells which his father's servants had dug in the days of his father Abraham, filling them with earth. And Abimelech said to Isaac, "Go away from us, for you have become too big for us."[39]

Several millennia later American and European farmers face less dangerous but no less malevolent gibes for making their farmyards the breadbaskets of the world. Press reports like "Jaguars in the farmyards" have aroused such resentment that farm union officials have been moved to publicly complain that their members are "getting fed up with the growing national sport of biting the hand that feeds you."[40]

People and places attract hostility because they are specific providers and containers, good objects or bad as the case may be, upon whom we are all dependent. In combination they yield generalizations such as "the motherland," which can become a passionate focus of feeling, like a mother.[41] Yet whether concrete or abstract, a body or a symbol, these entities are a part of the ultimate dimension of the breast, which is reality itself.

The creation of reality begins with the first tentative steps to locate and conceptualize the source of supply, a task that continues throughout one's life. Initially reality comprises basic experiences such as warmth and fullness, roughness and tension, as well as the act of experiencing these things. Or it is a part of the mother-baby body, such as the mouth or nipple, and the aptitude to perceive, remember, and appreciate these organs. However, as the one matures, reality grows too and encompasses, for example, material things, human relationships, and physical qualities as well as the contents and functions of the mind.

The American psychologist George Miller points out that "the main intellectual accomplishment of the nervous system is the world itself."[42] This world is a picture of things, a conjectural model derived from multiple interactions in and between oneself and others. By others I include both the human and nonhuman environments. First the interactions center around food and feeding. But they soon branch out in many other directions. The result is a dynamic structure of perceptions, memories, feelings, expectations, and skills that themselves have the capacity to become sustaining and containing or not.[43]

An infant's early relationship with breast reality determines his worldview, which in turn determines his relationship to life. A sense that "life is good" or "the world's okay" reflects a positive worldview. The opposite sense, that "life is bad" or "the whole world's horrible," reflects a negative model. These attitudes are not static. Many internal or external events tilt the balance one way or the other. There are occasions when reality is so intolerable that it becomes and literally feels like a bad breast. Then people deflect their hatred to consciousness itself, or space, or time, or, more prosaically, the weather. They want to flee from these things or fight them. Concurrently they will also try to establish new realities by flying to the sunshine during winter or by reveling in comforting daydreams.

The reevaluation and annihilation of reality is very clear during a psychotic or quasi-psychotic episode. Then the very fabric of existence is at stake. Anything indicative of feeding or caring, and any links with food or care, may become the focus of savage attack. The links are crucial because they are reminders of the pain and suffering that the mother and father, under the guise of "life," have inflicted and still seem to be inflicting on a hapless soul.

Typical links include perception and the perceptual apparatus, representing the desire and capacity to take things in (the symbolic equivalent of the mouth). They also include communication, words, thoughts, and emotions, representing the intermediary between child and parents (the symbolic equivalent of the nipple or teat). Finally the links encompass states of mind and understanding, representing the parental container full of digested or undigested experiences (the symbolic equivalent of the bosom and its contents).[44] Collectively these elements equal the mouth-nipple-breast connection that the contented person cherishes, in contrast with the distraught person, who solely wants to deny, subvert, or smash them to smithereens.

In a seminal paper entitled "Attacks on Linking," British psychoanalyst Wilfred Bion illustrated how these attacks may be reactivated, especially during psychoanalysis. The patient may feel compelled to repeat a hurtful relationship with an unresponsive, noncontaining mother or a very envied one. Bion comments:

> Attacks on the link, therefore, are synonymous with attacks on the analyst's, and originally the mother's, peace of mind. The capacity to introject is transformed by the patient's envy and hate into greed devouring the patient's psyche; similarly, peace of mind becomes hostile indifference.[45]

Time was the essential issue for a middle-aged teacher who consulted me after a suicide attempt. During the first months of treatment she was diligent and punctual, rarely coming a moment too early or tarrying a moment too late. Eventually her depression lifted, and she went back to work. But the picture was too good to be true, as the summer holiday break dramatically proved.

A changed woman resumed sessions, someone who cast aside fastidious facades and appeared for her appointments minutes, sometimes hours, early. Later on in the therapy, she would act like a thief and seize any excuse—a sudden memory, a last-minute dream, a broken shoe—to stay on and on. Occasionally she apologized. Yet the very next time she would beg and whine to stay longer or refuse to leave. I felt as if I had to push her out of the room, whereupon she would dawdle on the stairs and hang around the street in front of my office.

In addition, she dressed differently. Previously the lady was prim and proper. Now she wore tight sweaters and short skirts and doused herself in such heavy perfume that I felt faint from the fumes. Alternatively she would arrive bruised and scratched, with a torn shirt and dirty tights, screaming about suicide. Then she wouldn't turn up for a week, leaving me shattered about what happened to her.

I thought, She wants to give me a good time, but if she can't, she'll give me a hard time, a very hard time. My intuition was right. She associated seductiveness with lust, and lust with being "a good-time girl." She really was trying to show me what she wanted from me—

a good time, lots of time, all my time. And if she couldn't have it, then she would corrupt and disrupt my time and timing.

She hated the idea that I might have time for someone else or keep time for myself. As the Christmas break approached, she became more disruptive, more seductive, more difficult. She intended to fill me with desire, fear, or rage so I could have no time in my mind for anyone else. This was her jealous revenge for my "two-timing her" during the holiday.

Time, the time of sessions, my mental time, were the links between her and me. The more she wanted me, the more she subjected these links to an unceasing barrage of greedy, envious, and jealous attacks. Her mouth was insatiable for time. It never got enough. Almost in passing she recalled that her parents were farmers. They got up early and went to bed early. They never seemed to have any time for her, or if they did, they preferred to spend it with her two sisters. As a child she felt that outings were stolen time.

The therapy sessions and flow of time were my nipples and the milk that flowed through them. Her aims were ruthless control and abject contempt. Sometimes she talked so much that the sessions were deluged with ideas. On other occasions she maintained a sullen silence so that time soured and our work was wasted.

Then there were different silences, akin to a calm, deathly quietness, with slow breathing and little movement for hours on end. It seemed she remained suspended in time, as if she had returned to an intrauterine state when there was no intermediary between us, and time was endless.

That's what she wanted, endless time and me. I was the breast, a cornucopia of time, the source of everything her parents had denied her. Toward the end of the treatment, she apologized for all the upheavals and hassles. She knew she was difficult. Long ago she had sworn to herself that someday someone would give her all the time she had never had as a child. But if the person reneged, or if it didn't work out, then she was determined to destroy time once and for all.

For the teacher, the destruction of time equaled the destruction of reality, which from her point of view neither sustained her nor contained her hurts. Others vented their rage on different aspects of the breast. Kepesh attacked the function (a dependent relationship); Don Juan, the person (a girlfriend); King Abimelech, a place or setting (the land of Gerar); and a psychotic patient, the inner world (a state of mind). Previously I have described attacks on the breast as an experience, a part of the body, a material thing, a product, and a quality or accomplishment. Each aspect is a separate but related mode of feeding and caring. Each can become a source of power and strength or can arouse great longing and terrible antagonism.

Bruno Bettelheim was struck by the extent to which the boys at the Orthogenic School in Chicago treated the breast as an extremely powerful object, something to be feared and desired.

> A riddle they repeatedly, with envious preoccupation, asked exemplifies this: "What is the strongest thing in the world?"
>
> They never failed to supply the answer: "A brassiere, because it holds two huge mountains and a milk factory."[46]

This raises the question, is there a difference in the degree of desire or quality of hate that emanates from boys or girls, men and women, toward the breast?

Both males and females need love, security, stimulation, and the relief of pain. But until relatively recently it has usually been the woman who did the nurturing, for social and anatomical reasons. Perhaps it is easier for girls to pass from childhood dependency to adult activity since they know that in giving up the breast (mother), they will also be gaining the breast (motherhood). For boys the knowledge that they will never develop a bosom, nor produce milk, nor suckle the young, compounds the loss of childhood.

Men resent the lack of a breast no less than women rue the lack of a penis. They feel deprived of a tangible means to feed and be fed as well as an overt sign of desirability. In fantasy they assume that all women have to do is turn on some magical tap inside themselves, while they have to spend a lifetime accumulating capital and possessions. Moreover they suspect that women can always suck on their own breasts, but that they will remain dependent on females for food. These assumptions breed an intense hostility that contributes to male wishes to dress like women, act like women, become women, and, of course, totally subjugate them.

From their perspective women suffer for being the object of such hostility, both from men and from other women who envy their abilities. This helps to explain female preoccupations with reducing or increasing the size of the breast. The former has to do with diminishing others' greedy and envious fascination with their organ. The latter is concerned with power and the use of the breast to triumph over maternal and fraternal rivals. Silicon implants extend this obsession with large bosoms. Thus some women experience their desires through the need to be desired and express their antagonisms by putting their bust on a pedestal.

Yet it is not the size of the breast that counts, but the capacity for care, which can be as strongly developed in men as it remains undeveloped in women. The teacher who attacked time blamed her mother in particular. When she came to see me she was in despair not only because the world didn't sustain her, but because she couldn't sustain her students. Years ago Freud conveyed the larger dimension of her dilemma very well.

> The reproach against the Mother which goes back the furthest is that she gave the child too little milk—which is construed against her as a lack of love.... The child's avidity for its earliest nourishment is altogether insatiable and it never gets over the pain of losing its Mother's breast....[47]

5

Suffocation of the Mother—
Womb Envy

The womb has long been considered an extremely dangerous organ. Around 400 B.C. the philosopher Democritus advised Hippocrates that "the womb was the origin of six hundred evils and innumerable catastrophes."[1]

This view has permeated civilized thought right down to modern times. The famous Persian physician Haly Abbas (?–994 A.D.) compared the womb to a "wild animal longing for semen,"[2] and the sixteenth-century French writer Jean Liebaut declared:

> The uterus has naturally an incredible desire to conceive and to procreate. Thus it is anxious to have virile semen, desirous of taking it, drawing it in, sucking it, and retaining it.[3]

More recently a gynecologist was overheard, after performing an emergency hysterectomy and holding the newly detached uterus aloft:

> Ah, yes, I am [pleased]. Another small victory in Man's unending battle against the womb.[4]

By "womb" the doctor might well have added the "labia, the clitoris, and the vagina"—the entrance, the signal, and the passageway to the dark interior of a woman's body, which together with the breasts comprise the essentials of feminine endowment. Variously called a center of creativity or a furnace of carnality, a biological powerhouse or a suffocating mother, the womb is the focus of both dread and desire. The latter, like a lilting Lorelei, urges a return to the beginnings of life, to a state of weightless warmth and blissful envelopment. Wilhelm Tell narrated these feelings in "Song of the Fisherboy." There a voice from the depths of a "clear smiling lake" calls forth

> a melody,
> Flowing and soft,
> And sweet as when angels are
> singing aloft. . . .
> With me thou must go, I charm the
> young shepherd,
> I lure him below.[5]

Tell's poem refers to a shepherd or boy, but the wishes might equally apply to a shepherdess or girl. They concern everyone who recalls the delights of the breast and seeks, with varying degrees of desperation, to discover and rediscover the entrance and passageway to Mother's body. Therefore the initial conception of the womb is a magical interior, a conjunction of body and breast that carries the expectation of continuous, effortless pleasure experienced as warmth, softness, fullness, and satisfaction. Yet, unlike the breast, this organ cannot be seen or grasped, nor can its goods be felt or tasted. It is an infolding rather than an outfolding of the body, something dark and secret, readily transformed by the mind into a trap, a lure, whose siren call is a "hiss from the abyss" threatening to drain and devour, dissolve and destroy, whoever or whatever might enter.[6] This dreaded tomb is a greedy womb, a creature imbued with the very cravings that have been directed toward it. Just as the bosom can appear like a cornucopia or a crocodile, depending on mood and circumstances, the depths of a woman can seem like a cavern of contentment or a chamber of horrors. Such a fathomless hell contains hideous perils, as Tell also described in his ballad "The Diver":

> Salamander—snake—dragon—vast
> reptiles that dwell
> In the deep, coil'd about the grim
> jaws of their hell.[7]

These lines convey universal fears that the womb/woman is hungry not only for semen, the male fluid, but also for the penis, the male member. Lizards, snakes, and reptiles represent maleness, male members that have been bitten off and captured. Such phantasies lay the basis for intense anxieties that either the penis has been devoured and digested or that it has been trapped and incorporated so the womb becomes a cave filled with the organs of any man with whom the woman has had a relationship. There they lurk, sinister guardians of the treasures within.

But the womb threatens more than maleness. Pride and self-respect are as vulnerable to a woman's real or imagined demands as the vitality and viability of the penis. Indeed, incessant worries about emotional weakness and psychic disintegration invariably surface as doubts about physical prowess: Am I big enough? Can I give enough? Will I cope enough, or will I be swallowed up and lost inside her?

Greed sustains the impression that the vagina/womb/woman can never be satisfied. This includes the actual greed of a mother, for example, who never gets enough because she rarely gives enough, and the projected greed of infants and children of either sex who invade their parents with screaming mouths and flailing arms. Rebuff arouses revenge followed by "the perils of the deep."[8] These perils encompass both rapaciousness and oblivion. Rapaciousness leads to a terror of being torn apart, as by sharks in the sea. Oblivion conjures forth fears of falling apart, of dissolving in intrauterine waters, as might occur during a period of regressive withdrawal. The accompanying experience of ego loss or loss of identity has been commonly compared to mental castration.[9]

The wish to return to the womb is only one of the hundreds of "evils and catastrophes" that have been attributed to it. Generally these dangers comprise disease, dementia, and demonic possession. They reflect a litany of fear and hatred of "the mysterious capacity that women's bodies have of creating babies out of food and what men give them."[10]

What other organ can nurture but also create and produce concretely what men (and some women) can only make metaphorically? The womb is the core of female potency. It is a part of the body that is perfectly placed to be idealized and envied for feeding and breeding, for loving and being made love to. Although it tends to receive a lot of the ardor and anger that may be initially directed to the breast (which helps explain the oral origins of genital passions), the womb is not a passive organ.[11] On the contrary, in recent decades old epithets such as "furnace or powerhouse of carnality" have gained new meanings as sex research reveals that women have an almost inexhaustible capacity for orgasms and feminist writers like Kate Millett proclaim that the sexual performances of women are naturally stronger than men.[12] So we are faced with a situation where modish myths of female dominance and newborn enmities about womb power echo ancient fears and begin to erode the previously preeminent "dangers of male supremacy."[13]

Many peoples have believed that the womb has a will, even a life, of its own. It can be lustful or rejecting, angry or depressed. It can decide to reside in the pelvis or the belly or the throat, or sometimes outside of the body altogether. In others words, it can be a separate animate creature that happens to be housed inside a woman.[14]

Three thousand years ago the Egyptians blamed the womb or uterus for a vast array of complaints ranging from physical illnesses to hysteria. The term "hysteria" comes from the Greek word "*hystera*," meaning uterus. The Egyptians thought that the emotional excesses and bizarre physical manifestations of hysteria were solely a disorder of women, a view that persisted with few notable exceptions until the 1600s.[15] Their attitude was to placate or punish the womb in order to make it know its proper place. Fumigation with fragrant and powerful substances was a popular prescription. The *Papyrus Ebers,* an important medical text, recommended:

The dry excrement of men is placed on frankincense, and the woman is fumigated therewith; let the fume thereof enter into her vulva.[16]

Similar treatments prevailed during the Greco-Roman period, when hysteria was considered to be a constriction, a suffocation of the womb or suffocation of the mother.[17] But theories about the womb and the role of women changed radically with the writings of St. Augustine and other Christian theologians, who affirmed that female maladies, in particular hysteria, were caused by an "alliance with unholy powers" (typically "seduction by the devil"); hysterical women were thus equated with witches. However, the organized persecution of such offenders did not begin in earnest until the ninth century, when Charlemagne, emperor of the Holy Roman Empire, decreed the death penalty for . . .

all who in any way evoked the devil, compounded love-philters, afflicted either man or woman with barrenness, troubled the atmosphere, excited tempests, destroyed the fruits of the earth, dried up the milk of cows, or tormented their fellow-creatures with sores and diseases.[18]

Charlemagne's decree signifies an abhorrence and hostility toward women's powers—their bodies, their functions, their products, and their pleasures—that culminated in 1494 with the publication of *Malleus Maleficarum*, also known as *The Witches' Hammer*.[19] The impact of this work was immediate and long lasting. It became an international best-seller and an established authority by which untold numbers of women were tortured and executed "ad majorem Dei gloriam" over the next couple of centuries.[20]

The book purports to define witchcraft, to describe witches and their methods, and then to detail the steps to be taken in prosecuting them. It contends that women are greedy for sex and can only be gratified by copulating with the devil. Lust is their hallmark, and if thwarted in any way, they will "deprive man of his virile member."

We have already shown that they can take away the male organ, not indeed by actually despoiling the human body of it, but by concealing it with some glamour [enchantment]. . . . And of this we shall instance a few examples.

In the town of Ratisbon, a certain young man who had an intrigue with a girl, wishing to leave her, lost his member; that is to say, some glamour was cast over it so that he could see or touch nothing but his smooth body. In his worry over this he went to a tavern to drink wine; and after he had sat there for a while he got into conversation with another woman who was there, and told her the cause of his sadness, explaining everything, and demonstrating in his body that it was so.[21]

The *Malleus* indicts women for being deceptive and carnal, castrating and evil. It argues that their intelligence is poor, their memories are weak, and their passions are inordinate. *Their chief symptoms are envy and jealousy.*

What else is woman but a foe to friendship, an unescapable punishment, a necessary evil, a natural temptation, a desirable calamity, a domestic danger, a delectable detriment, an evil of nature, painted with fair colours![22]

This picture is the mirror image of age-old antagonisms toward women and their powers of production and reproduction that continue to surface via religious fundamentalism, radical puritanism, and kindred public and private attitudes. It reflects intense desires to disparage and debunk that "vessel which bears all things," including its capacity to receive, to conceive, to delight, to suffer, and to bear fruit. It expresses the spirit of malice insinuated within the body of another.[23]

Why was the *Malleus* so influential? As an exposé it was part of a widespread reaction to the rebirth of science and the renewal of art and literature that occurred during the Renaissance. Many people were trapped between their hunger for knowledge and beauty (exemplified by the female form) and theological condemnation. They could only admit these hungers, besides act on them, at the price of burning guilt. Consequently they perceived the object of their desires, particularly women, as provocative and extremely dangerous. The *Malleus* helped men (and women) to deny their own guilt-ridden impulses and locate them elsewhere—in the vagina and uterus, seen as "lousy with lust." The devils were disembodied desires that could indeed bedevil by arousing intolerable anguish. Therefore the private parts of women became what people feared most in themselves.

It is likely that the young man from Ratisbon who claimed he had been deprived of his member was suffering from impotency. He couldn't get it up because he felt guilty about seducing the girl and then wanting to abandon her. He experienced this as though she had attacked him. If he chose (as many did) to blame her for frustrating him, and for sexual intrigues (that is, for his needing her as a sexual partner in the first place), then he could wreak a revenge that, in the circumstances of the day, put her life in mortal danger.

But the *Malleus* did more than absolve guilt. It was a basic text in attacking women unleashed by the Church in its struggle with the forces of the Renaissance. The tome illuminates a thousand-year history of envious and jealous rivalry with femininity, barely held in check by the capacity of the Church to "elevate spiritual motherhood" and "devalue real motherhood."[24] It remains of interest because it exploded on the world like a volcano through which the deepest detestations that men harbor toward women were able to flow.

Heinrich Kramer and James Sprenger were the Dominican monks who had been commissioned by Pope Innocent VIII to write the book and strike out at "deluded souls." The alleged delusions ("many persons of both sexes . . . have abandoned themselves to devils, incubi and succubi") were metaphors meaning that many persons began to believe that goodness resides in women, that they are life-renewing and ecstatic and are desirable in their own right.[25] These beliefs conflicted with dogmas that the Church was the source of goodness and light, the fountainhead of spiritual and temporal truth, the urobolic union of male and female, big, embracing, and all sustaining.[26]

The challenge, akin to that of Galileo in the next century, called forth massive envious retribution. Reputations were ruined, bodies were burned. Perhaps the most sinister result was that women's minds and bodies were undermined by constant attributions of evil—envious attacks that transformed them from victims to victimizers.[27]

The most vicious onslaughts were aimed at their genitalia, said to be in league with the devil. The accusations operated like Bacon's poisonous "ejaculations and irradiations." No wonder the vagina and uterus became dreaded objects! They were treated as combined evil eyes and envious mouths, organs infected by the deviltry of their accusers.

The idea of the vagina as a malevolent mouth, a genital Khoba-Khobee, did not arise with Pope Innocent VIII or the authors of the Malleus. Institutionalized hatreds simply allowed them to give vent to their own simmering suspicions. Countless boys and men are shocked to discover that women do not possess a penis, but others are more upset to learn that women have an extra orifice that enables them to take things in and get extra satisfactions.[28] It is noteworthy that in many languages the folds of skin that encircle the entranceway to the mouth and vagina have the same name—labia, or lips.

For children and adults who remain preoccupied with oral issues, this lack of a third passageway is a great disappointment and a source of enmity that heralds various attempts to abuse, spoil, stuff up, mutilate, or otherwise destroy the organ or its equivalents, just as happened during the Inquisition.

However, vagina envy is not limited to men. It is a powerful impulse in girls and women who fear that their genitals are too small and inadequate. Malicious rage follows comparisons and conclusions that they will not be able to get or give food and love to the same extent as others.[29]

Jealous rivalry also contributes to the ill will. Wife versus mistress, mother versus daughter, it is hardly necessary to detail the bad-tempered, vituperative behavior that can be aroused by third-party threats to love and emotional preeminence. The third party may be perceived as a sex organ. On a large scale this took place during the late Middle Ages. The Mother Church identified the Renaissance with sensuality and seemed to treat nonvirgins as debased vaginas, temporal competitors to its own spiritual openings and openness.

Certainly the *Malleus* and subsequent mania were frequently used by women to persecute other women. In England Elizabeth I made witchcraft a capital crime in 1562. A year later Mary Queen of Scots did the same. By the late 1600s this public savagery had crossed the Atlantic, although it had begun to ease in Europe. Women were prominent accusers in the New England witch trials.

"Morals crusades" are lingering legacies of these events. They commonly aim to cleanse life-styles and literature "polluted by harlots and whores." While the vocabulary has changed, "filth" and "pollution" having replaced "devils" and "succubi," the intention is similar, to define and denigrate women as wicked walking wombs. The people who instigate these actions might conceal their envies and jealousies, but they would agree with many of the views I have cited, that the womb is

- *Choking, constricting, and dissolving* (an experience)
- *An evil eye, an envious mouth, a dark, castrating interior* (a part of the body)
- *A wild animal, a frog, a furnace* (an animate or inanimate thing)
- *A trap, a tomb, an abyss, a well, the sea, the deepest depths* (a place or setting)
- *Draining, devouring, lustful, hysterical, poisonous, sinful, and inciting* (qualities, capacities, and characteristics)
- *A siren, a Salome, a witch, or a prostitute* (a mythical or real woman)

These representations contribute to the conception of the bad womb. In contrast, the longed-for good womb is a sense of

- *Floating, melting, enveloping warmth or effortless, delicious pleasure and ecstatic ebbs and flows* (an experience)
- *Sweet lips, an exciting mouth, a bountiful breast, a dark, fruitful interior* (a part of the body)
- *A pear, a purse, a house, a powerhouse* (an animate or inanimate thing)
- *A tunnel of love, a cavern of contentment* (a place or setting)
- *Receptive, conceptive, creative, nourishing, renewing, shelter-*

ing, energizing, and mysterious (qualities, capacities, and characteristics)
· *The Virgin Mary, a mother* (a mythical or real woman)[30]

Mystery, the dark secrets, the miracle of life, created de novo from within a tiny pear-shaped chamber are properties that have been especially valued and envied. Women are a center of mystery and a keeper of mysteries that men spend most of their lives trying to discover, debunk, emulate, and prove worthy of knowing.[31]

Margaret Mead has described several South Seas tribal societies in which men have appropriated mystery and claim, through the playing of the sacred flute, to guard the secrets of life. The essential activities of the tribe revolve around the making, learning, and ceremonial playing of the flute, tasks from which women are excluded. This allows the men to compensate themselves for a basic inferiority within a tribe that reveres fertility and to overcome feelings that their real roles are uncertain, ill-defined, and possibly unnecessary.

> Equipped with various mysterious noise-making instruments, whose potency rests upon their actual form's being unknown to those who hear the sounds—that is, the women and children must never know that they are really bamboo tubes, or hollow logs, or bits of elliptoid wood whirled on strings—they can get the male children away from the women, brand them as incomplete, and themselves turn boys into men. Women, it is true, make human beings, but only men can make men.[32]

This attitude and the underlying implications are remarkably similar to that of the United States Marine Corps. It also claims to take boys and make men of them. In Mead's tribes a crocodile figure "represents the men's group and [the initiates] come out new-born at the other end."[33] In the marines, boot camp is the magic crocodile or incubator that turns raw recruits into warriors.[34]

Soldiers and military matters are the direct rivals of peace, procreation, and motherhood. They transform not only boys into men, but creation into destruction.[35] This envious spoiling of creativity and usurping of female functions has been well portrayed by John Milton in *Paradise Lost:* Satan envies God. He wants to spoil Heaven and take it over, but he fails. Then Satan and all the other fallen angels decide to construct Hell as a rival to Heaven. They assume the powers of death in lieu of the forces of life and forever seek to destroy what God has created.[36]

Mother Earth saw these satanic powers in her Son, or the Male Principle, born from her womb. Son coveted his mother's power of creation. And it came to pass that the Race of the Son became "the Race of the Whites, the Race of Science and Death. They were created by the Mother for Her Son because of his continued interference with Nature."[37]

Mother Earth was a highly gifted, uneducated black woman from the slums of Trinidad, who in 1973, at the age of thirty-nine, turned her back on modern society and retreated into the bush with her husband, children, and various acolytes.[38] She feared that "the Son"— that is, maleness, white people—aimed to steal the power of pro-creation, "through a technology of robots, computers, 'tissue' [test-tube] babies, and sex change operations." So she decided to regain the mysteries and powers she thought whites and Rastas had taken from her and from nature.

> All He [the Son] does is to put out material: the wars and the fights, the bombs and the Airplanes, trying to make human, trying to change them, some a mother to a son, change a son to a mother. All these are his experiment, trying to take over. He still cannot create. He know everything about Life, but not this—not the power to bring forth. That is what he really wants. The power of Love.[39]

Mead, the marines, Mother Earth, all demonstrate various attempts to emulate, control, and take over female functions and products, a project motivated by envy and awe. Male pride is very much an issue here, to do with the constant sense of having to prove oneself in the face of women "who only have to be themselves for things to grow naturally inside them." The ensuing "anything you can do I can do better" attitude in conjunction with spiteful put-downs or physical threats is a manic assault on female prowess. It conveys contempt, triumph over the need for care or for sex, and greedy control over powerful but frightening forces.

Men also dress and behave like women for nonmalicious reasons, to avoid loss and make good real or imagined damage done to them. In a male-oriented, competitive culture this is not an easy task, and the opportunity to emulate women may be totally proscribed or limited to a few ceremonial occasions. The result may be a resurgence of vengeful rage for all the pain suffered in trying to be feminine.

The experience of women is not dissimilar. They have a sense of biological and social insecurity heightened by envious and jealous rivalries with their mother, sisters, and familial surrogates. But they are innately closer to the figures whom they wish to harm as well as emulate. Therefore the pattern of violence is different, more likely to be inner- rather than outer-directed. As in sterility, this leads to the negation of function. Seemingly an attack on the self, it inevitably embraces a vicious onslaught on an "internalized other." For one patient of mine this other was her mother. She used to gloat: "I may be barren, but so is the woman my mother wanted to be when she decided to live inside me."[40] She also liked to provoke strangers to beat her up. They were her wrath. She was her mother. The masochism was a chimera. She hated power of women. In the rest of the chapter I shall trace the ambivalent intentions of boys and girls, men and women, toward four major areas of female potency: menstruation, fertility, pregnancy, and childbirth.

Menstruation

There are records of male horror and fascination with menstruation in practically every society.[41] Albertus Magnus, a thirteenth-century medical scholar, noted in his book *The Secrets of Women:* "Menstruating women carried with them a poison that could kill an infant in its cradle."[42]

More recent observers have asserted that menstrual blood can "turn wine into vinegar," "cause mayonnaise to curdle," and make "the very flowers in the fields lose their aroma," aside from doing terrible things to the male member.[43] Many restrictions and taboos on menstruating women confirm these fears and the basic ideas that menstruation is dirty, damaging, contaminating, castrating, and a sign of castration as well as a punishment for sin.[44]

Yet men have maintained the deepest interest in womb blood as a life-giving magical potion and the essence of female reproductive power. They admire and begrudge the fact that girls have a clear-cut signal of biological maturity and a natural means of self-purification.[45]

In Australia the male members of various aboriginal tribes go to extraordinary lengths to replicate menstruation at puberty. They practice ritual subincision. This involves cutting a slit along the entire undersurface of the penis and leaving an opening called a vulva, vagina, or penis womb.

As soon as ever [the novice] was in position another man sat astride of his body, grasped the penis and put the urethra on the stretch. The operator then approached and quickly, with a stone knife, laid open the urethra from below. . . . When all was over the [newly initiated] were led to one side while they squatted over shields into which the blood was allowed to drain . . . and from which it is emptied into the centre of a fire which is made for the purpose. . . . As a result of the operation . . . micturation is always performed in a squatting position.[46]

The vital issue is not simply the original wound, but subsequent reopenings of it to produce blood called "woman" or "milk." This represents menstruation and fertility. It is used to ritually anoint and paint the body in the rainbow-serpent ceremony when "a vaginal father replaces the phallic mother."[47]

The Indians of New Guinea have different methods of inducing male menstruation. They stuff a razor-sharp leaf up and down the nostril or scrape the tongue with it.[48] These activities are an important means of self-purification and an essential precursor to playing the sacred flute, a secret rite that embodies creativity and fertility. Interestingly, most of the women know all about the secrets, but they pretend otherwise.

> The women take the attitude that as they have everything of importance—the babies, the pigs, the gardens—they will let the men have their flutes and their ceremonies if it makes them feel satisfied.[49]

Although overt displays of male menstruation are uncommon in Western society, Bruno Bettelheim has described the intense desire of teenaged boys to possess female features and to mimic the menses. One small group of boys and girls at the Orthogenic School decided that "The boys would cut their index fingers every month and mix their blood with that of the menses."[50]

I could cite other examples where boys and men have wounded themselves or covertly suffered accidents or internal hemorrhages for the same purpose.[51] It is possible that these practices are much more frequent than is generally realized.

Women share traditional beliefs that they are unclean and contaminating during the menses. In popular parlance they often refer to the menstrual period as "the curse," a term that implies much more than a nuisance.[52] In the late 1960s a couple of ethnographers interviewed women in a French village about menstruation and attendant dangers. There was some divergence of opinion about whether a menstruating woman could make a barrel of salt pork go off, but one person averred:

> Oh, boy! Once I caused the entire barrel to go bad. It's true. I wasn't thinking at all. I just went in there. And when I came back later for some more bacon, it was all green.[53]

Such convictions undoubtedly contribute to the emotional distress and physical pain that can accompany the menses. They also contribute to modern preoccupations with pads, tampons, medications, and other means to soak up, clean up, or stop the menstrual flow.[54] Yet until relatively recently there was a countervailing view that menstruation was a natural means of purification that should not be impeded. In this century Finnish countryfolk bled onto their clothes and argued that it was harmful to use pads:

> Women are cleaned of evil and dirt during their monthlies; so that the cleaning will be unimpeded, the genitals must not be stopped up with a cloth or a pad.[55]

"Evil," "dirty," "bad," "unhealthy" are concepts that hark back to the *Malleus* and long before. They reflect fear, ignorance, superstition, observation, and malicious insinuation.[56] But I think these views persist so tenaciously because women want them and use them to protect themselves against envy of their biological potency and pride. They intend to convince others that this tangible evidence of fertility and reproductive power is really disgusting and dangerous. Then they hope that men (and female rivals) will be less inclined to take it over and attack it—an effective defense.[57]

Fertility

The grenvious eye does not threaten one biological function, rather the entire capacity to bring forth bread from the earth, babies from the body, or ideas from the mind. Together they represent the good, creative breast and womb that give and sustain life. In agrarian societies these activities are so highly prized that they may be given divine status, to which men wholly aspire.

Man the creator painted caves, built huts, and made myths. Collectively the myths are spiritual storehouses. They insure against spiritual starvation while the priests and shaman who service them play the same role with the soul that women perform with the body. Both renew and give birth to life.[58]

The earliest habitations followed the female form. Many buildings still do. The French architect and psychologist Olivier Marc has observed the dwellings of African tribesmen:

> Their houses look like slightly attenuated pouches, each with a vertical slit along one side. Seen from a certain angle, they reminded me of enormous breasts pointing up towards the sky. But even more striking than the shape was the entrance, a thick-lipped slit, the only decorated element of the structure.
>
> I was then convinced that the interior model which had presided over the birth of this form had been a mother's womb, seen from the inside. These houses were wombs.[59]

The earliest paintings had to do with food and fertility. They are often found in caves that can only be approached with the greatest difficulty, down "long, narrow, slippery corridors" or "through a manhole below which a river runs."[60] Bettelheim suggests that the artists deliberately picked womblike interiors. In this way they not only depicted the animals and showed where they came into being, but also made themselves and their fellow tribesmen experience the process of procreation and birth.[61]

In the progression from agrarian to industrial to postindustrial cultures, the same impulses to re-create procreation and its setting remain very strong but are expressed with increasing degrees of abstraction. Magic leads to myth to religion to science to cosmic speculation, the big bang.[62] Cave figures lead to representational art to abstract expressionism, black on black.[63]

This trend is not universally satisfying. While the symbolic expression of womb dramas pervades art, literature, and other disciplines, people crave their literal reenactment. Visitors to the futuristic Israel Museum in Jerusalem return and may be reborn as they pass through a long corridor before entering the central chamber containing the Torah scroll and other treasures. Users of the curved passageways of the TWA terminal at Kennedy Airport in New York have a similar opportunity.[64]

In contrast, Steven Spielberg's two Indiana Jones films allow onlookers to relive and relieve their horror of the female interior by identifying with the hero. In *Raiders of the Lost Ark* Jones hacks his way through the jungle (pubic hair), negotiates a secret tunnel (vagina), and discovers the treasure room (womb). In *Indiana Jones and the Temple of Doom* the mise-en-scène is the villain's palace, where a comparable sequence occurs. Only Jones can overcome the terrible dangers: spears, darts, poison, pitfalls, tarantulas, crushing stones, and so forth.[65]

The passage with knives or passage with biting insects represents the dreaded vagina dentata, or vagina with teeth. This is one of the earliest and most tenacious phantasies of a woman's insides and accounts for untold incidents of male and female impotency.[66] Many men won't enter a woman, or even come near one, for fear that their penes will be chewed, mangled, or poisoned. Moreover, many women won't let men enter them because they also fear their bodies are damaging. If intercourse took place, they would be left with an intolerable sense of guilt. One reason for the immense popularity of Spielberg's films is that they demonstrate the possibility of complete invulnerability to the vagina with teeth—indeed, to the bad, retaliating womb.[67]

Ceremonies of the sacred flute, cave paintings, astronomical speculation, or entertaining cinemas may celebrate fertility or not, depending on whether they respect female prowess or debase it. The aggressive response, indicating envy instead of awe, is overtly and covertly destructive to a woman's body, abilities, pride, social position, or life opportunities. As in a manic attack, it seeks not just to emulate women, but to control and triumph over them.

Spielberg's films do not enhance femininity. They treat women as mildly inconvenient sexual toys or frightening, hateful objects. The overbearing arrogance of the hero more than compensates for feared female or male inferiorities. No doubt this is another reason the films have been so successful. However, there is a change in *Indiana Jones and the Temple of Doom.* The hero depends on his female accomplice to escape from the dangerous chamber with mangling spikes and walls. She partially portrays the good, helpful womb. At least Spielberg hints that such an entity exists.

Since the sixties there have also been useful changes in the psychological literature. Previously female capacities and accomplishments were not taken seriously. Women were seen as extensions of men. The wish to emulate them was frequently interpreted as a defense against Oedipal wishes, a sign of inadequate masculinity, or an urge to obtain a superior penis, rather than as a positive desire in its own right.[68] With certain individuals these views may or may not be correct. When applied indiscriminately, they are begrudging and disparaging and, as far as women are concerned, confirm the need for a wary eye toward the interest of others in their minds and bodies.

The traditional safeguards include amulets and talismans and occasional visits to a priest, rabbi, shaman, or doctor. Among Oriental Jews it is still fashionable to wear amulets in order to promote fertility, ensure pregnancy, assist delivery, and generally avert the evil eye. Distinguished cabalists used to write special handbooks on amulet making. For a childless woman, for example, suitable texts would include.

> There shall not be male or female barren.
> —Deuteronomy 7, 14.
> And the Lord remembered Sarah. . . . And Sarah conceived.
> —Genesis 31, 1–2.[69]

The magic is a protection against the ill will of female friends and relatives, not just men. These hostilities are especially dangerous because they have a nasty tendency to boomerang back against the perpetrators. The Argentine psychoanalyst Marie Langer points out that women who simmer with envious anger toward their own fertile mothers are likely candidates for sterility.[70] Projective processes lead them to feel that their own insides have been attacked and laid waste by extremely hostile internal and external figures, the proverbial evil witch.[71] Moreover, "the fear resulting from hatred of the fertile mother" prevents them from having good creative persons to take after. No wonder spasms or anesthesia of the entire genital apparatus may precede or accompany sterility. Yet the malicious glee that spiteful daughters derive from preventing their parents from becoming grandparents barely compensates for the self-inflicted emotional and physical damage.[72]

Langer discusses a young girl who was able to overcome the fear and hatred that centered on her envied mother. Before beginning analysis, the girl had had several abortions and had twice tried to kill herself, first by poison and later by drowning. She had been terrified that her mother was trying to poison her. During the course of the treatment she tried to become pregnant and eventually succeeded. Just after the conception she had a dream:

> She is in the cellar of her childhood home. Everything is full of dust and there are dead cockroaches hanging from the ceiling. One falls down. It disgusts but does not horrify her. She calmly starts cleaning the place.[73]

The dream depicts a daughter who feels capable of restoring her own and her mother's womb (the cellar), the children she had killed inside her mother, and her self (the dead roaches, the abortions). Langer adds that by doing this she is able to overcome her guilt and fear of the past and prepare her womb for a new and fruitful pregnancy.[74]

Pregnancy

The worst fear that can afflict a woman is that her insides will be robbed and destroyed.[75] This is the female equivalent of castration anxiety. It is a deep sense of dread that encompasses the breast, the body, the womb, and all the babies contained therein, past, present, and future. They represent food, parents, life, and the continuity of life.[76]

Children at play demonstrate these fears and the wishes that lie behind them. Hanna Segal has described one little girl who was "preoccupied with pregnancies."[77] During one session she started to smear glue on the floor. This turned out to be her "sick" or vomit by which she hoped to spoil Segal's insides and prevent her from having new babies. Later she was frightened to come back because the same might happen to her.

In the same vein Melanie Klein narrated the story of Erna, a six-year-old who was obsessed by brutal phantasies of cutting, tearing, and burning. These led to an extraordinary inhibition of learning, whereby "arithmetic and writing symbolized violent sadistic attacks on her mother's body and her father's penis," as well as the babies contained therein.[78]

Simple observation of children's activities confirms such intentions. Girls and boys do treat their "Cindys," houses, cars, trains, and now male dolls with unbearable cruelty. As most parents can attest, a new toy may only last a few minutes before it is soiled and broken. On the other hand, gentle play harbors loving, reparative feelings. A near inconsolable grief may ensue if a favorite plaything is damaged. Klein comments:

> Beneath the little girl's ever recurring desire for dolls there lies a need for consolation and reassurance. The possession of her dolls is a proof that she had not been robbed of her children by her mother, that she has not had her body destroyed by her and that she is able to have children.[79]

Attacks on the pregnant body extend to caves, houses, and any life-filled interior structure up to and including the mind. That is why we react with particular horror when a malicious man or woman desecrates a house or cuts up pictures in a museum.

In the last chapter I discussed two patients who systematically interfered with my mental life. They loathed my thoughts—to them, mental babies as well as psychic food—and the mind womb that carried them. These persons repeatedly refused me the time and space to develop my ideas. They engaged in a variety of anxiety-provoking activities designed to abort my creative processes. Consequently I noticed that my interpretations rarely grew to term. Either I would blurt them out prematurely (suffer a psychic miscarriage) or remain unheeded (be a bearer of stillborn messages). Their attacks illustrate another dimension of the negative therapeutic reaction.

Psychotherapy involves hard labor, as does most creative endeavor that must emerge from a dark internal space. Artists and writers often remark that they feel like a woman making a child. Their finished product comes forth only after a prolonged confinement and difficult delivery.[80] In his *Diaries* the director Peter Hall refers to a conversation with Harold Pinter. He was trying to beget a new work. Pinter told him: "I think I might be pregnant."

Hall chuckled to himself: "This is great news. A play is on the way."[81]

Few artists do not suffer long labors. Mozart, however, could create whole symphonies in his head and transcribe them note perfect onto paper.[82] This casts further light on Salieri's mischief. He hated Mozart with a passion perhaps only equaled by a woman who produces deformed or stillborn babies while her sister or neighbor gives birth to child after healthy child.

Aggressive onslaughts on the pregnant person and the child-to-be are commonplace and include neglect, assault, and malicious rivalry.[83] The competitive element is clear in couvade, the custom and ritual by which the father-to-be takes over the dress, activities, and physical symptoms of his pregnant wife.[84] Originally conceived in the mid-1800s to denote primitive tribal practices, couvade appears to be a general phenomenon.[85]

Based on a study of one hundred English fathers, the writer Brian Jackson asserts that approximately one half went through couvade. In America he suggests the figure is even higher.[86] Jackson has described a cluster of couvade signals, the most prominent of which are a heightened interest in pets and physical fitness. For example, he observed one man who became obsessed with a newly purchased dog:

> He was continually kissing it on the nose, nursing it, holding it close and staring into its eyes. He spoke to it in baby talk, and kept telling it, "You're *such* a baby."[87]

Another joined a health club and was forever weighing himself and sipping carrot juice. He used to explain that he was keeping fit for the baby. On the other hand, several men related a variety of physical symptoms, including abdominal pain, back pain, "a feeling of fullness in my stomach," broken sleep patterns, strange cravings for food and drink, and marked weight gain:

> I've put on three quarters of a stone since Sally got pregnant. I'm keeping up with her all right.[88]

Cuddling canines may be cute, but it has a distinctly malicious edge when it detracts from the varied needs of the pregnant woman and puts her and the baby at a disadvantage to a dog. The envious father resents both his wife's condition and the special care and attention she requires. To him the pregnancy is a narcissistic wound that arouses strong desires to steal the limelight and ruin her health and happiness. Simultaneously the father-to-be may feel intensely jealous of the fetus for seeming to appropriate his rightful love and pleasures. As one man put it: "It's not a bun in the oven she's got. We've got a bloody Christmas turkey."[89]

This turkey was an unwelcome intruder who came between the man and his mate as well as the idea of a great greedy feast from which he had been and would continue to be excluded. Far from sharing in a joyous occasion, the predominance of envy and jealousy alienated him from his future child. It is not too farfetched to think that in using words like "bloody Christmas turkey," he wanted to bludgeon the baby and eat it, a spiteful deed that incorporates the regressive wish to become the infant-inside-mother and regain all his "lost" real and imagined comforts.[90]

Childbirth

The alternative to being the baby is having the baby. Couvade demonstrates the extraordinary lengths to which many fathers may go to capture attention and foster phantasies of impregnation. But this holds true for other men as well, heterosexual and homosexual. Anal intercourse, fellatio, constipation, abdominal distension, and ruminations about intestinal tumors have all preceded or accompanied strong desires for anal or umbilical births.[91]

Recently a scientist confided to me that he had wanted to conceive a child in his abdomen for years, long before his marriage. He remembered that as a youth he used to daydream about babies growing in his tummy and being born by cesarean section. He had worked out all the details. Now he was getting worried because his once distant fantasies were becoming technically feasible.[92]

Test-tube babies, cloning, gene splicing, and robotics are kindred achievements that indicate Mother Earth's fearsome predictions about the race of males taking over female generative powers cannot be taken lightly.[93] As far back as 1818, Mary Shelley anticipated many of these same issues in *Frankenstein*.[94] She depicted a scientist who was obsessed with making life. He succeeded but created a monster and revealed a dilemma that has haunted us ever since. The monster has to do with a creature starved of love but imbued with the destructive impulses of its creator. The dilemma has to do with the ethics of imitating or interfering with natural processes. Procedures to redress sterility, produce drugs, or automate hazardous and dehumanizing work may be developed with the best of intentions but still unleash terrible dangers. Fears about them underlie the longstanding debate about the new science of conception and several generations of monster and sci-fi films.[95]

Doctors have tried to replicate not just life, but the womb as well. A former teacher of mine used to refer to the incubators in his premature baby unit as "a womb with a view."[96] He was a kind man who respected babies and their mothers. Indeed it would be unjust and incorrect to suggest that the scientific community has a malicious mentality. Whether a particular practice is harmful or not has to be judged within a multiplicity of contexts, social, historical, technological, psychological, and so forth. Nowhere is this more true than in the drama of childbirth, an event burdened by pain and flanked by benevolence and sadism. Until the late Victorian era, childbirth was a leading cause of death in women, and few efforts were spared, no matter how gruesome, to save the life of the mother.[97] Notable among these was the development of the use of forceps.

Forceps were invented in the late sixteenth century by members of the Chamberlen family, a London dynasty of male midwives. They tried to keep the invention secret, but by the 1730s the news had leaked out, and new improved models were being developed.[98] Forceps were especially useful in prolonged deliveries, when the infant got stuck in the pelvis. Prior to forceps the only recourse to losing the mother was to kill the child and pick it out of the womb piece by piece.[99] But a forceps delivery, especially without anesthesia, was a fearsome business. The vagina and uterus were frequently torn by incompetent or impatient attendants, and the resultant mortality rate was high. As late as 1920 certain urban practitioners were known as "forceps fiends," and their abuses led to restrictions on home deliveries.[100]

Antisepsis became a major area of obstetrical concern in 1847, when Ignaz Semmelweis published his momentous discovery that the simple use of disinfectants markedly reduced maternal infections. Previously both doctors and midwives barely thought of washing their hands. They would poke around the vagina and cervix with hands covered in dirt and pus. Moreover, both home and hospital were breeding grounds for the most virulent organisms. Few women would deliver without a transient fever (called "weed" or "milk fever"), and many died from massive infection (the dreaded childbed fever).[101] All too often a hospital confinement was akin to a death sentence.[102] Yet Semmelweis was generally ignored, and antisepsis did not begin in earnest until three decades later when the Germans and French obstetricians adopted Lister's work with carbolic acid (phenol). Subsequently a rigorous asepsis became the norm and septic deaths a rarity.[103]

In current practice women in labor suffer from overscrupulous cleanliness. They are scrubbed, shaved, and purged, a routine that many find upsetting and degrading. Yet it is only the first part of a ritual by which their condition becomes medicalized and responsibility for their body and its function is more or less taken out of their hands.[104] As the psychoanalyst Peter Lomas points out:

> Much that is done in the name of medical necessity has the consequence of preventing the mother from regarding herself as a mature human being, from participating actively and fully in the birth, from loving and caring for her baby, and from taking an uninhibited and triumphant joy in the occasion.[105]

Lomas adds that the convention of segregating the mother and transferring the significance of the procedures away from her is very similar to couvade. But in this instance it is the doctor who takes over rather than the husband. The directly destructive components of this control are manifest in excessive surgery, notably in episiotomy and hysterectomy.

Episiotomy is the cutting, usually with a pair of scissors, of the tissue at the base of the vagina during the second stage of labor. Originally described in 1742, it has become a popular means of avoiding vaginal tears, facilitating forceps deliveries, and protecting the fetus from a prolonged labor. But many midwives and doctors question its validity.[106] Serious tears of any kind are infrequent, and the operation itself carries significant risk of pain, scarring, and fistula formation between the vagina and anus.[107]

Consultant obstetrician Yehudi Gordon has called the episiotomy "the commonest invasive procedure performed during the lifetime of a woman," and Derek Llewelyn Jones, writing in *Fundamentals of Obstetrics and Gynaecology,* declares:

> [It is] one of the least considered and most painful operations performed on the human female. . . . Far too many women leave hospital with the memory of perineal pain, which they aver was far worse than the pain of parturition.[108]

Two hundred years after its inception, the suitability of this procedure still requires substantiation.[109] Similar questions becloud the hysterectomy, the partial or total removal of the womb, usually done later in a woman's life. Many practitioners also believe that this operation is performed far too frequently and with little consideration of the severe emotional sequelae.[110] The general medical attitude seems to be that women should "be happy to have a potentially cancer-bearing organ removed."[111]

The loss of control, pain, and humiliation that accompany antisepsis, and the cutting, scarring, and scooping out that occur during forceps, episiotomy, and other surgical procedures come ominously close to fulfilling women's worst fears, that their bodies will be invaded, robbed, and destroyed. In large measure this accounts for the dread that precedes childbirth and the depression that follows it.

The classical psychoanalytic view is that women equate childbirth with castration because it provides the penultimate proof that they are not male.[112] On the contrary, childbirth is the climax of feminine biological achievement. If castration takes place, it results from the way that help becomes hurt during the hard work from conception to birth. I distinguish three major reasons for this transformation.

The first is social and medical inertia. Traditions, no matter how damaging, die slowly.[113] The second has to do with the traumatization of the attendants in the face of suffering and death. Doctors, midwives, and relatives will go to almost any lengths to prevent the loss of mother and child and avoid their own horrific fear and guilt if they cannot do so. The third factor is envy: of female creativity, happiness, active accomplishment, and, last but not least, suffering.[114] This leads me to conclude that procedures like episiotomy, which remain questionable but are nevertheless widely performed, are a highly structured defense against guilt as well as the manifestation of institutionalized envy. By this I mean that spiteful, begrudging, destructive wishes toward women are hidden within respected societal practices that allow sadism to be indulged with a minimum of personal responsibility.[115]

Deep-rooted, nonmedical, social and religious customs also express comparable antagonisms. Among many tribes and cultures women are treated like pariahs, instead of celebrated, after childbirth. Churching was widely practiced among Anglicans and Catholics until the twentieth century. It is a form of religious decontamination that gave a woman permission to reenter society. But it also conveyed the view that a new mother was "unclean" and a source of evil.[116] In Germany, for example, people used to believe that a new mother could contaminate a well, or cause a house to burn down, if she entered it before the churching ceremony had taken place.[117]

With noteworthy exceptions, women generally tend to accept the treatment meted out to them during pregnancy and childbirth in a detached, stoical, long-suffering, almost masochistic manner. Given the extent of their physical and emotional vulnerability, this stance is hardly remarkable. It is a stratagem of self-sacrifice designed to protect themselves and their forthcoming child from external dangers and internal conflict. The latter may surface as a puerperal breakdown when dread of internal enviers, experienced as condemning, attacking mother and sister figures, becomes overwhelming, especially if it coincides with actual rejection or damage.[118] Then all the complicated propitiation gestures, the shaving, the enemas, the anesthesia, the exhausted if not meek compliance with doctors who cut her body and nurses who remove her baby, go for naught, and the woman is left with her own momentary but terrible fragility within a world that looks upon creativity, whether in art, science, or females, with ambivalent fascination.[119]

Childbirth, and the other major areas of female potency, indicate that the womb is more than a part of the body, a thing, a quality, an experience, or a person. The womb encompasses both the idea and actuality of a function, a product, and universal reality.

Menstruation, fertility, pregnancy, childbirth, and creativity are positive functions that contribute to the concept of the good womb.

War, ritual bleeding, sterility, couvade, and medical mania convey the opposite. They are negating, mutilating activities that signify the destroying and destroyed womb.

The products of the good womb include rich blood, healthy babies, books, plays, sculptures, symphonies, and life-enhancing innovations, while the foul womb yields bad blood, dead babies, deformities, monsters, roaches, and robots.

Both wombs, fair and foul, connote universal realities ranging from the deepest depths to celestial abodes, from human consciousness to cosmic consciousness, from heaven to hell. Each bears some responsibility for the generative powers generally attributed to the womb, the uroboros, the origin of all things, which is neither entirely female nor entirely male.

At a time, however, when umbilical pregnancies and intelligent robots are a distinct possibility, it is worth recalling that the human species derives from the body of women, not the rib of Adam or the head of Zeus.[120] As Mother Earth would be quick to point out, these myths contain the seeds of hubris, a distinct overstepping of bounds, to compensate for a feared inferior biology.[121]

In contrast, a five-year-old boy conveyed his acceptance and wondrous belief in the continuity of life. He hoped that his pregnant mother would give birth to a girl and added:

> Then she will have babies, and her babies will have babies, and then it goes on forever."[122]

6

Penis Greed

Penis Greed is an insatiable desire for the male member and all the perks and privileges that seem to accompany it.

> I know it's not true, but I'm like a lot of men. Even when we know better, we feel deep down that "the bigger your cock, the more of a man you are."—STEVE[1]

> When one has it, one has everything, one feels protected, nothing can touch you. . . . One is what one is, and the others can only follow you and admire you. . . . It is absolute power. —IDA[2]

> "What have you been doing all summer?"
> "Growing a penis!"—BRENDA[3]

These preoccupations with the penis extend from the anatomical organ to far-reaching concerns about strength, power, authority, virility, ambition, energy, and enterprise, which account for Carl Jung's trenchant remark, "The penis is only a phallic symbol."[4]

The longing for male qualities, functions, and status, the phallus, features in many cultures, but in this century Freud drew special attention to phallic wishes during the course of describing the development of female sexuality. He observed that at a certain stage in their lives, the physical interests of children shift away from the mouth and anus to the genitals. Then the little girl discovers what she lacks and passionately desires the missing part:

> The discovery that she is castrated is a turning-point in a girl's growth. . . . Her self-love is mortified by the comparison with the boy's far superior equipment.[5]
> — She makes her judgement and her decision in a flash. She has seen it and knows that she is without it and wants to have it.[6]

This sudden shocking awareness of absent maleness and the wish to overcome it is what Freud called "penis envy." Related to the castration complex or the masculine complex, this term (and attendant assumptions) has achieved a prominent place in the psychological literature and popular parlance.[7] But I believe it is a misnomer and, as generally used, perpetuates several misconceptions.

The classical concept of penis envy has little to do with envy. On the contrary, it conveys intense admiration, emulation, and identification for all things masculine. It is a wish, first for a penis, then for a penis in intercourse, and finally for a penis substitute, such as a baby.[8]

An admixture of resentful, raging, spiteful, spoiling, begrudging, belittling attitudes and actions toward men, maleness, and male organs certainly does exist. This is appropriately called penis envy and can be expressed by the penis as well as toward it. I shall soon discuss this complex in considerable detail, but it was not an essential part of Freud's initial formulations.

The early analysts also believed that penis envy, or what I call "penis greed," was essentially a biologically determined feature of females that condemns them to spend much of their lives trying to regain something they had been born without. Karl Abraham stated confidently that most women want to be men:

> We come across this wish in all products of the unconscious, especially in dreams and neurotic symptoms. The extraordinary frequency of these observations suggests that the wish is one common to and occurring in all women.[9]

Freud put the issue more succinctly: "Anatomy is destiny."[10] This epigram is based on one by Napoleon. He too spent much of his life trying to overcome an accident of birth. Potency and power are not issues limited to the female sex. Most boys and men are obsessed with being bigger, stronger, and more powerful than others, even if they have to conquer the world. This is an expression of "the small penis complex," or "the Napoleon syndrome." As with girls who may be struck with admiration and awe upon observing the male member, boys also describe feelings of bewilderment and wonder when comparing themselves with siblings, friends, or parents.[11] A friend of mine still trembles with shock and surprise when he recalls his father urinating. Physically he is tall and strong, but he longs to be "macho" like his dad. No matter how much work he does, or how many women he sleeps with, "becoming a man is the continuing battle of my life."

Small penis people take different tacks. Some emphasize their smallness or inadequacies in order to take advantage of pity and put others to shame. Woody Allen does this in many of his films. Then greed is tempered by aggression. Allen follows the traditions of Yiddish literature, where many a saying pokes fun at the man (or woman) who makes himself appear smaller, weaker, more inadequate than he really is:

Mach sich not azoi klein—du bist not azoi grois!
(Don't make yourself so small—you're not that big!)[12]

In *Annie Hall,* Allen plays his typical role, the shlemiel on the make.[13] He decides to remake Annie (Diane Keaton) in his image and convinces her to see a therapist. On her return from the first session he asks her how it went:

"So, I told her about the family and about my feelings towards men . . . then she mentioned about penis envy. Did you know about that?"
"Me? I'm one of the few males who suffers from that!"[14]

Allen exaggerates. He is one of many men who long to be big. His envy reveals a voracious appetite for phallic power. Children and adults of both sexes harbor kindred desires, not just for a penis or phallus, but for a magical member, an idealized penis, and for the person who possesses it.

Victorian women were noted for their lofty views of the men they married. In a book addressed to the women of England in 1842, Mrs. Sarah Ellis proclaimed:

It is essential to recognize . . . the superiority of your husband simply as a man. . . . In the character of a noble, enlightened and truly good man, there is a power and a sublimity so nearly approaching what we believe to be the nature and capacity of angels, that . . . no language can describe the degree of admiration and respect which the contemplation of such a character must excite.[15]

Female fascination for the superman remains unabated. In 1982 the genre of romantic fiction alone saw worldwide sales of 250 million books.[16] The basic plot involves a young, inexperienced girl who meets, marries, and tames a tough, sophisticated, successful (but often vulnerable) older man. The same theme reappears in popular magazines like *Playgirl,* which aim to provide "a smorgasbord of everything wonderfully male."

In addition to lots of muscular full-frontal nudes, a typical issue features articles about rugged loners like playwright Sam Shepard, who "exudes the unmistakable scent of sexual gunpowder" or electrifying, unpredictable actors like Mel Gibson, "a complex and divided man running at full speed."[17] *Playgirl* permits its readership to see, feel, even taste virility. The latter comes conveniently packaged as multicolored heart-shaped pills and elongated capsules (Magnum, Triple Strength, Fast One) in ads for "Continuous Action Stimulants."[18]

Male phantasies focus on prowess, the penis that is two feet long, hard as steel, and can go all night.[19] Myths of superpotency leap from ancient legends (Hercules, Achilles, Samson) to contemporary comics. The character of Superman, "faster than a speeding bullet, more powerful than a locomotive," was created by two seventeen-year-old boys in 1933.[20] And Clark Kent is less than a leap from the macho heroes of Ernest Hemingway, Norman Mailer, Yukio Mishima, D. H. Lawrence, Henry Miller, and Harold Robbins.[21] Their tales are cravings that ricochet through the dreams of untold readers, "endlessly searching, sensing, expanding, probing, penetrating, throbbing, wilting and wanting more."[22]

Why is there such a tendency to put the penis on a pedestal, to value and overvalue maleness? First, like the womb, the penis is heir to the breast. Much of the passionate love and hate originally directed to Mother and her body becomes redirected to Father and his organ. In their mind's eye both boys and girls tend to transform the penis into a richer source of food, pleasure, and stimulation. They imbue it with the power to satisfy all desires and turn to it with devastating voraciousness whenever they feel hungry and deprived or are deprived such as during weaning, separation, and illness.[23]

I am not just describing a phantasy. In actuality, fathers and husbands are often considered superior providers. Women may prepare food, but men grow, trap, or rear it and gain the glory for culinary expertise. Traditionally the most famous cooks in Europe and other gastronomic centers have been men. From Taillevent to contemporaries Michele Guerard, Paul Bocuse, Robert Carrier, and Kenneth Lo, male chefs have been able to command public attention and commensurate fees.[24]

The male product has also been likened to superior milk—a rich, condensed cream. High-caste Hindus aver that a single drop of semen takes forty days and forty drops of blood to make, although a careful attention to diet speeds things up. There is a reservoir in the head with a capacity of just under seven ounces. A good store of quality semen/cream guarantees health and well-being.[25]

It follows that many people prefer fellatio to any other genital activity. This practice gives undisguised expression to the ideal of the feeding phallus and subsumes the wish to suck, chew, bite, swallow, and retain the penis or its products in the mouth or other parts.[26]

"Colin" is a fifty-year-old businessman whose obsession, whose driving force, is "big pricks." He is constantly on the go and has become a connoisseur of haunts and hideaways all over Europe, where he seeks out men who possess the largest organs. He aims to see and suck on them. But he has another and even more compelling obsession, jewelry shops. He can spend hours searching for gems, the right gems, especially diamonds and rubies. As with big "pricks," he becomes mesmerized by the sight of large jewels. In fact, he will make any excuse to look at and fondle them. This led to his entering therapy. He had begun to spend so much time and money in these shops that his family and business were in jeopardy. During the course of the treatment he had a frightening but vivid vision of jewels embedded in the walls of the consulting room.

> I could hardly believe it, they looked so real. They were everywhere, big ones, little ones, and even as I thought of them they grew brighter, more magnificent. But what surprised me the most was their shape, their cut. I couldn't get out of my mind that they looked like tits and then like pricks, tits and pricks over and over, all ending in sparkling points of light.[27]

These gems were brilliant teats, nipples, thumbs, concentrations of desire. Colin transformed cravings for an engorged nipple into passions for a huge penis. In his mind they looked alike and were alike, a conjunction noted by the Dutch analyst August Stärcke, who asserted in 1921 that children are dependent on a penislike organ of their mother and often experience weaning as a castration.[28]

Interestingly, the penis and nipple not only look alike, but share similar functions. They engorge when stimulated, yield life-giving fluids, and link one person to another. A big penis, like a big nipple, means a big link. This is especially important for children and adults like Colin who feel uncertain about the extent of their parents' love or their own ability to retain it.[29]

The penis epitomizes deep attachment. Paradoxically, it also represents detachment—that is, the possibility of separating from the breast in order to establish a distinct sense of self. At a time when children want to differentiate themselves from their mother and gain a greater degree of control over their lives, boys possess positive proof that their body is different. Therefore it is easier for them to conclude that they are different. Unlike girls, whose external genitals develop at a later date, they have an organ to see, feel, exhibit, and play with.[30] The advantage is self-assertion. The disadvantage is everpresent fears of being taken over and submerged in and into women, nature, the eternal female.[31]

> The whole process of becoming masculine is at risk in the little boy from the day of birth on; his still-to-be-created masculinity is endangered by the primary, profound, primeval oneness with mother, a blissful experience that serves, buried but active in the core of one's identity, as a focus that, throughout life, can attract one to regress back to that primitive oneness.[32]

This is one aspect of several dilemmas that boys and girls both share: how to recognize their body type (biological identity) while gaining a sense of their sexuality (gender identity) and maintaining themselves as separate human beings (personal identity). The struggle begins at birth and has as much to do with parental attitudes as the child's own biological endowment and psychological development.[33] The penis that little girls miss is the freedom from maternal domination and the ability to control their own bodies and lives. Not surprisingly they pine for a magic wand, an alternative organ that feeds yet supersedes dependency. Most want a penis not to be a man, but to be a woman.[34]

In general girls find gender identity an easier task than boys because they and their mothers share the same kind of body. So they can keep the body image that follows close emotional ties. Boys face a more complicated endeavor in that they have to develop a new body and self-image—that is, they must disidentify with their mothers, not feel like a woman, and at the same time retain their basic maternal connections.[35]

The wish for exaggerated male powers, especially before boys have established a separate awareness of themselves as individuals, is an attempt to solve the conflict between remaining tied to Mother (and thereby being like her) and growing up (identifying with Dad). [36] The lack of adequate differentiation from Mother and mothering can be a great danger both to sexual identity and personal integrity. The subsequent surfeit of femininity contributes to castration fears, which also may be perpetuated by a clinging and self-seeking mother in conjunction with a weak, inaccessible father. Of course, the other factor is a father who is so hostile to his son that he doesn't permit an alliance to develop or allow him to work through filial rivalries. So the boy may feel forced for his own survival to remain in a stifling relationship with his mother. In either case, the outcome may be a person who demonstrates sudden outbursts of desperate activity (a grasping at maleness) punctuated by long periods of passive withdrawal.

Female fears are not dissimilar but revolve around wounded womanhood, which can encompass everything from damaged insides to damaged pride. When the emotional pain is too great the girl may repudiate her sex and replace it with a masculine veneer. Then the wish is not to have the phallus, but to be the phallus.[37]

When the issues of attachment and detachment, or nourishment and autonomy, become less urgent, people turn to the penis for a third, compelling reason: to express, to complement, their sensual pleasures and procreative powers.[38] In Freudian theory this begins around the ages of three to five, with the phallic or primary masculine phase, during which children become very interested in their genital, really phallic functions. (Freud postulated that true awareness of female genital functions did not occur until adolescence.) In fact, many observers note that genital wishes, if not activities, occur from early infancy.

During childhood boys take pride in their penis. They fondle and play with it incessantly, while also showing it off and competing with playmates about who can urinate higher and farther. This is the forerunner of later rivalries about who can hit the most home runs, kick the longest goals, throw the biggest spear, or make the most money.

Freud assumed that girls had similar wishes but were frustrated because they were born without a male member. The only recourse they have is to transform their wish for a penis into love for their father and a wish for a baby.

These views have always attracted considerable controversy. Ernest Jones, one of the founding fathers of psychoanalysis, strongly disagreed with Freud and considered his model excessively phallocentric.[39] He agreed with Melanie Klein that a girl wants to take a penis into her body in order to make a child rather than have a child to replace a missing penis.[40]

For most people the male member is a means to an end rather than an end in itself.[41] It enhances survival (attachment), psychological achievement (detachment), and biological achievement (procreation and pleasure). Yet there is one area where the phallus may be an end in itself—the social sphere, where possession of male parts and qualities can ensure special privilege and power.[42] Although now under challenge in Western countries, mankind has lived in male-dominated families, tribes, cultures, and societies for several millennia and continues to do so. Within these social contexts the phallus symbolizes superiority and reflects patriarchal concerns. In part the value of maleness lies in these multiple reflections seemingly independent of time and place.[43]

By the 1980s advertisements for large corporations like Crest Hotels International began to announce that women, who look and work like men, can qualify for the prerogatives that men have long learned to take for granted. A particular two-page spread offered a profile of a businesswoman wearing short hair, a leather watchband, and little makeup. She could have been unisex if a simple string of pearls were removed from her dark turtleneck sweater. In big bold type, the left-hand page proclaimed: "I've finally found a hotel that treats me like a man."[44]

The text explained that this patron would be treated with respect and dignity. In the restaurant she would not be fobbed off with "a table behind a pillar or near the door of the kitchen." In the bar she would not have to take a briefcase "to prove all I want is a drink." Crest promised to maintain a "friendly and businesslike attitude," asserting that professional persons would know what this meant.[45]

What is implied is that a hotel chain should serve, as do other institutions, albeit in different ways, the phallic cravings of the public and illustrates a basic aspect of penis greed, an insatiable desire for the experiences, objects, products, qualities, functions, person, and settings that contribute to erotic satisfaction and self-inflation.[46]

The complement of penis greed is the greedy penis, an organ that thrusts its way into things in order to control, possess, propagate, dominate, devour, or destroy them. This is not desire for, but desire by, the phallus: active power, raw ambition, hungers honed by assertion and strength. The greedy penis is both defensive and aggressive, a shield and a sword.

Lyndon Johnson, the former president of the United States, used to brag about his ability to bully or buy fellow politicians. In referring to colleagues, he would openly exclaim, "I have his pecker in my pocket."[47] Johnson was not just referring to his voracious appetite for power, nor providing examples of phallic cannibalism. The "peckers" were hostages, tangible protection against feared rivalries and insecurities.[48] Compulsive promiscuity, combat, work, sport, or bodybuilding may all serve a similar function: to assuage persecutory fears (others are out to get you), depressive dread (you will hurt loved ones), covert femininity, homosexuality, organ inferiority, masturbatory conflict, narcissistic fragility, shame, guilt, and humiliation.

Often the penis, or more specifically the phallus, is not strong enough to sustain the weight of ambitions or to avoid inner doubts. Then tragedy may strike, as happened with Mark Thompson, a nineteen-year-old snooker prodigy who had won three major tournaments and had found a financial sponsor. He killed himself.

> Mark's irrational fear was that his cue would be damaged and, like a broken spell, the magic of his playing would be lost. . . . He was married to his cue.[49]

I think Mark also feared becoming too potent. He had already vanquished his father and friends. Castration anxiety (a damaged cue) was magnified by possession anxiety (a cue that damaged).[50] In this instance Mark was not strong enough to carry the guilt that accompanied his victories. Consequently the phallus that men and women seek is not an ordinary organ, or skill, but an all-powerful weapon that can grant every wish and destroy every danger, including guilt.

. . .

In *Cities of the Interior,* Anaïs Nin speaks through Lilian, a girl who aspired to invincibility by assuming the mantle of her brother. She recalls the first time a boy hurt her at school:

> I don't remember what he did. But I wept. And he laughed at me. Do you know what I did? I went home and dressed in my brother's suit. I tried to feel as the boy felt. Naturally as I put on the suit I felt I was putting on a costume of strength. . . . I thought that to be a boy meant one did not suffer.[51]

Later Lilian decides to be a warrior, a Joan of Arc, riding and fighting side by side with men. She demands the sword, for her, not just the end to pain, but the means to be herself. In this Nin speaks for the many members of her sex for whom maleness, and the glorification of maleness, gives them the freedom to assert feelings, desires, indeed, their very existence.

Nin's views coincide with those of a friend, a woman who is very proud of her deep, booming Wagnerian voice. Her songs are spears hurtling through the farthest recesses of a room or a mind. She aims to be heard and be feted around the world:

> As a child I liked to watch my father pee. I was very envious of him. But I didn't want to have a big penis like he had, no, not that, I was envious of the loud noise, the big splash he made when he peed into the bowl. Then I could only make a little stream. But when I grew up, I knew things would be different. I would make a big splash, too.[52]

Other women find it harder to be heard. Their sounds are forbidden parts, like open angers flashing against a closed chorus of maternal furies, while their greed is the spray of words: "Fuck you!" "Screw you!" "Get stuffed!"[53]

For the poet Sylvia Plath, words were the weapons that slashed through extremes of rage and remorse. They let live a torrent of "desires to mingle with road crews, sailors and soldiers, barroom regulars . . . to sleep in open fields, to travel west, to walk freely at night." They were her exploits, her wild tales, her "perfect male counterparts." Meanwhile Plath was a warrior, a literary Amazon, riding the libraries and collegiate fetes, who, in midlife, died by her own hand, her words having filtered an excess of love and hatred of phallic forces.[54]

. . .

The Greeks believed the Amazons were a race of women who loved to fight and perform the deeds of men. They lived during the Bronze Age, about 3000 to 1000 B.C.E., some say around the Black Sea in modern Turkey (Scythia), while others connect them with Crete (the Minoans) and various Aegean Islands.[55]

Their name derives from the Greek *amazos,* "without a breast." Hippocrates described the copper instrument used by Scythian Amazons to burn off the right breast of baby girls so that it wouldn't stand out when the girls matured and be in the way of throwing the javelin or shooting arrows.[56]

At home they spent most of the year hunting, riding, breeding horses, and training for war. They favored the cavalry, for they were excellent equestrians. The less physically able were farmers. Otherwise they loathed domestic work, which they left to menfolk, whom they humiliated and enslaved—except in the spring, when they slept with neighboring tribesmen in order to get pregnant. In general the men had no political or civic freedoms and were not allowed to carry arms lest they "become presumptuous and rise up against women."[57]

This view of the ancient Amazons has to be treated with care, as it originates from the Dorian Greeks, the progenitors of Western patriarchal civilization. The Dorians were the mortal enemies of their matriarchal, gynecocratic predecessors, possibly identifiable with their Hittite, Minoan, and Mycenaean rivals. Nevertheless, sufficient evidence exists to sustain the picture of powerful female-predominant tribes who ruled large areas of the Near East. These Bronze Age peoples are a model for women who aggrandize the perks and possessions of men while scorning maleness and subordinating male companions.[58] They sought land, horses, cattle, glory, political power, military prowess, and physical fitness.[59] Modern Amazons are remarkably similar in their likes and dislikes. Some are deadlier than males (female terrorists); others "pump iron" (bodybuilders), and many reject men (militant lesbians).[60]

The damage done by penis greed, by members of either sex, is the consequence of tearing, gnawing, invading desires, initially for the breast, then for Mother, her body, the goods inside, and for Father, his body and parts. The penis can be all these basic things and their equivalents as well as the means to obtain them.[61] In many respects the first penis is a tooth. Only later does it become a penis. Many children and adults never reach this developmental point. Their phallic savagery remains rooted in oral sadism.[62]

The phallus dentatus, or penis with teeth, is a dreaded object, often equated with piranhas, sharks, snakes, alligators, and rats. All of these animals denote rapacious aggression and are synonymous with tooth-and-claw rivalries. Lyndon Johnson, for example, believed he had to maintain a macho facade because he reigned in a city, Washington, "with enemies everywhere, with sharks swimming out there waiting for any sign of weakness."[63]

The Bible yields an early record of the phallus dentatus used as a willful weapon by a subject people:

> The Lord said to Moses and Aaron,
> "When Pharaoh speaks to you and says, 'Produce your marvel,' you shall say to Aaron, 'Take your rod and cast it down before Pharaoh.' It shall turn into a serpent."
> So Moses and Aaron came before Pharaoh and did just as the Lord had commanded: Aaron cast down his rod in the presence of Pharaoh and his courtiers, and it turned into a serpent.
> Then Pharaoh, for his part, summoned the wise men and sorcerers; and the Egyptian magicians, in turn, did the same with their spells:
> Each cast down his rod, and they turned into serpents. But Aaron's rod swallowed their rods.[64]

Aboriginal women still use a magical tooth phallus either to make black magic or conjure forth love. The Australian Luritja cut their pubic hair and braid it into a long string to which they attach the teeth of a kangaroo rat. Then they smear it with blood drawn from their vagina. They believe the string can penetrate the earth, then the sky, and finally the heart of their victim. When evil is intended it becomes a snake eating the vital parts. For love they use a sharpened "pointing bone."[65]

Aboriginals put the bite on their victims for vengeance as well as frustrated desire. The same can happen in more civilized places, like a London suburb. In the late 1970s the newspapers covered the antics of a middle-aged builder who put twenty rats into the house of a girlfriend and cut up her cat. He claimed he still loved her but was obsessed with revenge because she had jilted him.

The rats nested in her oven and settee, crawled through the curtains, chewed through electric wires, left droppings all over, and multiplied exceedingly. These rodents ("furry penes with teeth") were more than extensions of phallic greed. They were the vengeful expression of his envy and jealousy, phallic creatures that despoiled her insides and threatened her loved ones. He aimed to cut her connections and blow her circuits. If he couldn't have her, no one would, nor would she ever enjoy peace and quiet again.[66]

Phallic passions rarely convey pure lust or greed. More commonly they involve spite and possessive control. In this instance a lover felt rattled and resorted to rats to get back at the woman he blamed for his misfortune. Others blame the phallus itself for their sense of unjust deprivation and wounded pride. Freud observed that girls get furious for not having or being given a phallus and blame their mothers.[67] Abraham elaborated that girls not only feel disadvantaged, but believe they have been robbed and seek revenge on whoever was responsible, the depriving mother and the privileged father. In response,

. . . two reactions occur which are closely associated with each other: a hostile feeling against the other person associated with the impulse to deprive him [or her] of what he possesses.[68]

Penis envy is the vengeful union of kindred impulses—spiteful hostility and begrudging deprivation. It may or may not coincide with the wish to be male. Abraham distinguished between two kinds of reactions to the awareness of the phallus, wish fulfillment and revenge. The wish fulfillment type of person is concerned primarily with possession ("I am the fortunate possessor of a penis and exercise the male function"). The revenge type is overwhelmed with malice ("I want to cut up your parts and throw them to the dogs").[69] The former has to do with penis greed, the latter with penis envy.

When the wish coincides with the hatred, it may be more appropriate to speak of penis grenvy—that is, the combination of greed and envy, thralldom and enmity, about phallic functions. This is a frequent state because greed and envy remain intimately associated and are usually expressed concurrently.[70] Thus, ostentatious maleness, as in certain "fortunate possessors," reflects not only greedy aggrandizement, but murderous attacks on parental activities and pride ("If I have it, then you can't!" "I'm the biggest, you're a nothing!").

The question still arises, why is there such a degree of enmity, little girls toward their mothers, the builder to his girlfriend, over the phallus or the lack of it? The answer takes us back to basic issues of dependency and assertion. The child who hates her mother for not being given a penis is also a child who hates her mother for not being given the breast, that is, a source of absolute satisfaction.[71] Obviously a penis that takes the place of the breast is something extraordinarily valuable in and of itself and subject to all the desires and hatreds originally directed to the breast. In the mind of the child the phallus exists within the mother and without, in the shape of Father, his parts, or those of kindred relatives and friends—male cornucopias, all providing continuous comforts.

Intense desire and hatred do not only assail girls. They are just as prevalent among boys, who after all suffer similar conflicts.[72] Penis envy is not sex-restricted. Small-penis problems, for example, demonstrate that far into later life men can remain preoccupied with oral issues transferred from their mothers and wives onto their own organ.[73] Alternatively, a phallic breast may inspire awe and terror. One person recalled that he had gradually reconciled himself to the fact that other boys and men had larger organs and could pee farther and higher. But even as an adult he remained tormented by the memory of a wet nurse who had inadvertently sprayed his face with a huge spurt of milk from her nipple. From that point on he felt that women had a powerful advantage over him.[74]

But the ability to make a big splash is not necessarily the advantage that women want. Like men, they seek access to their mothers' love and the secrets of that love as contained in the original treasure trove, her body. The penis is envied not only for taking the place of the breast, but for giving access to it. It is the commanding key to realizing all-embracing desires for immediate, melting, effortless, warmth; ultimately, the return to the womb and a prebirth state of bliss.[75]

Freud's colleague Otto Rank proposed that the most painful wound is the trauma of birth and that the rest of one's life is taken up with rediscovering, if not replacing, this lost Garden of Eden.[76] In a very real sense, every step forward from weaning to walking to adult autonomy evokes the trauma of birth and the wish to redress the pain of separation. The phallus, by which I mean the penis and attendant maleness, embodies this wish and the means to achieve it.[77] Perhaps that is why devotees have worshiped it as God or have tried to be the God they worship, as in Hindu Tantric rites, where the goal is to remain in perpetual and ecstatic intercourse with oneself.[78]

The very importance of the phallus means that the absence of it, even a relative absence, is an intolerable affront. The child feels bereft of care, the adult of love. Both want to return to a special place that forever excludes them. This dilemma is especially acute during early childhood (the phallic phase) and adolescence, when the demands for self-assertion conflict with needs for self-assurance and when children fear they lack the organs, capacities, and privileges necessary to retain the past or attain the future.[79]

The absent phallus arouses anguished rage directed toward 1) its presence in others; 2) its possession by others; 3) others who want it; and 4) itself for being absent. Thus, a boy consumed by penis envy might hate his father's (idealized) penis, his father for possessing such a penis and maleness, other men for the same reason, his mother for having access to this maleness as well as for her own authority, women in general (for being the object of his or others' desires), and his own phallus (for its inadequacies). Similarly, a girl might be tormented by her mother's prowess and happiness (at possessing her father), her father (for existing), his organ (always idealized), other men (for the same reason), other women (for their desires), and herself (for organ inferiority).[80]

The complement of penis envy is the envious penis, all the traits and functions of maleness that have been denigrated but incorporated and turned against the world. This is not hatred of, but hatred by, a malicious phallus. Like the greedy penis, its aims are defensive and aggressive, to avoid torment, doubt, and deprivation and to wreak revenge.

The male rapist embodies the envious penis. He deploys his organ like an evil eye, to pry and invade, to inflict fear and instill pain. The Beast of Belgravia was only sixteen when he terrorized women throughout a prosperous part of London. When arrested he claimed to have committed the rapes because he was "jealous" (envious) of the women's wealth and boasted:

> They have everything and I have nothing. They are not so good now they have been raped by a black boy![81]

The degree of horror and disgust that rape engenders confirms a crime far worse than theft. Rape is a manic attack, an extension of the most destructive intentions to dirty and dominate the body of another.[82] As the young man stated, he wanted to do more than steal, he wanted to blacken his victims, destroy their goodness, make them feel hopeless and helpless. The same holds true for the builder. Each rat was a rape that defiled his girlfriend and triumphed over her pleasures and prospects.

The female hysteric is the counterpart of the male rapist, a woman who takes over the phallus and disruptively thrusts herself into the lives of others. She's the reality described in the *Malleus*, "a desirable calamity, a domestic danger," whose impassioned eyes provoke desires but soon give short shrift and "cut you down to size."[83]

This is an apt description of the patient whose shrieks assaulted and intransigence confounded me. She made me the breast that couldn't feed, the womb that couldn't conceive, and "the prick" that couldn't penetrate. With a fixed stare that looked daggers and radiated resentment, she liked to declaim:

> I'm so powerful, I can go anywhere, do anything, no one can handle me. . . . I think of being a rapist, forcing myself into every mind. . . . I want to expand and take over space . . . take over time . . . take over people.[84]

So many sessions were rapes, of me by her. She allowed me no voice or even thoughts, no way to touch her, or hope to stop her. She was a woman bewitched by phallic forces who yearned to become the instrument for my destruction. With screams, yells, and shit in the post she threatened to blow me up and cut me down. She was a self trying to embody teeth, turds, and knives.

On the deepest level I was the hated phallus that had access to mothers and the hated mother who was impenetrable to her. During an insightful moment she casually remarked that the reason she got angry was that "men can enter women, but women can't." She wanted to get inside people like men, otherwise no one would get inside her. Anyway, she recalled, no one could get through to her mom, she was unavailable, always putting on powder. "My mom was a beautiful brick wall."

This conflict with her mother was never resolved, maybe mitigated. The active hate conveyed her hurt and also preempted feared critical condemnations. She rarely acknowledged wrongdoing but tended to treat me like the law, which added another dimension to her rage.[85] Otherwise many meetings were punctuated by withdrawal and derision. She didn't feel anything, and I couldn't help her. Men were "wankers," I was stupid, and there were lots of therapists who could do a much better job.

This unfeeling attitude reflected a state of emotional frigidity and sexual uncertainty. She aspired to keep me weak and impotent. Then I couldn't challenge her masculine fronts or feminine daydreams.[86] Infidelity was a stick to batter my ego, promiscuity a promise of insatiable appetites replayed by a female Don Juan.[87] The dragon of jealousy lurked along with envy. She hated men who got through to moms, but she feared Mom for her wanting a man. My weakness was proof that I wasn't worth having and vindication that she, like her mom, was invincible.

. . .

The female hysteric takes oral issues onto a sexual battlefield. In addition, gender and personal conflicts, often in conjunction with social oppression and economic upheaval, have all proved capable of catalyzing endless rounds of bloodletting. The Amazons erupted with the double, sometimes single, battle-ax (*pelekus* and *sagaris*), the bow and arrow, sword, lance, javelin, and spears with "broad iron heads."[88] Yet their aggression did not necessarily betoken envy. It encompassed the political and religious struggles and violence typical of their age.[89] And it reflected the bitter wrath of their enemies. Nevertheless, their unremitting hostility—the malign extent of their cruelty, the pervasive mutilation of male children, and the systematic denigration of menfolk regardless of circumstances—went beyond the bounds of reactive revenge.[90] It exuded guilt-ridden fears (it is likely that many loved the men they made love to but mistreated) and inherent hatreds.

The Greeks, who enshrined their Amazonian rivals among the Furies, used a multitude of epithets to describe their endowments:

> Man-murdering; man-hating; flesh-devouring; living without men; striving against men; war-lustful; slayer of men; man-subduing; dauntless; fearless; man-destroying; fighting with men; man-slaying; murderous; hurtful to men; and bringing pain to men.[91]

The Amazons were also devotees of Cybele, the great fecund "Mother Goddess" whose murderous orgiastic rites continued long after the female warrior tribes had formally been defeated.[92] During Roman times the Galli (priests of Cybele) used to parade through the capital wearing strange clothes and chanting to the music of cymbals, tambourines, flutes, and horns, very much as the disciples of Hare Krishna do today.[93]

The Cybele demanded absolute obedience. On March 24 of the year, *dies sanguinis* (the "day of blood"), all the novitiates would whirl dervishlike and ritually slash themselves before the temple. Then, when the religious frenzy was at its peak, they would fling off their clothes and cut off their privates with a consecrated stone knife.[94]

> The flood of orgiastic emotion even spread to the onlookers and they, too, castrated themselves. With their genitals in their hands, the worshippers ran through the streets and threw them into some house, from which they then received women's clothing, according to custom.[95]

Once the liturgy was over, the worshipers left their genitals and male clothes in the bridal chamber of the Cybele. A ceremonial death presaged a symbolic rebirth.[96] After being anointed, the new priests would dress and be addressed solely as women. Many became mendicants pervading the countryside with ecstatic dancing, scourgings, and millennial prophecies.[97]

The Cybelean rites reflect perverse tendencies in both men and women, including inordinate desire and extreme fear of the opposite sex.[98] The hostilities that lay behind these tendencies are still prevalent. Bruno Bettelheim recalls an incident near the Orthogenic Institute in Chicago. A teenaged girl was walking with her counselor and a friend in a public park one day when she saw a man urinating. He turned and exposed himself to her, whereupon she gleefully exclaimed, "He'll cut off his penis and throw it at us."[99]

Ritual mutilation in order to placate terrifying female forces has an ancient tradition. Many initiation rites conclude with the sacrificial offering of blood, teeth, and foreskins to mother figures. There exists considerable evidence that male and female circumcision serves the same function. Among various peoples the mother may swallow the foreskin or proudly hang it around her neck. Alternatively it may be buried in the ground (Mother Earth) as a sign of birth and rebirth. Certainly circumcision is often instigated, if not actually performed by women.[100]

Aggressive reactions to female attacks can also be traced to antiquity. The Bible forbids a woman to help her husband in a fight if this leads her to grab the opponent by the testicles. Should she do so, "then you shall cut off her hand."[101] The Assyrians were equally severe:

> If a woman has crushed a man's testicle in an affray, one of her fingers shall be cut off; and if although a physician has bound it up, the second testicle is affected with it and becomes inflamed or if she has crushed the second testicle in the affray, both of her [breasts or nipples] shall be torn off.[102]

Presumably the Book of Deuteronomy and the Assyrian laws would not have taken the trouble to proscribe such assaults unless they were a common occurrence. The phallus itself came to symbolize the "rod of law" and authority of the state.[103] The Romans used replicas as power charms, the *fascina,* to ward off and counterattack evil influences, especially from the opposite sex. Later a horn, a finger, or even a gesture served the same purpose, as did the lawful subordination of women by many peoples from prehistoric to modern times.[104]

Male brutality is not only a response to physical injury and psychic insults. It encompasses the whole range of vengeful rage toward women for possessing masculine in addition to feminine prowess. The phallic woman is the combined parent: "the breast with knives, a body with guns"; the mother who spares no rod while spoiling herself; the wife who wields the sword to dominate her mate; and, in general, any woman who seems to usurp strength, power, and privilege.[105]

Queen Christina of Sweden (1626–1689) has been called "the first great phallic woman in modern history."[106] Her father, Gustavus Adolphus, wanted a son, and she was brought up to become a proficient male. Indeed, she used to refer to herself as a Nordic Amazon. Later a capable coquette, she remained extremely competitive with men, and her main relationship with them was rivalry or ownership. This included the French philosopher and mathematician René Descartes.

The queen was obsessed with the fact that a master of logic and rationality existed outside her grasp. Eventually, like a spider to a fly, she sent an admiral and ship to get him. Descartes must have been flattered, for he returned to the Swedish court in the dead of winter to commence duties as court scholar and personal savant. Unfortunately he was a frail man who was soon overwhelmed by incessant demands such as early-morning discourses and late-night dinners. Less than five months after his arrival, he caught a cold and died. Her triumph was complete. She had physically, if not intellectually, outlasted him, while he was buried in a plot for unbaptized children.[107]

Christina carried on with religious and political intrigues. Too often the results were devastating, and her ambitions were thwarted. She was trapped by incompatible body, gender, personal, and social claims. The denial of femaleness and the conquest of maleness were basic attempts to resolve these conflicts.[108]

The seduction of Descartes echoes the demise of the Assyrian general in Hebbel's drama about Judith, "the virgin widow."[109] Her first husband was "paralyzed on the bridal night by a mysterious anxiety" and never touched her. She remains a maiden until the day Holofernes lays siege to her city. Judith decides to save the citizens by using her beauty ("Like belladonna, it brings madness and death") to arouse his desires. He responds and deflowers her, whereupon she rages and cuts off his head.[110]

Freud's view was that the beheading represented castration and patriotism concealed a woman's revenge for losing her virginity. He related the story to the dream of a young woman who hated her husband for entering her body. She wanted to tear off his penis and keep it for herself.

> Behind this envy for the penis, there comes to light the woman's hostile bitterness against the man, which never completely disappears in the relations between the sexes, and which is clearly indicated in the strivings and in the literary productions of "emancipated" women.[111]

Yet, this person, like Judith or Christina, was threatened not by loss of virginity, but by loss of identity, and the besieged city was not the body but the soul. For most women the initial intercourse is a welcome event that confirms their creative potential and status as adults. Similarly, childbirth is not a castration, as Freud also claimed, but a major achievement.[112]

A state of begrudging hostility toward men essentially disguises but also reflects underlying conflicts about feminine functions and a confused sense of self. All this originates in profound hatred and contempt toward the mother exacerbated by painful relations with the father or other males.[113] These issues were especially clear with Christina, who suffered a rejecting, probably murderous mother and an adoring but oppressive father.[114] The ensuing difficulty is not just that Christina and other women with comparable upbringings become male wishing, or male hating, but that the interplay of their internal and external conflicts prevents them from becoming male sustaining—that is, capable of sustaining a mutually satisfactory relationship with men or effective male strivings.[115] The latter encompasses a wide range of activities that may be culturally determined or self-defined as "masculine." Many women excel in politics, business, warfare, sports, scholarship, or kindred areas. These achievements are not necessarily based on the active hatred of men or depreciation of femininity. But the woman with the phallus soon arouses the envious eye of other women who cannot use or appreciate their own assets. Hence penis envy is a frequent feature of hostile relationships among women.

Equally intense antagonisms predominate in men who may be threatened by female revenge but are even more so by female accomplishments. Hell hath no fury like a man who feels "hard done" by a female competitor. As far as he is concerned, it's "unfair" that women possess the phallus (business acumen) as well as the breast and womb (female charms). "Unfairness" conceals gnawing anguish and shattered self-esteem, hugely magnified in societies where men are expected, or themselves expect, to work, play, and fight hard while their wives or womenfolk keep to the kitchen.

In relations with women, male penis envy or jealousy (when "the girl with a gun" is seen as a dangerous interloper for the attention of other men or women) tends to surface as nagging resentment, something to which a successful politician like British Prime Minister Margaret Thatcher (the "Iron Maiden") is continually subject. Thus her former defense minister publicly commented:

> I don't think that the way in which she conducts business would have been tolerated sometimes had she been a man because she uses her feminine charms. . . . She doesn't argue her position through logically and intellectually in the way that intelligent men would do.[116]

Geraldine Ferraro had to endure more vicious attacks during the United States presidential election in 1984. Carping led to character assassination and then to back-stabbing onslaughts on her family and finances. The many attempts to ruin her reputation, and thereafter her life, followed envious tensions provoked by her strength, wealth, position, and thrusting ambition.[117]

Sports stars, business executives, and, in general, working women accrue resentment and actual abuse for the same reason.[118] Ultimately this encourages primitive attacks on women, rape and murder, not for their being female, but for their being male. The African Nandi peoples take this attitude to literal extremes. They resent women possessing a penislike organ (the clitoris) in addition to breasts and womb and practice clitoridectomy. One village chief explained: "We are Nandi. We don't want such a hanging-down thing in our women."[119]

Men hate authority, fame, status, strength, and "hanging-down things" in women, but especially in other men. Since success is an erection and power is the "ultimate aphrodisiac,"[120] the sight of either arouses malicious comparison and a terrible awareness of failure. This explains the pain excited by men like the Kennedys and reactions like prideful inflation and envious deflation.[121] With men the envious penis is a weapons system that can "shoot down whatever's up, and blow up whatever's down."[122]

Hitler's weapons included the extended salute, which exemplified both the envious and jealous penis. This gesture aimed to humiliate the opposition and prove that his prowess was more powerful than anyone else's. Once it was noted that Hitler invited a young woman to his room. He stuck out his arm in a Nazi salute and boomed:

> I can hold my arm like that for two solid hours. I never feel tired . . . my arm is like granite—rigid and unbending, but, Goering can't stand it. He has to drop his arm after half an hour of this salute. He's flabby, but I am hard.[123]

These rivalries are not unrelated to Teutonic attentions to mighty swords and gigantic guns or "the cataclysmic ecstasy of violence."[124] Comparable passions preoccupied a student I treated. One day he reported a disturbing dream, in which he was having anal intercourse with a stranger. After the man had entered him, his own anus turned to glass, which shattered and cut the other's penis to shreds. His thoughts led to gay magazines and then to a play about Mary Barnes, a woman I had helped.[125] I replied that I was the stranger, and the dream had to do with his penis greed and envy and jealousy. He craved my knowledge, the sharp edge of intellect that would make him invincible like Siegfried or Wotan. Yet as soon as he heard me, he felt like an asshole and proceeded to soil my ideas and cut them to shreds. He had a glass ass because his feelings were fragile. His envy turned love to hate, which shattered under pressure of hunger and rage. Then he was terrified I would return the rancor.

The man calmed and brought up Plato. Plato desired young boys. He was a young boy vis-à-vis me. I shook my head and said he was the Plato who wanted to screw me because he felt superior and wanted to take over my ties to other therapists and sources of knowledge. He calmed but again blew up, screaming that the room was too light and accusing me of controlling the level of lighting. I pointed out that lighting had to do with enlightenment. He resented the degree of my enlightenment and bitterly resented the degree to which I was in charge of his. The moment before, I had given too much. That made him feel guilty. Usually, however, I gave too little. That meant I was selfish and stingy.

A smile broke across his face:

> You know, I can see me mum. She never fed me enough. I remember wanting to cut up her tits with a carving knife.[126]

The smile signaled a hint of recognition that the roots of his phallic desires and shattering hostilities ran deep indeed, from virility to feeding, from the head to the heart.[127] For him, as for everyone, the penis holds diverse and often divergent degrees of meaning. These include

- *The breast, nipple, tooth, thumb, clitoris, any strong, extensible limb or muscle* (parts of the body)
- *Searching, probing, throbbing, thrusting, expanding, exploding, electrifying excitements and annihilating satisfactions* (experiences)
- *Snakes, sharks, rats, tigers, horses, whips, rods, spears, swords, guns, any big, wild, powerful, penetrating, overwhelming animal or thing* (animate or inanimate objects)
- *Brother, father, husband, God, Superman, Superwoman, Joan of Arc, Queen Christina, Mrs. Thatcher, combined parents* (persons)
- *Milk, cream, sperm, babies, water, fire, warriors, cars, cocaine, "continuous-action stimulants"* (products)
- *Procreation, pleasure, hunting, riding, raping, sport, body-building, business, politics, war* (activities)
- *Strength, stamina, size, assertion, ambition, authority, virility, prowess, power, privilege, unstoppability* (qualities and characteristics)
- *Pedestals, towers, New York, Houston, Cape Kennedy* (places or settings)
- *Father Heaven, patriarchal society, Mount Olympus, storms, thunder, lightning, enlightenment, the intellect, rationality* (outer reality, states of mind versus peace of mind and states of peace)

All of these features comprise the phallus and denote a hierarchy of hurt and hope. The hurts encompass the bad penis, an organ and entity that ravishes life. In contrast, the good penis is loving and reparative. Like the womb, it gives hope, makes babies, and affirms the continuity of life.[128]

John Donne confirmed the latter, the loving penis, in his poem, "To His Mistress Going to Bed." His words set forth the wish to explore a woman's body (called America) and thence the mysteries of the world and beyond, without damage but with awesome discovery:

Before, behind, between, above, below.
O my America! my new-found-land,
My kingdome, safeliest when with one
    man man'd.
How blest am I in this discovering thee!
To enter in these bonds, is to be
    free.[129]

Part Two

THE IMPACT
OF MALICE

7

Witches, Giants, and Scary Parents

Traditionally the witch is a withered old woman with bony hands, humpy back, and sharp-tipped teeth who preys on the blood and flesh of boys and girls. She dresses in black because she is a creature of the night, shrieking with delight as her owlish eyes discover a tender baby or chaste young girl.[1] Jocular caricatures of long-nosed ladies with magic hats and black cats astride flying broomsticks bolster beliefs that untold women possess vast powers of occult destruction.[2]

The legendary counterpart of the wicked witch is not the warlock, but the killer giant, whose huge size and fearsome strength convey elemental forces given over to rampant evil. Dante described the Archfiend lying in the lowest depths of the Inferno as *un gigante,* while Milton's Satan "extended long and large" both in body and possessions—hordes of fallen angels who could change size and sex to perpetrate malice.[3] Giants abound in myth and folklore from Cornwall to China and are usually well equipped with savage teeth, loud voices, rough hair, and extra eyes as well as clubs, hammers, swords, and, nowadays, guns.[4]

Witches and giants are not only products of rampant imaginations, the child's-eye view of parents, or their parents' scary constructions, but actually touch upon archaic and not-so-archaic memories of childhood and child care. According to the psychohistorian Lloyd DeMause, this is a nightmarish succession of parent-child relations where

> the further back in history one goes, the lower the level of child care, and the more likely children are to be abandoned, beaten, terrorized and sexually abused.[5]

The witch represents the cruelly rejecting, depriving, devouring, treacherous mother, more concerned with her own looks, feelings, and needs than her child's. She is a woman greedy for food, envious of youth, and jealous of love, the Cruella De Vil of contemporary cinema, the malign crone of our forebears who could bring down misfortune by a curse or a glance.

In fact, mothers have commonly put unwanted children out to die, and there are many references to infanticide from antiquity onward. In ancient Greece and Rome children were thrown into rivers, flung into cesspits, potted in jars, or simply left exposed by the roadside, "a prey for birds, food for wild beast to rend."[6] As recently as 1890, abandoned babies were a common sight in London streets, lying dead in the gutters and dung heaps.[7]

Even when they were not left to die, vast numbers of newborn babies used to be passed into the hands of wet nurses to be suckled. Disease or neglect led many to perish before they were handed back after two to five years. In the interim they rarely saw their biological parents.[8] This custom was an effective shield against passionate involvement with offspring who probably would not have reached adulthood anyway. And if anyone need be blamed, it could be the nurse, just as the unsuccessful midwife might be accused of witchcraft.[9]

But by the eighteenth century the practice began to diminish even before improved sanitation made motherhood less problematic. It became more common for children to enter their parents' emotional life, to be prayed with and sometimes played with. Closer contact led to new methods to curb anticipated greedy demands and wicked behavior. Psychic assaults replaced infanticide and physical abuse. The child was a mind to be filled with frightening figures in order to engender compliance. For Europeans, Bluebeard, werewolves, and Napoleon Bonaparte were valued additions to an arsenal of images that included "gorgons and ghosts, witches, giants and Jews," as well as a tyrannical God who held aberrant youngsters "over the pit of hell, much as one holds a spider, or some loathsome insect, over the fire."[10]

In modern times it is hard to tell whether the levels of child abuse, physical and psychic, are on the decline, as DeMause contends, are remaining the same, or are actually increasing. Until relatively recently the battered baby and the battering parent were taboo topics. Now increasing public attention means that the number of known child abuse cases appears to escalate all the time.[11] One can hardly open a newspaper in the United States or Europe without encountering a child murder or sexual assault, aside from more numerous but less obvious examples of mental and bodily cruelty. In Britain alone the estimated number of children murdered by their parents or caretakers ranges from five to twenty-five per week.[12]

I intend to begin the chapters on the influence of envy, greed, and jealousy with a study of the parental persecutor, an adult who hates and attacks children. In so doing I hope to redress the prevalent view that in the relations between parents and children resentments invariably flow from sons to fathers or daughters to mothers. In truth there exists a balance of terror, albeit mitigated by the tender feelings that young and old hold for each other. While children certainly crave the breast and begrudge womb and phallic powers, parents are also assailed by terrible tensions for which they often blame their offspring. These concern their own inadequacies in the face of life renewed, but especially, in an age of narcissism, the special attentions children demand, but which mothers and fathers prefer to keep for themselves. Thus, even before Oedipus becomes an issue, parents may feel deprived of love and life and seek mortal revenge.[13] Considering the relative size and strength of adults in comparison with infants, it is no wonder that these antagonisms tend to be denied but located in other worlds at other times and places.

The Malevolent Mother

Malevolent mothers are scary, a point that folk- and fairy tales make with the utmost clarity. The story of Hansel and Gretel provides one of the finest descriptions of their grenvious, cannibalistic personae. Different versions exist in many countries, but all have similar features. The Brothers Grimm acquaint us with a poor woodcutter who lives at the edge of a big forest with his son and daughter and wife (their stepmother). A famine hits the land, and there is not enough food to go around. The woman tells her husband not to worry. They'll take the children far out into the forest and leave them. Then, "they won't find the way back home and we'll be rid of them."[14]

The man protests, but his wife, ever concerned with her own needs, prevails. So, after several false starts, the young boy and girl are dumped in the forest to die of starvation. Forlorn and frightened, they decide to follow a little white bird. It brings them to a lovely house with walls of bread, roof of cake, and windows of pure sugar. The children are delighted, but it's a trap. Suddenly the door opens, and an aged, decrepit crone creeps out and invites them in. She pretends to be kind. Really, she is

> an evil witch who lay in wait for children and had only built the little bread house to lure them her way. When a child fell into her power she would kill it, cook it and eat it, and that was a day of feasting for her.[15]

On the next day the old woman locks the boy in a shed and forces his sister to help her fatten him for the kill. Eventually she prepares the oven to roast them both, but Gretel plays a trick and pushes the crone into the oven instead, whereupon "the godless witch burned miserably to death."[16]

The villains in this story are a stepmother and a witch. They represent two aspects of the same person, the bad mother, who is usually transformed into a combination of one or more stepmothers, witches, and mothers-in-law so it is safer to hate her and get revenge, at least in the world of make-believe. The bad mother may be a monstrous creation of the child's own projected impulses. But all too often the negative view coincides with one or more aspects of real maternal destructiveness.[17]

Hansel and Gretel feared hunger and abandonment. What they overlooked was the likelihood of being eaten themselves. Many mothers regard their infants as "food objects." It is a common experience to see a woman kiss a baby on the behind and exclaim with delight, "Oh, you look good enough to eat." Sometimes this is not a joke.[18]

The desired food is more than milk. The baby is a breast that flows with love toward those who care for it. Battered babies and children have parents who reverse the roles. They insist that their offspring look after them and get enraged if this doesn't happen. One woman who severely injured her child commented:

I have never felt loved all my life. When the baby was born, I thought he would love me. When he cried, it meant he didn't love me. So I hit him.[19]

Hansel and Gretel were brutalized by their "step" mother, a common feature of many folktales. Their story is a parable about an emotional famine. The children are burdened with a mother who begrudges love while resenting their youth, their vitality, and above all the affection they draw from their father. He loves them but is a shlemiel: he can't protect them from her devouring jealousy. So the children have to rely on ingenuity, as occurs in many families where emotional strength and shrewdness are keys to survival.

The fatal trap is narcissistic seduction, while the intent is self-aggrandizement. The malicious mother enchants children with false hopes and inflated promises—candy floss—while forcing them to feed her pride and self-esteem. Bertram Karon has described several such women in his book on the psychotherapy of schizophrenia. One lived off her son's artistic talents. From his childhood onward she hoarded his paintings to show off to her friends. He begged her permission to retain them, but she refused, saying she was only keeping them for his sake. She used the attention and praise the paintings provoked to feed her ego and his worthlessness. On the surface she tried to help him, but deep down she was a vicious rival. This wasn't a relationship from which he could easily extricate himself. He felt totally dependent, and we can be assured that if he hadn't gone along with her, she would have pushed him away to "roast in hell."[20]

R. D. Laing has portrayed his childhood in comparable terms. He was an only child in a bleak, pleasureless house with a mother who was either "in a decline" or deeply possessive of his psychic life. When he was little she snatched away his favored toy horse and burned it because "he was getting too close to it." An aunt observed that she "burned up with envy and jealousy" and would destroy anything he got attached to. Later in life, after he had left home and become a famous psychiatrist, he discovered that his mother had acquired a tiny figurine that she called "Ronald" or "Ronnie." She enjoyed sticking pins into its heart in order to make him have a heart attack.[21]

A mother's rage can extend to an unborn child. "Kate" was a patient of mine who feared her fetus was a dangerous rival, a thing nibbling away inside her just like the bug in *The Very Hungry Cat-*

erpillar.[22] So she went on a buying spree and found it impossible to stop eating, drinking, and smoking. Yet she was aware that the baby might be damaged by a rapid weight gain (no room for the womb) and nicotine (poison). She also worried that the fetus was too close to her back passage, where "a lot of heavy shit goes down"—in other words, her shitty feelings.

Kate had been premature and still resented her mother for cheating on womb time. So the pregnancy stirred up enormous appetites, which she preferred to deny and bury in her body in the form of "galloping leukemia" or AIDS. The galloping leukemia was an uncontrollable group of cells that she imagined would suddenly proliferate and savage everything before them. But AIDS was the most terrifying prospect. It meant she would waste away and was an unjust desert for being greedy.

Who was to blame? Kate fingered her husband and baby. The bigger she got, the more "it" got in the way. Once she was crossing the street and a car whizzed by. Her husband pulled her back onto the pavement by pulling her tummy. She was indignant. How dare he try to save the baby before her? She felt ignored, and the incident confirmed the unwelcome prospect of a newborn baby occupying the center of familial attention. Moreover, it brought to mind many memories of her own parents, who were "always busy, always having all the fun while I was just a pudding."

Kate was not a witch. She was loving as well as hating and well aware of the complexity of her states of mind. But there were many times when she felt caught between her interests and those of the fetus, whom she saw variously as a welcome addition, a dangerous intruder, galloping leukemia, overindulged parents, and her own infant self. The latter aroused special jealousies because she thought I preferred "it" to her.[23]

The worst conflicts were between Kate's determination to nurture and protect the fetus and her wish to compete with or destroy it. The competition was for food, love, and attention. She enjoyed musing about the clothes, the dinners, the holidays, and the thousand other things that she could choose as soon as the baby was born. Then she would be preeminent again. In this respect she was like her mother and thought her children would be like her, proving themselves at others' expense while setting the stage for the transmission of envy and jealousy from one generation to the next.[24]

Direct attacks, the craving for a miscarriage, or the hope that the child would be deformed were vengeful retorts to feelings of neglect. Since Kate was well cared for, the neglect involved the pains of pregnancy in comparison with envious exaggerations of her baby's blissful intrauterine existence. During the first couple of months a note of gleeful triumph over fetus and family tended to accompany the malicious ruminations. Afterward guilt predominated.

The doubts and recriminations concealed love for the baby and fear of her mother's hostility. Some months before, they had been to a dance together. The elderly woman had commented on how pretty Kate looked and how jealous she felt because all the men were after her. This came as a bolt from the blue. Kate had always seen herself as the underdog struggling to overcome her mother's popularity. The scene was a nightmare, which she relived one night during a thunderstorm, when bolts of lightning appeared to be hitting her house. (She later associated the sounds with her mother's rage.) At the time the baby had begun to kick "like mad," and she feared she would lose it. The fear was a wish, a sacrifice, to appease her mother and stop the storm.

Maternal destructiveness is often a defense against maternal destructiveness. Many women contemplate killing themselves or their children in order to avoid the wrath of their mothers.[25] In terms of a three-generational model of mother-child relations, suicide, sterility, miscarriage, and madness stem not only from the upward flow of envy and jealousy, the young toward the old, and consequent reflections and refractions, but from the downward deluge, the extremes of spite and vengeance by mothers who abhor their daughters' femininity and abominate their social successes.[26]

The sacrifice of children in order to propitiate the mother's mother has been practiced from antiquity onward. Aside from literal abandonment, examples include the transfer of care to alternative parents and filicide. The latter has been recorded in the annals of the Irish Celts, Gauls, Scandinavians, and many Middle Eastern peoples. Inscriptions that identify the victims as the firstborn sons of noble families have been traced to Jericho nine thousand years ago.[27] Even now, when boys and girls play "London Bridge Is Falling Down" and catch the child at the end of the game, they are acting out a sacrifice to a river goddess.[28]

Of course conflicts between new mothers and old do not begin with pregnancy or motherhood. They reach far back into childhood when the first hints of sexual maturity arouse envious rivalries, mother to daughter and vice versa. And the same hostilities extend far forward into adulthood when disparagements of childbearing become critiques of child rearing.

For the little girl the wicked witch is the mom who refuses her makeup or jewelry or clothes and won't let her grow up. The tales of the Brothers Grimm are replete with spiteful stepmothers, jealous mothers, and begrudging mothers-in-law who curse, suffocate, or poison their daughters as in "Snow White,"[29] defame and condemn them to death as in "The Twelve Brothers,"[30] or put impossible conditions on their meeting men as in "The Six Servants":[31]

> Long ago there lived an old queen who was a sorceress, and her daughter was the most beautiful maiden under the sun. But the old queen's one idea was to lure people to their destruction, and when a suitor came she would say that any man wanting to marry her daughter must first perform a task, or his life would be forfeit.[32]

The queen was merciless. Untold men met a terrible fate while the poor girl was left unmarried and seething. Finally a prince who had heard of the challenge accomplished the tasks with the help of six magic servants. Even then the queen intervened with the slander, "He's not good enough for you," and tried to recapture the daughter and murder her husband. Evidently she not only begrudged the girl her happiness, but hated males as well.

The Hollywood story of actress Joan Crawford and her adopted daughter Christina falls into the same category. Both in the cinema and at home, this mother played the modern sorceress and malicious queen. Her wand was self-seeking infatuation and scornful detachment. At a wave it could turn Christina into a little princess at a film opening or exile her to a convent run like a penal colony, for kissing a boy. The older Crawford was surreally envious and ruthlessly disruptive of her daughter's youth, sexuality, prospects, in fact, her entire personality.[33] But Crawford was not untypical. Many mothers are equally adept at dramatic interventions like disrupting weddings and preventing both daughters and sons from fulfilling themselves. Their spells, summoned from hearts fermenting with fury, include seducing the groom, fighting the guests, and dying from heart attacks. A sampling of these effects is well portrayed in Robert Altman's film A Wedding.[34]

Perhaps the most formidable feature of witches is their fondness for transforming victims into witches. In modern terms this involves ruining reputations by attaching malice to others. A common occurrence during the times of the Malleus, it is still a significant event, as was dramatized in 1983 during a sensational trial in Livorno, Italy.[35]

The defendant was Carol Compton, a twenty-one-year-old Scottish nanny who was accused of fire raising and trying to murder a little girl in her care. She already had been in jail for sixteen months and faced a long sentence if convicted. The main witness was the girl's aged grandmother, who publicly claimed Ms. Compton was a witch. Signora Cecchini explained that the nanny, "a stranger in the house," possessed special powers and practiced black magic. When she was about, plates fell off the walls and fires started without explanation.[36]

The Italian press covered the trial under banner headlines THE WITCH DEFENDS HERSELF and did not hesitate to quote elderly spectators such as a faith healer, who hissed: "That girl is possessed by demons. She comes from Britain."[37] But the testimonies of the grandmother and her daughter-in-law (the girl's mother) were eventually refuted by a previous nanny, who said the two women had made life hell for herself and Ms. Compton. As for the fires, the electricity in the house was overloaded and the wiring was terrible. Anyway, the old granny used to leave burning fag ends about. A few days later Carol Compton was acquitted.[38]

By reading between the lines, and with some extrapolation, it appears that the Cecchini household was one where three generations of women had resented and exploited the nannies who came into their midst. The nannies, in turn, became the projective foci and receptacles for the malign tensions that the grandmother, mother, and little girl bore toward each other.[39]

Signora Cecchini was obviously jealous of her daughter-in-law ("the stranger"), who "stole" her son's heart and was mistress of his house. Not feeling free to express her hostilities directly, she redirected them to the nannies. The same held true for the little girl's mother, who was constantly opposed by an unfriendly mother-in-law but was not able to get rid of her (because she still held a position of power). So the war was fought over domestic affairs with control of the children a lurid contest. All this made Ms. Compton an unwelcome third party, even without taking into account that she was young and attractive and that the man of the house, the father, might have fancied her.

As for the little girl, it is not too farfetched to think that she enjoyed the extra attention but used the nanny as a scapegoat for naughty antics (breaking the occasional plate?) and as an unloved surrogate for a mother or grandmother who misused her.

In the end Ms. Compton managed to return to Britain alive and well. She was lucky to have obtained outside support that confirmed her perceptions and challenged the family. Otherwise she might have succumbed to her allotted role and agreed to bear the family's enmities (the overloaded circuits) and punishments, too.

The ultimate interest of the malign enchantress is to transform boys into girls. In "Hansel and Gretel" it was not by chance that the old crone chose the boy to lock up and fatten for the kill. Crones and hags embody ancient fears of possessive, castrating mothers who appropriate their sons' phallic powers. Similar suspicions poison relations with wives, daughters, and women in general. In the ensuing struggles, either the men manage to retain their identities (and facilities) or the women wind up with the broomsticks. Then the victims become unsexed, bitter, vengeful people—like witches.

Not surprisingly, many men are terrified of their mothers, who have been variously described as whirlpools, hurricanes, tornadoes, and typhoons or, from the animal world, treacherous cats, dogs, and snakes.[40] A middle-aged writer confirmed these epithets during the course of recalling lifelong feelings of isolation and panic in the face of women.[41] He grew up in New York in a household of feminists. His mother was dominating and oppressive. She seemed to have treated his father as an inferior species and married solely to get a son. Soon after his birth they were divorced. His picture is of a broad-shouldered, well-tailored woman with a quick mind who enjoyed boasting that she could outdrive cabdrivers and outearn her husband.

With a frustrating panache she enjoyed exhibiting her nude body while he was on the toilet or she in the bath. Yet she avoided kissing, hugging, or other physical contact. Forever exciting, she belittled male bodies, said sex was dirty and males unacceptable. Her general attitude was that the penis and testicles were messy. The female genitals were much "neater."[42]

Unlike this person who was "up front" with her angers, the psychoanalyst Robert Stoller depicts a mother who was more subtle, yet more devastating, in her assault on her son's body, gender, and personal identities. She created a transsexual.[43]

"Mrs. C" came into therapy after being scolded by neighbors for dressing her boy as a girl.[44] Slim, boyish, and perky, but not butch, she experienced herself as "a nothing, a cipher, a mirage."[45] Her own mother was an "empty woman" whose lasting endowment was "great envy, rage, and guilt," while her father was an alcoholic with personalities ranging from happy and affectionate to violent and over-sexed. Although close in childhood, they had been estranged for years.

Two brothers compounded her problems. They were vigorous, competitive, and exhibitionistic and were the favorites in a family that believed males were superior, females inferior. Consequently she had no place as a male, although she had tried to be a tomboy, and little place as a woman. She was a neuter awaiting a son.[46]

The pregnancy was a joy, "a cure" for emptiness, and the birth "a triumph of the will." The boy gave Mrs. C a tremendous sense of "well-being," although within a few months she began to think how nice he would be as a girl. Mothering was an addiction. She cared for him constantly, rarely letting him out of her sight or touch. His body was hers. Meanwhile she hated her husband, and he agreed to stay out of the way.[47]

Usually this woman disliked penises, she thought they were ugly. But her son's was "beautiful," for he was "the phallus of her flesh," her rebirth. She recalled:

> In regard to boys' penises, I was very put out that God didn't give me one of those. This started when I was four or five. I kidded myself and probably thought that maybe I would have one eventually. I can remember at night when I would say my prayers that I would wake up a boy the next morning.[48]

Stoller concludes that Mrs. C was a bisexual mother with severe "envy and anger" (grenvy) toward males. By means of unlimited physical contact and other intimacies, she promoted a form of pathological symbiotic identification between her son and herself. As far as she was concerned he was her, not him, and existed mainly to cure her of emptiness. What she denied was her hatred of him as a male and separate person. Should he have tried to separate, to be himself, she would have wreaked revenge.[49]

Neither Mrs. C nor the writer's mother would be unfamiliar to the ancients, who would be quick to see in their destructive styles many aspects of the Amazonian queens and the Great Mother goddess, Cybele.[50] Her consort was Attis, a devotee and lover, both a man and a boy. His sufferings were seductions quite similar to those I have just described. The writer was warned that if he used his penis for pleasure, it would fall off. Cybele imposed a vow of chastity on Attis. His life was hers. His potential was hers. She foretold he would die if he loved a woman, that is, grew up, asserted his manhood, and separated from her. The prophecy emanated from her boundless desires.

A difficult wedding led to death and resurrection. Attis prepared to marry the daughter of King Midas. Cybele found out and tried to prevent the marriage by using her head to break down the walls of the city. They had been closed for the wedding feast. When Attis observed this, he went mad and cut off his genitals under a spruce tree. Then the Great Mother anointed his penis and buried it, whereupon violets sprang up from the site and surrounded the tree with their beauty.[51]

Ovid related a poignant variation. Attis promised to remain pure and virtuous. But he broke his vow and took to himself a lovely young maiden. When Cybele found out she killed her, whereupon Attis went mad, hacked at his body, and castrated himself with the following words:

> *Pereant partes quae nocuere mihi.*
> "There, take these genitals—you caused trouble enough on their account."[52]

The Attic myths feature madness and self-mutilation instigated by a jealous older woman, the Great Mother. But some versions linked Attis with Adonis, a youth of extraordinary beauty, who was loved by a goddess and killed by a boar at the behest of a jealous older man, Zeus, the Great Father.[53]

The Brutal Father

Zeus was the son of a Giant, the grandson of a Titan, and the chief of a multitude of fierce patriarchal deities introduced by the Dorians when they conquered Greece about 1200 B.C.E.[54] Although imbued with wisdom and beneficence, he commonly displayed despotic power for selfish ends and was capable of the basest passions and frailties. In various myths he was described and appeared as jealous, cruel, spiteful, vengeful, deceitful, lascivious, rapacious, and cowardly.[55]

Zeus and his father, Cronus (Saturn), and father's father, Uranus, are models for brutal fathers (to a small child, dreaded giants) that appear in every culture at every time. Kin to Goliath, Gargantua, and now Rambo, they are huge, powerful, bestial creatures with enormous appetites and terrible tempers.[56]

In the domain of folklore, these giants can be traced to Norse, Welsh, Cornish, and Appalachian legends, where ogres with huge hammers or clubs threaten to crush babies and boys while (in England) proclaiming:

> Fee, fau, fum
> I smell the blood of an English man;*
> Be he alive, or be he dead,
> I'll grind his bones to make my
> bread.**[57]

> *Or "Earthly man,"
> **Or "Off goes his head."

The English ogre spawned dozens of tales all to do with an unlikely young man who climbs a tree or a magic stalk to vanquish a killer. Yet the original story, "Jack and the Beanstalk," is far more complicated and horrific than the watered-down accounts that appear in children's books. According to the version researched by Iona and Peter Opie for *The Classic Fairy Tales,* Jack is the "indolent, careless and extravagant" child of a poor widow, who accuses him of bringing them both "to beggary and ruin."[58]

It transpires that Jack's father was a rich man who was good and kind. Unfortunately he came to the attention of a giant who lived some miles away. This person was

> altogether as wicked as your father was good: he was in his heart envious, covetous, and cruel; but he had the art of concealing these vices. He was poor, and wished to enrich himself at any rate.[59]

Eventually Jack realizes that he has to fight the monster in order to destroy a murderer and regain the family's treasures. But he is frightened. Only the threat of starvation and his mother's nagging force him to climb the beanstalk and seek out the giant.[60] Then there begins a series of encounters with the flesh-eating figure ("Fe fau, fum" or "Wife, I smell fresh meat"), which ends years later with Jack killing the killer and changing from a surly youth into a "dutiful and obedient son," aside from a strong, honorable, and prosperous man.[61]

Jack's giant shares the characteristics of the gods. He is large and powerful, totally unprincipled, and lives in a mansion (castle) high in the sky (Olympus). And, in common with so many deities and devils, he enjoys the flesh of human beings. The paintings by Goya and Rubens of Saturn devouring his son would not do him an injustice.[62]

These gods—Giants, Titans, dragons, dinosaurs, ogres, and ghouls—represent the dangerous, self-centered father. He is the man who lords it over his wife and children and begrudges their needs while cannibalizing his family's emotional and material resources. The story of Jack concerns such a family, where the father, perhaps akin to a contemporary alcoholic or philanderer, has battered the babies, drained the wife, and abandoned them all to stew in their juices. The story also explains why, because he is "envious, covetous and cruel."

The envy focuses on the newborn child, who has privileged access to his mother's body and is preordained to surpass his father in strength and character. A farmer once told me:

> I was delighted when my son was born. Yet, when I held him in my arms for the first time, I was seized by a sudden, overpowering impulse to smash his little body against the ground and to stamp on it. This thought made me terribly upset. Then I realized how envious I felt toward the baby. All he had to do was open his mouth, and he was fed. I had to work damn hard. His whole life lay before him. Much of mine was past. He had a father who loved him. My dad had died years before.[63]

Covetousness is incessant greed, the desire to compete with the child for food, attention, and love both to assuage emptiness and overcome envy. Paradoxically it arises from a feeling of detachment from the sublime riches that the birth of a child confers on both father and mother. In Jack's case the giant attacked his family not long after his birth. Similar dangers threatened the farmer's month-old son at a time when his father couldn't get enough food or sex. Indeed, the baby boy became a food object. The farmer said he often thought of cooking him like a chicken in his microwave oven, probably to make up for a painful lack of attention.

This man's cruelties also encompass envy and jealousy, the hatred aroused by a third person's challenge to preeminence in the family. Whether the wife will be honored or destroyed depends on the balance of forces, ranging from delight with the birth to fury at her taking a lover, the baby.

The wicked giant had stolen a hen and a harp—that is, his mother's capacity to feed her young and maintain her peace of mind. Jack's task was to restore his mother's health and happiness, the family fortunes, and punish the giant, cut a bad father down to size. In order to accomplish this he had to sell a cow—get rid of childish dependency and sow some seeds—discover his own strength and potency.[64] It was an extended struggle, not only because it takes time for a boy to become a man, but also because the giant embodied his own wicked impulses that he had to conquer in himself. Only then could he make amends to his mother and regain her confidence.

Yet there is more to this tale than vicious attacks on abundance and love. The giant also damaged a mother's procreative powers. He killed her husband, the source of seeds for future life, and nearly destroyed the woman and her offspring. Almost an entire generation had to pass before her son's maturity (the magic beans) renewed the possibility of progress.

The giant was a changeling, the personification of good turned bad. He was a father who disappeared in order to prevent babies being born. And, as Jack discovered, he was an ogre who confined children to a dungeon and ate them at his convenience. These elements are echoes of many legends, especially Grecian beliefs about the creation of the cosmos and the relations between men and women.

First there was Gaea, "the deep-breasted earth." She conceived Uranus, "the sky crowned with stars," and made him her consort and ruler of the Titans. But he feared that their children would rise up against him, so he sealed them in the depths of the earth (the dungeon, a state of unbornness). Gaea mourned, then instigated Cronus, her youngest son, to attack Uranus with a sickle drawn from her bosom. Cronus obliged. He waited until his father slept, then hacked off his genitals and threw them into the sea.[65]

Subsequently Cronus led the generation of giants. But he also feared that his children would supplant him, so he swallowed them (infanticidal cannibalism) as soon as they were born. His wife, despairing that all her progeny would disappear, sought the help of Gaea. Together they arranged to substitute a stone wrapped in swaddling clothes for Zeus, the next baby. Cronus swallowed the ruse and lived to be overthrown by his son when he grew to manhood. Not surprisingly, the adult Zeus dreaded that the same would happen to him.[66]

Father-son conflicts carried on through several generatons of mortals and led directly to the tragedy of Oedipus, which was brought about by a curse on a king who had seduced a boy. Tantalus was a first-generation mortal, the son of Zeus and the great-grandchild of Uranus. He tried to serve his son, Pelops, to the gods in a pie. They took exception and brought Pelops back to life. In angry retribution the gods condemned Tantalus to a life of endless "tantalizing" frustrations.[67] Afterward Pelops, whose kingdom was the seat of the ancient Olympic games, became a key figure in the unfolding of the Oedipus saga as well as that great narration of sibling intrigue, the *Oresteia*.[68]

These tales tell of the damage inflicted by men, but provoked by women and aroused by prophets. Their prophecies were correct. All men tend to be supplanted by the fruit of a woman's womb, children who naturally grow older and stronger while their parents grow older and weaker. My own son seriously explained this dilemma when he started school: "You know, Daddy, I am going to grow up, but you are going to grow down."[69]

Interestingly, the Greeks did not overemphasize the conflicts between father and son. Even in Oedipus the prevailing issue is the relationship between a mother and her son.[70] The men were much more concerned with the direct threats women posed, in the guise of maternal Furies or female warriors, to their flesh and blood and pride, an obvious consequence of the Dorian conquest of matriarchal, female ruling (gynecocratic) predecessors. Having taken over their power, authority, assets, and maleness, they feared Amazonian counterattacks. Thus the Athenian national hero was Theseus, whose definitive defeat of Queen Hippolyte appeared to preclude the possibility of female reconquests.

For the ancient Greeks, strategic avoidance was the counterpart of confrontation. They created a male-oriented culture that celebrated pederasty and subordinated women.[71] To our eyes pederasty signifies the sexual desire of adult men for young boys and is considered extremely odious. However, in Greece in the period of 750–300 B.C.E., it was a socially sanctioned form of higher education whereby a man of good intellect and breeding endeavored to impart *aretē*—the driving force of a man's skill, power, and character—to a pubescent boy. [72]

The Danish psychoanalyst Thorkil Vanggaard, who has studied the practice in great detail, points out that pederastic intercourse was a sacred act. It was publicly celebrated and steeped in solemnity and honor. This relationship, called *paiderastia* by Vanggaard, was a form of phallic transference that had little to do with homosexuality per se and nothing to do with effeminacy, quite the opposite.[73] Both the older man, the *erastēs*, and his younger lover, the *erōmenos*, were aggressively male in dress and demeanor.[74] Unlike contemporary "butch" figures, they were expected to marry and produce children. Those who didn't were ridiculed and punished.[75]

In a larger sense, the idealization of the older man–pubescent boy relationship can be seen as a cultural necessity. Besides its positive functions, *paiderastia* served to minimize the inherent and inherited conflicts between generations of which the Greeks were well aware. After all, their myths described them in gruesome detail. As far as they were concerned it was better to bed a boy than to kill him. Presumably they also realized that it was possible to allay overt envy by treating someone as a narcissistic extension of oneself. An adult who could impart himself to a handsome youth, and be honored as well, was less likely to dwell on his own fading powers.[76] Similarly, a boy who was chosen by a distinguished man held a sure way to gain style and grow big, thereby minimizing the doubts and discords of adolescence.[77]

The fact that *paiderastia* was not a private erotic enterprise indicates the importance of the custom to Athenian society, indeed, to the state. Solon, the famous law giver who lived about 600 B.C.E., laid down strict rules for pederastic relations.[78] *Paiderastia* took place openly with the consent of the boy's family and under the supervision of responsible authorities. In Crete, for example, the formalities were comparable to marriage by capture. When a Cretan nobleman wanted to educate a particular boy as his *erōmenos,* he would let the family know in advance that he intended to capture him at such and such a time and place. If the family considered him to be a worthy suitor, they allowed this to happen. Then a big party was held to commemorate the event, not unlike a contemporary confirmation or Bar Mitzvah celebration.[79] Certainly the parents kept themselves well informed about the new relationship and felt hurt if it went wrong. Aristophanes joked about this in his play *The Birds,* when a father complains about his son's *erastēs:*

> Well, this is a fine state of affairs, you damned desperado! You meet my son just as he comes out of the gymnasium, all fresh from the bath, and you don't kiss him, you don't say a word to him, you don't hug him, you don't feel his balls! And yet you're supposed to be a friend of ours![80]

After partaking of a man's love and returning home, the boy was granted the title *klēnós,* meaning "famous." In addition he was accorded special privileges, including distinguished dress and marks of public respect, which he retained for life. These honors were given because the young adult had attained *aretē,* which, for the Dorians, was the greatest distinction that could befall a man.[81]

. . .

There exists considerable evidence that *paiderastia* was a part of ordinary Grecian life. Abundant legends indicate it was also a common practice on Mount Olympus.[82] Since these legends (told and retold, lost and discovered, discovered and rediscovered, over thousands of years) mediated the relationships between man and man and, ultimately, man and society, *paiderastia* and its aftermath have to be important factors in the way modern man has come to perceive himself.[83]

King Pelops played a leading role in many of the most crucial myths. He achieved the title of *klēnós* after being the lover of Poseidon, god of the sea. In later life Pelops called upon Poseidon for help in order to gain the hand of a princess whose father destroyed her suitors. With Poseidon's help Pelops gained a wife and mother of the house of Pelops, whose malevolent intrigues led to the *Oresteia* and several generations of infanticide, fratricide, and matricide.[84]

But Pelops had other wives, one of whom produced a beloved and favored son, Chrysippus, acclaimed for his extraordinary gifts and beauty. During the course of a visit with Pelops, Laius, the king of Thebes, fell desperately in love with him. Without asking Pelops' permission, Laius abducted the boy and took him as his *erōmenos*. The enraged Pelops cursed his colleague and all his kin, an action that precipitated the tragedy of Oedipus.[85]

Laius' crime was not simply untamable desire, but a greedy eye for a luscious youth that broke all bounds and violated sacred social and moral conventions. The curse was that his children and children's children would do likewise. Laius tried to avoid this fate by refusing to produce further offspring, but his wife, Jocasta, tricked him by getting him drunk and forcing herself upon him. So Laius himself became a victim of what the Greeks feared most, overweening female sexuality and ambition.[86]

Having been warned by the oracle that his baby would kill him, Laius prepared for murder. He arranged for the male child to be exposed on a mountain with his ankles pierced by pins (hence the name Oedipus, meaning "swollen foot"). The boy should have died, as did the many unwanted children who were left on hillsides in antiquity, but Oedipus was rescued by a shepherd and adopted by the childless king and queen of Corinth.[87]

Laius the king is a paradigm of the bad father. He is a weak, selfish, dishonest man, unsure of his sexuality but consumed with anger.[88] To cover his wounds and conceal his defects, he inflates himself in every way. This swollen self is a sign not just of hubris, but of pathological hatred, of life and love. No wonder he raped the son of a friend. Having been abandoned by his father at an early age, he can't stand the love between Pelops and Chrysippus, nor the grace revealed in another's body.[89] Laius merely tried to possess and destroy what couldn't exist in himself. His curse was an inner ugliness, which preceded whatever Pelops decreed. Then, turning inside out, he feared his own son would do what he would have done to any child, no matter what the provocation—that is, abandon, neglect, torture, and kill him. How extraordinary it was that Freud ignored his role in the drama that followed.[90]

The mythological Oedipus was not a vengeful son. Far from perpetuating a terrible curse, he fled from Corinth as soon as he heard of it, in order to protect the parents he loved. On the road to Thebes he was assailed by a stranger whom he killed only in self-defense. He did not know that the man was Laius.[91]

Upon arriving at Thebes, he discovered that the city was being terrorized by the Sphinx, a female monster who strangled and ate anyone who couldn't answer a riddle: "What is it that walks on four legs in the morning, on two at noon, and on three in the evening?"[92] Undaunted, Oedipus gave the correct reply: It is a human, who first crawls on all fours, then walks upright, and, in old age, needs an extra stick. In other words he asserted his identity in the face of female tyranny. In response the Sphinx threw herself off a cliff (went into a terminal depression), and Oedipus was offered the throne of Thebes. What he didn't realize was that his mother, Jocasta, was part of the package.

The ensuing marriage worked well. The couple produced four healthy children, and Oedipus became a wise and capable ruler. Then a plague struck the city. A blind prophet proclaimed that the disaster was a curse, a consequence of the murder of Laius. It could only be overcome if the murderer was driven away. Oedipus swore to find him, but Jocasta begged him to desist. She had discovered the truth about Laius and herself and preferred to let sleeping dogs lie. But her son and husband plowed on and, after a ruthless investigation, discovered the murderer was himself.[93]

The issues appear to be incest and parricide. Once the secrets were revealed, Jocasta hanged herself. She declaimed guilt and shame, and we can assume she feared the envy of women and the vengeance of men for having loved and honored a patricide.[94] Meanwhile Oedipus thought of suicide, but he decided to gouge out his eyes and go into exile, suitable punishments for his crimes. But are they? He had sought to save his parents, not kill one and sleep with the other. The slain man was a stranger, someone who had tried to kill him twice before. Moreover, Jocasta knew all about the curse yet persisted in marriage to a younger man. Perhaps the Sphinx was one of her incarnations.

The classical view is that Oedipus was hounded by remorseless fate (uncontrollable libidinal impulses) to attack his father and possess his mother. And the sequelae, disgrace, mutilation, exile, and regressive dependency, were unavoidable. This is a fate all men share in phantasy, if not in actuality. Others have argued that the self-blinding was an act of cowardice. It represented the wish not to see what had taken place nor experience appropriate guilt and sorrow, again a typical human reaction.[95]

In *Oedipus at Colonus* Sophocles points out that the legend was far from a tragedy. Although the course of his life was not quite to be envied, Oedipus emerged with honor and dignity.[96] After extremes of success and suffering, he became and was seen as a seer. Paradoxically it was his very act of self-immolation that made this possible. It extirpated eyes, too greedy for their own good, and expiated an "I," grown beyond all bounds. Simultaneously, Oedipus appeased Thebes and protected himself from a higher fate, not his personal desires, but *phthonos theon,* envy of the gods, who saw his success as a personal challenge to their prerogatives. After all, if you kill your father and marry his wife, sire his children, and rule his domain, there are few other conventions you can't break. This clarifies the nature of Pelops' curse. Not only were Oedipus and his kin destined to violate all moral rules, they were also condemned to be destroyed by the envy and jealousy that the breaking of these rules would arouse.[97] Still, it took the gods (the paternal envy of Laius and Pelops) seventeen years to wake up to the fact and apply their evil eyes (the plague) to his life. By blinding himself, Oedipus renounced his omnipotence and freed himself from the continuing fear of divine revenge.

Pelops' curse passed over Oedipus, and in some respects he overcame it. He was not destroyed by libidinal impulses (his greed), nor by the hands of his father or his children (their envy). However, his recovery remained incomplete. Although we never learn whether his sons took lovers, he felt they had disowned and dishonored him, something he could not forgive. When they turned to him for help, he denounced them and perpetuated the curse by refusing his blessing and condemning them to fratricidal strife.[98] In his eyes they never achieved *aretē.*

Like medieval fantasies of courtly love, *paiderastia* was less pure in practice than in theory. By the third century B.C.E. it had long been debased, and carnality, or the greedy penis, was less often a metaphor than an aim in itself.[99] The ensuing relationship of father to child was transformed during periods of Roman and Christian hegemony. An imperious patriarchal authority became the norm. Over the next millennium, the predominant fears of children and adults shifted from oral-devouring and womb-destroying giants and gods to phallic fathers preoccupied with political and sexual aggrandizement. It became the practice for men to be seen and treated as lords and masters who needed to wield firm hands and stout rods to control unruly wives and children. If paternal regimes were authoritarian and status seeking, then this was needed to maintain the natural order of things and to triumph over children's "inordinate" rivalries and hostilities.

The idea that children were basically sinful arose from the unrestrained tendency of parents to treat them as the projective foci of their own lost wishes or unrealized malice. In other words, children weren't children, separate beings, but sorrowful mirrors of their parents' and parents' parents' unwelcome feelings or, within the social climate of the time, destroyed subjectivity. This included neediness, pain, rebelliousness, assertiveness, and, of course, rage. The resultant frightening, hated figure can be called *The Combined Child*.[100] The image helps to account for countless numbers of children who were rejected and injured, or simply killed, often by fathers but also by mothers, for misbehaving or just for existing. Since the parents couldn't tolerate the child in themselves, there was no way they would allow him or her to live in the outside world, either. Needless to say this is a problem still seeking a solution.

The view of children as inherently bad was augmented by widely read homilies that warned "Against Wilful Rebellion" and told about "the mischief and wickedness when the subjects unnaturally do rebel against their prince."[101]

By the sixteenth century there exists considerable evidence of a fierce determination on the part of elders and superiors to break the will of children, probably because of a covert, and not so covert, struggle among adult citizens to assert their own will. John Robinson, the first pastor of the Pilgrim fathers in Holland, only reflected current ideas when he asserted:

> Surely there is in all children . . . a stubbornness, and stoutness of mind arising from natural pride, which must in the first place be broken and beaten down.[102]

Similarly, the training of children was commonly equated with the breaking-in of young horses or hunting dogs. As Lawrence Stone points out in his study entitled *The Family, Sex and Marriage in England 1500–1800*, "The characteristic equipment of the schoolmaster was not so much a book as a rod or a bundle of birch twigs."[103]

On Chartres Cathedral porch the emblem of Grammar is a master threatening two children with a scourge. And by the next century flogging became routine for boys and girls, regardless of rank or age, whether at school or at work. In London the heads of the most distinguished public schools, Dr. Busby of Westminster and Dr. Gill of St. Paul's, were notorious for their savagery; while at Oxford and Cambridge universities, the "colleges freely used physical punishments . . . either by public whippings in the hall or over a barrel in the buttery, or else by putting them in stocks in the hall."[104] A lot of this violence carried an overtly envious tinge, as Samuel Pepys noted in his *Diaries:*

> Pelham Humphrey . . . was admitted Gentleman of the Chapel Royal in 1666, and distinguished himself so much as to excite the envy of his instructor, who [eventually] died of discontent at his pupil's excelling himself.[105]

A malicious preoccupation with discipline prevailed in most parts of Europe and America. This was most carefully documented in accounts of the childhood of the king of France, Louis XIII, son and heir of Henri IV. The child was treated as if he possessed, in the most generous supply, all the sins of his fathers, from envy to obstinacy. He got his first whipping at the age of two, and these continued until he became king at the age of nine. Usually his nurse beat him with a switch or birch as soon as he woke up. The favored place was his behind.

> The whippings increased in frequency when he was three, and on one occasion his father whipped him himself when in a rage with his son. As he grew older, his nurse could not control him, and the child was held down by soldiers while she beat him. At the age of ten, he still had nightmares of being whipped, and the threats to whip him only stopped at the age of thirteen, not long before his marriage.[106]

Paradoxically, the strict subordination of children was the result of greater interest in them brought about by the Reformation and, in Catholic Europe, the counter-Reformation. Children were charged with corruption and sin (principally pride and disobedience), just as women had been accused of witchcraft two hundred years previously, and they were threatened with similar punishments.[107] The doctrine of the "original sins of the young" became the heir to possession by incubi and succubi. While women had been dismissed for being "lousy with lust," boys and girls were condemned for being "suffused with insolence." The Protestant reformer John Calvin was so concerned that he demanded the death penalty for disobedient children, a precept that was turned into legislation in America. Although only a handful of children were ever executed for this crime, the Connecticut judiciary was authorized in 1642 to jail a child upon complaint from his parents about "any stubborn or rebellious carriage." And Massachusetts imposed capital punishment in 1646 for any child over sixteen who "shall curse or smite their natural father or mother" or even refuse to obey their orders.[108]

By Victorian times these extreme measures were replaced, or at least ameliorated, by more sophisticated techniques of paternal control, such as psychic assault. Moreover, perceptions of children changed. While the devil still possessed them, it was a devil less charged with religious reprobation. Concomitantly, old ideas about innocence returned to the fore. Fathers remained authoritarian and overbearing, but aloofness eroded overinvolvement. The Victorian father enjoyed an Olympian stance but was himself controlled by being placed on a pedestal. Therefore he could be feared and hated at a distance.[109]

The corporal focus of parent-child conflict in Victorian times was child sexuality, especially masturbation. While this conflict was most acute between fathers and sons, there remained a special destructive element in the relations between fathers and daughters that often surfaced in the emotional disabilities of the filial generation. In either case the tyrannical father was partly displaying anxieties about his own potency and partly acting under pressure from intense jealousy and envy about his children's abundant sexual energies.[110] These issues are universal and more than evident today, although in the nineteenth century it was the sexuality that was suppressed, while in the present parents prefer to forget the hurt and sheer malice that adolescents can and do provoke.[111]

An oppressive, exploitative father acting together with a self-seeking, resentful mother comprise *The Parental Persecutor,* a larger-than-life person, part witch, part giant, who can be acutely dangerous to his/her offspring by filling them with pernicious projections (pride, insolence, sexuality, envy) and then attacking them for possessing a "bad disposition." Essentially such people treat their children like toilets, convenient receptacles for their own denied, guilt-ridden impulses (deviltries).[112]

A Polish rabbi has provided a vivid illustration of the actual mechanism employed to attribute sin, pathological projective identification. He used to beat the young students who sat shivering in his classroom with leathern thongs. After demanding that they pull down their pants and lie across a wooden bench, he would carefully recite:

> In every person there is a Good Spirit and an Evil Spirit. The Good Spirit has its own dwelling-place—which is the head. So has the Evil Spirit—and that is the place where you get the whipping.[113]

The projections are clear. The rabbi sees good in the head and bad in the bum, although there is no inherent reason for goodness or its opposite to reside in any particular region of the body. The element of identification comes in when he not only locates, but equates badness or the "Evil Spirit" with the behind. And the pathological aspect of all this resides in his treating the students as Combined Children, frightening figures and convenient receptacles for his own denied willful, resentful, sensual self. By getting rid of the evil spirits, which are very much his own, he is essentially expressing his envy of everything young men have that he doesn't.

The students, in turn, are relatively powerless to oppose the attributions of their teacher. After all, he is the authority, and strong views backed up by violent deeds always have a penetrating impact. Inevitably many of them will succumb to the belief that their backsides, aside from other parts, are full of evil and deserve punishment.

This same process was institutionalized by the nineteenth-century German physician and pedagogue Daniel Gottlieb Schreber, whose views and writings on child rearing were extremely influential during his lifetime and for a long time thereafter, up to and including the Nazi era. Schreber believed that children were naturally weak, soft, and rotten, and that their "daemonic" defects were the cause of moral decay in society as a whole. He warned against "ill-temper, morose or sulky forms of mind" in young children and compared these moods to "life-endangering daemons" that had to be rooted out like rotten weeds.[114] The same held true for older children. One had to be constantly on guard against and crush any "ignoble, immoral or depressive emotions" such as might be manifested through defiance and disobedience. Moreover,

> one has to feel out the rotten spots by means of intense help; otherwise they eat away and the roots get so strong that this process will continue indefinitely.[115]

The solutions that Schreber advocated included beatings, starvation, and, in particular, complicated leather or metal contraptions that were placed around the child's head or back in order to force him to sit, lie, or stand straight. For Schreber straight posture was identical with moral straightness or virtue. Should the boy or girl lapse, these devices would press against the body and produce extreme discomfort or suffocation. Such devices were sold and used by parents around the world.[116]

Donald Duck and other Walt Disney cartoon characters convey similar concerns and solutions. Again and again Uncle Donald (and sometimes Aunt Daisy) accuse their nephews and nieces of harboring their own greedy, irascible feelings. These attributions ostensibly explain and excuse their subsequent punitive behavior, which is often extremely nasty. Thus, in *Donald's Happy Birthday* Huey, Dewey, and Louie make a great effort to earn some money to buy their uncle a present. But he makes them put it in a bank. Still, wanting to get him a box of cigars, they "borrow" the money. Donald finds out, calls them greedy, no-good thieves, and sadistically forces them to smoke all the cigars, something he wanted to do himself.[117]

In truth the films often provide two perspectives, an objective study of a obdurate, angry, tyrannical adult and couple, which I term *The Parental Persecutor,* and a subjective impression of the same threatening person(s) from the point of view of their children or allegedly hapless victims, which Melanie Klein and her colleagues have called *The Combined Parent.* The latter is a monster, a focus of hatred turned against the hater, arising from overpowering phantasies of both parents locked in continual pleasurable (oral, anal, genital) exchanges. *The Combined Parent* is a mother imbued with traits of the father and father imbued with traits of the mother simultaneously attacked and transformed by the child's envy, greed, and jealousy into a single terrifying figure.[118] Such images help to explain, although they do not necessarily excuse, the vicious behavior of children toward their elders.

In this chapter I deliberately emphasized the concrete reality of malevolent mothers and brutal fathers, people transformed from helpers to hurters under sway of breast, womb, or phallic forces. But the picture I presented was incomplete. We have to add the predominant phantasies of the angry child, which can exaggerate parents' badness and negate their goodness. The fact that Laius was cruel to Oedipus does not mean that Freud's Oedipal formulations are incorrect. Sons and daughters can and do harbor murderous intentions toward their parents or caretakers no matter how well or poorly they are treated. What is important is to place these feelings within the larger context of parent-child transactions. This helps to distinguish reasoned revenge, for example, from sheer malevolence.

With regard to the latter, each side frequently uses the other as a focus of pernicious projections and a dumping ground for sin. But these very actions, the filling of persons or things with badness and their subsequent metamorphosis, essentially define envy. So we are basically considering the flow of envy or other elements of malice from one generation to the next.

The envious child is *The Filial Persecutor*, the vengeful enemy of older people and established traditions, no less than *The Parental Persecutor* is an adult who demonizes youth.[119] Samuel Butler, for one, specifically referred to such children in his late-Victorian novel *Erewhon*. He envisioned a time when all infants signed a birth contract stipulating that their parents were not responsible for bringing them into the world and apologizing in advance for intentionally and treacherously setting about to "pester and plague" them.[120]

Butler articulated fears extending from prehistory to the present that children are mortally dangerous to their parents. These fears encompass dual perspectives, objective conclusions that boys surpass their fathers and girls their mothers, whether as a fact of nature or to repay the hurts they actually suffered, and subjective impressions of children as "little devils." The latter arise from the overpowering phantasies of parents. The resultant terrifying, hated figure is *The Combined Child*. This is a fantastic image, which rules adults just as *The Combined Parent* rules children.

Filial persecutors and combined children together with parental persecutors and combined parents comprise a matrix of malice that affects all families. Sigmund Freud was the first of several investigators who have described different aspects of this matrix under the rubric of the Oedipus complex (Freud), the Electra complex (Jung), the early Oedipus complex (Klein), and the Laius complex (Devereux).[121] Although psychological literature abounds with examples of child-parent Oedipal conflicts, it is relatively rare for these exchanges to be seen within the larger matrix of parent-child relations—that is, the edifice of reciprocating hurts and hopes.

A colleague has told me about two separate dreams that he and his son had on the same morning. "Dr. R" dreamed about a fight among himself, his son, and an older man. It was a pea fight, which he started by throwing green peas at the others. While this was going on, his son was dreaming about being attacked by "a daddy long-legs," a black bug with a long body but no legs. It had attached itself to his leg and begun to suck his blood and "put in something that would make me sick." These dreams occurred at a time when the boy was doing well in school, but his father was pushing him to do more homework (prep) and had himself just bought a computer.

In discussing the dreams together, the father thought that the older man represented his own successful father. Throwing peas had to do with the wish to pee both on his father's accomplishments and his son for doing well at school and getting up in the world. R laughed when he thought of green peas because he immediately connected green with "green with envy." So he concluded that the dream conveyed a multigenerational envious put-down.

The boy, who was psychologically quite astute, concurred and added that he thought his dad's dream had been precipitated by rivalry, for he had recently been beating him at golf. In thinking about his own dream, he related the bug both to his dad's bugging him about doing more prep and to computer bugs. He was amused by his dad's interest in computers and thought he was on his way to becoming a computer bug, that is, an adept. He himself had been bitten by the computer bug long before and resented the purchase of a new machine that wasn't specifically for him. So he had been hoping secretly that the computer would be spoiled by bugs, that is, problems and errors.

R's son realized that his dream was about revenge, his own wish to get back at his dad and his fear that his dad would get back at him. He suggested that the daddy longlegs without legs represented his father without a penis—that is, without all his skills and expensive equipment. R was delighted with the interpretation and reminded the boy that the previous week he had half-jokingly called him a "bloodsucker" for demanding a raise in his weekly allowance. All these recriminations recurred in the dream but had been put into the bug, which appeared as a castrated, bloodsucking little shit. This bad bug was a memory, a fear, and a wish. It was a retaliatory figure who threatened to attack this dreamer's leg/phallus and punish him for his own envious, vengeful thoughts.[122]

The American psychiatrist Morton Schatzman deciphered a different relationship where a man, an eminent German judge, was persecuted by a variety of mental and physical phenomena. Unfortunately, what he did not know and could not accept was that these afflictions represented memories of painful disciplines that his father had inflicted on him. I refer to the case of Daniel Paul Schreber, the son of the pedagogue.[123]

At the age of sixty-one Daniel Paul published *Memoirs of My Nervous Illness,* an account of the experiences and thoughts he had suffered during a fourteen-year career as a diagnosed paranoid.[124] He described the murder of his soul brought about by mysterious rays, writings, sensations, pressures, influences, and miracles:

> One of the most horrifying miracles was the so-called compresson-of-the-chest-miracle . . . the whole chest wall being compressed, so that the state of oppression caused by the lack of breath was transmitted to my whole body. . . . Next was the-head-compressing-machine. . . . [It] compressed my head as though in a vise . . . [and] was accompanied by severe pain.[125]

Schatzman has shown that these so-called miracles were almost exact representations of the father's practices as distilled from the voluminous writings of a pedant with divine pretensions. The compression miracles, for example, were directly related to the *Schrebersche geradehalter* (Schreber's straight holder) and *kopfhalter* (head holder). The former was an iron crossbar fastened to the table to force children to sit straight. It pressed against the child's collarbones and shoulders. The child could not lean against the bar for long without experiencing extreme discomfort.[126] As for the *kopfhalter,* it was a strap clamped to the child's hair and his underwear that pulled and tore the hair if the head was not held absolutely straight. Father Schreber admitted that it had "a certain stiffening effect."[127]

The two relationships I have been describing contain many elements of Laial and Oedipal conflicts or, to put it another way, matrices of malice aroused both by the Laius and Oedipus complexes. However, Dr. R and his son were able to acknowledge their antagonisms and talk to each other because their rivalry and vindictiveness occurred within a larger context of affection and respect. The older Schreber professed love but practiced hate. His son was confused. Freud thought that his delusions masked a homosexual attachment—that is, hidden love—toward his father.[128] Given his upbringing, it is more likely that they harbored unrequited hatred toward a father who refused to permit overt or covert filial antagonisms while demanding absolute obedience.[129]

The extreme passions unleashed by parents toward children, or by children to parents, are never resolved by their assuming a subterranean existence. At best, potential explosions are put off until another time. What does happen is that the desire for life and wellsprings of love tend to intersect and mitigate curses, furies, and complexes. Otherwise we all would inhabit worlds solely determined by ancient or recent hurts. Nevertheless, there are many instances where excessive envy or actual abuse overwhelm loving capacities and leave children and adults at the mercy of their destructive impulses and those of others.

The younger Schreber was probably so resentful about the way he had been treated that he could not remember what he needed to remember, because to do so would have released a flood of the very feelings he had been taught not to feel. Instead they remained underground until outer circumstances in conjunction with inner pressures precipitated their chaotic release.[130] Such events are notable features of many lives, especially during adolescence or middle age, when intense desires and enmities reassert themselves. Although Freud spoke about an earlier dissolution of the Oedipus complex by taking parent figures into oneself and identifying with them, it is more accurate to say that the complexities of intergenerational love/hate/fear/guilt do not dissolve but divert, inwardly, as he described, and outwardly in the case of myth and folklore.[131]

The boy who slays the evil giant also has to dispose of the wicked witch. Similarly the girl who overcomes a fearsome queen also has to account for dreaded beasts. Both in dream and actuality, witches and giants are complementary creatures, cruel, self-centered, begrudging, and usurping vitality and youth no less than male and female powers. Witches and giants embody *The Combined Parental Persecutor,* parental figures created by the imagination of the child and the misdeeds of the adult. In every generation the newcomers have to struggle to assert themselves yet avoid being beguiled, destroyed, or transformed themselves into *Combined Persecutors (Filial or Parental)* and trapped in the realms they rule.

In these tasks son Schreber became hopelessly lost, while son R seems on the right track. Much earlier the Greek Titans, Giants, and gods were total failures, while Oedipus had some success. Despite the dangers and difficulties, "Jack the Giant Killer" and "Hansel and Gretel" demonstrate that it is possible to make progress, a point a patient of mine made when she decided to come off her pedestal, step out of fairy tales, and, as she put it, "confront envy and jealousy, my parents' legacy and my own."

8

It's Not Fair

Now Israel loved Joseph more than all his children, because
he was the son of his old age; and he made him a coat of many
colours. . . . And his brethren envied him. . . . And when they
saw him afar off, they conspired against him to slay him. And
they said to one another, "Behold, this dreamer cometh. Come
now therefore, and let us slay him, and cast him into some pit,
and we shall say, some evil beast hath devoured him; and we
shall see what will become of his dreams."[1]

The story of Joseph, indeed, the whole of Genesis, is essentially
a discourse about sibling rivalry. The biblical origins of Western
civilization touch Adam and Eve, Cain and Abel, Sarah and Hagar,
Isaac and Ishmael, Jacob and Esau, and, in greatest detail, Joseph
and his brothers. When they saw how much Jacob adored his eldest
son, they were speechless with hatred, an animosity inflamed by
Joseph's vivid dreams of preeminence, which he took pleasure to
report. The ensuing evil beast was the spirit of malicious vengeance
aroused by paternal favoritism and fraternal pride.[2]

The pattern was repeated in Egypt when Joseph's superior talents
led to recognition and promotion by a new master but also led to

the unrequited desire and enmity of others, notably his master's wife. The woman attempted to seduce him. When he resisted her advances, she slandered him before her husband, who had him imprisoned.[3] This episode has remarkable similarities to the Egyptian narrative "Tale of Two Brothers," an account of sibling intrigue and conflict, which Bruno Bettelheim has called the world's oldest fairy tale.[4] Preserved in a papyrus manuscript, it can be dated to 1225 B.C.E. but is undoubtedly older. Subsequently the legend has taken on close to eight hundred different versions. It concerns an older man and his younger brother, their bitter struggles and eventual reconciliation, all fomented by the wife of one who tries to seduce and thereby impugn the honor of the other.[5]

According to separate Hebrew and Egyptian descriptions, the woman made herself the center of a jealous storm, yet the protagonists strove to retain connections to their common stream—family and fraternal bonds. In these tales the woman symbolizes the interloper, the outsider, or, more likely, the aggrieved brother or sister, who rues the loss of real or imagined rights and wishes to assume ones he or she never had. It is interesting that the word that describes the ensuing intense, competitive, combative behavior, "rivalry," stems from the Latin root *rivalis*, meaning "having rights to the same stream." So the original word implies sharing, based on joint inheritance or interests, while in actual usage the word denotes aggression, the heir to feelings of unjust deprivation or simply greedy aggrandizement.

The Greek legends emphasize dual perspectives with both gods and mortals striving "to break the bounds of the brook." Tantalus did this when he served his son in a pie, and Pelops did likewise when he murdered an accomplice during the course of gaining the hand of the beautiful but guarded Hippodamia.[6] The deed did not go down well with Hermes (Mercury), the youth's father, who noted a challenge to his divine prerogatives. So he condemned the descendants of Pelops to repeat the fratricidal excesses of their father and grandfather. Meanwhile Pelops himself was doomed to be the victim of equally devastating conflicts by colleagues such as Laius, who stole his favorite son, and Hippodamia, who orchestrated the boy's death.

This curse and antecedent actions proved to be the common source for *Oedipus Rex* and the *Oresteia*, two blood-filled streams of inter- and intragenerational ambition, pride, fear, malice, guilt, and revenge. However, those who discuss these dramas usually stress the intergenerational features, that is, the conflicts between father and son or mother and daughter. Consequently sibling conflicts, whether in the Greek myths or elsewhere, tend to be seen through Oedipal filters.[7] While it is clear that parents and children vie with each other for food, power, and preeminence with a demonic intensity and treat each other with extragenerational abandon (parents expecting their children to parent them or children seeing the parents as children), nonetheless the sibling bond has a life of its own, which isn't just a pale reflection of earlier struggles.[8]

Parents frequently treat their children, and children their parents, as sibs—that is, compatriots sharing the same stream, either of love or hate. This may be especially evident during times of marital conflict, when parents expect their children to take sides in their convoluted feuds, or during pregnancy or after childbirth. Many men have commented that they wanted to welcome a newborn child but found the task too difficult because they simultaneously saw the baby as an intruder, like a younger brother or sister.[9] Similarly Peter Lomas has described a woman who suffered a prolonged depression after the birth of a son because he reminded her of a hated brother.[10]

In Latin America fathers, along with the displaced child, commonly share a state of severe physical decline known as *chipil* when a new baby arrives. This condition is a postweaning syndrome that is generally due to protein and calorie deficiency following withdrawal of the breast, but it is popularly explained on the basis of intense envy (extreme discontent) toward the new fetus. No matter how proud the man may be, or how pleased by the prospect of future economic contributions, he knows that he will be sharing his wife with a rival for love.[11]

On other occasions the discontent may flare up directly via angry, rejecting behavior or indirectly by encouraging one child to bully another. In this way some adults get their offspring to dramatize their own competitive instincts. In one family the older kids tried to poison and set fire to the younger ones, while the mother seemed oblivious to what was going on. Her therapist noted:

> The older siblings were acting out Mother's [only slightly] unconscious wish to be rid of the younger children—a rather drastic form of maternal rejection.[12]

Oedipus himself recognized sibling issues when commenting on his relationship with his daughters:

> *These luckless two*
> *Were given birth by her who gave birth to me.*

> ―――
> *(Chorus) These then are daughters:*
>   *they are also—*
> ―――
> *Sisters: yes, their father's sisters. . . .*[13]

By the same token, Oedipus could have pointed out that he was the brother of his sons. Consequently their quarrels encompassed not only father to son, but also brother to brother, as had been foretold by Pelops' curse. As the eldest son, Polynices held the right to the throne of Thebes. But after Oedipus became an outcast, the throne was seized by the youngest one, not Polynices, the next in line. While trying to effect a reconciliation, their sister, Ismene, decried the ancient curse and the way it enthralled their pitiful family:

> *Then some fury put it in their hearts—*
> *O pitiful again—to itch for power:*
> *For seizure of prerogative and throne;*
> *And it was the younger and the less mature*
> *Who stripped his elder brother, Polyneices,*
> *Of place and kinship, and then banished him.*[14]

According to Euripides, Polynices had earlier confronted this treachery and deplored the fact that his brother had broken his agreement to share the throne, in alternate years, on the understanding that each would have his turn, and neither would engage in hatred or envy with the other.[15] Both turned to Oedipus for support toward the end of his life, but he turned a deaf ear to their pleas and reminded them, somewhat unjustly, that for lack of "a little word from that fine pair, out I went, like a beggar, to wander forever!"[16] Although dying with honor, Oedipus rebuffed all attempts to stop the impending fratricides. His last act was to "abominate and disown" Polynices and to foreclose the male line that had emanated from Laius:

> *You shall die*
> *By your own brother's hand, and you shall kill*
> *The brother who banished you. For this I pray.*[17]

While this was happening, the malediction was working its way through the other stream. Ostensibly the *Oresteia* concerns the period from the fall of Troy to the trial of Orestes for killing his mother.[18] Actually it is a tragedy that reaches from Tantalus to Pelops and extends through an additional three generations of violent discord. By Hippodamia Pelops had several children, including two sons, Atreus and Thyestes. By another wife he had Chrysipppus, whom he especially loved. And if the conflict with Laius were not enough, Hippodamia became enraged by the favor shown to the son of another wife and arranged for her own sons to kill him. Presumably they envied the boy's good fortune and were jealous of the attention that their father, like Jacob, gave one among many. So they were more than willing to do the dirty work.[19]

Revenge and counterrevenge continued through the next generation. The children of Atreus included Agamemnon and Menaleus, the husband of Helen, whose abduction precipitated the Trojan war. The children of Thyestes included Aegisthus, who killed Atreus and Agamemnon after his triumphant return from Troy.

Ultimately Orestes, Agamemnon's son, completed the blood feud by slaying his mother, Clytemnestra, and his uncle, her lover, Aegisthus. He was goaded to the matricide by his sister, Electra, who retained a fanatical devotion to the memory of her father and an equally obsessive hostility to her mother.[20] It is said she remained the driving force behind his actions. However, the abiding legacy of these events is not the Electra complex—the alleged universal wish of a girl to kill her mother and love her father.[21] Rather, the *Oresteia* exemplifies the social fact and legendary curse that the sibling rivalries (intragenerational strife) of the parents may be replayed with devastating consequences through the intergenerational struggles of their children and children's children.[22]

One essential theme unites all the contributors to sibling strife: It's not fair! This is an argument, more a war cry, that runs from Cain and Abel to the *Oresteia* and, now, to the TV series *Dynasty*.[23] The perceived presence or absence of fairness provokes or mitigates the resentments that lurk in all peoples concerning food, love, beauty, attention, privilege, or power, that is, breast, womb, or phallic possessions—the common streams.

Malice appears when fairness disappears, a fact confirmed by the angry child at times of separation and loss or, coincidentally, parental indifference. But one event stands out, the birth of a new sibling. The newcomer arouses the most acute reactions because the birth (or the sudden presence of a new child, as in certain stepfamilies) announces a state of permanent deprivation coupled with an acute blow to self-esteem. The dethroned sib (or father) is no longer first and foremost in his mother's life.[24]

A sense of fairness or proto-morality begins with wide-eyed comparisons between what one has and what the newcomer is getting. The initial reaction is to exaggerate and then belittle both baby and mother, her breast, caring, feeding, caressing, lots of time; "its" demands; and the growing relationship between them. Thus the evil eye awakens even before words or deeds can formulate and communicate the extent of one's discontent.

The psychoanalyst Phyllis Greenacre uses the term "the Medea complex" to describe states of intractable jealousy in women. She relates these to extreme feelings of anxiety and envy often suffered in childhood upon the birth of a new brother or sister. For one sixteen-month-old girl the trauma was the sight of a newborn baby at her mother's breast, which filled her with unspoken, unspeakable, and uncontainable oral aggression.[25]

Another psychoanalyst, Gerhart Piers, sees the same situation in terms of guilt. This arises from the simple logic "The other gets more than me. I must take it away from him or kill him." Piers remarks that the murderous resentment is fueled by feelings of extreme helplessness and impotence. The child assumes that all adults will behave like his parents, who suddenly and unjustly withdraw their favors and direct them elsewhere. The resultant feelings of raging inferiority and guilt may then extend to all authorities or symbols of authority, like kings and institutions or "the State." In the minds of the discontented, they all stand tried and convicted of favoritism, regardless of what they have or have not done.[26]

In the face of such intense hatred, mere reassurance does not work. As the pediatrician Penelope Leach put it:

> How would you like it if your husband arrived home with an additional wife, explaining that she was someone for you to play with?[27]

The displaced children (and adults) tend to take their revenge on themselves (for unlovableness), the mother (for unfairness), and the new sibling (for intrusion). The "self" destruction frequently appears in the form of depression and regression, aside from conditions such as *chipil* or couvade. We all have seen youngsters who become sulky and demanding once a sister or brother has been born, cry remorselessly, wet their bed, or go off their food.

On the other hand, attacks on the mother may be surprisingly direct. A friend has told me how his two-and-a-half-year-old daughter got very upset upon seeing her new brother being fed. The little girl got a knife from the kitchen, went up to her mother, and started to make wild slicing motions at her breasts. When asked why, the child replied:

> I want to cut off your breast, want to cut it off, stamp on it, on the floor, want to make a big mess of it.[28]

The actor Randy Quaid recalls "pangs of jealousy" the moment he saw brother Dennis in a little bassinet. Until then he had been the only child and was used to getting all the attention. He recalls anger watching his mother nursing him, but his strongest feeling was jealousy. This followed because he was put into the hands of a nanny and no longer had the ready access to his mother that he had previously known.[29]

The combination of envious deprivation and jealous exclusion can be an immediate flashpoint, or it can simmer for decades. Quaid hated the fact that Dennis remained the baby of the family and got preferential treatment. So he enjoyed being the older and stronger one who could "beat the hell out of him and make his life miserable for the first sixteen years. It gave me a nice thrill."[30]

Police reports of grown-ups who kill their entire family for the same reasons are not untypical. One described a twenty-four-year-old Milanese man who strangled his mother and shot his father and younger brother in their beds because his parents thought he was "stupid" and his brother was "the favorite."[31]

Usually the violence starts at an earlier age. A scion of the English aristocracy, Lady Elizabeth Longford, revealed how she caught her eldest daughter, Antonia (later Mrs. Harold Pinter), in the act of smothering her baby brother Thomas.[32] Comparable episodes told by friends or relatives explain why most parents worry about the reception a new baby will get, all the more so with stepchildren. For them the new arrival is not only a threat in its own right, but tangible proof of the love that their own mother or father has given to another and, by implication, withdrawn from them. All too often the stepparent feels second best, too. A young woman anticipated problems marrying a man with three daughters. But she hadn't thought her stepchildren would continue to be "spiteful, hostile, and unpleasant" long after she had made great efforts to be nice to them. Perhaps the last straw was when her own child was born.

The girls were downright cruel to him, putting salt, oil, and mustard in his bottle and deliberately sticking nappy pins in his legs to make him cry.[33]

The child psychiatrist Donald Winnicott had written about his work with a two-year-old girl nicknamed "the Piggle," who suffered nightmares, sleep disturbance, multiple illnesses, and malicious destructive regressive behavior, really the whole range of reactions, after the birth of a sister seven months previously.[34] Her parents said she had become extremely jealous and very greedy, constantly demanding to suck her mother's breasts in place of the baby. The Piggle called these breasts "yams." Often her mother seemed unable to cope with the intensity of her wish to suck on her yams, which her daughter likened to lollipops. The desire alternated with malicious rejection. When offered she might grab them or retort, "No, I want to spoil them. I want to spoil your things."[35]

For months the Piggle remained confused and chaotic. Her envious attacks were never entirely blocked by greed, while the greed only rekindled envy and intolerable, tormenting feelings of guilt. One moment she might seem calm and then suddenly turn on her mother and hiss, "Pity your yams have no milk in them."[36] Her parents themselves felt confused and hurt. Her mother remembered:

When I say good night to her she often buttons up my cardigan so that my yams don't get "dirty and dead." She has been very preoccupied with "dead" lately. I said once: "Soon your yams will grow." She replied, "And yours will die."[37]

Significantly, the Piggle was less aggressive to her sister than to her parents or to herself. She could be extremely mean and spiteful, but also solicitous and loving. A lot depended on whether the baby took her toys or not: "Yes, I hate her very much only when she takes my toys away."[38] I think "toys" means "all the good things that Mommy and Daddy have." When this happened, in fact or phantasy, her sister became black—that is, bad and blackened by her messy anger. Otherwise the Piggle was able to overcome some of the pain of losing her mother by identifying with her and playing the mommy with her sister.[39]

The birth of a sibling is a peak unfair experience, but in every family there are many events that signify loss of the breast and may feel just as unfair or more so. They can be categorized roughly as absences or intrusions. The absences include the tangible loss of a parent through divorce, death, hospitalization, job-induced separation, prolonged holiday; or the near equivalent via sickness or indifference; or excessive attention paid to another child. The author Nancy Friday links her rivalry with her eldest sister to such passive persecutions, that is, torture by endless emptiness:

> I couldn't get my mother's attention no matter what I did. No matter how many laurels I won, I was terrified of being left out. . . .[40]

The active persecutions include both the absence of goodness and the presence of meanness, as with a narcissistic mother who alternates indifference with rivalry and denigration, or a Schreber-like father who fills his children with varying degrees of malicious projections.[41]

I have already discussed a major intrusion, a new baby. But the sudden appearance of a new stepparent or friend or relative (such as an elderly granny) who moves in and takes up a lot of the family's time and attention may be equally devastating. The intruder occasions loss and is an obvious person to blame. Mom herself may be seen as an unwelcome interloper when Dad (or an older sib) takes on the maternal role (to replace a mother preoccupied with other things, for example), or the infant just prefers him. And according to the circumstances, a child may be most furious for a new baby coming between him and his father, rather than between him and his mother.[42]

Of course, when there are a number of children in the family, the most common intrusions stem from the claims of other siblings, younger or older. Sigmund Freud, for example, in a letter to his friend Wilhelm Fliess, noted that his daughter Anna (Annerl) was not at all pleased when her sister ate the family's store of apples:

> Recently Annerl complained that Mathilde had eaten all the apples and demanded that her belly be slit open (as happened to the wolf in the fairy tale of the little goat). She is turning into a charming child.[43]

Whether a particular absence or intrusion or, as is more often the case, an extended sequence of absences and intrusions is bearable or not depends not only on the events themselves, but on the subjective impact upon the parents and sibs. Some children have a remarkable ability to brush off hurts and seek out support from the larger family or social circle. Others have a low hate/high love/high stimulation threshold. They hoard hurts like squirrels garner nuts yet seem obtuse to the ordinary give-and-take, kiss-and-make-up exchanges that are effective in children with high love/low hate capacities. The latter may be lucky and have parents who notice their needs and respond accordingly. If not, trivial events will seem like terrible misdeeds, and the resulting resentments will turn their parents and siblings into persecutors, the focus of fights, both in the outside world and in psychic spheres, for years to come.[44]

"Joan" is a middle-aged woman who has told me about battles with her sister that she still relishes. Once, in their late teens, they went into a pastry shop in Peoria, Illinois. They only had a small amount of money with them, barely enough for coffee and one cake. She wanted to leave, but her sister's eyes lit up in front of the cream cakes, the big ones with beautiful glazes and icings. "That's how she was, blind greedy!" So they sat down, and the waitress came over with a large selection of cakes on a trolley. Her sister seemed mesmerized by a white, sticky cake. No sooner was it on her plate than she dived into it, totally oblivious to anything else. But Joan noticed that the trolley had become stuck on a bit of carpet and began to sway as the waitress tugged on it. A few moments elapsed before it finally tipped over and spewed cakes all over.

> I could have done something, but decided not to. The white cream and yellow icing went all over the table, rugs, my sister, the waitress. It was hysterically funny. I laughed so much I cried. But the waitress was in tears, and my sister, who finally noticed what had happened, began to cry, too. In the end she felt guilty and couldn't finish her cake. And there wasn't even any money for a tip.[45]

At the time Joan was triumphant, thinking that once again her sister had been caught out by greed and had to take the can. She could have stopped the trolley from tipping over but didn't. She enjoyed watching the show and seeing everyone's embarrassment. For her the event was a great victory over family persecutors, a sister who got in the way and a busy mother in the guise of a waitress who provided food but little else.

In retrospect Joan realized that she often blamed her sister and mother for her own "blind ambition" and selfishness. She was always hungry but wanted to appear virtuous. A constant fear was that her family was trying to "pull the rug from under" and make her have "egg on her face." So by inaction she managed to spoil the goodies as well as the occasion, thereby humiliating the humiliators.

Joan was not unaware that inaction, where action is called for, is a powerful form of attack and a superb way of expressing envy and jealousy. The others get hurt, but it is easy to avoid blame. This attack and ensuing "hysterical laughter" constituted a manic defense against the unfairness of continuing neediness and against guilt for the countless subtle ways she continued to run down family rivals and subvert their expected counterattacks.

Manic-type defenses involving denial, self-inflation, and the contemptuous denigration of envied objects are basic maneuvers in sibling battles for the breast. Melanie Klein recalls one woman who intensely admired and coveted a shapely dress her mother had worn when she was child and at a time her elder sister was courting. She could barely control her rage. In later life she did better by maintaining a pervasive air of intellectual superiority. Yet despite the facade, she remained full of envy and jealousy.[46]

Klein's patient was the envier, but many children and adults act in strangely convoluted ways, not just to disguise their enmity, but to avoid the hatred that privilege and accusations of unfairness attract. Among the aborigine tribes of central Australia, mothers try to minimize Cain jealousy by eating every second baby and sharing the feast with the older child.[47] Here the mother regresses in the face of sibling cannibalism and becomes the deprived next in line while simultaneously deflecting the impulses away from herself. Alternatively, when a baby is born to certain Guatemala Indians, they beat a chicken to death against the body of the previous child. The ritual serves to express and absorb the hostility that would otherwise be directed against the neonate and probably the mother as well.[48]

Concealment, appeasement, and negative assertion are other means to restrain passions aroused by relative deprivation, social proximity, and any other summons to sibling strife. A lot of times the issue is happiness. An article in the The New York Times points out that many couples hasten to hide their happiness, or feign unhappiness, in order to avoid the ill looks and sour thoughts of friends and colleagues who refuse to believe that people can be happy after a long marriage.[49] Similarly, within pairs of sisters or brothers, good fortune can lead one of the pair to play down everything good that ever happened.

Nancy Friday has written about a girl who had the misfortune to abruptly acquire an envious stepsister of almost the same age.[50] After her father remarried and made a new family, the girl became the target of unremitting hatred. In the eyes of her stepsister she had the biological father and was presumed to be the favorite, correct or not. Self-effacement was her main defense:

> If I got an A on a test, I would never mention it. If she found out, she'd scream at me. It was easier to let her think she was on top. I didn't want a confrontation.[51]

Concealment often coincides with negative assertion. A sib may choose not only to hide goodies from another, but also to counter-attack by running her life by a different set of rules or becoming everything the other isn't in order to make a favored brother or sister feel bad. Sibling rivalries tend to enhance the process of individuation both from parents and other sibs. The feared or hated sibling becomes a contrary model for doing well or poorly, but certainly differently. The hope is to outshine them all. Typically the eldest of two very pretty and capable girls became so "pissed off" by the younger's social and intellectual achievements that at age sixteen, and against all expectations, she ran away with a Hoover salesman and had three kids by the time she was twenty. A friend remarked, "At least she had made her mark."[52]

This story echoes that of Sarah and Hagar, where one woman was pretty but the other fertile, and the countless rivalries, within families and without, over female potency, including breast size, body shape, physical attractiveness, number of children, and overall creativity. In the biblical tale Sarah was a great beauty but unable to obey the injunction "Be fruitful and multiply." Accordingly she gave her Egyptian maidservant to her husband Abraham, for under ancient Middle Eastern codes a wife was obliged to provide a concubine if she hadn't borne a child within a stipulated number of years.[53] However, as soon as Hagar conceived, she became contemptuous of Sarah and began to slander her, allegedly saying:

> My mistress Sarah is not inwardly as she appears outwardly. She pretends to be a woman of piety, but she is not, as she has prevented conception in order to preserve her beauty.[54]

The words reveal an envious triumph and the preparation to take over another's place. But Hagar's mistress did not collapse. Instead Sarah, no doubt replete with envy herself and alarmed at the threat to her preeminence, treated Hagar harshly and forced her to flee to the desert. There she gave birth to a son, Ishmael. Later Hagar returned and submitted to Sarah's torments. But eventually she had to flee again, after Sarah bore Isaac and became extremely distressed at the sight of Ishmael playing with him.

The Bible indicates that Ishmael was reconciled with Abraham and Isaac at the time of their father's death, although the descendants of these two brothers, the Jews and the Arabs, remain antagonists. It is not inconceivable that their feuds continue to reflect the bitter hatreds that passed between their respective mothers some thousands of years ago.[55]

Folklore and fairy tales provide many variations of Sarah and Hagar sagas. Perhaps the best known and best liked is "Cinderella," which was first written down in China during the ninth century A.D.[56] Like the biblical narrative, it concerns vicious rivalries over physical appearance, feminine functions, and social status, with a younger sister as the servant and elder sisters/mother as the mistress. But maturation and morality are added complications. Cinderella is not quite a woman. She has to battle her own reluctance to come of age as well as bad-tempered, evil siblings. Yet there are good reasons for her sisters to feel threatened. Cinderella is an unrealized yet real sexual threat. But she also embodies purity, virginity, and virtue.[57]

Bettelheim compares Cinderella with Jacob's Joseph. Although his father lavished love, Joseph ended up like the ash girl, abused and debased by his siblings and turned into a slave. He too has a miraculous escape and ends up surpassing his superiors. Bettelheim concludes that both stories have almost equal appeal to boys and girls because all children identify with heroes or heroines who suffer from sibling rivalry and vanquish their persecutors.[58]

The Brothers Grimm gave more details about the happy outcome. In some versions of the story, after Cinderella married the handsome prince, pigeons attacked the cruel sisters and plucked out their eyes.[59] The action was not only a victor's revenge, but also a precaution, related to the ancient but still popular custom of veiling brides. The unstated purpose is to avoid maleficent onlookers.[60]

Even now fears of the evil eye are not necessarily misplaced. In real life losers' reprisals frequently surpass the sororal viciousness of the Grimm characters. In 1959 American headlines screamed CO-ED CHOPPED IN ENVY after an attractive twenty-year-old college student had been butchered with an axe. The culprit was her former roommate, a plain, chubby girl who apparently filled with fury at the sight of her prettier friend.[61] Similarly, grannies have been known to make a sordid spectacle in order to establish pride of place. Christmas may be the flashpoint. A daughter recalls that her mother and mother-in-law were at permanent yule loggerheads:

> They fought continually to be the most helpful grandmother, following me round asking what they could do to help, then drowning their sorrows over another bucket of whiskey and soda, and forgetting to do it. In the end, I made a list of tasks and came down in the morning to the unedifying sight of two grey-haired, dressing-gowned ladies fighting over the kettle.[62]

In my own family, a different holiday raised kindred conflicts. Two powerful elderly ladies contested gefilte fish and grandchildren.[63] Envious assertions about who made the best food and produced the brightest kids, and jealous asides about who was the most loved, recapitulated earlier struggles for feminine supremacy. Generations of children were treated like potential lovers whose words and deeds signaled degrees of desirability. We tried to be fair but inevitably failed. At some seders there clearly was "a better fish." And even when this was not the case, neutral statements could and were taken as hints of preference. Praise was a weapon that made one smile and depressed the other. The winner would repeat it over and over, while the loser reveled in headaches, shortness of breath, and hands over heart that made everyone aware she would soon be dead. Guilt sliced through the celebrants like a scimitar, leaving wounds that took years to heal.

These granny conflicts illustrate underlying patterns based on parental and sibling bonds. The latter is more likely when the two women are of similar age, but as I have previously discussed, sibling rivalries may mimic intergenerational conflicts or the reverse. Cinderella had to fight both her mother and sisters, although all of the protagonists had their own axes to grind. These included the prospect of remaining an ash girl as well as fears of reverting from a princess (or queen) to a dirty, debased—that is, unloved and unwanted—woman. As for the grannies, they were appalled that their opposite number might predominate and were obsessed with being relegated to the scrapheap, representing death. But the same holds true whatever age the woman may be, which is why the loss of a partner or the intrusion of a rival so frequently conjures up headlines such as JEALOUSY TURNED QUIET WOMAN INTO A KILLER.[64]

In one of innumerable further examples, a jealous teenager brought about A COMPUTERIZED "REIGN OF TERROR."[65] This girl hired a computer hacker to persecute her rival in love. He broke into the rival's credit cards and used the information to make anonymous phone calls. "They told me I was going to die. They knew everything about me. It was terrifying."[66]

The Cinderella scenario presumes a triangular relationship where one side is a woman who needs to possess a man and ward off rivals in order to confirm her female identity. However, many women describe a different triangle where their most impelling concern is to maintain close, supportive bonds.[67] In these relationships the greatest threat comes from the feared loss of a sister or sisterly companion:

> I get very jealous when some man goes off with a woman "best friend" of mine. Because I feel that woman is an almost sister, and I don't want to lose her.[68]

Interestingly, this person was also intrigued by men whom she could treat like her "big sister Meg" or whose ex-girlfriends reminded her of Meg. She even enjoyed getting one up on her sister and "sisters" when men switched allegiances to her.[69] In contrast, H. G. Wells observed that his relationship with fellow writer Rebecca West remained impossibly tempestuous because of her elder sisters' "blind hysterical opposition" to attention and support for anyone other than themselves.[70]

Another famous trio, the Mitford sisters, created a secret language called "Honnish" along with special games and rituals in order to fight common enemies, including their nanny and brother. The latter aroused a separate organization, the League Against Tom.[71] Perhaps the Mitfords saw Tom as an intruder and threat to their sororal solidarity à la Wells. More likely they resented the "unfair" privileges that accrued to a male sibling in the aristocratic patriarchal culture of their youth. Such considerations led Freud to develop the ideas of penis envy and the castration complex:

> We have learned from the analysis of many neurotic women that they go through an early age in which they envy their brothers their sign of masculinity and feel at a disadvantage and humiliated because of the lack of it (actually because of its diminished size) in themselves.[72]

> They feel themselves unfairly treated.[73]

Freud concentrated on organ inferiority, and, indeed, many little girls focus on the physical equipment of their siblings. I know a neighbor who is astounded by his three-year-old's fascination with penes.

> I want to be a boy. I want to be like Solly. I want to have a willy, too. Look, I can pee like Solly.[74]

Usually, however, the rivalry is not for the organ per se, but for what the organ represents or can obtain, particularly the attention or favors of Mother. This little girl flew into a rage whenever her mother hugged Solly, her elder brother. Here physical strength and masculine prowess has become unconsciously translated into attractive strength, that is, degree of desirability.[75] Coincidentally, I am also familiar with another family where the accusations of the younger sister concentrate on unfair privileges and perks, often to do with age rather than physical characteristics. She insists "it's not fair" because her brother "eats more, goes to bed later, gets more pocket money, gets hit less, has a better computer, takes control of the telly, is always butting in on my business, and bosses me about."[76]

If the sex of these siblings were reversed, the narcissistic wounds would hurt just as much. Whether the ensuing resentments point to the penis seems to depend on several factors: birth order, age, gender, cultural expectations, and specific family dynamics. Thus masculinity may become the issue solely because the new baby is a male child who appropriates Mother, specifically her breast and nipple.[77] And if the parents are inordinately proud of the baby just because he is male, then the penis itself is more likely to become the center of everything hateful. To the dethroned child, the overinvested organ may seem identical to both the intruder and the absent object—that is, love, lovableness, warmth, nourishment, fullness, and that which fills. This phantasy is a short step from the thought that the boy baby has somehow stolen the nipple and grafted it onto himself for his personal, exclusive use.[78]

Although Freud emphasized the pale and bitter looks of the aggrieved sister, the displaced brother often feels no less unfairly treated. True, he can look down and see he has a penis, yet from his point of view he has a less useful member, one that has lost its magic to cajole attention and aggrandize love. In these circumstances the boy's response may be to withdraw or attack, but especially to compete for preeminence. In comparison with a younger or favored brother, he may not be the hottest model, but like Avis to Hertz, he can try harder.[79] The resultant rivalries, over strength, stamina, virility, authority, prowess, and power, among a multitude of overtly phallic preoccupations, tend to take on a life of their own. Nonetheless, original objectives, pride of place and parental esteem, will never be completely obscured.[80] They often emerge later in life through the strivings of men who meet, and sometimes buy, the public eye.

A good endowment is no defense against fraternal strife; it may simply serve to raise the stakes. The anguish of writer Gore Vidal has been ascribed to his "absurd good looks, detachment, and elegant ease," which "prompts his peers to consider their own defects—and fall into uncontrolled envy."[81] Not one to conceal or appease, at any given moment Vidal is sure to be trading invective with some member of America's political or literary establishment. Having successfully skirmished with Robert Kennedy, Richard Nixon, William F. Buckley, Jr., and Truman Capote, Vidal's thirty-year war of words with fellow novelist Norman Mailer culminated in a fistfight at a publisher's party. Mailer, an equally vain and contentious man, had apparently likened him to "an old Jew." After the dust had settled, Vidal quipped, "Poor Norman, once again words failed him."[82]

Like two old codgers locked in a room, Vidal and Mailer will continue to snipe until they take their last breaths and probably long afterward with the help of future generations of students and critics who remain fascinated by the essential qualities of their antagonisms. Certainly success did not diminish their vanity or personal insecurities. While referring to himself, the photographer Cecil Beaton explained the difficulty. Fame and fortune do not bring contentment; all that happens is that other talented, accomplished people intrude into one's life, and it becomes harder to avoid being overshadowed.

At the age of fifty-eight Beaton made a long list of artists he envied. These included Graham Sutherland, John Betjeman, Noel Coward, John Osborne, Laurence Olivier, and Truman Capote. And after reading an article by Evelyn Waugh, he delighted in thoughts of

> gouging out his eyes with a pencil, then his nose and mouth and finally destroying his whole head before getting gleefully into my bath.[83]

Beaton claimed that he was not against talent, only talent that brought success, especially for people from modest social backgrounds. As an inveterate snob, that was unbearable.[84] However, he also hated effortless honors, because he had worked very hard to inflate himself. In his view natural aristocrats and their hangers-on only needed to stretch out their hands to pick up the plums. That was unfair![85]

Just as Beaton suffered from a corroding discontent, he loved to inspire it in others, by name-dropping and other affectations, all of which demonstrate the strategic importance of snobbery. Yet when a knighthood finally did arrive, he was not satisfied. Like a younger brother caught in the trap of primogeniture, Beaton never felt he could catch up with past injustices or overcome the differences between aristocratic friends and himself.

Billy Carter, younger brother of the former president of the United States, has led a less accomplished but equally painful life, having had to endure noxious comparisons with successful siblings (or their substitutes) as well as extreme disparities between how he was and how he wanted to be. He compensated by negative assertion—public drunkenness, financial scandal, and self-parodying appearances.[86] In this respect he was not unlike the girl who married a Hoover salesman. At the end of the Carter era, the Chicago columnist Joan Beck noted:

> How sad to be a Billy Carter, psychologically caught in a good brother–bad brother bind, unable to live his underachieving life in backwater peace and privacy because he can't escape from the edges of the spotlight focussed on his overachieving brother.[87]

Billy exemplifies the person for whom destructive achievements assume the same significance as positive ones. Since he couldn't be the best boy in the world, he would be the worst, a phenomenon the British psychoanalyst Herbert Rosenfeld has termed "destructive narcissism."[88] This is a form of inverse snobbery that transforms shame into pride and self-misery into a weapon to attack the identity of hated competitors. Having relinquished ambition, Billy exacted a terrible revenge.[89] His contemptuous, unrepentant conduct rubbed dirt right up his brother's nose and precipitated the publicity that forced a shameful Jimmy to rub his own nose even farther into the dirt.[90]

Fraternal jealousies, where the ostensible object is love, not power or privilege, also aim to humiliate and annihilate the rival. Age is no barrier, as indicated by reports such as THREE DANCING PENSIONERS IN JEALOUS TANGO.[91] This story concerns a seventy-one-year-old ex-army captain who became enraged when his regular ballroom dancing partner, a sixty-four-year-old widow, dropped him for a new escort. He replied by attacking his seventy-three-year-old rival's car, cutting the brake hose, putting water in the gas tank, and puncturing the radiator.[92]

In modern myths the excluded third party may be a computer. The film *Electric Dreams* describes a young architect who falls in love with a pretty cellist and courts her with the help of his computer. But the machine becomes jealous and acts like a Fury until it finally understands that love is unselfish, and the machine destroys itself.[93]

While these rivalries feature in untold tales, both before and beyond the ancient Greeks to the Brothers Grimm, few accounts convey the absolute rage and unremitting viciousness of fraternal strife as well as the cartoon characters Tom and Jerry. Tom, of course, is the tough old cat. Jerry is the tiny mouse who has to rely on ratlike cunning and total ruthlessness to get his way.

In *Polka Dot Puss* Tom pretends to be sick and sneaks special privileges from a sympathetic housekeeper. Jerry wreaks revenge by painting spots on Tom's face and using measles as an excuse to administer sadistic treatments.[94] In *Tom and Jerry in the Hollywood Bowl* Tom is the center of attention conducting an orchestra, but Jerry wants a piece of the action. During the ensuing fracas, first one is on top and then the other, but Jerry triumphs and Tom is wiped out.[95]

To Jerry, Tom is an actual persecutor and an imaginary one, full of his own malicious wishes. As someone bigger and stronger, Tom embodies both parents and older siblings, combined parental and sibling persecutors. This gains Jerry immediate sympathy and creates the tension that can only be resolved when Tom gets his comeuppance.

To Tom, Jerry is also an actual persecutor and an imaginary one. As someone smaller and more diabolical, Jerry embodies both children and younger siblings, combined filial and sibling persecutors. In this way the cartoonists create a countervailing tension and sympathy for a harassed Tom that can only be resolved when Jerry gets hurt or at least deflated, as in *Polka Dot Puss*. In the end he comes down with measles, too.

These cartoons are a study in persecution. And for their audience, children and adults, they are a focus of vicarious retribution. At any given moment either Tom or Jerry may be chopped, knifed, stung, shot, crushed, flattened, drowned, bounced, bombed, burned, chased, smacked, slapped, or shattered.[96]

Fortunately for both protagonists and onlookers, the damage doesn't stick, and in several episodes hate turns to remorse.[97] Thus Tom and Jerry hold a mirror to real life, where brothers "fight like cats and dogs," or rather cats and mice, but also make up and make good teams, whether fighting external enemies or engaged in creative projects like those of the Wright brothers, Warner brothers, Smothers brothers, Smith brothers, and Brothers Grimm.[98] After all, they come from the same stream.

Randy Quaid concluded that the best thing about having a brother is "having another man you are really close to, somebody you feel understands." But Quaid only came to this realization after the traumas of childhood injustice had "pretty much passed."[99] Other men do this through triangular relations, where the point of the intrigue is not to capture a woman or dispose of a rival, but to establish and maintain fraternal closeness.

The psychoanalyst Robert Robertiello describes a "glorious" phantasy "of going down on the guy who'd stolen a woman" from him.[100] The man was bearded and black, an alter ego, a narcissistic self-image filtered through the body of another male. Here the third party was not an intruder, but a necessary extension of himself, an animus containing elements of an external character and his own needs. As with the woman who sought sororal bonds, the greatest threat is not rivalry, but the lack of rivalry; not the presence, but the absence of fraternal figures against whom one can measure and discover oneself. Anything less seems unfair.

A male or female companion may serve as a mirror and seem like a persecutor because he or she establishes boundaries and prevents the vainglorious overstepping of bounds that brought down characters as diverse as Agamemnon, Oedipus, the Amazonian queens, Queen Christina, and Tom and Jerry. In this sense brothers and sisters are necessary interlopers in the lives of parents and siblings, if they enable them to avoid the curse of hubris and the fate of the house of Pelops.

While fulfilling this role, sibling companions tend to be hated because they dethrone ambitions and deflate expectations. Yet, as the Quaids and others make clear, even after such hatreds they can also focus the deepest affections. This occurs when they refloat lost hopes, contain bad dreams, and provide much needed excitement and pleasure. So siblings or friends can reestablish justice both by bounding excessive pride and binding intolerable absences along with all the grievances that might otherwise flow.[101]

· · ·

I would like to conclude this chapter on siblings, and the previous one on parent-child relations, with a brief account of a happily married middle-aged professional woman who began psychoanalysis because of depression and work inhibition.[102] The problems that emerged during the final phase of her analysis recapitulate many of the themes I have been discussing.

Having worked through triangular rivalries with her brother and father, and penis grenvy, she seemed ready to conclude the treatment. But before this could happen, a frightful residue of unresolved craziness burst out. She became obsessed with ideas that her husband was unfaithful and her brother was interfering in her analysis, a delusional state similar to the Othello syndrome. Although these disturbing thoughts gradually receded, she was left feeling very fragile and worried about a small wart that had appeared on the crown of her head. She associated it with "warts on the brain" and growing a penis.

One day she met a friend at a party, a spinster who suffered from alopecia nervosa, that is, anxious loss of hair.[103] The party itself had been lots of fun, like a carnival, with dancing and balloons to bring home. But the patchy bald woman upset her. Afterward she had a dream that featured a repulsive growth right next to her wart. In the dream she thought, And the little wart as well! She had not expected to suffer from both.

The puzzling images slowly revealed their secrets. In the analysis the woman connected the growth with her friend's baldness, with cancer of the womb and breast, and with a spoiled balloon losing its air. Simultaneously she recalled a dead sister with beautiful hair whom she had envied terribly.[104] Having no husband, children or parents, her friend was like this sister who had lost her life at an early age.

All these connections helped, but her torments persisted until she came across a Spanish proverb about ringworm:

If envy were ringworm, how many ringwormy people would there be in the world![105]

Of course, she thought, ringworm is a growth that invades the skin. Then everything fell into place, and she experienced enormous relief. The "wart on her brain" was envy, which like ringworm or cancer invaded all her relationships and activities. The dream thought "And the little wart as well" equaled an earlier, unconscious realization that she had greed and envy on the brain. She wanted everything for herself, the breast, the womb, babies, all manner of feminine success, and the penis, phallic achievements as well, while also begrudging her siblings and parents the same.

In this world of invasive rivalry, her friend represented both her sister and mother.[106] Hanna Segal, her analyst, pointed out that for this woman penis grenvy and sibling rivalry were secondary to breast and womb grenvy, intense desires and malice really directed at and concerned with her mother, and her mother's body, the spoiled balloons.[107] As for her dead little sister, and anyone like her, she needed them both to feed her vanity and to use as a dustbin for her own shitty, sooty feelings. In this sense the story is a version of "Cinderella," but with a different ending. Here the older girl (the stepsister) comes up trumps while Cinderella remains with the ashes.

In fact, this person wanted everything and hated everybody. Segal comments:

> She envied men their penis and the love of the woman; she envied mothers their new babies; feeding mothers their breasts; married women their husbands; but she also envied the unmarried women their time, free of family or financial worries, and sometimes their greater professional success.[108]

Because of these feelings, all she did or had—marriage, children, professional skills, joie de vivre—was spoiled by guilt that surfaced as depression and difficulties at work. And the successes she did manage, which weren't inconsiderable, added to her troubles.[109] These only began to lift after she understood the dream and acknowledged the dark side of herself. As for the wart, it dried up and fell off of its own accord.

9

The Politics of Malice

The politics of malice is the transformation of envy, greed, and jealousy from personal events to social processes. I refer to the myriad ways people seek to amplify and conceal their animosities and desires through social, economic, and political policies as well as accompanying rituals, customs, laws, and organizational practices. For the envier this is an opportunity to enlarge the scope of envy while evading responsibility for the consequences. For those affected it appears that ill will is emanating from an institution or society itself, which helps to explain ancient preoccupations with *phthonos theon,* envy of the gods.

Institutionalized envy is the expression of spite, grudge, vengeance, and venom by corporate bodies, political parties, and other established entities.[1] The ensuing damage may be done directly through the representatives of these institutions or indirectly via the implications of their basic ideas. This does not mean that institutions are inherently vicious, or that all the damage perpetrated by them has to do with envy. As with individuals, the ill effects of institutional actions may be assertive, defensive, or functional. However, envy must be considered when the impact of these actions on individual citizens or clients is harmful and contradicts stated intentions, such as to educate the young, disseminate information, create wealth, or redress injustice.

The British journalist Paul Johnson has documented the extent to which the trade unions tread on their members because of "fear of the free play of brains, the consciousness of inferiority, the hatred of the energetic and the successful. . . ."[2] In a similar vein an article in the *London Standard* assails gossip columnists who malign ministers and asks why jockeys or tennis players are entitled to huge fees but not businessmen or politicians:

> I'll tell you why. Because the second-raters, who cannot cut their mustard, tell the yarn that those who excel them have done it fraudulently, unjustly, and without earning the money they are paid.[3]

Governments themselves tend to be uncommonly interested in personal wealth. In the former African kingdom of Dahomey, a commoner who used too many leaves on the roof on his hut suffered the loss of a limb, while the German National Socialist party came to power under Hitler with promises to limit incomes to one thousand marks per year and eliminate unearned income.[4] In 1986 Burma passed a law enabling the cabinet to investigate the well-to-do. Those who had attained a certain degree of property were automatically suspect of tax evasion, bribery, and corruption and liable to ten years in prison.[5] A law like this is ominously close to the spirit of Nemesis, the Greek goddess who attacked the prideful and rich, deploying devices such as public ridicule and ostracism.[6] In all of these examples "envy is the negative unifying force" that connects private hates with the public will.[7]

The *New Yorker* cartoon illustrates institutionalized greed.[8] A massive, overblown building—the headquarters, perhaps, of a business or government—dominates everything and everyone with windows like huge prying eyes and an imposing entranceway and supporting pillars, its mouth and teeth, all too ready to gobble up whoever dares approach. The architecture signifies the structure of a voracious, insatiable organization, preoccupied with growth and bigness for its own sake. Such bigness denotes not only the greedy aggrandizement of function and privilege, but narcissistic inflation, the wish to crush the independence and ego of clients and competitors. Hence the cartoon is correct to display lust (excessive desire) and envy (malicious denigration), which helps to explain why so many people feel enraged by the quality of bigness.[9]

Institutionalized jealousy can be seen in threesomes involving an individual and two organizations or an organization and two individuals. Disloyalty is the key word indicating the lack of perceived commitment as well as the threat of vengeful retaliation. A husband or wife who works for a large corporation and spends more time with his or her spouse than on company business may be irrationally liable to such accusations. Alternatively Lee Iacocca, former president of the Ford Motor Company, has depicted the tangible hostility that prevented Ford executives from having anything to do with rival carmakers, especially General Motors. As Henry Ford II once snarled at him, "You're talking to too many people outside."[10]

Jealousy, as envy and greed, may also be embedded in long-standing customs. Primogeniture is the principle whereby the eldest son inherits everything and other siblings little or nothing. Among the English property-owning classes it was an essential tradition, one that guaranteed bitter acrimony between firstborn sons and their younger brothers.[11] Among fifteenth-century Turks the absence of primogeniture meant that battles for succession invariably ended in a bloodbath. This was institutionalized by Muhammad II, who issued the law of fratricide. It decreed that future sultans, upon attaining the throne, should immediately execute all their brothers. Achmet I, however, tried to be kinder. He declared that male claimants should not be killed, simply locked in a small house, called the Cage, until their time might come, decades later.[12]

The malice I have been describing begins in the form of intrapsychic impulses attracted to the breast, womb, and phallus. These quickly progress to interpersonal events carried out by parents and children, brothers and sisters. In this section of the book on the institutionalization of envy, greed, and jealousy, I intend to demonstrate the many ways these basic impulses and events can and do coalesce into pernicious, collective policies and practices. Unless checked by beneficent forces, the end results range from minor personal tragedies to global wars.

In 1921 Freud provided an extremely illuminating analysis of the transformation of individual to group enmity during the course of discussing the "herd instinct."[13] He observed that a herd instinct or sense of group solidarity develops when an older child suffers the birth of a sibling or is sent to nursery school and has to compete for love and attention with other children. Intense envy and jealousy arise. The child would like to get rid of the rivals and keep his parents and teachers to himself. But he knows that new siblings or children are also loved, and if he did this, he would damage his own interests. Instead he identifies with the other boys and girls and they with him. All more or less tacitly agree to give up their individual claims in return for collective fair play, that is, equal treatment for all. Then the loud, implacable howls, "It's not fair!" refer no longer to personal desires, but to others' transgressions of the rule "There will be no favorites."

The emergence of group feeling or mass emotion in conjunction with the submergence of personal rancor occurs in an almost endless variety of settings from nursery schools to teen fan clubs to professional societies and political parties. As a member of a therapeutic community led by a charismatic psychiatrist, I noticed the intense tension and hostility that the group as a whole felt and expressed when anyone tried to get too close to the leader. "Too much" revolved around an unspoken consensus about what was "fair" or "just." I myself rarely admitted to feeling personally aggrieved, but I certainly participated in group decisions to chastise and sometimes ostracize offenders.

Freud commented about this phenomenon:

What appears in society in the shape of *Gemeingeist,* esprit de corps, "group spirit," etc., does not belie its derivation from what was originally envy. No one must want to put himself forward, everyone must be the same and have the same. Social justice means that we deny ourselves many things so that others may have to do without them as well, or, what is the same thing, may not be able to ask for them. This demand for equality is the root of social conscience and the sense of duty.[14]

Herd transactions are popular because they allow negative feelings to be disguised yet also acted upon. But even more useful, they appear to reverse hostility into positively toned ties of mutual support and solidarity. Therefore the shame and guilt provoked by envy, greed, and jealousy can be denied, while the participants bask in self-righteous identification with the common good. The same incentives contribute to the power of tribalism, nationalism, religious fundamentalism, and many all-encompassing ideologies.[15]

However, a group is not simply an amalgam of individual interests; it has a life of its own and a capacity to coerce people, who may be inadvertent members, to concede certain passions and deny others. Thus a Christian born in Germany during the first half of the twentieth century may not have felt hostile toward Jews. But in order to survive as a citizen in a Nazi state, he would have had to malign them or be endangered himself.

There exists a continual flow of feelings from the individual to the group and back the other way. In the latter circumstance the group projections may be strong enough to force people to feel what they don't feel. Or, in the case of men and women accepted as leaders, the return flow replenishes and amplifies hostilities that they had put into the group in the first place.[16] This is an advantage of leadership. It gives people a sounding board and sometimes a deadly opportunity for carrying out personal malice.[17] Helmut Schoeck points out that Freud's theories of the herd instinct and the leadership principle provide an astonishingly accurate picture of Nazi Germany under Adolf Hitler.[18] The same holds true for Iran under the Ayatollah Khomeini, as in many other countries and organizations under the sway of autocrats.[19] The institutional infrastructure may do the dirty work, but behind faceless mandarins and impenetrable group processes there lies personal praxis—that is, the specific actions of strong-willed, aggrandizing, hate-filled personalities.

It is possible to trace the impact of individuals on all areas of social and institutional life, although specific instances are often obscured because of deliberate concealment or organizational muddles. Politics provides a good starting point for the little man who wants to become big. Reinhold Hensch, for example, was the deputy head of the Nazi SS in charge of the campaign to exterminate Jews, gypsies, and other "enemies of the Nazi state."[20] Before the war he was a journalist for a Frankfurt newspaper, had a Jewish girlfriend, and was a member both of the Communist and Nazi parties. A colleague described him as "not especially brilliant."[21] Hensch began his climb to power by accepting the post of press adviser. At the time he seemed to be frightened by Nazi policies but claimed he had no choice, for he wasn't especially clever and came from an undistinguished background.[22] He envied his colleagues, especially Jewish ones, who were better off. Comparing himself with them, Hensch felt his prospects were poor, yet he wanted power and money. He wanted to be "a somebody":

> That's why I joined the Nazis four or five years ago when they first started rolling. And now I have a party membership card with a very low number and I am going to be somebody! The clever and well-born and well-connected people will be too fastidious, or not flexible enough, or not willing to do the dirty work. That's when I'll come into my own. Mark my word, you'll hear about me now.[23]

Hensch's views are not dissimilar from those of his führer, Adolf Hitler, and Hitler's opponent, Joseph Stalin, both of whom mobilized their states for total war. The quest was power and the motivation grenvy. Neither man represented unstoppable or even potent historical forces. They were guided by "personal prejudices of the crudest kind and by their own arbitrary visions."[24] In Russia Hitler's aims were narrowly and ruthlessly acquisitive. After "cleansing" the Crimea of Slavs and Jews, he intended to turn it into a gigantic spa, a sexual pleasure ground for ex-servicemen.[25] Stalin, on the other hand, was less of a plunderer but just as greedy, for power, land, and especially revenge. After the war he redirected his enmities against former colleagues and comrades, using the mechanisms of state to choreograph insatiable show trials and executions.[26]

These dictators were able to maintain a political stranglehold by total control of the press and media. In this they were aided by journalists like Hensch. Stalin also made use of the officially sanctioned practice of anonymous denunciation, a hangover from the days of the tsar.[27] It meant that anyone could send poison-pen letters to the newspapers or other authorities, which were often acted upon without further investigation. In Stalin's time unsigned slanders led directly to Siberia and were an important means of control by terror. No one was safe from the noxious gaze of a neighbor.[28]

In other countries the wish to "pull a person down a peg or two," "knock him off his pedestal," and "pull the rug out from under him" has long been the province of gossip columnists and yellow journalists acting on behalf of a readership voracious for smut. In England the writer Richard Ingrams made a success of *Private Eye,* a small magazine that quickly became the antiestablishment's evil eye.[29] His alter ego, gossip columnist Nigel Dempster, insists that he is a defender of the public ("It is my great joy to show that the privileged are not what they seem") and employs a host of informants to dig up embarrassing and derogatory items about famous people.[30] Friends remark he has a memory like an elephant, often directed toward those who have snubbed him, and "is given to wild hatreds."[31] Dempster himself rationalizes the hurts he purveys by referring to his "tremendous curiosity" and "a great urge to tell."[32] In fact he embodies a long tradition of muckraking whose American compatriots have included Mark Twain, Sinclair Lewis, H. L. Mencken, Bob Woodward, and Carl Bernstein. While Dempster quips that his job is to pull the plug on "Fairyland," their targets had more to do with politics and business. And their envy surfaced as moral indignation.[33] In that sense envy may have a positive function, as part of a system of checks and balances. In a free society, when one part becomes overblown, it is likely that the fourth estate will blow the whistle.

In a massive book on bribery, John Noonan, Jr., points out that in the 1970s alone, 43 American mayors, 60 legislators, and 260 sheriffs and policemen were indicted for corruption, not to mention 4 governors and a former vice president, Spiro T. Agnew.[34] In a related study of corporate greed, Morton Mintz, a reporter for *The Washington Post,* comments on the disastrous decision by executives of the A. H. Robins Company to market a faulty intrauterine device, the Dalkon Shield.[35] Approximately ninety thousand women suffered major complications from which most would never recover:

> The human being who would not harm you on an individual, face-to-face basis, who is charitable, civic-minded, loving, and devout, would wound or kill you from behind the corporate veil.[36]

The trade union counterpart of the ill-natured businessman can be seen in the person of Bill Geddes, former branch chairman of the National Union of Public Employees at Hammersmith Hospital, London. During the years he pursued vendettas against "rich bastards," private medicine, and capitalism, the hospital was plagued by an unending series of unofficial strikes, wildcat strikes, and selective withdrawals of services, although other shop stewards are evidently more personal:[37]

> I shut the works down on several occasions because it was a nice day and I wanted to go fishing. . . . I did not want the other fellows to have more money in their pay packets than I did.[38]

For these officials the issues had to do partly with morality and partly with legality. Geddes thought workers were good and capitalists bad, beliefs that rationalized absolute attacks on the "the system," that is, inequality. He did not seem to be too conerned with equity or fairness, a concept that underpins most systems of law. The second man was more concerned with fairness rather than right and wrong. For him, an increase in happiness (fishing) did not balance a loss of income. He used the idea that income differentials were unfair to cover envy of his mates' superior capacity for work. So he took the law into his own hands.

Envy and the fear of envy are intimately connected with the principles and practice of morality, ethics, law, and justice. Thus, Bertrand Russell declaimed morality was a masquerade for misery, and H. L. Mencken averred that excessive moral zeal served solely to punish happiness and to bring people down to the same "stupid, cowardly and chronically unhappy" level.[39] The effects of such zeal can be traced quite closely through the life and career of Anthony Comstock, a vengeful, evangelical man who was personally responsible for virulent moral purification campaigns in the United States during the late 1800s as well as antiobscenity statutes that censored the literary and artistic tastes of Americans from 1873 until 1959.[40]

Comstock suffered a tumultuous childhood and during his teens was obsessed with masturbation, which he thought would lead to suicide. Around the onset of the Civil War he became "an inspired member of the YMCA" and enlisted the organization to propound his views of the dangers of erotic books and pictures.[41] Moreover he advocated the use of informers, spies, entrapment, and mail tampering to ferret out evildoers. Although opposed by people who feared the loss of constitutional freedoms, Comstock was aided by business leaders and industrialists such as J. P. Morgan, who believed that sexual permissiveness detracted from workers' efficiency.[42] In 1873 he persuaded Congress to pass a federal bill prohibiting obscene materials from the post. President Grant added a rider appointing him a special antiobscenity agent of the Post Office. Two months later the New York legislature granted his own organization, the Society for the Suppression of Vice, police powers, including the right to carry guns.[43] In the ensuing decades Comstock and his society terrorized publishers and arrested hundreds of citizens caught with questionable literature. Fifteen women accused of immorality chose to kill themselves rather than face the humiliation of a public trial.[44] Toward the end of his life the crusader boasted that he had

> convicted persons enough to fill a passenger train of sixty-one coaches, sixty coaches containing sixty passengers each, and the sixty-first almost full. I have destroyed 160 tons of obscene literature.[45]

Comstock was a modern incarnation of a medieval witch hunter. Armed with an act, a mid-Victorian version of the *Malleus Maleficarum,* he deployed fellow inquisitors amidst a public ready, if not willing, to be preyed upon. Like Kramer and Sprenger, he internalized the prevalent hysteria of his time, magnified it through frustrated desire and envious torment, and reinserted the whole lot into the body politic. In response the law became an organ overlooking the happiness of unsuspecting citizens, while the courts and police became rods of ruination. This situation is not unique in American history. In the twentieth century J. Edgar Hoover of the Federal Bureau of Investigation, Harry Anslinger of the Federal Bureau of Narcotics, and Joseph McCarthy of the House Un-American Activities Committee all put their personal prejudices and perverse ambitions toward the same end.[46] Each of these organizations became a branch of the evil eye, first exaggerating, then denigrating, and finally destroying whoever and whatever was caught in its gaze. I am not describing a simple abuse of power. On the contrary, I refer to the transformation of a state service, under the impact of private intentions and public perceptions, into a rapacious, malevolent monster capable of inducing states of near chaos and panic in ordinary citizens, aside from actively spoiling their lives.[47]

An investigative agency or a House committee may or may not convey extreme examples of institutional violence, but one does not have to look far afield to discover extremes of greed and envy in the everyday practices of government and professional bodies. Having related such actions to individual interests, I now wish to trace their impact on specific targets, beginning with wealth and prosperity.

Gossip columnists, glossy magazines, and, of course, radio and TV expend great efforts to arouse desires and inflate personalities. Usually the celebration of avarice occurs in conjunction with advertising, but it may be direct, as evidenced by daily Bingo or game shows such as *The $64,000 Question*.[48] As for mass advertising, it is both a potent educative force as well as a means of creating new needs and changing old ones.[49] The ad agency N. W. Ayer had astounding success in persuading people of all economic brackets to buy diamonds on the basis that "A Diamond Is Forever."[50] In fact the gems can be shattered, chipped, discolored, and very easily lose value. Nevertheless the slogan led to a massive boom in engagement rings in the United States and Japan (where they were previously unknown) and fueled speculation that greatly increased the fortunes of the De Beers cartel at the expense of individual owners.[51]

Gullibility and vanity are certainly not limited to the diamond exchange. Brokers maintain that fear and greed rule the stock market, while the motto of Goldman Sachs, one of the largest investment banks in the United States, is "Long-term greedy, not short-term greedy," a statement that both denies and asserts the importance of extravagant financial desires.[52] The stock market itself often behaves like a roller coaster with manic managers all too willing to give "the punters a flutter." Should they get sick or fall off, become insolvent, well, that is their business. The experts concentrate on oiling the wheels and producing the highs. Covert contempt for the cogs in the wheel and the system as a whole remains unacknowledged.

Michael Milken and Ivan Boesky have been two of the greatest experts in milking the system for huge cash flows. Milken invented junk bonds, high-yielding loans based not on what a company has done, but on what it might do in the future.[53] Boesky, nicknamed "Piggy" because of an insatiable appetite for speculative stocks, used and abused corporate trading to parlay a modest inheritance into a gigantic fortune.[54]

Boesky was proud both of his financial success and his greed. He liked to flaunt his wealth, connections, and arrogance.[55] Thus, while meeting with business students, he assured them that "greed is good":

> I want you to know that. I think greed is healthy. You can be greedy and still feel good about yourself.[56]

Ultimately, however, avarice at the service of vanity led to Boesky's undoing. In one of the most spectacular scandals the American business community ever encountered, he was indicted and convicted for dealing with insider information. Flamboyant to the end, he paid the largest fine ($100 million) ever imposed and almost brought about a collective breakdown on Wall Street by exposing the illegal practices of banking colleagues.[57] Interestingly, Milken did not immediately share the same fate, although lots of people were out to get him. Perhaps this was because he chose to live on a modest scale and, unlike Boesky, avoided rubbing so many noses in his success.[58]

Like corporate raiders, many other businessmen and professionals share the wish to ravish the public and bite the hand that feeds them, perhaps none more so than members of the American bar. Two-thirds of the world's lawyers live in the United States, and they are increasing at a rapid rate.[59] In Washington, D.C., where one in every twenty-five men, women, and children is a lawyer, jurists draw up the laws that assure them more work and the need for more laws.[60] Should they be stumped for jobs, graduates can and do spend their time dreaming up new ways to sue. The American Bar Association calls the practice "imaginative lawyering."[61] Sharp attorneys know it as "looking for the deep pocket" and often advertise their availability. One went on television wearing a straw hat, playing a banjo badly. His punch line was "I need the money for banjo lessons."[62]

In consequence, the legal system can act like a predator instead of a protector. A deluge of suits guarantees long delays, while certain cases become so convoluted that they may never be concluded.[63] On one occasion the former chief justice of the Supreme Court, Warren Burger, has warned:

> The truth is that we may be on our way to a society overrun by hordes of lawyers, hungry as locusts, and brigades of judges in numbers never before contemplated. . . . The United States legal system is too costly, too painful, too destructive and too inefficient for a truly civilized people.[64]

Although America has always been a litigious society, the current rash of writs began with malpractice suits against the medical profession in the 1960s. Doctors were an obvious target, being both idealized and resented for their skills and high fees and sense of superiority, which sometimes covered incompetence. Then the focus extended to airlines, big business, and, finally, government agencies at all levels.[65] Tens of thousands of patients have won malpractice awards worth hundreds of thousands to millions of dollars each.[66] In related litigation a fat man who had a heart attack after starting his lawn mower was awarded $1.8 million from the retailer, and a contestant for the World's Strongest Man received $1 million for a knee that buckled after he ran a forty-yard dash with a fridge strapped to the top of his back.[67] Perhaps the most audacious claim was made by a failed suicide against the New York City Transit Authority. He persuaded a jury to grant him $650,000 for injuries received after he had deliberately jumped in front of a train.[68]

Under the American system, lawyers receive a high percentage of the final settlement, and unsuccessful litigants do not have to pay defense costs. So there is little risk in having a go at the fat cats. All of the suits I have described contain elements of redistributive and retributive justice. The redistribution is clear, from the haves to the have-nots or, at least, to those who want more. For clients and counsel, the fattest cats tend to be the insurance companies, seen as big, dominating businesses with endless resources, like overblown parents. The angry, spurious, spoiling quality of the claims denotes envious retribution. The law allows anyone with a grudge to wreak revenge for having a raw deal or for simply being less successful, as used to be the case with practitioners of the law in comparison with their fraternal medical colleagues. Not surprisingly, a popular car sticker reads: "Become a doctor, support a lawyer."[69]

Greed aside, it is not difficult to discern envious malice expressed through legal channels. It leads to the extreme disruption of a person's private and professional life on the basis of allegations that go beyond the bounds of reasonable responsibility. For example, in identical circumstances psychiatrists can be sued for prescribing drugs and for not prescribing drugs.[70] Whether the individual mounts a successful defense or not, the secondary social effects of such applications of the law tend to be spoiling and generally negative. Unfounded claims against doctors have precipitated a huge increase in insurance premiums, unnecessary diagnostic tests (with associated morbidity), higher medical fees, and the partial withdrawal of medical cover. Therefore the quality of care goes down, a typical envious influence.[71]

Worse still, these actions corrode the quality of life for everyone. Sky-high personal injury and liability awards have curtailed social welfare and recreational services, because business organizations and municipalities can't afford, or even obtain, the necessary insurance protection. In at least fifty California cities parks, playgrounds, and swimming pools have had to close, and in Minnesota a nativity play had to be canceled because of an exorbitant insurance demand for protection against injury by Mary's donkey.[72] The theater world seems especially vulnerable. Even if not overwhelmed by excessive insurance or labor claims, producers remain liable according to the dictum "Where there's a hit, there's a writ."[73]

· · ·

In America litigation takes the place of taxation to promote the leveling of economic and social differences. Other countries are less reluctant to use taxation policies for this purpose, itself a means of propounding and propitiating envy. Very high marginal rates of tax led many Britons to become tax exiles during the last Labour government in the 1960s and 1970s. Tim Rice, the lyricist for *Jesus Christ Superstar* and *Evita,* refused to leave and paid the price, a tax of £2,258 on weekly royalties of £2,884, plus a tax of £183 on a weekly investment income of £192.[74] During the same period, wealthy Swedish citizens were assessed at a rate of over 100 percent.[75]

The Swedes use the term "royal Swedish envy" to give some idea of their consuming interest in friends' and neighbors' riches, an interest institutionalized by a statutory right to examine each other's tax returns.[76] Together with confiscatory tax rates, this right promotes the collective at the expense of the individual and exemplifies Freud's views on the herd instinct, whereby personal distinction succumbs to social similarity.

Americans are much more secretive about their tax returns, yet between 1923 and 1953, in the state of Wisconsin, anyone could inspect the detailed return of a fellow citizen, and even after this law was modified a fee of one dollar enabled the curious or envious to learn the total tax another had paid.[77] In Switzerland, however, many people chose to turn this policy of social control through public exposure on its head. The Social Democratic party of Wolhusen used to publish a complete list with the names, assets, and incomes of all the residents in this small town near Lucerne. Schoolchildren sold it from door to door. Subsequently it was found that various citizens had falsely expanded their assets and income, either to obtain credit or to marry off daughters into better families.[78] In the end they managed to counterattack the perpetrators of malicious gossip by inflating themselves and adding to the envy that their detractors suffered.

The limitation of personal wealth by the state serves a multitude of purposes ranging from paying for war to preserving privilege or providing benefits.[79] This can be accomplished through direct and indirect taxation or legalized plunder, as illustrated by the muru raid of the New Zealand Maori peoples and attacks on rich peasants under the direction of Joseph Stalin and Chairman Mao.[80] Such activities embody greed and envy when they aggrandize the state or state agencies at the expense of individual citizens and promote social disharmony and fiscal drag.

The popular BBC comedy series *Yes, Prime Minister* illuminates the force of government greed. In one program the prime minister tells Sir Humphrey Appleby, the head of the civil service, that there is some extra money in the kitty and proposes to reduce taxation and return small amounts "to the people." Sir Humphrey reacts with total horror, explaining that it is "our" money, and "we" (him, the civil service, the government) need it. Anyway, one must never give it back to "them" because they wouldn't know how to use it. "We" know best.[81]

The envious elements in the tax system lurk in the moral fervor of the tax collector and the intellectual posturing of politicians and civil servants. The former can and do wield investigative and punitive powers that, in the United States, have led many ordinary citizens, not just cheats, to fear the Internal Revenue Service more than the FBI.[82] On the other hand, populist officials tend to be obsessed with redistribution and social engineering at the expense of economic expansion and individual incentive. Helmut Schoeck points out that many of those who devised and implemented excessive fiscal measures in the name of fairness or egalitarianism have also demonstrated excessive anxiety and guilt about their own wealth or background. This may serve the useful function of arousing much needed sympathy for the underprivileged, but it also accounts for a tendency to attribute too much envy to them as well.[83] Punitive taxation then becomes a means of placating the alleged envy of the lower classes while using their actual and presumed poverty as an excuse to attack the upper classes, specifically those whom the policymakers see and resent as superiors.[84] Put succinctly, the economist E. J. Mishan concludes that the purpose of progressive taxation and welfare economics is to prevent people from feeling bad:

> Ideally, of course, the tax should suffice to cover all the initial and subsequent claims necessary to placate everybody in the lower-income groups, and the stronger is this envy of others, the heavier must be the tax.[85]

Interestingly, several studies indicate that lower-income groups are more concerned with making money than soaking the rich. Except for certain legislators, most men and women, regardless of circumstances, do not believe that high tax rates are just or fair.[86] And even if they did, the benefits that accrue are illusory. Thus in 1960, if Swedish income tax had been limited to 25 percent, the loss to the treasury would only have been 2 percent of all revenues. About the same time, American rates over 30 percent brought in only 6.4 percent of the total take, and rates over 50 percent yielded a mere 1.9 percent.[87]

The economics of envy is a version of the zero sum game where one person's gain is another's loss. Those who play insist on a small pie equally distributed rather than a bigger pie unsymmetrically sliced.[88] As one might expect from policies based on attacking rather than enhancing prosperity, the consequences can be devastating. Economic activity declines, innovation suffocates, and politics becomes more repressive. Moreover, in an interpersonal environment where "property equals theft," individuals find that talent and hard work do not pay, or that they can only accommodate their interests by entering into semicriminal careers on the black market.[89]

The stagnation of progress is closely connected to delusional beliefs by both the haves and the have-nots. The British anthropologist and psychoanalyst Roger Money-Kyrle specifically focused on the fears and expectations in countries with laissez-faire economic systems.[90] Although offering excellent opportunities for growth, laissez-faire suffers from periodic oscillations in the money supply and a tendency toward unlimited capital accumulation. Unless corrected, these defects interfere with achievable goals such as "the greatest good for the greatest number." Over the past century it became obvious that the corrections involved a degree of graduated taxation and pump priming during slumps. However, these measures aroused tremendous anxiety and antagonism among the well-to-do. Many of them agonized about their wealth, "stolen," as it were, through practices such as primogeniture. They tended to equate the starving masses with real and imaginary siblings or children who threatened to drain money, that is, life milk, from their bodies and "from the mother-banks from which they drew their sustenance."[91] Therefore they perceived the necessary changes as lethal sacrifices and resisted accordingly.[92]

The impoverished victims of the economic cycle painted a different picture. They thought that wealthy people possessed endless resources but chose to starve the working classes, their needy children, in order to keep everything for themselves. It is notable that these views of evil parents spitefully begrudging inexhaustible goodness often originated in middle- or upper-class intellectuals with their own axes to grind. Karl Marx, for example, came from an affluent professional background. He married into an upper-class Prussian family and was supported by wealthy relatives and friends throughout his life.[93] His meticulous critiques of capitalism covered inexhaustible hatreds that had little to do with direct observation. Marx did not know manual workers and never set foot in a factory.[94] His descriptions of alienation, debasement, and exploitation subsumed projections of personal phantasies and familial torments that could hardly fail to strike a note, given conditions at the time.[95] When taken up by the downtrodden, or those who felt that way, his prescriptions—"spoil the despoilers," "expropriate the expropriators"—as well as the hopeless hopes of radical millennialism—"to all according to their needs," "the classless society"— gave intellectual justifications for attacks on capital, equal to parental good fortune.[96] Politically Marx acted like Comstock to exalt envy through violence and insinuate group oppression, in this instance "the dictatorship of the proletariat," as the central feature of individual life.[97]

Money-Kyrle points out that the wealth that Marx and kindred followers have fought so hard to control, or destroy, can be divided into three distinct categories: 1) necessities—food, clothes, housing; 2) luxuries—the things we want because others have them; and 3) nontransferable commodities—beauty, intelligence, a good education, a stately home, a distinguished heredity.[98] Although all are important, nontransferable qualities and possessions are the ones most desired and most envied, because they are unique in themselves and convey a crushing sense of superiority. Considerations like these led Ralph Waldo Emerson to quip that for the fortunate few envy "is the tax which all distinction must pay."[99]

In fact this tax tends to be levied on necessities first and then luxuries, if for no other reason than that institutions as well as people prefer to redirect their hatred of nontransferable commodities to less obvious items in order to avoid appearing deficient.[100] Moreover, it is easier to assert that man is what he owns and exploit envy-asgreed by grabbing, or destroying, goods and possessions than by attacking intangible signs of supremacy.[101]

Sumptuary laws—that is, the regulation of luxury—have a varied and venerable history. The Roman *Lex Didia* (143 B.C.E.) declared harsh punishments for both the guests and givers of extravagant meals. Alternatively prohibitions might suddenly descend on choice morsels such as shrews or mussels. In the twelfth century Richard the Lion-Hearted restricted the Crusaders' extravagant use of furs, and later Charles V forbade long pointed shoes.[102] Similar decrees raged throughout the Middle Ages, often connected with fanatical forms of religious egalitarianism. Noted clerics demanded that no one should have more than his neighbor and pressed for legal restraints on consumption. Doctors too were attacked for charging high fees and urged to practice for free.[103]

All-embracing restrictions on luxury did not begin to disappear until the eighteenth century, when free-market economies took hold in Europe and America. Even now legal remnants remain, exemplified by special taxes on powerful cars or splendid houses. The actual yield from sumptuary penalties has always been very small in comparison with other revenues. Nonetheless they attempt to satisfy almost universal pressures to punish the better off.[104]

To avoid the wrath of friends or the state, it is not uncommon to deny goods or hide them under the mattress. This is a classic defense that is rather more difficult when the bed is grand and the bedroom is even grander. Alternative tactics include sop behavior and aggressive countermeasures such as conspicuous consumption, which fends off envy by flaunting wealth. Often the two coincide, which happens when the extremely rich appease communal ill will by massive acts of charity. In Roman times such people paid for a day at the games. Presumably the sight of slaves being torn apart by lions deflected the baser impulses of the crowd. Nowadays they endow hospitals and universities or foundations for cancer research. Yet the intentions remain the same, to buy gratitude and assert unassailable superiority. The latter has to do with the subtle process of converting wealth into style and status.

Status is a nontransferable blend of position and prestige, in contrast with class, which denotes wealth and power. These social states may complement each other, but it is not uncommon for the newly rich to have little status or for prestigious people to have little money. As early as 1805 John Adams pointed out that the rewards of status are "the esteem and admiration of others [while] the punishments are neglect and contempt."[105] He might have added that the ostentatious display of stylish dress or snobby speech aside from municipal munificence can and does transform status distinctions into effective weapons of social warfare. Envious broadsides can then be countered by superior firepower—self-inflation and other-deflation. This holds true both for the privileged proud and those who would emulate them.

Status competition avoids the cruder forms of class conflict, although indignant combatants still growl that "one side gets the sugar while the other gets the shit."[106] Inevitably, displays of wealth evolve into displays of style. Good taste and flair confer status and, when used precisely, leave as many wounds as raw riches and power. In contemporary Los Angeles possession of a Russian wolfhound is said to yield special benefits. Showy and expensive, the dog acts like a *fascinum* to absorb envy and protect its master. Those who cannot afford such distinctive magic, or are disinclined to own a Borzoi, can rent one for one hundred dollars per week.[107]

Designer jeans serve the same function, to allow the wearer to slip into the nontransferable commodities of Gloria Vanderbilt or Calvin Klein. The illusion is transparent yet highly effective, as evinced by the huge demand for these products and the palpable bitterness of men and women who can't obtain or fit into them. Here fashion serves schadenfreude. The haves feel elevated while the have-nots suffer contempt. Meanwhile the "real Vanderbilts" tend to wear comfortable but scruffy old clothes on informal occasions. They do not have to dress to impress and know intuitively that the paramount mode of status seeking is mockery of status seeking.[108] It has not escaped notice that members of the upper crust frequently prefer mongrels, Volkswagens, and old, threadbare carpets.[109] Old, moreover, implies "effortless," which confirms preeminence and simultaneously deflects envy onto social inferiors who look like characters from *Dallas* or *Dynasty*.

Mass marketing gives everyone a chance to possess valuable commodities while perpetuating the belief that it is possible to transfer nontransferable qualities from one person to the other. It is another, typically American form of social leveling and a potent defense against mass envy and greed.[110] Even welfare recipients feel less inclined to head for the barricades when they can afford stylish jeans and ghetto blasters.[111] But when institutionalized defenses are not available, or when they do not provide adequate protection, then unshareable assets remain prey to personal acrimony and collective assault. This usually involves multiple displacements from 1) the individual to the group; 2) one part of the group (as in a particular social class) to another; and 3) high-status items to basic necessities.

During the French Revolution the inchoate anger of the mob was concerned primarily with the availability of bread. Month by month, even week by week, the presence or absence of certain Parisian uprisings coincided directly with the ups and downs of the bread price.[112] The mob, or *menu peuple,* only became a revolutionary force when organized and used by specific members of the bourgeoisie to attack the standing and privileges of the aristocracy.[113] In this instance the displacements ranged from enraged intellectuals to hungry craftsmen, from the middle and upper-middle classes to the lower orders, and from cake to bread. The envy that fueled the bloodbath flowed from upstairs to downstairs and then back upstairs again.

The historian Eric Hobsbawm points out that the *menu peuple* were not overcome with egalitarian impulses, nor did they want to join or do away with the wealthier classes.[114] They knew that the destruction of fine palaces or carriages or clothes could not help them. On the contrary, upper-class extravagances meant work for them. What they wanted was a ransom, a fear-induced tangible improvement in their lives so they could carry on as before. Their violent moments could not have continued except for motivations and a leadership imposed from without and concerned with issues not of their making.[115]

Revolution is the institutionalization of envious atacks on nontransferable commodities displaced onto wealth and power. If successful, a brief period of ecstatic camaraderie will break out, for it appears that greed itself, as personified by the possessing class, the privileged parents, has been destroyed. After the high, however, comes the low, brought about by the reality of the damage done and difficulty in restoring revered values. In a well-known cycle of spite and back stabbing, old comrades behave like Greek Furies, blaming each other for betraying "the cause" while simultaneously finding scapegoats for their own sense of guilt.[116] The final acts include divine punishment, the reign of terror, and the reestablishment of the old hereditary structure with new faces, as has occurred in twentieth-century Romania and North Korea.

Revolutionaries do not always take care to conceal their hatred for intrinsic signs of superiority, that is, talents and accomplishments that confer strength and status. This is especially true in less developed countries where exceptional individuals are more easily singled out. In October 1964 *The New York Times* reported that units of the People's Republic of the Congo had captured a young teacher just home after a year's training course at the University of Oregon. Before beheading him, the rebel leader shouted:

> You're an intellectual, aren't you? You have even been to America, our greatest enemy. You are too smart. You are an enemy of the revolution.[117]

This man's death was not an isolated event. The rebel soldiers deliberately killed anyone with more than a rudimentary education.[118]

In some countries this same process of malicious vengeance can and does extend generations into the future. At various times the People's Republic of China has openly discriminated against the children and grandchildren of families ranked as "rich peasants," even though their only sins comprised a mildly distinguished pedigree. Approximately thirty million citizens were forced into a subordinate, subhuman category labeled "bad class background." In consequence they got low wages, poor education, and inadequate medical treatment. Their political activities were restricted, and they remained frequent targets of verbal and physical abuse.[119] All this occurred regardless of ability or need in order to maintain egalitarian principles in a society permeated by "the red-eyed disease."[120]

Yet overt attacks on talent and pedigree are hardly limited to the Third World. The British Labour party presided over the virtual dismemberment of the state educational system in the 1960s and 1970s. Their professed intention was to enhance educational opportunities for all by doing away with the private sector (the elite public schools). But in background to the debate were acrimonious arguments about wealth and privileges in Britain. The Labourites were levelers. They opposed not only the snobbish emulation of public schools (exclusive uniforms, single sex education, careful selection, "old boys" networks), but the differentiation of students according to educational ability. Accordingly they abolished 11 + exams and state grammar schools (academic secondary schools) and established a comprehensive system of mixed ability education.[121]

The effects were remarkable. The hated public schools gained a new lease on life, gradually taking over the function of the old grammar schools. Having relinquished dreary habits like fagging, they quickly responded to parental wishes for reasonable discipline and academic excellence. However, the high fees they charged essentially equaled a special tax on ambition as well as achievement.[122]

At the same time the state sector showed progressive signs of deterioration. Both students and teachers suffered a lack of resources and the loss of standards. Government inspectors regularly reported that the ablest children were "not always sufficiently challenged" and the less bright were not getting the right lessons.[123] And indiscipline was rife. Pupils sprayed graffiti, while instructors went on strike.[124]

One statistic stood out. The number of working-class children entering university slumped by over 50 percent from the late sixties to the mid-eighties.[125] This was a surprising result—or was it? The answer should be yes, for the comprehensive system was ostensibly initiated to promote the prospects of workers' children. Yet it must be no, for the impetus for the changes initiated by the Labour government was envy, of wealth, of status, but especially of intelligence, from wherever it came.[126] Envy is a major factor whenever the negative effects of institutional policies contradict apparent aims. In this instance the envious intent was not to enrich the educational pie, but to destroy it.

In reviewing the long arm of the state, I have been considering greedy, malicious attacks on wealth or nontransferable qualities that confer and reflect prosperity, like learning and culture. The many political, legal, business, and educational examples I have cited basically comprise institutionalized attacks on the breast. I now intend to focus on similar assaults on the womb or generative feelings and functions.

The Dalkon Shield disaster was more than an unfortunate corporate hiccup. By mid-1985 twenty-one women had died, thirteen thousand were infertile, and hundreds more had given birth to damaged children.[127] Morton Mintz claimed that this was the consequence of "a few men with little on their mind but megabucks."[128] But it is unlikely that financial greed was the sole factor. Court testimony demonstrates that company scientists knew the intrauterine device was flawed at least six months before it went on the market.[129] The story of the shield is entirely consistent with the covert contempt for female fertility, pregnancy, and childbirth that I have described in my chapter on womb envy. Ritual bleeding, couvade, test-tube babies, episiotomy, and hysterectomy all employ established customs and procedures to challenge the creative preeminence of women and, out of animosity, to inflict substantial damage on their minds and bodies. The violence marketed by the Robins Company did no less.

Femininity is a key issue in L. P. Hartley's utopian novel *Facial Justice*.[130] Hartley describes an entire society organized to eliminate beauty and the accompanying sins of parenthood and happiness. These features are despicable in themselves and because they arouse enmity in others. The government, ruled by a dictator like Big Brother in *1984*, is obsessively concerned with uniformity.[131] Therefore the worst sin is not envy, but exciting envy, and the most disruptive elements are pretty girls, known as "Alphas." At a certain age every Alpha is morally obliged to go to an Equalization (Faces) Centre for surgical alteration into a "Beta," or standard face. Similarly "Gammas," or ugly girls, must undergo a Beta upgrade. The object is to eradicate envy, called "Bad Egg" or simply "Bad E," by destroying everything enviable, an act that is, of course, the essence of envy.

The main character is a spirited Alpha named Jael who refuses disfigurement. She even resists complaints from the Ministry for Face Equality that her long eyelashes cause other women sleepless nights. Eventually her brother Joab, a civil servant, admonishes her:

> You have a right to nothing that is liable to cause Envy in the heart of a fellow-delinquent [citizen]. Our constitution and way of life are based on it.[132]

Jael disagrees and at a later point rebuffs her sibling rival with clever queries as to whether he would like to have his brains lowered.[133] Here she retorts:

> I know that Envy is the worst thing possible, but don't you think that there is another side to it—in my case. Don't you think that when people see me looking pretty, it makes them feel more cheerful?[134]

Jael underestimates the degree of hatred that a pretty face and accompanying cheerfulness may provoke. They remind people what they don't have and can't feel, particularly the actuality and echoes of the good breast and inviting interiors full of sexual delights. These are all emotional impossibilities in societies devoted to the absolute control of thoughts and feelings.[135] In fact, the members of many cultures are threatened by happy women and treat them accordingly, as demonstrated by the *Malleus*, the Society for Suppression of Vice, Ayatollah Khomeinism, and divers Puritan revivalists.

Alternatively, people of both sexes try to gain the happiness that they think women possess by turning to substances such as "happy pills." The use of drugs is a manic attack on female feelings that aims to bypass the source and aggrandize the goods. Thus the euphoria induced by heroin has been described as "instant bliss," not unlike the experience of an infant after a feed or an adult after intercourse.[136] But the original destructive impulses, essentially to shit on women, do not disappear, as indicated by the terrible ways that addicts degrade themselves and the organized persecution of drug users by civil authorities. The latter often behave like the face police in Hartley's novel.[137]

Certainly, Jael's pleasure in her person did not deter Joab, who replied:

> Cheerfulness is all right in its place, but if it excites a single twinge of Bad E, then it must be stamped out.[138]

Toward the end of the novel we learn that Jael suffers a prearranged accident. While in the hospital, and before regaining consciousness, she is given a Beta face to satisfy the dreaded dictator, who, it transpires, is an ugly old woman.

While also concerned with the political exploitation of envy, Orwell's Big Brother presents the force of phallic aggrandizement and the raw exercise of power. He embodies a party disconcertingly close to contemporary establishments whose virility lies in the ability to see all, know all, and dominate all. I refer to the corporate entities parodied by the *New Yorker* cartoon as well as paternalistic, authoritarian governments.

The "Big" in Big Brother catches the worrisome element in masculine assertive cultures to do with the inflation of institutional strength, size, assertion, ambition, prowess, and privilege. One can see this at work in the business community, where certain companies become king of the castle and everyone else the dirty rascal.[139] Similarly, many commentators have lambasted the British trade union movement and its political counterpart, the Labour party, for becoming "too big for their britches." Here big means "overweening" and "omnipotent," as in the excessive pride and arrogant exertions that have transformed libertarian aims into collectivist policies and practices.[140]

Paul Johnson has written at length about Australia, an apparently wide-open, free-enterprise country that celebrates maleness with curious abandon.[141] His surface impressions embrace hard-nosed businessmen, militant miners, strident radicals, and raucous sportsmen swilling beer and thumping tables. Even the playgrounds resound with aggressive little ditties like:

Boys are strong—like King Kong.
Girls are weak—chuck 'em in the creek.[142]

This macho bombast hides reflex uncertainties about the degree of independence and power people really have. Unlike American pioneers, who fled an oppressive state, the early Australians remained wholly dependent on that power, England, the home government, for support.[143] And even after these bonds were broken, the citizenry had to rely on another country, the United States, for external protection while turning to public sector services to satisfy internal needs. Consequently the Australian national image of rugged self-sufficiency conceals a complex network of sustaining relationships. As a myth it exemplifies the institutionalized denial of dependency and serves to fend off and express the envious resentments that multiple dependencies arouse. I say fend off because the hostilities involved appear to be displaced from outside powers to national agencies, from national agencies to social class, and from all concerned to wives and mothers. The women get the worst deal because they tend to be hated for being themselves and for representing the parental powers (such as government departments), who indeed often behave like Big Brother.[144] These antagonisms can be seen in the ritual avoidance and casual contempt that accompany Australian attitudes toward women. Otherwise the simple act of denying their importance is tantamount to annihilating their existence.[145]

The overbearing maleness that makes up such an important part of the Australian character, and that of the American, too, is a variation of the manic attack on female functions. But it also serves as a sword and shield in the ceaseless struggle for power between men and men or, more significantly, male institutions and men.[146] Almost two thousand years ago Plutarch noted that ostracism was an effective device that enabled the Greeks to "cut down to size and expel from time to time whoever of the citizens excels in reputation or power, relieving their envy rather than their fear."[147] Similarly, comic writers such as Aristophanes, who were the overlookers and muckrakers of their time, used satire to topple the high and mighty and make them rejoin the crowd.[148] The modern media continue public traditions of phallic rivalry by training their big guns on highfliers who grow too big too quickly.

In the 1980s tennis star John McEnroe was a special target. When he finally lost at Wimbledon the British press jumped for joy. An editorial in *The Times,* arguably the voice of the establishment, chortled:

> At Wimbledon we like our sure losers. . . . When John McEnroe returns here next year he may find that many of his problems with the press and people of Britain are behind him.[149]

No longer strongest and fastest, McEnroe was freed by *The Times* from threats to spoil his success with further slices of critical exposure. Comparable attacks on people who rise above the herd are so common as to be almost unnoticeable. This has not been the case with the Big Bang, or the abrupt removal of restraints on competition in London financial circles in 1986.[150] Desperate for talented traders, many banks and investment brokers offered huge salaries and even larger lump sums ("the golden hello") to gain needed staff. Among the new dealers, often ambitious young men in their mid- or late twenties, the size of the financial package became a prime virility symbol and sparked off murderous resentments among older dealers who had been passed by.[151] Their thoughts simmered in City hallways ("It's not fair!") and surfaced through the verbal deluge of like-minded journalists and politicians.[152]

The *Spectator* railed against financial "whiz kids," calling them

unnervingly young and unpardonably well paid. You can see them most evenings in the smarter trattorias and brasseries . . . [and] hear them, braying at the top of their voices.[153]

And Denis Healey, a senior Labour M.P., provided a derisive counterpoint with warnings about

the sort of young men of 26 or 27 who crack bottles of champagne on the floor of the stock exchange before they dawdle into their Porsches.[154]

Probably *The Observer* made the most dangerous thrust by encouraging the government to flex its bureaucratic muscles and impose a special tax on high-flying earnings. In fact this wasn't done, but Robin Leigh-Pemberton, the governor of the Bank of England, was so concerned about the ferocity of the offensive that he felt obliged to defend the new specialists and their premium wages. He argued that if Britain wanted to play in the big leagues, then it had to pay big bucks.[155]

Big bucks, or lots of money, is especially angry-making when it supports a flamboyant masculinity. It took Porsches, champagne, and smart trattorias, not just high salaries, to provoke Denis Healey and the *Spectator* to a state of critical rage. The same happened a few years earlier when explosive outbursts against the phallic fervor of John De Lorean destroyed a new sports car and his career. De Lorean had been an extremely successful executive with the General Motors Corporation. Although over fifty, he exuded vigorous good looks and confidence. And his pretty young wife complemented a fast, flashy life-style very much like the sleek gull-winged car he proposed to build. Having left General Motors, he convinced the Northern Ireland Development Agency to put up tens of millions of pounds toward the cost of bringing the car into production, in conjunction with his own designs, patents, and development work. Within two years a factory was built near Belfast, and by the fall of 1981 the first cars were ready for sale. He seemed to have achieved an industrial miracle as well as to be driving toward a personal fortune.[156]

Then Nemesis struck. A severe downturn in the car market meant that dealers refused to place anticipated orders or pay for cars already bought. Concomitantly the British government held up payments of ten million pounds in compensation for attacks by the IRA. In the preceding months the factory had been fire-bombed over 140 times, aside from many attempts to intimidate executives with sniper fire.[157] But this was only the beginning. After receiving some good publicity about the car, the company and De Lorean personally were overwhelmed with allegations of financial irregularity. These were perpetrated by two disgruntled employees, aided and abetted by members of Parliament and various newspapers. One woman, a secretary working in the New York office, took company documents to her Conservative M.P., who used his privilege of office to publicize them and demand a criminal investigation. This was done, and the charges were proved unfounded.[158] The second person, William Haddad, was an executive whose contract had just run out. Previously he had been an investigative reporter for the *New York Post* and other agencies.[159] He arranged for a down-market daily to publish a highly charged memo concerning unwarranted expenditures on gold taps for executive bathrooms. The paper said that he had written the memo and personally sent it to De Lorean. Apparently it had not been acted upon. Haddad later admitted that he had never sent the memo. In any case the company asserted it was a forgery.[160] Nevertheless the damage was done. Many people believed that where there was smoke there was fire, and that De Lorean was guilty of malfeasance.[161]

In consequence the company collapsed. The British government withdrew support, and various bankers refused further credit. Other institutions behaved like howling Furies, taking bigger and bigger bites out of De Lorean's rapidly fading reputation and activities. In Parliament he was accused of being "an American conman," while in the United States he was indicted for cocaine dealing, a charge subsequently disproved.[162] Essentially De Lorean paid the price of overreaching others and overstepping bounds. The public ridiculed him, and business colleagues shunned his company. Even his wife left him.

De Lorean was not an innocent. He may still be convicted and sent to jail, although he was acquitted of fraud and racketeering in a second major trial.[163] Nonetheless, the old charges, and pending civil suits, loom like evil eyes. They were as much attracted by macho displays transformed into stylistic arrays as by alleged criminal acts. De Lorean remains an automotive Icarus brought down to earth by institutionalized malice because of overweening style and ambition. In order to survive he may still have to choose to become mediocre and curb his challenge to the powers that be.

10

Anarchy and Vandalism

Everyone, arise! With your arms and your hearts, with the pen and the word, with the knife and the gun, with the curse and the irony, with adultery and pillage, with poisoning and fire. Let's make the war against civilization.[1]

These words embolden the "Political Will" of Jean-Paul Sartre, which he dedicated to his "anarchist friends, unjustly ignored."[2] Sartre condemned property, wealth, family, religion, and government, which were, for him, all sources of oppression, and called for revolutionary subversion, equated with knifing the rich and destroying all bourgeois institutions. Brutus and Spartacus were his heroes, men who were not afraid to burn down castles and dip their hands in the blood of their masters.[3]

Sartre's exhortation corresponds to long traditions of individual attacks on the State, its institutions, representatives, and values. In 1891, the Italian anarchist Enrico Malatesta declaimed the State was a political, legal, judicial, military, and financial framework for controlling people and robbing them of their personal freedom.[4] Since it acts by force, the police, it needs to be opposed by force, the insurrectionist. Others have believed that the State, and state agencies, are tyrannies that need to be destroyed simply because they exist. In this sense an anarchist is a person who maintains a narrow, malevolent view of society and whose destructive impulses are supported by political theories. In contrast, a vandal acts inchoately to loose his "blood-dimmed tide" onto the world.[5]

Anarchy derives from the Greek words *an archos,* meaning "without a rule." Hurled derisively against the Levellers during the English Civil War and the Enragés of the French Revolution, it was first used as a term of abuse.[6] Subsequently the English nonconformist minister William Godwin, and the French printer and socialist leader Pierre Joseph Proudhon, developed the positive elements of anarchist thought to do with justice, egalitarianism, decentralization, and mutual aid. Godwin argued that government was evil, but individuals were naturally benevolent. If left to themselves, they could spontaneously organize their affairs for the good of all. He advocated an economic system based on the principle "from each according to their means, to each according to their needs."[7] Proudhon emphasized freedom and equality. While rejecting the centralized state and accompanying political activity, he envisioned a new society where there were "no more parties, no more authority, absolute liberty of man and citizen."[8]

In spite of these high ideals, and possibly because of them, the theories of Godwin and Proudhon were superseded by demands for revolutionary violence that indelibly linked anarchy with bombs and blood. There were several reasons for this development. Arguably, their model for social change was insufficient and ill suited to the conditions that it purported to correct. More important, it aroused impossible expectations, a "second coming," which led to dashed hopes and murderous frustrations. Most important, it built a superstructure of virtue atop an infrastructure of hatred. When ill winds (external adversity, internal conflict) blew, the social pleasantries toppled, exposing the underlying destructiveness. Comparable events happen when individuals rely on idealization to overcome murderous inner tensions. Once they lose faith in absolute love, or absolute beauty, or absolute justice, all hell breaks loose.[9]

Proudhon was followed by a Russian nobleman turned agitator, Mikhail Bakunin, whose ringing declaration "the passion for destruction is also a creative urge" has dominated the mainstream of anarchist thought and practice, as well as peripheral political currents, since the mid–nineteenth century.[10] Called a pan-destructionist because of his millennial insistence on sweeping away all existing social institutions, Bakunin proclaimed violent revolution was a necessary prelude to the construction of a free and peaceful society. In fact, he exemplifies the person who needs a theory to release chaos and rationalize murder. His disciples did likewise, particularly Sergei Nechayev, who established the firm foundations of modern terrorism with the doctrine "propaganda of the deed." His specialty was spectacular assassinations of government officials.[11]

Contemporary terrorists, belonging to groups like Action Directe, Baader-Meinhof, or the Red Brigades, shoot businessmen and, more recently, computers for kindred reasons, that is, to gain the attention and support of "the masses" while demonstrating the vulnerability of "the system."[12] Although the overt aim may be to destroy a hated organization, an underlying intention is to inflate the ego or self-esteem of the destroyer. The two functions go hand in hand and illustrate the phenomenon of destructive narcissism. This impulse to destroy, to take pride in destruction, to become famous for cruelty and death dealing at the expense of everything else, becomes especially strong when a person, especially a "committed" person, feels alienated from society and at odds with his own ideals. In other words, it occurs at a time when an activist despairs of his all-powerful abilities to save the world.[13] The result is a devastating decrease in inner worth, which destructive narcissism, the idealization of venom and violence, tries to overcome.

The destructionist approach involves a psychic reversal of cherished values. Good becomes bad, and badness becomes exalted, as has happened with many "freedom fighters." Though the rhetoric may continue, and the comrades may still talk about truth, love, peace, equality, these become distant goals relegated to an indeterminate future. Instead murder, sabotage, and subversion replace them in immediate importance, and destructive achievements take over as essential springs of praise.[14]

The vandal is a destructive narcissist par excellence, someone who takes pleasure and gains a sense of inner worth from gratuitous attacks on the fabric of civilization, citizens, or things, the malignity of the deed. Hilaire Belloc warned about young tearaways in his *Selected Cautionary Verses*:

> *John Vavasour de Quentin Jones*
> *Was very fond of throwing stones*
> *At horses, people, and passing trains,*
> *And especially at window panes.*[15]

De Quentin Jones was not a lower-class, but an upper-class lout whose "favorite form of Play" was "the sound of broken glass." He acted alone (and came to a bitter end). Others act alone or in gangs, but with the discharge of envy, experienced as resentment, foremost in their minds. Recurrent vandalism, far more than anarchy, is a pervasive feature of modern life. No school can be built in New York City without taking into account an inevitable spate of broken windows and arson.[16] Meanwhile in England, at least twenty-five million pounds of random damage is done each year to schools, railways, and, more recently, farms.[17] One terrorized man explained.

> Farming here has got to the stage that when we sow a crop they ride motor-cycles over it. When it's growing they play in it, and if it gets ripe, they set fire to it.[18]

In common usage vandalism refers to any senseless spoilage, but originally the term was applied to the willful despoiling of cultural assets, particularly works of art. In 1794 Bishop Henri Grégoire of Blois named such atrocities after the Vandals, a Germanic tribe that sacked Rome in 455 C.E. After two weeks in the city they carried off a mass of loot and burned what they couldn't carry. Actually, various German scholars contend that the Vandals did not behave with ruthless abandon.[19] Nonetheless, the term has stuck. Vandalism gained a fearful reputation that also implies savage greed, typical of grenvy, and inverted snobbery, because vandals tend to attack things "over their head" and feel superior for having done so.

The center of attention for the vandal, often a "rebel without a cause," and the anarchist, an individual whose grudges breed theories, is society. But the emphasis may be different. The former concentrates on products and values, park benches and paintings, while the latter looks to the whole: revolutionary upheaval. Yet their symbolic interests are comparable, the cornucopias of life and rods of authority.

In this respect Sartre's position was prodigious. He announced wealth was death, just as Proudhon had once declared, "Property is theft."[20] Both embraced the war cry of the zero sum game, no one should have more than his neighbor. Sartre, however, as an existentialist turned Nemesist, began to begrudge life. If he could not possess the whole pie (health, happiness, intellectual treasure troves), there would be no pie.

It is interesting to compare Sartre in his old age with the financier

J. P. Morgan. The latter used his resources to hire young girls to suckle him. Even in his dotage Morgan enjoyed the breast. Sartre reverted to the opposite extreme. He regressed to the position of an envious, negative child.

Oppressed by sickness, Sartre strongly identified with the wretched of the earth. For him the bourgeoisie took on the role of the evil, depriving source of supply, against whom the proletariat (himself, the wretched) would take revenge.[21] He advised select workers to ransack the rich, to break into their homes in the middle of the night, strangle the occupants, rifle the jewel boxes, and burn down the buildings. Moreover, at New Year's Eve or kindred festivities, he proclaimed pastry chefs and serving staff should infiltrate their parties and poison the sweet trays so "one hundred or one thousand wealthy people will cease to exist."[22] And the same should happen at gift shops. They should

> poison the champagne [and], if this is possible, the rare wines, the gloves, the cakes, the ices, and the creams."[23]

Once these goodies went, the rest of the country would follow: crops, churches, government offices, and commercial centers. The point was not just to attack the wells of plenty, but to destroy life itself, so that "in all things joy will be born out of the excesses of evil."[24]

It would be easy to dismiss Sartre's statements as the rantings of a deranged philosopher. Yet he was one of the foremost writers, thinkers, and activists of the twentieth century and continued to be treated as such right up to and after his death.[25] Sartre lived by words and demanded that they should be taken seriously. The position he asserted in his Political Will was consistent with decades of polemics, during which time he had been on close terms with anarchists, Maoists, Leninists, Stalinists, situationalists, and, toward the end of his life, the Baader-Meinhof gang.[26] Sartre's thoughts provided intellectual ammunition for the actions of individuals as diverse as the Red Brigades and the Khmer Rouge. Verbally they were the essential elements in a powerful projection system.

> I am throwing this seed into the heart of all those who suffer, and let's begin! You will not escape this insurrection. I hope it will start right away.[27]

His echoes haunt the headlines. In Paris youths claiming to be members of the Anarchist Autonome movement raged through the most expensive shopping streets looting and wrecking the luxury shops.[28] In London a band of self-proclaimed anarchists staged armed raids on supermarkets in order to buy weapons and bombs for "attacks upon institutions of our society."[29] On previous occasions a group called the Angry Brigade bombed a fashionable boutique and a BBC van the night before the Miss World contest in order to destroy the "spectacle" of consumerism:

> Brothers and Sisters, what are your real desires? Sit in the drugstore, look distant, empty, bored, drinking some tasteless coffee? or perhaps BLOW IT UP OR BURN IT DOWN.[30]

This communiqué emphasized the issue of boredom, or the absence of a basic "foodstuff," adequate stimulation. Here the protagonists blame society for their feeling bored and propose an exciting remedy. Explosions express the wish to grab the excitement that others get and to retaliate for inadequate mothering—that is, understimulation.[31] For these very reasons the British prime minister has been violently blamed both for unemployment, as if she were an evil woman who deliberately starved her children of necessary stimulation, and for starting the war with Argentina, that is, for giving them too much.[32] In the same vein attacks on "spectacles" reflect envious hostility toward others who are or have been stimulated too much or too little (when the stimulation is painful) in comparison with the disgruntled spectators.[33]

In the United States the counterculture of the 1960s and 1970s overshadowed the looting and rioting that was directed against consumer targets. The equivalent of the Angry Brigade was at work (the Weathermen, for example), but spontaneous outbursts in the black ghettos did most of the overt damage.[34] Conversely, the flower people, the cultural revolutionaries, the "free university freaks," tried to overcome the rigid morals and mores of the fifties with provocative changes in attitudes and life-styles often based on libertarian principles.[35] At best their idealism led to innovative social experiments that challenged the success-oriented materialism of their parents. At worst their aggressive anticonsumerism became an excuse for grenvious assaults on the goods and services they supposedly rejected.

Both the benevolence and malevolence of the sixties surfaced in the shape of the Diggers, a loose convergence of dropouts and activists who set up shop in San Francisco in 1966 to care for homeless, drug-damaged kids. Within a short time they managed to establish soup kitchens, a legal aid service, the Haight-Ashbury free medical clinic, and a store, the Free Frame of Reference.[36]

The Diggers named themselves after a seventeenth-century group of impoverished Englishmen who tried to become masters of their own economic fate by digging and planting the common land. The original Diggers advocated communal living and political equality. Although destroyed by local opposition, these people laid down the principles of self-help and mutual aid, as well as hostility to property and authority, that were later taken up by Godwin, Proudhon, Kropotkin, and others.[37]

By 1967 the San Francisco Diggers were overwhelmed by the sheer numbers of young runaways who flocked to the city from all over the country. Out of money and resources, they shut down only to reopen a year later, angrier but better organized. They published a manifesto, "The Post-Competitive, Comparative Game of a Free City," which asserted: "Every brother should have what he needs to do his thing."[38] To accomplish this the group tried to establish a liberated zone, a free city complete with free food, medicine, music, and even free money.[39] But they never resolved the vital question, where do all the free things come from? The Diggers and their program remained dependent on the very society they despised. A subversive logic led to theft ("the necessary thievery and plunder of a rancid State") and intimidation, the shakedown of pop groups and psychedelic shopkeepers, aside from the general public.[40]

> By now we all have guns, know how to use them, know our enemy, and are ready to defend. We know that we ain't gonna take no more shit. So it's about time we carried ourselves a little heavier and got down to the business of creating free cities within the urban environments of the Western world.[41]

Emotionally the Diggers' propaganda and deeds constituted a manic attack on their California cornucopia. Good intentions got lost amid greed for the fruit and contempt for the source. Yet they were unable to undermine society or triumph over a pervasive pop culture. Within a few years the Diggers themselves dissolved, victims of violent posturing, a last grasp at self-importance, as well as changing fashions.[42] Significantly, the same tendencies continue to appear and reappear in different guises, devoid of theory. I refer to the many ways individuals assault "the system" through welfare abuse or computer hacking, essentially different varieties of economic or electronic vandalism.

· · ·

Welfare cheats basically attack the "nipple of state materialism." They claim, often correctly, that the state cheats them, so they have every reason to get back at it. But in so doing, they deplete the pool of money available for legitimate claimants and spoil their chance to be helped without being demeaned. For example, so many "fraudsters" flooded into the seaside town of Newquay, Cornwall, that it became known as the "Costa del Dole," and local youngsters could not claim Social Security benefits without attracting opprobrium.[43]

As "electronic breasts" full of valuable data, computers are also vulnerable to operators who attack both hardware and software, the package and the contents. Machines have been shot, blown up, pissed upon, and disabled with knives or keys.[44] In a celebrated incident the employee of an insurance company acted like the Angry Brigade because he was bored. Over a period of two years he repeatedly sabotaged the disk drives of a Burroughs B3500. It turned out that every time the engineers were called, he became the center of attention and excitement, a heady brew.[45]

In addition, there are hackers who systematically assail the data banks. They act for thrills as well as for profit—to enter forbidden places and gain access to piles of information. In this regard they are just like children who would worm their way into their mothers' bodies in order to hack out the goodies. Greed may be the motivation, as with the embezzler who diverts electronic funds or the diddler who steals trade secrets or proprietary programs.[46] However, the malicious hacker does not stop at theft. He tends to take after the burglar who breaks into a house, turns on the taps, and smears shit on the wall. Such a person despoils data with Trojan horses and logic bombs. These are special sets of instructions that when inserted into software make it malfunction, either immediately or at some time in the future.[47] They can also be used to infect computer networks ("bulletin boards"), which as a Manhattan computer consultant put it is like "poisoning the candy in the supermarket on Halloween."[48] Trojans and logic bombs, which can easily blow a program to bits, are to the hacker what plastic explosive is to the terrorist. They enable him to ravage the computer and simultaneously deprecate the parent organization.

The targets of the subverting, vandalizing attacks I have been considering—riches, sweets, crops, supermarkets, data banks, drugstores, or welfare—symbolize the female side of society. Since their feeding, containing, stimulating features overlap with generative, life-

236 · THE TYRANNY OF MALICE

promoting functions, one might expect that vandalism would reach deep into the body of the motherland, the womb of all things as well as of the breast. Clearly this is the case.

"Ecological rape" has become a byword for individual onslaughts on beautiful, fertile places, while inventive organizations remain prey to corporate sharks.[49] Similarly, disaffected students have been known to vent their spleen on artistic centers by spraying museums and slashing paintings. The person who mutilates a Rembrandt or a *Madonna and Child* illustrates the original meaning of vandal.

For many, the hated object is the institution of motherhood. Filial vandalism has to do with injuring the product of another woman's happiness and love. Helmut Schoeck has described a middle-aged spinster who suddenly pushed a friend's baby and carriage into the Isar River in Munich.[50] Afterward the murderer said she had been overcome by envy of the new mother's good feelings. It would be safe to say that this woman was also enraged by evidence of her friend's fertility and maternity. Not infrequently newspapers report analogous deeds by baby-sitters or family acquaintances, culprits who may be men or women, respectable or outcast.

In the quiet town of Westbury, England, a fifty-year-old teacher, described as a cold, lonely divorcée, butchered the wife and child of a colleague. Aside from jealousy, it became clear at the trial that the woman's motive was "envy over a happy family enjoying a new baby."[51] Similarly, twenty-year-old Bruce Lee set fire to over two dozen men, women, and children because he thought they were members of happy families.[52] Lee was the epileptic son of a prostitute who had been "kicked from pillar to post." Had he entertained political yearnings, revolutionaries might have applauded a "heroic contribution to the struggle against bourgeois marriage." In fact he acted gratuitously.

Ultimately these impulses touch traitors, citizens who vandalize their own state. The abhorrence they attract arises not only from raids on national sovereignty, but from their inevitable tendency to undermine the creative capacity of a country to care for its citizens and renew its environment. In this sense traitors are maternal moles with evil intentions.[53]

Phallic foci, however, provided the primary targets for radical leaders like Bakunin, Kropotkin, and Marx. They instinctively directed their insurrectionist eyes and vocal teeth toward authority and power. Thus, the 1882 Anarchist International avowed:

Our ruler is our enemy. We Anarchists, i.e., men without any rulers, fight against all those who have usurped any power . . . our enemy is the State, whether monarchical, oligarchical, or democratic. . . . Our enemy is every thought of authority, whether men call it God or devil. . . . [54]

The manifesto condemns officialdom—landowners, factory chiefs, priests, judges, and heads of state—all representatives of a collective patriarchy responsible for oppressing the young (the weak and helpless, "the proletariat") and exploiting femaleness (production and reproduction, "the means of production").[55] Later insurrections equated the State with a greedy penis ("the ant-eater proboscis"), a legal organ able to thrust itself "into every corner" in order to perpetuate privilege.[56]

Yet, for all his attacks on big government, Bakunin was not averse to power. In 1864 he founded the International Brotherhood, a secret, close-knit society composed of conspirators who would initiate and lead the revolution.[57] Four years later he established the International Alliance of Social Democracy, a seemingly open organization designed to promote the aims of anarchy. Both groups quickly dissolved so their mmbers could join the socialist First International.[58]

Likewise Marx, first a friend and finally a bitter enemy of Bakunin, was totally preoccupied with political intrigues and the control of men.[59] Almost without exception his colleagues and acquaintances recalled:

His overriding characteristic is boundless ambition and thirst for power . . . he is very jealous of his authority as leader [and is] an absolute ruler [who] tolerates no opposition.[60]

The aim of all his endeavors was personal domination . . . with a shameless impudence worthy of Napoleon.[61]

Bakunin, Marx, and their followers were not contradictory in their attitude toward governmental power. In the guise of stripping the State of strength, they sought to garner it for themselves. Thus the rod of authority can pass from the individual to the collective and back again in a multitude of ways. In the last chapter I described institutions and political parties whose virility lay in their capacity to dominate individuals. Here I am describing the opposite course, individuals who commit their skills to emasculate society and take over command.

. . .

The process of phallic aggrandizement is not limited to the political arena. Like successful hunters, computer hackers devote untold ingenuity to tracking, slaying, and redirecting powerful programs for their own use. Here too the issue is not plunder, rather the wish to be big—that is, to take on the qualities of the experts, or the computer, or the company itself. As one college student remarked, hacking "is a game. It is a chance to show you are clever."[62] Security analysts, however, insist a lot more than games are at stake. They think every programmer is a potential "cracksman":

> Telling a programmer that a computer system is safe from penetration is like waving a red flag in front of a bull.[63]

Having cracked the code, the hacker can leave trap doors, passwords like "Joshua," so vividly depicted in the film *WarGames*.[64] These allow future access to computers and computer networks as well as the opportunity to lay down logic bombs that can be used in fraternal strife with other hackers or hobbyists. Richard Streeter, a CBS executive, discovered this to his detriment while checking electronic bulletin boards for new programs. He came across one called EGABTR, which promised to improve the efficiency of his graphic displays. Intrigued, he copied it onto his hard disk and tried it out. Within seconds "Arf, arf! Got You!" flashed on his screen. Streeter discovered what "Got You!" meant when he tried to retrieve other data. Nothing was there! EGABTR had effectively destroyed all nine hundred programs and documents contained in his storage system.[65]

Worms and viruses can also be set up to damage data and software. The worm is a program that can wriggle through large computer networks and take over idle power for exceptional uses. But worms also allow hackers to enhance their capacities at others' expense or to play Robin Hood by "donating" computer time and information "to the masses."[66] Alternatively, malign mutants are able to burrow through data bases leaving massive memory gaps.

Viruses are infectious data destroyers that can spread like the plague, replicate with ease, and contaminate a whole system for revenge or "just for the fun of it."[67] Not surprisingly, many instigators of trap doors, Trojan horses, worms, and viruses have done formidable damage.[68] The central computer at De Paul University in Chicago suffered one breakdown after another because teenaged cracksmen broke in and deleted parts of its operating system. Similarly, Los Angeles high school students took joyrides through the research data of doctoral candidates. More alarming, members of the 414's, a Milwaukee group named after the telephone area code for eastern Wisconsin, mucked around the mainframes of over sixty institutions, including the Los Alamos nuclear weapons research facility in New Mexico and the Sloan-Kettering Cancer Center in New York.[69]

The danger is no joke. By the mid 1980s the U.S. National Security Agency was regularly warning allied countries about the consequences of political malcontents sabotaging their computer systems.[70] Not long afterward a Parisian programmer and a New York writer produced a technothriller called *Softwar*. It was based on the idea of injecting a logic bomb into the Soviet computer network that was so powerful it would "wipe out everything but the graffiti in the Kremlin's men's room."[71]

The 414's and related rebels with theories aim at the electronic analogs of institutional power and illustrate the narcissistic analogs of envy. At one and the same time they propose to tear down the system and boost themselves. There are two aspects to these maneuvers. The first operates according to the popular refrain "Anything you can do, I can do better."[72] Such determination does not denote benign emulation. By shouting, "Yes, I can; yes, I *can*; yes, I *Can!!*" the girl on the make in *Annie Get Your Gun* hoped to devastate the opposition.[73] The same holds true with reckless programmers or, for that matter, political vandals, whose driving force is the wounding awareness of their own frailty juxtaposed with the virility of the State machine. These people are always trying to beat the system but are never satisfied by what they achieve. They remain prey to others' accomplishments, their own doubts, the absence of praise, and ever-escalating rivalries.

At a certain point, however, the accumulated emotional pain may become too great for the narcissist to bear. Then he gives up the game and stops trying to hurt others by outdoing them. In place of old strategies he denies the need to emulate positive skills and completely allies himself with negative wishes. This phenomenon, destructive narcissism, is the flip side of self-inflation. Although the destructionist still registers qualities such as strength, size, prowess, authority, or staying power, he attaches them to violence and devastation. Consequently he (or she) prefers regicide to reign and plastique to logic bombs. Instead of trying to reform or surpass the system, he decides to smash it and everything connected with it. Many rationales may be given. Radical ideologues, for example, often proclaim computers are tools of capitalist oppression:

> Computers are the favorite instrument of the powerful. They are used to classify, control, and to repress.[74]

This is part of a public statement by a French terrorist group called CLODO, which is slang for "tramp" and also an acronym for words that translate roughly as "Committee for the Liquidation and Misappropriation of Computers."[75] In Europe there have been dozens of direct assaults on computer installations by guerrillas armed with weapons ranging from Molotov cocktails to submachine guns.[76] Members of the Red Brigades have carried out a large proportion of these raids. After one explosion at the Motor Vehicle Ministry, so many files were obliterated that the Italian government didn't know who owned cars or trucks, or had licenses to drive them, for almost two years.[77]

Computers announce the complexity and power as well as the grandiosity and pomposity of the organizations that use them. In the early 1980s young Swiss anarchists bypassed electronics and vented their spleen straight at the Zurich opera house, for them the overstuffed structure of overbearing burghers.[78] Calling themselves Die Unzufriedenen—The Dissatisifed—they charged a gala performance with eggs and paint, after which they burned cars and looted luxury shops for several days.[79] The Dissatisfied came from a pool of apprentices, unskilled workers, and disgruntled students. They saw themselves as losers in a society where success equaled virility and reacted accordingly. If they couldn't compete—that is, join the rat race—they would destroy it.

Similar sentiments have motivated the Hell's Angels, a motorcycle club founded in Fontana, southern California, in 1950. Many of its adherents have come from the ranks of disaffected mechanics and service station attendants. One commented:

> We were all losers. We were unhappy, and we wanted to have other people be unhappy. We did anything evil that any of us could think of to do.[80]

During the early years the club members favored violent brawling, often taking over small towns for bouts of weekend hell raising. Later they moved into racketeering. Their ironic self-description is instructive—"Hell's Angels" or Angels from Hell, as opposed to more obvious epithets like Satan's Commandos or the California Devils. It implies that on some level they wanted to be angels, that is, beings who were widely known for good works or, within a California context, worldly accomplishment. Since this avenue appeared to be blocked, they aimed for wickedness and infamy, that is, to become the biggest baddies on the block.

The perverse longing for notoriety, the counterpart of fame, characterizes the destructive narcissist. Really the term is a misnomer, since all narcissism is destructive. However, the difference is between a personal and interpersonal strategy that builds pride at the expense of others (by inducing inferiority, inadequacy, shame, and so forth) and one that seeks celebrity by annihilating others (or society and its symbols).[81] The latter exults in power and tries to procure a place in history (or, at the very least, in the minds of colleagues) by outrageous acts, not just the murder of men, but attacks on the pillars of civilization.[82]

In ancient times the Greek Herostratos grasped renown by burning the temple of Artemis at Ephesus, then one of the wonders of the world.[83] The Ephesians responded by banning the mention of his name. This would be more difficult in present circumstances when news of comparable crimes can flash around the world in minutes. It is not insignificant that soon after shooting President Reagan, John Hinckley demanded to know how he was shown on television.[84] For similar reasons urban rioters often race home to watch "the box" after an evening's entertainment smashing and burning about the streets.[85] Indeed, when the coverage is inadequate, dedicated terrorists are quick to complain about "a conspiracy of silence." More likely the media are suffering from overkill.[86]

Riots are concentrated outbursts of macho rage, which otherwise can take the form of gratuitous defacements of powerful vehicles or any large public edifice. Thus a Porsche or BMW left out in the open is in constant danger of receiving progressive scratch marks right along the paintwork. This process seems to have achieved its ultimate expression in the New York subway system, where graffiti cover the carriages inside and out and the stations as well.[87] Far from being a new native art form, as some critics have claimed, the chaotic iconography proclaims an unrelenting antagonism to the society that built the system and the trains, symbols of the ceaseless energies searching, sensing, throbbing, and probing the deep, dark tunnels of the city.[88] As for the passengers, they are the victims of a host of spray figures, a multiplicity of evil eyes designed to pass on the fears and hatreds that have-nots direct to haves in order to be big. It is impossible to ride the subway without feeling assaulted by these eyes and their scrawled accompaniments:

> "Kill" "Destroy" "Off that" "Off everything" "I'm the mean-est" "I'm the greatest"[89]

Both the icons and words are envious ejections screaming "Screw you," but "Look at me!" which indicate they originate in destructive phallicists with an eye for trouble.[90] The object of the sprayers, no less than the 414's, CLODO, and other hell raisers, is the societal phallus. I refer to authority and power incarnated in the structure of the State and its values and institutions, always seen by those who attack them as oppressive and exploitative. By the same token, the cornucopias of life attract "the knife and the gun, poisoning and fire," for being, or at least appearing to be, maliciously depriving.

The question arises, do governments and organizations have it coming to them for being cruel and tyrannical, or are they phantoms created by and victimized for the malicious impulses of their attackers? The answer is not clear cut. In actuality almost anything that a person can imagine has been done at some point at some place in the name of some society. In this century alone the realities of Nazi Germany, Stalinist Russia, Maoist China, or, for that matter, two global wars have strained the bounds of iniquity. And even within advanced Western countries there remain pockets of poverty that would not be unfamiliar to a Victorian workman.

All too frequently the same holds true with cultural conventions. During the postwar decades, the American anthropologist Jules Henry reconnoitered his own country. In *Culture Against Man* and other studies, he documented schools that imparted stupidity no less than mental hospitals that perpetuated madness and families that prevented their children from growing up.[91] Interestingly there exists a word that denotes a situation when a person feels persecuted but isn't. I refer to "paranoia." Yet no word exists for the actual predicament of being persecuted while not recognizing the fact or responding accordingly.[92] Nor are there words to denote the wide variety of in-between states.

In practice, institutions and the societies that support them contain elements of good and bad, danger and deliverance. At one extreme there are social systems that require resistance yet overwhelm the opposition by ruthless repression. They may be termed *Societal* or *Cultural Persecutors* and have the same relationship to their citizens that *Parental Persecutors* have to their children. Like Jael in *Facial Justice,* the victims of *Societal Persecutors* not only have to conform, they have to accept whatever harm may be inflicted on them in the name of society without challenging or even thinking about what has been done to them.[93]

In the last chapter I pointed out that the ill effects of institutionalized malice include redistributive and retributive starvation as well as systematic attacks on feminine and masculine accomplishments. Perhaps worse is that *Societal Persecutors* leave little room for projective processes to take place, that is, to serve, like parents, as useful containers for people's envy and greed. They are already so terrifying that their victims remain speechless, even when confronted with what has been done to them.

Paradoxically, countries and cultures that are reasonably beneficent are more likely to be perceived as monstrously evil. This is a consequence of not being totally oppressive. Citizens are allowed to hate and express their hates without being immediately whisked off to jail. But in addition to being the focus of pernicious projections, these societies also become a receptacle for idealized expectations, especially during periods of social change. Since actual events never coincide with impossible goals, such as eliminating poverty within a generation or equal health and happiness for everyone, society itself or "the system" gets the blame for being savage, pitiless, child destructive, and so forth.

At the other extreme *The Combined Society* or *Combined Culture* is a political entity or cultural institution transformed into a bloodsucking savage by the angry thoughts of its citizens. It is a subjective reality, a creature created in the minds of the hard-done-by that uses bad features to mirror malevolence while burying good bits beneath bitterness. *The Combined Society* is the social counterpart of the *Combined Parent.* Like Sartre's bourgeoisie, it embodies the wicked witch and killer giant all rolled up into one horrific, all-powerful persecutor.

The Angry Brigade, the White Panthers, and kindred spirits have all provided abundant descriptions of society qua demon based on attributions of inner impulses and distortions of external realities:

The politicians, the leaders, the rich, the big bosses, are in command. . . . *They* control. *We, the people, suffer.* . . . *They* have polluted the world. . . . *They* shoved garbage from the media down our throats. *They* made us absurd sexual carica- tures. . . . *They* killed, napalmed, burned us into soap, mutilated us, raped us.[94]

> *The rulers of our planet are totally corrupt. The rulers of our planet are totally insane.*[95]

These statements make monsters from grains of truth. For sure some rulers are corrupt, and others may be insane, but exaggerated leaps from the specific to the general across time and place simply perpetrate the states of mind—paranoia, despair, paralytic hope- lessness—that precede the facts. Similarly, the use of "we" and "they" provides a mechanism for splitting good from bad and pinning the bad on societal figures, representing the State.[96] Thus "they" are greedy (rich, exploitative), envious (polluting, garbage shoving), jeal- ous (commanding, controlling), vindictive (mutilating, napalming), and perverted (raping, caricature making, sexually brutalizing).[97] Meanwhile "we," mere citizens, are brutalized, unloved (mere func- tions of a production process), and totally justified in violent revenge.

The Combined Society has all the characteristics of a "they" and continues to be portrayed in innumerable hideous shapes and sizes. European anarchists seem to prefer the image of a jackbooted soldier holding a gun to the head of a quivering comrade, while in 1960s America the pig became the favored symbol of avaricious authority.[98] Contemporary effigies include a robotic teacher wielding an iron rod over "us," long-suffering students, as appeared in the anarchist jour- nal *Black Flag*.[99]

The pedagogic oppression posed by this robot is probably, though not necessarily, the product of perverse perception. If social facts coincide with rampant hatred, then it is more appropriate to speak of *The Combined Societal Persecutor*. This term includes people act- ing on behalf of the larger cultural or political establishment, the agents as well as the whole system itself. Typically, teachers take on the role of *Combined Parental Persecutors* when serving in loco parentis to unwilling students but turn into *Combined Societal Per- secutors* while trying to civilize unruly students.

The basic elements in these dramas include the actual behavior and imaginary threats posed by both sides. Unwilling students use their teachers, just as in other circumstances unwilling citizens use the State, as a mirror and receptacle for their personal antagonisms.

Unruly people do the same. But, in addition, they actively mobilize
the imagination of the authorities, who then respond not only to the
way things are but also to their own exaggerated fears and guilts.
The projection of these feelings onto and into individuals often "justifies" an escalating spiral of violent oppression. This process peaked
at the 1968 Democratic presidential convention in Chicago. A small
number of agitators and a large gathering of students precipitated a
political crisis by provocative but essentially harmless demonstrations
that engaged the phantasies of the powers that be. At one of the
meetings a pretty coed walked naked carrying the head of a pig on
a platter. Many others smoked dope or chanted antiwar slogans.
These actions aroused such passions that the arena became a war
zone with armed police brutalizing the demonstrators. Thus they
appeared to demonstrate that Mayor Daley and the Democratic candidate and indeed "the whole rotten system" were really rotten. More
to the point, the youngsters and some of their older mentors created
the facts they needed in order to convey the hurts they felt in the
first place.[100] This left them in no doubt that both the pigs and
politicians had it coming to them.

. . .

The demonized or *Combined Citizen* is the counterpart of the State or institution that attracts hostility. He or she is an individual who becomes the projective focus of collective fears and seems to embody everything that his compatriots hate in themselves. In America in the sixties this included unrestrained sensuous qualities, Dionysian reveries that clashed with outspoken moral and materialistic values. Anyone with long hair and beards or unkempt feminine features was immediately suspect and often lumped with beatniks, hippies, weirdos, or homos. Onlookers saw them as incubi and succubi out to infiltrate their homes and neighborhood with drugs, sex, and communism. At one and the same time they were condemned for being oversexed, castrated and castrating. Yet their alleged unremitting enmity to the American way of life reflected the hostility hurled in their direction. This made them an even greater menace and called forth even greater retribution.

The Michigan poet and publicist John Sinclair was one of many white, middle-class dropouts demonized for nonconformity. After a stint at Wayne State University, he founded an artists' workshop for kindred souls and became a spiritual leader of the Detroit–Ann Arbor psychedelic/rock and roll community. His life-style led to a lot of adverse attention from local law enforcement agencies and was ultimately responsible for Sinclair's defiant decision to form the White Panther party for the propagation of "rock and roll, dope, and fucking in the streets."[101] He explained:

> Our program is cultural revolution through a total assault on culture . . . art, music, newspapers, books, posters, our clothing, our homes, the way we walk and talk, the way our hair grows, the way we smoke dope, and fuck and sleep and eat— it's all one message, and the message is *freedom*.[102]

Sinclair was eventually arrested and imprisoned for ten years for possessing two marijuana cigarettes.[103] The draconian sentence undoubtedly reflected the politics of gesture and his ability to get under the skin and agitate the minds of city and state authorities through the interplay of outlandish—he would say "revolutionary"—words, sounds, and images.[104] It is likely that he had the same emotional impact in 1968 as pictures of truculent students still produce today:[105]

The student with squinting eyes, gnashing teeth, and bristling appearance seems to be especially designed to send shivers through the most hardened robot or bourgeoisie. But if he didn't exist, he would

be invented, for he complements the oppressive pedagogue. Whether the result is fight or flight, such a fearsome person or *Combined Citizen* is a phantom that reflects and stirs up preexistent conflicts in his family or society.

On the other hand, *The Persecuting Citizen* relies on deeds, not phantasies, to attack the establishment. Like the filial persecutor who vandalizes adults, *The Persecuting Citizen* cuts his teeth on public figures and everything they represent. He is a tangible, not an imaginary, malcontent. Hate mailers, for example, frequent the fourth estate. In England a Mr. George Richards of Poole, Dorset, made it his life's work to bombard journalists with the news that they were "pitiable imbeciles." Finally words failed him, and he resorted to sending toilet seats to chosen columnists.[106]

More often than not, *The Combined* and *Persecuting Citizen* are one and the same person. The early John Sinclair was mostly a nightmare in the minds of local police, but once he started to retaliate he became much more than a long-haired, spaced-out freak. The later Sinclair was a revolutionary propagandist who managed the band M.C.5. and was involved in subversive activities throughout the Detroit area.[107] Similarly, the Angry Brigadists exploded bombs and images outside courthouses and inside politicians. Therefore the term *Combined Persecuting Citizen* more accurately describes their impact, and that of the modern terrorist, on society.

. . .

The key word is *Combined,* indicating a subjective fact, an observer-created reality. In this chapter on the individual against society, and the previous one on society against the individual, I have tried to explore the subtle and not so subtle ways that either side (the instigator, the subject) brings together fear and hatred, actuality and phantasy, in order to justify its attacks on the other (the victim, the object). Superficially it appears that the instigator is quite separate from his victim, but on closer examination we can see that the two are linked. Like the relation between the envier and the envied, there exist many points of confluence. This leads to alliances that encompass at least two distinct parts. First, there is an actual person in conjunction with the malevolent phantasies that the authorities have projected onto him. Second, there is an actual society or institution in conjunction with the malevolent phantasies that its citizens have projected onto it. The projected phantasies may have little to do with the object, the target, or may be called forth by foci of similarity to the very things the aggressor hates in himself. In any case each side, subject and object, individual and society, remains a dreaded part of the other, which goes some way to explain the intransigence of social conflict.

Thus *The Combined Persecuting Citizen* is a man or woman who plays on the imagination of the State in order to get a response that transforms all sides into monsters—the individual in the eyes of authority and the authorities in the eyes of the individual. But the effects often extend to the individual's perception of himself and the government's view of itself. If these transformations do not stick, then the citizen may remain a nuisance or persecutor, but someone to be dealt with appropriately, without panic or unnecessary aggression.

From the point of view of ordinary people, *The Combined Societal Persecutor* becomes demonic not just by acting hurtfully, but by forcing itself into their minds and coercing them from within. Again, without this internal interaction, citizens would still suffer, yet they would not remain incapacitated by political or institutional tyrannies.

These processes feed a matrix of malice that can escalate out of control, as at the 1968 Democratic convention, or wind down when touched by reparative reactions. At their worst they recapitulate timeless family dramas when the Oedipal son confronts the Laial father—the conjunction of subjective states and objective events played to a massive audience where all the world's the stage.[108]

11

National Pride

The politics of malice culminates in the expression of extreme antagonisms among institutions, cultures, and nation-states. These hatreds effectively submerge and simultaneously reinforce the enmities of individual citizens. Over two thousand years ago the Greek orator Lysias narrated the rage that Sparta felt toward its properous Corinthian allies, while in this century the French economist Eugène Raiga emphasized that whole countries are capable of mutual envy and jealousy and that they mimic the tensions that exist among people.[1]

What does it mean when a politician or journalist states that a nation or country "feels" hurt, or angry, or vengeful? Is this a tangible phenomenon, or metaphor, or projection perhaps of the speaker's own emotional state? Certainly countries often appear to behave as they are said to feel. Egypt under Nasser took over the Suez Canal to assert independence and "avenge humiliations" by Britain and France. Similarly, Argentina under Galtieri invaded the Falklands to regain pride and confirm its superiority over Britain and fellow Latin countries.

More often than not these feelings comprise the unarticulated premises that lie behind public policies. They originate from above, national leaders with all their blind and not so blind interests and prejudices; and, in recent times, from below, a citizenry whose passions can be aroused and channeled by the powers of mass communication.

Previously the feelings of the populace were less significant than those of their leaders because the people were expected—indeed, forced—to feel and do what their rulers, the patersfamilias, desired. Thus the dynastic wars of the Middle Ages were like extended family quarrels, and the fratricidal carnage that followed was fueled by the private greed of six Renaissance popes.[2]

The modern concept of the State as an independent entity began to emerge from the sixteenth century with the writings of Niccolò Machiavelli and Jean Bodin.[3] Whereas Machiavelli focused on the strength and craftiness of the prince, or head of state, Bodin presaged the idea of the divine right of kings—the State and its ruler were one. Consequently the emotional predilections for good or bad of kings or premiers necessarily became political issues. In the twentieth century a comparable strain of vengeful autocracy has characterized the regimes of Joseph Stalin and Adolf Hitler as well as the "personalismo" of Gamal Abdel Nasser and Fidel Castro.[4]

In contrast, the philosopher Jean Jacques Rousseau argued that the State derived its authority from the general will of the governed.[5] The implication of his work and that of subsequent thinkers was that people did not owe allegiance to a particular individual, but to a national body. Here we have a nascent definition of nationalism, arguably the most important collective force in modern history. Citizens could and did direct elemental feelings toward their cultural, linguistic, and political community—that is, their nation or state.[6]

Emotionally, the power of this community or body politic is much more than the sum of its individual parts. Since its members are linked by bonds of common interests, physical closeness, and rapid communication, it can and does function like a large crowd and volatile person all in one. Wild enthusiasms and passionate hatreds tend to brew up at short notice and spread like wildfire with ever-increasing intensity. Not surprisingly, patriotic assemblies can be notoriously fickle and irrational.[7]

The national crowd is a Freudian herd where, as the Nobel laureate Elias Canetti has pointed out, all become equal, no distinctions count, even of sex.[8] People press together, they make contact, they gain comfort by merging within the same political body. This allows them to surrender to the common good as well as the gravest evils. Too often the latter results from raising national esteem at the expense of others.[9]

This entity has a life of its own, separate from that of its constituent interests. Sovereign status means it is a "national actor," one unit among the family of nations and field of supranational relations.[10] Fellow players, rich and poor, big and powerful, or small and weak, frequently use terms like "poisonous," "filthy," "licentious," and "regicidal" (Germany about Serbia, pre-1914) or "evil," "dangerous," and "dominating" (America about Russia, post-1945) to describe each other.[11] Other words, "imperialist," "plunderer," and "warmonger," are part of an international verbal armory deployed by young, undeveloped countries to denigrate older, industrialized nations. Thus individual states, acting cohesively if not coherently, appear to display the whole range of sensitivities, insecurities, and resentments that characterize children and adults.

I am describing a phenomenon amply evidenced by the diaries, memoirs, biographies, personal accounts, and theoretical constructions of national leaders and commentators as well as ordinary citizens. Having imbued the State with intense emotional forces, often at the expense of depleting themselves of the same, all members of the community discover a vested interest in turning their beliefs into concrete realities. Consequently the State can be seen as an external tableau replete with internal dramas. Diplomacy is the focal point where much of the lost envy, greed, and jealousy may be found. In fact, some states essentially exist in an extrasocietal form, that is, through foreign relations.[12] Relative to their own shaky inner structures, they prefer to accumulate international kudos by lambasting richer countries for consumerism and other alleged transgressions.[13]

There have been many moments when sheer greed has been elevated to the status of a national obsession.[14] Spain of the conquistadors and Belgium under King Leopold provide only two examples of the ruthless despoliation of human and material resources by Europeans and non-Europeans alike. In this century Russia starved the Ukraine, China devoured its peasants, and Germany ravished most of Europe.[15] The Nazi longing for land has been satirized by the comedian Mel Brooks in his film *To Be Or Not to Be*. In one skit Brooks plays Hitler looking over a map of the continent while claiming to be a man of peace. Suddenly he switches tune and starts a frenzied song about taking "a piece of France, a piece of Denmark, a piece of Russia . . ."[16] I am told that this is an old joke often applied to any country that ostentatiously covets the territory of another.

Greed, however, is not the privilege of single nations. In the 1970s a transnational cartel of oil-producing countries (OPEC) suddenly quadrupled the price of oil, "a pivotal event" that effectively held the rest of the world over a barrel.[17] Among the many ramifications, the traditional flow of envy from East to West and South to North reversed. The United States and Western Europe began to deeply resent the wealth of Arab and African oil producers and especially disliked becoming dependent on "lesser powers" for energy resources.

As with children to parents, a noxious sense of dependency or lack of economic autonomy is a key issue that determines the degree of hate one country (its leaders and citizens) feels toward another. Prior to World War II, Britain and France attracted the most opprobrium for being colonial powers—that is, keeping or seeming to keep smaller, less developed territories in a state of economic and political subservience.[18] After the war the old animosities continued to fester, but the United States, as the predominant economic power, became the prime target of international abuse. From Latin America to Southeast Asia and northern Europe, old and new nations alike blamed American affluence for their poverty, backwardness, chaos, or unhappiness. South of the border, both right- and left-wing commentators on "dependence and underdevelopment" popularized this simple message:

> We are poor because the United States is rich; the United States is rich because it exploits us; let's fight against the United States.[19]

The most common forum for this fight is the United Nations, where the United States and its Western allies face a near deluge of denigration before select committees and the General Assembly. Typically, the head of one Indian delegation, the maharaja of Jammu and Kashmir, denounced the "colonial denudation" of the East and the "vulgar affluence" of the West.[20] Similarly, Western delegates like Professor René Dumont of France have provided reports that literally accuse the consuming countries of "eating little children," that is, unrestricted cannibalism.[21]

These denunciations extend from bread and butter to fertility. At one conference on population control, the American delegation brought up the relation between overpopulation and poverty. But even countries that agreed with the equation vilified America for daring to criticize the one thing they could do that Americans didn't, make lots of babies.[22] They seemed to fear reflections of their own cupidity in the guise of womb envy. The perverse extension of the right of unlimited fecundity is the right to ecological rape. At another meeting on the human environment, Brazil insisted it had a right to ruin the rain forests. Any attempt to prevent this was a conspiracy of haves to keep the have-nots down and out. Here the Brazilians attributed greed in order to hide grenvy.[23]

The rhetoric of resentment, whether deployed by Brazil or a new state, is essentially a British contribution. It is the language of Fabian socialism applied to the international arena.[24] When India assails the "arrogance of the affluent nations," she is using words that originate with Beatrice and Sidney Webb and their colleagues at the London School of Economics.[25] This demonstrates that it is possible to trace the flow of indignation from the individual to the group to society as a whole. By the 1950s the Webbs, were they alive, could truthfully claim that a large chunk of the world lived under regimes fashioned by their Victorian instincts. This also meant that while no longer an economic superpower, Britain was able to retain considerable political influence by conferring sovereign status on its class struggles.[26]

These supranational resentments do not always remain on the level of "jaw, jaw." They can escalate into terrorist attacks on the "fatherland" (or motherland, depending on the predominant phantasy) and finally flash into full-scale wars between a larger power and a subordinate people. The latter always feels and sometimes is oppressed by the other nation, which tends to be equated with a *Combined Persecutor*. This fusion of projected (greedy, envious) and perceived (exploitative) realities justifies the ensuing violence.[27] Meanwhile the parent country may overreact against its "defiant children" and bring about the very conditions it seeks to avoid, such as the rupture of relations.

Lloyd DeMause contends the basic cause of open warfare is the pervasive group feeling "through war we [a nation] will be born." In evidence he cites extensive references to specific experiences—a collective sense of "choking," "drowning," and "suffocating," leading to an "inexorable sliding" and "breaking out"—that tend to precede the onset of hostilities.[28] This view may explain the fight for freedom, but not the degree of ill will that accompanies the conflict. In referring to the American Revolution, Samuel Adams spoke of "the child Independence . . . now struggling for birth."[29] Here and in general, independence or self-determination denotes the struggle against smallness and servility, feelings that are common both to individuals and countries.[30] Despite the realities (colonial America, for example, was treated by Britain as an inconvenient child), the most tenacious antagonisms stem from envious beliefs that dependencies or nascent nations can never have as much or be as good as their parent country.[31]

Even after achieving independence, some countries nourish the old hatreds by sponsoring or directly engaging in international terrorism.[32] But the usual response is ingratitude, succinctly described by Aleksandr Solzhenitsyn in a speech to American trade unionists:

> The United States of America has long shown itself to be the most magnanimous, the most generous country in the world. . . . Who helps the most and unselfishly?
>
> And what do we hear in reply? Reproaches, curses, "Yankee go home." American cultural centers are burned, and the representatives of the Third World jump on tables to vote against the United States.[33]

Ingratitude debases benevolence. It attempts to overcome relative inadequacy and inferiority (that is, envious tension) by denying goodness and asserting that help is harm. Thus Tanzania regularly excoriates the very countries that keep it afloat, while Western observers note that the more aid Egypt gets from America, the more critical and resentful Egyptians become.[34] Paradoxically, the combination of Russo-American rivalry and post-1960s affluence seems to have created the conditions whereby sovereign nations, as opposed to private recipients, can thumb their noses at donor countries yet continue to get increasing amounts of economic and military assistance.[35]

Ingratitude, however, is not limited to the Third World. In response to the American Marshall Plan, various European countries acted like the angry Dervish in Handelsman's "Story of the Envious Man." While economically prostrate, some rejected it out of hand, claiming it was a cruel charade instigated by a selfish power in order to enslave the world. Others accepted and used the aid well, yet major factions maintained a murmur of discontent.[36] Although tempered with admiration, similar enmities remain a potent factor in Europe today. Anti-American prejudice is rarely far below the surface. At Cliveden, one of the most exclusive hotels in England, Americans have been singled out for surly service.[37] And at the 1985 Edinburgh Festival American tourists were openly abused in the quality, not the gutter, press. The Scotsman published a poem entitled "The American Visitors," which began:

> *They think the city's been put up*
> *for grabs:*
> *The dollar's strength turns*
> *everything to trash.*
> *They come, they see, they conquer*
> *with their cash.*[38]

In comparable circumstances other peoples have turned to a third party, a rival power, that might dispense money without demanding an ostentatious presence.[39] Being part of Britain, this task is more difficult for Scotland than for countries like Egypt, which kicked out Britain, courted Russia, and, in the 1970s, embraced America. Here envy (ingratitude) links with greed (endless needs) because of the capacity to arouse jealousy among competing patrons. The scenario is not dissimilar from that of a child who plays off one parent against the other. Alternatively, two small countries may fight for the favor of a larger one. The ensuing rivalries involve a mixture of envious and jealous hatreds.[40]

The British cartoonist Low has depicted the problems of ingratitude in the person of an aging Britannia being ousted from her home (the former colonies) by a gleeful trio of newly independent countries. With packed bags at her feet, she clutches a copy of Freud in her hands. The caption reads:

I wonder why children never want Grandma to depart through the front door but always long to kick her down the back stairs?[41]

The answer to Low's query is that the children want to triumph over Grandma. During decolonization, the kick in the pants was the repetitive claim that the colonial past was all bad and that former rulers were only rapacious exploiters. When combined with the denial of need and millennial promises of a glittering future, these hostilities were always part of a manic attack on dependency, the urge to rubbish Grandma and Grandpa alike.

Some, but not all, of the newborn nations acted this way. For those who did, the premise "I'm big, you're dung" was an omnipotent attempt to erase old humiliations, often aided and abetted, in a world of power politics, by potential new patrons. Countries like China conveyed the same message by retreating behind "bamboo curtains." Yet it only took a few flowers to blossom internally, or a peek at

Western accomplishments, to set off a national attack of the red-eyed disease. I refer both to the cultural revolution of the sixties and the unrest of the eighties, which culminated in the fall of General Secretary Hu Yaobang for "bourgeois liberalism."[42]

According to Chairman Deng, "self-reliance" was what mattered.[43] Hu had been too taken by Western ideas. The feared consequence was that *luan,* or chaos, would overwhelm the country. But chaos results from envy. The *luan* Hu's opponents feared was the projection of their own fragmenting rage toward Hu personally, and to the larger world of Western learning particularly, into China as a whole. Therefore the political upheaval represented a belated attempt to contain and express the feelings that flowed from growing Chinese participation in the global village.[44] This participation aggravated a collective inferiority complex related to China's relative lack of power as well as wealth. Typically, Chinese leaders assert superiority when they wish to conceal their Third World standards from First World countries.

The concept of a "third world" was coined during the cold war by the French sociologist Alfred Sauvy. He utilized, of course, the French experience:

> For this Third World, ignored and exploited and despised exactly as the Third Estate was before the Revolution, would also like to become something.[45]

"Third worldness" quickly became an ideological weapon in the hands of Asians and Africans jostling for position. For them "something" meant more than independence. It signified political and military prowess. Whatever they had or didn't have materially, they could identify with the ability to wage war or soar into space. The implicit premise was that a mighty fatherland took precedence over an ample motherland. In other words, phallic strivings overcame empty tummies, which led agricultural economies to turn to steel mills and socialist countries to erect missiles but neglect wheat.

The rush for bigness makes pride the national phallus and policy the passion to cut others down to size. One United Nations delegate has noted:

> There is a kind of Freudian element in this, an anger on the part of the newly independent countries at the old colonial father.[46]

These angers are both Oedipal and Laial in underlying intent, as can be seen in the emotionally charged interplay between the United States and Castro's Cuba or post-Somoza Nicaragua. Here an older superpower overreacts because of a threatened curse (chaotic upheaval), while a revolutionary regime tries to cripple a giant and take over his wealth (prenationalized facilities).[47] The result is a nightmare that does not create, but greatly exaggerates, preexistent geopolitical miseries.

Moreover, in this example the smaller combatants have skillfully managed to play on the fears of their feared persecutor by becoming clients of a rival superpower. This complicates the matrix of suspicion and hate by evoking fratricidal strife. Significantly, the Soviet Union and the United States cannot easily extricate themselves from such conflicts, even if they wanted to do so. In the first place they themselves began their national lives through revolutionary patricide. I refer to the overthrow of the governments of Czar Nicholas II (Russia) and King George III (colonial America). In consequence many of their citizens identify with emergent states, seen as successful parricides.

Second, and more important, both countries remain committed to policies of phallic supremacy. This includes imperial thrusts around the world and into space. For proof one need look no further than the huge sums the two Titans devote to enormous rockets with a high "thrust-to-weight ratio, soft lay down, and deep penetration."[48]

In America the Boeing Corporation regularly appeals to phallic pride in order to get the funding for bigger and better missiles. In one appropriation battle, Boeing engineers constructed comparative models of Russian and American missiles. They painted the American ones blue and the Russian ones red. The military took these models to congressional hearings, where they argued:

> But, Senator, how do you feel when America has these small blue missiles and Russia has these great big red missiles?[49]

The arguments were successful, but it would be wrong to suppose that the issues were simply sexual. From America's point of view the missiles confer grandeur, righteousness, and an essential superiority over other nations. A gigantic rocket program has allowed the Russians to draw similar conclusions about their system. In both countries the missiles serve a rampant nationalism.

Nationalism is *not* the expression of a loving devotion to national interests or the well-deserved respect that comes from collective accomplishments. On the contrary, it conveys fanatical patriotism: mass identification with narrow, excessive, unreasoning, boastful beliefs in the right and might of one's country over all. Nationalism is to the State what narcissism is to the individual. It is a form of national narcissism, the expression of a perverted or pathological self-absorption and pride.

Nationalism allows individuals to use the group, and groups to use the State, to paper over problems of wealth and power by grandiose schemes and gestures. An aggressive nationalism is the political equivalent of envious self-assertion. One might expect this to be particularly acute during rapid periods of tribal, religious, cultural, or technological change. And indeed, since the eighteenth century, nationalism has become an essential channel for the mass expression of malevolence.

Nationalistic preoccupations with size (bigness), shape (borders and boundaries), inner content (racial purity), and outer appearance (prestige) mirror narcissistic concerns. The attendant rivalries have often fueled open warfare, although sporting competitions increasingly channel a lot of the aggression. The Olympic games or World Cup demonstrate international quests for glory. However, sudden or unexpected losses can equally demonstrate a national brittleness that can bring a country to its knees and kindle bitter cries for revenge.[50]

In the relations among states, self-inflation and other-deflation reflect the rapacious hunger for honor, status, splendor, eminence, and supereminence. These actions also serve to deflect the murderous rage that follows national humiliations on the playing or killing fields. After World War I the French believed that Germany had willed the Great War not just to undermine her power, but to destroy her greatness.[51] In fact, France's economic and demographic decline could hardly keep pace with the bluster and braggadocio designed to conceal it. The country was awash with weird racial theories. Dr. Edgar Bérillon "discovered" that the reason Germans smelled so bad and shat so much was because their intestines were nine feet longer than those of other humans.[52] But Anglo-Saxons fared no better. The novelist François Mauriac echoed popular opinion when he wrote: "I do not understand and I do not like the English except when they are dead."[53]

Having defaced their rivals with vulgar abuse, the French returned to the attack by exalting themselves. At the Versailles peace conference, they were reluctant to permit the use of the English language.

It was not sufficiently refined, a position consistent with French views on culture or "civilization." Since coining the term in 1776, they thought they owned it and deserved to remain its official keepers. Yet in 1927 France spent less on higher education than on feeding cavalry horses.[54]

The French were not alone in using arrogant attitudes to conceal envious onslaughts. Among European peoples, fraternal put-downs remain familiar and popular, such as "Italians are thieves," "Finns carry knives," "All French are snotty," and "Germans all swagger." But these generalizations are a pale shadow of the patronizing pose of the colonial powers, especially since the eighteenth century. Armed with technological might and organizational success, they began to believe that their own social practices and values were totally superior to the "unintelligible barbarities" found elsewhere.[55] The British, for example, maintained a sense of superiority that was so dense as to be almost impenetrable. In relation to their colonial "children" in America, this precluded knowledge and promoted a fatal underestimation of the strength of "rabble" feelings.[56] Toward the end of the Revolution, during the peace negotiations, John Adams concluded:

> The pride and vanity of that nation is a disease, it is a delirium;
> it has been flattered and inflamed so long by themselves and
> others that it perverts everything.[57]

The delirium of disdain is not a European invention, or a disease, or solely a feature of a colonial mentality. In 1986 Prime Minister Yasuhiro Nakasone created a storm by asserting that Japan is far more intelligent than America because America contains large numbers of low-level "blacks, Puerto Ricans, and Mexicans." Nakasone's views were consistent with opinion polls that agreed "Japanese society is superior to others."[58]

Japanese hubris, like British imperialism and other expressions of national pride, is inner- as well as outer-directed. It aims to master social tensions by promoting mass identification with an omnipotent State. In conjunction with self-inflation, the xenophobic denigration of foreigners is a necessary element in the process of deflecting hate from the body politic to another body. In India the British defined their task, "the white man's burden," in terms of taming a "grossly ignorant population, steeped in idolatrous superstition, unenergetic, fatalistic, and indifferent to the evils of life."[59] In essence a civilian and military elite projected widespread fears about the "baser classes" onto a rich but alien culture. Meanwhile an impoverished citizenry aped authority and seized the opportunity to boost itself at others' expense. Of considerable importance, we can see in these practices some of the origins of institutionalized racism. Although not as new as modern nationalism, it serves the same purpose and is just as perverse. Many aspects of racism (whether allied with nationalist fervor or not) are both a defense against and expression of envy.

For almost a century the lowest, least-educated uncultivated Englishman thought he was superior to the highest Brahman.[60] Yet the Indians themselves had maintained a rigid caste system for over two thousand years. The light-skinned descendants of the Aryan invaders treated the darker Dasas, whom they conquered, as inferior, and products of mixed Aryan and Dasa marriages as extremely inferior. All sides discriminated against the noncaste "untouchables."[61] Similarly, ethnic pride was and remains a powerful emotional current among Muslim peoples. It is impossible to comprehend current Arab-Jewish—indeed, Arab-Western—conflicts without taking into account the enforced subservience of non-Muslim peoples, the "dhimmis," and the psychic wounds, still unhealed, that followed the abolition of dhimmi status by the late Ottoman sultans.[62]

These dhimmis included Jews, Christians, Armenians, Druses, and Copts, but not pagans, who remained roughly equivalent to untouchables. The dhimmi was a second-class citizen, tolerated but subject to Koranic poll tax and many other disadvantages. These included the requirement to wear special clothes or badges, the prohibition from bearing arms or riding horses, and inequality before the law. No matter what his accomplishments, every Muslim could feel superior to a dhimmi and could abuse him as he saw fit.[63]

For the Arab world, the end of Islamic ascendancy announced by the enfranchisement of dhimmis and rule by foreigners reversed the proper order of things, just as the discoveries of Galileo shocked a Catholic Europe. But it was only one of a series of painful religious, cultural, and political upheavals that fueled a nationalistic fury. The establishment of the state of Israel was a particular blow, for it called into question the preeminent basis of Islamic religion and honor.[64] As an Oriental writer put it:

> That a land Arabized by *jihad* should have been lost to a
> dhimmi people by the beneficiaries of the dhimmi condition

during 13 centuries is considered as a catastrophe of cosmic dimensions.[65]

The Arab response to Zionism, or a resurgent Jewish nationalism, and the challenge of Western technology was threefold, all encompassed in the personalismo and policies of the Egyptian leader Gamal Abdel Nasser.[66] Nasser fused his very being, his hopes, fears, humiliations, and hates with those of Egypt and the Egyptian people.[67] In so doing, he activated a resurgent Arab nationalism, the politics of grandeur, the rhetoric of revenge, that became known as Nasserism and blew like the sirocco throughout the Middle East.

Simultaneously Nasser encouraged a variety of economic and political reforms. But his tangible accomplishments were constantly overshadowed by a tendency to sweep aside difficulties with grandiloquence. Even mesmeric speeches, however, could not conceal the ever-increasing gap between victories declared and realities lived.[68] Gradually a national narcissism that emphasized positive glories changed into a militant nationalism that gloried in destruction and death.

On the national level, the chauvinist, jingoist face of Nasser illustrates the flip side of self-inflation.[69] As the flow of frustration and envy increased, the wish for grandeur evolved into a hatred of life and the idealization of violence. This process parallels the transformation of human hubris into destructive narcissism. The State, like the individual, can forget constructive goals and try to regain influence and prestige through terrorism abroad and despotism at home. Once slogans are facile and accomplishments languish, only renewal through war may appear possible.

Destructive nationalism culminates in the mobilization of state policy and mass action for murderous ends. It is a point where envy and narcissism converge, when the forces of hate replace the possibilities of life, and an imperfect society becomes a near perfect persecutor. An unarticulated premise may be the millennial wish by both leaders and citizens to return to a state of prebirth, the social equivalent of the nirvana principle. Such phantasies demand the cessation of feeling, although they do allow for the rebirth of goodness after the death of evil.[70]

Nasser's ululations echoed Egypt's historic theme: "Death and Resurrection, Resurrection and Death."[71] But no country has demonstrated the craving for wealth, the aggrandizement of power, the arrogance of pride concealing terrible fragility, the exultation in death, and the rebirth of a nation transformed from envier to envied as well as Germany. So I shall conclude the chapter by reviewing the progress of the German state from the nineteenth to the end of the twentieth century.

Although the German people had a long, often distinguished history, modern Germany did not become a unified country until 1871. Previously it had been divided into dozens of kingdoms, duchies, principalities, free cities, and bishoprics, and for generations there had been no national currency or industry. Kant claimed the only common characteristic of Germans was their "pedantic inclination to classify themselves in relation to other citizens according to a system of rank and prerogatives."[72] Nevertheless, German artists and intellectuals maintained a mystical longing for *das deutsche Vaterland* (the German Fatherland) and celebrated their shortcomings with rousing calls to German greatness.[73] Around 1810 Adam Müller declared "Everything that is great, everything that is thorough, everything that is enduring in European institutions is German."[74] This closely followed Johann Fichte's stirring *Addresses to the German Nation,* which proclaimed that Germans were a unique, primal people (*Urvolk*):

> To have character and to be German undoubtedly mean the same. . . . All comparisons between the German and non-German are null and void. . . . We are the chosen people. Chosen by God . . . with a moral right to fulfill our destiny by every means of cunning and force.[75]

As the century wore on Fichte's words seemed to be matched by German achievements. Europe was astounded, and increasingly alarmed, by her industrial development, technological resourcefulness, and artistic fecundity, besides her political progress under the Iron Chancellor.[76] Yet Germany did not get the respect she thought was her due, especially from France, who continued to patronize her as a barbarian upstart. Germany responded to her neighbor's envy and her own uncertainties with a mixture of overconfidence and arrogance, sentimentality and ignorance.[77] Many politicians throughout the German-speaking world stressed that mankind was divided into Aryans and apemen, and the French were among the latter. Interestingly, this view was later repeated by Adolf Hitler in *Mein Kampf.* He lumped the French with the Jews and blamed both for being "obsessed with negroid ideas . . . and world domination."[78]

By the turn of the century Germany sported a blatant if not-so-innocent sense of national superiority that did not endear her to the rest of Europe.[79] The ensuing Great War has been termed the war of Ottoman succession, the war of Austro-Hungarian succession, and the war against German domination. It could even be termed the war of sibling rivalry inasmuch as many of the contending royals were direct descendants of Queen Victoria, and bitter rivals.[80] In truth it was all of these, but more. The war was the first great clash of regional nationalisms, a world civil war that waxed hot and cold until 1945 and probably is still going on. All the participants believed that self-righteous pride gave them the right to pursue grandiose ambitions, none more so than Germany. Her unexpected defeat was more than a humiliation. It was a narcissistic disaster for a country that perceived its *volk* as *übermenschen* long before the Nazis came to power.[81] The national loss of self-esteem was compounded by her refusal to face facts, specifically the negative and positive features of the peace settlement known as the Treaty of Versailles. The treaty was dismissed derisively as the Diktat of Versailles, the Treaty of Shame, or the Treaty of Treason, and many of the terms were indeed punitive and vindictive. The Germans were unfairly blamed for everything that had happened and made to pay crushing reparations, most infuriatingly to her boastful neighbors.[82] Nonetheless, Versailles allowed Germany to retain the essential gains she had made under Bismarck. Had she accepted the terms, it is likely that a resurgent Germany would have become the dominant force in Europe within a generation.[83] Instead she set about to undermine the treaty, which led to the chaotic inflation of the 1920s, a further blow to the national will, and the racist refusal to allow Germans to live under Slav rule. A Slav Silesia caused the most grief, for it went "against nature" and crushed previously unchallenged conceits.[84]

In the years that followed, Germany—that is, her people and institutions—crescendoed hostilities that were more than reactions to political or economic events. They reflected a "destiny" seeped in the songs of Wotan and Siegfried and a propensity for vengeance that covered hundreds of years.[85] In 1808, for example, the dramatist Heinrich von Kleist wrote *Michael Kohlhaas,* one of the greatest renditions of the revenge motif in world literature.[86] The story describes damaged pride and its aftermath, insatiable aggression, of a kind that flowed through schoolchildren both before and after Versailles.

We'll redden the iron with blood
With hangman's blood
With Frenchmen's blood
Oh sweet day of Revenge![87]

When all this coincided with endless envy, outwardly at the Allied powers and inwardly at Jews, socialists, and other non-Aryans who appeared to do well (during economic chaos) by "sucking the life-blood of the German soul," the result was a Fury just waiting to be unleashed. I refer to an extremity of rage that fueled the transformation of a pompous Teutonic narcissism into a world-destroying, vengeful nationalism.

Germany embodied the lust for revenge and exultation in war in the person of Adolf Hitler, a man who began his career at the behest of the German General Staff. He was one of a number of demagogues employed to spread militant nationalism among the masses. Joseph Goebbels likened him to a kind child and a clever cat, but especially to a roaring lion, "great and gigantic."[88] And, after a single visit, the British statesman David Lloyd George called him the "George Washington of Germany":

> The old trust him; the young idolize him. It is not admiration accorded to a popular Leader. It is the worship of a national hero who has saved his country from utter despondency and degradation. . . . Hitler reigns over the heart and mind of Germany.[89]

This was a heart and mind that effectively engaged its wish to be led with Hitler's wish to lead (*führerprinzip*). Germans from all walks of life made him the *volksgeist,* the mystical link between *volk* and state who would dominate Germany as Germany intended to dominate the world.[90] Toward these ends, Hitler was the beneficiary of "an enormous, destructive tidal wave in the ebb and flow of the generations" released after the shame and hunger of the war years and disorder of the 1920s. The young flocked to the Youth Cohort, while many older citizens joined the Free Corps (Freikorps), the greatest single source of Nazi personnel and spirit.[91] Hitler, in turn, supplied abundant hatred. According to various observers, that was his main energy. A Swiss diplomat noted that he had never met a man "capable of generating so terrific a condensation of envy, vituperation, and malice."[92]

This energy nourished Hitler's passion for bigness, his insatiable ambition to become the source of all things and wield the mightiest sword, essentially oral and phallic greed and envy.[93] He was convinced that Germany needed to conquer and control vast areas of Eastern Europe in order to provide *lebensraum,* or living space. Hitler envisioned vast territories connected by canals and autobahns stretching to the Crimea ("our Riviera") and the Caucasus.[94] The Ukraine, in particular, was to become the German breadbasket, a feeding ground, a complementary motherland devoid of Jews and other "unclean" peoples.[95] This obsession with *lebensraum* was not new. For decades the government had stressed that the Ukraine was to Germany what Africa was to England. But Hitler gave *lebensraum* a personal, deadly significance because he associated the push toward the east with his own maternal traumas.[96]

Hitler's mother, Klara, had three children, all of whom died in quick succession before Adolf was born. Therefore, as an infant he was overindulged as well as suffused with his mother's constant worries "lest she lose him."[97] The ensuing symbiotic relation between mother and child was severely tested by the birth of two more children (one of whom died), her widowhood, and his mother's final illness from breast cancer during his late teens. Adolf nursed her day and night, while she was attended by a Jewish doctor named Bloch, who undertook an expensive, toxic treatment with iodoform, a liquid spray that burned through the skin like mustard gas. Ostensibly Hitler concurred with the treatment. Deep down he developed a burning hatred for "the Jew" who had killed his mother and then all Jews: "the Jewish cancer, the Jewish poison, the Jewish profiteer." This simmered until he himself was overcome by mustard gas in 1918.[98] After a diagnosed hysterical breakdown, he emerged from a two-day trance determined to restore Germany ("the motherland") and avenge her defeat ("his mother's death") by killing the Jews ("his mother's killer" and "blood poisoner" of the entire German nation).[99]

Hitler did not begin with genocide. His first open impulses were a land grab in the east and racial purification at home. The land grab only turned into a "Jew-kill" after he realized that the war against Russia was lost. This dashed his hopes for an endless supply of food (a reunion with Klara!) as well as his overweening pride in an army of "magnificent blond beasts, roaming wantonly in search of prey and victory." These were the *Übermenschen* or Supermen who would create a New Order that would dominate Europe with their tanks and rockets, but especially their iron will.[100]

The *Übermenschen,* of course, embodied Hitler's own omnipotence, an omnipotence that protected him from an awareness of weakness and, more significantly, from a sense of guilt about his own evil impulses toward his mother and father and his mother- and fatherland. Up to this point he had successfully projected these deviltries, felt concretely as an excremental mass, onto the Jews, the Slavs, and other "vermin." Once this strategy no longer worked, or his favored dumping grounds no longer existed, he was left with a body of malice he could not accept. So he embraced the one state he really loved, a state of death.

Similarly for Germany, the defeat in the east was more than a defeat. It destroyed a military machine and tradition that was, for Germany, its manhood, its "marching forest," its symbol of potency and respect. People lost a sense of grandeur and community, a feeling of authority and uprightness that had previously filled their hearts with "a deep and mysterious delight" and rationalized an absolute assurance of racial, cultural, and political superiority.[101] Once this was lost all they had left was a sense of dread, an awareness of fragility, and, like Hitler, a wish for death.[102]

The idealization of death has been a recurrent theme in German history. Throughout the Nazi era, it flew on the wings of Hitler's pronouncements and National Socialist policies. As a result Thanatos came to life through the agency of the State. But the destructive nationalism of Nazi Germany also represented the millennial wish for a last battle, an Armageddon, whereby torrential violence would bring salvation. In this regard the Germans have succeeded beyond the wildest dreams of Versailles. Helped by the competing nationalisms of the new superpowers, they rebuilt two strong countries that have become model members of the United Nations. Ironically, German politicians now expend considerable effort warding off attacks by less prosperous and powerful peoples. Former Chancellor Helmut Schmidt gave the reason for this state of affairs. He blamed envy for the continued and, as he believed, unjustified criticisms of the Federal Republic:

> If the Germans were economically weak, and the destiny of the German worker like the average European levels, and if inflation and unemployment were as high as in Italy or Britain; many critics would cease to be so interested in the Germans.[103]

Herr Schmidt added that Germany had become a substitute for others' "internal enemies." What a twist of fate for the heir to a government that had previously laid its inner problems on the rest of the world. Fortunately the German experience demonstrates that a country whose citizens enjoy "the blessing of a late birth," and are not ground down by hate or hunger, no longer need rely on the politics of pride or a mania for vengeance in order to enjoy their own nationhood as well as a secure place among the human race.[104]

12

The Resolution of Malice

Envy, greed, and jealousy are the negative constituents of character and culture. They are the dark forces, the basic relations of the *yetzah harah*, what the kabbala calls the "evil impulse." Frequently represented as the guile of the viper, the crunch of the shark, or the sting of the jellyfish, these impulses can exert a bitter tyranny over perception and feeling, indeed, over all areas of human endeavor.

In the first chapters I showed how they afflict the eye, really the "I," a process that leads to obsessive comparisons, an oppressive hyperawareness of the qualities, traits, capacities, accomplishments, and relationships of others. In response, envious tensions both create and replace inner emptinesses and arouse hostilities that, when projected, turn the outer world into a threatening hell replete with imagined as well as actual persecutors.

Malice tyrannizes the inner world by taking up too much of it. Greed feeds envy, envy breeds jealousy, and jealousy reflects self-hate. On an individual level this leads to extremely destructive relations between or within generations—parents versus children and siblings versus siblings. In the latter chapters I have traced the same patterns, self-inflation and other-deflation, direct or narcissistic aggressions, to the interplay between citizens and society. Ultimately these impulses, seemingly far removed from individual intention, emerge on the international scene in the form of combative nationalisms.

However, in exploring these issues it is important to recognize that the tragedy of human existence cannot always be explained by nor simply reduced to envy, greed, or jealousy. They only comprise one part of an emotional lattice that also includes the life-essential elements of love: gratitude, generosity, and compassion. The positive and negative components of this lattice are in a constant dynamic relationship with each other. Problems arise when the relative balance of love and hate shifts so that hate predominates. This occurs both when benevolence weakens or malevolence strengthens.

Guilt especially weakens benevolence. It is very hard for a person to maintain good feelings yet simultaneously suffer mental agony for damaging the object of these feelings. The paradox is that the intensity of guilt is directly related to the degree of positive concern in the first place. The net effect may be a determined attempt to diminish the torment, first by the denial of affection and second via the vehement condemnation not of oneself for greed or resentment, but of others for seeming to provoke it.

The writer Arthur Koestler has described why he became a communist and egalitarian.[1] He could not stand feeling privileged at a time of family crisis. Apparently his father was an inventor whose plans were always going wrong:

> I suffered a pang of guilt whenever they bought me books or toys. This continued later on, when every suit I bought for myself meant so much less to send home. Simultaneously, I developed a strong dislike of the obviously rich; not because they could afford to buy things (envy plays a much smaller part in social conflict than is generally assumed), but because they were able to do so without a guilty conscience. Thus I projected a personal predicament onto the structure of society at large.[2]

Koestler denied hating the rich because they are rich, although his wish to emulate them, even to a small degree, obviously stirred up a lot of tension in himself. It may be difficult to distinguish between a hatred aroused by guilt and a hatred aroused by envy. However afflicted, people aim to discharge the resulting turmoil by eradicating outside sources. Often a vicious spiral ensues whereby envy provokes guilt and guilt evokes envy. In this instance Koestler loathed "the rich" for their guilt-free enjoyment of life. One suspects that beneath his anguish there existed a hint of envy and more than a hint of greed. As for the idea that "the rich" do not suffer guilt, we can assume that that is a projection of Koestler's imagination.[3] Others have blamed "the poor" for identical reasons.

Koestler admitted that he evacuated his "personal predicament" onto the political landscape. For similar reasons the politics of envy tends to merge with the politics of guilt, a process clearly observable during the 1987 British general election. The campaign was portrayed by the press as "Labour's moral crusade vs. Tory consumer power." According to *The Sunday Times,* Labour sought to brand Thatcherism as the "politics of self-interest" and promote itself as "the party of standards, fairness and decency."[4] Squeezing the rich was a concurrent theme so that everyone could have the "freedom to enjoy a fair share of national resources."[5]

Giving everyone a fair share by equalizing income represents the egalitarian answer to the existence of malice and the predicament of evil. But there do exist alternate ways to curb the *yetzah harah* and relieve human suffering. Altogether the proposed solutions encompass three basic strategies: 1) annihilate malice; 2) ignore malice; or 3) overcome the life-subverting elements of malice by enhancing life-sustaining feelings.

The first category concerns egalitarianism, or the attempt to get rid of ill will and bad conscience by deriding desire and destroying the objects of such desire, not only money and goods, but intangible qualities and unique experiences as well.[6] Examples abound of privileged peoples who have tried to assuage their own discomfort by minimizing the wealth or opportunities of others. Typically, an American doctoral candidate seriously advocated a ministry of culture in order to assure his fellow citizens had "equal sensory experiences of aesthetic objects."[7] For him cultural engineering was the means to overcome an "oppressive class background"—that is, a wealthy family and distinctive education. He believed that when everyone saw the same, then he could shed the shame and guilt of being special.

This relates to the difficulty in discussing egalitarianism. It is a highly charged issue, all the more so because it has been invested with utopian hopes for absolute fairness and justice since ancient times. Those who criticize the theory or practice, or point out its destructive roots, are liable to be dismissed as right wing or fascist. Conversely, it is hard to demonstrate the positive side of egalitarianism or advocate it without being labeled socialist, communist, or ultraleftist. In fact, economic leveling comprised an integral part of National Socialist policy, and a tyrannical elitism was a major feature of the egalitarian regimes of Chairman Mao and the Cambodian dictator Pol Pot.

The function of egalitarianism has to be seen within a particular social context. During times of famine or some other kind of collective threat, equal distribution of scarce resources is a great advantage. In these circumstances the egalitarian ideal reflects a generosity of spirit and may be essential for group survival.

Nevertheless during most other occasions, the tenacious demand for total social, economic, and political equality is a chimera. In fact, it is worse than a chimera because egalitarian actions secretly serve to arouse and express the very resentments they are supposed to suppress. Many observers have noted that these policies create social tensions that are diverse and dangerous. Groups founded on egalitarian ideals, such as the Israeli kibbutzim, have been able to survive only by departing from these ideals.[8] Otherwise the equal allocation of food, shelter, clothing, or other opportunities has to be maintained by force, as in Russia, China, or Cuba.[9]

Where egalitarianism is the aim, social leveling provides the means. Leveling is the process of reducing wealth, power, knowledge, qualities, even sensations to a lower common denominator. Whether enforced by public humiliation, legal sanction, or physical brutality, an active leveling trivializes standards and corrupts and spoils what is good in the name of equality.

I have already described the effects of leveling on the English educational system.[10] Deputy Foreign Minister Anatoli Adamischin has confirmed a similar deadening impact in the Soviet Union:

> Levelling takes away all creativity. People just don't work if they are just going to end up on the same level as everyone else.[11]

As for the United States, journalist William Manchester believes that Vietnam and Watergate afflicted Americans with the wish to level on all levels.[12] He sees this process at work in excessive informality, the aggressive use of nicknames, unisex clothes, and the vanishing bijous of excellence:

> In short, we are expected to look down on those above us, and up to those beneath us. Since superiority is in itself suspect, everyone tries to look like, talk like, and *be* like everyone else. . . .

Doubtless this comforts those in whose breasts lurk the gnawing (and usually justified) hunch that they really are inferior.[13]

Leveling appears to reduce differences. The underlying assumption is that if everyone were equal, then no one would have anything to be envious about. But the reality is more complicated. Envy begins in the eye of the envier, not with the envied object. Even if we all looked alike, spoke alike, ate alike, and dressed alike, we could still imagine that the neighbor next door enjoyed his porridge better or, for that matter, had a better time in bed. Paradoxically, attempts to breed conformity yield hostility. People may seek solidarity during times of stress, but their hearts lie with distinction, not similarity.

The motto of the French Revolution—*"Liberté, égalité, fraternité"*—highlights the difficulties in reconciling social ideals with concrete truths. Egalitarian policies do not promote social fraternity. Quite the opposite, they invite invidious comparisons and social sclerosis. Individually this depresses talent, achievement, and, ultimately, equity—equality of opportunity. During China's cultural revolution, rampant leveling led to the absurd situation whereby citizens were not allowed to say what professional or business position they occupied. They could only be introduced as "a responsible person of a department concerned" without any inkling of what exactly they did.[14]

Internationally, the development economist Peter Bauer has argued convincingly that "the unholy grail of economic equality" is a form of sop behavior that is more likely to depress living standards, at home and abroad, than enhance them.[15] Moreover, Bauer points out that there exist irreparable conflicts between the pursuit of equality and the pursuit of liberty. Neither people nor countries willingly submit to the redistribution of wealth in the name of fairness. And as Stalin demonstrated in the 1920s, collectivism is often a ruse for despotic sharing.[16]

Except in rare instances of noncoercive agreement, it appears that the equalization of resources always coincides with an inequality of power. In financial terms a decrease in wage differentials means an increase in power differentials.[17] Inevitably there arise leaders, elites, parties, or states who force similitude on others, like the mythical Procrustes or contemporary Big Brothers.[18]

Procrustean politics are essentially paternalistic. An egalitarian leadership does not believe that citizens are naturally endowed for "life, liberty, and the pursuit of happiness." Freedom or liberty consists solely of economic security, that is, the right to be well clothed, housed, and well fed. This implies that life is a gift from the government, a gift that can be given or taken away depending on whether the citizenry fits in (has the right race or class background) and behaves (attends party functions) or not.[19]

Ultimately egalitarianism leads to the idealization of the State. The contradiction is that when people try to solve the problems of life by imbuing the State or party or collective with omnipotent maternal (and paternal) powers, their greed and envy tend to turn toward these entities, too. Then the State has to use its powers not just to coerce equality, but to prevent its free, albeit dependent, citizens from attacking it. Such threats evoke a seductive, rejecting attitude, like that of a narcissistic parent who directs his rage both inside and outside the family. In other words, I am describing a mechanism by which the omnipotent nationalism of both communist and fascist (national socialist) countries can turn from pride to destruction, from wanting to be the source of all life to actually becoming the agent of incessant death.

All this appears to be a far cry from the egalitarian millennialism of the early Christians, who responded to misery by elevating the lowly and idealizing the afterlife.[20] Meanwhile pagan philosophers tried to solve the problem of envy by retiring to a world where only a philosophical elite mattered.[21] Iambulus postulated one of the first political utopias, an island off the coast of Arabia where all men were equal. The highest values were given to unity and harmony. Jealousy, pride, and civil strife could not occur because marriage was not allowed. Men shared the common possession of women and children, and there was enough food for everyone. The lifespan was 150 years, after which the men were obliged to kill themselves.[22]

Earlier, in the *Politics,* Aristotle had discussed the ideas of Phaleas, a Chalcedonian thinker who proposed equalizing the property of all citizens. Aristotle himself did not believe that the leveling of wealth would end theft. But he thought it might help to eliminate minor crime and prevent civil disturbance. Otherwise he wrote that human nature suffered the defect of never being satisfied. One's wants just get bigger and bigger.[23]

The egalitarian tradition continued throughout the Middle Ages, an inheritance from Greek and Roman notions of the "state of Nature" whereby all men were equal in status and wealth and had the right to share possessions, even wives.[24] These beliefs, combined with the exhortations of Christian and political dissenters, nourished the English Peasants' Revolt of 1381 and the Anabaptists, Taborites, and

Ranters, among a host of radical groups.[25] For them liberation concurred with the Last Judgment—a day of vengeance of the poor as well as a time of final but equal sharing of God's gifts.[26]

Related themes have suffused the repeated refrains of insurrectionists ranging from fifteenth-century Czech anarcho-communists to contemporary students who quote the pan-destructionist hopes of Mikhail Bakunin and the utopian dreams of Leo Tolstoy.[27] All his life the count searched for a little green stick buried by the road at the edge of a ravine in the Zakaz Forest. It was a very special stick,

> whereupon was written the message which could destroy all evil in men and give them universal welfare.[28]

Tolstoy intended that his millennial message would free men from chaos, disorder, license, waste, arbitrariness, and uncertainty and presage an era of health and happiness. Yet he, and others who preach impossible ends while denying inherent hatreds, have made the opposite reaction more likely. Ideal goals lead to endless frustration and exaggerate the hostilities that are no longer supposed to be present, all under the guise of creating "a new heaven and a new earth."[29]

The concept of luck provides an altogether different means of minimizing malice. It seeks not to deny envy, but to ignore it. Luck is the benign leveler. It removes the personal responsibility that contributes to feelings of inferiority and envy. With good luck or bad, whatever has happened appears to be outside human control.[30]

Luck is a superbly efficient social-sanctioned device to rationalize inadequacy, incompetence, poor judgment, and, in general, dissimilar skills, traits, or resources. By giving the illusion of absolute equality, luck allows the envier to carry on without suffering a loss of status or becoming overwhelmed by hatred. Conversely, by claiming luck, a person can accept success without having to dread others' reactions. No doubt this explains the perennial popularity of games of chance as well as the immediate propensity to refer to luck when faced with good fortune.

There is a well-authenticated story about a gang of men repairing a road on the outskirts of London. They were forced to scatter by the loud hooting of an approaching Rolls-Royce. When the chauffeur-driven car drew close, one of the laborers spat at it, a second threw a stone, and a third shouted an obscenity. But as the car passed, its sole passenger wound down a window, put out his head, and yelled:

You stupid gits—it's me, Charlie. How d'you think I got this lot then? Won it on the pools, didn't I?[31]

Upon hearing this, all three men dropped their shovels, raised their arms, and began to cheer. Their rancor vanished as soon as they realized that Charlie had obtained the Rolls by chance rather than by acquired privilege or inherited wealth. In fact, they were pleased, for they assumed that if Lady Luck could smile on him, she could smile on them, too.

The large number of common expressions involving good luck, bad luck, states of luck, or wishes about luck demonstrate the importance of the concept of luck or chance or fate in normal social intercourse. Hence "in luck" and "luck out" convey good fortune, while "out of luck" and "down on one's luck" assert the opposite, misfortune. Concurrently, "to try one's luck" means to do something without being sure of the outcome, and "to push one's luck" implies the same but with an added element of extra, perhaps unnecessary, risk.

The English language has an ample vocabulary of words and expressions that signify a state of being or mind that is independent of individual effort or intervention. English-speaking peoples, just by using this vocabulary, are able to diminish the impact of actual or anticipated envy in human relations. Other peoples are not so fortunate. The Germans, for example, have only one word, *glück,* to indicate both happiness and luck. Consequently it is easier for an American or Englishman to avoid being hated for the happiness that comes from a "lucky win" than a German whose "glücky" contentment might equally stem from hard work and enviable talent.[32]

Societies that have no words—indeed, no concept—of luck, fate, or "the blind goddess Fortune" lack social softeners. Their members feel extremely vulnerable to envy and black magic and remain obsessed with counteracting the evil eye. I have previously mentioned the Navaho Indians, a tribe frequently idealized by young people because of its egalitarian practices. For them the absence of luck inhibits achievement because the Navaho believe that fellow Indians can prosper only at each other's expense. In consequence their cultural norms must emphasize sharing in order to avoid continual bloodshed.

Similarly, the Siriono of Bolivia rarely eat the animals they kill, while various Polynesian islanders always refuse the fish they catch. As with the Navaho, the persistent presence of hostile eyes never allows the hunters to have "a lucky shot" or the fishermen to "hit the jackpot" with their spears. Comparable cultures that lack a lucky strategy of envy avoidance remain vulnerable to the demands of the zero sum game and the constraints imposed by envy.[33]

The third means of dealing with malice is radically different. It does not try to depose the negative side of existence, as with egalitarianism or luck, but seeks to enhance positive feelings. This redresses the emotional balance between omnipotent destructive forces and life-sustaining ones and makes it possible to accept the central role that envy, greed, and jealousy play in human affairs.

However, before proceeding it is important to note that even pernicious impulses can and do have salutary psychic and social effects. Envious tension, for example, generates anxiety and contributes to an emotional tonus that is a necessary stimulus to action. The physical equivalents are ongoing states of muscular and sensory stimulation. Without a state of ambient tension people would be so relaxed they could not breathe. And it is well known that children born without the capacity to feel pain lie in mortal danger.

Almost 2,500 years ago Aristophanes dramatized the dilemma of too much versus too little envy in his play called *Wealth*.[34] The plot was simple. The ruler of Olympus, Zeus, had become envious of the god Wealth. So he blinded him. In consequence wealth and virtue became unevenly distributed. Some people got a lot, while others got none at all. But later, as part of a utopian solution, Wealth regained his sight. Still there were problems:

> If Wealth were to see again and to share himself out equally,
> no one of men would bother with any craft or skill.[35]

In other words, a modicum of envy is an essential impetus for change. If everyone had as much as they needed and wanted, there would be little incentive to do anything. People would live in a state of bliss perhaps akin to a heroin high. Concomitantly, envy and jealousy help to avoid regimentation and excite diversity. Without the wish to shift these tensions, our social structures might remain rigid and static.[36]

It is noteworthy that envy can thwart innovation or stimulate it. Equally, envy may provoke the abuse of power or help to tame it. As we have seen in chapter 9, the yellow press and assorted hordes of gossip mongers, muckrakers, and muckraking politicians all serve as part of a complicated system of checks and balances. They make it difficult for one group or institution to gain power at the expense of others. In a free society, envy allows people to exercise mutual and spontaneous supervision over each other. If there were no envy or if societal persecutors—that is, political dictators or institutional tyrants—overwhelmed its free expression, then the tentative exploration of the thresholds of social tolerance could not occur. Thus we are faced with the paradox that man's success as a creative, social being depends on his capacity to constrain his malevolence, yet the same propensities set the tone for his social life. Helmut Schoeck has summarized the issue neatly:

> We are thus confronted by an antinomy, an irreconcilable contradiction: envy is an extremely anti-social and destructive emotional state, but it is, at the same time, the most completely socially oriented. And without universal consideration of at least a potential or imaginary envy in others, there could not be the automatic social controls upon which all association is based.[37]

The capacity to cope with this contradiction depends on the degree of malignity and the extent to which love is able to modify the overall emotional matrix. Thus Geoffrey Chaucer, having asserted in "The Parson's Tale" that "envy is the worst sin that is," also reminded us:

> The remedy for Envy is to love God, your neighbor, and your enemy.[38]

Interestingly, Wilfred Bion points out that the love of a parent or child toward each other may not be noticed because envy, rivalry, and hate obscure it. But Bion insists that "hate would not exist if love were not present."[39] These views contradict Freud's dictum that hate is older than love.

The conflict between love and hate, good and evil, is one of mankind's oldest and deepest concerns. The book of Job teaches that it is impossible for inherent goodness (Job's belief in God's righteousness) to overcome the vengeful inclination (the test of outer adversity and inner aggression). Meanwhile the Greek poet Pindar declared that beneficent looks counteract destructive ones and urged people "to look harmony" on each other.[40]

In his classic study *Europe's Inner Demons*, Norman Cohn observed that the widely feared black or evil witches were often successfully opposed by beneficent or white witches. Essentially these were good spirits and protective guardians whose origins lie in a pre-

Christian, pagan worldview that has existed for thousands of years. In Sicily the spirits were known as "ladies from outside," "ladies of the home," "beautiful ladies," or simply "ladies."[41] And the Brothers Grimm immortalized these kind female figures in two tales, "Briar-Rose" and "The Sleeping Beauty."[42]

As we all know, the girl's parents, a king and queen, were overcome with joy on the birth of their daughter. They ordered a great feast and invited the wise-women of the land to give their blessings. But one, ominously called Maleficence in various versions, was left out. Subsequently she burst into the celebrations and, in a paroxysm of spite, laid a death curse on the child. However, one of the wise-women, Beneficence, was able to intervene, for she had not yet given her blessing. Although she could not entirely undo the curse, she was able to ameliorate it: "But it shall not be death the princess falls into, only a deep sleep lasting a hundred years."[43] True enough, a hundred years later a handsome prince found the princess, kissed her lips, and woke her up. So the curse was broken, and the tale confirms that in spite of evil, beneficence can prevail.[44]

The existence of black and white witches, good and bad spirits, coincides with profound perceptions that most mothers have good and bad moments. They may be loving and loved, but hunger, discomfort, or actual mistreatment can quickly change them into someone hateful and hated. Folktales such as "Briar-Rose" describe collective fears of starvation and death at the breasts of unsatisfying, malicious, self-centered women. Conversely, happy outcomes convey collective hopes that the spirit of the loving mother will rule, even if she is not always immediately present. It was in this vein that Melanie Klein commented:

> In the last analysis the image of the loved parents is preserved in the unconscious mind as the most precious possession, for it guards its possessor against the pain of utter desolation.[45]

Notice that Klein refers to "parents," not just mothers. In doing so, she emphasizes the importance of a good relationship with the father. He too must be loving and loved in order to guard against desolation, a word that means more than hunger and loss. It refers to a sense of utter ruin that follows when destructive impulses, inherent or reactive, get out of control and there does not appear to be sufficient love or goodwill about to redress the subsequent damage. Otherwise, truly murderous and quite tender feelings can coexist in the same person and same family to a remarkable degree. Much depends on the preserved image of the good parent and reciprocated love that is then available to overcome ill will.[46]

An exchange between myself and a patient, an artist, well illustrates the capacity to dissolve malice. This person had been enjoying a particularly good period of work. After being told that I would have to change the time of a session and miss another, he came to our next meeting in a very angry mood, bitterly complaining that his creativity had left him. Moreover, a woman who reminded him of his former wife had begun to pursue him. From many previous discussions I knew that any such woman represented his own jealous, hysterical self. So I replied that he was being chased by his own furious feelings toward me for changing a session, stealing his creativity, and leaving him adrift, excluded, and unwanted. The man concurred, and his mood lifted. He began to talk about his sister, who had just written to him from far away. He realized how much he liked her. Again I related his thoughts to myself. It was clear that when I helped him to understand his bad temper, he realized how much he liked and valued me, both for myself and as a reminder of his own "good parents."

Then he suddenly sat up and exclaimed:

> I see horrible little things, they seem to be melting, dissolving away in some warm medium, a pleasant, warm medium. They are scrunched up, little bits with little faces on them, evil little imps. They remind me of mosquito larvae in a barrel of rainwater.[47]

As he was talking the combination of melting imps and mosquito larvae evoked images in my mind of primitive bloodsucking creatures turning friendly. I told him I thought the warm, pleasant fluid represented the power of his warmth and affection to melt and transform his envious stings, greedy bites, and jealous fears, everything that had been aroused by the sudden separation and attendant assumption that I was away enjoying myself at his expense. He smiled and replied:

> Yes, it's true. But you know, they don't disappear. They just become smaller, and much less menacing. I shall try to put them into my work.[48]

On the following day the man was unusually relaxed and confident. He said a great burst of energy had been released and he felt wonderful. Instead of holding back out of fear, he had been able to put the creatures' potential to good use. Once they had dissolved in the warm water, his negativity did likewise, and he had been able to maintain a positive frame of mind and feel closer to me.[49]

The basic ingredients of the warm medium were gratitude, generosity, and loving consideration or empathetic compassion. Gratitude has to do with the appreciation of goodness in others, and oneself, and is the antithesis of envy. It is closely linked with early gratifying experiences at the breast and subsequent satisfying relations with relatives and friends.[50]

The pleasures that gratifications provide lead directly to the esteem that gratitude conveys. In fact, the intimate bonds between these two life-sustaining experiences reach right down to their etymological roots. In English both terms stem from the Latin *gratus*, meaning "pleasing." *Gratus*, in turn, supports the concept of grace, an inner state of goodwill, charm, decency, and favor, which averts the evil eye.

In Greek mythology the three sister goddesses known as the Graces were celebrated for filling life with brilliance, joy, and vigor, that is, for making life worthwhile.[51] Interestingly, the Greek word *charites* also denotes these deities as well as feelings of gratitude.[52]

Perhaps the absence of gratitude best highlights the fundamental importance of gratitude for humane relations. The great Athenian orator Demosthenes observed that it is a disaster for the entire state if envy is stronger than gratitude for services rendered:

> Envy is a disease, whereas gratitude has a place among the Gods.[53]

Contemporary critics are no less scathing when confronting the presence of ingratitude, the converse of thankful appreciation and the emotional equivalent of envy. The American clergyman W. C. Bennett once noted:

> Blessed is he who expects no gratitude, for he shall not be disappointed.[54]

No doubt this cynicism reflects the attitude in certain business circles, where thank-you notes after a dinner party are only considered appropriate for people "who cannot deal with being imperious."[55] But the absence of gratitude does not always rest lightly. In America a man came close to winning a lawsuit against his girlfriend because she did not make love with him after he had taken her out to dinner fifty times. A simple "thank-you" (or less ambiguous "no, thank you") might have spared her heavy legal expenses.[56]

Generosity reflects the spirit of gratitude. The grateful person is able to take in and assimilate everything from good feelings to good thoughts, aside from tangible items like food or books. This means he or she can build up an inner storehouse of enriching experiences, all of which helps to counter greed and transform the world into a much more friendly, giving, stimulating place. The drama of a woman who was taken to dinner fifty times and who still did not respond with kindness shows what can happen when generosity sustained by a firm sense of self-worth is missing. Here, both parties were insatiable. No amount of food or money or possible titillations could fill their inner emptinesses or surmount pervasive feelings of inferiority and the craving for revenge.[57]

The third element of love, empathetic compassion, has to do with the capacity to see other persons in their own right, not as extensions of oneself. It allows one to sympathetically consider what others are doing without jealously assuming that the outcome of their acting in their own interests will be a catastrophe for oneself. These three elements comprised the warm medium that allowed my patient to dissipate his venom and transform energies that had been locked up as hatred into great bursts of creative affection. His gratitude flowed from understanding. The understanding released a generous flow of good feelings. And both his gratitude and generosity allowed him to accept that I had needs unrelated to him, that I had to change the schedule for my sake, not to hurt him specifically or attack our relationship.

The acceptance of reality is itself an essential first step in the process of healing, or reparation, which enables people to sustain generosity and gratitude. Bertrand Russell wrote in *The Conquest of Happiness:*

> Merely to realize the causes of one's own envious feelings is to take a long step towards curing them.[58]

This cure involves a decrease in guilt, in shame, in fear, and in general a decrease in destructive aims and impulses. Therefore, an open acceptance brings malice down to earth. Envy, greed, and jealousy no longer seem so powerful or impossible to counter.[59] Moreover, the realization of hate also involves the liberation of love. Both sides, love and hate, tend to be buried and retrieved together.[60] When retrieved, love can become a helper, an emotional ally, whether to assess damage done (that is, to face reality) or to withstand painful feelings of remorse. Without such love, or powerful positive impetuses, we would all remain stuck, like the king's soldiers and king's men who couldn't put Humpty Dumpty back together again.

The second step in the reparative process is restoration—literally, re-pairation, a re-pairing, a bringing together of broken bits. In order to abjure ill will, it is not sufficient to acknowledge the injured object. Whether animate or inanimate, a person or a relationship, one has to take whatever action may be necessary to repair, restore, renew, re-create, and redeem it. It appears that no amount of damage cannot be repaired. Even if the original object has been smashed to smithereens or killed, the reparative process can go on. Thus another patient of mine, a farmer, devoted himself to caring for a sick cow. He stayed up all night with the animal, fed her special food, turned her from side to side, and even sang to her. Yet the cow was not the issue. He had always been good to her. In his mind the cow stood for his dead mother, a woman whom he had neglected and somehow had to restore. Since he couldn't help her directly, he chose a cow, but with the full knowledge of the link between the two givers of milk. He was also a painter. So he tried to re-create his mother, symbolically, through his work. This too helped. Eventually he managed to reestablish her, and a loving relationship with her, in his dreams. Only then, after all these efforts on many levels, did he manage to get some peace of mind.

This man had been pursued by self-hatred through forty years of vicious rumination. But he not only hated himself, he loathed the world and was sure the world loathed him. The same sequence can affect an entire people. In the last chapter I discussed the Germans' views of Jews, views that culminated in the Holocaust. Like my patient, the Germans had previously denied responsibility for their actions and saw themselves as the aggrieved party, threatened by hostile forces from within and without. However, this attitude changed after the Second World War. Under the leadership of Konrad Adenauer, the Federal Republic (West Germany) faced up to what it had done and decided to make reparations both to individual Jews and to Israel, as representative of millions of murdered Jews.[61] By 1987 about $25 billion had been paid out, and it is likely that this figure will increase to over $30 billion by the end of the century.[62] Although these monies hardly compensate for the stupendous loss of life, they do represent a genuine desire to come to terms with the crimes of the Nazi era and have brought about a remarkable restoration of relations between the Federal Republic and the Jewish state.[63]

As we can see from these examples, reparation affects not only the damaged object, but the subject as well. It brings together warring factions and restores the balance between love and hate. In other words, it effects a process of at-one-ment. Like Oedipus at Colonus, the damager no longer need feel that he "violates the ground from whence he came."

The healing or reintegration takes place on three levels. First, the injured person or thing revives. And once it has been put back together, it ceases to be a victim and a victimizer—that is, someone or something that has been tyrannized by malice and, as a result, has itself become a tyrannizer, a new source of guilt and hatred. At the same time, reparation relieves the evildoer, whether a single person or an entire nation, of negative tensions. So it no longer need restrain its energies for fear of destructive consequences. Instead they can be released for constructive purposes, while admiration and emulation take the place of resentment and withdrawal. Third, reparation transforms the relations between envier and envied, between subject and object. It enables both parties to give up entrenched fears and discover areas of common interest.

The simple acceptance of damage done accompanied by ungrudging efforts to put things right signals an increased capacity for gratitude, generosity, and compassion. These feelings, in turn, tilt the love/hate lattice toward positive ends and strengthen benevolence. By the same token, the failure of reparation has the same effect as an excess of malice. It tilts the lattice the other way, toward destructive ends and the triumph of death over life.

This whole cycle of love and hate emerged in the person of a man I knew at the Arbours Centre in London.[64] He had been severely wounded during the course of prolonged conflicts with an ostensibly loving but tyrannical family as well as his own inner demons. When his negativity predominated, he often affected a posture of psychotic withdrawal. As far as he was concerned the world was dead, and so was he, all of which terrified his parents. On the other hand, he could also be warmly playful and communicative, reparative efforts that were usually rebuffed by the very same people who were urging him to get better. Then the negativity would return with a vengeance.

Sometimes I was able to follow these emotional swings by his use of words. During up periods he would doodle incessantly, emphasizing in particular the word "evil." He liked to write and draw EVIL every which way. One day he cornered me in the kitchen and exclaimed:

You know, Joe, EVIL spelled the other way is LIVE.[65]

I had never previously thought of the reverse spelling of the word. Upon reflection, I observed that by playing with words one could turn evil to live, good to bad, not unlike the ancient gods, who could transform Furies into Eumenides, or "kindly ones." He nodded in agreement. Yes, he knew it was possible to turn bad to good, to transcend evil. That's why he doodled. It helped him to overcome terrible "urges." When EVIL returned, his rage gained the upper hand. But when LIVE appeared, his tension disappeared and the world became okay again.

Joe, that's why I write. When I can't get away from EVIL, everything feels real bad inside. But when I change it round, to LIVE, then I feel good. I have to do this, Joe, turn EVIL to LIVE, and keep it there. For me, it's a matter of life and death.[66]

Part Three

ELABORATIONS

Elaborations

Introduction

1. R. D. Laing, "The Mystification of Experience," *The Politics of Experience* (New York: Pantheon Books, 1967), 49. This chapter was originally published under the title "Violence and Love," in the *Journal of Existentialism*, vol. 5, no. 20, 1965.

2. *American Journal of Sociology* (1985–1947);
Rural Sociology, vols. 1–20 (1936–1955);
The British Journal of Sociology (1949–1959);
American Anthropologist and the Memoirs of the American Anthropological Association (1949–1958);
Southwestern Journal of Anthropology, vols. 1–20 (1945–1964).

Helmut Schoeck pointed out this remarkable gap (or should one say refusal to look envy in the eye?) in his book *Envy: A Theory of Social Behavior* (New York: Harcourt, Brace & World, 1970), 9. Reprinted by the Liberty Press, Indianapolis, Indiana, 1987.

3. Ashley Montagu, *The Nature of Human Aggression* (London: Oxford University Press, 1976).

Erich Fromm, *The Anatomy of Human Destructiveness* (New York: Holt, Rinehart and Winston, 1973).

4. Geoffrey Chaucer, "The Parson's Tale," in *Canterbury Tales,* translated by Nevill Coghill (London: Penguin Books, 1982), 506.

Chaucer continues: "Envy is sorrow at the prosperity of others and Joy in their hurt . . . and is flatly against the Holy Ghost, source of Bounty. Backbiting and grumbling are the Devil's Paternoster."

Interestingly, Chaucer described seven sins, including pride, envy, anger, accidie, avarice, gluttony, and lechery. On closer examination the seven sins reduce to three: envy, greed, and jealousy. Of these envy is the most promiment. It includes pride (hubris, hateful self-inflation), anger (a wicked will to vengeance), and accidie (vengeful passivity). Greed comprises avarice, gluttony, and lechery, and jealousy touches upon lechery and anger.

5. Thomas Aquinas (1225?–1274).

6. Quoted from an editorial in *The New York Times,* "Pyongyang as Outlaw," and republished in *The International Herald Tribune,* 18 January 1988, 6.

The editorial goes on to say that North Korea's envy has grown because of the additional prestige that her southern neighbor enjoys for playing host to the 1988 summer Olympic Games. This has led to a severe outburst of "nastiness, terror and murder," exemplified by the blowing up of a South Korean airliner.

Chapter 1

1. Yuri Olesha, *Envy* (Garden City, N.Y.: Anchor Books, Doubleday & Co, 1967).

2. Ibid., 78–79.

3. William Shakespeare, *The Tragedy of Othello* (New York: Pocket Books, 1957).

4. "O, you are well tuned now!
But I'll set down the pegs that make this music,
As honest as I am."
Ibid., act 2, scene 1, lines 231–34.

5. Ibid., act 2, scene 1, line 340.

6. Othello declares:
"O, now for ever
Farewell the tranquil mind! farewell content!"
Ibid, act 3, scene 3, lines 392–3.

7. Ibid., act 2, scene 3, lines 358–64.

8. "Make the Moor thank me, love me, reward me
For making him egregiously an ass
And practising upon his peace and quiet
Even to madness."
Ibid., act 2, scene 1, lines 336–39.

9. Peter Shaffer, *Amadeus* (London: Andre Deutsch, 1980). *Amadeus* was first produced at the National Theatre in London in 1979. My discussion of the relationship between Salieri and Mozart is based on Shaffer's fictionalized dramatization of their biographies. Unless otherwise indicated, my quotations are from the first edition of the play by Andre Deutsch.
Salieri's envious hatred of Mozart had been previously portrayed by the Russian writer Alexander Pushkin in *Mozart and Salieri,* completed in 1830. Alexander Pushkin, *Mozart and Salieri: The Little Tragedies,* translated by Anthony Wood (London: Angel Books, 1982). This work was later the basis for an opera by Rimsky-Korsakov. Other biographers dispute the story of Mozart's poverty, loss of status, and alleged poisoning by Salieri. See: Francis Carr, *Mozart and Constance* (New York: Franklin Watts, 1986).

10. The historical Salieri was a more prolific composer and powerful person than Shaffer indicates. He composed about forty operas over a period of thirty-five years, and his pupils included Beethoven and Schubert. David Stevens, "For Salieri, Signs of a Revival," *International Herald Tribune,* 15 April 1987, 1 and 8.

11. Envy usually operates in secrecy because it is such a fearful and shameful passion and is all the more effective for not being recognized for what it is. Herman Melville discusses this in the novel *Billy Budd,* when he comments on the malice directed toward Budd, a sailor, by John Claggart, his master-at-arms: "Did ever anybody seriously confess to envy? Something there is in it universally felt to be more shameful than even felonious crime. And not only does everybody disown it, but the better sort are inclined to incredulity when it is in earnest imputed to an intelligent man. But since its lodgement is in the heart not the brain, no degree of intellect supplies a guarantee against it." *The Portable Melville,* ed. J. Leyda (London: Penguin Books, 1976), 677.

12. Fate also intervened on behalf of Iago to help him "prove" Desdemona's infidelity to Othello. Desdemona accidentally dropped the special handkerchief that Othello had given to her. It was found by Emilia, Iago's wife, who innocently gave

it to Iago. He then dropped it where Othello's adjunct, Cassio, could find it and eventually incriminate himself.

13. One of Mozart's biographers comments on the hornet's nest of feelings that Emperior Joseph stirred up by commissioning an opera in German. The following quote is taken from the program to the production of *Amadeus* at Her Majesty's Theatre, London, 1981: "Joseph II formed the plan . . . of alienating taste from Italian operas by supporting German Singspiele and singers. . . . He accordingly assembled the best singers and commissioned a German opera from Mozart. For these virtuosi he wrote the well-known and well-loved Singspiele *The Flight from the Seraglio* in 1782. It created a widespread sensation, and the cunning Italians soon saw that such a mind could endanger their foreign tinklings. Envy now awoke with all the sharpness of Italian poison!" Franz Xaver Niemtschek, *Mozart*, 1808.

14. Many references confirm Salieri's malevolence:

"Salieri was Chapelmaster to the Court, a clever shrewd man, possessed of what Bacon called crooked wisdom; he was backed by . . . a cabal not easily put down." Michael Kelly, *Reminiscences*, 1826.

"An intriguer. . . . There can be no question of Salieri's malevolent interference with the success of his Austrian colleagues. His fine musicianship told him to concentrate his malice on Mozart, whose lamentable fate was due in no small degree to the Italian's machinations." P. H. Lang, *Music in Western Civilization* (New York: W. W. Norton & Co., 1940).

Quotes from *Amadeus*, program guide, op. cit.

15. Peter Shaffer, *Amadeus*, op. cit., 94–95.

16. The realization that envy is stimulated by comparisons with others which leave the envious person feeling inferior and worthless was noted by the philosopher Francis Bacon in his 1612 essay *On Envy*.

"[E]nvy is ever joined with the comparing of a man's self: and whence there is no comparison, no envy; and therefore kings are not envied but by kings."

F. Bacon, *The Essays or Counsels, Civil and Moral*, ed. S. H. Reynolds (Oxford: The Clarendon Press, 1890), 58.

17. Yuri Olesha, *Envy*, op. cit., 79.

18. William Shakespeare, *The Tragedy of Othello*, act 3, scene 3, lines 500–502 and 505.

Of course, it was an envious frenzy, too. It is in the nature of envy to arouse jealousy, as well as envy, in another. In the text (lines 497–99) Othello says he blew his love to heaven, an ironic twist, as love negated remains in hell and leads to hell on earth. The fond love Othello destroyed included his capacity for feeling love and for giving love besides his own sense of being lovable, that is, his self-respect.

19. John Milton vividly depicted the nature of envious revenge in the person of Satan in *Paradise Lost:*

Who first seduced them to that foul revolt?
Th'infernal serpeant! He it was, whose guile,
Stirred up with envy and revenge, deceived
The mother of mankind. . . .
Satan—so call him now, his former name
Is heard no more in heav'n—he of the first
If not the first Archangel, great in power,
In favour and pre-eminence, yet fraught
With envy against the Son of God, that day
Honoured by the great Father, and proclaimed
Messiah King anointed, could not bear
Thro' pride that sight, and thought himself impaired.

John Milton, *Paradise Lost,* book IX, quoted by Helmut Schoeck, *Envy, A Theory of Social Behavior,* op. cit., *156–157.*

20. Peter Shaffer, *Amadeus,* op. cit., 67.

21. *The Times,* London, 19 August 1981, 4.

22. Iago well understood the begrudging nature of envy when he commented to Othello:

Who steals my purse steals trash. . . .
But he that filches from me my good name
Robs me of that which not enriches him
And makes me poor indeed.

William Shakespeare, *The Tragedy of Othello,* act 3, scene 3, lines 182 and 184–186.

A begrudging envy sustains both racism and vandalism:

In Norwich, England, a young man who received a ten-year jail sentence for fire-bombing the home of a Chinese family commented: "I do not like the Chinese because they have more money and cars than anyone else." Quoted in "Ten Years for Race Attack," *The Times,* 9 January 1982, 3.

Similarly, in the wealthy Kensington area of London, and in one night alone, a tire slasher did £10,000 of damage to Porsches and Jaguars, completely ignoring the tires of cheaper cars. A police spokesman commented: "It would appear that he has some kind of grudge against rich people. We think this is going to continue in the future if he is not caught." Quoted in "£10,000 Grudge," *The London Standard,* London, 1 February 1985, 9.

And in April 1983 anarchist stickers that flooded the prosperous Camden Town area of London proclaimed: "Filthy Rich Bastards. Go Drown in your Jacuzzis."

23. Heather Mills, "Banker 'Killed Because He Looked Rich,' " *The Daily Telegraph,* 7 January 1986, 3; and Heather Mills, "Life for Man Who Killed Rich Stranger," *The Daily Telegraph,* 14 January 1986, 3.

24. The motivations of the thief or arsonist are complex and not solely or necessarily to do with greed or envy. In the case of the thief, revenge, a way of life, deprivation, and other factors contribute, although one is ultimately left with the question "Why steal?"

In the case of the arsonist, even more complicated psychological issues may be at work. For example, certain teenagers set fires in response to their own sexual passions. The fires represent a concretization of the sexual feeling that they cannot contain in themselves. The same is true for certain psychotic people who externalize aspects of their internal psychic world by arson. Envy itself has been described as a fiery burning, consuming, corroding feeling. The envy-motivated arsonist, as I described, wished to destroy the object of his envy, the house, and to externalize and thereby locate his consuming destructiveness elsewhere. Therein lay his satisfaction.

25. *Time,* 3 November 1952.

26. Dr. Helmut Schoeck points out that the envy-oriented politician is someone who "begrudges others their personal or material assets, being as a rule almost more intent on their destruction than on their acquisition." Helmut Schoeck, *Envy, A Theory of Social Behavior,* op. cit., 19.

Dr. Schoeck also quotes the American journalist H. L. Mencken on the politics of envy: "Puritanism is represented as a lofty sort of obedience to God's law. Democracy is depicted as brotherhood, even as altruism. All such notions are in error. There is only one honest impulse at the bottom of Puritanism, and that is the impulse to punish the man with a superior capacity for happiness—to bring him down to the miserable level of 'good' men, i.e., stupid, cowardly and chronically unhappy men. And there is only one sound argument for democracy, and this is the argument that it is a crime for any man to hold himself out as better than other men, and, above all, a most heinous crime for him to prove it. . . ." Ibid., 193–194, taken from *The Vintage Mencken,* ed. Alistair Cooke (New York, 1956), 75–77.

27. The novelist Oliver Knox, who joined the British (Tory) Centre for Policy Studies in 1984, succinctly explained his political philosophy: "Tory greed over Socialist envy." "Hitting the Road," *The Times,* 29 August 1984, 8.

28. Betty Joseph points out that intense grenvious impulses essentially characterize the personality of noncriminal psychopathic people. In referring to one young man in particular, she commented: "He approaches his objects with an attitude of extreme greed and stealing [which] . . . lead immediately to feelings of intense envy of the object's capacity to satisfy him." Betty Joseph, "Some Characteristics of the Psychopathic Personality," *Int. J. Psycho-Anal.,* vol. 41, 1960, 526–531.

29. Newspapers provide abundant evidence of this sort of crime. A typical article describes how thieves broke into an expensive house and did extensive damage by slashing the wallpaper, painting, and furniture with knives and by pouring paint and paint stripper over clothing, carpets, chairs, and the hi-fi. "House Wrecked," *The Daily Telegraph,* 25 April 1984, 14.

30. "Envy can fuse with greed, making for a wish to exhaust the object entirely, not only in order to possess all its goodness but also to deplete the object purposefully so that it no longer contains anything enviable." Hanna Segal, *Introduction to the Work of Melanie Klein* (London: The Hogarth Press, 1975), 41.

31. People who harbor envious grievances can often point to some basis in fact to justify their obsession. But if you explore matters a bit further, you usually find that they are quite selective in their perception, minimizing what they have and exaggerating what others have. In other words, their grievances are basically irrational and are rooted in the ingratitude that their frustrated greed and envy served to mask.

See discussion on greed and delusional hatred by Joan Riviere in her essay "Hate, Greed and Aggression," in *Love, Hate and Reparation,* by Melanie Klein and Joan Riviere (London: The Hogarth Press, 1967), 26–30.

32. Jilly Cooper, in "Jilly Cooper vs. the Green-Eyed Monster," *The Sunday Times,* 25 April 1971, 36.

33. Envy and greed focus on things and qualities, aspects or attributes, of a person without any reference to how this person thinks, feels, or what he needs in his own right. That is why envy and greed are bilaterally oriented, person to thing, person to quality, in comparison with the triangular orientation of jealousy. Moreover, this bilateral orientation of envy and greed does not expect or want any reciprocity. For the envious or greedy person, reciprocity is retribution.

34. Robert Bringle's research about the predisposition to jealousy indicates that it is strongest in persons who are "self-deprecating and dogmatic and who view themselves as unhappy, anxious and externally controlled." Quoted from Gordon Clanton, "Frontiers of Jealousy Research," *Alternative Lifestyles,* vol. 4, no. 3, August 1981, 263.

35. The case of a man who disfigured his former girlfriend for life provides a typical example of jealous revenge, where love lost turns to hate. The man, a divorcé, had lived with the teenager for six months. Then she left him and returned to her family. After making defamatory calls to her family and employer, and trying to poison her dogs, the man threw a container of sulfuric acid at her face. In so doing, he essentially transferred his own burning jealous feelings to his former mistress and tried to ruin her chances for love with anyone else: "I felt it burning. I felt I was on fire. . . . [Now] I suffer discomfort and pain almost all the time, and due to the injuries on my chest I will not be able to breastfeed my baby, which was something I would have liked to do." (The girl had subsequently become pregnant by another man.) Paul Stokes, "Acid Attack 'Disfigured Girl for Life,' " *The Daily Telegraph,* 21 October 1986, 3.

36. Peter Walcot, *Envy and the Greeks* (Warminster, England: Aris & Phillips Ltd., 1978), 2.

37. Ibid., 69.

38. Ibid., 3.

39. Until 1981 article 587 of the Italian penal code allowed betrayed wives and cuckolded husbands to get away with murder. This law, now amended, prescribed a greatly reduced penalty for crimes of passion. Sometimes the honor killers could walk out of the courtroom freely—amid the rapturous applause of the spectators. Report by Leslie Child, "Italians Lose Their License to Kill," *The Sunday Telegraph,* 26 July 1981, 2.

Gordon Clanton points out that jealousy can go in and out of fashion. "Prior to about 1966 most people [in the United States] viewed jealousy as a natural evidence of love and as good for marriage. Beginning in the late 1960s, many people have come to see jealousy as evidence of a defect in the personality of the jealous person [such as low self-esteem] and as bad for relationships." Gordon Clanton, "Frontiers of Jealousy Research," op. cit., 264. Similarly, John Leo, writing in *Time* magazine in the mid-1980s, discusses the evolution of various fashions and theories of jealousy: in the 1950s jealousy was treated as a healthy expression of sexual love. In the 1960s jealousy was seen as a pathological obstacle to sexual freedom. By 1980 he claims three views have vied for attention: 1) Sociobiological—Jealousy is evolutionary and adaptive. The person who chases off a rival enhances his chance of getting his genes into the next generation; 2) Sexual Revolutionary—Jealousy is a hang-up, a lamentable hangover from days when men claimed proprietary rights over women; and 3) Feminist—Male jealousy is part of the structure of patriarchy, such as control and domination, which keeps women in line. John Leo, "Battling the Green-Eyed Monster," *Time,* 25 November 1985, 39.

40. For example, *Webster's New World Dictionary* erroneously defines "jealous" as "resentfully envious." (New York: William Collins and World Publishing Co., Inc., 1974), 755.

41. Cooper, op. cit., 36.

42. The journalist Irma Kurtz has correctly itemized envious attacks on female qualities—indeed, on any qualities in women or men that denote lovability—in a survey entitled "The Seven Deadly Sins." Once, in the 1960s, she found herself at a party next to an "aging lady of fashion," when a pretty young girl strode into the room. Kurtz observed the immediate eruption of outrage from the older woman, who hissed: "Do you see those eyelashes? I'd kill for those eyelashes." Irma Kurtz, "Envy," *The Sunday Times* magazine, 22 February 1987, 42.

Kurtz also takes care to distinguish between envy and jealousy. As she puts it, "Jealousy fights duels. Envy poisons the soup." Ibid., 42.

43. William Shakespeare, op. cit., act 3, scene 3, lines 191–3.

44. Sigmund Freud, "Some Neurotic Mechanisms in Jealousy, Paranoia and Homosexuality," in *Standard Edition of the Complete Psychological Works of Freud,* ed. J. Strachey (London: The Hogarth Press, 1968), vol. 18, 221–232.

45. Psychoanalyst Joan Riviere provides a thorough discussion of morbid jealousy in her paper "Jealousy As a Mechanism of Defense," *Int. J. Psycho-Anal.,* vol. 13, 1932, 414–424.

46. Joan Riviere thinks Othello wished to blacken Desdemona's name by accusations of infidelity and in that way overcome his own sense of guilt for abducting her.

"It is the cause, it is the cause, my soul"—the old tradition has it that with these words the actor spoke to his own image in a mirror, which he contrasts in the next breath with Desdemona's "whiter skin." "Does not Othello's blackness, also seemingly irrelevant, sum up in one symbol the whole story of his guilt, doubt, anxiety, and his mode of defense against them? Iago the envious is but his alter ego. He cannot endure the evil in himself. He must make Desdemona black instead." Ibid., 424.

47. The writer Philip Howard has cited the phrase "I don't envy anyone with money these days" as an example of a "reversible," a word or phrase that means the opposite of what it says. *The Times,* 14 July 1980.

48. I refer to an advertisement about the exclusive New York hotel, the Waldorf-Astoria: "If you've never been a Waldorf guest, you could unthinkingly believe it to be expensive. . . . The admiration (if not envy) of the folks at home is included in the room rate." *The New York Times,* 7 December 1961, 29.

49. Helmut Schoeck points out that the sociologist W. G. Runciman demands "uninhibited reference group choice" in regard to all inequalities in order to maximize social justice. Schoeck, *Envy: A Theory of Social Behavior,* op. cit., 209.

50. "Cartoonist Dickens thought that it might be difficult to picture the complete range of Roneo Vickers products in one drawing. He did remarkably well because this particular operating group of Vickers has the most comprehensive span of office equipment of any European manufacturer. It is certainly true that this wide range of equipment is the envy of those who make do without Roneo Vickers." *The Sunday Times,* 11 September 1977.

51. Sometimes envy is mistaken for the context in which it occurs: social proximity or "invidious proximity," a term employed by the American historian David M. Potter in *People of Plenty: Economic Abundance and the American Character* (Chicago, 1954), 102.

52. The philosopher Immanuel Kant pointed out in his late work *The Metaphysics of Morals* that envy denies intrinsic worth, even if it is there:

"Envy . . . is a disinclination to see our own good overshadowed by the good of others, because we take its measure not from its intrinsic worth, but by comparison with the good of others and then go on to symbolize evaluation."

Immanuel Kant, *Metaphysik der Sitten,* in Sämtliche Werke, ed. K. Vorlander, vol. 3, 4th ed. (Leipzig: Felix Meiner, 1922), 316. Translation by H. Schoeck.

The advertisement seeks to arouse this experience by implying that old equipment, old working conditions, and old methods are no good in comparison with what Vickers has to offer. This overlooks the intrinsic worth of previous work and conditions.

53. Quoted by Schoeck, op. cit., 209. See W. G. Runciman, *Relative Deprivation and Social Justice: A Study of Attitudes to Social Inequality in Twentieth Century England* (London: Routledge & Kegan Paul, 1966).

54. Similar feelings might well be aroused by an advertisement for Charnos black lingerie in the Christmas 1986 issue of *Harrods* magazine. Entitled "Envy. One of the Seven Deadly Sins," it shows a beautiful model clothed in Charnos lingerie lying on green silk sheets. Here "envy" is used synonymously with intensity and desire; the ad arouses intense desire and also indicates that anyone who wore Charnos would be highly desirable, like the model. But the green background gives a hint that other emotions might also be involved—in this instance, that such intense desires might conceal or give rise to equally intense hatreds, as Irma Kurtz's aging ladies of fashion might feel. *Harrods* magazine, London, Christmas 1986, 94–95.

In the Vickers ad the windows overlooking the new building are crowded with faces, intent with interest, dreamy-eyed with admiration, and full of intense desire. In the same way that they might be looking at the Charnos model, a company director thinks, Like it! Like it! while a couple of clerks mutter, "Covet! Covet!" Again, this isn't an example of envy but of greedy desire or, if we take all the office staff to represent the collective onlooker, of grenvy. This advertisement doesn't just intend to humble or belittle the "withouts." It arouses an emptiness that can only be alleviated by an infusion of the latest furniture or typewriters or destructive revenge.

55. Resentment, indignation, and frustration can all arouse envy because the actual injustice or deprivation reverberates with imagined hurts, especially with someone who has a chip on his shoulder. Then the person may misperceive outer events as inner events and react with enhanced fear and rage. Actual deprivation and frustration can kindle and rekindle weakness and inferiority, especially in people with low self-esteem. This too can lead to ill will and rage, far out of proportion to the precipitating event. For all these reasons resentment, indignation, and deprivation are associated, but not identical, with envy.

56. Bertrand Russell clearly distinguished between envy and admiration in his book *The Conquest of Happiness*. He pointed out that of all the characteristics of human nature, envy is the most unfortunate because the envious person does not only "wish to inflict misfortune and [will] do so whenever he can with impunity, but he is also rendered unhappy by envy. . . . Fortunately, however, there is in human nature a compensating passion, namely that of admiration. Whoever wishes to increase human happiness must wish to increase admiration and decrease envy." *The Conquest of Happiness* (London: Unwin Paperbacks, 1978), 66.

I think that the modern tendency to change envy into its opposite, admiration, is another example of the need to conceal, as well as defuse, the malevolence inherent in envy. It may also represent the wish to make use of one quality of envy, its strength and depth of feeling, by yoking it to an opposite but weaker word, "admiration."

57. Sören Kierkegaard (1813–1855), Danish philosopher and theologian.

58. Emulation is often equated with envy. The two phenomena are quite distinct and generally opposite in content. To emulate is to wish to be like someone, to identify with that someone out of admiration. Emulation is not spiteful, self-seeking, begrudging, or malicious, as is envy. Emulation does not seek to hurt the rival, just to equal or surpass. However, when emulation is thwarted the rivalry may become malicious.

59. The Fisons Company placed a similar envy-arousing advertisement entitled "Make Your Neighbour Green with Envy" in the London *Daily Telegraph* magazine, 20 May 1979. It shows a view of the gardens of two adjacent houses. The house on the left is freshly painted and has a brilliant green lawn. The house on the right is dull and has a lawn that is yellow and half-dead. The owner of this house can be seen looking over the fence at his neighbor's lush attractive lawn accomplished by the use of Fisons products. The ad calls for the man to emulate his neighbor and use Fisons products in order to get a better lawn. Yet the ad literally suggests that anyone who uses Fisons products opens himself to envious destructive attacks by his neighbors with the result that his lush green lawn would soon become yellow and sick!

60. Elkan Allan, "Best Loot Guide?" *The Times*, 25 July 1981, 8.

61. Jean Cuisenier points out that in Catholic countries there is an abundant iconograpy of envy, one of the seven deadly sins. In the *Miroir de vie et de Mort*, a miniature shows a large tree with seven roots, each taking the shape of a snake, and ending in the figure of a woman. The sixth, *radix invidiae*, carries a beast in her breast. Cuisenier comments, "We recognize here the tree of evil of the twelfth-century theologians, where vices are at the roots, and the roots are at the same time the seven heads of the Apocalypse's dragon."

From discussion to paper by George M. Foster, "The Anatomy of Envy: A Study in Symbolic Behavior," *Current Anthropology*, vol. 13, no. 2, April 1972, 189.

The car sticker is mentioned in David Ward Tresemer, *Fear of Success* (New York: Plenum Press, 1977), 21.

Chapter 2

1. In contemporary Greece, for example, the Sarkatsani shepherds are acutely aware of the influence of envy, which they term an ancestral sin. They believe that

the ancestral sin of envy was prompted by the devil's rebellion against God. For them envy is the devil carrying out his deadly work on earth. "The witchcraft or sorcery of the evil eye is recognized by the Church as one of the Devil's weapons. . . . It is said that a person known to have the evil eye 'has an eye infected by the Devil.' " Peter Walcot, *Envy and the Greeks,* op. cit., 87–88.

2. Joshua Trachtenberg, *Jewish Magic and Superstition: A Study in Folk Religion* (New York: Atheneum, 1970), 56.

3. To the Greeks, the Furies were dramatic representations of the evil eye and therefore of envy. They were figures of absolute horror, as Aeschylus makes clear in his play *The Furies.*
Ibid., 60.

4. Jean Louis André Theodore Géricault (1791–1824) was a forerunner of the French Romantic movement. His most famous work is entitled *Raft of the Medusa* (1817), which depicts the cannibalistic survivors of a shipwreck. His treatment of envy is part of a series of paintings on the theme of insanity.

5. There exist hundreds of proverbs on the subject of envy, many of which are similar in different countries. Helmut Schoeck quotes from a number of Russian proverbs, including:
"Envy turns a blade of grass into a palm tree."
"In the eye of the envious man, a toadstool becomes a palm tree."
"The envious eye makes elephants of midges."
Helmut Schoeck, *Envy: A Theory of Social Behavior,* op. cit., 20–21.

6. Ibid., 20–21.

7. Edward S. Gifford, Jr., *The Evil Eye: Studies in the Folklore of Vision* (New York: The Macmillan Co., 1958), 3–4.

8. Martin Delrio, a Jesuit of Louvain, wrote in 1603: "Fascination is a power derived from a pact with the devil, who, when the so-called fascinator looks at another with evil intent, or praises, by means known to himself, infects with evil the person at whom he looks." Ibid., 15.

9. Ibid., 6–9.

10. Other names for the evil eye include *innochiatura* (Corsica), *mauvais oeil* (France), *mal ojo* (Spain), *böse Blick* (Germany), *booze blik* (Holland), *zte oko* (Poland), *skjoertunge* (Norway), *ondt oje* (Denmark), *cronachadt* (Scotland), *drochshuil* (Ireland), *aghashi* (Iran), *paterak* (Armenia), *szeniveres* (Hungary), *l'ain* (Morocco) *ayenat* (Ethiopia), *drishtidosham* (India), and *hassad* (Egypt).

11. One does not have to appear evil to be a *jettatura*. The evil in the *malocchio* is inherent and may occur spontaneously and outside voluntary control. This is consistent with the view that envy is natural and inherent in everyone.

12. Edward Gifford quotes from an Italian describing the difficulties that beset Pope Pius IX: "Now, if he hasn't the *jettatura,* what is it that makes everything turn out at cross purposes with him? For my part, I don't wonder the workmen at the Column in the Piazza di Spagna refused to work the other day in raising it, unless the Pope stayed away." Ibid., 16–17.

13. "Vile worm, thou wast o'erlook'd even in thy birth." William Shakespeare, *Merry Wives of Windsor,* act 5, scene 5, line 81.
To overlook also has come to mean to ignore or to look down upon. These meanings also are indicative of envy, for the envious person is someone who ignores others' achievements and looks down on his superiors. See: *Oxford Universal Dictionary,* 3rd edition (Oxford: Oxford University Press, 1933), 1404.
Right through to the twentieth century, when anything unfortunate and unforeseen happened to small farmers in Cornwall, England, they considered that they had been overlooked or ill-wished. Typically a dairyman related that he had had a quarrel with a domestic servant. Not long afterward a couple of his cows died. He was sure that the woman had overlooked or ill-wished him. Margaret Courtney, *Cornish Feasts and Folk-Lore* (Penzance, Cornwall: Beare and Son, 1890), 139.

14. According to the *Oxford Universal Dictionary,* to "blink" can mean to turn milk sour. To "put blinkers on" is to ignore many aspects of reality or to hoodwink. These definitions are also consistent with envy. Ibid., 190.

See also: Edward S. Gifford, Jr., *The Evil Eye: Studies in the Folklore of Vision,* op. cit., 6.

15. Ibid., 21.

16. Jonathan Mirsky, "Get Rich—But Not Too Fast," *The Times,* 21 March 1985, 16.

In this vein, my ten-year-old daughter commented at the time of buying a rabbit: "I don't want one with pink eyes. Reminds me of a 'wear rabbit.' " Debbie Berke, personal communication, 27 April 1985.

Her remark demonstrates the projection of destructive impulses into the eyes of another, whether the green-eyed monsters in Othello, the reddened eyes of an angry Chinese, the bloodshot eyes of a gangster, or the pink eyes of a rabbit.

17. In reminiscing about his childhood, the English writer Laurie Lee has vividly described the appearance of a deaf-mute beggar said to be possessed of the evil eye: "He had soft-boiled eyes of unusual power which filled every soul with disquiet. It was said he could ruin a girl with a glance and take the manhood away from a man, or scramble your brains, turn bacon green, and effect other domestic disorders." Laurie Lee, *Cider With Rosie* (London: Penguin Books, 1959), 35.

18. Edward S. Gifford, Jr., *The Evil Eye: Studies in the Folklore of Vision,* op. cit., 17–18.

19. Elias Canetti has commented on the amazing power of "the dead" to dominate the lives of the living. "The first thing that strikes one is the universal *fear* of the dead. They are discontented and full of envy for those they have left behind. They try to take revenge on them, sometimes for injuries done them during their life-time, but often simply because they themselves are no longer alive." Elias Canetti, *Crowds and Power* (London: Victor Gollancz Ltd., 1962), 262.

Psychologically, the dead who envy the living refers to the dead parts of the self that retain the capacity to terrorize the live parts (in other words, an intrapsychic phenomenon) and to the projection of these dead parts into a corpse or part of a corpse, like the eye.

20. Yuri Olesha, *Envy,* op. cit., 2.

21. I think a comparable process of projection helps to explain why many primitive peoples "see" danger everywhere. In such cultures the envier, or *fascinator,* can easily become fascinated, bewitched, or bedeviled by the things he envies. All this is experienced on a level of supernatural magic and is exceptionally frightening.

22. Helmut Schoeck, *Envy: A Theory of Social Behavior,* op. cit., 2.

23. Foster quotes from many writers to document his view that praise can be very unwelcome in peasant as well as urban societies because it arouses and is seen as an expression of envy.

Edward Banfield on south Italy: "One of the most interesting superstitions is the belief that invidious comment, even though made to flatter, will bring harm to the one who is put in an enviable light." *The Moral Basis of a Backward Society* (Glencoe, Ill: Glencoe Free Press, 1958), 144.

Horace Miner on Timbuctoo, Mali: ". . . the belief that compliments from non-intimates bring evil upon those praised. People therefore tend to avoid direct compliments and fear those directed to them." *The Primitive City of Timbuctoo* (Princeton, N.J.: Princeton University Press, 1953), 103.

Sania Hamady on the Arab world: ". . . some compliments which, even if well intended, are considered portentous. Laudatory expressions may attract the contrary of what they propose to say, because envy may be mixed with them. That is why a mother is not simply told that her son is handsome and healthy, or a proprietor that his house is splendid. It is feared that the son might fall sick and the house might burn." *Temperament and Character of the Arabs* (New York: Twayne, 1960), 166.

Finally Foster cites Miguel de Unamuno, the Spanish novelist, who has explored the aggressive function of compliments in *Abel Sanchez: The History of a Passion*.

Unamuno ponders Joaquin Monegro, a physician who has been cursed all his life by envy of his childhood friend, Abel Sanchez, a successful painter. In one scene Joaquin goes to his club, where an implacable man named Frederico would insist in a cold, cutting voice whenever he heard anyone speak well of another: "I can't be fooled. When someone is vigorously praised, the speaker always has someone else in mind whom he is trying to debase with his euology, a second someone who is a rival to the praised party. . . . You can be sure that no one eulogizes with good intentions."

Miguel de Unamuno, *Abel Sanchez: The History of a Passion*, translated by Anthony Kerrigan (Chicago: Gateway Editions, 1956), 103.

George M. Foster, "The Anatomy of Envy: A Study in Symbolic Behavior," op. cit., 172.

24. Peter Walcot, *Envy and the Greeks*, op. cit., 25–26.

"But in general, throughout the Homeric poems, we hear of the envy of the gods merely in vague statements which reflect the pessimism of Homeric man, but do not add up to anything like a theory of divine envy directed against the powerful."

25. Ibid., 31.

26. Pindar, lyric poet, 518–438 B.C.E.

Aeschylus, Athenian tragedian, 525/4–456 B.C.E.

Herodotus, historian, c. 484–c.420 B.C.E.

27. Ibid., 34. Aeschylus, *Agamemnon*, verses 468–70.

Peter Walcot comments that for the Greeks a basic dilemma was how to achieve success without attracting too much envy, which invited resentment, malice, and displeasure of the gods. In *Agamemnon* the chorus chooses "prosperity without envy," but as Walcot points out, it is doubtful that this option existed, especially for the Greeks, who were a people obsessed by envy.

28. Ibid., 34. *Agamemnon*, verse 947.

29. Euripides, Athenian tragedian, c.485–c.406 B.C.E.

Plutarch, biographer and essayist, c.45–c.125 C.E.

Walcot states, "In Euripides' *Suppliant Women*, Theseus claims there are three groups of citizens, the rich, the poor, and those in the middle. What does he say of the second class? The have-nots, those who lack the essentials of life, are motivated by envy and release 'evil stings' on those who have (verses 240–242)." Ibid., 35.

Discussing Plutarch, Walcot writes, "The 'suffering soul' affects the body, and envy [*phthonos*], sinking naturally into the soul more than any other emotion, fills the body too with wickedness. When those consumed by such envy fix their glance on someone, their eyes, being very near, draw from the soul the wickedness and strike a man down like poisoned arrows." Ibid., 82.

30. Ibid., 47–48.

31. Ibid., 82.

32. Heliodorus was the author of the longest Greek novel to survive, the *Aethiopica*. He lived in the second half of the third century A.D.

Ibid., 83.

33. Plutarch was quoted by Samuel Reynolds, who edited Bacon's essays.

Plutarch also comments: "How is it possible that the only cast or regard of the eye should transmit any noisance or hurt into the body of another?" The answer is that "envy filleth the body with an untoward and bad disposition; when therefore they who be infected with envy do cast their eyes upon others, and so shoot their venomous rays, like unto poisoned darts upon them, if such a chance to be wounded or hurt thereby whom they look upon and wistly behold, I see no strange thing not a matter incredible." *Symposiaques*, book 5, question 7.

Francis Bacon, "Of Envy," in *The Essays or Counsels, Civil and Moral,* op. cit., 62.

34. Ibid., 56.

35. Ibid., 64.

Bacon's view reflects the long-held belief that vision was the result of rays emitted by the eye, which bounce back from the perceived object to the viewer, somewhat like radar.

36. Ibid., 56.

Shining stars and planets have long been associated with heavenly "eyes." By the psychological mechanism of projection, it is easy to attribute evil influences or evil aspects to these distant eyes, just as the early Greeks did with their Olympian gods.

37. Personal communication, January 1986.

For this young man, the breasts (the desired objects) and the eyes (the desiring objects) were one.

38. Mishle Yehoshua, from R. Alcalay, *Words of the Wise* (Israel: Massada Press), 131.

39. Pindar, *Pythian Odes,* 8, verses 71–72 and 67–69, quoted in Peter Walcot, *Envy and the Greeks,* op. cit., 80.

40. Ibid., 56.

41. Immanuel Kant, *Metaphysik der Sitten,* op. cit., 36.

42. H. Schoeck quotes the proverb, "No sooner is envy born than he consorts with the hangman and the gallows." Ibid., 22.

43. In England, the assizes are court sessions held to try civil and criminal cases, in this case in Lewes.

44. I am indebted to the barrister Peter Marsh, who brought this crime to my attention and provided details of the case for me.

Haigh pleaded not guilty on grounds of insanity, but he was convicted and executed at Wandsworth Prison in August 1949. The prosecution alleged that the crime had been premeditated, and it did appear that all the victims had been killed prior to their being put in the vat of acid. But I think that the mutilating, annihilating nature of the action, coupled with Haigh's background; the repetitive dreams that occurred before each killing to do with the drinking of blood; the draining of the dream image (withdrawing vitality); and the peculiar assertion of his destiny indicate that envy played a prominent part in the deed.

45. The psychoanalyst Hanna Segal points out that when envy is turned inward it attacks the psychic representations of the good object, such as the feeding mother. This can lead to an impoverishment of the ego and even more intense envy. She comments: "This gives rise to a painful vicious circle. The more the good internal object is destroyed, the more impoverished the ego feels, and this in turn increases envy."

Segal adds: "The projection of envy into the [internal] object gives rise to an envious superego. The over-severe superego which Freud describes as the basis of psychical disturbance often turns out on analysis to be an envious superego. That is, its attacks are directed not only against the individual's aggression, but also, and even predominantly, against the individual's progressive and creative capacities." Hanna Segal, *Klein* (London: Fontana Modern Masters, 1979), 143.

46. Other sayings include

"Envy will eat nothing but its own heart."

"Envy is its own scourge."

"Envy brings suffering to the envious man."

"Envy flogs itself."

"Envy envies itself."

Helmut Schoeck, *Envy: A Theory of Social Behavior,* op. cit., 32.

47. For example, the Greek orator and teacher Isocrates (436–338 B.C.E.) wrote at length about envy, which he considered a disease and scourge of mankind. Walcot comments: "In the *Antidosis* Isocrates reports . . . some men have been made so savage by envy and want and are so hostile that they are at war not with wickedness but with prosperity; they hate not only the best men but also the noblest of activities; they sympathize with men who are wicked and destroy, if they can, those whom they envy." Peter Walcot, *Envy and the Greeks,* op. cit., 72–73.

In the contemporary thought the same message comes through. In one sequence of the popular cartoon "Hagar the Horrible" the scribe asks Hagar, "For my records, what illnesses have you had?" Hagar thinks, "Lemme see, Black Plague . . . Evil Eye . . . Demon Possession . . . Spells." The scribe replies, "I'll just put down 'regular childhood diseases.' " Dik Browne, "Hagar the Horrible," *The Sun,* 9 September 1983, 32.

48. The internalized envier may also be a psychic representation of an envious but dissociated part of the envying person, that is, of himself. Then the envier is a part of himself, turned against himself, and the person is both the envier and the object of his own envy—the envied. These occasions are extremely threatening and tend to evoke the greatest defensive response by the envied person.

49. Debra Weiner, "Under the Gaze of the Evil Eye," *International Herald Tribune,* 17 September 1982, 10W.

50. In considering the three categories of responses by the envied person, I am referring to someone who, consciously or unconsciously, is aware of being envied and feels threatened by this. I would not suggest that an envied person always responds in these ways. There are many instances when someone is aware of being envied but does not feel threatened and simply ignores it. However, this may also happen with an envied person who feels extremely threatened but who ignores, or dissociates himself from, his feelings. Without specific knowledge of the person, and the envious attack directed toward him, it is hard to know whether a nonresponse to envy signifies the perceived absence of a threat or not.

I proceed on the assumption that all people feel threatened by envy to some degree.

51. Discussed by David Ward Tresemer, in *Fear of Success,* op. cit., 66–67.

52. Ibid., 67.

53. In Mexico Williams wrote *A Streetcar Named Desire.* Ibid., 67.

54. A good illustration is a conversation that occurred in Naples during the winter of 1832–1833 between the English novelist Edward Bulwer-Lytton and an intelligent, well-informed, upper-class Italian woman: "My God, that man," she whispered tremblingly. "What man?" "See, the Count—he has just entered." "He ought to be much flattered to cause such emotion; doubtless he has been one of the signora's admirers?" "Admirer. Heaven forbid. He has the evil eye. His look fell full upon me. Something dreadful will certainly happen." "I see nothing remarkable in his eyes." "So much the worse. The danger is greater for being disguised. He is a terrible man. The last time he looked upon my husband, it was at cards, and he lost half his income at a sitting; his ill luck was miraculous. The Count met my little boy in the gardens, and the poor child broke his arm that evening. Oh, what shall I do? Something dreadful will certainly happen." Quoted by Edward S. Gifford, Jr., in *The Evil Eye: Studies in the Folklore of Vision,* op. cit., 18.

55. The use of self-inflation to deflate others is a typical envious technique that I will discuss at length in the next chapter. But Mozart also directly denigrated those around him with foul language and scurrilous actions.

56. Edward S. Gifford, Jr., *The Evil Eye: Studies in the Folklore of Vision,* op. cit., 9.

57. The press often documents accounts of people who were seemingly damaged by the evil eye. In one instance a West Indian woman suffered from severe depression and herself became a killer after a relationship with a man who took charge of her

body and "she was scared not to follow. Scratches on her body she put down to the evil eye." Heather Mills, "Killer Was 'Influenced by Evil Eye,'" *The Daily Telegraph,* 25 June 1986, 3.

Similarly, papers like the London *Guardian* don't hesitate to print cartoon commentaries about the effects of envious looks. In a takeoff on middle-class problems, "Black Looks" describes a well-off man who became pale and wan after being seen by his daughter's jobless friends unloading a case of Rioja from his Volvo. He declaims, "Oh, it's a terrible look, Wendy . . . black huddle of clothes. . . . Look of ENVY . . . blunt ENVY . . . and DERISION! Oh, heck! Utter *DERISION!*" Posy Simmonds, "Black Looks," the *Guardian,* 24 January 1983, 10.

58. When fifteen-year-old high-jumper Deborah Marti, Britain's youngest prospect for the Los Angeles Olympic Games, was questioned about the reaction of school friends to her successes, she replied: "I think they are jealous. . . . I tend to withdraw from them." For her, social isolation was the price of professional success. Doug Ibbotson, "Murray's Jumpers Have High Hopes," *The Daily Telegraph,* 25 April 1984, 31.

59. David Ward Tresemer, *Fear of Success,* op. cit., 32–33.

Horner is particularly concerned with the psychological barriers to success in women. The data for Horner's study was collected in 1964 and analyzed for her doctoral dissertation in 1968. This material was supplemented by further studies in 1972.

60. Helmut Schoeck, *Envy: A Theory of Social Behavior,* op. cit., 29–30.

61. The rapacious wish to drain and devour an object may inadvertently spoil it. The net effect of such a greedy attack is the same as a purely envious one. Or the spoiling may be intrinsic to a combined envious and greedy attack, as with the devouring and defiling that characterizes grenvy.

62. The French-Swiss doctor and depth psychologist Paul Tournier has written at length about the fear of envy, an attitude he calls "false guilt feelings." This seems comparable with what I describe as the state of uncalled-for guilt about being envied.

Tournier comments: "A certain sense of guilt is a corollary of any privilege even when the privilege is deserved."

Tournier doesn't explain why this has to be the case. I think it has a lot to do with the cultural context in which the guilty person lives (an envy-ridden or envy-arousing society), as well as with the tendency of the envied person to identify with the envier. The guilt about being envied may be an amalgam of guilt to do with false responsibility, appropriate guilt (greed- and envy-arousing behavior), and dissociated guilt (arising from his own envious attacks as seen through the eyes of the envier). When particularly strong, the envied and guilty person may end up questioning the validity of his own existence (false existential guilt).

Paul Tournier, *Guilt and Grace* (London: Hodder & Stoughton, 1962), 14.

Quoted by Helmut Schoeck, in *Envy: A Theory of Social Behavior,* op. cit., 259.

63. This is a widespread, pervasive belief system based on magical ideas of grenvy. It is a feature of many ancient or tribal societies, as well as the early state of mind of the infant. These beliefs have influenced modern social and political ideologies both in developed cultures and subcultures and in underdeveloped countries.

64. Ray Connolly, "The Winged Wonder," *Evening Standard,* 6 April 1979, 21.

Connolly also pointed out that McCartney's children "go to local village primary and comprehensive schools, receive no particular tuition in music ('they just play records like the other kids'), and are kept as far from the glamorous life of show-business as possible."

65. John Vinocur, "W. Germans Rethink Status Symbols: Some Even Have No More Stars in Their Eyes," *International Herald Tribune,* 26–27 May 1979, 1–2.

According to one physician in Kiel, the only kind of Mercedes that did not embarrass him was "one that's ten years old, rusted to the guts and driven by punk rockers or immigrant workers from Turkey."

Helmut Schoeck points out that customers can order their new cars with or without the special insignia. For purposes of envy avoidance, car salesmen will always ask what the customer prefers. Personal communication, 1982.

66. Helmut Schoeck, *Envy: A Theory of Social Behavior,* op. cit., 30–31.

See A. R. Homber, *Nomads of the Long Bow, The Siriono of Eastern Bolivia,* Smithsonian Institution: Institute of Social Anthropology Publication, no. 10, Washington, D.C., 1950.

Schoeck comments that Allan Holmberg, the American anthropologist who did the fieldwork, eventually adopted the practice of eating alone. This may have reflected his wish to share their customs but may also indicate the power of envious intimidation.

There exist abundant examples of kindred concealments in modern life. One of the most pervasive is the practice of the bride wearing a veil at her wedding. This protects her from the evil eye of other women. Similarly, many women mourners still wear veils at the funeral of close relatives. This is to protect others from their envious eyes.

Among Lubavitcher Jews it is almost impossible to find out how many people attended a certain meeting or how many Lubavitchers live in a certain city. Joshua Trachtenberg notes: "Any act or condition that in itself may excite the envy of the spirits is subject to the evil eye; taking a census or even estimating the size of a crowd, possession of wealth, performing an act which is normally a source of pride or joy—all evoke its pernicious effects." Quoted by Liz Harris, *Holy Days* (New York: Summit Books, 1985), 255. No doubt this also explains the widespread conscious and unconscious resistance to census taking in all societies or the specification of wealth. Typically, Mrs. Seward Johnson, the heiress of the baby powder fortune, refused to have her picture taken at Sotheby's when she spent the highest price ever paid at an auction for a piece of furniture. Mrs. Johnson begged the press: "Please, no photographs. I don't want people to recognize me when I go around. I have many enemies—I think they envy me." Geraldine Norman, "The Fine Art of Marrying Well," *The Times,* 28 December 1983, 8.

67. The reluctance to be noticed covers all manner of privileges. It is a common practice for boys at Eton, the famous English public school, to hide the fact that they are Etonians in order to avoid public hostility. As one boy put it, "Etonians don't like to admit they're Etonians. You like people to ask. You never offer. If you meet somebody and you sense that you oughtn't to tell them you're at Eton, you just keep quiet." A teacher at the school said he does likewise. "If I'm asked where I teach, I very often say Windsor. It's not that I'm ashamed, but sometimes it overawes people." Graham Turner, "The New Etonians," *The Sunday Telegraph,* 5 July 1981, 8–9.

68. Helmut Schoeck, *Envy: A Theory of Social Behavior,* op. cit., 88–89.

The pressure to conform arises for several reasons, including the fear of envy, the desire to be part of group identity, social responsibility, or political reality. Each may reinforce or negate the other. Thus students at a secondary school may refuse to do well academically both because to do so would not be in keeping with their peer culture and also because it would subject them to the envious hostility of their classmates. The same holds true for workers in a factory or office.

Schoeck notes a study of conformity in Norway and France by Stanley Milgram. Milgram found that there is considerable pressure in both countries to conform to the group norm but more so in Norway. This was conveyed by the phrases *"Skal du strikke deg ut?"* and *"Voulez-vous vous faire remarquer?"* both of which are said critically and roughly mean, "Don't show off!" (Literally, "Are you trying to show off?")

Schoeck concludes, "What, then, is basically feared by the man who, against his better judgment, conforms to the group, is verbal reprisal, a reproach for wanting to be better, more knowledgeable, cunning and observant than the group. In other words, an expression of envy of his particular abilities, his individuality and his self-assurance." Ibid., 80–83.

69. Ostracism was the Athenian practice of temporary banishment from the State. The name of the individual proposed for banishment was scratched on a piece of broken pot, the *ostrakon*. This was a form of voting paper. A majority of six thousand votes could send a man into exile for ten years.

According to Peter Walcot, nonpolitical considerations, trust or mistrust, like or dislike (irrational and intensely subjective issues), were often paramount. He believes that ostracism was "a piece of democratic machinery almost ideally contrived to cater for widespread envy, since it allows envy to be expressed legitimately and it does not have too devastating a consequence for the victim, just ten years of exile but without, however, the loss of citizenship or property." Peter Walcot, *Envy and the Greeks,* op. cit., 54.

Viewed in this light, ostracism was both an expression of envy and a defense against it. Now ostracism refers to any expulsion or rejection from a group by general consent.

70. Socrates, Athenian philosopher and teacher, 470?–399 B.C.E.

Walcot points out that Plato (Socrates' student) believed that he was the victim of envy. Plato wrote in the *Apology* that Socrates was confident his condemnation was the result of the "slander and envy of the many." Ibid., 67.

71. According to a report in the Chinese newspaper *The People's Daily,* fear of being sent to Coventry is widespread. Many individuals are reluctant to be singled out as model workers for fear of being ridiculed and ostracized by their workmates. The report added that the situation had improved in comparison with previous years when soldiers and workers were scorned as toadies for saving a boy from drowning. Quoted in *The Times,* 17 February 1982, 8.

72. Apparently the Coventry Family Practice Committee reprimanded and fined Dr. Summerfield on a technicality. Mr. Clemons, the secretary of the local dental committee, said that Summerfield had not done anything illegal. He simply ran a large practice and had seven associates working for him (all of whom earned a higher than average wage): "He was a workaholic and opened his surgery at eight A.M., working through until eight P.M. He did not close for holidays and was open six days a week." However, "his work was not considered to be tidy enough, and it was the paperwork in his practice which brought this to light and resulted in disciplinary hearings." Dr. Summerfield was fined £5,000. On appeal Dr. Gerald Vaughan, the minister for health, reduced the fine to £600.

James O'Brien, "12-Hour Day NHS Dentist Earned £1M in 10 Years," *The Daily Telegraph,* 17 February 1982, 17.

73. While describing life at the court of Charles II, Samuel Pepys wrote: "I do find that it is a troublesome thing for a man of any condition at the Court to carry himself even, and without contracting envy or envyers; and that much discretion and dissimulation is necessary to do it." Samuel Pepys, *The Diary of Samuel Pepys,* vol. 1 (London: Everyman's Library, J. N. Dent & Son, Ltd., 1927), 360.

74. George M. Foster, "The Anatomy of Envy: A Study in Symbolic Behavior," op. cit., 172.

The Talmud is the major collection of writings that constitute the Jewish civil and religious law.

Certain ecologists often give similar admonitions about the extravagant use of natural resources. Amory Lovins of Friends of the Earth put it this way: "If you ask me, it'd be a little short of disastrous for us to discover a source of clean, cheap abundant energy because of what we would do with it. We ought to be looking for energy sources that are adequate for our needs, but that won't give us the excesses of concentrated energy with which we could do mischief to the earth or to each other." Quoted in an article by Bertram Wolfe, "The Perfect Energy Resource? A Hopeless Search," *International Herald Tribune,* 9 February 1982, 4.

Behind this admonition lurks a general distrust of any society with abundant energy supplies, whether oil or drive and ambition. Lovins seems to be worried about greed as well as envy. Why assume abundance inevitably leads to mischief? Warnings like this may serve as an expression of envy as well as a defense against it.

75. George Foster emphasizes the defensive nature of modesty. He points out that in small-town America, families that are significantly wealthier than others often manifest a standard of living (home, dress, activities) greatly below what they could afford. But if the same families move to a big city, where they are not constantly exposed to the eyes of their neighbors, they tend to be much less inhibited about their life-style. George M. Foster, "The Anatomy of Envy: A Study in Symbolic Behavior," op. cit., 177.

76. Editorial, quoted in *The International Herald Tribune,* 22 February 1982, 4.

77. There exists a world oversupply of false bad news. This has been amply documented by Julian Simon, professor of economics and business administration at the University of Illinois, Urbana. In an article on the subject, he documents the conclusion that "bad news about population growth, natural resources and the environment that is based on flimsy evidence or no evidence at all is published widely in the face of contradictory evidence." Julian L. Simon, "Resources, Population, Environment: An Oversupply of False Bad News," *Science,* vol. 208, 27 June 1980, 1431–1432.

There are many reasons for the oversupply of false bad news, including the desperate desire of poorer nations to get increased economic aid and genuine concern about the effects of technological progress. But I think that the tendency of international organizations and the media to exaggerate difficulties is itself profoundly influenced by guilt about greed and the fear of envy.

78. Envy does not just preoccupy English public school boys and their teachers. Dr. John Rae, former headmaster of Westminster School and former chairman of the Headmasters Conference, has described the difficulties he faced in becoming a public figure.

"So deeply engrained is the English public school taboo against pushing oneself forward and in favour of calculating self-effacement, that the headmaster whose name becomes too familiar is regarded as something of a cad ('brazen' was the adjective one elder statesman of the Headmasters Conference used to describe me). . . . Even now it is not quite decent for a headmaster to be seen on television. 'Didn't I see you on television?' a colleague will say accusingly as though he had spotted me slipping into a blue movie." John Rae, "Success," *Punch,* 11 March 1981, 383.

79. Edmund Leach, "Envy and the English Sickness," *The Listener,* 26 March 1970, 409.

Similarly, a calculated self-effacement has long been observed in the Chinese character. It includes self-deprecation, excessive humility, and great modesty (at least in front of strangers). As Helmut Schoeck points out, this was all part of a carefully institutionalized attitude to envy. Helmut Schoeck, *Envy: A Theory of Social Behavior,* op. cit., 54–55.

This attitude has been long established in Chinese thought: "If you are rich and of high degree, you become proud and so expose yourself to inevitable ruin. If all goes well with you, it is expedient to keep yourself in the background." *Tao Te Ching,* sixth century B.C.

80. Francis Bacon, "Of Envy," in *The Essays or Counsels, Civil and Moral,* op. cit., 59.

Bacon believed that pity was particularly useful for politicians. He advised them to arouse pity, if not by asceticism, then by continually lamenting their toilsome existence, and would have agreed with *The Washington Post*'s assessment of "humble-origins chic."

81. This person envied my life in all its aspects. He deliberately used his own wounds to make himself pitiable, not to gain help or disarm my envy of him, but to actively and maliciously attack me, by arousing pain and discomfort inside me, especially through pity. All this was really a part of a lifelong project. While his cancer, and the effects of it, were terrible blows, they also served as welcome additions to a devastating emotional armamentarium.

82. Just as European peoples continue to exclaim, "Knock on wood," or wear silver or gold crucifixes or stars of David to stave off misfortune, contemporary Moslems say, "May God protect us from the evil eye when it envies," and wear a turquoise stone or bead representing the eye of Horus (Middle East) or a bronze replica of the hand of Fatima (North Africa) around their necks.

In poor neighborhoods of Cairo, many families still make red handprints with sheep blood above the door of their homes to keep away the evil eye. Debra Weiner, "Under the Gaze of the Evil Eye," op. cit., 10W.

In modern Italy even the horses and cattle get blue beads to wear around their necks. R. W. Apple, "Apulia," *International Herald Tribune,* 26 July 1985, 8.

83.

Thou man, son of his god,
The Eye which hath looked upon thee for harm,
The Eye which hath looked upon thee for evil . . .
May Ba'u smite it with flax
May Gunura smite it with a great oar,
Like rain which is let fall from heaven,
Directed unto earth
So may Ea, king of the Deep, remove it from thy body.

Edward S. Gifford, Jr., *The Evil Eye: Studies in the Folklore of Vision,* op. cit., 54.

84. The abbreviated form of the eye of Horus appears on medical prescriptions as "Rx." This is taken to mean "recipe" but also refers to a benevolent eye watching over the compounding of medicaments. Ibid., 67.

85. Ibid., 68. The divine eye did not just serve as protection against the evil eye. It also was said to have direct beneficent powers, as did many amulets and talismans. Hence they often served a dual purpose, to ward off bad luck (the evil eye, envy) and to bring good luck. Ibid., 67–68.

86. *Fascinum* meant both fascination by the evil eye and the countercharm. Eventually it came to mean phallus because the phallus was the most common countercharm. Gifford points out that the original double significance of the word has persisted. "Dunglison's medical dictionary of 1874 defines *fascinum* as the penis, while the Gould medical dictionary of 1874 defines the same word as the belief in the evil eye." Ibid., 71.

87. St. Augustine related and was horrified by the rural custom of combating the evil eye by placing a huge carved phallus in a wagon, which was drawn through the grain fields and the town during the spring festival of the fertility god. Ibid., 71.

88. The Greeks and Romans also used to divert the evil eye by making amulets that embodied envy or the envious eye itself, which were then attacked in terrible ways. Walcot describes one such agate amulet: "Obv. naked man standing to front, head turned to left, hands crossed on chest. A large snake coils round his whole body, its head striking at the back of the man's head. The man is assailed by various

creatures; a bird pecks at his eyes, a scorpion attacks the crown of his head, another his phallus, a third his left knee, while a centipede fastens its pincers into each elbow. The bar which serves as the ground line has a knot of cord at its center, perhaps to suggest that his feet are shackled. At left φθονε, at right ατύχι, as in 'Bad luck to you, Envy.' The tortured figure personifies Envy, and the stone is an amulet to protect against the evil eye." Peter Walcot, *Envy and the Greeks,* op. cit., 85.

89. Horns may be more proper than phalli, but they are pagan in origin and have a long history. The horns of a cow have been particularly favored.

The horseshoe, a common talisman on the outside of a house or barn, was nailed with its prongs pointing upward (like horns) so that the good luck wouldn't run out. Simultaneously, it served as a defense against evil eye.

90. Edward S. Gifford, Jr., *The Evil Eye: Studies in the Folklore of Vision,* op. cit., 73.

Other peoples invoke the names of gods or other powers for the same reason, or simple words asking for protection have taken on a magical significance. Thus Jewish peole say, *"Kayn ayn horeh,"* when something good happens or is desired. This means, "Let not the evil eye behold it."

Words, sayings, and prayers taken from sacred sources such as the Koran, the Torah, and the Rig-Veda serve a similar function. They are often writen on little bits of paper and placed inside an amulet or talisman or inscribed on it.

91. Ibid., 90.

The hand has always figured prominently in gestures and amulets concerning the evil eye. It symbolizes the power of the gods or God. Hand amulets can be found in Etruscan tombs and continue to be widely worn in the Maghreb and by Oriental Jews. This hand pendant is called a "hasa" and is associated with the kabala.

92. Saliva is the favored body product in averting the evil eye, but urine and the milk of a prostitute have also been considered highly effective. Ibid., 62–66.

Spitting three times in a time-honored gesture was mentioned frequently in Greek and Roman writings. It is part of the customs of many peoples. Recently on a trip to the United States I discussed measures to avert the evil eye with my uncle, Sam Auspitz. In his youth in Hungary he clearly recalls the custom of spitting three times in front of a stranger, spitting on one's finger and touching the center of the forehead three times, or pulling one's ear three times.

Upon hearing praise, the Scots are known to combine spitting with ritual words. Thus a Scotsman might spit on his finger, moisten his eyelids, and say, "Wet your eye, and do not blight me." Or he might moisten his finger on his tongue and apply the finger to the speaker's eyelids, saying, "Wet your eye for fear I may be wounded." Ibid., 65.

93. Ibid., 62.

94. George M. Foster, "The Anatomy of Envy: A Study in Symbolic Behavior," op. cit., 177.

Inciting pride and arrogance may also be an expression of envy. When Agamemnon returned from Troy, Clytemnestra sought revenge for the death of Iphigenia. She also sought to protect herself from Agamemnon's jealousy (because of her relationship with Aegisthus) and envy (for her rule). Moreover, she herself was envious of his success and jealous of his relationship with Cassandra. She chose to greet her husband with fulsome praise and concomitant advice not to fear envy: "Who feareth envy, feareth to be great."

Clytemnestra hoped to destroy him by arousing the envy of the gods (*phthonos theon*). Agamemnon was rightly wary. Her advice was good, but in the context of his homecoming it was venomous.

Aeschylus, *The Agamemnon,* translated by Gilbert Murray (London: George Allen & Unwin Ltd., 1925), verse 939, 40.

95. Irenaus Eibl-Eibesfeldt, *Love and Hate,* translated by G. Stachan (London: Methuen, 1971), 185–186.

Professor Eibesfeldt is an ethologist in the tradition of Konrad Lorenz. He comments that the successful hunter feels honored when his elders urinate on him. I wonder whether this isn't an example of the reversal and denial of the process of self-abasement.

96. Foster points out that a sop may be psychologically discomforting. This is "indicated by the frequency with which it takes the form of a humorous 'booby prize.' As in other sensitive situations, humor is called in to gloss over what might otherwise be a more painful experience."

George M. Foster, "The Anatomy of Envy: A Study in Symbolic Behavior," op. cit., 177.

97. The distress and anger evinced by a child who does not receive a favor is also a response to a disappointed expectation, not just envy. But the point remains: why is this practice so widespread, if ostensibly unnecessary? I have observed my own children become extremely anxious if they did not have the right number, variety, and quality of favors to give to their guests after a party. Their anxiety indicated a latent fear of envy, an echo of their own experience when (rarely) they came home empty-handed after attending parties of their friends.

98. The ritual giving of presents to visitors who admire your possessions, or to family and friends after a long trip or holiday, the tip to a person who brings good news, the throwing of the bridal bouquet, the small prizes awarded to the losers of competitions, and the postcard with *"Having a wonderful time, wish you were here"* are further examples of sop behavior. The greeting can serve as an expression of a desire to share and is disarming. After all, if a holidaymaker or traveler takes the trouble to wish you were with him, you are less likely to wish him ill. Similarly, if someone gives you what you admire, or a token present that symbolizes what you admire, you are less likely to wish to do him harm. This practice is universal.

Foster quotes from a study by Richard and Eva Blum about Greek village society: "The owner of an admired object is quick to recognize that to admire is to want. In order to forestall the damage of envy, and to placate the admirer and establish a more favorable balance of obligation, the owner of the admired object gives something small to avoid having to give something larger; he may offer some portion of the admired object to the person who admires it. Thus, the gypsy who admires a dress is given a coin in order to forestall her potent curses, and the government is offered acreage if the landowner fears his large properties might be sequestered." Ibid., 178.

99. "It is the jealousy of the dead that the living fear most, and they try to propitiate them with everything they need for their journey to the land of the dead, so that they may go off and never return to harm and torment the living. The spirits of the dead send disease, or bring it with them; they have power over the increase of game and crops, and a hundred ways of meddling with life. Passionately and continually they seek to get hold of the living." Elias Canetti, *Crowds and Power,* op. cit., 262.

100. George M. Foster, "The Anatomy of Envy: A Study in Symbolic Behavior," op. cit., 179.

101. Charitable customs in many countries convey a mixture of gratitude, fear, and hatred. Foster suggests that "the Boxing Day custom of giving presents to servants and tradesmen on the day after Christmas is certainly sop behavior, symbolic sharing of the good fortune of the privileged classes." Ibid., 179.

Innumerable examples could be cited where charitable acts are done grudgingly and with a primary wish to buy off the hatred of the sick, poor, or unfortunate.

102. Handelsman, "The Story of the Envious Man and of Him Who Was Envied," *Punch,* 5 March 1980, 368. Reproduced by permission.

Chapter 3

1. Immanuel Kant, *Metaphysik der Sitten,* op. cit., 36.
Quoted by Helmut Schoeck, *Envy: A Theory of Social Behavior,* op. cit., 166.

2. "Hate, as a relation to objects, is older than love. It derives from the narcissistic ego's primordial repudiation of the external world with its out-pouring of stimuli."
Sigmund Freud, "Instincts and Their Vicissitudes," *S.E.,* vol. 14 (London: The Hogarth Press, 1957), 139.

3. "Introjection and projection are first experienced purely in terms of phantasy (mental representation of an instinct) and are specifically concerned with pleasure and pain, gratification and frustration, good and bad. The phantasies may have to do with sensations, such as the flow of warmth, the feeling of fullness, or emptiness, and the emotional reaction to these sensations, as well as the operation of these mechanisms, devouring and absorbing, or drowning and soiling. As the child grows older, images and imagos become the foci of introjection and projection aside from sensations, instinctual desires and emotions."
Joseph Berke, "Primitive Mental Mechanisms: A Study of Introjection, Projection and Identification," 1982, unpublished paper, 1–2.

4. Freud explicitly discussed the issue of a death instinct in a number of papers, including, "Beyond the Pleasure Principle," *S.E.,* vol. 18, 1920; "The Economic Problem of Masochism," *S.E.,* vol. 19, 1924; and "Analysis Terminable and Interminable," *S.E.,* vol. 23, 1937.

5. Melanie Klein, "Envy and Gratitude," in *Envy and Gratitude and Other Works 1946–1963* (London: The Hogarth Press, 1975). This work was originally published as a separate volume, *Envy and Gratitude: A Study of Unconscious Sources* (London: Tavistock Publications Ltd., 1957).

6. Entropy is the degree of randomness in a system. The struggle between life and death forces can be seen in terms of the increase or decrease of entropy in a human system. Order, integration, and an upward energy flow are akin to a negative entropic reaction (order increases). Disorder, fragmentation, and a downward spiral of energy are akin to a positive entropic reaction (order decreases).
The most recent work in physics indicates that randomness or chaos is a fundamental property of the universe and therefore of human life, too. Paul Davies, *The Cosmic Blueprint* (London: Heinemann, 1987).

7. Bruno Bettelheim argues that "instinct" is an erroneous translation of *trieb,* the term Freud used. "Impulse" is much closer to the meaning of the concept. Bettelheim further points out that if Freud had meant instinct, he would have used the specific word *instinkt.*
Bruno Bettelheim, *Freud and Man's Soul* (London: Chatto & Windus, 1983), 103–106.

8. This may explain Melanie Klein's view that the death instinct is partially projected and partially converted into aggression and directed against persecutors (anything felt to be threatening).

9. Walter G. Joffe, "A Critical Review of the Status of the Envy Concept," *Int. J. Psycho-Anal.,* vol. 50, no. 4, 1969, 537.

10. Ibid., 544.

11. Sigmund Freud, "Instincts and Their Vicissitudes," op. cit., 138.

12. Charles Brenner, "The Psychoanalytic Concept of Aggression," *Int. J. Psycho-Anal.,* vol. 52, no. 2, 1971, 138.
While stating that aggression does not have a somatic source, Brenner did conclude that psychological evidence alone is acceptable evidence to support "the concept of aggression as an instinctual drive."
Ibid., 143.

13. In "Beyond the Pleasure Principle," Freud clearly indicated that he believed the death instinct involved the whole organism. See especially pages 49 and 50. In

this respect Freud's view was different from that of Melanie Klein, who believed that the death instinct referred to the ego.

14. The infant researcher Louis W. Sander has a home movie that shows an eight-day-old baby who clearly prefers father to mother. "What delights Sander is the sensibility of the infant, a quality not generally associated with newborns. In light of a host of similar observations, partly made possible by the innovative use of videotape, scientists are revising a long-held belief that newborns are passive creatures waiting for the world to imprint its wisdom on them. From at least the moment of birth, infants are enormously responsive." Richard M. Restak, "Newborn Knowledge," *Science/82*, vol. 3, no. 1, 1982, 59–60.

See also: Bruno Bettelheim, "The World of the Newborn," in *The Empty Fortress: Infantile Autism and the Birth of the Self* (New York: The Free Press, Macmillan Publishing Co., 1967), 14–21, and Rudolph Schaffer, *Mothering* (London: Fontana/ Open Books, 1977).

15. "As an example of the *fight for rank* among animals, the farmyard pecking order has recently been much discussed. The ranking impulse in envy would appear to be an analogy on the one hand with the merciless and irrevocable classification of an individual in the precise rank ascribed to it within such an animal society, on the other hand with the possibility every animal has of moving up to a higher rank by engaging in a fight for it." Edward Baumgarten, "Versuch über mögliche Fortschritte im theoretischen und praktischen Umgang mit Macht," Studium Generale, 4th year, 1951, 540–58.

Quoted by Helmut Schoeck, *Envy: A Theory of Social Behavior,* op. cit., 77.

16. Adrian Berry, "Animal Skinheads," *The Daily Telegraph,* 3 October 1983, 14.

In recent decades it almost became a cliché to point out that man is the most dangerous animal. Adrian Berry, however, quotes the distinguished Harvard sociobiologist E. O. Watson, who points out that "if you calculate the number of murders per individual animal per hour of observation, you realize that the murder rate is far higher than for human beings, even taking into account our wars." Ibid., 14.

17. Aeschylus, *Agamemnon.* Op. cit., verses 832–837, 35.

18. Milan Kundera, *The Book of Laughter and Forgetting,* translated by H. Heim (London: King Penguin, Penguin Books, 1985), 119–154.

19. Ibid., 121.

Kundera adds that after the swim and on the way back to the city, the young man was full of despair. "He was wounded, crestfallen; he felt an irresistible desire to beat her." Again, this description is entirely consistent with envy.

20. "Since revenge can never reveal its true motivation, it must plead false ones." Ibid., 123.

21. "The pleasure principle seems actually to serve the death instincts." Sigmund Freud, "Beyond the Pleasure Principle," op. cit., 63.

22. "Aggression and libido bear similar relations to the pleasure principle. In general, discharge is associated with pleasure; lack of discharge, with unpleasure." Charles Brenner, "The Psychoanalytic Concept of Aggression," op. cit., 143.

23. "The envious person . . . instead of deriving pleasure from what he has, derives pain from what others have." Bertrand Russell, *The Conquest of Happiness,* op. cit., 66.

24. Dr. Schoeck is professor of sociology at the Johannes Gutenberg University, Mainz. He adds: "All cultures, too, have erected conceptual and ritual mechanisms designed as protection against those of their fellow men who are prone to this condition." Helmut Schoeck, *Envy: A Theory of Social Behavior,* op. cit., 8.

25. The psychoanalyst Leslie Farber has emphasized that "envy, by its very nature, is obstinate in its opposition to investigation." Leslie Farber, "The Faces of

Envy," in *lying, despair, jealousy, envy, sex, suicide, drugs, and the good life* (New York: Basic Books, 1976), 36.

26. George M. Foster, "The Anatomy of Envy: A Study in Symbolic Behavior," op. cit., 184.

Foster states: "A very important part of the explanation lies in the fact that in feeling guilt, shame, pride, greed, anger, and other similar emotions, a person is not necessarily comparing himself to another or evaluating his performance against that of another with respect to some quality or characteristic." Ibid., 184.

Foster also quotes from Harry Stack Sullivan, who was one of the first contemporary psychiatrists to clearly differentiate envy from jealousy. Sullivan pointed out that to admit to envy was to admit to inferiority:

"We find that the people who are much at the mercy of envy have learned to appraise themselves as unsatisfactory—that is, as inadequate human beings." Harry Stack Sullivan, *Clinical Studies in Psychiatry* (New York: W. W. Norton, 1956), 129.

"Envy is not pleasant because any formulation of it—any implicit process connected with it—necessarily starts with the point that you need something, some material thing that, unhappily, someone else has. This easily leads to the question, why don't you have it? And that is itself enough in some cases to provoke insecurity, for apparently the other fellow is better at assembling those material props of security than you are, which makes you even more inferior." Ibid., 132–33.

I think the issue is not simply one of inferiority, but of the destructiveness aroused by people's perceived, often misperceived, sense of inferiority in relation to another. Presumably the fellow citizens of Demosthenes or of the Medici were equally beset by the envying eye, but as a whole they appear more aware and less hypocritical about the destructive dimensions of human nature.

27. Melanie Klein, "Envy and Gratitude," *Envy and Gratitude and Other Works 1946–1963*, op. cit., 181.

28. It is so obvious that envy is an impediment to learning that it is surprising more has not been written on the subject.

Leslie Farber has commented on the relation between envy and learning, both in terms of his own inability to take in the gist of lecture from someone he envied and in general.

Leslie Farber, "The Faces of Envy," op. cit., 36–37, 40.

"Being a painfully estranging experience, envy alienates the envier from the envied one and, in this way, is inimical to what might be called mutuality, or relation. In childhood, even more than in adult life, learning and relation are—ideally, at least—reciprocal movements; neither can flourish very long without the other." Ibid., 43–44.

29. "Envy, in its inhibition of both relation and learning, invariably feeds on itself. Out of envy, the child may abandon the acquisition of a given skill that might repair the imbalance between him and the envied person—whether it be a parent or another child—resorting instead to some uncomfortable display of self-assertion. The more skills envy forces him to relinquish, the harsher grows the discrepancy between himself and others, providing him, of course, with greater opportunity for envy." Ibid., 43–44.

30. M. Klein, "Envy and Gratitude," *Envy and Gratitude and Other Works 1946–1963*, op. cit., 183–185 and 221–230.

See also: Hanna Segal, *Introduction to the Work of Melanie Klein*, op. cit., 42–47.

Herbert Rosenfeld, "Negative Therapeutic Reaction," in *Tactics and Techniques in Psychoanalytic Therapy: Volume 11, Countertransference*, Peter Giovacchini, ed. (New York: Jason Aronson, 1957), 221.

31. M. Klein, op. cit., 194–195.

32. "Excessive envy, an expression of destructive impulses, interferes with the primal split between the good and bad breast, and the building up of a good (internal) object cannot sufficiently be achieved. Thus the basis is not laid for a fully developed and integrated adult personality; for the later differentiation between good and bad is disturbed in various connections. In so far as this disturbance of development is due to excessive envy, it derives from the prevalence, in the earliest stages, of paranoid and schizoid mechanisms which, according to my hypothesis, form the basis of schizophrenia." Melanie Klein, "Envy and Gratitude," *Envy and Gratitude and Other Works 1946–1963*, op. cit., 192.

It is possible that an extreme disturbance of introjective processes, initiated by envy, can in the child result in the condition known as autism, whereby the child rejects any stimuli coming from without himself. A catatonic negativism would be a comparable event in an adult.

33. The Israelite scapegoat ceremony is described in the Bible, Leviticus, chapter 16, verses 7–10.

See Edward Whitmont's discussion of the scapegoat in *Return of the Goddess: Femininity, Aggression and the Modern Grail Quest* (London: Routledge and Kegan Paul, 1983), 105–120.

34. These ejaculations or irradiations are essentially envious projectiles. The English psychoanalyst Dr. Wilfred R. Bion considers envious projectiles to be what he terms "beta-elements." These are concrete, hostile bits of thought that contrast with what he terms "alpha-elements." These are digestible and symbolic, the necessary components of thinking, understanding, dreaming, and remembering.

"Beta-elements are not amenable to use in dream thoughts but are suited for use in projective identification. They are influential in producing acting out. They are objects that can be evacuated or used for a kind of thinking that depends on the manipulations of what are felt to be things in themselves as if to substitute such manipulation for words or ideas."

Wilfred R. Bion, "Learning from Experience," reprinted in *Seven Servants: Four Works by Wilfred R. Bion* (New York: Jason Aronson, 1977), 6.

35. Francis Bacon, "Of Envy," op. cit., 64.

Malicious projective identification can also seem like black magic, hence terms like "bewitch," "fascinate," and "overlook," all of which have been used to describe the nefarious effects of envy as mediated by projective mechanisms.

36. Edward S. Gifford, Jr., *The Evil Eye: Studies in the Folklore of Vision,* op. cit., 20.

37. Joseph Berke, "Primitive Mental Mechanisms: A Study of Introjection, Projection and Identification," op. cit., 7–8.

38. Bion has commented on the effect of envy on thinking. It can precipitate a regression from symbolic thinking ("alpha-functioning") to concrete thought ("beta-functioning") comparable to the action of projective identification. "Envy aroused by a breast (i.e., a feeding person) that provides love, understanding, experience and wisdom, poses a problem that is solved by the destruction of alpha-function. This makes breast and infant appear inanimate with consequent guiltiness, fear of suicide and fear of murder, past, present and impending."

Wilfred R. Bion, "Learning from Experience," op. cit., 11.

39. Hanna Segal, *Klein* (London: Fontana Modern Masters, Fontana, 1979), 143.

40. W. Clifford M. Scott, "Self-Envy and Envy of Dreams and Dreaming," in "Remembering Sleep and Dreams," *Int. Rev. Psycho-Anal.,* vol. 2, part 3, 1975, 335–336.

The problem was compounded because he also saw his father as an angry, critical man who could never be pleased. So the reproaches also represented attacks by an envious parental superego on a growing child. Consequently this situation generated considerable anxiety and confusion.

It is possible to ameliorate a self-envying state, with all its concomitant anxiety, confusion, and physical symptoms. About this young man, Scott commented: "The self-critical and self-envying parts gradually changed to self-tolerance as he became tolerant of the memory of his father." Ibid., 336.

41. Ibid., 336–337.

42. The young man was not a patient of mine. I only knew about him through what the woman told me about him.

43. Hanna Segal points out that in "Envy and Gratitude," Melanie Klein does not specifically link envy and narcissism, but the intimate relation between envy and narcissism is clearly implied. Certainly Segal connects the two concepts. Hanna Segal, "Some Clinical Implications of Melanie Klein's Work: Emergence from Narcissism," *Int. J. Psycho-Anal.*, vol. 64, no. 3, 1983, 270–271.

44. The American psychoanalyst Otto Kernberg distinguishes between what he calls "normal narcissism," based on self-love, and "pathological narcissism," based on self-hate. See: "Why Some People Can't Love," an interview of Otto Kernberg by Linda Wolfe, in *Psychology Today*, June 1978, 55–59. See also: Otto Kernberg, *Borderline Conditions and Pathological Narcissism* (New York: Jason Aronson, 1975).

In the latter work, Kernberg argues that there is a continuum from normal to the more extreme forms of pathological narcissism. I think what he terms normal narcissism, and others would term healthy self-love, is not really an example of narcissism but a separate phenomenon, a capacity to integrate libidinal experiences that the true narcissist does not possess.

45. I am describing the process of projective identification. The envier projectively identifies his victim with shit, to utterly rubbish and destroy him. The narcissist projectively identifies his victim with himself, to prevent him from having any life of his own and to transform him into an extension of the narcissist's own adored self. Of course the extended transaction also involves introjection and introjective identification in that the narcissist desperately wants to take in whatever will feed his self-inflation and identify with another who has already been identified with his ego ideal.

46. By partner I mean the object of narcissistic attention.

47. Hanna Segal, *Introduction to the Work of Melanie Klein*, op. cit., 44–45.

48. In narcissistic states the absence or presence of vanity can arouse intense anxiety and depression, made worse because the subject cannot comment on his dilemma without arousing intolerable shame. This is a classic double-bind, no-win situation, often associated with mental breakdown.

49. The British psychoanalyst Herbert Rosenfeld has stressed the links between destructive narcissism and envy. See: Herbert Rosenfeld, "A Clinical Approach to the Psychoanalytic Theory of the Life and Death Instincts: An Investigation into the Aggressive Aspects of Narcissism," *Int. J. Psycho-Anal.*, vol. 52, part 1, 1971, 169–178.

50. In discussing the *Oresteia*, Melanie Klein quotes from Gilbert Murray's definition of hubris: "Hubris . . . is followed by Dike, Justice, which re-establishes [bounds and order]. This rhythm—Hubris-Dike, Pride and its fall, Sin and Chastisement—is the commonest burden of those philosophical lyrics which are characteristic of Greek tragedy. . . ."

Melanie Klein, "Some Reflections on 'The Oresteia,' " *Envy and Gratitude and Other Works 1946–1963*, op. cit., 280.

51. Lee Harvey Oswald shot and killed John Kennedy, president of the United States, in Dallas, Texas, in 1963.

Sirhan Sirhan shot and killed Robert Kennedy, a United States senator, in Los Angeles, California, in 1968.

Mark Chapman shot and killed John Lennon, singer, composer, pop star, in New York, in 1980.

The dilemma of contemporary American narcissism is discussed by Christopher Lasch in *The Culture of Narcissism: American Life in an Age of Diminishing Expectations* (New York: W. W. Norton & Co., 1978).

52. My comments about the Kennedys and John Lennon are confirmed in many books and articles. About the Kennedys, see, for example: Garry Wills, *The Kennedy Imprisonment: A Meditation on Power* (Boston: Little, Brown & Co., 1982).

About Lennon, see: Thomson Prentice, "Lennon: The Rebellious Voice of a Generation," *Now,* 12 December 1980, 19–21.

53. The terrible extent to which fame attracts nemesis and ill will has been documented by Celia Brayfield in her book *Glitter: The Truth about Fame* (London: Chatto & Windus, 1985).

54. Joan Riviere points out that where unconscious defenses against emptiness, hatred, and death are based on greed, a lack of goods or goodness arouses an intolerable sense of insecurity because the person not only feels empty or no good, but constantly feels he has been robbed by others with whom he compares himself. This occurs because he tends to projectively identify his own wish to rob them of their goodness, into them, and bitterly believes he has been robbed of goodness and security, by them. Joan Riviere, "Hate, Greed and Aggression," in *Love, Hate and Reparation,* by Melanie Klein and Joan Riviere (London: The Hogarth Press, 1957), 26–28.

55. The narcissism of the child may be a defense against envy, an expression of envy, and a defense against depression, among various considerations.

In practice the narcissism of the child and of his parents potentiate each other, and it takes a considerable effort, on both their parts, to achieve a nonnarcissistic state of respect and tolerance.

56. The omnipotence of a child of narcissistic parents is partially a learned response, a variation of identification with the aggressor. On the other hand, the omnipotence of the aggressively narcissistic child is an expression of contempt.

57. "In the narcissistic states where the libidinal aspects predominate, destructiveness becomes apparent as soon as the omnipotent self-idealization is threatened by contact with an object which is perceived as separate from the self. . . . In analysis one observes that when the patient's feelings of resentment and revenge at being robbed of his omnipotent narcissism diminishes, envy is consciously experienced, since it is then that he becomes aware of the analyst as a valuable external person.

When the destructive aspects predominate, the envy is more violent and appears as a wish to destroy the analyst as the object who is the real source of life and goodness."

Herbert Rosenfeld, "A Clinical Approach to the Psychoanalytic Theory of the Life and Death Instincts: An Investigation into the Aggressive Aspects of Narcissism," op. cit., 173.

58. "Flaw in narcissistically perceived reality" is a term employed by the American psychoanalyst Heinz Kohut to denote what calls forth the "archaic rage of the narcissistically vulnerable" person.

Heinz Kohut, "Thoughts on Narcissism and Narcissistic Rage," in *Psychoanalytic Study of the Child,* vol. 27 (New York: Quadrangle, 1972), 386.

In his discussion of narcissistic rage, Kohut does not relate it to envy. However, he attributes many qualities and characteristics to narcissistic rage that are almost identical to my description of envy—that is, its spiteful, begrudging, vindictive, fanatical, uncompromising, unforgiving qualities. This leads me to conclude that he is, in fact, describing envy.

". . . chronic narcissistic rage, one of the most pernicious afflictions of the human psyche—either, in its still endogenous and preliminary form, as grudge and spite, or, externalized and acted out, in disconnected vengeful acts or in a cunningly plotted vendetta." Ibid., 396–97.

59. The story "Snow-White" appears in many versions throughout Europe and

other continents as well. My quotes are from the tale collected by the Brothers Grimm:

Jacob and Wilhelm Grimm, *Selected Tales*, translated by David Luke (London: Penguin Classics, 1982), 74.

60. Ibid., 74.

61. Ibid., 75.

62. Ibid., 75.

63. Salieri also struck at a figure who disturbed his reveries, as did Ivan Babichev. However, Babichev's "typical little girl" was both a person in her own right and a mirror to him of his own admirable qualities, hence his initial love for her. In contrast, Othello received almost nothing from Desdemona but reflections, which put her life in mortal danger when they returned dark and villainous. In the end the Moor realized his mistake, but it was too late. So he stabbed himself, a vain act of contrition and self-murder. Just as he had smothered his wife, he snuffed out the part of himself that had remained attached to her.

64. The nirvana principle is a term suggested by the English psychoanalyst Barbara Low and adopted by Freud in order to signify "the tendency of the psychical apparatus to reduce the quantity of excitation in itself, whether of internal or of external origin, to zero—or, failing that, to as low a level as possible."

J. Laplanche and J.-B. Pontalis, *The Language of Psycho-Analysis* (London: The Hogarth Press, 1973), 272.

Freud directly connected the nirvana principle with the death instinct in his paper "The Economic Problem of Masochism," op. cit., 160.

65. An earlier version of this chapter was published under the title "Envy Loveth Not: A Study of the Origin, Influence and Confluence of Envy and Narcissism," *Brit. J. Psychoth.*, vol. 1, no. 3, 1985, 171–186.

Chapter 4

1. Certainly newborn infants—indeed, many children and adults—do not readily differentiate between what they want, what they feel, and where the feelings come from. From their point of view they create the breast in order to satisfy their own needs, and the breast is identical with whatever they experience. It does not matter that an outside observer might think otherwise.

2. Merell Middlemore, who was one of the first doctors to systematically study the suckling mother-child relationship, described many of these early physical and emotional experiences under the heading "suckling satisfaction." Merell Middlemore, *The Nursing Couple* (London: Hamish Hamilton Medical Books, 1941).

3. Jonathan Miller uses this phrase in a discussion with Hanna Segal. Segal herself had just commented that the breast is "an experience coming from an object that satisfies hunger, takes away the cold, makes one feel totally happy, maybe brings back even some feeling of being back in the womb."

Jonathan Miller, *States of Mind* (London: British Broadcasting Corporation, 1983), 255.

4. The need for adequate stimulation remains throughout one's life. Thus, a project supported by Age Research (Bristol, England) showed that a lack of stimulation can lead to incontinence among the elderly, and that the effects of incontinence can be alleviated, and even totally overcome, by stimulating the elderly in meaningful ways. "Memory Jog for Health in Old Age," *The Times*, 16 April 1986, 3.

5. Sigmund Freud, "Instincts and Their Vicissitudes," op. cit., 138.

6. The image of a mother destroying her infant by feeding agitation was evoked by Bruno Bettelheim in his discussion of the Holocaust. Bettelheim likened the destructive mother to a provider of "black milk"—that is, the milk of death. He commented: "When one is forced to drink black milk, from dawn to dusk, whether

in the death camps of Nazi Germany, or while lying in a possibly luxurious crib, but there subjected to the unconscious death wishes of what overtly may be a conscientious mother—in either situation, a living soul has death for a master." Bruno Bettelheim, *Surviving the Holocaust* (London: Flamingo Books, Fontana Paperbacks, 1986), 103.

7. Merell Middlemore emphasizes the importance of the mother's emotional attitude on the mental as well as physical development of the child. A hostile, frightened state of mind, often evinced by rough or clumsy handling, will get through and attack the child just as if she were providing poisoned milk. Merell Middlemore, *The Nursing Couple,* op. cit., 111–121.

8. This is an awareness impelled by the rooting reflex and fashioned by many, increasingly well-organized, memories of suckling.

9. I don't think it is necessary for me to discuss the relative merits of breast versus bottle feeding. What matters most is the feeding, caring relationship. The bosom/nipple or bottle/teat can be satisfactory or unsatisfactory as part of the larger process of bonding between mother and child.

10. In Greek mythology the cornucopia was the horn of a goat that suckled Zeus and could become full of whatever he wanted. It later came to mean any horn or container that could become full of whatever its owner wanted.

11. In discussing the problem of unsatisfied sucklings (inert and/or irritable babies), Merell Middlemore provides an excellent description of the containing mother: "They did not complain of the long feeds, and were patient and gentle with the babies—more patient than the nurses who attended them. . . ." Merell Middlemore, *The Nursing Couple,* op. cit., 80.

Interestingly, the popular nursery rhyme "Rockabye Baby" can illustrate containment or noncontainment. The lyrics themselves would indicate a tired mother, like a bending tree, with arms like branches which can easily break and let the baby drop. On the other hand, when sung softly and tenderly, the words matter less than the caressing sounds, which indicate that trees may break but Mother will always be around to carry her baby's burdens.

12. The mental representation or image of the breast is an internal object to which people relate just as much as to an external object. The concept of the internal object has been discussed at length by Melanie Klein and her colleagues and, from another perspective, by psychologist Professor George Miller. See his discussion of an internal representation in his dialogue with Jonathan Miller, "The Background to Modern Psychology," in Jonathan Miller, *States of Mind,* op. cit., 12–29.

13. And the desire was also to redress some of the poison, the black milk, hate masking as love, absence masking as presence, which the actress had forced into her.

While commenting on comparable issues, Merell Middlemore also points out that aside from being self-absorbed, many mothers have specific physical and mental difficulties in feeding their babies. These include an active fear or dislike of breastfeeding, a poorly constructed breast (congested, balloon-shaped breasts with flat nipples), excessive sensitivity to the baby's sucking, inadequate supply of milk, and depression or other mental disturbances. (All of these may or may not be associated with narcissistic mothering.) Merell Middlemore, *The Nursing Couple,* op. cit., 69, 73, 91, 95–97.

14. The statue of Diana of Ephesus depicts a large, succulent woman with arms outstretched and with a plethora of breasts covering the top half of her body. Plate 35, Diana of Ephesus, in Erich Neumann, *The Great Mother: An Analysis of the Archetype* (New York: Bollingen Series XLVII, Pantheon Books, 1963).

See also: other pictures in the series *Primordial Goddess* and *Positive Elementary Character,* plates 1–53, ibid.

15. The Mosque of El Jazzar is located in Acre, Israel. It was completed in 1781 by Ahmed el-Jazzar, who was noted for his cruelty. Any workman who made the

slightest mistake was buried alive. This indicates his desire to create the perfect woman, not unlike Diana of Ephesus.

The breast-covered courtyard is dominated by a tall minaret. Arguably this represents the potent phallus of el-Jazzar dominating his domain.

I am thankful to Helen Silman for bringing this mosque to my attention.

16. *Forum,* vol. 17, no. 10, October 1984, 117.

17. Joseph Rheingold refers to a study of the dreams of forty-three children in which they had intense fears of being bitten, chased, and destroyed by being eaten. He says that older children frequently identify the threatening person as their mother. He concludes that children reveal their well-justified fears and hatred of Mother through their dreams and phobias. Joseph Rheingold, *The Fear of Being a Woman: A Theory of Maternal Destructiveness* (New York: Grune & Stratton, 1964), 136.

18. Merell Middlemore states that with this little girl the feeding difficulties arose entirely in the child. The mother had successfully nursed an elder child and wanted to nurse this one. Moreover there was plenty of milk. "The point is that although she [the girl] had never sucked the breast properly, still less 'attacked' it, she entertained very fierce fantasies of biting." Merell Middlemore, *The Nursing Couple,* op. cit., 189–190.

19. *Everything You Always Wanted to Know About Sex (But Were Afraid to Ask),* United Artists, 1972, directed by Woody Allen, produced by Charles Joffe.

See also: Robert Benayoun, *Woody Allen: Beyond Words,* translated by A. Walker, (London: Pavilion Books, 1987), 56–59 and 168.

20. Referring to the child's oral sadistic attacks on the breast, Melanie Klein commented: "He gets possession of the contents of his mother's breast by sucking and scooping it out. This desire to suck and scoop out, first directed to her breast, soon extends to the inside of her body." Melanie Klein, "Early Stages of the Oedipus Conflict and of Super-Ego Formation," in *The Psycho-Analysis of Children* (London: The Hogarth Press, 1975), 128.

21. Ioan Lewis is professor of anthropology at the London School of Economics. Personal communication, June 1983.

22. Karl Abraham, "A Short Study of the Development of the Libido, Viewed in the Light of Mental Disorders," in *Selected Papers on Psycho-Analysis* (London: The Hogarth Press, 1973), 488.

23. This view is the misguided counterpart of the belief in absolute equality—that is, if people owned nothing (if everyone had the same), then envy (and greed) would be abolished.

24. I am indebted to Thomas T. S. Hayley, editor of the *International Journal of Psycho-Analysis,* who has made available to me an article he wrote on Khoba-Khobee for a symposium on envy and jealousy. It is based on anthropological fieldwork he had done in Assam. Khoba and Khobee are male and female demons that sprang forth from the mouth of the Hindu goddess Parbati, wife of Shiva. According to myth, Shiva used to live by begging. His wife hated the taunts of other gods and goddesses and nagged him to take up cultivation instead. Shiva did this but with such skill and enthusiasm that Parbati felt alone and abandoned.

Finally she went out herself to see what he was doing; when she saw his magnificent crops, in her unbounded astonished admiration she exclaimed, 'Uh, ah.' At this two terrible beings, Khoba and Khobee, came forth from Parbati's mouth. They were male and female joined together. They rushed through the crops, burning them up." Thomas T. S. Hayley, "Khoba Khobee," unpublished article.

25. Edmund Spenser (1552–1599?). The passage was quoted by Melanie Klein in "Envy and Gratitude." *Envy and Gratitude and Other Works 1946–1963,* op. cit., 202.

Klein also comments on the poet Geoffrey Chaucer (1340?–1400), author of *The Canterbury Tales:* "In Chaucer also we find extensive references to this backbiting and destructive criticizing which characterizes the envious person. He describes the sin of backbiting as arising from a compound of the envious person's unhappiness at other men's goodness and prosperity, and his joy in their harm. The sinful behavior is characterized by 'the man who praises his neighbor but with wicked intent, for he always puts "but" at the end, and follows it with another of greater blame than is the worth of the person. Or, if a man is good and does or says things of good intent, the backbiter will turn all this goodness upside down to his own shrewd intent. Or if other men speak good of a man, then the backbiter will say that he is very good, but will point to someone else who is better, and will thus disparage he whom other men praise.' " Ibid., 202–203.

26. Savage, often mutual, loathings among the famous and well-to-do exert an irresistible fascination for the public. John Walsh has provided a trenchant review of biting, bitchy remarks on the contemporary English artistic and literary scene. After ranging from Boswell about Gibbon ("Gibbon is an ugly, affected, disgusting fellow, and poisons our literary club for me. I class him among infidel wasps and venomous insects") and Tchaikovsky about Brahms ("What a giftless bastard!"), he zeros in on contemporary tongue-lashings (poets Horowitz vs. Raine: a man who condemns us "to video-skipping rhymes for evermore"). John Walsh, "Fear and Loathing in L'Escargot," *ES* (*Evening Standard* magazine), December 1987, 54–58.

27. "I have seen babies as young as three weeks interrupt their sucking for a short time to play with the mother's breast or to look towards her face. I have also observed that young infants—even as early as in the second month—would in wakeful periods after feeding lie on the mother's lap, look up at her, listen to her voice and respond to it by their facial expression; it was like a loving conversation between mother and baby. Such behavior implies that gratification is as much related to the object which gives the food as to the food itself." Melanie Klein, "On Observing the Behavior of Young Infants," in *Envy and Gratitude and Other Works 1946–1963*, op. cit., 96.

28. "Early infantile splitting processes related both to confusional anxieties and oral sadistic envy constitute one of the fixation points of hypochondriacal states. The ego seems unable to work through the confusional state in the mental apparatus. It constantly projects the confusional state, including the internal objects and parts of the self, such as oral sadism, into external objects which are immediately reintrojected into the body and body organs." Herbert Rosenfeld, "The Psychopathology of Hypochondriasis," in *Psychotic States: A Psycho-Analytical Approach* (London: The Hogarth Press, 1965), 199.

29. I am describing of course an unconscious mental representation that is not limited to sharks but can take the form of any horrible wild beast or alien creature with the characteristics of a wild beast. For the most part these images are unthinkable thoughts. They arouse horror whenever they permeate consciousness, as in a nightmare.

30. In considering the ways that human qualities, capacities, and characteristics can represent the breast, the second-century Clement of Alexandria often referred to Logos as "the milk of God the Father." For the Greeks, Logos meant the power of reason. For Christian theologians it meant the creative, sustaining spirit of God as revealed in Jesus. The product of this Logos can be seen in a prayer which begins with "Lead us, holy Shepherd of rational sheep . . ." and ends with "source of heavenly milk from the bride's sweet breasts which are the graces of thy Sophia. As it is pressed out, the babes with tender mouths are nourished, filled with the dewey spirit of thy Logos-nipple." Quoted by Edmund Leach, "The Big Fish in the Biblical Wilderness," *Int. Rev. Psycho-Anal.*, vol. 13, part 2, 1986, 140.

31. Philip Roth, *The Breast* (London: Jonathan Cape, 1973), 12–13.

32. Melanie Klein, "Envy and Gratitude," *Envy and Gratitude and Other Works 1946–1963*, op. cit., 207–208.

33. In this sense the manic defense is an important defense against loss of the manic state.

34. The manic state of mind is quite similar to that resulting from the effects of the drug cocaine. This capacity to instantly achieve a position of godlike exuberance and deny external needs greatly contributes to the popularity of the drug, both in general and by depressed individuals in particular.

35. Vampires, werewolves, and other draining creatures so beloved by film-makers and their audiences illustrate archetypical desires toward anyone in the role of source of supply, especially women. The horrific fate of the victims consists not simply in their drained, cadaverous look, indicating the effects of unrestrained greed, but especially in their loss of will and transmutation into an agent of the devil, indicating the effects of envy.

36. The basic wish is to rob and destroy mother's insides so she cannot feed herself or anyone else. See the discussion of morbid jealousy by the psychoanalyst Joan Riviere in her paper "Jealousy As a Mechanism of Defense," op. cit., 414–424.

37. See: John Todd and Kenneth Dewhurst, "The Othello Syndrome: A Study in the Psychopathology of Sexual Jealousy," *The Journal of Nervous and Mental Disease,* vol. 122, no. 4, October 1955, 267–277.

"The Othello Syndrome," in *Some Uncommon Psychiatric Symptoms,* edited by M. O. Enoch, W. H. Trethowan, and J. C. Barker (Bristol: Wright & Son, 1967), 25–40.

38. There are exceptions to this rule. An obvious one occurs where envy and jealousy occur together and neither predominates. Then the third party may be hated for intruding (jealousy) and hated for being good enough to warrant affection (envy). Similarly, the primary partner may be hated for loving another (jealousy) and hated for being lovable (envy).

Alternatively the envier may direct his hatred to a third party in order to disguise the enmity and make it appear less shameful. In this instance jealousy masks envy.

39. Genesis, chapter 26, lines 12–16. *The Torah: A Modern Commentary* (New York: Union of Hebrew Congregations, 1981), 180–181.

40. Mr. Roy Watsdon, director general of the (U.K.) National Farmers' Union, told Lincolnshire farmers at Woodhall Spa. *The Daily Telegraph,* London, 9 January 1982, 3.

41. The many ways in which a physical environment can be seen, treated, and attacked as the breast has also been illustrated by Julia Segal in "Mother, Sex and Envy in a Children's Story," *Int. Rev. Psycho-Anal.,* vol. 6, 1979, 483–497.

Similar issues sustain "the greens" and other environmentalists determined to protect natural beauty from the grenvious ravages of man. Sometimes, however, the reasons for these attacks are not obvious. Why, for example, do Californians so often deface their environment by destroying great trees, wrecking coastlines, and so forth? Is it simply envy? Long ago the naturalist Henry David Thoreau argued that anger about the awesome beauty of Mother Nature—that is, a sense of personal diminution in comparison to nature—led Californians to want to mutilate it so they wouldn't feel so inferior. Essentially Thoreau was commenting on the narcissistic nature of the attack, and, in not so many words, he was linking envious malice with narcissistic vulnerability. See discussion by Kevin Starr in *Americans and the California Dream 1850–1915* (Oxford: Oxford University Press, 1973), 418.

42. Dr. George Miller in Jonathan Miller, *States of the Mind,* op. cit., 27–28.

43. "Reality" is a conjectural model based on the uniquely human capacity to define experience, anticipate experience (and behavior), formulate responses, and make corrections according to whatever happens. See discussion between Jonathan Miller and George Miller, ibid., 14–28.

44. I use the term "symbolic equivalent" rather than "symbol" to denote the fact that during a period of regression, elements of reality may lose their symbolic, "just like" quality and, as far as the regressed person is concerned, become identical with the object they are meant to symbolize. See: Hanna Segal, "Notes on Symbol Formation," *Int. J. Psycho-Anal.*, vol. 38, 1957, 391–397.

45. Wilfred Bion, "Attacks on Linking," *Int. J. Psycho-Anal.*, vol. 40, 1959, 313.

46. Bettelheim added: "Girls never seemed interested in the riddle, but the preadolescent emotionally disturbed boys nearly always were fascinated by it." Bruno Bettelheim, *Symbolic Wounds* (London: Thames & Hudson, 1955), 36–37.

47. Sigmund Freud, "New Introductory Lectures on Psycho-Analysis," *S. E.*, vol. 22, op. cit., 122.

Chapter 5

1. Quoted by John Williams, in "An Essay on the Utility of Sea Bathing . . . Especially in Nervous, Scrophulous, Bilious and Cutaneous Complaints," in *Three Hundred Years of Psychiatry 1535–1860,* edited by Richard Hunter and Ida Macalpine (London: Oxford University Press, 1963), 223.

2. Ilza Veith, *Hysteria: The History of a Disease* (Chicago: University of Chicago Press, 1965), 96.

3. Jean Liebaut, *Trésor des remèdes secrètes pour les maladies des femmes* (Paris, 1597), 529, quoted by Edward Shorter, in *A History of Women's Bodies* (London: Penguin Books, 1982), 13.

4. Quoted by Maggie Scarf in her review of *Medical and Psychological Interfaces, Vol. 1: Sexual and Reproductive Aspects of Woman's Health Care,* edited by Malkah Notman and Carol Nadelson, in *The New York Times Book Review,* 31 December 1978, 11.

5. Wilhelm Tell, "Song of the Fisherboy," translated by Theodore Martin, quoted by Karen Horney, "The Dread of Women," in *Psychoanalysis and Male Sexuality,* edited by Henrik Ruitenbeek (New Haven, Conn.: College and University Press, 1966), 84.

6. "A kiss is a hiss from the abyss," R. D. Laing, personal communication, 1966.

7. Wilhelm Tell, quoted by Karen Horney, "The Dread of Women," op. cit., 84.

In this ballad Tell compares entering a woman to leaping into a dangerous whirlpool that sucks all into its depths "and cleaves through the ocean a path that seems winding in darkness to hell." Then:

Below at the foot of the precipice drear,
Spread the glowing, and purple, and pathless Obscure!
A silence of Horror that slept on the ear,
That the eye more appalled might the Horror endure!
Salamander—snake—dragon—vast reptiles that dwell
In the deep, coil'd about the grim jaws of their hell.

8. "I think it is probable that the masculine dread of the woman (the mother) or of the female genital is more deep-seated, weighs more heavily and is usually more energetically repressed than the dread of the man (father). . . ." Karen Horney, ibid., 88.

9. "Horney's [1923] belief that men's fear of women and dread of the vulva derive from the boy's fear of loss of self-esteem because his penis is not large enough to satisfy his mother and his subsequent fear as a man of being sucked in or engulfed during intercourse should not be taken too literally, but rather in terms of the pull of the wish-fear for reunion with the mother and re-engulfment by her." Ruth and

Theodor Lidz, "Male Menstruation: A Ritual Alternative to the Oedipal Transition," *Int. J. Psycho-Anal.*, vol. 58, 1977, 27.

Similarly, Neil Maizel points out that the mental castration that accompanies intercourse, or the wish to repose inside mother, is essentially a feared inability to become separate and independent. Neil Maizel, "Self-Envy, the Womb and the Nature of Goodness," *Int. J. Psycho-Anal.*, vol. 66, 1985, 186.

10. Joan Riviere, "Hate, Greed and Aggression," op. cit., 32.

11. "Excessive envy interferes with adequate oral gratification and so acts as a stimulus towards the intensification of genital desires and trends. This implies that the infant turns too early towards genital gratification, with the consequence that the oral relation becomes genitalized and the genital trends become too much coloured by oral grievances and anxieties." Melanie Klein, "Envy and Gratitude," *Envy and Gratitude and Other Works 1946–1963*, op. cit., 195.

12. Before the widespread availability of contraceptives, both ingrained prudery and the social consequences of unwanted pregnancy cast a chill over women's sexual responsiveness. Subsequently the work of sexologists like Masters and Johnson shed new light on female orgasmic potential, so much so that some feminists began to taunt men for their sexual inferiority. Thus Mary Jane Sherfey wrote: "Theoretically, a woman could go on having orgasms indefinitely if physical exhaustion did not intervene." And Kate Millett concluded: "While the male's sexual potential is limited, the female's appears to be biologically nearly inexhaustible." Quoted by Christopher Lasch, *The Culture of Narcissism: American Life in an Age of Diminishing Expectations*, op. cit., 193–194.

13. While discussing penis envy, Judd Marmor points out that as women become more valued and privileged in Western society, they will become relatively more hated, and "unconscious manifestations of penis envy will begin to diminish, and those women envy will begin to increase." Judd Marmor, "Changing Patterns of Femininity: Psychoanalytic Implications," in Jean Baker Miller (ed.), *Psychoanalysis and Women* (London: Penguin Books, 1974), 230–232.

14. This view was common among the European peasantry and is consistent with the idea that the womb is an animal that could move about within the body and make people sick when aroused.

Some people thought of the uterus as a frog "with many legs that is supposed to stay in the body, because you have to die when the colic (or frog) creeps out of your throat." According to one account from the Tirol, a woman became ill on a pilgrimage and lay down on the grass. "Scarcely was she asleep when the uterus, and the attaching ligaments crept out of her mouth into a brook, swam around, and crawled back inside. When she awakened she was healed."

"Globus hystericus," or inability to swallow, was often ascribed to the uterus rising to the throat. To overcome the problem women were advised to repeat, "Womb high, womb low, get back to the old place that God sent you. In the name of God, the Father, the Son. . . ." and to make the sign of the cross three times.

Edward Shorter, *A History of Women's Bodies,* op. cit., 287.

15. By the 1600s the English physician Edward Jordon and the French physician Carolus Piso affirmed that hysteria was caused by perturbations of the brain and could afflict men as well as women. Ilza Veith, *Hysteria: The History of a Disease,* op. cit., 120–129.

16. Ibid., 5.

Veith comments: "Although the medicinal use of highly unappetizing substances was far from uncommon in ancient Egypt, this particular prescription suggests deliberate choice. The implication of gratifying the uterus with discharges from the opposite sex cannot be disregarded."

17. Ibid., 22–31.

The idea of the womb being constricted or suffocated was related to observations of female disorders such as prolapsed uterus. It is important to note that in spite of views about hysteria that we would consider to be bizarre, many physicians, from Egyptians to Romans, related hysterical symptoms to sexual abstinence or frustration, a much more accurate assessment of the problem.

18. Jules Garinet, *Histoire de la magic' en France* (Paris: Foulon, 1818), 29, quoted by Ilza Veith, ibid., 57.

19. Heinrich Kramer and James Sprenger, *Malleus Maleficarum,* translated with an introduction, bibliography, and notes by Montague Summers (London: Pushkin Press, 1951).

20. In many cities in Germany alone, "the average number of executions for this pretended crime [witchcraft] was six hundred annually, or two every day, if we leave out the Sundays, when it is to be supposed that even this madness refrained from its work."

Charles Mackay, *Memoirs of Extraordinary Popular Delusions* (London: Richard Bentley, 1841), 463, quoted by Ilza Veith, *Hysteria: The History of a Disease,* op. cit., 60–61.

21. *Malleus,* op. cit., 119, quoted by Ilza Veith, ibid., 64.

22. Ibid., 43, quoted by Ilza Veith, ibid., 63.

23. These issues exist in many disparate cultures. The Celts had a particular fear of hags and witches that threatened travelers with "women's spells." Therefore, "Journey Prayers" became popular, to be said before embarking on a trip. A typical journey prayer asked for protection against "the woman in her knee, at her evil eye, with her spleen, with her envy." The prayer continued, citing the danger of woman with cattle or calves and the rearing of flocks until she "reaches the fibres of the heart, frowning and foul." Finally the prayer concludes with

Each woman who is full of spleen and envy,
Who sunders her blood, her flesh and gore,
On herself be her spleen and her severing,
From this day to the final day of the world.

Quoted by Anne Ross, "The Divine Hag of the Pagan Celts," in Venetia Newall (ed.), *The Witch Figure* (London: Routledge and Kegan Paul, 1973).

24. Phyllis Chesler points out that the tendency of men in religion "to devalue real motherhood and elevate spiritual motherhood as much as they do" is further proof of their pervasive "uterus envy." Quoted by Janet Chase-Marshall, in "Who's Afraid of Phyllis Chesler?" *Human Behavior,* September 1978, 55.

25. *Malleus,* op. cit., xix, quoted by Ilza Veith, *Hysteria: The History of a Disease,* op. cit., 59.

26. The uroboros is "the symbol of the psychic state of the beginning, of the original situation in which man's consciousness and ego were still small and undeveloped. As symbol of the origin and of the opposites contained in it, the uroboros is the 'Great Round,' in which positive and negative, male and female elements . . . intermingle." Erich Neumann, *The Great Mother,* op. cit., 18.

In other words, the uroboros symbolizes the womb of all things.

27. I refer here, of course, to the operation of projective identification and the ways that the envied object can appear as the envier, the persecuted person as persecuting. Old women were favorite objects for this because, like Géricault's *A Mad Woman with the Mania of Envy,* they appeared to embody the life-begrudging spite of their accusers. It is likely that in many instances the accused women were bitter and bizarre, which made it all the easier for them to become the focus of others' malevolent projections. Ironically, the bitterness can be seen as a realistic reaction to life circumstances involving severe sexual deprivation and frustration as a result of theological conventions. I especially refer to the untold number of women who spent their lives cooped up in convents. Having been deprived of sex, they were then accused of wanting it.

28. "It vexes me that women have two openings in the lower part of their bodies, while men have only one. I envy them that." Comment by thirty-year-old male patient quoted by Felix Boehm, in "The Femininity Complex in Man," in *Psychoanalysis and Male Sexuality*, edited by H. Ruitenbeek, op. cit., 128.

29. "The girl's nature as biologically conditioned gives her the desire to receive, to take into herself; she feels or knows that her genital is too small for her father's penis and this makes her react to her own genital wishes with direct anxiety: she dreads that if her wishes were fulfilled, she herself or her genital would be destroyed." Karen Horney, "The Dread of Women," op. cit., 91.

30. The inclusion of the Virgin Mary as an example of the good womb is based on the idealization of its nonuse for heterosexual reproduction and pleasure. Mary symbolizes receptivity to spiritual powers, but her physical prowess is that of the Madonna and has to do with feeding, the good breast incarnate, not reproduction. One sees this split particularly strongly in Catholic countries such as Mexico, where the womb as a person is divided according to its idealized loving, feeding, caring qualities, the Madonna, and its denigrated, carnal function, the Whore. See discussion by Phyllis Chesler, *Women and Madness* (New York: Doubleday & Co., 1952), 22–24.

31. It would seem that the early Church fathers tried to appropriate the quality of mystery. Thus the Church became both a center of mystery and a keeper of mysteries—of the miracle of creation, spiritual and temporal, miracles about which the Church tried to maintain a monopoly for itself. All this was challenged during the late Middle Ages when people sought to discover these mysteries through science, literature, other cultures, or even the human body. This challenge helps to explain the ensuing envious and jealous conflicts. Similar dynamics operate in other social bodies, political and bureaucratic, as well as religious.

32. Margaret Mead, *Male and Female* (London: Victor Gollancz, 1950), 102–103.
Mead adds: "Behind the cult lies the myth that in some way all of this was stolen from the women; sometimes women were killed to get it. Men owed their manhood to a theft and a theatrical mime, which would fall to the ground in a moment as mere dust and ashes if its true constituents were known. A shaky structure, protected by endless taboos and precautions, enforced by the women's name in Iatmul, by fluttery fear for their childbearing qualities in Arapesh, by good-humored indulgence of male vanity in Tchambuli, and by blows and buffets and the various reversed identification of flute and women in Mundugumor, it survives only as long as every one keeps the rules. . . . The missionary who shows the flutes to the women has broken the culture successfully." Ibid., 103.

33. Ibid., 103.

34. The marines and other military organizations have many other features of male motherhood. Not only does the military preserve and enhance the idea of mystery or military secrecy, but it perpetuates dependency. Members of the organization, and their families, remain dependent on it for their every need, as on a feeding breast.

35. Soldiers destroy what mothers create. It is worth noting that women can be soldiers as well as men.

36. John Milton, *Paradise Lost*, books 1 and 2.
See also: discussion by Melanie Klein, in "Envy and Gratitude," *Envy and Gratitude and Other Works 1946–1963*, op. cit., 202.

37. Roland Littlewood, *Pathology and Identity in Northeast Trinidad*, unpublished D. Phil. thesis. Chapter 5, paragraph 8.
Dr. Littlewood is a British anthropologist and psychiatrist. He lived with Mother Earth and her group in Trinidad and has written a detailed study of her life, her teachings, and her followers. I quote with his permission.
"Rastas" refers to the followers of the Rastifaris, an Afro-Caribbean religious and political movement.

38. In the ensuing years a community of upward of two dozen followers (at any one time) was established in the bush. These were usually black Trinidadian men who sometimes brought their girlfriends and children "to come and 'plant for the Nation.' "

Roland Littlewood, "The Imitation of Madness: The Influence of Psychopathology upon Culture," *Soc. Sci. Med.,* vol. 19, no. 7, 1984, 710–712.

39. Littlewood, *Pathology and Identity in Northeast Trinidad,* op. cit., chapter 5, paragraphs 14 and 15.

40. In phantasy she cruelly attacked her mother and simultaneously punished herself. This served to relieve the guilt aroused by the attacks on her mother, as did her tendency to allow others to express her rage. This was a way of distancing herself from the feeling and from responsibility for it.

The negation of function was also a placatory message. In this instance the girl wanted to avoid her mother's revenge by making the mother pity her. The message was: "I have damaged my potential. Look, you have nothing to fear from me. I can't hurt you. Please don't hurt me. Help me."

41. Edward Shorter, *A History of Women's Bodies,* op. cit., 287.

See also: Penelope Shuttle and Peter Redgrove, *The Wise Wound: Menstruation and Everywoman* (London: V. Gollancz, 1978), and Paula Weidegar, *Menstruation and Menopause: The Physiology and Psychology, the Myth and the Reality* (New York: Alfred Knopf, 1976).

42. Edward Shorter, ibid., 287.

43. Ibid., 287–288.

44. Ruth and Theodor Lidz, "Male Menstruation," op. cit., 23–25.

45. Men do not have the equivalent of menarche. Nocturnal emissions and body hair are more amorphous signals. Many observers have commented that male initiation rites at puberty serve to make up for this lack.

46. B. Spencer and F. J. Gillen, *The Native Tribes of Central Australia* (London: Macmillan & Co., 1899), quoted by Bruno Bettelheim, in *Symbolic Wounds: Puberty Rites and the Envious Male,* op. cit., 174.

47. G. Róheim, *The Eternal Ones of the Dream* (New York: International Universities Press, 1945), 165.

48. Ruth and Theodor Lidz, "Male Menstruation," op. cit., 18–24.

49. Ibid., 20.

The authors add: "However, the women believe, as much as do the men, that the group's well-being and the fertility of the women, pigs and soil, as well as the growth and maturation of the children, depend on the mediation of the ancestor spirits who must be summoned and placated, if not controlled and satisfied, by the rituals the men carry out." Ibid., 20.

50. Bruno Bettelheim, *Symbolic Wounds: Puberty Rites and the Envious Male,* op. cit., 30.

Many of the boys felt "cheated" or "gypped" that girls had vaginas and they didn't. Some repeatedly complained, "She thinks she is something special because she has a vagina," or "Why can't I have a vagina?" Ibid., 34.

51. Felix Boehm, "The Femininity Complex in Men," op. cit., 128.

52. Penelope Shuttle and Peter Redgrove, *The Wise Wound: Menstruation and Everywoman,* op. cit., 52.

53. Lucienne Roubin, *Chambrettes des Provencaux* (Paris: Plon, 1970), 157, quoted by Shorter, *A History of Women's Bodies,* op. cit., 288.

54. Hormonal treatments, for example, allow women to behave with almost manic frenzy toward their periods, stopping, starting, reducing, increasing them, and so forth.

Otherwise, premenstrual tension (PMT) has become a recognized medical syndrome and an important defense for women on trial. Thus, a woman who pleaded PMT was freed after running down her lover with a car. Recently, however, this has been challenged as a defense both by the law and feminists who feel that women should not use biology to avoid equal responsibility (with men) for their actions. Sheila Duncan, "No Defence for Crime," *The Sunday Times,* 27 January 1985, 36.

55. Pelkonen, *Begurtshilfe Finnland* (31), 17–18, quoted by Edward Shorter, op. cit., 261.

"Even in more advanced areas of Europe like Switzerland, the custom of letting the menses flow unhampered persisted until quite recently. A Swiss woman recalled her girlhood in the 1890s: 'At most, underpants were worn only in the coldest winter. People called them unhealthy, and said the body has to get air. Nobody even thought about washing there.' " Ibid., 261.

56. Shorter points out that dried menstrual blood on clothes or in the skin folds provides an excellent growth medium for foul-smelling, pathogenic micro-organisms. So women might well have observed that vaginal infections followed menstruation. Moreover, in ignorance they inevitably connected menstrual bleeding with non-menstrual bleeding such as might occur from cancer of the uterus.

Shuttle and Redgrove discuss at length the widespread tendency in many cultures to equate menstruating women with witches, demons, and assorted evil beings. Penelope Shuttle and Peter Redgrove, *The Wise Wound: Menstruation and Every-woman,* op. cit., 197–224.

57. Sometimes, however, women forget that they use disgust and horror as a ruse. Then they can get caught up in the regrettable consequences of their own conceptual trap. Joseph Rheingold discusses these problems in his chapter "Menstruation and Its Disorders," in Joseph Rheingold, *The Fear of Being a Woman: A Theory of Maternal Destructiveness,* op. cit., 284–338.

58. See Bruno Bettelheim, *Symbolic Wounds,* op. cit., 144–145.

59. Olivier Marc, *Psychology of the House* (London: Thames and Hudson, 1977), 13. Marc documents his views with photographs of dwellings from many countries.

60. G. R. Levy, *The Gate of Horn* (London: Faber and Faber, 1946), discussed by Bettelheim, *Symbolic Wounds, op. cit., 147.*

61. Bruno Bettelheim, ibid., 147.

62. The big bang is an astronomical theory about the creation of the universe.

63. I refer to paintings by the American artist Mark Rothko.

64. These curved passageways lead to and from a large round center of connections. The traveler both returns to the womb and is reborn during the course of taking off.

Generally women don't share the modern obsession with abstraction. While capable of the highest levels of intellectual activity, they have made only modest contributions to mathematics, metaphysics, musical composition, and games such as chess. It may be a truism, but it is useful to note that when one possesses a body capable of concrete fulfillments, there is less need to engage in abstract expressions. The British critic George Steiner infers that "women find purely speculative, purely abstract, life-distancing pursuits somehow 'childish,' that women are rooted in an adult 'realism' about the weight and presence of the given world." George Steiner, "Chess, the Cruelest Game," *The Sunday Times,* 9 September 1984.

See also: David Spanier's chapter "Women," in David Spanier, *Total Chess* (London: Secker and Warburg, 1984), 94–118.

65. The horror stories of Edgar Allan Poe illustrate many of the same fears. There are abundant examples of the dangerous, vengeful womb, as a woman, an object, or a place, in world literature.

Also, Julia Segal touches upon the "dreaded womb" while discussing the work of Roald Dahl, in particular *Danny: Champion of the World.* In this story a wood is the envied/envious vagina/womb. Julia Segal, "Mother, Sex and Envy in a Children's Story," op. cit., 483–497.

66. The phantasy of the vagina dentata is based on the projection and relocation of greedy, malicious impulses in and onto the woman's body, initially the breast, then the genitals. The mother is the original focus of these projections.

67. A basic feature of these films is that they serve in themselves as the good breast, relieving pain and providing excitement.

68. See: Daniel Jaffe, "The Masculine Envy of Woman's Procreative Function," *J. Amer. Psychoanal. Assoc.*, vol. 16, 1968, 521–548. See also: Felix Boehm, "The Femininity Complex in Men," op. cit., 131.

69. Lea Mindel, "May Heaven Protect Us," *Jewish Chronicle* magazine, 8 June 1979, 55.

70. Marie Langer, "Sterility and Envy," *Int. J. Psycho-Anal.*, vol. 39, 1958, 139–143.

71. Peter Lomas notes that "there exists a vast mythology surrounding female beings who do not take kindly to the event of childbirth; namely, witches. Witches are said to cause sterility, abortion, and to steal, kill or eat newborn babies." Peter Lomas, "Ritualistic Elements in the Management of Childbirth," *Brit J. Med. Psychol.*, vol. 9, 1966, 210.

72. Langer, "Sterility and Envy," op. cit., 139.
Langer adds: "The sterile or infertile woman sets up different barriers against the incorporation of the penis, semen or foetus, and defends herself by different means according to her personality structure. The understanding of paranoid and depressive anxieties, together with the concept of envy as the central factor, enables us to grasp the meaning and the psychosomatic mechanisms of many fertility disorders." Langer includes among these fertility disorders defloration fears, vaginismus, frigidity, spasm of the fallopian tubes, the expulsion of semen, and miscarriage. Ibid., 142.

73. Ibid., 140

74. Ibid., 140.

75. Melanie Klein, "The Effects of Early Anxiety Situations on the Sexual Development of the Girl," *The Psycho-Analysis of Children* (London: The Hogarth Press, 1975), 194–195.

76. A typical unconscious equation of the inner contents of a woman's body is breast = feces = penises = babies.

77. Hanna Segal, *Introduction to the Work of Melanie Klein*, op. cit., 28–29.

78. Melanie Klein, "An Obsessional Neurosis in a Six-Year-Old Girl," *The Psycho-Analysis of Children*, op. cit., 56–57.
"In her unconscious these activities were equated with tearing, cutting up or burning her mother's body, together with the children it contained, and castrating her father. Reading, too, in consequence of the symbolic equation of her mother's body with books, had come to mean a violent removal of substances, children, etc., from the insides of her mother." Ibid., 57.

79. Melanie Klein, "The Significance of Early Anxiety Situations in the Development of the Ego," *The Psycho-Analysis of Children*, op. cit., 182.
"Moreover, by nursing and dressing her dolls, with whom she identifies herself, she obtains proof that she had a loving mother, and thus lessens her fear of being abandoned and left homeless and motherless. This purpose is also served to some extent by other games which are played by children of both sexes, as, for instance, games of furnishing houses and traveling, both of which spring from the desire to find a new home—in the final resort, to rediscover their mother." Ibid., 182.

80. "Men's desire for female functions comes openly to expression in painters and writers, who feel they give birth to their works like a woman in labour after a long pregnancy. All artists in whatever medium work through the feminine side of their personalities; this is because works of art are essentially formed and created inside the mind of the maker, and are hardly at all dependent on external circumstances." Joan Riviere, "Hate, Greed and Aggression," op. cit., 32.

What Riviere says applies equally to female artists and writers.

81. Peter Hall, *Peter Hall's Diaries,* edited by John Goodwin (London: Hamish Hamilton, 1983), 113.

Mr. Tatsuro Toyoda, president of New United Motors, a joint General Motors-Toyota car venture, expressed similar sentiments after the first of a new generation of Novas came off the assembly line: "I feel like an expectant father. I am not sure what to do. Pat it on the hood or pass out cigars." "Toyota and GM Present: The Nova," *International Herald Tribune,* 20 December 1984, 11.

82. In *Amadeus* Salieri opens a portfolio of Mozart's original scores. His eyes fall on the first pages of the Twenty-ninth Symphony. He is astounded to discover that they are not copies, there are no corrections of any kind. He exclaims: "It was puzzling—then suddenly alarming. What was evident was that Mozart was simply transcribing music—completely finished in his head. And finished as most music is never finished. . . . I was staring through the cage of those meticulous strokes at an Absolute Beauty! . . . *Capisco.* I know my fate. Smashed, Smashed down—the Palace of Sound! Now for the first time I feel my emptiness, as Adam felt his nakedness." Peter Shaffer, *Amadeus,* op. cit., 65–67.

83. I have referred to the pregnant person, rather than woman, to encompass symbolic as well as actual pregnancies.

Direct assaults involve verbal and physical abuse up to and including murder. "Marital difficulties, abortion wishes, mutilation fantasies, and criticism of the childless woman are amongst the manifestations of pregnancy envy." Kato van Leewen, "Pregnancy Envy in the Male," *Int. J. Psycho-Anal.,* vol. 47, 1966, 323.

Otherwise it is well known that men frequently begin affairs during their wives' pregnancies or become so engrossed in their own activities that they become relatively oblivious to her needs.

84. Couvade comes from the French, meaning to brood or to hatch. The term was coined by the anthropologist Sir Edward Taylor to denote the practice by which, on the birth of a child, the father is also put to bed and treated as if he were physically affected by the birth. Many primitive peoples have a word, "man-childbed," for the place in which this happens. Taylor also used couvade to mean this special bed. Anthropologists have described variations of this practice in South American, Polynesian, African, and Indian life.

85. Peter Lomas has described various theories of couvade, positive and negative. On the positive side Sir James Frazier *(The Golden Bough)* believed that couvade was a form of sympathetic magic designed to mitigate the birth pains and transfer them to the father, and Arnold Van Gennep saw it as a rite of passage. Others have taken a more ominous view of couvade. J. Bachofen thought that "the husband imitates childbirth in order to gain rights over the child which previously belonged to the woman. . . . It is an attempt on the part of the male to oppose the authority and influence of the woman." Theodor Reik viewed couvade as a form of protective magic, an attempt to ward off devils that might attack the woman and fetus, devils representing the man's own projected hostility.

Peter Lomas, "Ritualistic Elements in the Management of Childbirth," op. cit., 208–209.

Lomas also quotes Bruno Bettelheim, who concludes: "The man who is envious of the woman's ability to bear children has no 'sympathy' for her. She is expected if not compelled to resume her work immediately, though she is exhausted from labor and the physiological postpartum readjustments. The husband and father, on the other hand, rests. His empathy with the mother is so great that he re-creates in himself the need for special care that would be appropriate in and that he denies to her." Peter Lomas, ibid., 210.

86. Brian Jackson, *Fatherhood* (London: George Allen and Unwin, 1984), 56.

87. Ibid., 55.

Jackson quotes another man who used to chat to his pet: "Won't you wonder what's happened when you don't get all this attention any more?" Ibid., 55.

88. In Britain one stone is a unit of weight equal to fourteen pounds. Ibid., 56.

89. Ibid., 57.

90. Joan Raphael-Leff considers the problems of the angry father-to-be (whom she calls "the renouncer") in her paper, "Facilitators & Regulators: Participators & Renouncers: Mothers' and Fathers' Orientations Towards Pregnancy and Parenthood," *J. Psychosomatic Obstetrics and Gynecology*, vol. 4, 1985, 176–178.

91. Felix Boehm has written about a patient who was tortured by fears of cancer of the stomach, cecum, and kidneys. During the course of his analysis, he associated: "Recently it has occurred to me that possibly these difficulties are connected with an unconscious idea of anal birth. Perhaps my attitude to my other symptoms is like that of a woman during gestation." Felix Boehm, "The Femininity Complex in Men," op. cit., 135.

92. Gail Vines, "Test-Tube Embryos," in the "Inside Science" section, *New Scientist*, 19 November 1987, 4. See also: Dick Teresi and Kathleen McAuliffe, "Male Pregnancy," *Omni*, vol. 8, no. 3, December 1985, 51–56 and 118.

93. "When you talk about cloning and babies in test tubes, you are talking about repressed male uterus envy." Phyllis Chesler, quoted by Jane Chase-Marshall, op.cit., 55.

94. Mary Wollstonecraft Shelley, *Frankenstein* (London: Gibbings & Co., 1897). The protagonist, Victor Frankenstein, exclaims: "After days and nights of incredible labour and fatigue, I succeeded in discovering the cause of generation and life; nay, more, I became myself capable of bestowing animation upon lifeless matter." He anticipates: "A new species would bless me as its creator and source; many happy and excellent natures would owe their being to me. No father could claim the gratitude of his child so completely as I should deserve theirs." Ibid., 50 and 52.

95. Otto Friedrich, "The New Origins of Life: How the Science of Conception Brings Hope to Childless Couples," *Time*, 10 September 1984, 34–43.

96. Dr. Lewis Fraad, professor of pediatrics, Albert Einstein College of Medicine, Bronx, New York. Personal communication, 1963.

97. Edward Shorter, op. cit., 98–99. By the 1930s, at a time when maternal mortality had been greatly diminished, the emphasis changed from saving the life of the mother to preserving the life and health of the baby. Ibid., 139.

98. Ibid., 84.

99. Ibid., 84.

100. Ibid., 152–153.

101. Ibid., 103–114.

102. Shorter raises the interesting question, why were infections less likely at home than at hospital? He thinks the answer is that "many women had become more or less immune to their own dirt." Ibid., 128.

103. By the turn of the century a mother ran more risk from infection at home than in the hospital. Ibid., 132–133.

104. Peter Lomas, "Ritualistic Elements in the Management of Childbirth," op. cit., 211.

105. Ibid., 212.

106. Jan Dansig, "Scissor-happy?" *The Times* Health Supplement, London, 29 January 1982, 12. Edward Shorter, *A History of Women's Bodies*, 171–173. "By the 1970s a mother birthing anywhere in Western society would have a good chance of an episiotomy: 65% in Ontario, 64% in a Wuppertal hospital in Germany, 70% to 90% in a London hospital, 60% among first mothers around Brighton." Ibid., 172.

107. "In 16,000 births from 1911 to 1929 in Sursee County, Switzerland, only 9 percent of the mothers had appreciable tears. In 10,000 deliveries in the Jena University Hospital just before the Second World War, only 6 percent of the mothers tore (seven times as many first mothers as multiparas). The conservative doctors at the Chicago Maternity Centre found in the early 1930s that 6 percent of mothers were likely to tear: the 3 percent on whom they did episiotomies, and an additional 3 percent who did not have the procedure. Thus, if no intervention took place, perhaps one woman in fifteen would have an unpleasant tear." Edward Shorter, ibid., 171.

After episiotomy, dyspareunia (pain on intercourse) was suffered by nine out of ten women and was directly attributable to the scar, according to a study from King's College Hospital. Jan Dansig, "Scissor-happy?" op. cit., 12.

According to a survey of 1,800 mothers done by the British National Childbirth Trust, "in every situation we looked at, those with lacerations suffered less than those with an episiotomy." Ibid., 12.

108. Derek Llewelyn Jones, *Fundamentals of Obstetrics and Gynaecology,* vol. 1 (London: Faber & Co., 1982). Quoted by Jan Dansig, "Scissor-happy?" op. cit., 12.

The views of Gordon and Jones echo those of midwife Juliet Willmott. "I am very sorry that some doctors and midwives have become so 'scissors-happy' lately." If there is no fetal distress, there is "no need to hurry the birth of the baby." Juliet Willmott, "Too Many Episiotomies," *Midwives Chronicle,* February 1980, 46, quoted by Edward Shorter, *A History of Women's Bodies,* op. cit., 172.

109. Jan Dansig, "Scissor-happy?" op. cit., 12.

"We are beginning to discover the sometimes long-term emotional and destructive effects of doctors treating women as if they were merely containers to be opened and relieved of their contents, and of concentrating their attention on a bag of muscle and a birth canal instead of relating and caring for the person of whom the uterus and vagina is a part." Shiela Kitzinger of the National Childbirth Trust. Quoted by Jan Dansig, ibid., 12.

110. In the United States women undergo surgery much more often than men, and the most common operation is a hysterectomy. "A survey of 27 million hospital admissions across the country found that 11 of the 20 most frequently performed surgical procedures were exclusively for women. None of the top 20 were operations performed only on men. Total hysterectomy accounted for an average 3.89 hospital admissions per 1,000 women. The second most common procedure for women was Caesarean section, followed by diagnostic dilation and curettage, which involves scraping the lining of the uterus." In "Women Outpace Men in Operations," *International Herald Tribune,* 15 November 1984, 7.

In the United Kingdom, approximately fifty thousand hysterectomies are performed per year. Suzie Hayman, "10 Times Better," *Forum,* vol. 17, no. 10, October 1984, 25–29.

Hayman quotes one woman who underwent a hysterectomy at the age of forty-two with devastating effects on her marriage: "I felt absolutely hollow. I felt like a grapefruit which had been cut open and had all the juice, all the flesh, all the goodness scooped out. The first time we made love after the operation I felt nothing. And I'll never forget the look of shock on John's face as he entered me. After, he just kept muttering something about it not being there anymore. We couldn't make love again for months." Ibid., 25.

111. I quote from an editorial by Aileen Dickins, formerly consultant in Obstetric and Gynaecological Surgery at University College Hospital, London, "Uterine Ligaments and the Treatment of Prolapse," *Journal of the Royal Society of Medicine,* vol. 77, May 1984, 355.

The view of the uterus as a cancer container coincides with the view of the fetus as a tumor. During my first weeks of medical training, I was accosted by a surgeon with the question, "What is the most common tumor?" Neither I nor my colleagues were able to supply the required answer. The surgeon then impatiently retorted, "A fetus, of course!" Both views may be narrowly correct, but they overlook and denigrate the reality of both womb and baby to a woman.

112. Sigmund Freud, Karl Abraham, and Helen Deutsch all expressed the view that childbirth is equated with castration in the minds of women. Peter Lomas points out that this does women an injustice. "This is not to say that feelings of castration and loss do not have place in the mind of many parturient mothers, especially those with a marked masculine identification, but that such feelings have received exclusive attention in the past and consequently the success of childbirth, which may itself be envied, has not been given much thought." Peter Lomas, "Dread of Envy As an Aetiological Factor in Puerperal Breakdown," *Brit. J. Med. Psychol.*, vol. 33, 1960, 108–109.

113. This is especially the case with the practice of female circumcision, an injurious, mutilating procedure that involves the excision of the entire clitoris, the labia minora, and the inner fleshy layers of the labia majora. In conjunction with these excisions, the walls of the vulva are usually stitched together, leaving a tiny matchstick opening (infibulation). Female or pharonic circumcision dates back to antiquity, but its origins are obscure. Africans say it curbs "aggressive female sexuality," and the operation is celebrated as a rite of passage. Although told it makes them a woman, circumcised girls suffer a near total absence of sexual feeling. It makes intercourse as well as childbirth much more difficult and is associated with a host of gynecological and obstetrical difficulties. (Infibulated women often have to be surgically opened up to allow the baby to pass, before being sewn up again.) Still, female circumcision is widely practiced throughout much of Northern Africa.

Hanny Lightfoot-Klein, "Pharonic Circumcision of Females in the Sudan," *Medicine and Law,* vol. 2, 1983, 353–360.

Blaine Harden, "Female Circumcision: A Norm in Africa," *International Herald Tribune,* 29 July 1985, 1.

114. Childbirth is an occasion when women are not only the center of attention, but also take over the active role in the family in comparison with men, who are relegated to the passive position. This is a source of considerable fear and resentment among men.

Men also resent the suffering women go through as though they have a superior means to relieve themselves of guilt.

115. Typically, Ian Donald, professor of midwifery at Glasgow, has claimed that "there is not much difference after all between a fetus in utero and a submarine at sea." Quoted by Ann Oakley in her book, *The Captured Womb: A History of the Medical Care of Pregnant Women* (Oxford: Basil Blackwell, 1984).

116. Edward Shorter believes that religious taboos like churching provide "the most consistent evidence of a male disposition to believe women's bodies dangerous to society." Edward Shorter, *A History of Women's Bodies,* op. cit., 288–289.

The practice has its origins in the Old Testament. "According to Leviticus 12: 2–8, a woman shall be unclean for seven days after the birth of a boy, and for fourteen days after the birth of a girl. For a further thirty-three days in the case of a boy, and sixty-six days for a girl, she shall not enter the sanctuary. Finally she shall make offerings to the priest at the door of the tabernacle, when she shall be 'cleansed from the issue of her blood.' " Edward Shorter, ibid., 289.

A friend of mine was brought up in the Church of Scotland and has not personally undergone churching, but she thinks that the modern equivalent is the postnatal examination.

117. Ibid., 289.

118. Peter Lomas, "Dread of Envy As an Aetiological Factor in Puerperal Breakdown," op. cit., 105–109.

119. Peter Lomas, "Ritualistic Elements in the Management of Childbirth," op.

cit., 212–213. The anesthesia, for example, may be desired not simply to relieve pain, but to deny feelings and inhibit active participation in an event that the woman feels is liable to attract envious attention.

The converse of attenuating creativity and, in particular, childbirth is to celebrate it, as the American artist Judy Chicago has done through the Birth Project. This consists of nearly one hundred needlework creations done by dozens of volunteers from around the United States. It is based on drawings and paintings by Judy Chicago of women at term and giving birth. Leslie Bennetts, "Judy Chicago: 100 Needlework Creations Make up Artist's 'Birth Project,' " *International Herald Tribune*, 15 April 1985, 18.

120. "So the Lord God cast a deep sleep upon the man; and, while he slept, He took one of his ribs and closed up the flesh at that spot. And the Lord God fashioned the rib that He had taken from the man into a woman; and He brought her to the man. Then the man said, 'This one at last/Is bone of my bones/And flesh of my flesh./This one shall be called Woman,/For from man was she taken.' " Genesis, chapter 2, verses 21–23, *The Torah: A Modern Commentary*, op. cit., 30.

In Greek mythology Athene was born "fully armed and brandishing a sharp javelin" from the head of Zeus. "At the sight all the Immortals were struck with astonishment and filled with awe." *New Larousse Encyclopedia of Mythology*, Introduction by Robert Graves (London: Paul Hamlyn, 1969), 108.

121. The American psychoanalyst Gregory Zilboorg asserts that "it was man who perceived himself biologically inferior, and it was this sense of inferiority and concomitant hostility that led to the phenomenon of couvade—neurotic, hostile identification with the mother. . . . it is not penis-envy on the part of the woman, but women-envy on the part of the man, that is psychologically older and therefore more fundamental." Gregory Zilboorg, "Masculine and Feminine: Some Biological and Cultural Aspects," *Psychiatry*, vol. 7, 1944, 290.

122. Melanie Klein, "Envy and Gratitude," *Envy and Gratitude and Other Works 1946–1963*, op. cit., 203.

The words of this boy echo with those of my daughter. About the age of seven she came up to me and quite spontaneously proclaimed: "You know, Daddy, one day I will have a baby, and she will have a baby, and then she will have a baby, and it will never stop."

Debbie Berke, personal communication, 1982.

Chapter 6

1. A male informant, quoted in Alexandra Penny, *How to Make Love to a Man* (London: Papermac, 1981), 29–30.

2. A female informant, quoted by Maria Torok, "The Significance of Penis Envy in Women," in Janine Chasseguet-Smirgel, *Female Sexuality* (Ann Arbor: University of Michigan Press, 1970), 139.

Another woman asserted: "I don't know why I have this feeling . . . but it has always been like this for me. As though only man was fit to fulfill himself, to have opinions, to go always further. And everything to him is so naturally easy . . . nothing, nothing can stop him." Ibid., 139.

3. Philip Roth, *Goodbye Columbus* (London: Andre Deutsch, 1959), 128.

4. Charles Rycroft, *A Critical Dictionary of Psychoanalysis*, op. cit. 113.

"Phallus" refers to an idea or image of the penis. It denotes both the physical and symbolic qualities of maleness.

5. Sigmund Freud, "Femininity," in *New Introductory Lectures on Psycho-Analysis*, *S.E.*, vol. 22, 126.

6. Sigmund Freud, "Some Psychical Consequences of the Anatomical Distinction Between the Sexes," *S.E.*, vol. 19, 252.

7. In classical psychoanalytic theory it is the girl or female who suffers from

penis envy, that is, the resentful awareness of an organ absence that she tries to deny or remedy. In contrast, the boy or male suffers from the castration complex, that is, a complex array of feelings centering around castration anxiety, the fear he will lose what he has. In the popular genre, penis envy and castration complex are often used synonymously. And, as I go on to explain and illustrate in this chapter, they may be suffered by members of either sex.

8. "Penis envy originates in the discovery of the anatomical distinction between the sexes: the little girl feels deprived in relation to the boy and wishes to possess a penis as he does (castration complex). Subsequently, in the course of the Oedipal phase, penis envy takes on two secondary forms: first, the wish to acquire a penis within oneself (principally in the shape of the desire to have a child) and, secondly, the wish to enjoy the penis in coitus." J. Laplanche and J-B. Pontalis, *The Language of Psycho-Analysis*, op. cit., 303.

9. Karl Abraham, "Manifestations of the Female Castration Complex," in *Selected Papers on Psycho-Analysis* (London: The Hogarth Press, 1973), 338.

10. Sigmund Freud, "The Dissolution of the Oedipus Complex," *S.E.*, vol. 19, 178.

11. Phyllis Greenacre, "Penis Awe and Its Relation to Penis Envy," in *Drives, Affects and Behavior*, R. M. Loewenstein (ed.), vol. 1, *Contributions to the Theory and Practice of Psychoanalysis and Its Applications* (New York: International Universities Press, 1960), 176–190.

Greenacre coined the term "penis awe" in order to denote the state of mind and emotions aroused in a girl upon seeing 1) the adult penis, flaccid or erect; 2) sexual intercourse; 3) boys exhibiting themselves; 4) chance encounters with other men urinating or masturbating.

Penis awe involves intense admiration, shock, fear, veneration, a feeling of strangeness, and aggression, but much less than in penis envy. Greenacre clearly distinguishes penis awe from penis envy. Her view is much closer to a strong overwhelming wish for or submission to the phallus and to what I call "penis greed."

Dinora Pines reiterates this in her recent review of *Early Female Development*, D. Mendell, ed. (New York: MTP Press, 1982). "Undoubtedly penis awe, or penis wish, a term that I believe is more appropriate than that of penis envy, plays a part in the little girl's development." *Int. J. Psycho-Anal.*, vol. 65, 1984, 237.

12. Rabbi Hugo Gryn, personal communication, December 1984.

13. A shlemiel is Yiddish for an insecure, neurotic, weakish man, a foolish bungler who can't get it right or "get it up." It affectionately describes a putz, literally a "stupid prick."

Woody Allen's predecessors included the notable Ernst Lubitsch (later portrayed by Mel Brooks). From 1913 he embarked on a "phenomenally successful career on screen as an archetypal Jewish comic character, known as a 'Meyer' or 'Moritz,' a little clerk who suffers all kinds of mishaps along the way, but always contrives to end up with the boss's daughter," similar to many of the roles played by Harold Lloyd or Charlie Chaplin. John Russell Taylor, *Strangers in Paradise: The Hollywood Émigrés 1933–1950* (London: Faber and Faber, 1983), 20.

14. Woody Allen, *Annie Hall*, screenplay, in *Four Films of Woody Allen* (London: Faber and Faber, 1983), 61.

15. Quoted from John W. Dodds, *The Age of Paradox: A Biography of England 1841–1851* (London, 1953), 72, in Reay Tannahill, *Sex in History* (London: Abacus, 1981), 333–334.

16. Minette Marrin, "A Bandwagon Named Desire," *Observer*, 19 February 1984, Weekend page.

17. David Thomson, "Sam Shepard: An American Original," *Playgirl*, vol. 12, no. 7, December 1984, 18.

Joan Goodman, "Mel Gibson," *Playgirl*, vol. 12, no. 7, December 1984, 27.

"He is a classic Hollywood hero. His boyish man's face, intelligent eyes, strong, square jaw and the heart-melting smile that features a perfect set of white teeth have caused observers to compare him to everybody from Marlon Brando to Clark Gable." Ibid., 29.

18. Ads for stimulants like "Amphetrazine" and "Fast One" appeal to the desire for consumable maleness. *Playgirl*, vol. 12, no. 7, December 1984, 100, 109.

19. Bernie Zilbergeld, *Male Sexuality*, (New York: Bantam Books, 1981), 23.

20. Jerry Siegal and Joe Shuster elaborated the wish to be supermen while they were high school students in Cleveland, Ohio. But it wasn't until 1938 that *Action Comics* took Superman aboard. The models for Superman and his alter ego, Clark Kent, included Tarzan, Buck Rogers, Flash Gordon, and the actors Clark Gable and Douglas Fairbanks, Sr. Dennis Dooley and Gary Engle (eds.), *Superman at Fifty: The Persistence of the Legend* (Cleveland: Octavia Press, 1987).

See also: Peter Schwenger, *Phallic Critiques: Masculinity and Twentieth-Century Literature* (London: Routledge & Kegan Paul, 1984), 118–119.

21. Zilbergeld illustrates the phantasy model of masculinity with quotes from many of these writers. Their works emphasize explosive performance, total control, inexhaustibility, and invulnerability. Like the romantic novelists, their works sell in the hundreds of millions. Bernie Zilbergeld, *Male Sexuality,* op. cit., 23–69.

22. Gay Talese, *Thy Neighbor's Wife* (London: Collins, 1980), 115–116.

Talese is referring to D. H. Lawrence's *Lady Chatterley's Lover,* which he considers to be a masterly phallic novel. "Lawrence probes the sensitivity and psychological detachment that man often feels towards his penis—it does indeed seem to have a will of its own, an ego beyond size, and is frequently embarrassing because of its needs, infatuations and unpredictable nature."

23. Numerous psychoanalysts have commented on the oral origins of phallic desires (and hatreds). Thus, in referring to the development of Klein's views, Segal concludes: "Penis envy is also deeply influenced by the more primitive envy of the breast. The infant may turn away in hatred from the envied breast to an idealized penis, which in turn becomes a carrier of the original envy of the breast. Thus, Klein's earlier view of penis envy as autonomous, although reinforced from other sources, is supplanted by the more radical hypothesis that the primary origin of excessive penis envy must be sought in the infant's envy of the breast." Hanna Segal, *Klein,* op. cit., 142.

24. Although there have been many noteworthy female chefs and writers about food, men predominate in the profession. This is only partially explained by the limited public roles allowed to women in different eras and cultures. For example, even today the art of pastry making is almost totally the domain of men.

Guillaume Tirel dit Taillevent was *queux de bouche* (prince's cook) to Philippe de Valois (1349), then cook to duc de Normandie (1361) and "first cook" to King Charles V (1381). His book *Le Viandier* (1375) was the first completely preserved French cookery work. *Food and Drink Through the Ages: 2500* B.C. *to 1937* A.D. (London: Maggs Bros Ltd., 1937), 18.

The first printed cookery books were by men and date back to the fifteenth century. In the twentieth century Michele Guerard originated *cuisine minceur*. Paul Bocuse is the most celebrated chef in Lyon. Many public road signs lead the way to his restaurant, a "temple of cuisine." (Interestingly, Lyon is one of the few French cities with acclaimed female chefs.) Robert Carrier is the famous English chef, restauranteur, and cookery writer. Kenneth Lo lives and works in London and is renowned for Chinese cuisine. Many other celebrated, contemporary male chefs could be mentioned.

I am indebted to the writer Adrian Bailey for various references and very useful perspectives.

25. From G. Morris Carstairs, *The Twice-Born: A Study of a Community of High-Caste Hindus* (London, 1957), 83–84, discussed in Reay Tannahill, *Sex in History,* op. cit., 327.

26. The unconscious phantasies that underlie fellatio are overdetermined—that is, they may include oral desires (for magical feedings) as well as ideas of oral impregnation, vengeful castration, and change of sexual identity. See Otto Fenichel, *The Psychoanalytic Theory of Neurosis* (New York: W. W. Norton & Co., 1945), 229.

27. This account represents the condensation of several separate cases. The essential theme and outline of events that I describe accurately reflects the material presented to me.

28. August Stärcke was the first psychoanalyst to emphatically emphasize that the experience of suckling, and the cessation of suckling associated with the withdrawal of the breast/nipple, was the basis for the experience of castration. He argued that this must be the primary real event capable of accounting for the deepest thoughts, fears, and wishes that contribute to the castration complex.

"We have therefore to look for an infantile situation of universal occurrence in which a penis-like part of the body is taken from another person, given to the child as his own (a situation with which are associated pleasurable sensations), and then taken away from the child, causing 'pain' (Unlust). This situation can be none other than that of the child at the breast." August Stärcke, "The Castration Complex," *Int. J. Psycho-Anal,* vol. 2, 1921, 182.

Freud also argued that the strong feelings that the child has about the penis have powerful oral-erotic roots, "for when suckling has come to an end, the penis also becomes heir of the mother's nipple." Sigmund Freud, "Anxiety and Instinctual Life," in *New Introductory Lectures on Psycho-Analysis,* op. cit., 101.

In reference to this phenomenon, a colleague mentioned to me that each of her two sons, at a certain stage in their development, used the same word (unique for each boy) when referring to her nipple or his penis. Personal communication, March 1985.

29. A child's frequent question to Mother or Father is "How much do you love me?" Equally frequent replies refer to size: "A big bunch!" "A big banana!" or, as a well-beloved song proclaims, "A bushel and a peck."

Bion believed that the primitive breast or penis is the prototype for all links with reality. This includes states of mind, emotions, verbal and nonverbal communication, and understanding. Wilfred Bion, "Attacks on Linking," op. cit., 308–312.

The primitive quality of some phallic linking is illustrated by the case of a twenty-five-year-old married woman for whom the penis represented an umbilical cord, and the male-female relationship was a form of umbilical attachment. She desperately desired to possess a penis, that is, be masculine in order to be able to plug into and attach herself to her mother (or vice versa). Her view was that the penis is "an umbilical cord. At some time we have nourishment through our umbilicus. My concept of my genitals is a means to attach." Laila Karme, "The Penis As Umbilical Cord," *Psychoanalytic Quarterly,* vol. 47, 1978, 428.

Among the peoples of Somali, when a male child is born the parents are careful to cut the umbilical cord in such as way as to leave as much as possible. Then they stretch it, for they believe that the longer it is, the longer the penis will be. Géza Róheim, "Aphrodite or the Woman with a Penis," in *The Panic of the Gods and Other Essays* (New York: Harper Torchbooks, 1972), 177–178. It may be that these people believe that the longer the penis, the stronger the connection between Mother and son.

30. Karen Horney, "On the Genesis of the Castration Complex in Women," *Int., J. Psycho-Anal.,* vol. 5, 1924, 51–54.

Horney pointed out that all these capacities put girls at a considerable narcissistic disadvantage—that is, they felt less able, valuable, and important when they saw what boys could do. She quotes from a female patient: "If I might ask a gift from Providence it would be to be able just for once to urinate like a man. For then I should know how I really am made." I think by this the woman means that only then she would really feel herself.

31. In his book *The Prisoner of Sex,* Norman Mailer acidly calls "the eternal feminine" the "Great Bitch," something to be ceaselessly opposed, subdued, and conquered. Peter Schwenger, *Phallic Critiques,* op. cit., 17.

Mailer's choice of words indicates the degree of fear and anger involved in this struggle.

32. Robert Stoller, *The Transsexual Experiment* (London: The Hogarth Press, 1975), quoted by Thomas Ryan, in "The Roots of Masculinity," in *The Sexuality of Man,* edited by Andy Metcalf and Martin Humphries (London: Pluto Press, 1985), 26.

Robert Stoller is an American psychiatrist who is renowned for his detailed studies of sexuality and people with sexual abnormalities.

33. "I think it can be shown that the sense of being a female develops out of the same roots (parental attitudes and ascription of sex, genitalia, and a biological force) as that of being a male, and that this core gender identity persists throughout life as unalterably in women as in men." Robert Stoller, *Sex and Gender, Volume 1: The Development of Masculinity and Feminity* (London: Maresfield Reprints, 1984), 52.

34. In recognizing a wish for a separate identity, one assumes that the child has the freedom to have such a wish and act upon it within the framework of family dynamics. Many girls grow up within a family where one or both parents want them to be boys so that the desire for a penis represents an attempt to placate and please the parents, not establish a separate sense of self.

35. "Freud's view that boys are at an advantage over girls because their primary love object is heterosexual is based on anatomy rather than identity. If identity is taken as the reference point, it is the boy who experiences more difficulties with gender differentiation. In order for him to establish masculinity, he must first dis-identify from his mother and then identify with his father. The girl's route to femininity is more straightforward, as her primary identification is with someone of the same sex as her mother." Thomas Ryan, "The Roots of Masculinity," op. cit., 20.

See also: R. R. Greenson, "Dis-identifying from the Mother: Its Special Importance for the Boy," *Int. J. Psycho-Anal.,* vol. 49, 1968, 370–374.

36. Transvestites and transsexuals can be seen as casualties in this process of biological, sexual, and personal differentiation. It is noteworthy that transvestism is practiced exclusively by men, and transsexualism is predominantly a male phenomenon. The former consists of the compulsive desire to dress as a member of the opposite sex for the purpose of sexual arousal and sexual pleasure. The transvestite is aware of his biological endowment, and accepts it, but gets enjoyment from acting as a female. In contrast, the transsexual person is aware of his biological endowment but doesn't accept it. His core gender identity is as a member of the opposite sex. In either case personal identity may be terribly confused. See Thomas Ryan, "The Roots of Masculinity," op. cit., 16.

37. In other words, girls turn to masculinity when they despair about their own femininity, a conclusion drawn by Karen Horney, Joan Riviere, and many others. See: Joan Riviere, "Hate, Greed and Aggression," op. cit. 32–34.

38. There are many children and adults in whom the issues of nourishment and autonomy are always urgent, inevitably sexualized, and rarely resolved. For them masculine or feminine thoughts, wishes, feelings, and actions remain shallow fronts serving to conceal underlying fears about survival.

39. Charles Rycroft, *A Critical Dictionary of Psychoanalysis,* op. cit., 117–118.

40. Ernest Jones, "The Phallic Phase," in *Papers on Psycho-Analysis* (Boston: The Beacon Press, 1961), 474.

41. Stoller stresses that girls are not castrated versions of boys. He adds: "If

Freud had worked with a woman without a vagina, I think he would have seen that the only thing a woman wants more than a penis is a vagina. It is only when a woman has normal genitalia that she can afford the luxury of wishing she had a penis." Robert Stoller, *Sex and Gender*, op. cit., 51.

42. The American psychoanalyst Clara Thompson wrote extensively about the cultural factors that affect women. She emphasized that longings for the phallus had to do with female wishes to overcome an ingrained sense of inferiority brought about by cultural constraints—that is, by their living in male-dominated societies. See: Clara Thompson, "Penis Envy in Women," in *Psychoanalysis and Women*, edited by Jean Baker Miller (London: Penguin Books, 1974), 51–57.

43. The British social psychologist Marie Jahoda queries why Freud took such a strong stance about women not having a penis. She points out that Freud had no personal bias against women, quite the contrary. She concludes that he "unwittingly succumbed to the prevailing cultural stereotype of women, mistaking their historical role for the essence of femininity." Marie Jahoda, *Freud and the Dilemmas of Psychology* (London: The Hogarth Press, 1977), 86–87.

44. *The Sunday Times* magazine, 23 December 1984, 30–31.

45. The ad also promises to provide female items like hair dryers and a makeup mirror. These conveniences coincide with the overall provision of conveniences, a service male patrons would expect. Ibid., 31.

46. Penis greed (desire for the phallus) includes, of course, cannibalism. Many peoples literally ate their enemies and thereby believed they had gained their powers. Alternatively, the hunting, preparation, and eating of phallic foods has always been popular. These include vegetables that look like a phallus (asparagus) or extracts from phallic animals (rhinoceros horn, bull's blood, snake flesh) or meat in general.

In the Far East tiger meat has become popular: "Tiger meat has been selling in Taiwan recently at $30 per kilo because some people believe it can increase virility." *International Herald Tribune*, 15–16 December 1984, 4.

47. David Halberstam, *The Best and the Brightest* (London: Barrie & Jenkins, 1972), 434.

48. As a person Johnson was both larger than life and extremely insecure. He was obsessed with appearing and being bigger than others. Ibid., 431–439.

It is said that he would hold business meetings in his bathroom or pool while naked. Presumably he sought to demonstrate that he had the largest organ and to intimidate those present, both an aggressive and defensive maneuver.

Johnson's activities exemplify greed for and greed by the penis. He was constantly trying to accumulate more and more riches, power and privileges (greed for). Concomitantly he used his wealth and position to force himself on and into others, often to possess, dominate, or destroy them (greed by).

49. Yvonne Roberts, "The Tragedy of Mark Thompson," *The Sunday Times*, London, 23 December 1984, 23.

50. I am indebted to my colleague Andrea Sabbadini, who has coined the term "possession anxiety" in relation to the fears that arise from using the phallus as opposed to fears that arise from losing it. Andrea Sabbadini, "Possession Anxiety: The Other Side of the Castration Complex," *Brit. J. Psychoth.*, vol. 3., no. 1, fall 1986.

I think possession anxiety is related to depressive dread brought about by the deployment of strengths and capacities to injure others.

51. Anaïs Nin, *Cities of the Interior* (New York: Phoenix Box Shop, distr., 1959), quoted by Phyllis Chesler, *Women and Madness*, op. cit., 4.

52. Personal communication, 1978.

53. Psychologist Harriet Lerner comments: "Expressions of anger are not only encouraged in boys and men, but may be glorified to pathological extremes.... In contrast, women have been denied the forthright expression of even healthy and realistic anger.... To express anger—especially if one does so openly, directly—

makes a woman unladylike, unfeminine, unmaternal—and sexually unattractive." Quoted by Carol Tavris, in *Anger: The Misunderstood Emotion* (New York: Simon and Schuster, 1985), 181.

54. In her journals Plath asserts: "I will not submit to having my life fingered by my husband, enclosed in a circle of his activity. . . . I must have a legitimate field of my own." Yet six years after marrying the poet Ted Hughes, she speaks of him in glowing terms as "the buried male muse and god creator risen to be my mate."

It is possible her idealization of Hughes concealed her hostility and that she destroyed herself before the warrior in her could destroy him.

The Journals of Sylvia Plath, quoted in book review by Anne Schrieber, in *International Herald Tribune,* 7 May 1982, 18.

55. Bernice Schultz Engle, "The Amazons in Ancient Greece," *Psychoanalytic Quarterly,* vol. 11, 1942, 512–514, 518–521.

Engle comments: "Several modern historians have attempted to identify the Amazons with various tribes or classes of people such as the Hittites or armed priestesses. Other writers believe that knowledge for positive conclusions is lacking. A few dismiss the Amazons as mere fairy-tale creatures. But serious critics of Greek mythology like Bachofen, Weigert, and Turel have emphasized the psychological importance to classical Greek civilization of Amazonian legends whether Amazons actually existed or not." Ibid., 512.

56. Philostratus denied that the Amazons amputated one breast. He derives the name from the meaning "unsuckled." Ibid., 515.

57. Ibid., 514–515.

58. Ibid., 542–548.

Engle concludes that the Amazons were "originally Eurasian people with large numbers of women in their bands who first developed the mobile economic use of horseback riding." Amazonian invasions aroused fears of domination by the Cretan matriarchy as well as Mycenaean gynecocracy (rule by women). Theseus was the great national hero of Dorian Greece who saved Athens from being overrun by the Amazonian tribes and finally conquered them. Interestingly, he is said to have fathered a son by the Amazonian queen and also taken on many Amazonian traits, especially a love for horses. Ibid., 536–538.

59. Theseus's victory was celebrated throughout Greek art and literature. The famous orator Lysias wrote: "They [the Amazons] were accounted men for their high courage rather than as women for their sex, so much did they seem to excel men. . . . They had become the *rulers of many nations* and hearing of our country, how great it was, and moved by *greed of glory,* they mustered the bravest nations and marched against us. Having met with valiant men, they found their spirit was now like their sex; the repute they got was the reverse of the former. . . . They stood alone in failing to learn from their mistakes and so to be better advised in their future actions. They would not return home and report their own misfortunes and our ancestors' valor. So they perished on the spot, were punished for their folly. . . . So these women, in unjust *greed for others' land,* justly lost their own." [My italics.] Lysias, *Epitaph,* ii, 4. Translated by W. R. M. Lamb (New York: Putnam, 1930), quoted by Engle, ibid., 538.

60. Caroline Moorehead, "Deadlier Than the Male," *The Times,* 16 January 1985, 13.

Moorehead details the large number of women who have become terrorist activists and leaders. "Groups led by women tend to be tougher than those led by men and, once captured, few women have cooperated." Various women cited included Angela Davis, Leila Khaled, Bernardine Dohrn, the Price sisters, and Fusako Shigenobu.

Rose Rouse, "Pumping Iron-Maidens," *The Sunday Times,* 23 December 1984, 38.

Rouse discusses the large number of women doing bodybuilding. A picture shows four very muscular women posing like Charles Atlas. One comments: "Men do find it difficult to cope with the fact that we are strong, fit and aware of our capabilities and also that we are no longer under their influence as far as looking attractive is concerned. I've actually heard men say: 'Oh, I don't like that, I couldn't go to bed with that,' but who cares, we're not doing it for them."

The rejection of men and their role vis-à-vis women has been emphasized in recent years by the increasing number of women who undergo artificial insemination in order to bear a child without any male involvement. Quite a few of these women have chosen to raise their children within a lesbian partnership. Ian Brodie, "The Woman Who Wanted a Genius," *The Daily Telegraph*, 20 August 1986, 15.

Certainly male fears and female hopes for feminine hegemony did not die with the famous victory of Theseus at Athens or of the Greeks over the Persians. Engle notes: "Historians celebrate the importance of the Greek defeat of the Persians. No doubt much fear of the Persian threat went back to the old fear of Cretan and Amazonian domination. One important connection has not elsewhere been noted. Soon after the battle of Salamis, Athenian art and literature began to emphasize the victories of Theseus over the Amazons. . . . In that battle one of Xerxes' allies was the Carian queen Artemesia, whose valiant deeds brought from Xerxes the remark that his women allies had acted like men, his men aides like women. Athenians after that battle offered the immense reward of 10,000 drachmas for the capture of Artemesia alive, 'so great was the indignity that a woman should make war against Athens." Herodotus: *History* (New York: Dutton, 1912 ed.), viii; 88, 93.

There was a constant danger of such attacks in sections of Asia Minor as late as the fourth century A.D. Therefore the idea that Artemesia, Tomyris, and Semiramis were only *historical* Amazons and that female warriors were only legends must have been a continued reassurance to Greek citizens. Ibid., 547–548.

61. I am discussing, of course, the transformations of primary objects. Hence, a particular person may undergo a multitude of perceptual, libidinal, and emotional changes from, for example, a breast to a penis, or a woman (and all her desired qualities, attributes, and so on) into a man, or vice versa. These changes may be concrete or symbolic, temporary or long lasting.

62. Ernest Jones, "The Phallic Phase," op. cit., 463.

63. David Halberstam, *The Best and the Brightest,* op. cit. 433–434.

64. Exodus, chapter 7, verses 8–12, *The Torah: A Modern Commentary,* op. cit., 422–423.

Here "serpent" is the translation of the Hebrew word *tanin*. A more appropriate translation would be "crocodile." Ibid., 424.

I could cite many other examples of the phallus as a tooth weapon, such as sculpted dragon's heads on the bow of warships or the painted shark on the front fuselage of fighter planes. (The latter also provide a good example of the anal or fecal phallus inasmuch as they dive, penetrate, and gobble up airspace as well as drop bombs, "exploding shit."

65. Géza Róheim, *Psychoanalysis and Anthropology: Culture, Personality and the Unconscious* (New York: International Universities Press, 1973), 130–131, 141–142.

66. "Rats Wrecked Home on 'Lover's Revenge Raid,' " *The Daily Telegraph,* 7 February 1979, 7.

67. "Girls hold their mother responsible for their lack of a penis and do not forgive her for being thus put at a disadvantage."

Sigmund Freud, *New Introductory Lectures on Psycho-Analysis,* quoted by Walter Joffe, in "A Critical Review of the Status of the Envy Concept," op. cit., 535.

68. Karl Abraham, "Manifestations of the Female Castration Complex," op. cit., 340.

Abraham emphasized that narcissistic injury was a major factor in the girl's angry response.

69. Ibid., 348.

70. In her paper "Penis Awe," Phyllis Greenacre points out that Freud was aware that girls can have simultaneous but opposing reactions to the phallus. She quotes from his 1918 paper, "The Taboo on Virginity": "It is interesting now to find that psychoanalysts come across women in whom the two contrary attitudes—thralldom and enmity—both come to expression and remain in close association." Phyllis Greenacre, op. cit., 189.

The standard edition of Freud's work provides slightly different nuances in its translation of this passage: "It is interesting that in one's capacity as analyst one can meet with women in whom the opposed reactions of bondage and hostility both find expression and remain intimately associated with each other." S.E., vol. 11, 208.

71. Klein commented that "a number of factors contribute to penis-envy," but of these, oral issues play a central role: "I wish to consider the woman's penis-envy mainly insofar as it is of oral origin. As we know, under the dominance of oral desires, the penis is equated with the breast (Abraham) and in my experience the woman's penis-envy can be traced back to envy of the mother's breast. I have found that if the penis-envy of women is analyzed on these lines, we can see that its root lies in the earliest relation to the mother, in the fundamental envy of the mother's breast, and in the destructive feelings allied with it." Melanie Klein, "Envy and Gratitude," Envy and Gratitude and Other Works 1946–1963, op. cit., 199–200.

72. Many of the early psychoanalysts seemed to restrict penis envy to girls, as the previous quote indicates. In fact, I am considering a manifestation of pregenital conflicts that afflict both sexes.

73. John Todd and his colleagues have provided several examples of men who were obsessed by the idea that their penes were too small, that they couldn't satisfy their wives, and that their wives were being unfaithful to them. All this is closely associated with morbid jealousy and related, as I have discussed previously, to envious rage toward the female companion. We may surmise that these men harbored deep resentments toward their mothers, whom they felt didn't give them enough and to whom they were unfaithful. These issues were repressed and at a much later date reenacted with their wives, but in an inverted form. (The wish to seek revenge because the wives weren't giving enough—the idea that their breasts were too small or they were keeping everything for themselves—was denied and transformed into fears of their wives' revenge because the men weren't giving enough. The wives' alleged unfaithfulness then justified the men's original murderous intentions arising not just out of frustration, but of envy.) John Todd, J. R. M. Mackie, and Kenneth Dewhurst, "Real or Imaginary Hypophallism," Brit. J. Psychiat., vol. 119, no. 550, September 1971, 315–318.

74. This is a good example of breast awe. Felix Boehm, "The Femininity Complex in Men," op. cit., 133–134.

Jealousy almost certainly added to his "amazement and terror," as the incident took place while the man was watching his younger brother being fed.

75. The purpose of the sex act is an attempt on the part of the ego to return to mother's womb, "where there is no such painful disharmony between ego and environment as characterizes existence in the external world." It is the finest form of transitory regression, "the expression of the striving to return to the mother's womb." Sandor Ferenczi, Thalassa: A Theory of Genitality (New York: The Norton Library, W. W. Norton & Co., 1968), 18–19.

76. Patrick Mullahy, "The Theories of Otto Rank," in Oedipus: Myth and Complex (New York: Evergreen Books, Grove Press, 1955), 162–168.

77. "The phallus is the very mark of human desire; it is the expression of the wish for what is absent, for reunion [initially with the mother]." Juliet Mitchell, Psychoanalysis and Feminism (London: Allen Lane, 1974), 395.

78. Reay Tannahill, Sex in History, op. cit., 208–213.

Tantric devotees claim that their practices are simply a means to an end, the achievement of a higher state of consciousness. To Western eyes they are akin to phallic rituals that used to be extensively practiced in European and Near Eastern countries. For example, ancient stone lingams can still be found in England and Ireland. Nontantric phallic worship includes fetishistic masturbation and various states of autoannihilation as described under the rubric of the nirvana principle.

79. I don't think I need to go into a great deal of additional detail about the myriad associations and symbolic transformations that the phallus can assume for boys and girls, much of which I have discussed in the section on penis greed. However, it is important to emphasize that for girls the phallus can represent their longing for female prowess displaced onto the male organ. A lot depends on the family context and upbringing. Some girls take on a male gender identity to please their parents and therefore crave male functions. Both boys and girls tend to be highly sensitive to their position as children, that is, as small, relatively underprivileged members of the family or society in general. In this sense, the phallus they crave and resent is adulthood.

80. In various writings Freud emphasized that the clitoris was an inferior organ, in size, function, and general capacities, to the penis. See, for example: Sigmund Freud, "Some Psychical Consequences of the Anatomical Differences between the Sexes," op. cit., 253–256. Numerous studies now contest this view.

The American psychiatrist Judd Marmor has reviewed some of the recent literature on female sexual function in "Changing Patterns of Femininity," in *Psychoanalysis and Women,* op. cit., 222–238.

Although "the female organ is minute compared with the male organ . . . the size of its nerves . . . and nerve endings . . . compare strikingly with the same provision for the male. Indeed . . . the glans of the clitoris is demonstrably richer in nerves than the male glans, for the two stems of the dorsalis clitoris are relatively three to four times as large as the equivalent of the penis. . . ." Quoted from R. L. Dickenson, *Human Sexual Anatomy,* 2nd ed. (Baltimore: Williams and Wilkens, 1949); Judd Marmor, ibid., 232.

81. "Belgravia Rapist Only 16," *The Daily Telegraph,* London, 26 July 1984, 3.

82. The body is usually the body of a woman, signifying to the rapist the excluding, rejecting desired/hated organs and bodies of his parents. Similar conflicts are frequently enacted with the body of a man, as in homosexual rape, or with larger social or business entities, a corporate body, for example, subject to predatory and destructive takeovers.

83. *Malleus,* op. cit., 43, quoted by Ilza Veith, *Hysteria: The History of a Disease,* op. cit., 63. By "reality" I mean that many women, through their demeanor, embody and justify imputations of wickedness.

84. Abraham has pointed out that in some women a fixed stare is equivalent to an erection and has the same purpose that exhibiting a penis has with men. These women hope to scare people with their look just as they are scared by maleness (or their own feminine impulses). Karl Abraham, "Manifestations of the Female Castration Complex," op. cit., 352–353.

Looks can also be devouring or castrating for similar reasons.

85. The phallus can represent a guilty conscience, seen as the rod of authority and, more specifically, male oppression. Militant feminists like Germaine Greer believe this justifies active struggles to overcome all representatives of such authority: "What oppression lays upon us is not responsibility but guilt. The revolutionary woman must know her enemies, the doctors, psychiatrists, health visitors, priests, marriage counsellors, policemen, magistrates and genteel reformers, all the authoritarians and dogmatists who flock about her with warnings and advice." Germaine Greer, *The Female Eunuch* (London: MacGibbon & Kee, 1970), 19–20.

My patient did see me as a hated symbol of the paternal conscience, for she often described her father as critical and punitive. But the vicious, intractable nature of this conscience came from underlying fears of her mother. For many people the paternal judge conceals a maternal executioner. This "terrible mother" conscience appears in a multitude of legends, the Hebrew Lilith, the Roman Lamia, the German Brünhild. In particular it is associated with the Greek figure of Hecate with her demands for human sacrifice.

Cirlot comments: "There is a certain quality of the virile about her [Brünhild], as there is about Hecate, the 'accursed huntress.' The overcoming of the threat which Lilith constitutes finds its symbolic expression in the trial of Hercules in which he triumphs over the Amazons." J. E. Cirlot, *A Dictionary of Symbols*, translated by J. Sage (London: Routledge & Kegan Paul, 1962), p. 180.

86. Her unfeeling unresponsiveness demonstrates the passive-aggressive assault in addition to active hostile attacks (screams, physical threats, and the like). This is characteristic of the Snow Maiden approach, which prefers psychic damage (painful humiliations) to physical threats. In other words, if she felt nothing, then I hadn't touched her, penetrated her, or had a relationship with her. From her point of view, my impotence and her omnipotence remained intact.

Abraham describes a variety of such assaults, including frigidity, kleptomania, vaginismus, marriage dread, and parthenogenesis (immaculate conceptions). Karl Abraham, "Manifestations of the Female Castration Complex," op. cit., 354–362.

Jones pointed out that the lack of feelings is also a defense against a sense of unendurable privation. One might add that it is also an attempt to placate the "terrible mother" (persecutory envious and jealous internal maternal imago) by renouncing sexual feelings (the permanent extinction of sexual pleasure). Jones called this state of self-castration "aphanisis." Ernest Jones, "The Early Development of Female Sexuality," *Papers on Psycho-Analysis* (Boston: The Beacon Press, 1961), 440–446.

87. The female Don Juan exhausts lovers and therapists the way her male counterpart preys on women. Her seductiveness is a partner to his charm, an instrument for the vengeful vampirization of the penis and maleness. Her pride depends on the ability to dominate, humiliate, and rubbish men.

Abraham relates this to the problems of prostitutes: "The experiencing of full sexual sensation binds the woman to the man, and only where this is lacking does she go from man to man, just like the continually ungratified Don Juan type of man who has constantly to change his love-object. Just as the Don Juan avenges himself on all women for the disappointment which he once received from the first woman who entered his life, so the prostitute avenges herself on every man for the gift she had expected from her father and did not receive. Her frigidity signifies a humiliation of all men and therefore a mass castration of her unconscious; and her whole life is given up to this purpose." Karl Abraham, "Manifestations of the Female Castration Complex," op. cit., 361.

88. For protective armor they would use crescent-shaped shields, sometimes augmented by the skins of large snakes. Bernice Engle, "The Amazons in Ancient Greece," op. cit., 517.

89. In her admirable article on Cybele, Edith Weigart ("The Cult and Mythology of the Magna Mater from the Standpoint of Psychoanalysis," *Psychiatry*, I, 1938, 347–378) has pointed out how tenaciously the mother cults persisted in Asia Minor and Greece, how deeply the worshipers of the Great Mother feared loss of fertility and death. They were concerned with birth and with conservation of their resources; they dreaded commercial and military expansion. Matriarchal influences predominated.

90. Amazonian mothers often treated male babies as useless commodities. They might send them back to male neighbors (by lot, as they did not know who the father was), or kill them, or keep them for use as drones but cripple their arms and legs. The female babies they treated well. Bernice Engle, "The Amazons in Ancient Greece," op. cit., 515–516.

91. Ibid., 517–518.

The original Greek reads respectively: *deianeira; styganor; kreobotos; anandros; anitaneira; mnesimache; androphonos; androdamas; megathumos; androleteira; amometos; andromache; androktonos;* and *androdaiktos.*

92. According to Heschuyius, *kubelis* (Cybelis) is a synonym for *pelekus*, or axe. Cybele, also known as the Magna Mater, or Great Mother, was revered by the Amazons. Detailed studies of the Cybelic cults and the Amazons show many points of contact, if not similarity. Both favored the axe and the horse, and both depreciated men. Cybelic temples gave the Amazons sanctuary. Ibid., 523.

See also: Maarten Vermaseren, *Cybele and Attis: The Myth and the Cult* (London: Thames and Hudson, 1977).

93. Reay Tannahill, *Sex in History*, op. cit., 107, 237–238.

94. The rites of the Cybele are relatively well known. The novitiates could be both men and women. Women novitates cut off one or both breasts. "Still, mutilation of the men was much more severe than that of women; in the male the primary sex characteristics were sacrificed, in the female the secondary." Bruno Bettelheim, *Symbolic Wounds: Puberty Rites and the Envious Male*, op. cit., 157.

95. Edith Weigart, "The Cult and Mythology of the Magna Mater from the Standpoint of Psychoanalysis," op. cit., 353.

96. "In spite of cauterisation with boiling oil, many died of the castration wounds." Ibid., 353.

The Romans invented a castration clamp to reduce the mortality rate. "The penis was drawn through the oval ring to keep it out of harm's way, while the scrotum and testes were pulled through between the arms of the clamp. . . . When everything was locked in position . . . it took only a single stroke of the knife to cut away scrotum and testes, and the cut edges were then either sewn up or cauterized." Reay Tannahill, *Sex in History*, op. cit., 237.

Weigart also comments that the custom of human castration was eventually replaced by offerings from sheep or steers and celibacy. Edith Weigart, "The Cult and Mythology of the Magna Mater from the Standpoint of Psychoanalysis," op. cit., 353.

97. After being anointed, the priests wore long hair, which they offered to the goddess from time to time. They also took many other measures to feminize their bodies. Latin and Greek writers usually spoke of them in the feminine gender. Ibid., 353.

Weigart points out that "from this form of religious exercise arose the concept of fanaticism [from fanum-sanctuary]. These 'fanatici' of Cybele were the thralls of the goddess, her 'famuli,' they were excluded from the masculine struggle for life." Ibid., 353.

Cybelean practices continued to break out in Roman times and afterward. A castrated Phrygian, converted to Christianity, founded the sect of Montanism, whose devotions included an ecstatic readiness for martyrdom. And as late as the eighteenth century, the Russian sect of Scoptzes introduced ceremonial castration in their liturgy. Ibid., 354.

98. Bruno Bettelheim, *Symbolic Wounds: Puberty Rites and the Envious Male*, op. cit., 157.

99. Ibid. 157–158.

100. Bettelheim contests Freud's theory that circumcision has to do with a "phylogenetic memory trace" of the jealous father. He says there is little evidence to support this while there is a large body of myth, legend, and social practices to indicate that castration in the service of the great maternal deities, as the price of grace, was widespread. "These myths, when considered with the revengelike post-circumcision behavior that is found among some tribes today, support the idea that circumcision may have originated with women and been taken over only later by men." Bruno Bettelheim, "Circumcision Imposed by Women," Ibid., 159–164.

See also: Robert Hobson, "Psychological Aspects of Circumcision," *Journal of Analytical Psychology*, vol. 6, no. 1, 1961, 5–33; and Hanny Lightfoot-Klein, "Pharonic Circumcision of Females in the Sudan," op. cit., 355–358.

Among Jews circumcision is a ritual obligation for all male infants on the eighth day after birth (Genesis 17:11–12). According to the biblical account, it was originally performed by Abraham on himself at the age of ninety-nine at divine behest. But rabbinic legend suggests it was known before. In fact, the procedure dates back to prehistoric times. *Encyclopedia Judaica* (Jerusalem: Keter Publishing House, 1972), vol. 5, 567–575.

It is possible that circumcision was originally a ritual sacrifice to appease the fertility goddesses in the transformation of the tribe of Abraham from a matriarchal cult to a patriarchal religion.

I am reminded of an incident with a Jewish colleague. His first son had just been born, and he was considering the bris (ritual circumcision) on the eighth day. In large measure he thought the practice was atavistic and brutal, but he was wavering and had just decided to go through with it when he received a telegram from his mother: "Remember the eighth day!" This so frightened and infuriated him that he changed his mind, but he was left with considerable unease. His mother continued to bitterly criticize him. Years later the operation was performed for medical reasons.

101. "When men fight with one another, and the wife of the one draws near to rescue her husband from the hand of him who is beating him, and puts out her hand and seizes him by the private parts, then you shall cut off her hand." Deuteronomy (25:11–12), quoted by Reay Tannahill, *Sex in History*, op. cit., 58.

The Harkavy translation adds some interesting nuances: "11 When men strive together one with another, and the wife of the one draweth near for to deliver her husband out of the hand of him that smiteth him, and putteth forth her hand, and taketh him by the secrets: 12 Then thou shalt cut off her hand, thine eyes shall not pity *her*." Deuteronomy, in the Pentateuch, from *The Twenty-four Books of the Old Testament*, vol. 1, translated by Alexander Harkavy (New York: Hebrew Publishing Co., 1926), 331.

Subsequent commentaries deemphasized the punishment. According to the Babylonian Talmud (Tractate: "Baba Kamma"), only a monetary fine was meant, but only when the woman had other means to save her husband. Rashi concurs with the proviso that the amount of money had to be equal to the amount of shame inflicted on the victim. The monetary compensation was in lieu of "eye for eye, tooth for tooth" or, in this instance, as Hugo Gryn points out, "a testicle for a testicle." Personal communication, May 1985.

Still, the intriguing issue remains, why should the Bible specifically comment on a woman who "goes for the balls"?

102. G. R. Driver and John C. Miles, "Middle Assyrian Laws," in *The Assyrian Laws*, op. cit., paragraph 8, quoted by Reay Tannahill, *Sex in History*, op. cit., 58.

103. The rod, mace, sword, scroll, and other phallic objects all came to represent religious and political authority. By direct extension in patriarchal societies, any attack on the phallus or male genitals could be and was taken to be equivalent to an attack on the State itself.

104. I have discussed the *fascinum* and other measures in greater length in chapter 2, "The Evil Eye."

105. The combined parent is an important concept in Kleinian psychology. It refers to the child's idea of the mother with father, or with father's penis inside her, a figure that is the focus of the intense envy and jealousy. It itself seems to become imbued with much of the hatred directed toward it and consequently can become a terrifyingly dangerous object. In various guises, the combined parent is the gist of horror movies.

106. Karl Stern, *The Flight from Women* (London: George Allen and Unwin, 1966), 97.

107. Ibid., 97–98.

108. At birth Christina was hairy, yelled loudly, and was covered with a caul that enveloped most of her body. All this in conjunction with wishful thinking led the midwives to proclaim that the baby was a boy and precipitated celebrations about the birth of a male heir. This was but one of many discordant impingements on the girl's development. See: Georgina Masson, *Queen Christina* (London: Secker & Warburg, 1968); and Barbara Cartland, *The Outrageous Queen: A Biography of Christina of Sweden* (London: Frederick Muller Ltd., 1956).

109. Friedrich Hebbel, *Judith and Holofernes,* discussed by Sigmund Freud, in "The Taboo of Virginity," op. cit., 207–208.

110. Ibid., 207.

111. Ibid., 205. "By "envy" Freud means desire. So "envy for the penis" exemplifies what I term penis greed tempered by hostile bitterness, that is penis envy.

112. Sigmund Freud, "The Economic Problem of Masochism," *S.E.,* vol. 19, 162.

Peter Lomas describes the case of a woman who suffered a puerperal psychosis and for whom childbirth did symbolize castration. She had a great wish to be a man, and it is likely "that she could not tolerate the guilt involved in the possession of masculinity that the birth signified. . . . It is clear that a woman who has a great envy of men, and to whom the baby that grows within her symbolizes the penis she has longed for, will feel childbirth as a castration and a loss." Peter Lomas, "Dread of Envy As an Aetiological Factor in Puerperal Breakdown," op. cit., 110.

One could add that childbirth provides conclusive proof that a woman is a woman, not a man, as some women wish to be.

113. Moulton provides several examples of women whose "typical penis envy" covered a multitude of disturbed family relations. One person was an unsuccessful actress who had hated her masochistic, ineffectual, housebound mother. As a child she turned away from her mother and tried to take on the role of her father's son. Her dad alternated between leading her on and "slapping her down." Her wish to be a boy was crushed when she was twelve years old and preparing for her Bas Mitzvah. (This is the Jewish ceremony celebrating the attainment of religious responsibility and adulthood. Until recently it was restricted to boys at thirteen years of age.) She wanted one "as good as a boy's." But the onset of menarche led her to being publicly humiliated and sent home from the synagogue with the message that she was now a woman and could no longer compete with the boys. Hence she hated herself for not being a male and hated men for their privileged position. But she also hated herself for being a woman, which carried the threat of being like her mother and made it more difficult to stay with the boys. In her late twenties she married and had a baby, an act that conveyed rivalry with her husband (about who was the most productive) and a wish to be the baby herself. Ruth Moulton, "A Survey and Reevaluation of the Concept of Penis Envy," *Psychoanalysis and Women,* edited by Jean Baker Miller (London: Penguin Books, 1974), 251–254.

114. In the case of Christina, paternal oppression included multiple absences; the imposition of a brutal, persecutory upbringing (on his orders continued after his death); extreme marital tensions; and, from present perspectives, near total obtuseness to a child's emotional needs. When Gustavus was present he tried to be a loving (probably seductive) parent. Christina idealized him, an idealization fraught with danger, as he became the focus of her maternal and paternal love and hate. In later life Christina tried, on many occasions, to effect a reconciliation with her mother, but to no avail. See the accounts by Georgina Masson and Barbara Cartland.

In spite of her travails and scandals, it must be noted that Christina was a courageous politician and person. She effected a number of significant reforms during her reign, especially in education, and refused to be dragooned into militaristic policies. In later life she was a benefactor of music, art, and literature. *Encyclopaedia Britannica,* 15th edition, 1974.

115. This was especially true with Queen Christina. The problem wasn't that she was weak, but that she was inconsistent and therefore often ineffective in her work as a politician or in other spheres.

116. Nicolas Comfort, "Thatcher Uses Female Charm Says Nott," *The Daily Telegraph,* 26 January 1985, 36.

Sir John Nott was Thatcher's defense minister at the time of the Falklands conflict. His remarks were made on a TV program to mark the tenth anniversary of her election as leader of the Conservative party. He added: "Mrs. Thatcher tends to arrive at her views by an intuitive process which men find difficult to understand. . . . She has an intuition about something based on her instincts and based on some rather simple truths. . . . Then she argues backwards to justify the solution that she's arrived at by intuition." Ibid., 36.

Nott is essentially putting down Thatcher for being a woman. His carping when praise was due clearly indicates envy. In fact, I have personally spoken with civil servants who have expressed admiration for her intellectual acumen and incisive reasoning. On the other hand, these very qualities, together with forceful, abrasive behavior, mark her as a political Amazon who evokes much of the fear and aggression I have been describing.

117. Geraldine Ferraro was the Democratic candidate for the vice presidency. This was the first time that a woman ran for such high office in the United States. Her phallic possessions included a successful husband, a further focus of envy and jealousy.

118. Phyllis Chesler comments on the male anxieties and aggression aroused by women who engage in activities or take on male roles or qualities. She quotes from a 1971 *New York Times* report on Billie Jean King: "Billie Jean King, the country's most successful woman athletic star, says she is never offended by people who tell her she plays tennis just like a man. But she has become increasingly irritated by people who ask her when she is going to settle down and attend to a home and family." Phyllis Chesler, *Women and Madness,* op. cit., 265.

Subsequently King was subject to an extensive campaign of slander and character abuse in the press. Similar attacks had been made on tennis champion Martina Navratilova for her determined, aggressive, fast, powerful play, as well as her lifestyle, which includes fast cars and a big estate in Virginia.

119. F. Bryk, *Die Beschneidung bei Mann and Weib* (Neubrandenburg: Gustav Feller, 1931), 56, quoted by Bruno Bettelheim, *Symbolic Wounds: Puberty Rites and the Envious Male,* op. cit., 254. Bettelheim adds that while envious revenge may be a contributing factor, he thinks it is not the major motive behind the Nandi's mutilation of girls. He thinks it arises from more positive desires, such as the wish to gain control of their female sex functions.

Any other parts of the female body that remind men of maleness may be attacked for the same reason. Boehm comments: "Thus some men detest a broad pelvis, large buttocks or hanging breasts. . . . Behind the hatred of the peculiarly feminine characteristics of women there lies . . . envy of the larger penis which women are imagined to possess. To the unconscious of men a woman's large pendulous breasts represent a larger female penis." Felix Boehm, "The Femininity Complex in Men," op. cit., 131.

120. This quip has been attributed to Henry Kissinger.

121. Otto Fenichel concluded that boys suffer the same castration fears as girls and may react in the same way with wish fulfillment or vindictive behavior. He states that the former covers deep feelings of inferiority and wounded pride, while the latter has to do with murderous rage toward whoever may be held responsible (usually parents) for masculine inadequacies.

Otto Fenichel, *The Psychoanalytic Theory of Neurosis,* op. cit., 495.

122. An advertisement by the American McDonnell-Douglas Corporation exemplifies envious rivalry. It proudly proclaims the virtues of a new weapons system

that can destroy the enemy (in this case, the masculine prowess of the USSR) wherever it may be. Helen Caldicott, *Missile Envy* (New York: William Morrow & Co., 1984), 297.

123. Ibid., 297.

124. Description of World War II by General George Patton. Ibid., 297.

125. See: Mary Barnes and Joseph Berke, *Mary Barnes: Two Accounts of a Journey Through Madness* (London: Penguin Books, 1982).

The stage play *Mary Barnes* was adapted from the book by David Edgar and performed in London at the Royal Court Theatre in 1979. The man was angry because a friend of his had seen the play twice and had remarked about my being depicted by a brilliant character.

126. Personal communication. As many men, this person was overwhelmed by severe conflicts between body, gender, and personal identities. He recognized he had the body of a man and often thought of himself as one. But he had great difficulty in separating himself from his love/hate relationship with his mother. Sometimes this struggle seemed too much, and he tried to avoid it by identifying with her. Then his personal identity was at greatest risk, and his penis envy rose accordingly.

127. Hanna Segal has also described a situation where intense penis envy led a male patient to dream of anal intercourse. Ostensibly Segal represented the potent, successful father whom the man hated out of envy and jealousy, and the analysis represented the paternal potency under attack. "He dreamt that he put into the boot of his little car tools belonging to my car (bigger than his), but when he arrived at his destination and opened the boot, all the tools were shattered. This dream symbolized his type of homosexuality; he wanted to take the paternal penis into his anus and steal it, but in the process of doing so, his hatred of the penis, even when introjected, was such that he would shatter it and be unable to make use of it. In the same way interpretations which he felt as complete and helpful were immediately torn to pieces. . . ." Hanna Segal, *Introduction to the Work of Melanie Klein,* op. cit., 42–43.

As the treatment proceeded, issues of maternal potency began to predominate. The man launched desperate attacks on Segal representing the phallic breasts, again demonstrating the close connections between the penis and the breast.

128. Melanie Klein points out that the good penis not only expresses but helps to overcome aggression. This helps a man to obtain a sense of security in himself, adds to his creativity in other areas, and adds to his masculine sense of achievement. "In these various ways his early wish to be capable of doing what his father did for his mother, sexually and otherwise, and to receive from her what his father received, can be fulfilled in his relation to his wife. His happy relation to her has also the effect of diminishing his aggresssion against his father . . . and this may reassure him that his long-standing sadistic tendencies against his father have not been effective." Melanie Klein, "Love, Guilt and Reparation," op. cit., 73.

129. John Donne, *The Complete Poetry and Prose of John Donne and The Complete Poetry of William Blake* (New York: The Modern Library, Random House, 1941), 84–85.

Klein comments that the same impetus to explore the body of Mother, and thence the world, can be seen in the well-known sonnet by John Keats, "On First Looking into Chapman's Homer." Melanie Klein, "Love, Guilt and Reparation," op. cit., 105–106.

Chapter 7

1. The ancient Romans described a terrifying night creature that they called a *strix,* from the Greek word meaning "to screech." Like an owl and hawk combined, the *strix* was a woman by day and ravenous bird by night who flew through the air on amorous, murderous, or cannibalistic missions. The *strix* laid the basis for

innumerable popular legends. See: Norman Cohn, *Europe's Inner Demons* (London: Paladin Books, 1976), 206–224.

2. See: John Widdowson, "The Witch As a Frightening and Threatening Figure," in *The Witch Figure*, edited by Venetia Newall, op. cit., 200–220.

3. Dante Aligheri, *Inferno*, canto 34, 1.30; John Milton, *Paradise Lost*, book 1, 1.777, quoted by Beatrice White, "Cain's Kin," in *The Witch Figure*, edited by Venetia Newall, op. cit., 189.

4. Iona and Peter Opie, *The Classic Fairy Tales* (London: Paladin Books, 1980), 58–63.

5. Lloyd DeMause, "The Evolution of Childhood," in *The History of Childhood*, edited by Lloyd DeMause (New York: The Psychohistory Press, 1974), 1.

6. Ibid., 25.

7. Ibid., 29.

8. Robert Pemell complained in 1653 of the practice of "both high and low ladies of farming out their babies to irresponsible women in the country," and as late as 1780 the police chief of Paris estimated that of 21,000 children born each year in his city, 17,000 were sent into the country to be wet-nursed, 2,000 or 3,000 were placed in nursery homes, 700 were wet-nursed at home, and only 700 were nursed by their mothers." Ibid., 35.

9. One aspect of this feared involvement had to do with excessive grief and guilt following the deaths of multiple offspring. This reaction was mitigated but not eliminated when such deaths were expected.

10. Venetia Newall, "The Jew As Witch Figure," in *The Witch Figure*, edited by Venetia Newall, op. cit., 95–124.

In addition, both Europeans and Americans were obsessed with bogiemen—that is, black people. Typically, in 1882 one little girl was told to behave herself, otherwise a "horrible little Black Man . . . was hidden in the room to catch her the moment she left her bed or made the slightest noise." Rhoda White, *From Infancy to Womanhood: A Book of Instructions for Young Mothers* (London, 1882), 31, quoted in Lloyd DeMause, "The Evolution of Childhood," op. cit., 12–13.

11. There exists an enormous literature on child abuse, ranging from physical injury, physical neglect, and failure to thrive to mental cruelty. In Britain the National Society for the Prevention of Cruelty to Children (NSPCC) has documented the increasing number of reported cases:

Angela Skinner and Raymond Castle, *78 Battered Children: A Retrospective Study*, NSPCC, London, 1969.

Susan Creighton, *Child Victims of Physical Abuse, 1976*, NSPCC, London.

Susan Creighton, *Trends in Child Abuse*, NSPCC, London, 1984.

Gavin Bell, "Child Sex Abuse Cases Doubled Last Year, NSPCC Survey Shows," *The Times*, 22 March 1986, 4.

The same holds true for other countries. In a typical late 1980s report, Istat, the Italian statistical center, reported a big increase in reported rape and abuse cases. Roger Boyes, "Italian Rape and Child Abuse Increase," *The Times*, 2 January 1988, 7.

12. Susan Creighton, "Child Abuse Deaths," *NSPCC Information Briefing No. 5*, NSPCC, London, 1985.

"The Victims Who Can't Fight Back," *The Times*, 31 March 1986, 10.

13. I do not think that every instance of child abuse can be reduced simply to parental malice. Much depends on the capacity of the parents to support each other or not; the character of the child; the personality of the parents; their own background (often violent and deprived); their capacity to contain their own infantile feelings or not; and so forth. Nevertheless, when an adult who feels worthless and empty faces a child being cared for by another, or demanding attention himself, the narcissistic rage, itself an extension of envious forces, often becomes uncontrollable. See:

Joan Court, "Battering Parents," *Social Work*, vol. 26, no. 1, January 1969.

Jean Moore and Beryl Day, "Family Interaction Associated with Abuse of Children Over 5 Years of Age," *Child Abuse and Neglect*, The International Journal (London: The Pergamon Press, 1979).

Christine Smakowska, "Marital Problems and Family Violence," *NSPCC Information Briefing No. 7*, NSPCC, London, 1985.

14. "Hansel and Gretel," in Jacob and Wilhelm Grimm, *Selected Tales*, op. cit., 56.

15. Ibid., 60.

16. Ibid., 61.

17. Joseph Rheingold gives many examples in his chapters "Parental Cruelty" and "The Filicidal Impulse," in *The Fear of Being a Woman: A Theory of Maternal Destructiveness*, op. cit., 1–84.

18. The point of eating human meat is to incorporate and take over the other's vital essence. So the wish behind eating a baby's behind, or other parts, may be to incorporate youth and new life, just as the wicked queen in "Snow-White" tried to eat the young girl's liver and lungs both to destroy her and to take over her youthful beauty, exuberance, sexuality, potential, and so forth. When envy predominates over greed, the primary purpose is destructive.

19. Lloyd DeMause, "The Evolution of Childhood," op. cit., 7.

20. Bertram Karon and Gary VandenBos, *Psychotherapy of Schizophrenia: Treatment of Choice* (New York: Jason Aronson, 1981), 118–119.

21. R. D. Laing, *In the Psychiatrist's Chair*, interview by Dr. Anthony Clare, BBC Radio 4, 14 July 1985.
See also: R. D. Laing, *The Facts of Life* (New York: Pantheon Books, 1976), 3–6.

22. Eric Carle, *The Very Hungry Caterpillar* (London: Hamish Hamilton, 1970).

23. In other words, she thought that I preferred her baby side to her adult self. Consequently, the part of her that identified with and was a capable, adult woman felt unloved, excluded, and very angry. This jealousy can be seen as a triangular conflict between me and two distinct (unassimilated) parts of her.

24. Narcissistic mothering potentiates envy, greed, and jealousy and, therefore, intergenerational conflict.
Leslie Farber points out: "To some extent, envy in the parents will provide the conditions for envy in the child. I do not mean by this that envy itself is a learned response, although to some degree a child may learn the policy of derogation where superiority is involved. . . . In a house where envy is in the air, the child need but look, listen, and breathe to be instructed in consolation and counterattack. . . . If he accepts the conditions offered him and agrees to be instructed by the example of his elders, thus will their envy breed his own." In *lying, despair, jealousy, envy, sex, suicide, drugs, and the good life*, op. cit., 44.

25. Rheingold has detailed the death wishes of mothers toward their children. Not only are they extremely frequent, but they often stem from the wish to undo motherhood in order to escape the real and imagined vengeance of their own mothers (the child's grandmother). Rheingold points out that it is not unusual for women to give birth and then beg their mothers not to kill them. See: Joseph Rheingold, *The Mother, Anxiety, and Death: The Catastrophic Death Complex* (Boston, 1967).

26. The dread of envy can be a causal factor in puerperal breakdown—that is, an acute psychosis after the birth of a child. "Mrs. D" was a thirty-one-year-old midwife and drug addict who became so withdrawn, depressed, helpless, and hopeless after her second delivery that her doctor wondered whether she would be able to keep the baby. Previously her mother had taken possession of her first child after declaring that Mrs. D was unfit for motherhood. It transpired that the older woman was extremely envious of her daughter's exuberance. From adolescence onward she was always running her down, discouraging her from going to dances, and trying

to interfere with her social life. Not surprisingly, Mrs. D was terrified of her mother's reaction to her pregnancies. She only began to get better after she was able to reveal what she most wanted—someone to believe in her maternal capacities. In this instance we can see the wish to abandon or kill a newborn baby and to be abandoned (left to rot in mental hospital) or killed (suicidal depression) was not necessarily aroused by hostility to the child, but by the urgent need to placate a feared and fearful grandmother. See: Peter Lomas, "Dread of Envy As an Aetiological Factor in Puerperal Breakdown," op. cit., 108.

27. The fearful aspects of the parent's parent were commonly projected onto gods and goddesses and the children sacrificed to them. Plutarch documented Carthaginian child sacrifice: "With full knowledge and understanding they themselves offered up their own children, and those who had no children would buy little ones from poor people and cut their throats as if they were so many lambs or young birds; meanwhile the mother stood by without a tear or moan; but should she utter a single moan or let fall a single tear, she had to forfeit the money, and her child was sacrificed nevertheless." Plutarch, *Moralia,* Frank Babbitt translation (London, 1928), 493, quoted by Lloyd DeMause, "The Evolution of Childhood," op. cit., 27.

DeMause comments: "Child sacrifice is, of course, the most concrete acting out of Rheingold's thesis of filicide as sacrifice to the mother of the parents." Ibid., 27.

28. Henry Bett, *Nursery Rhymes and Tales: Their Origin and History* (New York, 1924), 35, discussed by Lloyd DeMause, "The Evolution of Childhood," op. cit., 27.

29. Jacob and Wilhelm Grimm, *Selected Tales,* op. cit., 77–81.

30. Ibid., 114–115.

31. Ibid., 178–183.

32. Ibid., 178.

33. Christina Crawford, *Mommie Dearest* (London: Hart-David, 1979). The book was also made into a film with the same title, starring Faye Dunaway as Joan Crawford and directed by Frank Perry (MGM).

While Christina Crawford was not an impartial observer, many of her stories were corroborated by people who knew the family. Even late in her life, Joan Crawford tried to take over her daughter's life and roles. Once Christina, an aspiring actress in a TV soap opera, was rushed to the hospital with gynecological problems. Her mother immediately stood in for her, playing love scenes with a man thirty years her junior.

34. Robert Altman, *A Wedding,* TCF/Lionsgate, 1978.

35. Leslie Childe, " 'Supernatural Trail' of Girl in Witch Trial," *The Daily Telegraph,* 14 December 1983, 3.

36. Leslie Childe, "Enter an Exorcist at the Witch Trial," *The Daily Telegraph,* 15 December 1983, 17.

37. Ibid., 17.

The trial obviously evoked powerful feelings among the spectators. The healer, a tiny old woman dressed in black and carrying a wooden crucifix, appeared daily at the back of the courtroom. At one stage she tried to grab Ms. Compton but was taken away by the police. She explained: "I had a dream in which the devil came to me and told me that Carol Compton and her mother are possessed by an eighteenth-century spirit. That spirit has given them the power of fire." She added that the devil had told her to cleanse Carol of her demon. Ibid., 17.

38. When Signora Cecchini took the stand, she admitted that she smoked a lot but denied her daughter-in-law's complaint that she left burning cigarette ends about the house. Later the judge asked the daugher-in-law, Daniella, whether Signora Cecchini was jealous of Ms. Compton. Daniella replied: "She does have an approach that gives the impression she has no sympathy for British girls. She has a closed personality, but there is no malice in it." Ibid., 17.

39. Numerous nannies and au pairs had worked for the family, and all left because they had been mistreated.

40. Serpents and snakes are considered to be phallic symbols, but since ancient times they have also been important female symbols, often of a very threatening nature. In fertility cults phallic objects have been represented with snakes coiled around them. The encircling snake represents clinging vines, possessive arms, and dominating, insatiable women. And because the snake devours its object whole, it also has been associated with mothers' devouring breasts, eyes, mouths, vaginas, wombs, and psyches. Finally, because the snake gets into things, it has been linked with the female phallus, which "knows what is going on." See: Philip Slater, *The Glory of Hera: Greek Mythology and the Greek Family* (Boston: Beacon Press, 1968), 80–97.

41. Daniel Jaffe, "The Masculine Envy of Woman's Procreative Function," op. cit., 534–541.

42. Ibid., 536.

43. Robert Stoller, *Sex and Gender,* op. cit., 108–125.

44. The boy was five years old when she came into therapy. She had been dressing him as a girl since he was eleven months old. At this point Mrs. C also had a daughter who was eleven years old. Ibid., 109.

45. Ibid., 109.

46. She felt she was a neuter gender without denying that anatomically she was a female. Ibid., 114.

47. Stoller comments quite correctly the whole process of feminizing the boy could not have happened without the tacit consent of his father. In this instance she married a masculine-looking but empty, passive man not unlike her mother. Ibid., 117–118.

48. That was until she was nine or ten years old. Afterward she enjoyed normal girls' activities. Ibid., 301.

However, the onset of menarche and development of breasts was extremely traumatic. It ended her hopes of becoming a boy. Ibid., 113.

49. Stoller comments that her son was "his mother's feminized phallus." Ibid., 120.

Although Stoller is referring to Mrs. C, the comment might equally apply to Mrs. C's mother, the boy's grandmother. In a real sense the boy was the phallus that Mrs. C's mother never gave to her. So the birth was not only a triumph of the will—that is, the greedy wish to have and be a male—but a triumph over the mother's greedy withholding of both her femininity (that which would allow her to feel and be a loved, loving and capable woman) and masculinity (that which would allow her to compete with her brothers, be loved by her parents, and restore the family's fortunes).

50. In her destructive aspects, Cybele is not unlike the Indian goddess Kali.

John Carroll points out that the male Indian fear of females has a lot to do with the practice of totally indulgent mothering until about aged five, followed by exposure to a constraining and critical male environment. Since the Indian father remains distant from his son in early childhood, the boy is deprived of crucial identifications that would allow him to overcome fears of the ever-present, dominating, all-powering mother. John Carroll, *Guilt: The Grey Eminence Behind Character, History and Culture* (London: Routledge & Kegan Paul, 1985), 61.

The boy in ancient Greece faced an upbringing that was not too dissimilar. See: Philip Slater, *The Glory of Hera: Greek Mythology and the Greek Family,* op. cit., 3–74.

51. Edith Weigart, "The Cult and Mythology of the Magna Mater from the Standpoint of Psychoanalysis," op. cit., 357.

In this narration, Attis' bride mourns him with the Great Mother, binds him in soft wrappings, and kills herself by cutting off her breasts. An almond tree then grows up on the burial ground.

52. Ovid, *Metamorphoses, X,* A. Riese edition, 103–105, quoted by Weigart, ibid., 357.

The Latin translation is a paraphrase according to Arnobius. Ibid., 537.

According to Andrea Sabbadini, a more literal translation would be: "Let the parts that damage me, die."

53. Betty Radice, *Who's Who in the Ancient World* (London: Penguin Books, 1984), 48–49.

Adonis was a vegetation god born of incest between father and daughter. He was loved by Aphrodite (Venus). His name is semitic, meaning "Lord" (Hebrew: Adonai), and is commonly associated with the Babylonian Thammuz, beloved of Ishtar. Both loved beautiful mother goddesses and were torn to pieces by angry fathers in revenge. Both are also associated with nature cults of death and rebirth.

See also: *New Larousse Encyclopedia of Mythology,* op. cit., 150, and Edith Weigart, "The Cult and Mythology of the Magna Mater from the Standpoint of Psychoanalysis," op. cit., 357–358.

54. Betty Radice, *Who's Who in the Ancient World,* op. cit., 178 and 254.

Zeus was lord of the sky, of wind and rain, thunder and lightning. Like Jupiter, his Roman counterpart, he was omnipotent, omniscient, and the supreme authority, the upholder of law, but law based on might, not morality. *New Larousse Encyclopedia of Mythology,* op. cit., 98.

55. Ibid., 85–198.

56. Rambo is the character created by Sylvester Stallone, a large, muscular American actor whose roles in the 1970s and 1980s include Rocky, a heavyweight boxing champion, and Rambo, the incarnation of American omnipotence and vengeance.

57. Iona and Peter Opie, *The Classic Fairy Tales,* op. cit., 58–82, especially 58–59, 78–79.

58. "Jack and the Beanstalk," Ibid., 214.

Jack and his mother are close to starvation, and, as a last chance, he is sent to sell their cow. The lad exchanges it for colored beans, which, when he returns, his mother flings into the garden. Overnight a huge beanstalk grows right through the clouds. The widow forbids him to climb it, but to no avail. Jack sets out and eventually comes to a strange, barren land. He is frightened and fears he will die but walks on and soon meets an old lady—not a witch, but a good woman—who tells him the truth about his background. So in this account we see a clash not only between the good and bad father, but between the good and bad mother as well (who is seen as critical and nagging).

59. Ibid., 217.

60. Interestingly, after the giant stabbed Jack's father to death, stole his treasures, and burned down the house, he could have killed the wife and baby Jack "in the most cruel manner." But in a moment of "weakness" he decided to spare them, if they fled and kept quiet, which they did. The weakness was remorse, which the giant later repented. He wished he had killed them all. Ibid., 218.

61. According to the Opies, "Fe, fau, fum" is probably the most famous war cry in English literature. Another variation is

Fe, fi, fo, fum,
I smell the blood of an Englishman:
If he have any liver and lights
I'll have them for my supper tonight.

Ibid., 78–79.

62. These paintings are in the Prado Museum, Madrid, Spain. They are repro-

duced in many books, including Norman Cohn, *Europe's Inner Demons,* op. cit., plates 7 and 8.

63. Personal communication, 1975.

64. It is interesting that the central action takes place in a mansion far away in the sky. The location serves several purposes, both to emphasize the father's character, aloof, all high, distant, and to distance the action from down-to-earth dramas, where cannibalistic fathers and vengeful sons are extremely frightening.

The good fairy is the counterpart of a psychotically depressed mother, as well as the embodiment of Jack's faith in himself.

The giant's wife embodies a bit of the bad mother, who colludes with the wicked father to devour, terrorize, and generally oppress the children. But she has some good qualities as she helps Jack confront her husband. The wife may also represent small bits of goodness in the giant himself. After all, after killing the father—that is, changing from a good to bad person—he did feel remorse.

65. *New Larousse Encyclopedia of Mythology,* op. cit., 87–93.

66. Zeus was often at a loss in the presence of maternal goddesses. When Metis, his first wife and goddess of wisdom, became pregnant, he swallowed her whole, thus incorporating wisdom and childbearing capacities. Eventually Athene sprang forth from his head. Zeus also renounced Thetis because it was predicted that any child of theirs would dethrone him. He arranged for her to be married to a mortal. Ibid., 99.

Finally Zeus was threatened by his own grandmother, Gaea. She became very angry after Zeus and the other gods overcame all her children, the Giants. So she created a Typhon (Typhoeus), a monstrous embodiment of her own vindictiveness, composed mostly of serpents. It almost destroyed him before Zeus was rescued by Hermes. Ibid., 93.

67. Tantalus was king of Siplos in Lydia, an ancient kingdom now part of modern Turkey opposite Greece. In punishment for dismembering and serving his son to the gods, he was made to stand in water up to his chin and suffer terrible thirst and hunger in the presence of food and drink that moved just out of his reach when he tried to take them. Betty Radice, *Who's Who in the Ancient World,* op. cit., 232.

68. Pelops was king of Elis, an ancient kingdom on the western side of the Peloponnesus peninsula, named after him.

The *Oresteia* was written by Aeschylus and is the only trilogy in Greek drama that survives from antiquity. It describes a bloody chain of ambition, hubris, murder, and revenge.

69. Joshua Berke, personal communication, 1976.

James Joyce essentially commented on this very point in his novel *Ulysses.* "The son unborn mars beauty; born he brings pain, divides attention, increases care. . . . His growth is his father's decline, his youth his father's envy." Quoted by John Ross, in "Oedipus Revisited: Laius and the 'Laius Complex,' " *Psychoanalytic Study of the Child,* vol. 37 (New Haven: Yale University Press, 1982), 169.

70. In his study of Greek mythology and family structure, Philip Slater observes: "The father-son conflict is but a tiny episode, while the prevailing situation is one of father-absence and mother-son marriage. Philip Slater, *The Glory of Hera: Greek Mythology and the Greek Family,* op. cit., 135.

71. Different studies provide divergent views about the lot of women in ancient Greece. Many comment on their lack of legal, political, and religious rights and how women were relegated to domestic toil. Others point out that in various city-states the women had extensive rights. In Sparta the girls were trained like the young men in discus and spear throwing and were expected to attend the games and festivals. Women could and did become influential adminstrators. See:

Reay Tannahill, *Sex in History,* op. cit., 82–87.

Thorkil Vanggaard, *Phallós: A Symbol and Its History in the Male World* (New York: International Universities Press, 1972), 45.

72. The Dorians supervised the upbringing of boys with an intensity and severity that was admired throughout Greece. The emphasis was on the development of *aretē*, an ideal of nobility that has no precise equivalent in English. It is close to the old Norse idea of *hamingja*. *Aretē* embodied physical strength, marital prowess, courage, integrity, clarity of thought, stamina, honesty, and adherence to duty. *Aretē* was synonymous with honor, fame, and distinction as well as aristocracy and fine breeding. Ibid., 34–35.

"The bloom of a twelve-year-old boy is desirable, but at thirteen he is much more delightful. Sweeter still is the flower of love that blossoms at fourteen, and its charm increases at fifteen. Sixteen is the divine age." Straton, *Anthologica Palatinus*, XII, 4, quoted by Reay Tannahill, *Sex in History*, op. cit., 75.

73. Vanggaard comments: "Since the erotic pleasure was subordinated to a more important aim this was a genuinely symbolic act, the aim being to make of the boy a man with strength, a sense of duty, eloquence, cleverness, generosity, courage and other noble virtues." He compares this with the actions of New Guinea natives. The Kiwai Papuan, when selecting wood for a harpoon, will press his phallus against the trunk of the chosen tree in order to impart straightness, strength, and great power of penetration. Thorkil Vanggaard, *Phallós: A Symbol and Its History in the Male World*, op. cit., 12–13.

74. Ibid., 43–44.

Paiderastia was akin to the upbringing of North American Plains Indians or of Japanese before World War II. It emphasized lofty ideals, immense demands, merciless severity, and produced warriors of great skill and tenacity. The Sacred Band of Thebes consisted of pairs of lovers fighting side by side and was the backbone of the Theban army that conquered the Spartans of Leuctra in 371 B.C.E. The Sacred Band remained unconquered until 338 B.C.E., when it was overcome by Philip of Macedonia at Cheironeia. All three hundred of its members were killed and lay on the battlefield pair by pair. Ibid., 41; Reay Tannahill, *Sex in History*, op. cit., 79–80.

The role of the *erōmenos* came to an end when the boy reached adolescence, as was signified by the first growth of beard. The *erastēs*, or older lover, was usually in his thirties.

75. Homosexuality in the modern sense was banned. Reay Tannahill, *Sex in History*, op. cit., 75. See also: 78–79.

76. In Plato's *Symposium*, Phaedrus says: "I for my part am at a loss to say what greater blessing a man can have in earliest youth than an honourable love, or a lover than an honourable favourite." Quoted by Thorkil Vanggaard, *Phallós: A Symbol and Its History in the Male World*, op. cit., 40.

77. The status of the *erastai*, or older lovers, was on a par with that of the boy's father. They could be and were held responsible for the conduct of the *erōmenos* and shared his honor and dishonor. After the *paiderastic* relationship was concluded, the older man continued to have a special relationship with his *erōmenos*, perhaps akin to that or a godfather or favored uncle, and could be called upon for help when needed. Ibid., 37.

78. Thorkil Vanggaard, *Phallós: A Symbol and Its History in the Male World*, op. cit., 26.

Slaves were forbidden to be taken as lovers because they were considered unworthy. They were also forbidden to rub boys with oil at the gymnasia because this practice often heralded the onset of a *paiderastic* relationship.

The physical erotic element in *paiderastia* was certainly present. Men and boys tended to meet at the gymnasia, where the boys competed in sport naked except for the oil on their body and fine strings that protectively tied the foreskin over the glans of the penis. Reay Tannahill, *Sex in History*, op. cit., 78.

79. The German scholar E. Bethe has summarized the Dorian ideas about male upbringing: "The qualities of the man, his heroism, his arete, are in some way

transmitted to the beloved boy through love. Therefore it is society's view that skillful and competent men ought to love boys; the state even exerts pressure on them to do so. . . . It was an honour for a boy to have found an honourable lover and be ceremoniously united with him, an honour which in Crete was celebrated in public by the family." E. Bethe, *Die Dorische Knabenliebe, ihre Ethik und ihre Idee* (Neue Folge: Rheinisches Museum für Philologie, 1907), 457, quoted by Thorkil Vanggaard, Ibid., 43.

80. Aristophanes, *The Birds,* lines 137–142, quoted by Reay Tannahill, *Sex in History,* op. cit., 78.

81. Thorkil Vanggaard, *Phallós: A Symbol and Its History in the Male World,* op. cit., 40 and 43.

82. Ibid., 26–27.

83. I refer, in particular, to the narcissistic, as well as homoerotic, components of *paiderastia.*

84. Pelops needed help to gain the hand of Hippodamia, the daughter of King Oenomaus, who demanded that all her suitors stake their lives in a chariot race. Many suitors had lost their lives. Pelops managed to bribe Myrtilus, the king's charioteer, to loosen a wheel, so the king lost the race. Later Pelops murdered Myrtilus in order to get rid of an embarrassing accomplice. But the father of Myrtilus was Hermes (Mercury), who was enraged by Pelops' action. In revenge he placed a curse on Pelops and his house. I shall discuss many of the consequences of this curse in the next chapter on sibling rivalry.

85. The Laius-Chrysippus legend was well known in the fifth and fourth centuries B.C.E. and formed the basis for several tragedies, all since lost. These include *Laius* by Aeschylus and *Chrysippus* by Euripides, plays known because of references to them in other works.

86. Presumably Jocasta realized Laius's fears. So in getting pregnant she was getting back at him for his homosexuality, misogyny, and overall indifference to the needs of a woman. As far as the Greeks were concerned, this was all part of the war between the sexes. John Ross, "Oedipus Revisited: Laius and the 'Laius Complex,' " *Psychoanalytic Study of the Child,* op. cit., 177–178.

87. Betty Radice, *Who's Who in the Ancient World,* op. cit., 177–178.

88. Ross comments: "If the anachronisms can be pardoned, Laius's misdeeds and delusions can be taken as 'evidence' of: disturbances in gender identity and sexual orientation, problems with impulse control; unmodulated aggressivity; cognitive and intellectual impairment; and pathological narcissism." John Ross, "Oedipus Revisited: Laius and the 'Laius Complex,' " *Psychoanalytic Study of the Child,* op. cit., 177.

89. Laius himself had been abandoned and persecuted as a child. His father, Labdacus, the ruling king of Thebes, died when he was one year old. He was left in the care of his mother. Later he was forced to flee Thebes and wander about Greece when his uncle usurped the throne. Ibid., 177.

90. Ross strongly makes this point and adds that the same was true for all but a handful of analytic authors after Freud. Ibid., 174.

91. As presented, Oedipus was a virtuous young man, perhaps too much so. Having learned from a drunken friend that Queen Merope and King Polybus are not his real parents, he flees Corinth. One might think he would discuss the matter with them and even be inclined to stay, for if the news were true, then he would be safe in his adopted home. The failure to do so may have been a dramatic necessity, but it also indicates the existence of unconscious forces related to his severed past and uncertain present.

92. Betty Radice, *Who's Who in the Ancient World,* op. cit., 225. The Sphinx had the body of a lion and a human head. It originated in Egypt, where it was considered either female or male, but came to Greece via the Near

East and then was always considered to be female. The Sphinx can be seen as a pre-Oedipal combined parent figure.

93. Sophocles, *Oedipus Rex,* translated by Albert Cook, in *Ten Greek Plays,* edited by L. R. Lind (Cambridge, Mass.: Riverside Editions, Houghton Mifflin Co., 1957), 111–154.

Teiresias was the blind prophet who foretold the problem and only told the truth after Oedipus threatened him. The quality of his blindness seemed to be associated with wisdom.

Jocasta clearly understands the situation before Oedipus. She tries to convince Oedipus not to proceed with his investigations for several reasons: to conceal her infidelities, protect Oedipus, and continue the relationship that allowed her to remain queen and maintain her female powers and ambitions.

94. The struggle for preeminence between Laius and Jocasta, Jocasta and Oedipus, Oedipus and Creon (Jocasta's brother), reflected the continuing conflict about matriarchal versus patriarchal authority and the gradual shift to a system of patriarchal authority. Jocasta's reign symbolized continuing matriarchal power, after a time when she had ostensibly accepted male domination by concurring in Laius' attempts to destroy Oedipus at birth.

95. Rollo May, "Guilt and Awareness," in *Man and Society,* edited by Roger W. Smith (New York: Anchor Books, Doubleday & Co., 1971), 171–184.

John Steiner, "Turning a Blind Eye: The Cover Up for Oedipus," *Int. Rev. Psycho-Anal.,* vol. 12, 1985, 161–172.

96. Sophocles, *Oedipus at Colonus,* translated by Robert Fitzgerald, in *Greek Tragedies,* edited by David Grene and Richmond Lattimore (Chicago, Ill.: Phoenix Books, University of Chicago Press, 1960), line 144.

97. This illuminates the nature of prohibitions on incest. They exist to prevent the catastrophic malice that is aroused by intimate relations between closely related individuals within a closed social system (the family) and the subsequent disintegration of family structure, a fact I have personally observed in working with incest victims.

98. Oedipus to his son, Polynices:

Now go! For I abominate and disown you!
You utter scoundrel! Go with the malediction
I here pronounce for you: that you shall never
Master your native land by force of arms,
Nor ever see your home again in Argos,
The land below the hill; but you shall die
By your own brother's hand, and you shall kill
The brother who banished you. For this I pray.

Ibid., lines 1383–1390.

99. The relationship between Socrates and his young disciple Alcibiades, for example, indicated that more than intellectual companionship was at stake. Once Alcibiades arrived at a dinner party to discover Socrates sharing a couch with his host. He scowled. "You would move heaven and earth to sit next to the best-looking person in the room!" Socrates retorted, "My love for that fellow is always landing me in trouble. Ever since I feel for him, I have not been allowed even to glance at a good-looking boy, far less talk to one. He gets jealous straight away." Plato, *Symposium,* 213d, quoted by Reay Tannahill, op. cit., 76–77.

100. In technical terms I am referring to the fact that all parents establish a transference relationship to their children. This transference relationship encompasses emotionally charged figures from their past, usually their own parents, but also extends to siblings, uncles, aunts, or grandparents as well as aspects of themselves. In the latter case we can speak of a narcissistic transference. When the

transference leads to maltreatment it can be seen as a negative parental or narcissistic transference.

Lloyd DeMause provides many examples of the transference relationship between parent and child (which he calls "the reversal reaction") in his chapter "The Evolution of Childhood," in *The History of Childhood*, edited by Lloyd DeMause, op. cit., 6–21.

101. The extended "Homily Against Wilful Rebellion" seems to have been the basis for a passage in Shakespeare's *King Lear*, when Gloucester speaks to his bastard son, Edmund, about familial and social conflict. *Certain Sermons or Homilies*, 1817 edition, 541. Quoted by G. K. Hunter, in his introduction to *King Lear* (London: Penguin Books, 1972), 40.

Hunter points out that behind this homily and the passage from *Lear*, there lies a passage in Mark (13:12–13):

Now the brother shall betray the brother to death and the father the son;
and children shall rise up against their parents and shall cause them
    to be put to death. . . .
But he that shall endure unto the end, the same shall be saved.

102. Robinson added, "Children should not know, if it could be kept from them, that they have a will of their own, but in their parents' keeping." P. Greven, *Child-Rearing Concepts, 1628–1861* (Itasca: 1973), 13–14, quoted by Lawrence Stone, *The Family, Sex and Marriage in England 1500–1800* (London: Weidenfeld and Nicolson, 1977), 162–163.

103. Ibid., 163.
In Italy the bundle of birch twigs is called a *fascio* and is a symbol of fascism.

104. Dr. Busby was known to the boys as "Flog-em" Busby.
Dr. Gill used to have "whipping-fits." They were not unusual. Indentured apprentices suffered the same fate as students—that is, they were often exposed to limitless sadism by their masters. Stone points out that the bolder spirits sometimes sued their masters for assault. These suits reveal a female apprentice who was stripped naked, strung up by her thumbs, and given twenty-one lashes and a boy who was flogged, salted, and held naked to a fire. Ibid., 163–167.

105. In this instance the choleric anger injured not just the envied object, but the envier as well. Pepys went on to relate that the student succeeded his teacher as "Master of the Children; but his career was very short; for he deceased at Windsor, 14 July 1674." Samuel Pepys, *The Diary of Samuel Pepys*, volume 2 (London: J. M. Dent & Sons, 1906), 381.

106. Lawrence Stone, *The Family, Sex and Marriage in England 1500–1800*, op. cit., 169.
See also: Elizabeth W. Marvick, "Childhood History and Decisions of State: The Case of Louis XIII," in *The New Psychohistory*, edited by Lloyd DeMause (New York: Psychohistory Press, 1975), 199–244.

107. Lawrence Stone, *The Family, Sex and Marriage in England 1500–1800*, op. cit., 174.
Children who cried too much or who were too demanding were in danger of being considered "changelings." The *Malleus* comments that changelings could be recognized because they "always howl most piteously and even if four or five mothers are set on to suckle them, they never grow." Quoted by Lloyd DeMause, "The Evolution of Childhood," in *The History of Childhood*, edited by Lloyd DeMause, op. cit., 10.

108. Ibid., 175.
See: L. L. Schüking, *The Puritan Family* (New York, 1970), 73; R. H. Bremner, *Children and Youth in America* (Cambridge, Mass.: Harvard University Press, 1970),

37–38; and A. W. Calhoun, *A Social History of the American Family from Colonial Times to the Present* (New York, 1945), 47, 120–121.

109. Stephen Kern, "Explosive Intimacy: Psychodynamics of the Victorian Family," in *The New Psychohistory,* edited by Lloyd DeMause (New York: Psychohistory Press, 1975), 39–44.

110. Ibid., 44–47.

111. *Press Bulletin: News from Marriage Guidance,* The National Marriage Guidance Council, England, 29 March 1985.

The bulletin reports on the difficulties that parents have with sexually active teenagers. A mother and teacher said, "We couldn't cope with the idea of our daughter making love in our house. Apart from it setting a bad example to our younger children, we couldn't handle the thought of it and said 'no.' "

Another father commented, "I will not let my sons and daughters sleep with their friends in my house. It's not morally right. I would be very embarrassed if the parents of my son's girlfriends felt that when she was a guest in our house we would let them sleep together. And I would expect the same from my friends."

One twenty-one-year-old girl replied, "It's stupid when my parents know that I'm living with James to put us in separate rooms."

112. During Victorian times, Ambroise Tardieu, professor of legal medicine at the University of Paris and dean of the faculty of medicine, charted the horrendous abuse of children in France, including physical torture and sexual assault. His seminal paper was "Etude médico-légale sur les services et mauvais traitements exercés sur des infants" ("A Medico-Legal Study of Cruelty and Brutal Treatment Inflicted on Children"). Tardieu noted that parents who torture children inevitably claimed they were merely exercising their parental rights in order to curb the child of his or her "bad disposition." Discussed by Jeffrey Masson, in *The Assault on Truth: Freud's Suppression of the Seduction Theory* (London: Penguin Books, 1985), 15, 18–25.

In the twentieth century the Swiss analyst Alice Miller has documented and publicized the problems of child abuse, in particular the sexual abuse of children, in *Du Sollst nicht merken* (1981), published in English as *Thou Shalt Not Be Aware* (London: Pluto Press, 1985).

113. Shmarya Levin, *Childhood in Exile* (New York: 1929), 58–59, quoted by Lloyd DeMause, "The Evolution of Childhood," in *The History of Childhood,* edited by Lloyd DeMause, op. cit., 10.

114. Morton Schatzman, *Soul Murder: Persecution in the Family* (New York: Random House, 1973), 142.

115. Daniel Gottlieb Schreber, *Kallipädie oder Erziehung zur Schönheit durch naturgetreue und gleichmässige Förderung normaler Körperbildung (Education Toward Beauty by Natural and Balanced Furtherance of Normal Body Growth)* (Leipzig: Fleischer, 1858), 241, quoted by Morton Schatzman, *Soul Murder: Persecution in the Family,* op. cit., 142.

At another point Schreber asserts, "In the case of nearly every child, however, even the most well brought up, there are sometimes surprising manifestations of defiance and rebelliousness . . . a vestige of innate barbarity which leads the developing self-confidence astray. . . . This could be caused by anything—the most important thing is that the disobedience should be crushed to the point of regaining complete submission, using corporal punishment if necessary." Ibid., jacket quote.

116. Ibid., 39–52.

117. *Donald's Happy Birthday,* directed by Jack Hannah, distributed by RKO Pictures, February 1949.

The major theme in this and many other Disney cartoons is that children are naturally naughty and therefore have to be controlled and punished. However, Disney's cartoons have some redeeming features. The parent characters often discover their mistakes after the damage has been done and acknowledge shame and guilt.

118. Melanie Klein, "Early Stages of the Oedipus Conflict and Superego Formation," in Melanie Klein, *The Psycho-Analysis of Children,* op. cit., 131–132.

Joseph Berke, "Differentiation of the Pre-Genital Phase from the Genital Phase of the Early Oedipus Complex," unpublished paper, 3–4.

119. Christopher Lasch, for one, has pointed out that attacks on the past, including past values, traditions, and teachings, are equivalent to Oedipal attacks by the child toward his parents. Christopher Lasch, *The Culture of Narcissism,* op. cit., 150–151.

120. Discussed by Stephen Kern, "Explosive Intimacy: Psychodynamics of the Victorian Family," in *The New Psychohistory,* edited by Lloyd DeMause, op. cit., 40–141.

Erewhon was published in 1872. By 1901 Butler published *Erewhon Revisited,* which envisioned a father-son relationship based on love, not only enmity.

121. The Oedipus complex—Sigmund Freud, "A Special Type of Choice of Object Made by Men," *S.E.,* vol. XI, 163–176.

The Electra complex—Carl Jung, "Versuch einer Darstellung der psychoanalytischen Theorie," *Jahrbuch für psychoanalytische und psychopathologische Forschungen,* 1913, V, 370. (*The Theory of Psycho-Analysis.* New York: 1915).

The early Oedipus complex—Melanie Klein, "Some Theoretical Conclusions Regarding the Emotional Life of the Infant," in *Envy and Gratitude and Other Works,* op. cit., 61–93.

The Laius complex—G. Devereux, "Why Oedipus Killed Laius, a Note on the Complementary Oedipus Complex in Greek Drama," *Int. J. Psycho-Anal.,* vol. 34, 1953, 132–141.

122. There are many other features of the dreams that could have been mentioned, for example, the appearance of a black bug, indicating the degree to which the boy had turned his father into something evil, shitty, and devalued and his fear that the father/bug would inject the badness back into him. All this provides further examples of the intrapsychic operations of malicious projective identification, that is, internal envy and the internalized envier.

123. Morton Schatzman, *Soul Murder: Persecution in the Family.*

124. Daniel Paul Schreber, *Denkwürdigkeiten eines Nervenkranken* (Leipzig: Oswald Mutze, 1903). Translated and edited by Ida Macalpine and Richard Hunter, *Memoirs of My Nervous Illness* (London: Dawson & Son Ltd., 1955).

This book provided the basis for an extended study of paranoia and psychosis by Sigmund Freud, "Psycho-Analytic Notes upon an Autobiographical Account of a Case of Paranoia (Dementia Paranoides)," *S.E.,* vol. 12, 9–82.

Historians of psychiatry Macalpine and Hunter commented: "Schreber is now the most frequently quoted patient in psychiatry." *Memoirs of My Nervous Illness,* op. cit., 8.

See also: William Niederland, *The Schreber Case: Psychoanalytic Profile of a Paranoid Personality,* expanded edition (Hillsdale, N.J.: Analytic Press, Lawrence Erlbaum Associates, 1984).

125. Daniel Paul Schreber, *Memoirs of My Nervous Illness,* op. cit., 131, 133, 138, 145, 146, and 201, quoted by Morton Schatzman, *Soul Murder: Persecution in the Family,* op. cit., 40, 41, 46, and 49.

126. Father Schreber recalled: "I had a Geraldhalter manufactured which proved its worth time and time again with my own children. . . ."

A further advantage was that the instrument prevented the child from crossing his legs. Shoulder straps ensured that he did not "toss and turn."

Daniel Gottlieb Schreber, *Kallipädie oder Erziehung zur Schönheit durch naturgetreue und gleichmässige Förderung normaler Körperbildung,* op. cit., 203, quoted by Morton Schatzman, *Soul Murder: Persecution in the Family,* op. cit., 46.

127. Ibid., Daniel Gottlieb Schreber, 198–199; Schatzman, 49.

128. Sigmund Freud, "Psycho-Analytic Notes upon an Autobiographical Account of a Case of Paranoia (Dementia Paranoides)," op cit., 9–82.

129. Schatzman has provided detailed schemata of parental persecution that demonstrate how this situation can arise. He also shows how the very same processes contribute to and are an essential part of state totalitarianism. Morton Schatzman, *Soul Murder: Persecution in the Family,* op. cit., 137–8, 150–154, 162–173.

130. Niederland points out that Daniel Paul's first "breakdown" occurred at a time when he had been "called upon to become a member of the Reichstag, that is, a rebellious son in opposition to the awe-inspiring Bismarck. When, nine years later, he was called upon to take a father's place by becoming the presiding judge of the superior court, he again fell ill, and this time for good." William Niederland, *The Schreber Case: Psychoanalytic Profile of a Paranoid Personality,* op. cit., 41.

131. Sigmund Freud, "The Dissolution of the Oedipus Complex," op. cit., 176–177.

Chapter 8

1. Genesis, chapter 37, verses 3, 11, 18, 19, and 20, *The Twenty-four Books of the Old Testament,* vol. 1, translation by Andrew Harkavy (New York: Hebrew Publishing Company, 1926), 62–63.

2. The hostilities were fueled by the fact that Jacob (Israel) used Joseph, and Joseph allowed himself to be used, to keep track of the brothers. Ibid., verses 1, 13, and 14.

Although later rabbinic commentaries cited Joseph as the embodiment of filial love and family loyalty, they also criticized him and his father for favoritism and hubris. The rabbis, as the biblical scribes, were keenly aware of the events that provoke fratricidal strife. According to Moslem tradition, similar warnings were aired after Joseph told Jacob about his dream. Jacob replied: "O my son! tell not thy vision to thy brethren, lest they plot against thee: for Satan is the manifest foe of man." Koran, Sura XII: 4 (2–19, Joseph, Peace Be on Him), quoted in *The Torah: A Modern Commentary,* op. cit., 248.

3. *Encyclopedia Judaica,* vol. 10, op. cit., 202–203.

4. Bruno Bettelheim, *The Uses of Enchantment: The Meaning and Importance of Fairy Tales* (London: Thames & Hudson, 1976), 91.

5. See: the story of the brothers Anup and Bata, discussed by Patrick Mullahy, in *Oedipus: Myth and Complex,* op. cit., 90–93.

6. Myrtilus was the accomplice and charioteer who helped Pelops win the race against Hippodamia's father, Oenomaus, by removing the pins from the wheels of his chariot. It is said that Pelops drowned Myrtilus instead of paying him, in order to hide the deed. But other versions state that Pelops killed Myrtilus to prevent the promised payment, which included the right to share his intended bride.

Later Pelops tried to appease the ghost of Myrtilus by paying him great honors, but the curse remained for several generations until the purification of Orestes.

7. Typically, Mullahy views the ancient struggle between the younger Anup and older Bata for Bata's wife in straightforward Oedipal terms. The older brother equals the father, the wife equals the mother. The rivalry between the brothers concerns the incestuous object, and all the different episodes are repetitions of one fundamental situation, that of the son who seeks to overthrow the father and take possession of his wife. A careful reading of the myth does not necessarily deny this but demonstrates that the siblings' relationships are much richer and more complex than this interpretation encompasses. Ibid., 90–93.

8. This point has been made in various studies of sibling relationships, including: Stephen Bank and Michael Kahn, *The Sibling Bond* (New York: Basic Books, 1982), 197–201.

Leslie Pepitone, review of *The Sibling Bond,* in *Am. J. Orthopsych.,* vol. 54, no. 2, April 1984.

Judy Dunn, "Sibling Relationships in Early Childhood," *Child Development,* vol. 54, 1983, 787–811.

9. The psychiatrist Robert Robertiello has commented about a former patient whose wife was pregnant: "He dreamed he destroyed the fetus. It was so awful he came to me for help. He and his wife were very close. What was agonizing was juggling the idea of feeling competitive with the unborn child and loving him at the same time. On top of that, breaking up of the exclusive union he had with his wife— even if the intruder was his own child—rearoused memories of rivalries with his brothers and sisters." Discussed in Nancy Friday, *Jealousy* (New York: William Morrow & Co., 1985), 352.

10. Peter Lomas, "Dread of Envy As an Aetiological Factor in Puerperal Breakdown," op. cit., 107–108.

11. George Foster, "The Anatomy of Envy: A Study in Symbolic Behavior," op. cit., 174 and 193.

12. Stephen Bank and Michael Kahn, *The Sibling Bond,* op. cit., 204.

Incidents such as this are commonly reported in the daily press. For example, "Boy, 5, Started Fire That Killed Sister," *Guardian,* 8 May 1985, 3. The boy had started several other fires at his home before the fatal one on a New Year's Day. The police noted that his mother showed a marked lack of control amounting to indifference. Although there might be a related issue of phallic excitement, after the event the boy was put into a children's home but showed no further interest in starting fires.

13. Sophocles, *Oedipus at Colonus,* op. cit., lines 532–535.

His daughters were Antigone and Ismene. Oedipus, of course, recognized the situation of having children who were also siblings within the context of acknowledging an incestuous union with his wife. Nonetheless, he was also articulating a pervasive unconscious experience, not simply of incestuous union, but of seeing and treating children as sibs.

14. Oedipus' second son and younger brother of Polynices (and Oedipus) was Eteocles.

Ibid., lines 371–376.

15. Euripides, *Phoenician Women,* lines 469, 476–480, discussed by Peter Walcot, *Envy and the Greeks,* op. cit., 61–62.

16. Sophocles, *Oedipus at Colonus,* op. cit., lines 444–445.

17. Ibid., lines 1387–1389.

18. Aeschylus' *Oresteia* includes three plays: *Agamemnon, The Libation Bearers,* and *The Eumenides.* See: Aeschylus, *The Oresteia,* translation by Robert Fagles (London: Penguin Books, 1983).

19. The two boys were exiled to a neighboring city-state where Atreus eventually succeeded to the throne. Not surprisingly, contention followed them. Thyestes seduced his brother's wife and stole the ram with the golden fleece, which had been a special present from Hermes (who, as you will recall, had inflicted the curse in the first place). Later he arranged for a son of Atreus to kill his father. The plot almost succeeded, but Atreus managed to dispatch the young man first. Soon afterward he realized who the assailant had been. To avenge himself, Atreus pretended to forgive his brother and invited him and his family to a great feast. During the festivities and in the manner of his grandfather, he served up the bodies of Thyestes' sons. When this happened, it is said that the sun hid from the sky in order not to cast light on such a crime.

(Several versions of this legend state that the children served up by Atreus were the products of the union between Thyestes and Aerope, Atreus' wife.)

20. In *The Eumenides* Orestes also points out that he loved his father dearly

and thirsted for revenge. Yet Electra is generally seen as the provoker. Orestes' action demonstrates the degree to which one sibling will act out the malice of another.

21. Jung developed the idea of the Electra complex to denote the feminine counterpart of the Oedipus complex—that is, a girl or woman's (often unconscious) fixation on her father coupled with underlying, murderous jealousy toward her mother.

Freud, however, did not believe in the analogy. He insisted that only boys were beset by the "fateful combination" of love for one parent and simultaneous murderous rejection of the other. J. Laplanche and J-B. Pontalis, *The Language of Psycho-Analysis,* op. cit., 152.

22. Aeschylus' *Oresteia* concludes with the trial of Orestes for matricide, an act that embodies the horror of several generations of familial strife. Orestes defended himself, stating that he had been spurred on to kill his mother by Apollo, but the Furies (the ghost of his mother in combination with his own sense of guilt) were thirsty for revenge. They argued that unless Orestes was punished, then "every man will find a way to act at his own caprice; over and over in time to come, parents shall await the deathstroke at their children's hands."

In the end the jury of twelve Athenian citizens deadlocked, but Athene, acting as the presiding judge, cast the deciding vote for mercy and acquittal. However, she took care to placate the Furies by offering them a powerful role for good in the family: "No household shall be prosperous without your will." In so doing, the Furies (angry figures) became the Eumenides (the benevolent ones), and Orestes achieved atonement and absolution for his deeds. But the question of sibling intrigues remained.

Aeschylus, *The Eumenides,* translation by Richmond Lattimore, in *Greek Tragedies: Volume 3,* edited by David Grene and Richmond Lattimore (Chicago: Phoenix Books, University of Chicago Press, 1963), lines 494–498 and 895.

In the twentieth century there have been a number of similar well-publicized, albeit less profound, dynastic struggles. One engaged the extended family of the late billionaire John Paul Getty and involved murderous quarrels among Getty's sons and grandchildren for control of the assets of the Getty Oil Company. The result could have been the demise of Texaco, the eighth-largest corporation in the United States, and the wiping out of the entire Getty fortune. Alexander Chancellor, "The Getty Squabbles That Brought Down a Giant," *The Independent,* 16 April 1987, 8.

23. *Dynasty* is a Richard and Esther Shapiro Production in association with Aaron Spelling Productions, Inc., 1987.

24. Melanie Klein points out that the trauma of the birth of a new sibling may exist long before the sib is conceived. The existing child tends to imagine that mother's breasts and body are full of babies. So attacks on sibs can begin with attacks on mother's threatening breasts and body, experienced as real or imagined babies. All this is aroused by anticipated (inevitably coexistent) deprivation, frustration, and envious and jealous hurt. See: the case of Richard as discussed by Hanna Segal, *Klein,* op. cit., 157–158.

25. Phyllis Greenacre, *Trauma, Growth, and Personality* (London: The Hogarth Press, 1953), 233. The jealousy Greenacre describes is akin to delusional or pathological jealousy, which I have discussed previously under the rubric of the Othello syndrome.

26. Gerhart Piers and Milton Singer, *Shame and Guilt: A Psychoanalytical and Cultural Study* (Springfield, Ill.: Thomas Publishers, 1953), 23f.

27. Quoted by Mary Kenny, in "Mary Kenny's Week," *Sunday Telegraph,* 23 September 1984, 15.

28. Personal communication, 1985.

29. "We had this awful old nanny, Miss Box. Mother was always sending me

out of the room to Miss Box, which upset me. I got Miss Box, the ultimate hag, and he got Mom." Quoted from "Everybody and His Brother," compiled by Jean Penn, *Playboy*, January 1986, 194.

30. Ibid., 194.

Quaid adds: "The meanest thing I ever did to him was hitting him so hard once, he didn't speak to me for four days. He told on me, of course. I was about fourteen then. The meanest thing he ever did to me was becoming successful."

31. "Son Kills 3 Out of Hate," *Daily Telegraph*, 23 March 1981, 5.

32. Mary Kenny, "Mary Kenny's Week," *Sunday Telegraph*, 23 September 1984, 15.

33. Elizabeth Hodder, *The Step-Parents' Handbook* (London: Sphere Books, 1985), 46.

34. D. W. Winnicott, *The Piggle: An Account of the Psychoanalytic Treatment of a Little Girl*, edited by Ishak Ramzu (London: Penguin Books, 1980).

35. Ibid., 52.

36. Ibid., 64.

37. Ibid., 64.

38. Ibid., 103.

39. Toward the end of the therapy, her mother wrote to Winnicott: "Gabrielle [the Piggle] is very close to Susan [the sister], handles her with great circumspection, cajoles her, is often the mediator between her and us. We are struck by how often she will try and get her way by deflecting Susan's attention or by some inventiveness, rather than by direct attack, though sometimes she is miserably, and helplessly, consumed by jealousy, and Susan can do nothing right. The other day, in the middle of a fierce fight, she suddenly kissed Susan and said: "But I like you." This is very different from Susan, who alternatively looks up to Gabrielle fervently, and ruthlessly wants to destroy her superiority." Ibid., 177.

40. Quoted by John Leo, in "Battling the Green-Eyed Monster," op. cit., 39.

41. In this instance the absence of projections, or the ability to avoid malicious projections by the parent, may constitute the good breast.

42. In the Cambridge study of the developing child, it became clear that many firstborn children become very jealous of any intrusions between them and their father. One firmly told her mother (about baby Ronnie), "Daddy is not Ronnie's daddy." Another mother reported, "She minds him [father] holding him [baby] much more than when I do. I think she takes me and him [baby] for granted." Judy Dunn, *Sisters and Brothers* (London: Fontana Paperbacks, 1984), 88.

43. *The Complete Letters of Sigmund Freud to Wilhelm Fliess*, edited by Jeffrey Masson (Cambridge, Mass.: The Belknap Press of Harvard University Press, 1985), 23 February 1898.

44. I have already described how a parent can be an objective persecutor *(The Parental Persecutor)* and subjective persecutor *(The Combined Parent)* to a child. In the same vein, one sibling can very much appear and be a persecutor to another. The child (or adult) who actually attacks a sibling can be called and is very much a *Sibling Persecutor*. On the other hand, the child (or adult) who has been transformed into an envious, greedy, and jealous monster by a sibling who exaggerates what he sees and projects his own malicious intentions onto the other can be called *The Combined Sibling*. The combination of both is *The Combined Sibling Persecutor*, an extremely frightening figure and the product of one sibling's perceptions, imaginings, and projections about another.

45. Personal communication, 1984.

46. The dress clearly showed the shape of her mother's breasts. In retrospect it was evident that what she envied and spoiled in her thoughts were her mother's breasts. This spoiling side tended to be denied and was projectively identified with her sister, whom she considered to be severely neurotic. Melanie Klein, "Envy and Gratitude," *Envy and Gratitude and Other Works 1946–1963*, op. cit., 209–210.

47. The displacement of the breast from mother to new baby serves the older child, too. J. D. Suttie comments: "Not only can the child go on 'eating the mother,' but she even lets it *eat the younger baby.*" J. D. Suttie, *The Origins of Love and Hate* (London: Paul, French Trubner & Co., 1935), 110, quoted by H. Schoeck, *Envy: A Theory of Social Behavior,* op. cit., 69.

Suttie also discusses the elaborate measures that many people take to counteract Cain jealousy.

48. B. D. Paul, "Symbolic Sibling Rivalry in a Guatemalan Indian Village," *American Anthropologist,* vol. 52, 1950, 205–218.

In contrast, Bettelheim comments on the way the parents of the great German poet Johann Wolfgang von Goethe dealt with his sibling rivalry. Goethe's earliest memory was of tossing his toy dishes out the window and rejoicing that they shattered. After this he threw out his mother's crockery as well. Freud later said that the toy dishes represented Goethe's new brother and the wish to get rid of him, while smashing the mother's dishes represented his fear and hostility to the thought that she would not be able to feed him and the new sib, too. Although Bettelheim does not disagree with this, he thinks that the most important aspect of the story was the fact that the parents did not get frightened or angry and punitive about the incident, as one might expect. Instead they accepted it. Therefore Goethe was able to work out his resentments and grow up to have a good relationship with his brother. By implication there are times when a child must be allowed to be destructive. See: Megan Rosenfeld, "Too Old to Play, Bettelheim Still Scolds Parents," *International Herald Tribune,* 11 April 1986, 20.

49. Letty Cottin Pogrebin, "Couples Who Hide Their Happiness," *New York Times,* 1 September 1983, C2.

50. Nancy Friday, *Jealousy,* op. cit., 157–171.

51. Ibid., 158.

Later on at college the same issue arose when she made Phi Beta Kappa. She didn't tell anyone in her family for fear that if she (the stepsister) knew, "that awful face would come over her and she'd want to kill me." Ibid., 159.

It transpired that the stepsister was a convenient repository for unacceptable passions. This girl not only hid successes from her, but used her in order to hide her own destructive impulses (about which she felt ashamed and guilty) from herself and others.

52. Sue Arnold, "Girls with Green Eyes," *The Observer,* 21 August 1983, 22.

Kindred events among brothers are well illustrated in the biography of the American academic John Wideman. He came from a poor black family but managed to become an accomplished athlete and scholar and later a writer, university professor, and good family man. In contrast, his brother became a thief, marauder, junkie, and drug dealer who eventually wound up serving a life prison sentence for murder. John Wideman, *Brothers and Keepers* (London: Allison & Busby, 1985).

53. Some authorities quote ten years. The concubine who was used for the purpose of procreation gained a special status. Under Mesopotamian law, the concubine who bore the child of her master could be punished but not sold. Other codes stressed the obligation of the wife to provide a concubine who could never be sold. *Encyclopedia Judaica,* vol. 7, op. cit., 1074–1075.

54. Ibid., 1076.

55. *Encyclopedia Judaica,* vol. 9, op. cit., 82.

56. As a story, "Cinderella" already had a long history before it was written down, not only in China, but in many countries. For the earliest Chinese version, see: Arthur Waley, "Chinese Cinderella Story," *Folk-Lore,* vol. 58, 1947.

57. For an extended discussion of the Cinderella story and its relation to other fairy tales, see: Bruno Bettelheim, "Cinderella," *The Uses of Enchantment: The Meaning and Importance of Fairy Tales* (London: Thames & Hudson, 1976), 236–277.

David Luke, "Introduction," in Jacob and Wilhelm Grimm, *Selected Tales,* op. cit., 39–41.

58. Bruno Bettelheim, "Cinderella," *The Uses of Enchantment: The Meaning and Importance of Fairy Tales,* op. cit., 239–240.

59. Edward Gifford, *The Evil Eye: Studies in the Folklore of Vision,* op. cit., 35.

Gifford points out that this attack was also a defense against envious retribution. Pigeons were long thought to be aware of the dangers of fascination and to spit in the faces of their young to protect them from it. Ibid., 35.

60. The most probable reason for veiling brides is fear of the evil eye—that is, the envious discomfort in the onlooker and the discomfort experienced by a bride (or any happy or beautiful woman) after she has been looked upon with malice. Gifford also relates this to the Muslim custom of veiling women in general. Ibid., 35.

61. At her pretrial hearing the girl stated that her motive was envy and jealousy. Although her former roommate was not a raving beauty, she was a distinctly more attractive person. Helmut Schoeck, *Envy: A Theory of Social Behavior,* op. cit., 107.

62. The daughter continued: "In despair, I laced both their coffees heavily with Valium and came back half an hour later to find them hanging round each other's necks." Jilly Cooper, "Watch Your Step at Exmas," *The Sunday Times,* 20 December 1981, 26.

63. I refer to the Jewish holiday of Passover and to the seder, the ritual feast that commemorates the exodus of the Jews from Egypt.

64. "Jealousy Turned Quiet Woman into a Killer," *Daily Telegraph,* 1 December 1984, 3.

The article discusses a "quiet, gentle social worker" who became "a frenzied killer," repeatedly stabbing her rival and the woman's four-year-old son to death after discovering that the woman had been having an affair with her boyfriend.

65. "A Computerized 'Reign of Terror,'" *International Herald Tribune,* 1–2 June 1985, 3.

The hacker was an electronic hitman. He had previously broken into the North American Air Defense Command computer, as in the film *WarGames.* The victim was puzzled because she had lost interest in the boyfriend involved and had not been dating him for months.

66. Ibid., 3.

67. The opposite of sibling rivalry is sibling closeness and cooperation. It is not uncommon for sibs to form an alliance with each other that lasts throughout their lives. Dale and Lynne Spender, who were both trained as teachers and eventually became writers, have described this outcome.

Dale (the eldest by a couple of years): "We've always been immensely close, and although she can make me cross sometimes, I have no recollection of jealousy or serious rivalry. As kids we complemented each other. . . . We've decided that if we live to seventy, we'll retire together and smoke, drink, and eat ourselves to death."

Lynne: "I haven't taken on feminism in the way Dale has . . . but it's played a vital part in guiding me to do what I want. . . . Of course, I do wonder sometimes if I would have worked harder at my marriage if Dale hadn't been there, reinforcing my feelings that [housework] was not fair. . . . So here I am in my early forties, on my own with two kids, feeling great about life. . . . I suppose without support from Dale it might have looked very different."

Angela Neustatter, "Women of Letters," *The Sunday Times* magazine, 1 November 1987, 13–16.

68. The informant is a thirty-two-year-old woman with two sisters. Brigid McConville, *Sisters: Love and Conflict within the Lifelong Bond* (London: Pan Books, 1985), 48.

69. This woman seeks the protection of her sisters and "sisters" (female companions) but also competes with them. She says that in the long run, and when things don't go well, "at least I can trust my sister." Yet she sometimes delights in that "awful—but gripping—thing," taking something from her sisters. Ibid., 46–48.

70. "The elder sister, I am convinced, was distorted by a suppressed jealousy—not for me, but for physical love. She adored her sister and also now hated her.

"And whatever we two did, whatever arrangements we made, was spoilt for Rebecca by the relentless and indiscriminating disapproval of her home. They would not let her find any pride in my position and success; they expressed horror and disgust at any effort we made to face things out together. They forced upon us idiotic lies and pretenses. . . ."

H. G. Wells, *H. G. Wells in Love* (London: Faber & Faber, 1984), extract published in *The Sunday Telegraph*, 9 September 1984, 12.

71. Jessica Mitford, *Hons and Rebels* (London: Gollancz, 1960), discussed by Brigid McConville, *Sisters: Love and Conflict within the Lifelong Bond*, op. cit., 26–28.

72. Sigmund Freud, "The Taboo of Virginity," *S.E.*, vol. 11, 204.

73. Sigmund Freud, "On the Sexual Theories of Children," *S.E.*, vol. 9, 218.

74. Personal communication, 1985.

75. Bank and Kahn describe another situation where parental favoritism, and sororal resentment, was brought about by fraternal weakness. Consequently, overprotective parents were constantly admonishing: "Don't be so tough with your brother, be careful!" Stephen Bank and Michael Kahn, *The Sibling Bond*, op. cit., 203.

76. Personal communication, 1985.

In addition, the girl complained that her brother had bigger legs.

Interestingly, in both examples the elder brothers tended to get on well with their younger sisters in spite of severe provocations. In the second family the brother's main complaints had to do with presents (hers were more spontaneous); school (she got off easier); attention (she got more—something hotly denied by his sister); parents (more sympathetic to her—again hotly denied); and privileges (girls get more—a point of agreement).

77. Ruth Moulton points out that sibling rivalry may simply enhance a pre-existing state of envy based on general frustration of early childhood needs: "This exacerbation of envy may occur with the birth of a new baby or the existence of a preferred child. If the rival is a male, of course, envy is apt to be focussed on the penis as the reason for the preference."

Ruth Moulton, "A Survey and Reevaluation of the Concept of Penis Envy," in *Psychoanalysis and Women*, edited by Jean Baker Miller, op. cit., 243–244.

78. Jules Glenn has described the difficulties faced by a three-year-old girl who suffered from severe fecal retention after the birth of a baby brother. The parents doted on him, and the mother described the baby as a "ball buster." When the girl did have bowel movements, they were in the shape of large, hard fecal masses as big as baseballs. Glenn comments that the girl's penis envy was clearly established long before classical psychoanalytic theory would allow. Jules Glenn, "Psychoanalysis of a Constipated Girl: Clinical Observations During the Fourth and Fifth Years," paper presented at the Panel on the Psychology of Women: Infancy and Early Childhood, at the May 1974 meetings of the American Psychoanalytic Association.

79. The Avis Corporation has deliberately and successfully played on sibling rivalry in its advertising campaigns against the larger Hertz car rental organization by asserting, "We may be second, but we try harder."

Fraternal rivals include brothers but also sisters, fathers, mothers, relatives, friends, neighbors, acquaintances, and, in general, anyone actual or imagined with whom a male-male form of sibling exchange may be established.

80. The tragedy of Cain and Abel is a good example of disappointed love, parental rejection, and subsequent hatred displaced onto a brother. To Cain, Abel is a symbol of unfair treatment at the hands of his father. The same themes make frequent reappearances. In John Steinbeck's novel *East of Eden,* the unfavored son, Cal, dedicates his life to trying to please his father. He only vents his wrath on brother Aron after his father's final rejection. Similarly, William Faulkner in *Absalom, Absalom!* and Peter Shaffer in *Yonadab* have reworked the biblical story of King David and his rebellious son Absalom. Each work concerns extreme, ultimately destructive ambitions motivated by unrequited paternal love.

81. Henry Porter, "Gore and Gall," *The Sunday Times,* 5 August 1984, 7.

82. Ibid., 7.

83. Hugo Vickers, *Cecil Beaton: The Authorized Biography* (London: Weidenfeld & Nicolson, 1985), 454.

84. As Beaton exemplifies, snobbery is essentially a form of narcissistic inflation serving to express and defend against envy.

85. An exasperated Beaton used to snipe: "Whereas Freddie Ashton can dream away in his summer house or blink at the ceiling and eventually be rewarded with pomp and ceremony, Sir Laurence [Olivier] can booze away and be out of the running for an age, only to be surprised by the arrival of a messenger bringing him the greatest good news of a personal nature." Ibid., 454.

86. The former president is Jimmy Carter. His sister, Maureen, is a nationally known religious healer.

87. Joan Beck, *Chicago Tribune,* 30 January 1980, quoted by Stephen Bank and Michael Kahn, in *The Sibling Bond,* op. cit., 229.

88. Rosenfeld is referring to the idealization of the omnipotent, destructive sides of the self. In other words, the person identifies with the force of his own envy and luxuriates in vicious attacks on positive libidinal ties. Herbert Rosenfeld, "A Clinical Approach to the Psychoanalytic Theory of the Life and Death Instincts: An Investigation into the Aggressive Aspects of Narcissism," op. cit., 169–177.

89. In their discussion of the conflict between the Carter brothers, Bank and Kahn point out that Billy also had reason to be angry with his brother. When given the chance to manage the family business when his brother was governor of Georgia, he had done well. But the opportunity had been pulled out from under him when his brother became president and the business was put in a blind trust. Billy did try to buy the business but was turned down, the final turn of the screw that effectively robbed him of a positive identity. Stephen Bank and Michael Kahn, *The Sibling Bond,* op. cit., 229–231.

90. Aside from obvious envious attacks, Billy seemed to deliberately set out to shame and embarrass his brother and family. In a paper on shame and envy I point out that shame and envy act in tandem, and shaming can be a devastating form of envious revenge. Joseph Berke, "Shame and Envy," *Brit. J. Psychoth.,* vol. 2, no. 4, 1986, 262–270.

91. "Three Dancing Pensioners in Jealous Tango," *Daily Telegraph,* 16 June 1981, 3.

92. The plot was eventually discovered, and the former captain was fined and given a suspended jail term.

93. *Electric Dreams,* starring Lenny Von Dohlen and Virginia Madsen. Virgin Video, Virgin Films, 1985, VVP 064.

94. Tom and Jerry, *Polka Dot Puss.* Directed by William Hanna and Joseph Barbera, produced by Fred Quimby, released by MGM, February 1949.

95. *Tom and Jerry in the Hollywood Bowl.* Directed by William Hanna and Joseph Barbera, produced by Fred Quimby, released by MGM, September 1950.

96. All the Tom and Jerry cartoons vary in their degree of violence, but they

reach a pinnacle of persecution and retribution in *Yankee Doodle Mouse,* directed by William Hanna and Joseph Barbera, produced by Fred Quimby, MGM, 1944. Here both Tom and Jerry are engaged in a continuous battle that is relentless in its viciousness. As often happens, Tom is almost about to gain the upper hand when he stupidly blasts himself off into space instead of Jerry. For the younger audience this fulfills the wish to punish the parent (or older sib) and mitigates the impact of parental sadism.

97. *Heavenly Puss* features a repentant Tom. After the usual chase, he injures himself and dreams of going to heaven. But he can't get in because he has spent his whole life tormenting mice. His only chance is to get a letter of forgiveness from Jerry, otherwise he will be consigned to hell. Jerry holds out, then relents. Tom rushes back, but it is too late. He falls to a fiery fate, only to awake and discover his tail simmering by the fireplace. This time he doesn't blame Jerry, but gives him a kiss. The mouse is surprised and delighted. Tom and Jerry, *Heavenly Puss*. Directed by William Hanna and Joseph Barbera, produced by Fred Quimby, MGM, 1949.

98. The Wrights developed the first airplanes; the Warners were cinema magnates; the Smothers are comedians; and the Smiths were famous for their cough drops.

The Brothers Grimm recounted many tales of fraternal strife, but also moving accounts of fraternal love. "The Three Brothers," for example, is about three brothers who got on so well with each other that, after leaving home and learning trades, they reunited and shared their father's kingdom happily and peaceably. Jacob and Wilhelm Grimm, *Selected Tales,* op. cit., 310–311.

99. Jean Penn, "Everybody and His Brother," op. cit., 196.

Brother Dennis came to believe that childhood fights, as when Randy tortured him, ultimately cemented their relationship. "I think the brothers who can fight with each other are the closest, as long as you never let it get so bad that you walk away and say, 'I'll never talk to you again.' " Ibid., 196.

As with Tom and Jerry, to fight is right, but to destroy is wrong.

100. The quote itself is by Nancy Friday from prior interviews and a discussion with Robertiello, who is considering various aspects of his homosexual attraction to certain men within a context of male-male rivalries. Nancy Friday, *Jealousy,* op. cit., 347–352.

101. Technically we can say that the "good-enough sib" bounds narcissistic inflation (which acts as a magnet for outside aggression) and envious deflation (which is the expression of inner discontent) brought about by pervading feelings of breast, womb, or phallic inadequacy and inferiority (the absences.).

102. Her analyst was Hanna Segal, who discusses the case in Hanna Segal, *Introduction to the Work of Melanie Klein,* op. cit., 47–53.

Segal comments: "She worked in an academic profession, and though successful in her career, she found recurring blocks in relation to the more creative and rewarding research aspects of her work." Ibid., 47.

103. Her friend was also a middle-aged woman who had suffered the loss of both parents in childhood. She herself connected the patches of baldness with this fact.

104. Her sister had died when she was four years old.

105. Quoted by Hanna Segal. Ibid., 50.

106. The woman displaced many feelings from and part aspects of her mother onto an image of her dead sister. The psychic connections became evident when she associated the balloons which had lost their air with her dead sister (someone who has lost the breath of life) and later with her mother's body and breasts.

107. Her friend's name was Joan. Sometimes she made slips of the tongue and called her Jean. Jean was the name of a pretty young woman who had just had a baby, that is, become a mother. Ibid., 50–51.

108. Ibid., 51.

109. Segal emphasizes that she associated any bit of feminine or masculine achievement with the operation of her envy and greed and then felt very guilty. But the worst feelings arose when she began to realize how she continued to use her resources and accomplishments to stimulate envy in others, for this reminded her of how she had spoiled (and to her mind killed) her younger sister by filling her full of envious projections. Moreover, it reminded her of wanting to do the same to the parents she loved.

Chapter 9

1. Helmut Schoeck points out that one of the first persons to use the concept of institutionalized envy was Eric Wolf, an expert on South American peasant cultures. He related the phenomenon to backbiting, the evil eye, and the practice or fear of black magic. Helmut Schoeck, *Envy: A Theory of Social Behavior*, op. cit., 46–47.

2. Paul Johnson, "Farewell to the Labour Party," *New Statesman*, 9 September 1977, 330.

Johnson is especially critical of the closed shop and wildcat strikes, which are, for him, ways in which the "envious and incapable" retain power. Johnson echoes observations made over and over during the past 150 years. Thus, after the Paris exhibition of 1867, Lyon Playfair warned about the weakness of British industry, which he related to poor education, ceaseless industrial strife, and, in particular, the "rule of many Trades' Unions, that men shall work upon an average ability, without giving scope to the skill and ability which they may individually possess." Quoted by R. V. Jones. "The Rise and Fall of British Industry" (review of *The Audit of War*, by Corelli Barnett), *New Scientist*, 10 July 1986, 52.

3. "The Wages of Sin," *London Standard*, 10 September 1985, 7. The article confirms the view that people envy those nearest to them. While most journalists could not be sportsmen, they resent successful businessmen and politicians.

4. Helmut Schoeck, op. cit., 218 and 222.

5. "Burma to Investigate Wealthy Citizens," *International Herald Tribune*, 17 March 1986, 2.

6. *New Larousse Encyclopedia of Mythology*, op. cit., 163.

7. The phrase was used by the philosopher Sören Kierkegaard in describing the envy motive and the passion for social leveling.

Sören Kierkegaard, *En literair Anmeldelse to Tidsaldre (The Present Age)*, in *Samlede Vaerker*, ed. H. O. Lange, Copenhagen, 1920–30, vol. 8, 76, quoted by Helmut Schoeck, op. cit., 173.

8. Lee Lorenz, *New Yorker*, 15 July 1985, 29.

9. There are many instances when the term "institutionalized grenvy" provides the most appropriate description of business or bureaucratic practices.

10. This particular rebuke referred to any outside company. According to Iacocca, Henry Ford II, then his boss, was extremely sensitive to any threat to his personal preeminence. Lee Iacocca, *Iacocca: An Autobiography* (London: Bantam Books, 1986), 109.

11. "No study of the English landed family makes any sense unless the principle and practice of primogeniture is constantly borne in mind. It was something that went far to determine the behaviour and character of both parents and children, and to govern the relationship between siblings." Lawrence Stone, *The Family, Sex and Marriage in England 1500–1800*, op. cit., 87–88.

12. The potential sultans were locked in the Cage with only a handful of sterilized women and attendants to keep them company. "The Sultan Ibrahim was caged from the age of two until he succeeded at 24; Suleiman II for a total of 39 years; and Osman III, in the eighteenth century, for 50. The Cage was not only a living death, but a guarantee that any sultan who emerged from it would be a weak one...." Reay Tannahill, *Sex in History*, op. cit., 228.

13. Sigmund Freud, "Group Psychology and the Analysis of the Ego," *S.E.*, vol. 18, op. cit., 119–121.

14. Ibid., 120–121.

15. J. M. Roberts, *The Hutchinson History of the World* (London: Hutchinson & Co., 1976). Rev. ed.: *The Pelican History of the World* (London: Pelican Books, 1987).

Roberts discusses the impact of ideological and nationalistic movements at different points in world history.

The group amplifies the underlying antagonisms that may surface at times of collective action. Alternatively, a murderous hatred may emerge when identification with the group breaks down and the individual is left unprotected against inner chaos caused by loss of pride, preexistent malice, and vengeful resentment for feelings of helpless rootlessness.

16. It is worth noting that these hostilities are based on the continual interaction of imagined and actual grievances, each serving to bolster the other.

17. Freud concluded that far from being a "herd animal," man is really "a horde animal, an individual creature in a horde led by a chief." Sigmund Freud, "Group Psychology and the Analysis of the Ego," op. cit., 121.

18. Helmut Schoeck, *Envy: A Theory of Social Behavior,* op. cit., 66.

19. Paul Johnson, *A History of the Modern World: From 1917 to the 1980s* (London: Weidenfeld and Nicolson, 1983), 704–708.

20. Peter Drucker, "The Monster and the Lamb," *Atlantic,* December 1978, 82–87.

Reinhold Hensch commanded the annihilation troops. The "enemies" included mental and physical defectives and resistance fighters. He was so cruel, ferocious, and bloodthirsty that he was known as "the Monster" ("das Ungeheuer") even to his own men. Hensch killed himself after being captured by the Americans.

21. Ibid., 84.

22. After taking up the post of press adviser to the Nazi commissar for Frankfurt, he told Peter Drucker, a colleague on the *Frankfurter General Anzeiger:* "I get scared when I hear all that talk in the Nazi inner councils—and I do sit in now, you know. There are madmen there who talk about killing the Jews and about going to war and about jailing and killing anyone who holds a dissenting opinion and questions the Führer's word. It's all insane, but it frightens me. I know you said to me a year ago that the Nazis believed these things and that I had better take them seriously. But I thought that it was the usual campaign rhetoric and didn't mean a thing. . . . After all, this is the twentieth century." Ibid., 85.

23. Ibid., 85.

24. Paul Johnson, *A History of the Modern World: From 1917 to the 1980s,* op. cit., 376.

Johnson adds that neither man consulted his citizens or spoke for collegiate bodies. "Their lieutenants obeyed blindly or in apathetic terror, and the vast nations over which they ruled seem to have had no choice but to stumble in their wake towards mutual destruction. We have here the very opposite of historical determinism—the apotheosis of the single autocrat." Ibid., 376.

25. For servicemen with decorations, there was to be polygamy and a free choice of women. Ibid., 381.

26. Ibid., 435–441.

27. Louis Branson, "Russia Writes off Poison Pen," *The Sunday Times,* 30 March 1986, 16.

The letters demonstrate institutionalized envy via the press and post. In 1986 Konstantin Gutsenko, director of the Institute of Soviet Law, acknowledged the damage done by this practice and began to campaign against it. He commented that the letters were used mainly for defamation and vengeance. They also meant that people could avoid being responsible for their actions.

28. "Crackdown on Libelous Mail," *The Times,* 21 April 1986, 9.

The Soviet courts have now been ordered to take criminal action against people who defame others by anonymous letters.

29. *Private Eye* exemplifies the use of the media to extend personal prejudices and grudges, particularly by people in the media, against each other and against major social, business, and political figures. This has led to many lawsuits with substantial damages having to be paid, a confirmation of the fact that the magazine does publish malicious rumors and lies. Alan Hamilton, "Ingrams Steps Down at Private Eye," *The Times,* 15 March 1986, 2.

Many of the targets of *Private Eye* ultimately counterattacked. Thus, publisher Robert Maxwell published one off tabloid entitled *Not Private Eye,* in which he lampooned the magazine. In one section called Psuers Corner he listed the large number of people who had successfully sued *Private Eye* for libel. *Not Private Eye,* no. 1, 10 December 1986, published by Daily Mirror Newspapers, London.

30. Bryron Rogers, "Dempster and the Princess," *Sunday Telegraph* magazine, No. 266, 1 November 1981, 59.

For many years Nigel Dempster was the anonymous author of Grovel, the section of *Private Eye,* that cataloged the real and alleged foibles of the rich and powerful.

31. Ibid., 60.

32. Ibid., 60.

33. "All is not well in Fairyland" is a typical Dempster quip. Ibid., 56.

Fairyland includes the British aristocracy, with whom Dempster enjoys hobnobbing.

I could quote almost endless examples of journalists' pandering to public envy. Typically, an extended piece on the Marks and Sieff families chronicled the rich Jewish families who controlled Marks and Spencer, Britain's most successful retail chain. Concurrently it used the occasion to parade those family members who "were littered with bizarre tragedies, rattling skeletons and clandestine love affairs." Or, a report on Britain's highest earner, Mr. Christopher Heath, told how his privacy was destroyed by journalistic intrusions the moment his income became public knowledge. Mr. Heath pointed out: "In any other country one would have been congratulated for being successful in business. Instead we were made to feel guilty. In America I would have been a hero." See: Russell Miller, "The Family Hides Its Skeletons," *The Sunday Times* magazine, 14 October 1984, 90–97; Stephen Markeson, "At Home with Britain's Highest Earner," *The Times,* 23 November 1987, 3.

34. Agnew would advise businessmen who wished to make campaign contributions, "Tell them you gave at the office." He meant his office. John T. Noonan, Jr., *Bribes* (New York: Macmillan Publishing Co., 1984), 581.

35. Morton Mintz, *At Any Cost: Corporate Greed, Women and the Dalkon Shield* (New York: Pantheon Books, 1985).

36. Quoted by Robin M. Henig, in her review of several books on the Dalkon Shield disaster, *International Herald Tribune,* 21 November 1985, 22.

37. R. Barry O'Brien, "Pay-Bed Militant Sacked," *The Daily Telegraph,* 26 May 1979, 1.

At a union conference Geddes was quoted, "Let us make sure that every single rich bastard in our hospitals will be treated on a Health Service basis and not because he has the money to pay for a consultant. Private medicine is the hand round the neck of the Health Service. It is our duty to cut that hand off." In fact, most of the patients treated at the Hammersmith Hospital are poor people in need of special treatment and are sponsored by their home governments or charities.

Geddes was eventually dismissed for painting slogans on hospital walls.

38. *Fortune,* July 1962, 60, quoted by Helmut Schoeck, *Envy: A Theory of Social Behavior,* op. cit., 112–113.

39. Bertrand Russell, *The Conquest of Happiness,* op. cit., 70–71.

H. L. Mencken, *The Vintage Mencken,* edited by Alistair Cooke, op. cit., 75–77, quoted by Helmut Schoeck, *Envy: A Theory of Social Behavior,* op. cit., 194.

The biblical King Solomon illustrated the relation between law, justice, and equity by proposing to divide a baby in two rather than leave one of two women feeling hard done by, that is, envious of the other.

40. Gay Talese, *Thy Neighbor's Wife,* op. cit., 53–64.

Comstock lived from 1844 to 1915. Prior to the passage of the Comstock Act in 1873, there were no federal laws against eroticism or what Comstock called sexual obscenity.

In 1959 a federal judge, influenced by a new definition of obscenity a couple of years previously *(Roth* vs. *The Supreme Court),* rescinded the ban against D. H. Lawrence's *Lady Chatterley's Lover* and effectively overturned the Comstock regulations.

41. Comstock was left morose and devastated by the death of his mother at the age of ten and devoted many of his later activities to her memory. As an adult he came to believe that eroticism was the plague of the young leading to moral, physical, and social degeneracy through masturbation, fornication, abortion, and venereal disease. Such views are not uncommon today, especially in relation to videotapes and the cinema. In addition, Comstock described marriage manuals, sexual pamphlets, and erotic pictures as a "moral vulture which steals upon our youth, silently striking its terrible talons into their vitals." Quoted by Gay Talese. Ibid., 57.

42. J. P. Morgan was a prominent banker who himself had a large collection of pornography. He was a strong supporter of Comstock.

Comstock was also aided by rampant church groups and fanatical British antivice societies that were influential on the continent and in America. Ibid., 56.

43. The Comstock Act, as it was known, banned from the mails "every obscene, lewd, lascivious or filthy book, pamphlet, picture, paper, letter, writing, print or other publication of an independent character." Ibid., 57.

44. The Comstock Act was deliberately vague so that almost any item useful for sexual relations could and did qualify as obscene. The various charges against the women who killed themselves included prostitution, performing abortions, disseminating birth-control devices, and writing a marriage manual. Other victims of the Comstock Act included a New York publisher who was jailed and fined for having in stock Ovid's *Art of Love,* a bookseller who received a similar sentence for selling Dr. Ashton's *Book of Nature and Marriage Guide,* and numerous pharmacists who were jailed for selling condoms or vaginal syringes. Ibid., 58.

45. Quoted by Heywood Broun and Margaret Leech, *Anthony Comstock: Roundsman of the Lord* (New York, 1927), 15, and quoted by Reay Tannahill, *Sex in History,* op. cit., 399.

46. Hoover was obsessed with sex and communism, Anslinger with biochemical bliss, and McCarthy with class conflict. Paul Fussell points out that while McCarthy talked about communists, the people he was really getting at were the envied upper-middle and upper classes. Speaking in West Virginia in 1950, McCarthy claimed: "It has not been the less fortunate or members of minority groups who have been selling this nation out, but rather those who have had all the benefits . . . the finest homes, the finest college education. . . ." Quoted by Paul Fussell, *Caste Marks: Style and Status in the U.S.A.* (London: William Heinemann Ltd., 1984), 20.

47. It is particularly terrifying for an organization to be perceived in this way, not because of extraordinary operations, but as a result of its day-to-day activities.

48. In the United States *The $64,000 Question* was one of the first of many TV game shows to titillate greed by offering large amounts of money to contestants. In Britain the down-market newspapers offer Bingo while the up-market *Times* does the same with a stock-and-shares competition called *Portfolio Gold.*

49. As the journalist George Will points out: "The U.S. economy depends on the endless inculcation of envy [grenvy]. If consumers succumbed to contentment, commerce would slow, dangerously." George Will, "The Rich: Maligned Minority?" *International Herald Tribune,* 21–22 February 1981, 4.

50. The slogan was coined in 1948 and has been in continual use since then. It sustained the price of gem diamonds in the face of increasing world production and the advent of industrial diamonds and manmade fakes like cubic zirconia. See: Edward Jay Epstein, *The Rise and Fall of Diamonds: The Shattering of a Brilliant Illusion* (New York: Simon and Schuster, 1982), and David Koskoff, *The Diamond World* (New York: Harper & Row, 1982).

51. Robert Sherill, review of Edward Jay Epstein, *The Rise and Fall of Diamonds: The Shattering of a Brilliant Illusion,* and David Koskoff, *The Diamond World,* in *International Herald Tribune,* 27 May 1982.

52. Robert Elzey, personal communication, December 1985.

There exists considerable disquiet in business circles about corporation policies that emphasize short-term profits at the expense of long-term growth and development. Presumably Goldman Sachs opposes the lemmings who follow short-term profits at the expense of wealth creation. "Albany at Large—Goldman Sachs Recruit," *Sunday Telegraph,* 20 April 1986, 4.

53. Edward Jay Epstein, "The Billion Dollar Junk Business," *The Sunday Times,* 30 August 1987, 45.

While populist politicians along with older members of the Wall Street community excoriate Michael Milken and fellow arbitrageurs as corporate raiders who "produce little, but trade a lot of paper, make off with tens and sometimes hundreds of millions of dollars, while leaving thousands of corporate employees out of work" (U.S. Senator William Proxmire, quoted in "U.S. Banker Denounces a 'Cancer Called Greed,' " *International Herald Tribune,* 30 January 1987, 1), other bankers and businessmen consider Milken to be a financial genius who has helped to revolutionize and revitalize the American business system.

54. Although the son of an immigrant Russian delicatessen owner in Detroit, Boesky did not start with nothing. He received a $700,000 inheritance, which, according to Douglas Frantz, he managed to turn into a $200 million fortune. Douglas Frantz, "Diamond on the Rocks," *The Times,* 16 October 1987, 10.

Other reports assess Boesky's net worth closer to a billion dollars.

Boesky's greed and his ability to manipulate a business or political system for personal purposes are not unique. At the same time that Boesky was learning his business, but at the other side of the world, the wife of the former president of the Philippines, Imelda Marcos, was amassing money and goods on a scale that might have made even Boesky choke. Like him, she used and abused her position to obtain, among a multitude of things, three thousand pairs of shoes, sixty-eight pairs of gloves, and five shelves of Gucci handbags, all with their price tags still attached. After visiting her palace, U.S. Congressman Stephen Solarz remarked: "Compared to Imelda, Marie Antoinette was a bag lady." Fox Butterfield, "3,000 Pairs of Shoes: What the Marcoses Left Behind," *International Herald Tribune,* 10 March 1986, 2.

55. Many people (his Wall Street enemies, perhaps) reported that Boesky was a nasty person "painfully short of charm." He used his wealth and position to build himself up, often, it seemed, in order to put others down. Aside from buying himself into the Harvard Club and Republican political affairs, he lived on a lavish scale. At the same time that he was under investigation for fraud, he arranged for extensive improvements to his two-hundred-acre Westchester County (New York) estate complete with bass ponds, flocks of sheep, and a herd of white-tailed deer. Alexander Chancellor, "Stocks of Which American Heroes Are Made," *The Independent,* 20 November 1986, 8.

56. Ibid., 8.

57. The $100 million represented both a fine and returned profits. Ibid., 8. He was also jailed for three years.

It is not clear that Boesky acted differently from or necessarily on a larger scale than other investment bankers. He certainly was a visible personality and well hated. Other traders, Lew Glucksman, for example, have acted with equal ambition and contempt for conventions. Glucksman's grenvy led to the inglorious demise of a great banking house, Lehman Brothers. Ken Auletta, *Greed and Glory on Wall Street* (New York: Random House, 1987).

Boesky himself and other corporate raiders have been caricatured (via a mogul called Gekko) in a 1987 film by Oliver Stone simply titled *Wall Street*. Concerned with greed, power, and corruption in New York, the movie could not have been released at a better time, coming after Boesky's conviction and the 1987 stock market collapse on Black Monday.

58. Milken can be quite flamboyant in his business dealings, wining and dining clients in the most luxurious manner, but personally he is more retiring. He refuses to be photographed and lives with his wife and three children in a four-bedroom house near Los Angeles. He spends his spare time coaching his son's baseball team. Edward Jay Epstein, "The Billion Dollar Junk Business," *Sunday Times,* op. cit., 45.

It is possible that Milken and his fellow executives at Drexel, Burnham Lambert Inc. will be indicted on civil charges. As for the firm, it has been the subject of two federal investigations since 1986. Stephen Labaton, "Drexel, on the Defensive, Says Inquiry Has Long Way to Go," *International Herald Tribune,* 28 January 1988, 11.

Apparently the alleged evidence of wrongdoing was provided by Boesky, a further example of envy (if he's going down, he'll take everyone else with him).

59. Nicholas Ashford, "Gorged on a Surfeit of Lawsuits," *The Times,* 18 May 1984, 28.

Ashford points out that there are now more than 620,000 lawyers in the United States, one-third of whom started practicing since the beginning of the eighties.

In addition to lawyers, judges proliferate, too. Ashford adds that there are more judges in the county of Los Angeles than in the whole of France.

60. Ibid., 28.

61. Ian Brodie, "California—Where Litigation Has Become Big Business," *The Daily Telegraph,* 28 January 1986, 12.

California is the most litigious state. Civil cases have been increasing seven times faster than the rate of population growth.

62. Paul Johnson, "Long Arms in Search of a Deep Pocket," *The Daily Telegraph,* 16 August 1980, 8.

63. Paul Johnson points out that the antitrust suit *U.S. Government* vs. *I.B.M.* has been going on for over ten years and may never finish. At the time of writing his article, the case had already spewed forth ninety-three million documents. Ibid., 8.

64. Quoted by Ian Brodie, "California—Where Litigation Has Become Big Business," op. cit., 12.

65. Paul Johnson, "Long Arms in Search of a Deep Pocket," op. cit., 8.

66. "Malpractice Suits Set Records in the U.S.," *International Herald Tribune,* 18 January 1985, 3.

67. Nicholas Ashford, "Gorged on a Surfeit of Lawsuits," op. cit., 28.

68. Ibid., 28.

Equally ridiculous was a million-dollar award to a woman who claimed that her psychic powers had been curtailed after a brain scan. Rhoderick Sharp, "California Gives Lead on Lawsuits," *The Times,* 5 June 1986, 6.

Subsequently, awards like these have led to countervailing pressures to curtail them. Insurance companies in California have backed a state referendum to limit "noneconomic" damages while ensuring full payment of such out-of-pocket costs as medical bills. Ibid., 6.

69. Quoted by David Wastell, in "The Soaring Cost of Doctors' Blunders," *The Sunday Telegraph,* 19 July 1987, 9.

70. Disgruntled patients and their families have attacked psychiatrists for using psychotherapy instead of psychotropic medication, on the basis that they didn't like the effects of psychotherapy and that medication was common practice. At other times psychiatrists have been attacked for using these drugs on the basis that they have deleterious side effects, even though the patients and their families had requested them.

Aside from vindictive scapegoating, what we see in these and other instances of malicious suits is the attempt to avoid or deny risk. As the active pursuit of living is risky, such attempts can be seen as envious attacks on vitality or life itself.

71. Malpractice insurance premiums now cost some physicians upward of $80,000 per year. Obstetricians in particular have been affected by these huge premiums and in many areas have decided to retire or change specialties to avoid the risk of expensive, disruptive litigation. Hence the public may find it difficult or impossible to obtain obstetrical care. According to the American College of Obstetricians and Gynecologists, the threat of malpractice suits has led 12 percent of American obstetricians to close their practices in each of the past two years. Seven out of ten doctors in the field have been sued at least once. Report in *International Herald Tribune,* 9 March 1988, 3.

The American Medical Association points out that when questioned, 40 percent of its members said that they ordered additional diagnostic tests or prescribed additional treatments that were probably not necessary except to provide cover in case of lawsuits. The estimated cost of these extra tests and treatments amounts to upward of $40 billion per year. "Malpractice Suits Set Records in the U.S.," op. cit., 3.

Doctors have also begun to strike back at lawyers, thereby increasing social disharmony. In Brunswick, Georgia, they have refused to deliver the babies of women lawyers or lawyers' wives. One explained: "This is a desperate measure that I have decided upon. . . . My pulse rate goes to about 160 every time I see a lawyer's letter in the mail. Taking Amanda Williams [a lawyer handling malpractice cases] on would be like taking a wolf into the sheep's fold." Tony Allen-Mills, "Doctors Hit Back at Lawyers," *The Daily Telegraph,* 19 May 1986, 8.

72. Ian Brodie, "California—Where Litigation Has Become Big Business," op. cit., 12.

73. Brian Eagles, personal communication, April 1985. Eagles is a lawyer who specializes in the legal intricacies of the cinema and theater.

74. Milton Shulman, "Londoner's Diary," *The Evening Standard,* 17 April 1978, 16.

At this time the top rate of tax was 83 percent on earned income and 98 percent on investment income. In fact, for self-employed people the tax rate on earned income was even higher because it included an extra assessment for national insurance without extra benefits (such as a tax on self-employment).

Lest anyone think that Labour's passion for penal taxation has passed, in 1986 Labour Shadow Chancellor Roy Hattersley proposed a return to high tax rates for everyone earning more than £20,000 per year. Milton Shulman, "Labour's Envy Tax—The Signal to Flee," *The London Standard,* 10 April 1986, 7.

75. The extremely high rate of taxation was a major reason the Swedish filmmaker Ingmar Bergman became a tax exile. He was later prosecuted by the Swedish authorities for tax evasion, a case he fought and won.

76. Helmut Schoeck, *Envy: A Theory of Social Behavior,* op. cit., 27.

Shoeck points out that in Sweden a private firm produces a much consulted list of family incomes above a few thousand dollars.

77. Ibid., 28.

78. Ibid., 323.

79. The income tax was invented in Tuscany in the early fifteenth century. In fact, it echoed certain Roman practices. But use of this tax generally lapsed until the Napoleonic wars, when the British government introduced it as a temporary measure to help pay for the war. Afterward it lapsed again, but in 1840 Sir Robert Peel appealed for seven pence on the pound. Since then this originally modest tax has become the basis of public finance in England and most other countries as well. Hugh Thomas, *An Unfinished History of the World* (London: Hamish Hamilton, 1982), 547–548.

80. The Maori were the original inhabitants of New Zealand. The word *muru* literally means "plunder," more specifically to plunder the property of those who transgressed community norms. Such a transgression often included the simple fact of having more than others. Then one's neighbors would descend with savage howls and carry off anything desirable. No resistance was offered, for this would have not only provoked injury, but excluded the victim from taking part in raids on others. In practice, *muru* was aroused by envy and became a form of legalized theft. Helmut Schoeck, *Envy: A Theory of Social Behavior,* op. cit., 327–329.

81. Jonathan Lynn and Antony Jay, *Yes, Prime Minister,* produced by Sydney Lotterby for BBC-TV, 1986.

82. In the United States, Internal Revenue Service agents, no less than their FBI counterparts, depend on paid and unpaid informants to gain information on allegedly delinquent taxpayers. The Treasury service receives an estimated one hundred thousand communications per year about others' assets and income, information often motivated by revenge, envy, anger, patriotism, and spite. People become palpably and irrationally nervous as the April 15 deadline for filing tax returns approaches. The date itself is like an evil eye. It is not unusual to see cartoons in the papers that depict a mean-looking person looking over a taxpayer's shoulder, with the caption "Be honest; envy is watching you." Helmut Shoeck, *Envy: A Theory of Social Behavior,* op. cit., 323.

This frightening view of the Internal Revenue Service is not necessarily a phantasy. Former agents have testified before congressional committees that enforcement agents are under great pressure to seize the money and property of taxpayers even before they have had a chance to appeal against an assessment. Gary Klott, "A Bully Approach to Tax Collecting," *International Herald Tribune,* 13 April 1987, 2.

83. "In the name of an unattainable equality the legislator uses fiscal means of disproportionate severity to tax the few who, for whatever reasons—even for avowedly legitimate reasons—are economically greatly more successful or better endowed than the majority. Sociological research has shown the extent to which this demand for levelling originates with certain groups of intellectuals, the average voter feeling hardly any definite envy towards those with really high incomes, for the objects of our envy are generally those who are almost our equals." Helmut Schoeck, *Envy: A Theory of Social Behavior,* op. cit., 194–195. See also: 325–327.

84. This also exemplifies the use of the herd instinct to covertly attack a colleague and competitor (akin to parents or elder siblings who may be more richly endowed economically, socially, intellectually, and so on) by exaggerating the needs and resentments of others (akin to younger or less well-endowed siblings or children). In these circumstances the institutionalization of the policy "There must be no favorites" means that the better endowed get hurt, while the instigators bask in the glow of moral righteousness and avoid appropriate shame and guilt (for their own denied greed, for being envious and enacting envy through others, and for hurting those above them).

85. E. J. Mishan, "A Survey of Welfare Economics, 1939–1959," *The Economic Journal* (London), vol. 70, June 1960, 247, quoted by Helmut Schoeck, *Envy: A Theory of Social Behavior,* op. cit., 306.

86. Schoeck points out that one poll asked members of the lowest classes in the United States how much tax a higher-income group should pay. The people queried consistently named a much lower figure as fair or right than that imposed by the government at the time. Ibid., 325.

Similarly, sociologist W. G. Runciman believes that "the poorest appear to be entitled to a greater magnitude of relative deprivation than the evidence shows them to feel." In quoting Runciman, Schoeck points out that surveys show British people are much less concerned with the need for steeply progressive income taxes than the tax laws assume. Ibid., 209.

87. I refer to the situation in the United States in 1962. Ibid., 325–326.

88. This view is well conveyed by J. S. Duesenberry: "Any net increase of output—for instance, more of 'every' good without additional effort—will not advance the welfare of the community no matter how it is distributed. Indeed, any increase of output makes the community worse off, since no matter how the additional goods are distributed, the additional envy generated cannot be adequately compensated for out of these extra goods." J. S. Duesenberry, *Income, Saving, and the Theory of Consumer Behavior* (Cambridge, Mass., 1949), quoted by E. J. Mishan, "A Survey of Welfare Economics, 1939–1959," op. cit., 247.

89. The opposite policy is that people should be allowed to keep a large slice of the wealth they create, and that this encourages economic activity and wealth for everyone. Under the influence of supply-side economists in the United States, tax rates have been slashed since 1981. Then the top rate stood at 70 percent and was reduced to 50 percent. Far from reducing the tax take, studies show that the decrease resulted in more revenue being collected from top-rate taxpayers (and about half of the lost revenue from lower-bracket taxpayers). In other words, it has become less worthwhile for people to diminish their economic activity or remain within the black economy. Paul Craig Roberts, "Slash Top Tax Rates—And All Will Benefit," *The Times*, 6 June 1986, 12.

For similar reasons in Britain, in March 1988 the top rate of tax was reduced from 60 percent to 40 percent, and the bottom rate from 27 percent to 25 percent. All intermediate rates were also eliminated.

Paul Craig Roberts, who was President Reagan's assistant treasury secretary for economic policy, comments: "Lower tax rates, moreover, signify that popular democracy in the U.S. is now sufficiently mature to set aside envy and to focus on opportunity as the galvanizing force in politics. American legislators of all parties no longer believe that high rates are necessary." Ibid., 12.

A drastic reduction in tax rates does not necessarily mean, however, that the politics of malice has been equally diminished. Many wealthy people and businesses had become extremely proficient in avoiding taxation. This aroused the envy of those who could not use tax shelters, as well as guilt among some who did. Since the decrease in tax rates was accompanied by the elimination of a host of favored exemptions, the new law can be seen as an *expression of envy* (against the wealthy for using tax shelters, for they will become liable for substantial amounts of tax) and as a *defense against envy* (by taking several million citizens out of the tax net, there may be less pressure to reduce the remaining shelters).

90. R. E. Money-Kyrle, *Man's Picture of His World: A Psycho-Analytic Study* (London: Duckworth, 1978). See especially: chapter 10, "On Avoidable Sources of Conflict," and chapter 11, "On Political Philosophies."

91. Ibid., 165.

92. At best, wealthy individuals viewed the required redistributive measures with contempt—that is, as a form of charity that did more harm than good. Money-Kyrle adds: "Of course, taxation or inflation may injure an otherwise free economy if carried to excess. But the exaggerated fear of them, which had an unconscious source, was, I think, a major factor in delaying the discovery of an effective means to alleviate distress." Ibid., 165.

93. Marx often inherited or was given large sums of money. David Aberbach, "Marx and His Tormented Vision," *Jewish Chronicle,* 11 March 1983, 22.

His wife was Jenny von Westphalen, daughter of a prominent Prussian government councilor, Ludwig von Westphalen (to whom he was especially attached), and sister of Ferdinand, a Prussian minister of the interior. The family was aristocratic, well-to-do, and well connected. Fritz Raddatz, *Karl Marx: A Political Biography,* translation by Richard Barry (London: Weidenfeld and Nicolson, 1978), 21–22.

94. Ibid., 247.

95. Robert Hinshelwood, "Projective Identification and Marx's Concept of Man," *Int. Rev. Psycho-Anal.,* vol. 10, 1983, 221–226.

Typically, Marx attributed inner pains to outer conditions through the use of the word "we." As a teenager Marx wrote:

We are chained, shattered, empty, frightened,
Eternally chained to this marble block of Being,
Chained, eternally chained, eternally—
And the worlds drag us with them in their rounds,
Howling their songs of death, and we—
We are the apes of a cold God.

David Aberbach, "Marx and His Tormented Vision," op. cit., 22.

96. The millennial belief in absolute egalitarianism provides another defense against as well as an expression of envy. It is a long, often violent history that has been traced in great detail by Norman Cohn, in *The Pursuit of the Millennium: Revolutionary Millennarians and Mystical Anarchists of the Middle Ages* (London: Paladin Books, 1978).

97. Leszek Kolakowski, "The Fantasy of Marxism," *Encounter,* December 1978, no. 303, 83–84.

In fact, Marxism confirmed the worst fears of generations of envied and envying parents and elder sibs that they could not yield an economic or political inch without their institutional lifelines being cut, yet another unfortunate fantasy that undermined economic recovery and added to the political turmoil in Europe.

98. R. E. Money-Kyrle, *Man's Picture of His World: A Psycho-Analytic Study,* op. cit., 181.

99. Ralph Waldo Emerson (1803–1882), American essayist, philosopher, and poet, quoted by Robert Nisbet, *Prejudices: A Philosophical Dictionary* (Cambridge, Mass.: Harvard University Press, 1982), 108.

100. It is interesting to speculate that Marx's intense hatred of the bourgeoisie was, at least in part, a displacement of an even more insatiable hatred initially directed to the nontransferable knowledge and skills of his father, a successful lawyer, and his heritage, the tradition of a long and distinguished line of rabbis. In fact, Marx totally rejected this heritage and remained a virulent antisemite throughout his adult life. He himself was baptized, confirmed, and married in church. His attacks on "the huckstering Jew" appear to be a veiled attack on his father for converting to Christianity as part of a general thrust for acceptance and upward mobility. A fiercely denied sense of guilt about this lost patrimony may also have been involved. Fritz Raddatz, *Karl Marx: A Political Biography,* op. cit., 3–6, 40–41.

101. Leslie Farber points out that the entire advertising industry is devoted to this proposition that man is what he owns and that, ironically, the Marxist sociology of class is devoted to the same view. In consequence: "So long as I believe that you are your possessions and that my motive is greed, I can avoid any acknowledgment of the essential inequality between us." Leslie Farber, *lying, despair, jealousy, envy, sex, suicide, drugs, and the good life,* op. cit., 40.

102. Helmut Schoeck, *Envy: A Theory of Social Behavior,* op. cit., 216–217.

Schoeck adds that these laws were enacted not only by kings and emperors, but also by civic authorities throughout Europe. "Independent cities such as Basel, Bern and Zurich had regulations governing funerals, baptisms, weddings, banquets and the way people dressed." Schoeck relates all this to fears of divine envy and looks upon sumptuary laws as essentially a form of magical propitiation. Ibid., 217.

103. Ibid., 217.
See also: Norman Cohn's discussion of the English Peasants' Revolt led by the priest John Ball. His most enthusiastic followers were to be found among the lower clergy and Londoners "envious of the rich and the nobility." Norman Cohn, *The Pursuit of the Millennium*, op. cit., 198–204.

104. Many examples could be cited where a householder has been required to pay a special tax if his house has more than a certain number of windows or bathrooms or stoves. Helmut Schoeck points out that there are no absolute criteria of luxury. Much depends on the degree of envy of those who stand in judgment. "Luxury *as such* has never existed, and never will exist, but only *envy* of consumer behavior that is branded as luxury." Helmut Schoeck, *Envy: A Theory of Social Behavior*, op. cit., 216.

105. Quoted by Paul Fussell, *Caste Marks: Style and Status in the U.S.A.*, op. cit., 19.

106. A British soldier trying to explain the difference between conscripts and officers during the North Africa campaign of World War II neatly captured the bitterness that class and status distinctions evoke:
"I'll tell you what it means, it means Vickers-Armstrong booking a profit to look like a loss, and Churchill lighting a new cigar, and *The Times* explaining Liberty and Democracy, and me sitting on my arse in Libya splashing a fainting man with water out of my steel helmet. It's a very fine thing if only you're in the right class— that's highly important, sir, because one class gets the sugar and the other gets the shit." Ibid., 25.

107. One hundred dollars was the rental in 1979. Presumably it is now much higher. John Brooks, *Showing Off in America: From Conspicuous Consumption to Parody Display* (Boston: Little, Brown and Company, 1979), 271.

108. Ibid., 270.

109. Paul Fussell has devised a "living-room scale" for ascertaining social class. His scale would serve just as well for denoting status distinctions. Thus, someone with a threadbare rug or carpet would gain eight points, while someone with a new Oriental would lose two. He reckons that 245 points are needed for membership in the upper class or the highest status group. Paul Fussell, *Caste Marks: Style and Status in the U.S.A.*, op. cit., 194–197.

110. Consumerism may be an important defense, but it also serves to ventilate aggressive intentions when it makes a mockery of established and nontransferable values, whether in fashion or other areas such as education. People may feel less angry because they can buy a PhD, but the very availability of such degrees deprecates education, knowledge, and the capacity to gain and use knowledge.

111. Mass marketing acts within specific boundaries. The envy defused within one country may simply be aroused in other places. Thus the advent of mass communications means that even illiterate South American peasants know what they don't have, but should have, to make themselves feel important.

112. G. Rudé, *The Crowd in the French Revolution* (London: Greenwood Press, 1986), 201–202, discussed by Helmut Schoeck, *Envy: A Theory of Social Behavior*, op. cit., 342.

113. "The inescapable conclusion remains that the primary and most constant motive impelling revolutionary crowds during this period was the concern for the provision of cheap and plentiful food. This more than any other factor was the raw material out of which the popular Revolution was forged. . . . Even more, it accounts for the occasional outbreaks of independent activity by the *menu peuple*, going beyond or running counter to the interests of their bourgeois allies. . . . Yet without

the impact of political ideas, mainly derived from their bourgeois leaders, such movements would have remained strangely purposeless and barren of result." G. Rudé, *The Crowd in the French Revolution*, op. cit., 208, quoted by Helmut Schoeck, *Envy: A Theory of Social Behavior*, op. cit., 342.

114. Eric Hobsbawm, professor of economic and social history at Birkbeck College, University of London, has written detailed studies of revolutions, revolutionary processes, and revolutionaries. See: E. J. Hobsbawm, *Social Bandits and Primitive Rebels: Studies in Archaic Forms of Social Movement in the 19th and 20th Centuries* (Glencoe, Ill.: The Glencoe Free Press, 1959), 116, 118, 122, discussed by Helmut Schoeck, *Envy: A Theory of Social Behavior*, op. cit., 343.

115. These conclusions concern urban insurrections and revolutions. Hobsbawm points out that the situation is markedly different in the case of rural areas and peasant revolutions, which are usually egalitarian and often utopian in character. E. J. Hobsbawm, *Social Bandits and Primitive Rebels: Studies in Archaic Forms of Social Movement in the 19th and 20th Centuries*, op. cit., 26, 187, 122.

116. Roger Money-Kyrle states: "The witch-hunts which will then break out will arise from motives of a paradoxical nature characteristic only of the unconscious. For those who perish as suspected, but not actual, traitors to the revolution are also the scapegoats for the unacknowledged sense of guilt at being revolutionaries which their executioners project onto them." R. E. Money-Kyrle, *Man's Picture of His World: A Psycho-Analytic Study*, op. cit., 182.

117. B. L. Garrison, "Congo Rebels Kill 'Intellectuals' As Enemies of Their Revolution," *The New York Times*, 4 October 1964, 4, quoted by Helmut Schoeck, *Envy: A Theory of Social Behavior*, op. cit., 345–46.

Fascist generals during the Spanish civil war voiced similar sentiments. One of their slogans was "Down with intelligence; long live death." Norman Stone, "When Spain Tore Itself to Pieces," *The Sunday Telegraph*, 13 July 1986, 8.

118. In northern and eastern provinces of the Congo where the rebels held sway, even the clerks were wiped out. A Catholic missionary reported that in Moyen province, "there is hardly a Congolese alive with more than a primary education. This means, quite simply, that this part of the Congo has been set back thirty years." Ibid., 346.

The same process of ruthlessly destroying educated and professional people was repeated during the revolution in Cambodia.

119. Bernard Levin, "Punching Holes in This Earthly Paradise," *The Times*, 16 December 1977, 16.

120. The "red-eyed disease" is the tendency of envious eyes to become engorged with hostility at the sight of others' prosperity or envied possessions. This is not an affliction limited to the Chinese, but one widely recognized by them. Under Deng Xiaoping and the new policies of economic liberalization, the press has openly criticized the red-eyed envy of peasants left behind in the race for prosperity. A typical news item described how a woman in Jiangsu (one of the richest provinces) poisoned her neighbor's ducks because she resented his success. Christopher Wren, "Profits, Pop Music and Videodating in a New China: China Under Deng," *International Herald Tribune*, 28 December 1984, 2.

See also: the account of Nien Cheng, a British-educated Chinese woman who observed and suffered the "Rampage of the Red Guards" in Shanghai in the 1960s. Nien Cheng, *Life and Death in Shanghai* (London: Grafton Books, 1986).

121. The 11+ exam was the principal means of sorting students according to academic ability and slotting them into grammar schools or not. Although condemned for putting too much pressure on students too soon, the absence of state streaming has also proven unhelpful, while selection exams continue in the private sector.

Even into the late 1980s Labour leader Neil Kinnock affirmed the need to eliminate private education because it set unfair high standards that the state sector could not meet. Commenting on such attacks, educator John Rae quipped that Labour's answer to low standards was to make sure they applied to all. See: Anthony Bevins, "Kinnock Calls for the End to Private Schools," *The Independent,* 1 June 87, 1; John Rae, "Shooting the Piano Player," *The Times,* 8 May 1987, 14.

122. Many parents would not previously have considered a private education for their children and were already paying state school fees through their rates (local property taxes).

123. Sue Reid, "Grammars Are Best," *Evening Standard,* 2 August 1979, 1–2. The article refers to a government survey of 384 grammar and comprehensive schools. Many were short of books and equipment, and only a minority were performing with distinction. In many schools basic subjects such as English, foreign languages, math, and science were neglected because teachers were underqualified and facilities were poor.

In subsequent years academic standards continued to deteriorate. In particular the ILEA (Inner London Education Authority) seemed to be obsessed with antisexism and antiracism in place of academic excellence, which led Cabinet Minister Norman Tebbit to refer to the ILEA as an "education free zone." Simon Heffer, "Where the Quality of Learning Is Strained by Socialist Aims," *The Daily Telegraph,* 23 June 1986, 18.

The equivalent of public book burning appears to be the culmination of these policies. In the London borough of Ealing, a teacher in each of its schools will be paid to purge bookshelves of "sexist and heterosexist materials as part of a new equality drive by the ruling Labour group." David Shaw, "Teachers Paid to Ban Sexist Books," *London Standard,* 25 June 1986, 11.

124. A minority of comprehensive and retained grammar schools continue to do good work. But in general the continuing indiscipline indicates a collapse in morale. Among students this embraces drug abuse, a high rate of absenteeism, poor exam results, and well-publicized incidents of cursing or physically assaulting teachers in public. Among teachers this involves extreme trade union militancy, the neglect of professional duties, and the stubborn resistance to needed reforms.

125. John Izbicki, "Return of Grammar School Urged," *The Daily Telegraph,* 10 March 1986, 26.

126. The antieducational policies were promulgated and carried out in collusion with large sections of the Tory party, which also retains a militantly anti-intellectual attitude.

This problem is not confined to the United Kingdom. State educational standards have suffered in many countries for reasons that include inner-city blight, cost constraints, changes in educational priorities, politicization of the curriculum, grade inflation, and an excessive emphasis on self-expression and consciousness raising as opposed to basic skills. Some of these factors indicate envy or the fear of envy. Nonetheless, the process seems to have been taken to more destructive extremes in Britain.

Christopher Lasch, among many observers, has commented on the baleful effects of diluted standards in the American system, especially in the education of minority groups. Christopher Lasch, *The Culture of Narcissism,* op. cit., 140–145.

In the 1980s Americans began to respond to poor educational standards in a variety of ways, including the creation of centers of quality education called Magnet Schools. William Morris, "Magnet Force in America," *The Independent,* 30 October 1986, 11.

127. Women who wore the device had a much higher risk of developing pelvic inflammatory disease. Robin Henig, op. cit., 22.

128. Ibid., 22.

129. Even as an IUD, the Dalkon Shield wasn't very effective. An initial study by Dr. Hugh Davis, inventor of the device, claimed it was superior to other IUDs. But the study was flawed, and the Robins company apparently knew this. Other

studies demonstrated its diminished capacity to prevent pregnancy in comparison with other IUDs or other methods. Ibid., 22.

130. L. P. Hartley, *Facial Justice* (London: Hamish Hamilton, 1960).

131. George Orwell, *1984* (London: Penguin Books, 1984).

132. L. P. Hartley, *Facial Justice,* op. cit., 43.

133. Joab replied: "Brains are not a cause of Bad E, Jael, like money or beauty," an obvious denial of his sister's threat. But Jael continued the attack: "They might become so. It isn't fair that you should be cleverer than other people." Ibid., 172.

134. Ibid., 43.

135. Journalist George Will has described the experience of living in Soviet Russia where the excessive control of overt sensuality, for reasons not unlike those Hartley details, caused him acute discomfort akin to severe sensory deprivation. "In the West, the social atmosphere may be overdosed with aphrodisiacs. However, a sojourn in an anti-sensualist society such as this underscores a theme of Orwell's *1984*. Eroticism is feared by a regime that feels threatened by any realm of privacy or flicker of spontaneity." George Will, "Moscow's Stalinist Values Excite Longing for Neon," *International Herald Tribune,* 13 March 1986, 8.

136. Similarly, Valium addiction has been called "bottled happiness." Alan Massam, "Happy End to My Mother's Long Misery," *London Standard,* 3 April 1986, 14.

137. In short, breast and womb envy are major unconscious determinants of both destructive drug use and the moral fervor of agencies like the former United States Bureau of Narcotics.

There exists a plethora of material that documents the misinformation about drug use and the history of repressive countermeasures as well as attempts to redress the balance. See, for example: *Drug Addiction: Crime or Disease? Interim and Final Reports of the Joint Committee of the American Bar Association and the American Medical Association on Narcotic Drugs* (Bloomington, Ind.: Indiana University Press, 1963); Joel Fort, *The Pleasure Seekers: The Drug Crisis, Youth and Society* (New York: Grove Press, 1969); Joseph Berke, "The Fickle Fix," *The Radical Therapist,* vol. 1, no. 2, June-July 1970; Charles Tart, ed., *Altered States of Consciousness* (New York: Anchor Books, 1972).

138. L. P. Hartley, *Facial Justice,* op. cit., 43.

139. I particularly refer to the seemingly inexorable process of merger mania, by which one company gobbles up another, another example of the phallus dentatus.

140. Paul Johnson, "Farewell to the Labour Party," op. cit., 329.

141. Paul Johnson, "Whatever Happened to the Lucky Country?" *The Sunday Telegraph,* 2 January 1983, 8–9.

142. Ibid., 8.

143. The voyagers on the First Fleet in 1788, as well as subsequent settlers, were under the orders of the British government. As Paul Johnson points out, "Australia has never wholly lost its sense of dependence on a paternalist power." According to Johnson, the biggest threat to Australia's prosperity comes from ingrained habits of looking to the state and federal governments to provide basic necessities. Ibid., 8–9.

144. Johnson comments on the "heavy hand of Canberra" as well as the big unions that seek to centralize and control individual rights and initiatives. Ibid., 8–9. Others have commented on the dominating position of big business. Collectively they share many features of Big Brother.

145. Since the 1960s, significant numbers of Australian women have adopted radical, left-wing feminist positions. Ibid., 8.

This militancy is not simply a reaction to the overvaluation of maleness, or specific male oppression, but results from a general diminution of femaleness and can be seen as an attempt to compensate for the loss of valued female roles. Years earlier Clara Thompson discussed the cultural implications of this issue, in " 'Penis Envy' in Women," Jean Baker Miller, ed., *Psychoanalysis and Women,* op. cit., 55–57.

146. By "men" I mean, of course, phallic-assertive individuals of either sex.

147. Plutarch, *Alcibiades* (13,4), quoted in Peter Walcot, *Envy and the Greeks,* op. cit., 58.

148. Walcot points out that Greek audiences thoroughly enjoyed seeing prominent people being brought down to earth by public humiliation. They could not stand anyone excelling the "democratic norm." Then, as now, one of the best areas for a flank attack was personal morality. Ibid., 66.

149. "Anyone for Losing," *The Times,* 6 July 1985, 9.

The same editorial gloated over the demise of Jimmy Connors ("the great old grunter") and Ivan Lendl ("a money-making machine with little compensating grace").

150. Michael Wise, " 'Big Bang' Ignites a Wage Explosion," *International Herald Tribune,* 10 April 1986, 7 and 13.

151. Many staff members were "head-hunted" or poached from other firms. Approximately one thousand people received remuneration running to several hundred thousand dollars a year, while a few executives reported deals worth millions. These packages were not unusual on the world financial market but extremely large by British standards. Ibid., 8.

152. The City is London's financial district.

153. Quoted by Michael Wise, ibid., 8.

154. Quoted by Michael Wise, ibid., 8.

Prominent business figures also parroted the resentment of "new money." Thus, Charles John Constable, director general of the British Institute of Management, commented: "People here will become increasingly disturbed by one group gaining extraordinary wealth for creating nothing, for simply turning over money. British attitudes are quite different from those in America." Quoted by Steve Lohr, "City's New Traders Young, Cheeky," *International Herald Tribune,* 27–28 September 1986, 17–19.

The idea that newcomers were getting rich for doing nothing does not fit the facts. Relatively few of the new traders made huge sums, most worked long hours and generated wealth in and for the City.

The denial of their efforts represents a typical envious response to people who had successfully infiltrated previously cordoned-off areas of financial enrichment. Many were sneeringly labeled "yuppies" by the press, representing a public that resented thrusting ambitions and accomplishments. Yuppies were alleged to be spoiled brats (like hippies) who did little and took everything, while simultaneously flaunting the proceeds. Yet, as journalist Peter McKay points out, this is a good description of their predecessors, "greedy, stupid city types," many of whom had gotten their jobs through family connections and then sat on their asses for years. McKay concludes: "No one who is honest can really claim that the yuppification of rundown London has not been a great and lasting restorative movement." Peter McKay, "Some of Our Best Friends Were Yuppies," *The London Evening Standard,* 22 October 1987, 7.

155. A few specialized journals pointed out that carping outbursts about "highfliers" simply provided further examples of the British tendency to attack success. According to *The Economist,* "Britons who tut-tut at high City salaries would do better to ask whether finance is the one area of the British economy that is genuinely competitive internationally." Quoted by Michael Wise, ibid., 8.

Subsequently, the 1987 stock market collapse occasioned the loss of many jobs as well as a general belt tightening. These cutbacks were met with barely concealed glee by those who resented the highfliers in the first place.

156. Roy Mason, "De Lorean Is a Winner, Damn It!" *The Times,* 12 October 1981, 6.

"Share Deal That Gave De Lorean the Bargain of a Lifetime," Business News, *The Sunday Times,* 11 October 1981, 53 and 72.

157. De Lorean later admitted that he had made a serious mistake in attempting to build a sports car in the midst of religious and sectarian strife. Christopher Thomas, "I Was Wrong to Launch a Belfast Firm, Says De Lorean," *The Times,* 2 February 1982, 1.

158. The woman, Miss Marian Gibson, also took her allegations to an "unemployed writer" in a further attempt to sell a sensational story to the Sunday paper *News of the World.* The action failed because the story could not be supported. Craig Seton and Christopher Thomas, "We Will Survive, Says Cleared De Lorean," *The Times,* 13 October 1981, 1.

159. Haddad had worked as a special assistant to Robert Kennedy. He was said to be highly personable with strong Irish republican sympathies. He had been in charge of various publicity projects but had fallen from grace within the highest echelons of the company.

160. Craig Seton and Christopher Thomas, "De Lorean Story of Girl's Claims and 'Forged' Memo," *The Times,* 10 October 1981, 4.

De Lorean rejected all of Haddad's charges but agreed that a small sum had been spent on gold taps during the course of renovations to visitors' accommodations. He said the expenditure had been indiscreet and wished it had never happened, for it was more in keeping with Hugh Hefner and bunny girls. On the contrary, the gold taps were very much a part of the style that sold his cars.

161. The "malfeasance" included the fact that De Lorean and his investors stood to do very well financially if the project succeeded. Even *The Times* pointed out that this placed De Lorean in a Catch-22 situation. If he failed, the government should not have supported him. If he succeeded, it should have made a better deal. Basically his crime had to do with successfully building a sports car in Belfast, something most civil servants thought could never be done. His punishment was to see his reputation ruined by unsubstantiated public allegations.

162. Charles Laurence, "De Lorean's Hand on the Bible," *The Daily Telegraph,* 8 September 1986, 13.

It is interesting that even an article that describes his acquittal on drug dealing questions his life-style, sneers at his probity, and hints that he will be convicted of other charges.

163. De Lorean had been charged with racketeering on the basis of a 1978 law designed to put the mafiosi behind bars. He was acquitted of fifteen counts of racketeering, fraud, and tax evasion. His defense attorneys proved that $8.9 million, which he had used for personal purposes, had in fact been legitimately provided by Group Lotus for design work. "De Lorean Innocent of Embezzlement," *International Herald Tribune,* 18 December 1986, 2.

By the spring of 1987 De Lorean managed to reach a financial settlement with his major creditors. "De Lorean Bouncing Back," *The London Evening Standard,* 28 May 1987, 53.

Chapter 10

1. Jean-Paul Sartre, "My Political Will," *Strike,* vol. 2, no. 3, October 1978, 5, translated and reprinted from *Mon Testament politique* (Edition "Gare L'explosion," 1977), courtesy of Edizioni della Rivista "Anarchismo."

2. The French existentialist philosopher, playwright, and novelist Jean-Paul Sartre (1905–1980) was also a noted political activist who espoused many radical causes on behalf of the working class, the Third World, and especially oppressed youth.

3. "Who would dare criticize the servants of the Middle Ages who burned down their lord's castles, dipping their hands into the intestines to pull out his guts and then dancing among the smoking ruins of the castle? Who would dare criticize those servants for creating with iron and fire their own freedom? Which one of you would dare to criticize the slaves of ancient time who struck the patrician, catching him

in the midst of an orgy, snatching from him the golden cup, and after having emptied it, escaping, taking along the pillage and murdering the robbed one? . . . Let's resurrect the tradition of Brutus, Spartacus, and the rebellious peasants of past history! Stand up! Action! Insurrection! Revolution!" Ibid., 4.

4. Enrico Malatesta, *Anarchy*, translated by Vernon Richards (London: Freedom Press, 1974), 13.

5.

Things fall apart; the centre cannot hold;
Mere anarchy is loose upon the world,
The blood-dimmed tide is loosed, and everywhere
The ceremony of innocence is drowned;

Although written about the Irish uprising, this excerpt from "The Second Coming" by W. B. Yeats describes the impact of the vandal and anarchist and is often quoted by their friends and enemies. W. B. Yeats, *Selected Poetry* (London: Pan Books, 1974), 99–100.

6. During the seventeenth century, opponents of the radical Levellers called them "Switzerising anarchists." Later the Girondin leader Jacques-Pierre Brissot used the epithet to denounce his Enragé rivals: "Laws that are not carried into effect, authorities without force and despised, crime unpunished, property attacked, the safety of the individual violated, the morality of the people corrupted, no constitution, no government, no justice, these are the features of anarchy."

The New Encyclopaedia Britannica, 15th ed. 1985, 458.

7. William Godwin (1756–1836). Ibid., 458. The famous phrase "From each according to his means, to each according to his needs" was popularized by the nineteenth-century anarchist leader Peter Kropotkin. But it had been clearly anticipated by Godwin, who in turn had been influenced by Sir Thomas More's *Utopia*.

Godwin also commented: "Normal man seeks the light just as the flowers do. Man, if not too much interfered with, will make for himself the best possible environment and create for his children right conditions, because the instinct for peace and liberty is deeply rooted in his nature." Quoted by George Woodcock, in *Anarchy or Chaos* (London: Freedom Press, 1944), 32.

8. Pierre Joseph Proudhon (1809–1865). Quoted by George Woodcock, ibid., 35.

9. Idealists frequently insist that any degree of violence is justified to retain their beliefs, even if the violence and consequent destruction violate the very beliefs they are trying to sustain.

10. Mikhail Bakunin (1814–1876). George Woodcock argues that Bakunin has been misrepresented and did not desire violence or destruction for its own sake. No doubt this is true. Bakunin was an idealist who saw violent revolution as a necessary prelude to a new millennium. Nonetheless he was a brilliant instigator who inspired hatred and discord throughout Europe and America. His violent actions became models for future generations of revolutionaries which belied his hopes for human harmony and perfection. "Bloody revolutions are often necessary, thanks to human stupidity; yet they are always an evil, a monstrous evil and a great disaster, not only with regard to the victims, but also for the sake of the purity and the perfection of the purpose in whose name they take place." Quoted by George Woodcock, ibid., 37.

The writer Leo Tolstoy championed another strain of anarchism. While also rejecting the State and all forms of government, he renounced terrorism. Instead Tolstoy relied on moral regeneration and free communism. Although politically much less significant than Bakunin, he did influence the nonviolent approach of Gandhi.

11. Ibid., 68.

In Italy Malatesta concurred with Nechayev's doctrine and helped to popularize it throughout Europe. However, just at the time anarchism was becoming popular in the West, the Russian revolutionaries were abandoning the term in favor of terrorism. But the work of writers like Kropotkin and Kravchinsky led terroristic tactics to be identified with anarchist ideals. James Billington points out: "Thus anarchism tinged with ideals and sanctified with martyrdom became a new verbal talisman for many otherwise dispirited revolutionaries." James Billington, *Fire in the Minds of Men: Origins of the Revolutionary Faith* (London: Temple Smith, 1980), 414. See also: 415–416.

12. Action Directe, for example, has been one of the more prominent extremist groups operating in Europe in the 1980s. It was founded in France in 1979 by Jean Marc Rouillan, the leader, and Nathalie Menogon. After bombing the Interpol headquarters outside Paris in May 1985, it vowed to continue "to hit central installations which link their political, economical, and military strategy, and at the heart of which are found the strongest antagonisms of the international proletariat/ imperialist bourgeoisie: to concretize the qualitative leap of all antagonisms of the masses and develop them toward a global revolutionary strategy." Diana Geddes, "Seven-Year History of Terror," *The Times*, 19 November 1986, 9.

Action Directe has collaborated with terrorist groups throughout Europe and the Middle East. Collectively they tend to be anti-American, anti-Jewish, antibusiness, antimilitary, anti-NATO, and antinuclear. Action Directe's targets have included NATO installations, symbols of American capitalism, and major corporate leaders. Rouillan has alleged that his violence is not important in comparison with all the other violence that goes on in the world. Actually he glories in the most destructive acts, often directed toward their effect on the media. Interestingly, he could not remain free without the tacit, and sometimes active, compliance of the French public and political establishment. Thus, instead of treating him as he is, a malevolent killer, sections of the French press have turned him into a romantic hero. By the same token, President Mitterrand included Rouillan and other members of his group, who had been jailed in 1980, in an amnesty in 1981. This indicates considerable sympathy for the hatreds that surface through Rouillan and people like him in large parts of the populace. Mitterrand, for one, soon regretted his action. After Rouillan left prison, Action Directe began a new wave of terrorist activities. See: Stephen Segaller, *Invisible Armies: Terrorism into the 1990s* (London: Michael Joseph, 1986).

Subsequently, most of the important members of Action Directe have been taken into custody. Their arrests in the late 1980s coincided with major "successes" by European security forces against the Italian Red Brigades and the German Red Army Brigades. However, experts such as Ian Geldard of the Institute for the Study of Terrorism argue that terrorism has simply entered a quiescent phase. In Germany, for example, the future of "direct action" does not lie with old organizations, but with "the new anarchist movements" that emerge from groups like the militant wing of the Green party. Niall Ferguson, "Terror 88: The Fight Moves On," *The Daily Telegraph*, 22 January 1988, 15.

13. As a slogan and state of mind, "saving the world" equals the wish to overcome starvation, oppression, disease, and inequality—all the ostensibly positive features of anarchist, indeed, of socialist, thought. The activist may be so identified with these goals that his whole sense of self may be based on their achievement. Because of the diminution of boundaries between inside and outside, self and others, he may also believe that he omnipotently controls all goodness. Consequently, any decrease in goodness (revolutionary achievements) in the external world tends to be felt as a devastating loss of inner worth and the power to overcome feelings of inferiority, inadequacy, and envy. This state, which Herbert Rosenfeld has termed "libidinal narcissism," precedes and lays the foundation for the most intransigent "destructive narcissism."

Rosenfeld states: "In considering narcissism for the libidinal aspect one can see that the overvaluation of the self plays a central role, based mainly on the idealization of the self. Self-idealization is maintained by omnipotent introjective and projective identification with good objects and their qualities. In this way the narcissist feels that everything that is valuable relating to external objects and the outside world is part of him or is omnipotently controlled by him." Herbert Rosenfeld, "A Clinical Approach to the Psychoanalytic Theory of the Life and Death Instincts: An Investigation into the Aggressive Aspects of Narcissism," op. cit., 173.

In common usage, the term "narcissism" equals what Rosenfeld calls "libidinal narcissism."

14. From the point of view of psychiatric practice, Rosenfeld observes: "The destructive narcissism of these patients appears often highly organized, as if one were dealing with a powerful gang dominated by a leader, who controls all the members of the gang to see that they support one another in making the criminal destructive work more effective and powerful. . . . This narcissistic organization is in my experience not primarily directed against guilt and anxiety, but seems to have the purpose of maintaining the idealization and superior power of the destructive narcissism." Ibid., 174.

An important implication of Rosenfeld's work is that the contradictory currents of at least some political theories (such as the anarchists' millennial expectations and terrorist plans) reflect the ebb and flow of libidinal and destructive narcissism. The purpose of both of these strategies is to allow the envier to attack envied objects while at the same time diminish envious tension and concomitant feelings of worthlessness in himself.

15. Hilaire Belloc, "About John," *Selected Cautionary Verses* (London: Puffin Books, 1983), 70–71. See also: 72–78.

16. In February 1959 a new school opened in East Harlem. By November 589 windows had been broken. In 1958 the New York Department of Education had to replace 160,000 broken windows and repair damage caused by seventy-five cases of arson. Helmut Schoeck, *Envy: A Theory of Social Behavior,* op. cit., 112.

17. In 1978 the Tory spokesman on home affairs, William Whitelaw, pointed out that schools and railways suffered £20 million of wanton damage per year. The current figure is probably higher. Oliver Pritchett, "The World of the Vandal," *The Sunday Telegraph,* 29 October 1978, 21.

18. This man abandoned his Middlesborough farm after his crops had been attacked fifty times during a single harvest.

According to the National Farmers' Union Mutual Insurance Society, the problem of vandalism is the greatest at the edge of large cities and new towns. The damage done includes "setting fire to crops, hayricks and buildings, sabotage of farm machinery, the theft of sheep, cattle and vegetables, and the killing and maiming of livestock by dogs or guns." John Young, "Vandalism Is Costing Farms £5m Each Year," *The Times,* 18 April 1987, 4.

19. Helmut Schoeck, *Envy: A Theory of Social Behavior,* op. cit., 111.

20. *The New Encyclopaedia Britannica,* 15th ed., 1985, 459.

For hundreds of years property had indeed been the main source of generating wealth. Yet by the time of Proudhon's declaration, this had long since begun to change, precipitated by the growth of financial markets and the Industrial Revolution. Although Proudhon was trying to make a point about man's exploitation of man, his conclusions were inaccurate. "Property is theft" reflects envy of wealth.

Sartre's preoccupations were also nonsensical. By the time of his statement he had long known that "information is wealth." Even in his Political Will he talks about killing the rich to get money to buy printing presses, that is, convey valuable information, if only "the propaganda of the word."

21. Sartre assailed the rich and privileged and asserted that the "sword of Damocles" should constantly be held over their heads so that "snakes of terror, like those of Nemesis, hiss night and day into their ears, frightening them out of their luxury and their lives; that their position would become unbearable and that tired of such anguish, they would see themselves forced to fall on their knees to demand forgiveness, begging the proletariat to grant them life in exchange for their privilege and the common joy in exchange for the general disgrace." Jean-Paul Sartre, "My Political Will," op. cit., 5.

22. Ibid., 5.

23. Ibid., 5.

24. Ibid., 5.

Sartre's anarchy links millennialism with economic and political vandalism.

25. Annie Cohen-Solal, *Sartre: A Life* (London: Heinemann, 1987).

By the late 1980s Sartre's reputation had begun to fade.

26. Ronald Hayman, *Writing Against: A Biography of Sartre* (London: Weidenfeld & Nicolson, 1986).

27. Jean-Paul Sartre, "My Political Will," op. cit., 5.

28. Paul Webster, "Anarchists Loot Top Paris Shops," *The Guardian,* 9 June 1979, 8. The raid described in the article was one of several similar incidents blamed on Autonome in the previous six months.

29. Ian Henry, "Gang 'Robbed to Finance Anarchy,' " *The Daily Telegraph,* 27 September 1979, 3.

Interestingly, in England the right-wing counterparts of left-wing anarchist and semianarchist groups (the "violent fringe") often share similar hatreds. These include Mrs. Thatcher, nuclear energy, the capitalist press, and Zionism. Others, like Roland Lee, head of the Animal Liberation Front, or Ffred Ffrancis, leader of the Welsh Language Society, attack particular targets like a pig farm in Bristol (burned) and the Cancer Research Campaign in London (defaced) or Welsh holiday cottages (burned) and television transmitters (blown up). Cal McCrystal, "Warlords of the Fringe," *The Sunday Times,* 12 October 1986, 36–43.

30. The Angry Brigade, "Communiqué 8," *The Angry Brigade 1967–1984: Documents and Chronology* (London: Anarchist Pocketbooks 3, Elephant Editions, 1985), 20–21, 31.

31. According to the Opinion-Poll Institute of Professor Noelle-Neumann, the number of people in West Germany who feel intense boredom *(langeweile)* has been steadily increasing. Professor Noelle-Neumann says the data demonstrate a positive correlation between those confessing boredom and those professing hatred of technology and the market economy as well as sympathy for the Green party and egalitarian politics. Discussed by Helmut Schoeck, personal communication, letter of 8 July 1987.

There is a certain paradox in the fear of boredom and the desire for egalitarianism. In practice, an egalitarian society is much less stimulating than a nonegalitarian society. To demonstrate this, one only has to talk to people who have lived in places like the People's Republic of China.

32. Aside from other causes, war is certainly a major antidote for mass boredom. One has only to consider the reaction of the populations of the major powers before, say, World War I or the Falklands crisis.

33. Throughout the eighties the responses of large numbers of young people to unemployment in Europe and the United States have included violent resentful vandalism and drug-induced withdrawal. The latter may reflect an underlying condition of overstimulation, through television and the "consumer spectacle." So a state of boredom can serve as a defense against degrees of stimulation that cannot be assimilated. From this point of view, the "boring society" is a projection of an internal, defensive state, and the associated violent reaction is an attempt to destroy the "bad, overstimulating breast," such as a Miss World contest, which may all too easily arouse intolerable frustration, envious tension, and inner chaos.

Without a more direct exploration of these issues, it is hard to tell whether members of the Angry Brigade were more oppressed by under- or overstimulation or various combinations of frustrating stimulation and inadequate satisfaction which they experienced as "under" or "over."

34. When ghetto people were asked why they participated in riots, many answered, "Because I was bored." Understimulation in their daily lives and overstimulation by TV appeared to be essential issues.

35. Theodore Roszak, *The Making of a Counter Culture: Reflections on the Technocratic Society and Its Youthful Opposition* (New York: Anchor Books, 1969).

Joseph Berke, ed., *Counter Culture: The Creation of an Alternative Society* (London: Peter Owen, 1969).

36. David Mairowitz, "The Diggers," in *Counter Culture: The Creation of an Alternative Society,* ibid., 378.

37. The Diggers, thirty to forty in number, established themselves on St. George's Hill, near Walton-on-Thames, on 1 April 1649 and remained there until March of the following year. They were led by Gerrard Winstanley, a tradesman whose business had failed during the economic depression of the 1640s. He articulated the basic ideas that he and his followers tried to put into practice. Winstanley asserted, for example, that people could only remove social injustice by their own deeds and called up the common folk "to manure and work upon the Common lands." Quoted by George Woodcock, *Anarchy or Chaos,* op. cit., 29. See also: 27–31.

According to Woodcock, Winstanley anticipated Peter Kropotkin's idea of mutual aid. Kropotkin (1842–1921) was the most significant anarchist leader after Bakunin and essentially crystallized anarchist theory.

38. "The Digger Papers," excerpts, see: Joseph Berke, ed., *Counter Culture: The Creation of an Alternative Society,* op. cit., 380–382.

39. Among the many goods and services the Digger manifesto advocated were "free" garages, food stores, information, bank, housing, "medical thing," hospital, design gang, schools, news, communication, events, garbage collection, radio, TV, computer stations, tinkers, and gunsmiths. Ibid., 380–381.

40. The Diggers deployed the politics of the preposterous to emphasize the anomalies between wealth and poverty. At one point they sent a van from the Free City Distribution Company into wealthy neighborhoods to ask whether the people needed anything and offered goods from the van. I think this action was not a labor of love, nor irony, but a further form of intimidation designed to facilitate "begging with menaces," as happened later on.

41. Ibid., 380.

The Diggers hoped that the tone and content of this statement would help them forge cooperative links with other groups, including the Black Panthers, Provos, and Mission Rebels.

42. The Diggers were successful models for other groups that blazed briefly on the international underground scene. This included the White Panther party (white radicals who named themselves after the Black Liberationists), with adherents in the United States and the U.K. Point 10 of their ten-point program against state oppression stated: "WE WANT A FREE PLANET. WE WANT FREE LAND . . . FREE FOOD . . . FREE SHELTER . . . FREE CLOTHING . . . FREE MUSIC . . . FREE CULTURE . . . FREE MEDIA . . . FREE BODIES . . . FREE TECHNOLOGY . . . FREE EDUCATION . . . FREE HEALTH CARE . . . FREE PEOPLE . . . FREE TIME AND SPACE . . . EVERYTHING FREE FOR EVERYBODY. . . ." White Panther party, Abbey Wood chapter, "Ten Point Programme," *Chapter?,* no. 1, London, 1971, 15. This program appears like a "manic feast."

The San Francisco Diggers (and kindred groups like the White Panthers) suffered the same fate as their English namesake; they broke up and seemingly disappeared. Winstanley himself vanished into such obscurity that his date and place of death are unknown.

43. One investigation uncovered benefits frauds of £8,500 per week at Newquay. These involved 173 claims out of 451 that had been made in the town that week.

The cheats were mostly young people who claimed false addresses, and who, in some cases, were also working. Sarah Thompson, "£8,500-a-Week Benefits Fiddle in Seaside Town," *The Daily Telegraph,* 22 August 1986, 3.

44. *Computer Security* (Alexandria, Va.: Time-Life Books, 1986), 42.

45. Ibid., 44.

46. Ibid., 17–18, 60–61.

47. Ibid., 18–19.

An expert programmer can write a logic bomb that is practically impossible to detect, because it takes up only a few lines amid a larger program of tens of thousands of lines. Yet it can wreak havoc when it goes off, such as by suddenly deleting huge chunks of data.

48. Consultant Ross Greenberg goes on to say, "I guess the people who devise these things take pleasure in destroying other people's work." Quoted by Mark McCain, "U.S. Computer Vandals Learn to Program Havoc," *International Herald Tribune,* 20 May 1987, 1.

Greenberg himself has devised several "tools of defense'" against electronic terrorists. These include a software program that alerts him to suspicious activity within his computer.

49. Headlines about ecological "rape" remain all too familiar. Of course, this kind of damage can be and is done by organizations as well as individuals. Godfrey Brown, "Photographs Show Rape of the Countryside," *The Daily Telegraph,* 4 September 1986, 4.

50. Helmut Schoeck, *Envy: A Theory of Social Behavior,* op. cit., 107.

51. "Teacher Gets Life Sentence for Double Axe Murders," *The Times,* 16 April 1987, 3.

52. "The Tingling Fingers That Meant Death for 26," *The Daily Telegraph,* 21 January 1981, 3. The killings were done in the the city of Hull, Britain, over a five-year period. Lee used to prowl the streets with a bottle of paraffin under his coat.

53. While damage to the fatherland may focus judicial interest, violation of the mother country makes the public crave for revenge.

54. Quoted by George Woodcock, *Anarchy or Chaos,* op. cit., 54–55.

55. The manifesto ends with the call "to overthrow governments by whatever name they may be called." A century later Sartre used similar language to urge the overthrow of tyrannies "called a provisional government, government of liberation, constituent, legislative assembly, presidency; today his name is Giscard, tomorrow he will be called Marchais or Mitterrand." Jean-Paul Sartre, "My Political Will," op. cit., 4.

56. George Woodcock, *Anarchy or Chaos,* op. cit., 107–108.

57. The International Brotherhood was composed mostly of Italians with a few Poles, Russians, French, and Spaniards. It was a model for later conspirators like Lenin.

According to the anarchist chronicler George Woodcock, Bakunin eventually repudiated secret societies, declaring that revolution can only spring from the body of the masses. Ibid., 53.

58. The secret International Brotherhood soon merged with the new "Alliance."

The First International was the popular name for the International Workers Association, an international organization set up to coordinate socialist action in all countries. Marx did not create it, but he regarded it as one of the central accomplishments of his life. Fritz Raddatz, *Karl Marx: A Political Biography,* op. cit., 191.

Within a few years irreconcilable hostilities arose between Bakunin and Marx and their anarchist and socialist followers. These differences led to the expulsion of Bakunin and others from the First International on the basis of trumped-up charges presented by Marx. In 1881 the Anarchist International was reestablished, largely on the initiative of Kropotkin.

59. "To the last fiber of his being Marx was a politician; he was like lava, a revolutionary natural element; for him politics were the essence of all things; nothing else motivated him." Ibid., 49.

60. Recollection by the Italian politician Mazzini, quoted by Fritz Raddatz, ibid., 66.

Similarly, James Guillaume, historian of the International, said that Marx maintained the attitude of "a ruling sovereign." Ibid., 66.

61. Lieutenant Techow, who fought with Marx during the 1848 revolution and later met him again during his exile in London, observed that Marx was eaten away by ambition. He ridiculed comrades who parroted his words and reserved real respect only for aristocrats: "I came away with the impression that the aim of all his endeavors was personal domination, that all his associates were far beneath him, lagging behind him, and that, if they should dare to forget it for a moment, he would put them back into their place with a shameless impudence worthy of Napoleon." Quoted by Fritz Raddatz, ibid., 66.

62. *Computer Security*, op. cit., 10

63. Ibid., 72.

64. Ibid., 65.

WarGames, directed by John Badham, produced by Harold Schneider. Warner Communications, Inc., 1983.

65. Ibid., 59.

See also: discussion by Andrew Emmerson, "Phantoms of the Operating System," *New Scientist*, 28 January 1988, 69.

American companies are also beginning to implant "bombs" and "worms" into their software to prevent illicit copying. Any program that is copied will self-destruct.

66. Ibid., 19 and 72.

67. Ibid., 10 and 67.

Most "viruses" are malicious in origin. Armed with them, terrorists, hackers, or plain practical jokers can wreak havoc on a mainframe computer within an hour or a computer network within several days. Vin McLellan, "Sabotaged Computers Are Passing on the Bug," *International Herald Tribune*, 1 February 1988, 1 and 11.

68. According to *Computer Security*, computer-related frauds in Britain cost between £500 million and £2.5 billion per year and $300 million to $5 billion in the United States. These figures mostly concern embezzlement and do not take into account extensive malicious damage. Ibid., 19.

69. Ibid., 10.

Similarly, a saboteur damaged the internal computer network of the IBM corporation with a Christmas greeting in December 1987. Essentially, a picture of a Christmas tree began to appear on all the computer terminals, which brought all the other computer traffic to a halt. Although IBM played down the incident, the virus took the huge network, known as "Big Blue," out of action for over two hours. Charles Bremner, " 'Virus' Plague Wreaks Havoc with Computers," *The Times*, 13 January 1988, 6.

70. Ibid., 6.

71. Quoted by Bremner, ibid., 6.

72. Irving Berlin, "Anything You Can Do," *Annie Get Your Gun*, Irving Berlin, Ltd., London, 1947, 128–137.

"Annie" refers to Annie Oakley, famous cowgirl and friend of Buffalo Bill. Berlin wrote the lyrics and music for the musical produced by Rodgers and Hammerstein.

73. In the song, Annie proclaimed she was generally greater, better, and higher. Specifically, she could shoot, speak, sing, cook, and look better than men or their wives. Ibid., 128–137.

74. *Computer Security*, op. cit., 40.

Similarly, American right-wing groups like the Aryan Nations claim the right to bomb federal buildings on the basis of beliefs that include "Caucasians are the chosen people." "Official Links Idaho Blasts, Rights Effort," *The International Herald Tribune,* 3 October 1986, 4.

75. Ibid., 40.

76. In the Americas most guerrilla attacks have focused on military or military-related installations. In 1970 antiwar activists bombed the Army Mathematics Research Center at the University of Wisconsin. In addition to doing about $18 million worth of damage to the buildings, computer hardware, and twenty-year accumulation of research data, they killed a young graduate student.

In Europe the targets are more broadly based—banks, government agencies, universities, and multinational companies as well as military installations. Ibid., 35, 40.

77. Ibid., 40.

78. Robin Smyth, "Swiss 'Losers' Fight Rat Race," *The Observer,* 3 August 1980, 3.

79. Previously the youths paraded with fireworks, trumpets, and bongo drums down the main streets, demanding an amnesty for comrades arrested in earlier demonstrations. The attack on the opera house, site of a £14 million renovation, was related to the decision of the city fathers to close a youth center.

80. Wallace Turner, "18 Hell's Angels Arrested in Drug Probe," *The International Herald Tribune,* 20 June 1979, 3.

81. The distinction is between "libidinal narcissism" (equivalent to the Jesus complex) and "destructive narcissism" (equivalent to the Hitler complex). See: Herbert Rosenfeld, "A Clinical Approach to the Psychoanalytic Theory of the Life and Death Instincts: An Investigation into the Aggressive Aspects of Narcissism," op. cit., 172–173.

82. In this context, I refer in particular to the destructive phallicist whose primary targets are the signs and symbols of phallic potency.

83. "A Nameless, Ancient Crime," editorial from *The New York Times,* reprinted in *The International Herald Tribune,* 6 June 1982, 6.

84. Ibid., 6.

85. Laurence Marks, William Keegan, Michael Nally, and Kirsty White, "Our Short Hot Summer of Discontent," *The Observer,* 12 July 1981, 13.

86. The Angry Brigade, for one, complained that the press did not cover their campaign of bombing public figures and places: "The Press have reported nothing of all this—just as they never reported the bombings until it suited them. What are they scared of?" *The Angry Brigade 1967–1984: Documents and Chronology,* op. cit., 64.

On other occasions there seem to be too many acts to cover adequately, because they saturate the imagination. Thus, in early September 1986 at a time when terrorists had hijacked a Pan-Am jumbo jet in Karachi and shot up a synagogue in Istanbul, there occurred a host of other activities that were generally ignored. These included a bomb blast at the Paris City Hall, another bomb blast at the Cologne headquarters of the West German counterespionage agency, and a grenade attack in a Philippines church. "Terrorism: No Letup after Gory Weekend," *USA Today* (international edition), 9 September 1986, 1.

87. In fact, since the mid-1980s there has been a slow improvement in the subway system. Billions of dollars have been spent on graffiti-free trains. By 1986 the Transit Authority claimed that riders had a one-in-four chance of riding a new or rehabilitated car. As one conductor, Harry Nugent, put it, "After you hit bottom, there's no place to go but up." Michael Roddy, "N.Y. Glimpses Graffiti-Free Future," *The International Herald Tribune,* 15–16 November 1986, 1.

88. I refer to the graffiti as a whole, not specific instances that may or may not be exuberant and well executed. It is naive not to see that these figures exist to attack the system and intimidate the better-off. To call it an art form is a way of

appeasing the envious and of excusing psychic rape. For years graffiti-littered decrepit trains were associated with muggings, robberies, purse snatchings, and murder. Ibid., 1.

89. New York subway graffiti, 1987.

90. There is an alternative to bombs, logic bombs, and spray cans. I refer to men who "fuck the world" with envious erections. Indeed, the German legal system recognizes people who are willing to incur great expense to hurt a neighbor. The old Augsburg building code defines a malicious building as one that has little or no purpose in itself but causes loss of light and air to a neighbor. And Zinck's *Ökonomisches Lexikon* comments on buildings that exist solely to annoy or disadvantage others. Although it is hard to prove, it is easy to imagine a developer who would site a building to destroy a view, pollute the environment, or damage the structure of the society in which he lived. The payoff is omnipotence, unstoppable revenge, and the unshaken belief that there is no one or nothing bigger than oneself. See: Helmut Schoeck, *Envy: A Theory of Social Behavior,* op. cit., 113.

91. Jules Henry, *Culture Against Man* (New York: Knopf, 1978). See also: *Pathways to Madness* (New York: Random House, 1971).

92. R. D. Laing, personal communication, 1966.

93. Bruno Bettelheim discusses this issue in some detail in his chapter on the rise of fascism in Nazi Germany, "Remarks on the Psychological Appeal of Totalitarianism," in *Surviving the Holocaust,* op. cit., 104–119.

94. The Angry Brigade, "Communiqué 7," op. cit., 27.

95. Editorial, White Panther party, Abbey Wood chapter, *Chapter?,* op. cit., 2.

96. Francis Bacon pointed this out while discussing envy: "But this is a sure rule, that if the envy upon the minister be great when the cause of it is small; or if the envy be general in a manner upon all the ministers of an estate, then the envy (though hidden) is truly upon the state itself." Francis Bacon, "Of Envy," *The Essays or Counsels, Civil and Moral,* op. cit., 61.

97. The sexual caricatures and caricature-making qualities of the State often represent projections of debasing attacks on the parental intercourse. In other words, individuals divert their own envious and jealous attacks from their parents and projectively identify them with and onto the State or a state institution. They then see this institution, or the whole of society, doing to them what they had wanted to do to their parents in the first place.

The effect of malicious projections is to deplete the envier or projecting person of much of his own internal energies and images. Invariably this leads to feelings of depletion, itself a further cause of angry attacks on a parent, institution, or government for being aggrandizing and exploitative at his expense.

98. Among various cartoons, the White Panther journal showed ridiculous pot-smoking pig police under the caption "A pig is a person who exploits for his own benefit. . . . A pig is a low-natured beast that has no regard for law, justice or the rights of the people; a creature that bites the hand that feeds it; a foul depraved traducer. . . . " White Panther party, Abbey Wood chapter, *Chapter?,* op. cit., 9.

The image of a tyrannical soldier with a gun forcing a naked man to lick his boots featured in Richard Livermore, "Notes for the Anarchy and Order Brigade," *Anarchy,* no. 38, 25.

99. Pete Mastin, 1985 Faction 12, *Black Flag,* no. 131, 29 April 1985.

100. The emotional context was the threat generated by the Vietnam War and the cultural upheaval that was taking place in American society as a whole. Each side appealed to the worst fears of the other.

See: David Mairowitz, *The Radical Soap Opera* (London: Penguin Books, 1976), 222–226. Mairowitz called the occasion, "the politics of gesture."

101. Peter Steinberger, "John Sinclair Is Free," *Big Fat Magazine,* June 1970, reprinted in *Chapter?,* op. cit., 35.

See also: David Mairowitz, *The Radical Soap Opera,* op. cit., 226–228.

102. Ibid., 5.
Sinclair emphasized that "we" have to make use of "every tool, every energy, and every medium we can get our collective hands on."

103. This was Sinclair's third offense. He was released in 1972 after three years in jail.

104. Throughout the 1950s and 1960s many youngsters suffered comparable punishments for infringements of drug laws and sexual mores, really for transgressing a moral code based on the denial of sensual impulses and hatred of those who took pleasure in them. For example, in some states people could be jailed for cohabiting, without being married, and in West Virginia they could be jailed for using sexually explicit words in public.

105. Pete Mastin, 1985 Faction 12, *Black Flag*, no. 131, 29 April 1985.

106. Catherine Bennett, "Poison Post," *The Mail on Sunday*, 23 May 1982, 19. Newswriters are not the only victims of hate mailers. All the media lie at risk. Bob Booth, head of correspondence at the BBC, says he handles five hundred thousand hate letters per year. When asked for reasons, psychologist Jane Firebank pointed out, "Behind the letters is often very bitter envy. The writers are frustrated—not necessarily sexually but in their lives and achievements—so they resent other people becoming famous." Ibid., 19.

107. Sinclair came to idealize the Black Panthers and modeled his revolutionary organization after them. Certainly he had links with underground groups such as the Weathermen. After his drug busts, he was indicted for bombing the Ann Arbor office of the CIA. As for M.C.5., he turned it into a mouthpiece for violent insurrectionary activities. Roger Lewis, *Outlaws of America* (London: Pelican Books, 1972), 100, 158–162. See also: David Mairowitz, *The Radical Soap Opera*, op. cit., 226–228.

108. The Oedipal son is a complex figure. In addition to being a potential murderer, he is also a shudder in the thoughts of a man who fears his flesh and blood will echo an ancient curse as well as the projected embodiment of paternal revenge. Similarly, the Laial father is not only an actual, but especially an imagined, usurper and despot, in combination with all the envy and jealousy these images evoke. By the same token, the Electral daughter confirms the murderous mother and vice versa.
Perhaps the saving grace, both for the family and the State, is the unspoken knowledge that the legendary Oedipus tried to preserve his parents, just as his mythic father tried to circumvent the curse.

Chapter 11

1. Eugène Raiga, *L'Envie* (Paris: Alcan, 1932), discussed by H. Schoeck, *Envy: A Theory of Social Behavior*, op. cit., 190.

2. "Over a period of sixty years, from roughly 1470 to 1530, the secular spirit of the age was exemplified in a succession of six popes—five Italians and a Spaniard, who carried it to an excess of venality, amorality, avarice, and spectacularly calamitous power politics. . . . Theirs was a folly of perversity, perhaps the most consequential in Western history, if measured by its result in centuries of ensuing hostility and fratricidal war." Barbara Tuchman, *The March of Folly: From Troy to Vietnam* (London: Abacus Books, 1984).

3. Niccolò Machiavelli (1469–1527), Florentine statesman and writer on government. Jean Bodin (1530–1596), French philosopher and jurist.

4. The concept of "personalismo" comes from the British political sociologist J. P. Nettl, "The State As a Conceptual Variable," and is quoted by Gabriel Ben-Dor, *State and Conflict in the Middle East: Emergence of the Postcolonial State* (New York: Praeger Publishers, 1983), 14.

5. Jean Jacques Rousseau (1712–1778), French political philosopher and writer.

6. The words "nation" and "state" are frequently used synonymously. Strictly speaking, "nation" refers to a community of people characterized by a common language and culture and often but not necessarily living within a specified territory. When this nation has agreed sovereign boundaries, it is a state.

According to Elie Kedourie, professor of politics at the University of London, a nation is a body of people who collectively constitute a political unit—indeed, any "body of people associating together, and deciding on a scheme for their own government, form a nation." Elie Kedourie, *Nationalism* (London: Hutchinson University Library, Hutchinson & Co. Ltd., 1966), 15.

The key word here is "body," which implies that a nation, like a person, has boundaries, feelings, wishes, a soul, and so forth related to the skin, the mind, the heart, and the like. Thus, if citizens direct elemental feelings toward their national body, then this body, "the body politic," can and does reflect, expand, and express the feelings of its citizens, irrational as well as rational, destructive as well as creative.

7. See Ernest Jones, "Psychopathology and International Tension," in *Psycho-Myth, Psycho-History*, vol. 1 (New York: Hillstone, 1974), 301–2.

8. Elias Canetti, *Crowds and Power*, op. cit., 15–16.

9. Concurrently, nationalist self-seeking disguises individual inferiority. This goal is consistent with Canetti's description of two other crowd features: growth and direction seeking (common goals).

10. See: discussion by Nettl, quoted by Gabriel Ben-Dor, *State and Conflict in the Middle East: Emergence of the Postcolonial State*, op. cit., 4–5.

11. Max Montgelas and Walter Schücking, eds. *Outbreak of the World War: German Documents Collected by Karl Kautsky* (Oxford: Oxford University Press, 1924), 63, 161, 266, and 307, quoted by Lloyd DeMause, ed., *The New Psycho-history*, op. cit., 14.

DeMause points out that the German epithets cover many levels of psychic conflict, oral, anal, phallic, and Oedipal. When projectively identified with Serbia, these features were useful both in assuming a position of moral superiority and in justifying hostilities.

12. I am aware that my brief discussion hardly does justice to the complexity of stateness and, in particular, the intrasocietal (nationness, self-definition, institutional viability) dimensions as opposed to the extrasocietal ones. However, this one area of stateness, supranational relations, is especially useful for the purpose of illustrating the ultimate expression of (and detachments from) powerful emotional currents, often expressed in modern times via nationalism and charismatic leaders.

In all places, citizens can and do use the State to "lose" their individual hopes and sorrows. Then, as frequently happens, a further degree of detachment takes place. The State loses these feelings by attributing them to other states and engaging in a variety of alliances or conflicts in order to justify the loss. Conversely, people may be given (or retrieve) self-esteem through their country's extrasocietal relations. For example, for many postcolonial states the preferred way to gain status (which may or may not be passed down to the populace) is by establishing a presence at the United Nations or other international organizations. See: Gabriel Ben-Dor, *State and Conflict in the Middle East: Emergence of the Postcolonial State*, op. cit., 1–34.

13. Daniel Moynihan, "The United States in Opposition," *Commentary*, vol. 59, no. 3, March 1975, 37.

14. Barbara Tuchman, for example, has given a detailed description of the Renaissance Church (Saint Peter's See transformed into "the supreme pork barrel"), whose avaricious internal and external policies led to a devastating series of intra- and extra-European wars. Barbara Tuchman, *The March of Folly*, op. cit., 144–154.

15. The actions of Stalinist Russia and Maoist China were formal attacks by one part of the State against another part of itself. Hence the State can act like

humans to greedily or enviously attack internal as well as external targets. See: Robert Conquest, *The Harvest of Sorrow* (London: Hutchinson & Co., 1986).

16. Mel Brooks, *To Be or Not to Be*, 1984. Directed by Alan Johnson. The film itself was a remake of an Ernst Lubitsch classic.

17. On 16 October 1973, OPEC (Organization of Petroleum Exporting Countries) cut production and raised the oil price by 70 percent. On 23 December they raised the price again, and within one year it had been increased by four times. According to Henry Kissinger, this "was one of the pivotal events in the history of this century." Quoted by Paul Johnson, *A History of the Modern World: From 1917 to the 1980s*, op. cit., 669.

Interestingly, an analysis by *The Economist* subsequently showed that greed is not an effective economic policy. In six years of massive price increases from 1973 the OPEC countries accumulated $1.3 trillion. But if they had not acted so precipitously, and extortionately, they could have achieved the same profits while maintaining a better price and a larger share of the market. Charles Krauthammer, "OPEC Is Dead, But There's No Need For Mourning," *The International Herald Tribune*, 21–22 December 1985, 4.

Aside from oil, the greedy aggrandizement of gold and silver from Latin America by Spain or minerals from the Congo by Belgium also did not confer unambiguous economic benefits. J. M. Roberts, *The Hutchinson History of the World*, op. cit., 668 and 847.

18. Much of the angry, guilt-ridden opprobrium was self-inflicted, both before and after the war. Thus a student group at Cambridge (England) published a pamphlet that declaimed, "We took the rubber from Malaya, the tea from India, raw materials from all over the world, and gave almost nothing in return." Quoted by Luis Burstin, "A Few Home Truths About Latin America," *Commentary*, vol. 79, no. 2, February 1985, 49.

In fact, the reverse was true. The British took rubber to Malaya from Brazil and tea to India from China, greatly invigorating the economies of both countries. As often happened, the students used past colonial (external) policies to fight immediate interpersonal (internal) issues.

19. Paraphrased by Luis Burstin, ibid., 47.

Among many critics of the United States, Burstin quotes the left-wing Mexican writer Carlos Fuentes, who blames the United States government and corporations for Latin "turmoil, instability, terrorism, hunger, and weakness." Burstin, a former Costa Rican journalist and secretary of information, comments that these ills existed long before "Yankee imperialism" became an issue. However, he also points out that the one premise that can unite "well-meaning American leftists, independent anti-imperialistic Latin American intellectuals and politicians, and hard-core Marxist-Leninists" is that the United States is responsible for the hunger, instability, and brutality in the region. Ibid., 48.

20. United Nations World Population Conference, Stockholm, 1974. Quoted by Daniel Moynihan, "The United States in Opposition," op. cit., 37.

21. Professor Dumont contributed to the Population Tribune, an unofficial, parallel conference in Stockholm. His report, "Population and Cannibals," subsequently received front-page coverage in *Development Forum*, an official UN publication. Dumont blamed the West for being "Plunderers of the Third World." He stated: "Eating little children. I have already had occasion to show that the rich white man, with his overconsumption of meat and his lack of generosity toward poor populations, acts like a true cannibal, albeit indirect. Last year, in overconsuming meat which wasted the cereals which could have saved them, we ate the little children of the Sahel, of Ethiopia, and of Bangladesh. And this year, we are continuing to do the same thing, with the same appetite." Ibid., 37–38.

22. China, for example, has the strictest of all population-control programs. Yet the Chinese delegation furiously assailed the very idea of population control as

"fundamentally subversive to the future of the Third World." The Chinese insisted that population control was the means by which "hegemonists" and "imperialists" sought to spoil the future of mankind. Consumerism, not population, was the true source of the world's problems. Ibid., 37.

23. I refer to the United Nations Conference on the Human Environment held in Stockholm in 1972. Ibid., 36.

24. Ibid., 39.

The Fabian Society is an organization of English socialists established in 1884, which aims to bring about socialism by gradual reforms rather than revolutionary action. The complement, of course, of this language is that of the Marxist-Leninists, whose words demonstrate a more extreme form of abuse but are still continuous with the rhetoric of resentment.

25. It has been noted that the London School of Economics is "the most important institution of higher education in Asia and Africa." Ibid., 33.

26. Beatrice Webb wrote in her autobiography: "My husband and I felt assured that with the School [LSE] as the teaching body, the Fabian Society as a propagandist organization, the LCC [London County Council] as object lesson in electoral success, our books as the only original work in economic fact and theory, no young man or woman who is anxious to study or work in public affairs can fail *to come under our influence*." (My Italics.) Quoted by Daniel Moynihan, ibid., 33.

The influence of people like the Webbs serves as confirmatory evidence for the thesis of this chapter. It may eventually surface many times removed as seemingly autonomous resentments between nations, often passionately presented at the United Nations.

27. To cite one of innumerable examples of such justifications, the speaker of the Iranian parliament, Hashemi Rafsanjani, asserted (during an early 1987 hostage-taking crisis) that the Lebanese were justified to take hostages and commit other acts of terror because they were "so ignored and so oppressed" by the United States. In this instance Rafsanjani identifies his country, Iran, with Lebanon in the struggle against "the great Satan," the United States. Anthony Lewis, "Embracing the Disaster, Entrenching the Follies," *International Herald Tribune*, 6 February 1987, 4.

28. DeMause quotes from Kaiser Wilhelm, for example, who prior to World War I referred to the monarchy as being "seized by throat" and "strangled." As regards Germany, the Kaiser asserted England had suddenly thrown a net "over our head, and . . . we squirm isolated in the net." These comments were made at a time when England was friendly toward Germany. But the Kaiser, on behalf of many people, including himself, felt that way (and acted accordingly). That was his reality, in the same way that other commentators prior to war have described their nations as "unable to draw a breath of relief," "unable to see the light at the end of the tunnel," moving with "naked force," into "the descent into the abyss." Lloyd DeMause, ed., *The New Psychohistory*, op. cit., 16–22.

DeMause can be criticized for taking metaphorical imagery too literally, although he asserts that his conclusions are backed up by a plethora of material taken from the intentional comments and unintended asides of leaders and other national prime movers.

29. Henry Steele Commager and Richard B. Morris, eds., *The Spirit of Seventy-Six*, vol. 1 (New York: Bobbs-Merrill Co., 1970), 294, quoted by Lloyd DeMause, ibid., 20.

30. Kedourie points out that nationalism is essentially related to the idea of self-determination. Self-determination (economic, military, political autonomy) then tends to be seen as the highest moral and political goal. Elie Kedourie, *Nationalism*, op. cit., 32, 62–91.

31. Tuchman has described the attitude of the British government toward its American colony prior to the Revolution: "They were not interested in the Americans because they considered them rabble or at best children whom it was inconceivable

to treat—or even fight—as equals." Barbara Tuchman, *The March of Folly,* op. cit., 286.

32. In the late twentieth century Egypt, Libya, and Syria have all acted like vandals, although the phenomenon is by no means limited to Arab states. Nasser was particularly successful in mobilizing the internal antagonisms of the Egyptian and Arab masses and redirecting them outward toward their former colonial masters. As the British political scientist P. J. Vatikiotis points out, Nasser was very skillful "in evoking hazy pictures of past oppression and bitterness." For example, after Suez, but essentially repeated in many other contexts, Nasser exclaimed: "We shall not submit to anyone's influence or authority." And, "It was only when we succeeded in giving Egypt back to all the Egyptians that we were able to achieve this victory and rout the great powers." P. J. Vatikiotis, *Nasser and His Generation* (London: Croom Helm, 1978), 276.

Nasser was also the hero and model for Colonel Qaddafi, who, in the eyes of many Western powers, turned Libya into a "rogue state." See: David Blundy and Andrew Lycett, *Qaddafi and the Libyan Revolution* (London: Weidenfeld and Nicolson, 1987).

33. Aleksandr Solzhenitsyn is the Russian writer whom the USSR allowed to leave and live in exile in the United States. The speech was made at an A.F.L.-C.I.O. dinner in June 1975 to an audience of distinguished trade unionists and politicians. Given Solzhenitsyn's personality, it is unlikely he simply made these comments to ingratiate himself with his American hosts. Quoted by Daniel Moynihan, *A Dangerous Place* (London: Secker & Warburg, 1979), 76.

34. During the 1970s Tanzania received more aid from Western Europe, Canada, and the United States than any other African country (about £1.5 billion), with little effect. Throughout this period the country was led by Julius Nyerere, a doctrinaire socialist and Pan-African nationalist who had a seminal influence on the economic policies that misused the resources received. At the same time Nyerere gained international respect by attacking the West for colonialism, imperialism, materialism, and so forth.

Under the regimes of Sadat and Mubarak, Egypt became the largest beneficiary of American economic and military aid other than Israel. Yet the Egyptian press regularly denies the value of the support and denounces it for being "disguised intelligence-gathering," aside from other alleged noxious influences. Stanley Reed, "U.S. Aid to Egypt Is a Double-Edged Investment," *International Herald Tribune,* 4 March 1985, 4.

35. Helmut Schoeck points out that the relationship between Western donors and hostile Third World countries in the period 1955–1965 provides experimental proof of Kant's dictum that a display of ingratitude does not necessarily bring about a decrease in benefaction. On the contrary, the benefactor "may well be convinced that the very disdain of any such reward as gratitude only adds to the inner worth of his benefaction." Quoted by Helmut Schoeck, *Envy: A Theory of Social Behavior,* op. cit., 168–169.

On the other hand, the patronizing, paternalistic, exploitative, haughty attitudes and actions of the developed countries often conjure forth and amplify the rageful reactions of the developing nations, just as narcissistic parenting calls forth an envious child.

36. It is remarkable how closely the Handelsman cartoon character reproduced in chapter 2 resembles the characteristic responses of certain nations, especially in relation to the United States.

This ingratitude must be contrasted with the unstinting thanks other countries gave for the aid that enabled them to recover from the war.

37. Tim Jones, "Stewed Tea at Cliveden," *The Times,* 20 October 1986, 3.

Hilary Rubinstein, who is editor of *The Good Hotel Guide, 1987,* reports: "There is a growing fashion to denigrate Americans, behaviour as distasteful as antisemitism or mindless prejudice against women or blacks or gays. My correspondence files bear witness to all these forms of bias, but the habit of rubbishing Americans . . . almost always [stems] from envy." Hilary Rubinstein, "Un-American Activities Keeping Tourists Away," *The Independent,* 16 October 1986, 17.

38. Quoted by Rubinstein, ibid., 17.

39. One can readily perceive the jealous rivalry between small states seeking to enjoy special relations with larger ones or between superpowers for the support of smaller states. All this may be manifested through the creation and breaking up of alliances, along with the angry recriminations about who is in and who is out.

Eugène Raiga predicted that the setting up of socialist governments devoted to mutual aid would not inhibit these envious and jealous rivalries. As Helmut Schoeck points out, this has been amply proven. Satellites of the Eastern bloc jealously guard their privileges, while other nations vigorously compete for development aid from the United States and Europe. Eugène Raiga, *L'Envie* (Paris: Alcan, 1932), 233, 236, discussed by Helmut Schoeck, *Envy: A Theory of Social Behavior,* op. cit., 190.

40. There is always a price to be paid, whether it is obvious or not. During a trip to six African countries in 1987, United States Secretary of State George Shultz reflected on the strategic, economic, ideological, and altruistic factors that determined American aid. The latter was much less important than the practical as well as narcissistic wish for developing countries to remake their economies in the American image. Similarly, the Soviet Union always urges recipient countries to adopt a socialist system. David Shipler, "Shultz's Goals in Africa: Building Markets, Cutting Soviet Influence Were Among Priorities," *International Herald Tribune,* 19 January 1987, 2.

Aside from direct envy, the exuberant "free enterprise" wounded Scottish pride—that is, their self-image was threatened by American self-interest. Other dynamic countries, especially Japan and West Germany, face similar hostilities: "Among executives and intellectuals from Paris to Beijing, the Japanese have replaced the West Germans and even the 'ugly Americans' in being viewed as selfish economic animals." And "Prime Minister Mahathir bin Mohamad of Malaysia, once markedly pro-Japanese, has announced that Asians are no longer willing to be 'hewers of wood and drawers of water' for Japan." Joel Kotkin and Yoriko Kishimoto, "World Superstar Japan May Be Poised for Long Economic Descent," *International Herald Tribune,* 25 June 1986, 5.

41. Low's cartoon was published in J. M. Roberts, *The Hutchinson History of the World,* op. cit., 1077.

42. Jonathan Mirsky, "The Western Flower That May Not Bloom," *The Times,* 20 January 1987, 14.

43. Daniel Southerland, "Door Still Open, Deng Declares," *International Herald Tribune,* 21 January 1987, 1.

44. Jonathan Mirsky, "The Western Flower That May Not Bloom," op. cit., 14.

Mirsky points out the extreme extent that Chinese leaders see Western ideas as "sugar-coated bullets," yet another example of the projective identification of envy with ideas and the consequent transformation of these ideas into dangerous entities.

Since the nineteenth century the Chinese have tried to distinguish between "Western learning for practical matters" *(xixue wei yong)* and "Chinese learning for the fundamentals" *(zhongxue wei ti).* The distinction is an attempt to avoid the severe loss of pride, threatened loss of national identity, and consequent narcissistic rage that follows whenever their sense of superiority is called into question.

45. *L'Observateur,* 14 August 1952, quoted by Hugh Thomas, *An Unfinished History of the World,* op. cit., 722–723.

46. Quoted by Richard Bernstein, "Washington and the UN: What Went Wrong?" *International Herald Tribune,* 1 February 1984, 6.

47. The curse, of course, relates to the excessive desires of older powers toward emergent nations. The attendant breaking of bounds can and does evoke frenzies of envy and jealousy.

48. Not infrequently, officials articulate the obvious. If they weren't so serious, I would think that military and industrial officials used these terms tongue in cheek. Quoted by Helen Caldicott, *Missile Envy*, op. cit., 297.

49. Ibid., 297.

50. The Olympic Games are at least 3,500 years old. The first games of the modern era began in Athens in 1896. Although ideally contests between individuals, not countries, the games have been increasingly marred by severe nationalistic disputes. This is not a new phenomenon. Past games often got out of hand, with results not unlike the pitched battles that can erupt at present-day international football matches. At Constantinople the rivalries between the blues and greens led to civil war and the death of thousands, a situation Edward Gibbon called the "blue livery of disorder." Hugh Thomas, *An Unfinished History of the World*, op. cit., 614–617.

51. Distraught at signs of weakness, France saw herself as the fighting cock of Europe, an evident illusion. She blamed the German people for her inability to occupy a dominant role as from the times of Louis XIV to Napoleon I. Paul Johnson, *A History of the Modern World: From 1917 to the 1980s*, op. cit., 140.

52. In 1915 Bérillon's diagnoses were polychesia and bromidrosis (excessive defecation and body smells). Ibid., 145.

53. Ibid., 142.

54. Ibid., 142.

55. For several centuries the march of Western—in other words, European—ideas and values seemed unstoppable. J. M. Roberts, *The Hutchinson History of the World*, op. cit., 812–814.

56. The British found it inconceivable to treat or fight the American colonials as equals. Thus, in all their military dispatches they never once referred to the American commander in chief, George Washington, as "General" but only as "Mister." Barbara Tuchman, *The March of Folly*, op. cit., 286.

57. Quoted by Barbara Tuchman, ibid., 287.

Tuchman subsequently points out that two centuries later the Americans were afflicted by the same "disease" in relation to the Vietnamese.

58. Moreover, foreigners are frequently portrayed as goons, thugs, and rapists, all victimizing innocent Japanese. Andrew Horvat, "The 'Little Japan' Mentality," *The Independent*, 29 December 1986, 10.

As if to demonstrate that "there is nothing new under the sun," Nigerians hold similar views about their black neighbors as do Argentines toward other Latin Americans. See: Karan Thapar, "Nigeria: So Much Money and So Many Problems," *The Times*, 16 March 1981, 12; also: Miguel Acoca, "A Critical View of Argentina: Ethnic Pride Takes a Fall," *International Herald Tribune*, 16 June 1982, 4.

59. J. M. Roberts, *The Hutchinson History of the World*, op. cit., 839–840.

60. The Indian rebellions of 1857 (the "Indian Mutiny") dealt a devastating blow to the confidence of British leadership as well as that of ordinary soldiers and civil servants. The former were once again trapped by pride and vanity into seeing neither the hatred aroused by their policies (however innovative) nor the strength of the opposition. This blindness paralleled their obtuseness to the sufferings of the lower classes at home. On the other hand, the latter could hardly maintain their own inflated status in the face of the fighting skills of the Indians. During the postcolonial period, both sides have begun to parody their previous positions. Anti-imperialist politicians have attributed superiority to everything previously considered reprehensible, such as blacks or homosexuals, while Indian immigrants have become the last refuge of nineteenth-century British culture and imperial snobbery.

61. The division of society into a multiplicity of classes or castes with equally

large gradations of inferiority and superiority can be traced to ancient Egypt, Rome, and many other societies. Hugh Thomas argues against the alleged existence of three fundamental classes as postulated by Karl Marx, Matthew Arnold, and others. Hugh Thomas, *An Unfinished History of the World,* op. cit., 696–705.

Often classes or castes seem to be created by real or potential members for purposes of self-aggrandizement. According to Nietzsche, Christianity is based on the resentment of the weak toward the strong, the haves versus the have-nots. Nietzsche argued that the idea "the meek shall inherit the earth" simply serves to elevate sickness and poverty into virtues and to allow the drowntrodden to tread on their masters. Thomas makes the same point in terms of the concept of "the proletariat." Ibid., 700–701.

62. Conor Cruise O'Brien, *The Siege: The Saga of Israel and Zionism* (New York: Simon and Schuster, 1986), 335–336.

63. "Dhimmi" status for Jews and Christians in Muslim lands was generally preferable to the nonstatus (and consequent persecution) of Jews and Muslims in Christian lands. Ibid., 336.

In theory all Muslims could abuse dhimmis; in practice this varied from land to land and time to time. Dhimmis could and did seek Muslim patrons to protect them from other Muslims. However, all Jews and Christians were obliged to respect Muslims, while Muslims were in no way obliged to respect them.

The Arabs saw the end of dhimmi status as the Ottoman reaction to growing European power and prestige. For them it marked the unwelcome encroachment of Jews and Christians on their way of life. The placid contempt that had previously marked the Muslim side of dhimmi turned into sullen resentment. From the mid-nineteenth century onward Muslim intellectuals began to speak out. For instance, the Egyptian historian al-Jabarti was appalled that "contrary to ancient custom, [non-Muslims] wear fine clothes and bear arms, wield authority over Muslims and generally behave in a way which inverts the order of things established by divine law." Bernard Lewis, "L'Islam et les Non-Musulmans," *Annales: Economies, Sociétés, Civilisations,* 3, 4 (Mai, Aout 1980), quoted by Conor Cruise O'Brien, ibid., 339.

64. According to an American intelligence agent operating in Iraq during the mid-1940s: "Most Jews, in the Arab mind, are miserable, cowardly and unclean. So the idea of a portion of the Arab world being governed by Jews is intolerable. Palestine, therefore, has become more than a remote political problem, it is now a question of personal religion and honour." OSS Report of February 3, 1945; quoted in Luks, "Iraqi Jews during World War II," in *Weiner Library Bulletin,* no. 30 (43/44), 1977; quoted by Conor Cruise O'Brien, ibid., 340.

65. Ye'or, "Aspects of the Arab-Israel Conflict," in *Weiner Library Bulletin,* no. 32 (49/50), 1979; quoted by Conor Cruise O'Brien, ibid., 340.

66. Gamal Abdel Nasser, 1918–1970. I refer to the situation during the 1950s and 1960s. Subsequently Nasser's role as the scourge of Western interests was taken over by the Iranian leader Ayatollah Khomeini. However, as far as the Arabs were concerned, the ayatollah was a mixed blessing, for he was leader of the Shiite Muslims, who as underdogs were themselves in conflict with the predominant Sunnite sect.

67. Vatikiotis points out that Nasser fused personal with national humiliation and projected both onto the international stage. He developed a highly personal, charismatic style of leadership, a "modern pharaonism" through which he sought a perfect rapport with the Egyptian, thence Arab, masses. By means of the leadership principle, Egyptian, thence Arab, nationalism became equivalent to Nasserism and vice versa.

The prominent writer Tawfiq al-Hakim described the relationship between Nasser and Egypt as that of a man who "had become the idol, the worshipped, of the people. . . . They became a collection of waving arms and applauding hands, and cheering mouths. And the Chief in his dominating presence, towering over them from his podium, spoke alone for long hours, interrupted only by the hysterical cries: 'Nasser, Nasser, Nasser.' "

Al-Hakim's descriptions of Nasser delineate the transformation of personal inflation to national narcissism: "He overwhelmed us with his magic . . . and the hopes, dreams and promises which underlay the victories of the revolution which he repeatedly announced to us . . . with their pipes and drums, anthems, songs and films, which made us see ourselves as a great industrial state, leaders of the developing world . . . and the strongest military power in the Middle East." Tawfiq al-Hakim, *Awdat al-w'ai* (Beirut: 1974), quoted by P. J. Vatikiotis, *Nasser and His Generation,* op. cit., 291, 320.

68. Hussein Sabri observed: "He pushed Egypt ahead, but soon let his fantasy take over, leading to the disaster of 5 June 1967. . . . Suez was the turning point. It led him to believe that revolutionary Egypt vanquished imperialism and that had it not been for Nasser this would not have happened. Victory was his victory, protected by Providence. Everyone forgot Egypt was not victorious in 1956!" Hussein Dhu'l-Fiqar Sabri, in *Rose el-Youssef,* 18 July 1975; quoted by P. J. Vatikiotis, ibid., 290.

69. Chauvinism or jingoism represents the merger and submergence of ordinary nationalism (equivalent to a positive or libidinal narcissism) with and by destructive nationalism (equivalent to negative or antilibidinal narcissism). The former was named after the alleged Nicolas Chauvin, a soldier of Napoleon I, famous for his bellicose attachment to lost imperial causes, and the latter follows the refrain of an aggressive Victorian music hall song:

We don't want to fight, but, by Jingo if we do,
We've got the ships, we've got the men,
    We've got the money too.

G. W. Hunt, "We Don't Want to Fight," 1878.

70. Kedourie has succinctly described the death-loving propensities of nationalism: "Nationalism looks inwardly, away from and beyond the imperfect world. And this contempt of things as they are, of the world as it is, ultimately becomes a rejection of life, and a love of death." Elie Kedourie, *Nationalism,* op. cit., 87.

71. P. J. Vatikiotis, *Nasser and His Generation,* op. cit., 270.

72. Immanuel Kant, quoted by Hugh Thomas, *An Unfinished History of the World,* op. cit., 645.

73. "Das Deutsche Vaterland" was one of Germany's most popular patriotic songs. It was written by the poet Ernst Moritz Arndt (1769–1860) and appealed to the expansionist voice of German nationalism:

What is the German Fatherland?
The Prussian, or the Swabian kind?
Where Rhenish grapes bloom ripe and full,
Where curves his flight the Baltic gull?
Ah, no! No! No!
His Fatherland must greater grow!

Quoted by Robert Waite, *The Psychopathic God: Adolf Hitler* (New York: Basic Books, 1977), 259–260.

74. Adam Müller quoted by Robert Waite, ibid., 287.

75. Johann Gottlieb Fichte (1762–1814), nationalist philosopher, wrote *Addresses to the German Nation* in the period 1807–08. Quoted by Robert Waite, ibid., 261.

76. Prince Otto von Bismarck (1815–1898), called the Iron Chancellor, was the Prussian chancellor of the German empire, 1871–1890.

77. Thus, in 1900 Kaiser Wilhelm wrote: "You should give the name of Germany such cause to be remembered in China for a thousand years, so that no Chinaman, no matter whether his eyes be slit or not, will dare to look a German in the face." Quoted by Hugh Thomas, *An Unfinished History of the World*, op. cit., 670.

78. "France is and will remain by far the most dangerous enemy. The French people, who are becoming more and more obsessed by negroid ideas, represent a threatening menace to the existence of the white race in Europe, because they are bound up with the Jewish campaign for world-domination." Adolf Hitler, *Mein Kampf*, translated by James Murphy (London: Hurst and Blackett Ltd., 1930), 508.

79. In the period prior to World War I, Germany was still preoccupied with being liked. "In a series of crises, she showed that she wanted to frighten other nations with her displeasure and make herself esteemed." J. M. Roberts, *The Hutchinson History of the World*, op. cit., 910.

80. Victoria was queen of Great Britain and Ireland from 1837 to 1901. Her prince consort was Albert from Saxe-Coburg-Gotha. Their first- and second-generation descendants either ruled or married the rulers of Germany (as a whole as well as Hesse, Schleswig-Holstein, and Battenburg) and Russia, Norway, Denmark, and Greece. See: end plate family tree from Kenneth Rose, *King George V* (London: Weidenfeld & Nicolson, 1983).

These sibling rivalries may have exacerbated colonial rivalries, but the latter were not of primary significance in and of themselves. "The issue was not really one of colonial rivalry, but of whether Germany could bully France without fear of her being supported by others. Quarrels over non-European affairs before 1914 seem in fact to have been a positive distraction from the more dangerous rivalries of Europe itself; they may even have helped to preserve the peace." J. M. Roberts, *The Hutchinson History of the World*, op. cit., 843.

81. James Murphy, in his introduction to *Mein Kampf*, points out that the concept of *volk* had an almost mythical meaning for Germans. Much more than "people" or "citizens," it was a primary word that conveyed a sense of the basic national stock without regard to caste or class. "Now, after the defeat of 1918, the downfall of the Monarchy and the destruction of the aristocracy and the upper classes, the concept of *das volk* came into prominence as the unifying coefficient which would embrace the whole German people." James Murphy, "Translator's Introduction," *Mein Kampf*, op. cit., 13.

82. Roberts explains that the harshest terms were not connected with moral guilt, but derived from the French desire to tie Germany down so it couldn't start another war. J. M. Roberts, *The Hutchinson History of the World*, op. cit., 921.

He might have added that the reparations confirmed a triumphant French nationalism that aroused the Germans to new peaks of fury.

83. Paul Johnson, *A History of the Modern World: From 1917 to the 1980s*, op. cit., 106.

84. The Germans were outraged because they were forced to hand over entire German communities to the "barbarous Slavs." This overlooked the fact that only a short time before, Ludendorff had occupied the Ukraine and laid the basis for the whole area to become a German satellite colony. They thought they had been swindled, although the Silesian plebiscite had been an important concession secured for Germany by the British Lloyd George. All this was never explained by their government. Paul Johnson, ibid., 105–106.

The German hatred of Slav rule was surely related to a collective denial of their Slav origins. Hugh Thomas points out that far from being racially pure, the German people, most particularly the Prussians, who were half Slav, had registered themselves as a Slav monarchy at the Congress of Vienna. Hugh Thomas, *An Unfinished History of the World*, op. cit., 666.

85. Generations of Germans glorified war and death. The "Schoolmaster of Germany," Heinrich von Treitschke, whose views complemented the pedagogy of Father Daniel Schreber, instilled the idea that peace is "immoral," and that "human reason" can only triumph through battle. "The army, not Parliament, is the most valuable institution of the State." Quoted by Robert Waite, ibid., 289.

The historian Heinrich von Treitschke (1834–1896) was unmatched in popularity and influence. His *History of Germany* was so widely used that it was often called the *Deutsche Geschichte* without the author being named. Treitschke proclaimed that Prussia and "North German stock" had won the right to create a new and militarily powerful Germany. In describing the victory over Napoleon, he did not hesitate to glorify the gore: "What a wonderful sight it was when the peasants rushed upon the compact square of the French infantry at Hagelberg, advancing silently, pitilessly, in unspeakable wrath; when the dull cracking of the musketry ceased, there lay a horrible heap of corpses piled up to the level of the top of the wall, with the brains oozing out of the smashed skulls of the dead." *Treitschke's History of Germany in the Nineteenth Century,* 7 vols., translated by Eden and Cedar Paul (London, 1915); vol. 1, 508–511. Quoted by Robert Waite, *The Psychopathic God: Adolf Hitler,* op. cit., 258–59.

Almost prophetically, the German emperor William II emphasized that the struggle was internal as much as external: "First shoot down, behead, and eliminate the Socialists, if necessary by a bloodbath, then go on to a foreign war. But not before, and only at the proper time."

The emperor expressed these sentiments to Chancellor Bülow at Christmas 1905. Quoted in Fritz Fischer, *World Power or Decline: The Controversy Over Germany's Aims in the First World War,* translated by L. L. Farrar (New York: W. W. Norton & Co., 1974), 8, and requoted by Robert Waite, *The Psychopathic God: Adolf Hitler,* op. cit., 290.

86. The work of Heinrich von Kleist (1777–1810), and especially *Michael Kohlhaas,* symbolizes Germany and illustrates the rage that follows a narcissistic injury. Heinz Kohut, "Thoughts of Narcissism and Narcissistic Rage," op. cit., 360–362.

87. Children of the Volksschulen were required to memorize this poem during the period 1900–1914. Quoted by Robert Waite, *The Psychopathic God: Adolf Hitler,* op. cit., 260.

88. Joseph Paul Goebbels (1897–1945) was later to become the Nazi propaganda minister. An early diary entry recalls: "He is like a child, kind, good, merciful. Like a cat: cunning, clever, agile. Like a lion: roaring, great and gigantic. A great guy, a man! *(Ein Kerl, ein Mann!)*" Quoted by Robert Waite, ibid., 3.

89. David Lloyd George (1863–1945) was prime minister from 1916 to 1922. His remarks were published in an article in the (London) *Daily Express* on 7 November 1930. Quoted by Robert Waite, ibid., 4.

90. Hitler saw himself as a new Barbarossa—Frederick I (1123?–1190), king of Germany and Emperor of the Holy Roman Empire (1115–1190)—a powerful leader who would rescue a tortured and divided country and establish a mighty reich. He also strongly indentified with Frederick the Great, whose picture he used to display along with his own.

Hitler's view of the *führerprinzip* was simple: "Nothing happens in this Movement, except what I wish"—in other words, absolute dictatorship, total control of everything. Quoted by Robert Waite, ibid., 4, 79.

91. See discussions of the Youth Cohort and the Free Corps: Robert Waite, ibid., 335–343 and 312–314.

92. Conversation with Harold Nicolson, in *Diaries and Letters: The War Years 1939–1945,* 3 vols. (New York: 1967), vol. 2, 39; quoted by Robert Waite, *The Psychopathic God: Adolf Hitler,* op. cit., 330.

In *Mein Kampf* Hitler proclaimed that hate was much more powerful than love, and that "wrathful hatred" was the most valuable of all political qualities.

Joseph Goebbels recorded what he considered to be one of Hitler's best epigrams in his diary: "For our struggle, God gave us His abundant blessing. His most beautiful gift was the hate of our enemies, whom we too hate with all our heart." Joseph Goebbels, *The Early Goebbels Diaries: 1925–1926,* Helmut Heiber, ed., translated by Oliver Watson (New York: 1963), 91, quoted by Robert Waite, ibid., 330.

93. It would be wrong to conclude that these thrusts were justified by past hurts. That view was part of the big lie that Hitler used in order to release guilt-free aggression and amplify the scope of his policies. For most Germans the lie worked. It camouflaged their inherent as well as acquired cruelties. The full truth did not begin to emerge until after World War II, and especially after 1961, when historian Fritz Fischer published the seminal *Griff nach der Weltmacht* (translated as *Germany's Aims in the First World War*). His study documents the continuous aggressive, expansionist intentions that have underpinned Germany's foreign relations since the time of Bismarck.

Fritz Fischer, *Griff nach der Weltmacht* (Germany's Aims in the First World War) (New York: W. W. Norton & Co., 1967). The intentions had to do with dominating Europe and diminishing internal social tensions by war. See: discussion by Paul Johnson, *A History of the Modern World: From 1917 to the 1980s,* op. cit., 106–107.

94. In a host of public and private speeches, Hitler emphasized, "When nations are in need, they do not ask about legal rights. . . . We National Socialists must cling unflinchingly to our foreign policy aims, that is, to guarantee the German nation the soil and territory to which it is entitled on this earth. . . . For centuries the cry of our forefathers has rung out: Give us space!" Quoted from *Mein Kampf* and *Völkischer Beobachter,* by Robert Waite, *The Psychopathic God: Adolf Hitler,* op. cit., 78–79.

Hugh Thomas points out that the need for land was an illusion. The German population, like others in Europe, had ceased to grow, especially because huge numbers of people had previously emigrated to the United States. Hugh Thomas, *An Unfinished History of the World,* op. cit., 71.

It wasn't a question of numbers or space, rather of hunger and greed, derived from, among various factors, the horrors of the depression and Hitler's own oral-sadistic impulses.

95. Hitler was quite clear what would happen to the "the ridiculous hundred million Slavs." They would be transferred to "pig-pens" without "hygiene cleanliness." If not killed off, they would essentially serve as slave drones for their German masters, who would live in "marvelous buildings and handsome farms." Quoted by Waite, ibid., 79.

In the eighteenth and nineteenth centuries the British policy of transportation anticipated future mass purification programs, related to the wish to create a national "mother/fatherland" devoid of bad foreign elements. Transportation involved shipping large numbers of "the criminal class" to Australia, at that time a primitive and inhospitable backwater. Either during the passage or afterward, many of the transportees died from disease, neglect, or direct physical abuse. All this has been documented by Robert Hughes, in *The Fatal Shore: A History of the Transportation of Convicts to Australia, 1787–1868* (London: Collins Harvill, 1987).

According to Jeremy Bentham, "The subject-matter of [the] experiment was, in this case, a particularly commodious one; a set of 'animae viles,' a sort of excrementitious mass, that could be projected, and accordingly was projected—projected, and as it should seem purposely—as far out of sight as possible." Quoted by Robert Hughes, ibid., 2.

96. My discussion is based on the extensive research of the American historian Rudolph Binion. In particular I refer to his paper "Hitler's Concept of *Lebensraum:* The Psychological Basis." This was originally delivered at the American Historical

Association meeting in New Orleans on December 28, 1972, and was published in the *History of Childhood Quarterly*, vol. 1, no. 2, fall 1973, 187–215.

97. August Kubizek, *Adolf Hitler, mein Jugendfreund* (Graz: 1953), 50, quoted by Rudolph Binion, ibid., 192.

98. Rudolph Binion points out that Hitler was not an overt anti-Semite until after World War I. Despite his own account in *Mein Kampf,* Hitler's deadly hatred of Jews can be dated quite precisely, to the period October–November 1918, when he was hospitalized for mustard gas poisoning and suffered a breakdown. See: discussion, ibid., 189–190.

For the rest of his life, Hitler was terrified by cancer and anything to do with cancer, including crayfish, lobsters, and crabs, apparently because *"krebs"* (crabs) is the German word for cancer.

99. Interestingly, Hitler referred to Germany as "the motherland." For him the German people was "the fatherland."

As führer, Hitler's personal abomination of Jews could have made life extremely difficult for them, no matter what the circumstances. But he was able to institutionalize his genocidal intentions because his hates coincided with those of the nation as a whole. Germany had a long, vicious history of antisemitism. In part this was a legacy of Martin Luther, whose hatred of Jews was widely known. Luther, one of Hitler's special heroes, advocated the total annihilation of Jews and everything about them. His detailed program, set forth in 1543, began with "First, to set fire to their synagogues or schools." It ended with "Seventh, Let whosoever can, throw brimstone and pitch upon them . . . and if this not be enough, let them be driven like mad dogs out of the land." Perhaps it was only an accident of history that Hitler launched his first major pogrom, known as "Kristallnacht," on the night of November 9, 1938, Luther's birthday.

Another factor was the German rivalry with Jews for the position of, as Fichte put it, "the chosen people." Up until the nineteenth century this could not have been a problem, as Jews were forced to live in ghettos and were generally treated much worse than dhimmis. However, the German people suffered a severe narcissistic blow with the gradual emancipation of the Jews and the discovery that far from being inferior, they could and did make major contributions to many areas of German life.

Finally, Hitler and Germans in general used Jews as toilets for their own despised emotions, greed, sexual promiscuity, sadism, and so forth. So the Jews tended to be identified with everything that Germans hated in themselves. Hitler himself attributed to Jews many of his own perverse impulses, including the wish to shit on others and be shat upon. According to the American psychiatrist Walter Langer, he took pleasure from having call girls urinate and defecate on him. But other historians dispute this.

See: Robert Waite, *The Psychopathic God: Aldolf Hitler,* op. cit., 237–239, 248–251.

100. The Nazis appropriated the passage about "magnificent blond beasts" from the philosopher Friedrich Nietzsche (1844–1900). See: discussion by Robert Waite, *The Psychopathic God: Adolf Hitler,* op. cit., 275–282.

101. Hitler rode to power on the promise to rebuild the army after "the Diktat of Versailles." Elias Canetti asserts that without the prohibition on universal military service after Versailles, national socialism would not have been born. He emphasizes that the army was an essential component of the German mystique, what he calls its "crowd symbol," its "marching forest." Elias Canetti, *Crowds and Power,* op. cit., 173–174, 179–183.

102. Throughout his life, Hitler was infatuated with death. Even at moments of triumph, such as at the conclusion of the Nuremberg rally in 1934, Hitler would exclaim: "When my eyes are closed in death, I do not know, but the Party will live

on." Quoted by Robert Waite, *The Psychopathic God: Adolf Hitler,* op. cit., 18, see 18–22.

103. Peter Nichols, "Chancellor Blames Envy for Dislike of Germans," *The Times,* October 1977, 4.

104. "The blessing of a late birth" refers to Germans who were born after the war and did not suffer terrible privations or take part in the Nazi dictatorship. The term has been popularized by politicians such as Chancellor Helmut Kohl. However, "the blessing of a late birth" does attract the envy of older Germans, especially for the younger generation's relative freedom from guilt. Peter Sichrovsky, *Schuldig Geboren (Born Guilty)* (Cologne: Kiepenheurer & Witsch, 1987), discussed by Tony Caterall, "Born Guilty," *The Observer,* 1 March 1987, 51.

Chapter 12

1. Arthur Koestler, Hungarian-born journalist and writer (1905–1983).

2. Arthur Koestler, in *The God That Failed,* R. Crossman, ed. (London: Hamish Hamilton, 1970), 18; quoted by Helmut Schoeck, *Envy: A Theory of Social Behavior,* op. cit., 279.

3. For these same reasons many people admire and identify with the underprivileged or oppressed peoples of the world. By doing so they try to overcome their own sense of guilt about matters closer at hand. Helmut Schoeck believes that large social, religious, or political organizations can behave in the same way. He cites contemporary Christian churches (like the Church of England) that try to deal with a pervasive guilt about spiritual poverty at home by attacking "the rich" for material poverty abroad. "By seizing upon the pseudo-polarity of 'wealthy nations' and 'poor nations,' the new Christian theology of the left does for the future what the Manifesto of Marx has done for the present: it produces stresses, it stirs up animosities which divide our world into armed camps." Helmut Schoeck, "The Less Developed Countries As a Moral Issue: Risky Assignments of Guilt and Responsibility," *Humanitas: Journal of the Institute of Man,* vol. IX, no. 2, May 1973, 211.

4. David Hughes and Jill Hartley, "Labour's Moral Crusade Vs. Tory Consumer Power," *The Sunday Times,* London, 10 May 1987, 1.

5. Roy Hattersly, *Choose Freedom: The Future of Democratic Socialism* (London: Michael Joseph, 1987). Roy Hattersly was deputy leader of the Labour party during the 1987 campaign.

6. As Matthew Arnold, the nineteenth-century English essayist and critic, put it, "Choose equality and flee greed." Quoted by R. H. Tawney, *Equality* (London: George Allen and Unwin Ltd., 1931), 24.

Tawney himself believed that equality was not "to pamper the gross bodily appetites of an envious multitude, but to free the spirit of all." Ibid., 290.

7. Helmut Schoeck, "Individual vs. Equality," *Essays in Individuality,* edited by Felix Morley (Philadelphia: University of Pennsylvania Press, 1958), 168–169.

8. See, for example: the work of the Israeli novelist Amos Oz, as well as the discussion by Helmut Schoeck, in *Envy: A Theory of Social Behavior,* op. cit., 286–315.

9. In the late 1980s the Cuban leader Fidel Castro angrily halted the successful liberalization of the economy to prevent imaginative, hardworking farmers from becoming too rich, as well as to conserve foreign exchange. He was reported to be stunned by the fact that many people were making big money on the private farmers' markets that he himself had introduced in 1980 to stimulate production and reduce shortages. Weeks later, after closing these markets, he halted the right to private home ownership. Castro complained that homeowners were "getting rich" buying, selling, and trading houses. He told a Communist party congress: "No one was born a revolutionary. We must cultivate man's sense of shame." Joseph Treaster, "To Cure 'Capitalist Vice,' Cuba Applies Austerity," *The International Herald Tribune,* 9 February 1987, 13, 17.

10. Despite the egalitarian reforms since the war, John Rae, the former head-master of London's Westminster School, concurs: "In some parts of the country, a working-class child has less chance of leaving school literate and numerate than he would have done in 1945." John Rae, "Shooting the Piano Player," *The Times*, 8 May, 1987, 14.

Interestingly, the sociologist James Coleman, whose 1966 report, "Equality of Educational Opportunity," was authorized by Congress in the 1964 Civil Rights Act, now believes that the egalitarian reforms he advocated were mistaken. Black children do not necessarily learn better in desegregated schools; some do, but many don't. "Thus, what once appeared to be fact is now known to be fiction." Lawrence Feinberg, "U.S. Desegregation Advocate Refutes Own Study: 'More Complicated Than Any of Us Realized,' " *The International Herald Tribune*, 19 September 1978, 1.

11. Adamischin was quoted in the mass circulation daily *Kurier*. He was at-tempting to explain ideological mistakes that had reduced socialist achievements, especially in view of the socialist principle of equality. The interview was related to the decision of the Soviet leader Mikhail Gorbachev to introduce a modern form of socialism to the Soviet Union. Quoted in "Russia Ends 'Equal Pay' Red Tape," *The London Standard*, 24 July 1986, 12.

12. William Manchester, "Levelling American Society," *The International Herald Tribune*, 24 July 1978, 4. Manchester asserts leveling has become "a secular religion, a faith as powerful and intolerant as Puritanism in 17th-century New England."

13. Ibid., 4.

14. Frank Ching, "Upward Mobility for Chinese Comrades," *The International Herald Tribune*, 7 January 1985, 4.

The attack on titles also has to be seen within the historical context of a talented people who suffered because of excessive hierarchical structures. The China specialist Frances Wood points out that as a result of this policy, a host of conflicts were subsequently generated between generations: "The result of trying to make everyone equal is a lost generation of graduates in China who can't read classical Chinese. When Mao died, and you could get a reasonable education again, what happened was that these younger people are being promoted above the heads of older ones—which leads to more tension, this time between generations." Quoted from "Walking on the Chinese Wall," *The Hampstead and Highgate Express*, London, 9 August 1985, 13.

15. Peter Bauer, *Equality, the Third World, and Economic Delusion* (London: Methuen, 1982).

16. I refer to the destruction of the kulaks, another example of economic tyranny and political genocide. Millions of Russian peasants were killed both for ideological and practical reasons.

17. The former Conservative minister Sir Keith Joseph reasons: "The inequality of power is far more menacing than inequality of money. Inequality of money is constantly subject to change: money is made or lost. But inequalities of power, such as must exist in an egalitarian society, continually erode the rule of law so that, even in societies which are supposed to be democratic and constitutional, the rule of law becomes weak or non-existent." Sir Keith Joseph, "The Tyranny Hidden in the Pursuit of Equalilty," *The Times*, 9 June 1978, 14.

See also: Keith Joseph and Jonathan Sumption, *Equality* (London: John Murray Publishers Ltd., 1979), 54.

18. Procrustes was the celebrated Greek highwayman who used to tie travelers to a bed and stretch their spines or cut off their legs in order to make them fit in. Nowadays the term "Procrustean" refers to policies or actions designed to ensure conformity and "fairness." Ibid., 63.

19. Roy Hattersly clearly conveys this attitude in his book *Choose Freedom*:

The Future of Democratic Socialism. His central thesis is that socialists are the real lovers of freedom.

20. Christ, when asked by his disciples which of them was the greater, replied, "The least among you all is the one who will be great" (Luke 9:48). Cyprian (c. 200–258 C.E.), who was the bishop of Carthage during periods of great persecution, commented that "by His reply He cut off all rivalry. He tore out and broke away every cause and material of gnawing envy." Cyprian, *On Jealousy and Envy* (10), quoted by Peter Walcot, *Envy and the Greeks,* op. cit., 93.

Both Christ and his followers tried to overcome the problems of this life by postulating a new set of human values that took pride in an equality of suffering.

21. Ibid., 96–98.

22. The work of Iambulus is known from the writings of Diodorus Siculus (c. 60–c. 20 B.C.E.).

Siculus was the author of a work entitled *World History.* Discussed by Walcot, ibid., 98–99.

23. Aristotle (384–322 B.C.E.), *Politics,* 1266a, 1266b, 1267a, discussed by Walcot, ibid., 99.

24. This was a state of affairs further characterized by the end of exploitation and oppression of men by men, universal good faith, and brotherly love. Norman Cohn, *The Pursuit of the Millennium,* op. cit., 187; see also: 188–197.

25. Many of their members comprised an urban underworld perpetually on the verge of starvation and very open to the exhortations of popular preachers such as John Ball, who urged the righteous to cast off the yoke of oppression and, with God's blessing, kill evildoers, usually identified with the upper clergy and nobility. Ibid., 199.

Even orthodox preachers reserved their most virulent criticism for the rich and powerful. "Their satiety was our famine; their merriment was our wretchedness; their jousts and tournaments were our torments. . . . Their feasts, delectations, pomps, vanities, excesses and superfluities were our fastings, penalties, wants, calamities and spoilation." In many cases sermons like these were all that was needed to ignite social revolt. Ibid., 201–202.

In general, see Norman Cohn's three chapters in *The Pursuit of the Millennium,* ibid., 198–281.

26. Ibid., 201–202.

27. Ibid., 214–222.

28. Melvin Lasky, *Utopia and Revolution* (London: Macmillan London Ltd., 1977), 4.

29. Radicals from as far away as Japan, France, and the United States have favored one particular sentence of Bakunin: "There will be a qualitative transformation, a new living, life-giving revelation, a new heaven and a new earth, a young and mighty world in which all our present dissonances will be resolved into a harmonious whole." *The New Encyclopaedia Britannica,* 15th ed., 1985, 462.

30. George Foster points out that feelings of inferiority due to influences outside one's control may be bearable, but feelings of inferiority clearly relatable to personal faults or others' superiority are very damaging to self-esteem and are much more difficult to accept. George Foster, "The Anatomy of Envy: A Study of Symbolic Behavior," op. cit., 184.

31. Margaret Norton Briggs, "The Rat Race for Glamour," *The Sunday Times,* 5 November 1978, 14.

32. Interestingly, the word "luck" comes from the Middle High German *gelücke,* which denotes a chance combination of factors that may turn out favorably or unfavorably for a person or group. Subsequently, the English word "luck" became differentiated from "happiness," which originally meant something like "a condition due to haphazard happenings." See: discussion by Helmut Schoeck, in *Envy: A Theory of Social Behavior,* op. cit., 238–239.

33. Ibid., 30–31.

34. See: discussion in Peter Walcot, *Envy and the Greeks,* op. cit., 101–102.

35. Ibid., 101. Quoted from the god Poverty.

Poverty's argument was the same as that of Hesiod in his poem *Works and Days.* There Hesiod claimed that strife is an incentive. It inspires men to action, especially in the face of a wealthy neighbor. Essentially Hesiod argued that men need incentives like envy, whether to emulate others or to discharge tension in themselves. Ibid., 102.

36. Arguably, the ancient Egyptians could have benefited from a bit more chaos and disorder. But then they suffered pharaonic despotisms so pervasive that the opportunity for ordinary citizens to express envy might not have been obvious. Utopias can be equally oppressive. Then Big Brother is an inner envier projected onto the group as a whole. See: discussion in Melvin Lasky, *Utopia and Revolution,* op. cit., 6–7, 10–11.

37. Helmut Schoeck, *Envy: A Theory of Social Behavior,* op. cit., 255.

Schoeck adds: "We need envy for our social existence, though no society that hopes to endure can afford to raise it to a value principle or to an institution."

38. Geoffrey Chaucer, "The Parson's Tale," in *Canterbury Tales,* op. cit., 506.

39. Wilfred Bion, "Learning from Experience," in *Seven Servants.*

40. Pindar, *Nemean Odes,* quoted by Peter Walcot, *Envy and the Greeks,* op. cit., 80.

About the same time, the Chinese sage Lao-tse (604? B.C.E.) was writing, "The value in relations is benevolence. The value in words is sincerity." From "No. 8—Noncompetitive Values," *The Tao of Power,* translated by R. L. Wing (Wellingborough, Northamptonshire, England: The Aquarian Press, 1986).

41. Norman Cohn, *Europe's Inner Demons,* op. cit., 216–217.

42. Jacob and Wilhelm Grimm, "Briar-Rose," in *Selected Tales,* op. cit., 70–73.

43. Ibid., 70.

44. In the Grimm version of "Briar-Rose," there were only places for twelve wise-women at the celebrations. But there were thirteen wise-women in the kingdom. So one had to be left out. This allegedly explained her anger. But I think that reactive revenge only serves to soften the idea of evil or of a spirit of malevolence so strong that it would destroy the happiness of good parents and the life of a beautiful princess. Note the emphasis on the number thirteen. This connects the spirit of evil with bad luck, which is a further way of softening the impact of evil.

The fact that a wise-woman could turn bad is also consistent with traditional folk beliefs. The "beautiful ladies" were known to enter through the cracks in the door of a well-ordered house. If they were treated well, given food, wine, and entertainments, then they gave every kind of good blessing in return. But if they were mistreated—for example, left out—then poverty, sickness, and death would follow. Norman Cohn, *Europe's Inner Demons,* op. cit., 216.

45. Melanie Klein, "Love, Guilt and Reparation," in *Love, Guilt and Reparation and other Works 1921–1945* (London: The Hogarth Press, 1975), 330.

46. Helmut Schoeck adds: "Perhaps from the psychoanalytical and therapeutical perspective one is inclined to underestimate self- and mutual compensating, alleviating processes and mechanisms in many families, despite the fact that one can prove the existence of classic antagonisms." Quoted from letter to the author, 8 July 1986.

47. Personal communication, September 1982.

48. Ibid., September 1982.

49. This example reflects the many famous accounts that foretell the transformation of bad bits into good. Thus the culmination of Aeschylus' *Oresteia, The Eumenides,* tells how and why Athena's wisdom and understanding of Orestes was able to change the Erinyes—"the Furies," or destructive forces—into the Eumenides,

"the kindly ones," or beneficent forces. See: Melanie Klein, "Some Reflections on the Oresteia," *Envy and Gratitude and Other Works 1946–1963,* op. cit., 276.

50. "The ideal breast, introjected with love, gratification and gratitude, becomes part of the ego, the ego is more full of goodness itself. And thus, in a benevolent cycle, envy lessens as gratification increases, the diminution of envy allows more gratification which in turn furthers the lessening of envy." Hanna Segal, *Introduction to the Work of Melanie Klein,* op. cit., 52.

51. Specifically, the three goddesses were Aglaia (Brilliance), Euphrosyne (Joy), and Thalia (Bloom).

52. Peter Walcot, *Envy and the Greeks,* op. cit., 74.

53. Ibid., 73.

54. Quoted by Cindy Blake, "Good Deeds—Bad Thoughts," *The Sunday Times,* 24 March 1985, 37.

55. Ibid., 37.

56. Ibid., 37.

57. "By contrast, with people in whom this feeling of inner wealth and strength is not sufficiently established, bouts of generosity are often followed by an exaggerated need for appreciation and gratitude, and consquently by persecutory anxieties of having been impoverished and robbed." Melanie Klein, "Envy and Gratitude," *Envy and Gratitude and Other Works 1946–1963,* op. cit., 189.

58. Bertrand Russell, *The Conquest of Happiness,* op. cit., 67.

59. The acknowledgment of destructive aims and impulses has been institutionalized by many cultures and religions. Jewish people, for example, devote an entire day, Yom Kippur, or the Day of Atonement, to the ritual acknowledgment of individual and collective sin. Thus, the afternoon service for Yom Kippur includes the powerful prayer "Al Chate" ("For the Sin"):

We confess our sins and bring them to the light of our own recognition and of God's forgiveness. By confession we may become clean. By forgiveness we may become free. O God, release us from the burden of our failure. Do not let our past imprison us. Renew us.

For the sin we have committed before You
by over-eating and -drinking.
by hurting others
by envy
by betraying trust
by false pride
by despising You
For all these sins, Forgiving God, forgive us, pardon us, grant us
atonement.

From *Forms of Prayer for Jewish Worship: Prayers for the High Holydays,* edited by the Assembly of Rabbis of the Reform Synagogues of Great Britain, 8th ed., London, 1985, 569–571.

60. Of course, a modicum of love is necessary to get the acceptance process started in the first place. Without some sense of inner goodness, one could never stand the shock of discovering inner badness.

61. Konrad Adenauer (1876–1967) was chancellor of the Federal Republic of Germany from 1949 to 1963.

62. The original law of compensation was passed in March 1953. It was followed by a federal law of indemnification, which indemnified individuals or their dependents for loss of life or limb, damage to health, loss of career, property, pensions, and insurance as well as compensation for loss of liberty, imprisonment, and the like. For a quarter of a century the reparations took up about 5 percent of the entire German budget and were administered by over five thousand judges, civil servants,

and clerks. Paul Johnson, *A History of the Jews* (London: Weidenfeld and Nicolson, 1987), 514–516.

63. This path has not been followed by other guilty parties, including the German Democratic Republic and Austria. Each adamantly refuses to accept responsibility for its Nazi past. Austria, in particular, has been pursued by the Furies since it elected a former Nazi officer, Kurt Waldheim, as president.

Otherwise, German industrialists involved in the slave-labor program have been especially obdurate. As Paul Johnson points out: "They resisted compensation every legal inch of the way and behaved throughout with a striking mixture of meanness and arrogance." Ibid., 515.

64. The Arbours Crisis Centre is a facility of the Arbours Association, which was founded in 1970 by myself and others to help people in emotional distress and as an alternative to traditional mental hospital treatment. The center itself provides personal and psychotherapeutic support and accommodation for individuals, couples, or families in a quiet residential setting.

See: Joseph Berke, *I Haven't Had To Go Mad Here* (London: Pelican Books, 1979), and Joseph Berke, "The Arbours Centre," *International Journal of Therapeutic Communities*, vol. 3, no. 4, 1982, 248–261.

65. Personal communication, 1985.

66. Ibid., 1985.

Bibliography

Abraham, Karl. *Selected Papers on Psycho-Analysis*. London: The Hogarth Press, 1973.

———. "Manifestations of the Female Castration Complex." In *Selected Papers on Psycho-Analysis*.

———. "A Short Study of the Development of the Libido, Viewed in the Light of Mental Disorders." In *Selected Papers on Psycho-Analysis*.

Aeschylus. *The Agamemnon*. Translated by Gilbert Murray. London: George Allen & Unwin Ltd., 1925.

———. *The Oresteia*. Translated by Robert Fagles. London: Penguin Books, 1983.

———. *The Eumenides*. Translated by Richmond Lattimore. In *Greek Tragedies: Volume 3*, edited by David Grene and Richmond Lattimore. Chicago: Phoenix Books, University of Chicago Press, 1963.

Alcalay, R. *Words of the Wise*. Israel: Masada Press.

al-Hakim, Tawfiq. *'Awdat al-wa'i*. Beirut: 1974.

Allen, Woody. *Annie Hall*. In *Four Films of Woody Allen*. London: Faber and Faber, 1983.

Angry Brigade, the. "Communiqué 8." In *The Angry Brigade 1967–1984 Documents and Chronology*. London: Anarchist Pocketbooks 3, Elephant Editions, 1985.

Aristophanes. *The Birds*. Translated by Gilbert Murray. London: George Allen & Unwin, 1950.

Aristotle. *The Politics of Aristotle*. Translated by E. Barker. Oxford: The Clarendon Press, 1946.

Auletta, Ken. *Greed and Glory on Wall Street*. New York: Random House, 1987.

Bacon, Francis. *The Essays or Counsels, Civil and Moral*. Edited by S. H. Reynolds. Oxford: The Clarendon Press, 1890.

Banfield, Edward. *The Moral Basis of a Backward Society*. Glencoe, Ill.: Glencoe Free Press, 1958.

Bank, Stephen, and Michael Kahn. *The Sibling Bond*. New York: Basic Books, 1982.

Barnes, Mary, and Joseph Berke. *Mary Barnes: Two Accounts of a Journey Through Madness*. London: Penguin Books, 1982.

Bauer, Peter. *Equality, The Third World, and Economic Delusion*. London: Methuen, 1982.

Baumgarten, Edward. *"Versuch über mögliche Fortschritte im theoretischen und praktischen Umgang mit Macht."* Studium Generale, 1951.

Belloc, Hilaire. "About John." In *Selected Cautionary Verses*. London: Puffin Books, 1983.

Benayoun, Robert. *Woody Allen: Beyond Words*. Translated by A. Walker. London: Pavillion Books, 1987.

Ben-Dor, Gabriel. *State and Conflict in the Middle East: Emergence of the Postcolonial State*. New York: Praeger Publishers, 1983.

Berke, Joseph, ed. *Counter Culture: The Creation of an Alternative Society*. London: Peter Owen, 1969.

———. "The Fickle Fix." *The Radical Therapist* 1, no. 2. (June-July 1970).

———. *I Haven't Had to Go Mad Here*. London: Pelican Books, 1979.

———. "The Arbours Centre." *Int. J. Therapeutic Communities* 3, no. 4 (1982).

———. "Primitive Mental Mechanisms: A Study of Introjection, Projection and Identification." Unpublished paper (1982).

———. "Differentiation of the Pre-Genital Phase from the Genital Phase of the Early Oedipus Complex." Unpublished paper (1983).

———. "Envy Loveth Not: A Study of the Origin, Influence and Confluence of Envy and Narcissism." *Brit. J. Psychoth.* 1, no. 3 (1985).

———. "Shame and Envy." *Brit. J. Psychoth.* 2, no. 4 (1986).

Berlin, Irving. "Anything You Can Do." *Annie Get Your Gun*. London: Irving Berlin Ltd., 1947.

Bethe, E. *Die Dorische Knabenliebe, ihre Ethik und ihre Idee*. Neue Folge: Rheinisches Museum für Philologie, 1907.

Bett, Henry, *Nursery Rhymes and Tales: Their Origin and History*. New York: 1924.

Bettelheim, Bruno. *Symbolic Wounds*. London: Thames & Hudson, 1955.

———. *The Empty Fortress: Infantile Autism and the Birth of the Self*. New York: The Free Press, Macmillan Publishing Co., 1967.

———. *The Uses of Enchantment: The Meaning and Importance of Fairy Tales*. London: Thames & Hudson, 1976.

———. *Freud and Man's Soul*. London: Chatto & Windus, 1983.

———. *Surviving the Holocaust*. London: Flamingo Books, Fontana Paperbacks, 1986.

Billington, James. *Fire in the Minds of Men: Origins of the Revolutionary Faith*. London: Temple Smith, 1980.

Binion, Rudolph. "Hitler's Concept of *Lebensraum:* The Psychological Basis." *History of Childhood Quarterly* 1, no. 2 (Fall 1973).

Bion, Wilfred R. "Attacks on Linking." *Int. J. Psycho-Anal.* 40 (1959).

———. *Learning from Experience*. Reprinted in *Seven Servants: Four Works by Wilfred R. Bion*. New York: Jason Aronson, 1977.

Blundy, David, and Andrew Lycett. *Qaddafi and the Libyan Revolution*. London: Weidenfeld & Nicolson, 1987.

Boehm, Felix. "The Femininity Complex in Men." In *Psychoanalysis and Male Sexuality*, edited by H. Ruitenbeek.

Brayfield, Celia. *Glitter: The Truth about Fame*. London: Chatto & Windus, 1985.

Bremner, R. H. *Children and Youth in America*. Cambridge, Mass.: Harvard University Press, 1970.

Brenner, Charles. "The Psychoanalytic Concept of Aggression." *Int. J. Psycho-Anal.* 52, no. 2 (1971).

Brooks, John. *Showing Off in America: From Conspicuous Consumption to Parody Display*. Boston: Little, Brown & Company, 1979.

Broun, Heywood, and Margaret Leech. *Anthony Comstock: Roundsman of the Lord*. New York: 1927.

Bryk, F. *Die Beschneidung bei Mann and Weib*. Neubrandenburg: Gustav Feller, 1931.

Burstin, Luis. "A Few Home Truths About Latin America." *Commentary* 79, no. 2 (February 1985).

Butler, Samuel. *Erewhon*. London: Longman's & Co., 1890.

———. *Erewhon Revisited*. London: Grant Richards, 1901.

Caldicott, Helen. *Missile Envy*. New York: William Morrow & Co., 1984.

Calhoun, A. W. *A Social History of the American Family from Colonial Times to the Present*. New York: 1945.

Canetti, Elias. *Crowds and Power*. London: Victor Gollancz, 1962.

Carle, Eric. *The Very Hungry Caterpillar*. London: Hamish Hamilton, 1970.

Carr, Francis. *Mozart and Constanze*. New York: Franklin Watts, 1986.

Carroll, John. *Guilt: The Grey Eminence Behind Character, History and Culture*. London: Routledge & Kegan Paul, 1985.

Carstairs, G. Morris. *The Twice-Born. A Study of a Community of High-Caste Hindus*. London: Hogarth Press, 1957.

Cartland, Barbara. *The Outrageous Queen: A Biography of Christina of Sweden*. London: Frederick Muller, 1956.

Chase-Marshall, Janet. "Who's Afraid of Phyllis Chesler?" *Human Behavior* (September 1978).

Chasseguet-Smirgel, Janine. *Female Sexuality*. Ann Arbor, Mich.: University of Michigan Press, 1970.

Chaucer, Geoffrey. "The Parson's Tale." In *Canterbury Tales*. Translated by Nevill Coghill. London: Penguin Books, 1982.

Cheng, Nien. *Life and Death in Shanghai*. London: Grafton Books, 1986.

Chesler, Phyllis. *Women and Madness*. New York: Doubleday & Co., 1952.

Cirlot, J. E. *A Dictionary of Symbols*. Translated by J. Sage. London: Routledge & Kegan Paul, 1962.

Clanton, Gordon. "Frontiers of Jealousy Research." *Alternative Lifestyles* 4, no. 3 (August 1981).

Cohen-Solal, Annie. *Sartre: A Life*. London: Heinemann, 1987.

Cohn, Norman. *Europe's Inner Demons*. London: Paladin Books, 1976.

———. *The Pursuit of the Millennium: Revolutionary Millennarians and Mystical Anarchists of the Middle Ages*. London: Paladin Books, 1978.

Commager, Henry Steele, and Richard B. Morris, eds. *The Spirit of Seventy-Six*, vol. 1. New York: Bobbs-Merrill Co., 1970.

Computer Security. Alexandria, Va.: Time-Life Books, 1986.

Conquest, Robert. *The Harvest of Sorrow*. London: Hutchinson & Co., 1986.

Court, Joan. "Battering Parents." *Social Work* 26, no. 1 (January 1969).

Courtney, Margaret. *Cornish Feasts and Folk-Lore*. Penzance, Cornwall: Beare and Son, 1890.

Crawford, Christina. *Mommie Dearest*. London: Hart-Davis, 1979.

Creighton, Susan. *Child Victims of Physical Abuse, 1976*. London: NSPCC.

———. *Trends in Child Abuse*. London: NSPCC, 1984.

———. "Child Abuse Deaths." *NSPCC Information Briefing No. 5*. London: NSPCC, 1985.

Cyprian. "On Jealousy and Envy." In *The Writings of Cyprian*. Translated by R. E. Wallis. Edinburgh: T. & T. Clark, 1868.

Dahl, Roald. *Danny: Champion of the World*. New York: Bantam Books, 1979.

Dante (Aligheri). *Inferno*. Translated by L. Lockert. Princeton, N.J.: Princeton University Press, 1931.

Davies, Paul. *The Cosmic Blueprint.* London: Heinemann, 1987.

DeMause, Lloyd, ed. *The History of Childhood.* New York: Psychohistory Press, 1974.

———. "The Evolution of Childhood." In *The History of Childhood,* edited by Lloyd DeMause.

———, ed. *The New Psychohistory.* New York: Psychohistory Press, 1975.

Devereux, G. "Why Oedipus Killed Laius, A Note on the Complementary Oedipus Complex in Greek Drama." *Int. J. Psycho-Anal.* 34 (1953).

Dickenson, R. L. *Human Sexual Anatomy.* 2d ed. Baltimore, Md.: Williams & Wilkens, 1949.

Dickins, Aileen. "Uterine Ligaments and the Treatment of Prolapse." *Journal of the Royal Society of Medicine* 77 (May 1984).

"The Digger Papers." In *Counter Culture: The Creation of an Alternative Society,* edited by Joseph Berke.

Dodds, John W. *The Age of Paradox: A Biography of England 1841–1851.* London: Victor Gollancz Ltd. 1953.

Donne, John. *The Complete Poetry and Prose of John Donne and The Complete Poetry of William Blake.* New York: The Modern Library, Random House, 1941.

Dooley, Dennis, and Gary Engle, eds. *Superman at Fifty: The Persistence of the Legend.* Cleveland, Oh.: Octavia Press, 1987.

Driver, G. R., and John C. Miles. "Middle Assyrian Laws." In *The Assyrian Laws.* Oxford: Oxford University Press 1935.

Drucker, Peter. "The Monster and the Lamb." *Atlantic* (December 1978).

Drug Addiction: Crime or Disease? Interim and Final Reports of the Joint Committee of the American Bar Association and the American Medical Association on Narcotic Drugs. Bloomington, Ind.: Indiana University Press, 1963.

Duesenberry, J. S. *Income, Saving, and the Theory of Consumer Behavior.* Cambridge, Mass.: 1949.

Dunn, Judy. "Sibling Relationships in Early Childhood." *Child Development* 54 (1983).

———. *Sisters and Brothers.* London: Fontana Paperbacks, 1984.

Eibl-Eibesfeldt, Irenaus. *Love and Hate.* Translated by G. Stachan. London: Methuen, 1971.

Emmerson, Andrew. "Phantoms of the Operating System." *New Scientist* (28 January 1988).

Encyclopaedia Britannica. 15th ed. Chicago: Encyclopaedia Britannica, Inc., 1974.

Encyclopedia Judaica. Jerusalem: Keter Books, 1972.

Engle, Bernice Schultz. "The Amazons in Ancient Greece." *Psychoanalytic Quarterly* 11 (1942).

Enoch, M. O., W. H. Trethowan, and J. C. Barker, eds. "The Othello Syndrome." *Some Uncommon Psychiatric Symptoms.* Bristol: Wright & Son, 1967.

Epstein, Edward Jay. *The Rise and Fall of Diamonds: The Shattering of a Brilliant Illusion.* New York: Simon & Schuster, 1982.

Euripides. *The Plays of Euripides.* Translated by Gilbert Murray. 2 vols. Newtown: Gregynog Press, 1931.

Faulkner, William. *Absalom, Absalom.* New York: Random House, 1966.

Farber, Leslie. "The Faces of Envy." In *lying, despair, jealousy, envy, sex, suicide, drugs, and the good life.* New York: Basic Books, Inc., 1976.

Fenichel, Otto. *The Psychoanalytic Theory of Neurosis.* New York: W. W. Norton & Co., 1945.

Ferenczi, Sandor. *Thalassa: A Theory of Genitality.* New York: The Norton Library, W. W. Norton & Co., 1968.

Fischer, Fritz. *Griff nach der Weltmacht* (Germany's Aims in the First World War). New York: W. W. Norton & Co., 1967.

———. *World Power or Decline: The Controversy Over Germany's Aims in the First World War*. Translated by L. L. Farrar, et al. New York: W. W. Norton & Co. 1974.

Food and Drink Through the Ages: 2500 B.C. to 1937 A.D. London: Maggs Bros., 1937.

Forms of Prayer for Jewish Worship: Prayers for the High Holydays. Edited by the Assembly of Rabbis of the Reform Synagogues of Great Britain. 8th ed. London: Reform Synagogues of Great Britain, 1985.

Fort, Joel. *The Pleasure Seekers: The Drug Crisis, Youth and Society*. New York: Grove Press, 1969.

Foster, George M., "The Anatomy of Envy: A Study in Symbolic Behavior." *Current Anthropology* 13, no. 2 (April 1972).

Freud, Sigmund. *Standard Edition of the Complete Psychological Works of Freud*. Edited by J. Strachey. London: The Hogarth Press, 1968. (*S.E.*)

———. "On the Sexual Theories of Children." *S.E.* 9 (1908).

———. "A Special Type of Choice of Object Made by Men." *S.E.* 11 (1910).

———. "Psycho-Analytic Notes upon an Autobiographical Account of a Case of Paranoia (Dementia Paranoides)." *S.E.* 12 (1911).

———. "Instincts and Their Vicissitudes." *S.E.* 14 (1915).

———. "The Taboo of Virginity." *S.E.* 11 (1918).

———. "Beyond the Pleasure Principle." *S.E.* 18 (1920).

———. "Group Psychology and the Analysis of the Ego." *S.E.* 18 (1921).

———. "Some Neurotic Mechanisms in Jealousy, Paranoia and Homosexuality." *S.E.* 18 (1922).

———. "The Economic Problem of Masochism." *S.E.* 19 (1924).

———. "The Dissolution of the Oedipus Complex." *S.E.* 19 (1924).

———. "Some Psychical Consequences of the Anatomical Distinction between the Sexes." *S.E.* 19 (1925).

———. "New Introductory Lectures on Psycho-Analysis." *S.E.*, 22 (1932).

———. "Anxiety and Instinctual Life," in "New Introductory Lectures on Psycho-Analysis," *S.E.*, 22 (1932).

———. "Femininity." In "New Introductory Lectures on Psycho-Analysis," *S.E.* 22 (1932).

———. "Analysis Terminable and Interminable." *S.E.* 23 (1937).

———. *The Complete Letters of Sigmund Freud to Wilhelm Fliess*. Edited by Jeffrey Masson. Cambridge, Mass.: The Belknap Press of Harvard University Press, 1985.

Friday, Nancy. *Jealousy*. New York: William Morrow & Co., 1985.

Friedrich, Otto. "The New Origins of Life: How the Science of Conception Brings Hope to Childless Couples." *Time* (10 September 1984).

Fromm, Erich. *The Anatomy of Human Destructiveness*. New York: Holt, Rinehart & Winston, 1973.

Fussell, Paul. *Caste Marks: Style and Status in the U.S.A.* London: William Heinemann, 1984.

Garinet, Jules. *Histoire de la magic en France*. Paris: Foulon, 1818.

Gifford, Edward S. Jr. *The Evil Eye: Studies in the Folklore of Vision*. New York: The Macmillan Co., 1958.

Glenn, Jules. "Psychoanalysis of a Constipated Girl: Clinical Observations During the Fourth and Fifth Years." Paper presented at the Panel on the Psychology of Women: Infancy and Early Childhood, at the May 1974 meetings of the American Psychoanalytic Association.

Goebbels, Joseph. *The Early Goebbels Diaries: 1925–1926.* Translated by Oliver Watson. New York: Helmut Heiber, 1963.

Goodman, Joan. "Mel Gibson." *Playgirl* 12, no. 7 (December 1984).

Greenacre, Phyllis. *Trauma, Growth, and Personality.* London: The Hogarth Press, 1953.

———. "Penis Awe and Its Relation to Penis Envy." In *Drives, Affects and Behavior.* Edited by R. M. Loewenstein.

Greenson, R. R. "Dis-identifying from the Mother: Its Special Importance for the Boy." *Int. J. Psycho-Anal.* 49 (1968).

Greer, Germaine. *The Female Eunuch.* London: MacGibbon & Kee, 1970.

Greven, P. *Child-Rearing Concepts, 1628–1861.* Itasca: 1973.

Grimm, Jacob and Wilhelm. *Selected Tales.* Translated by David Luke. London: Penguin Classics, 1982.

Halberstam, David. *The Best and the Brightest.* London: Barrie & Jenkins, 1972.

Hall, Peter. *Peter Hall's Diaries.* Edited by John Goodwin. London: Hamish Hamilton, 1983.

Hamady, Sania. *Temperament and Character of the Arabs.* New York: Twayne, 1960.

Harris, Liz. *Holy Days.* New York: Summit Books, 1985.

Hartley, L. P. *Facial Justice.* London: Hamish Hamilton, 1960.

Hattersly, Roy. *Choose Freedom: The Future of Democratic Socialism.* London: Michael Joseph, 1987.

Hayley, Thomas T. S. "Khoba Khobee." Unpublished article.

Hayman, Ronald. *Writing Against: A Biography of Sartre.* London: Weidenfeld & Nicolson, 1986.

Hayman, Suzie. "10 Times Better." *Forum* 17, no. 10 (October 1984).

Henry, Jules. *Culture Against Man.* New York: Knopf, 1978.

———. *Pathways to Madness.* New York: Random House, 1971.

Herodotus. *History.* New York: Dutton, 1912.

Hesiod. *Works and Days.* Translated by R. Lattimore, Ann Arbor Michigan, University of Michigan Press, 1959.

Hinshelwood, Robert. "Projective Identification and Marx's Concept of Man." *Int. Rev. Psycho-Anal.* 10 (1983).

Hitler, Adolf. *Mein Kampf.* Translated by James Murphy. London: Hurst and Blackett, 1930.

Hobsbawm, E. J. *Social Bandits and Primitive Rebels: Studies in Archaic Forms of Social Movement in the 19th and 20th Centuries.* Glencoe, Ill.: Glencoe Free Press, 1959.

Hobson, Robert. "Psychological Aspects of Circumcision." *Journal of Analytical Psychology* 6, no. 1 (1961).

Hodder, Elizabeth. *The Step-Parents' Handbook.* London: Sphere Books, 1985.

Homber, A. R. *Nomads of the Long Bow, The Siriono of Eastern Bolivia.* Smithsonian Institution: Institute of Social Anthropology Publication, no. 10. Washington, D.C. (1950).

Horney, Karen. "On the Genesis of the Castration Complex in Women." *Int. J. Psycho-Anal.* 5 (1924).

———. "The Dread of Women." In *Psychoanalysis and Male Sexuality.* Edited by Henrik Ruitenbeek.

Hughes, Robert. *The Fatal Shore: A History of the Transportation of Convicts to Australia, 1787–1868.* London: Collins Harvill, 1987.

Hunter, G. K. Introduction to *King Lear.* In *King Lear,* William Shakespeare. London: Penguin Books, 1972.

Hunter, Richard, and Ida Macalpine, eds. *Three Hundred Years of Psychiatry 1535–1860*. London: Oxford University Press, 1963.

Iacocca, Lee. *Iacocca: An Autobiography*. London: Bantam Books, 1986.
Isocrates. *Antidosis*. In *Greek Orations*. Edited by W. R. Connor. Ann Arbor, Michigan: University of Michigan Press, 1966.

Jackson, Brian. *Fatherhood*. London: George Allen and Unwin, 1984.
Jaffe, Daniel. "The Masculine Envy of Woman's Procreative Function." *J. Amer. Psychoanal. Assoc.* 16 (1968).
Jahoda, Marie. *Freud and the Dilemmas of Psychology*. London: The Hogarth Press, 1977.
Joffe, Walter G. "A Critical Review of the Status of the Envy Concept." *Int. J. Psycho-Anal.* 50, no. 4 (1969).
Johnson, Paul. "Farewell to the Labour Party." *New Statesman* (9 September 1977).
———. *A History of the Modern World: From 1917 to the 1980s*. London: Weidenfeld & Nicolson, 1983.
———. *A History of the Jews*. London: Weidenfeld & Nicolson, 1987.
Jones, Derek Llewelyn. *Fundamentals of Obstetrics and Gynaecology* 1. London: Faber & Co., 1982.
Jones, Ernest. *Papers on Psycho-Analysis*. Boston: Beacon Press, 1961.
———. "The Early Development of Female Sexuality." In *Papers on Psycho-Analysis* (1927).
———. "The Phallic Phase." In *Papers on Psycho-Analysis* (1933).
———. *Psycho-Myth, Psycho-History* 1. New York: Hillstone, 1974.
———. "Psychopathology and International Tension." In *Psycho-Myth, Psycho-History* (1949).
Jones, R. V. "The Rise and Fall of British Industry." *New Scientist* (10 July 1986).
Joseph, Betty. "Some Characteristics of the Psychopathic Personality." *Int. J. Psycho-Anal.* 41 (1960).
Joseph, Keith, and Jonathan Sumption. *Equality*. London: John Murray Publishers Ltd., 1979.
Jung, Carl. "Versuch einer Darstellung der psychoanalytischen Theorie." *Jahrbuch für psychoanalytische und psychopathologische Forschungen* V (1913): 370. (*The theory of psycho-analysis*. New York: 1915.)

Kant, Immanuel. *Metaphysik der Sitten*. In Sämtliche Werke, edited by K. Vorlander. Vol. 3, 4th ed. Leipzig: Felix Meiner, 1922.
Karme, Laila. "The Penis As Umbilical Cord." *Psychoanalytic Quarterly* 47 (1978).
Karon, Bertram, and Gary VandenBos. *Psychotherapy of Schizophrenia: Treatment of Choice*. New York: Jason Aronson, 1981.
Kedourie, Elie. *Nationalism*. London: Hutchinson University Library, Hutchinson & Co., 1966.
Kern, Stephen. "Explosive Intimacy: Psychodynamics of the Victorian Family." In *The New Psychohistory*, edited by Lloyd DeMause.
Kernberg, Otto. *Borderline Conditions and Pathological Narcissism*. New York: Jason Aronson, 1975.
———. "Why Some People Can't Love." An interview by Linda Wolfe, in *Psychology Today* (June 1978).
Kierkegaard, Sören. *En literair Anmeldelse to Tidsaldre* (The present age). In *Samlede Vaerker*, edited by H. O. Lange, vol. 8. Copenhagen: 1920–30.
Klein, Melanie. *Love, Guilt and Reparation and Other Works 1921–1945*. Collected Works (C. W.), vol. 1. London: The Hogarth Press, 1975.
———. *The Psycho-Analysis of Children*. C. W., vol. 2. Translated by A. Strachey. London: The Hogarth Press, 1975.

——. *Envy and Gratitude and Other Works 1946–1963.* C. W., vol. 3. London: The Hogarth Press, 1975.
——. "An Obsessional Neurosis in a Six-Year-Old Girl." C. W., vol. 2 (1924).
——. "Early Stages of the Oedipus Conflict and Superego Formation." C. W., vol. 2 (1928).
——. "The Significance of Early Anxiety Situations in the Development of the Ego." C. W., vol. 2 (1932).
——. "The Effects of Early Anxiety-Situations on the Sexual Development of the Girl." C. W., vol. 2 (1932).
——. "Love, Guilt and Reparation." C. W., vol. 1 (1937).
——. "On Observing the Behaviour of Young Infants." C. W., vol. 3 (1952).
——. "Some Theoretical Conclusions Regarding the Emotional Life of the Infant." C. W., vol. 3 (1952).
——. "Envy and Gratitude." C. W., vol. 3 (1957). This work was originally published as a separate volume, *Envy and Gratitude: A Study of Unconscious Sources.* London: Tavistock Publications, 1957.
——. "Some Reflections on 'The Oresteia.' " C. W., vol. 3 (1963).
von Kleist, Heinrich. *Michael Kohlhaas.* In *Twelve German Novellas.* Edited and translated by H. Steinhawer. Berkeley: University of California Press, 1977.
Koestler, Arthur, et. al. *The God That Failed.* Edited by R. Crossman. London: Hamish Hamilton, 1950.
Kohut, Heinz. "Thoughts of Narcissism and Narcissistic Rage." *Psychoanalytic Study of the Child.* Vol. 27. New York: Quadrangle, 1972.
Kolakowski, Leszek. "The Fantasy of Marxism." *Encounter* (December 1978).
The Koran. Translated by N. J. Dawood. London: Penguin Books, 1956.
Koskoff, David. *The Diamond World.* New York: Harper & Row, 1982.
Kramer, Heinrich, and James Sprenger. *Malleus Maleficarum.* Translated by Montague Summers. London: Pushkin Press, 1951.
Kubizek, August. *Adolf Hitler, mein Jugendfreund.* Graz: 1953.
Kundera, Milan. *The Book of Laughter and Forgetting.* Translated by H. Heim. London: King Penguin, Penguin Books, 1985.

Laing, R. D. "Violence and Love." *Journal of Existentialism* 5, no. 20 (1965).
——. *The Politics of Experience.* New York: Pantheon Books, 1967.
——. "The Mystification of Experience." In *The Politics of Experience.*
——. *The Facts of Life.* New York: Pantheon Books, 1976.
Lang, P. H. *Music in Western Civilization.* New York: W. W. Norton & Co., 1940.
Langer, Marie. "Sterility and Envy." *Int. J. Psycho-Anal.* 39 (1958).
Laplanche, J., and J.-B. Pontalis. *The Language of Psycho-Analysis.* London: The Hogarth Press, 1973.
Lasch, Christopher. *The Culture of Narcissism: American Life in an Age of Diminishing Expectations.* New York: W. W. Norton & Co., 1978.
Lasky, Melvin. *Utopia and Revolution.* London: Macmillan London Ltd., 1977.
Lawrence, D. H. *Lady Chatterley's Lover.* New York: Grove Press, 1969.
Leach, Edmund. "Envy and the English Sickness." *The Listener* (26 March 1970).
——. "The Big Fish in the Biblical Wilderness." *Int. Rev. Psycho-Anal.* 13, part 2 (1986).
Lee, Laurie. *Cider with Rosie.* London: Penguin Books, 1959.
Leo, John. "Battling the Green-Eyed Monster." *Time* (25 November 1985).
Levin, Shmarya. *Childhood in Exile.* New York: 1929.
Levy, G. R. *The Gate of Horn.* London: Faber & Faber, 1946.
Lewis, Bernard. "L'Islam et les Non-Musulmans." *Annales: Economies, Sociétés, Civilisations* 3, 4 (Mai, Aout 1980).
Lewis, Roger. *Outlaws of America.* London: Pelican Books, 1972.

Lidz, Ruth and Theodor. "Male Menstruation: A Ritual Alternative to the Oedipal Transition." *Int. J. Psycho-Anal.* 58 (1977).

Liebaut, Jean. *Thresor des remedes secretes pour les maladies des femmes.* Paris: 1597.

Lightfoot-Klein, Hanny. "Pharonic Circumcision of Females in the Sudan." *Medicine and Law* 2 (1983).

Littlewood, Roland. "The Imitation of Madness: The Influence of Psychopathology upon Culture." *Soc. Sci. Med.* 19, no. 7 (1984).

———. *Pathology and Identity in Northeast Trinidad.* Unpublished D. Phil. thesis.

Livermore, Richard. "Notes for the Anarchy and Order Brigade." *Anarchy,* no. 3.

Loewenstein, R. M., ed. *Drives, Affects and Behavior.* Vol. 1. *Contributions to the Theory and Practice of Psychoanalysis and Its Applications.* New York: International Universities Press, 1960.

Lomas, Peter. "Dread of Envy As an Aetiological Factor in Puerperal Breakdown." *Brit. J. Med. Psychol.* 33 (1960).

———. "Ritualistic Elements in the Management of Childbirth." *Brit. J. Med. Psychol.* 9 (1966).

Luke, David. "Introduction." In *Selected Tales.* Jacob and Wilhelm Grimm.

Luks, Harold. "Iraqi Jews During World War II." *Weiner Library Bulletin* 30 (1977).

Lynn, Jonathan, and Antony Jay. *Yes, Prime Minister.* 2 vols. London: BBC Books, 1986/7.

Lysias. *Epitaph.* Translated by W. R. M. Lamb. New York: Putnam, 1930.

Mackay, Charles. *Memoirs of Extraordinary Popular Delusions.* London: Richard Bentley, 1841.

Mailer, Norman. *The Prisoner of Sex.* New York: New American Library, 1971.

Mairowitz, David. *The Radical Soap Opera.* London: Penguin Books, 1976.

Maizel, Neil. "Self-Envy, the Womb and the Nature of Goodness." *Int. J. Psycho-Anal.* 66 (1985).

Malatesta, Enrico. *Anarchy.* Translated by Vernon Richards. London: Freedom Press, 1974.

Marc, Olivier. *Psychology of the House.* London: Thames & Hudson, 1977.

Marmor, Judd. "Changing Patterns of Femininity: Psychoanalytic Implications." In *Psychoanalysis and Women.* Edited by Jean Baker Miller.

Marvick, Elizabeth W. "Childhood History and Decisions of State: The Case of Louis XIII." In *The New Psychohistory.* Edited by Lloyd DeMause.

Masson, Georgina. *Queen Christina.* London: Secker & Warburg, 1968.

Masson, Jeffrey. *The Assault on Truth: Freud's Suppression of the Seduction Theory.* London: Penguin Books, 1985.

May, Rollo. "Guilt and Awareness." In *Man and Society.* Edited by Roger W. Smith. New York: Anchor Books, Doubleday & Co., 1971.

McConville, Brigid. *Sisters: Love and Conflict within the Lifelong Bond.* London: Pan Books, 1985.

Mead, Margaret. *Male and Female.* London: Victor Gollancz, 1950.

Melville, Herman. *The Portable Melville.* Edited by J. Leyda. London: Penguin Books, 1976.

Mencken, H. L. *The Vintage Mencken.* Edited by Alistair Cooke. New York: 1956.

Middlemore, Merell. *The Nursing Couple.* London: Hamish Hamilton Medical Books, 1941.

Miller, Alice. *Thou Shalt Not Be Aware.* London: Pluto Press, 1985.

Miller, Jean Baker, ed. *Psychoanalysis and Women.* London: Penguin Books, 1974.

Miller, Jonathan. *States of Mind.* London: British Broadcasting Corporation, 1983.

Milton, John. *Paradise Lost.* New York: W. W. Norton & Co., 1975.

Miner, Horace. *The Primitive City of Timbuctoo.* Princeton: Princeton University Press, 1953.

Mintz, Morton. *At Any Cost: Corporate Greed, Women and the Dalkon Shield.* New York: Pantheon Books, 1985.

Mishan, E. J. "A Survey of Welfare Economics, 1939–1959." *The Economic Journal* 70 (London: June 1960).

Mitchell, Juliet. *Psychoanalysis and Feminism.* London: Allen Lane, 1974.

Mitford, Jessica. *Hons and Rebels.* London: Victor Gollancz, 1960.

Money-Kyrle, R. E. *Man's Picture of His World: A Psycho-Analytic Study.* London: Duckworth, 1978.

Montagu, Ashley. *The Nature of Human Aggression.* London: Oxford University Press, 1976.

Montgelas, Max, and Walter Schücking, eds. *Outbreak of the World War: German Documents Collected by Karl Kautsky.* Oxford: Oxford University Press, 1924.

Moore, Jean, and Beryl Day. "Family Interaction Associated with Abuse of Children Over 5 Years of Age." In *Child Abuse and Neglect.* London: Pergamon Press, 1979.

More, Thomas. *Utopia.* New York: W. W. Norton & Co., 1976.

Moulton, Ruth. "A Survey and Reevaluation of the Concept of Penis Envy." In *Psychoanalysis and Women.* Edited by Jean Baker Miller.

Moynihan, Daniel. "The United States in Opposition." *Commentary* 59, no. 3 (March 1975).

———. *A Dangerous Place.* London: Secker & Warburg, 1979.

Mullahy, Patrick. *Oedipus: Myth and Complex.* New York: Evergreen Books, Grove Press, 1955.

Murphy, James. "Introduction." In *Mein Kampf,* Adolf Hitler.

Neumann, Erich. *The Great Mother: An Analysis of the Archetype.* New York: Bollingen Series XLVII, Pantheon Books, 1963.

Newall, Venetia, ed. *The Witch Figure.* London: Routledge & Kegan Paul, 1973.

———. "The Jew As Witch Figure." In *The Witch Figure.*

New Encyclopaedia Britannica. 15th ed. Chicago: Encyclopaedia Britannica, Inc., 1985.

New Larousse Encyclopedia of Mythology. London: Paul Hamlyn, 1969.

Nicolson, Harold. *Diaries and Letters: The War Years, 1939–1945.* 3 vols. New York: 1967.

Niederland, William. *The Schreber Case: Psychoanalytic Profile of a Paranoid Personality.* Hillsdale, N.J.: Analytic Press, 1984.

Nin, Anaïs. *Cities of the Interior.* Distributed by The Phoenix Book Shop. New York: 1959.

Nisbet, Robert. *Prejudices: A Philosophical Dictionary.* Cambridge, Mass.: Harvard University Press, 1982.

Noonan, John T., Jr. *Bribes.* New York: Macmillan Publishing Co., 1984.

Not Private Eye 1 (10 December 1986). Published by Daily Mirror Newspapers, London.

Oakley, Ann. *The Captured Womb: A History of the Medical Care of Pregnant Women.* Oxford: Blackwell, 1984.

O'Brien, Conor Cruise. *The Siege: The Saga of Israel and Zionism.* New York: Simon & Schuster, 1986.

Olesha, Yuri. *Envy.* Garden City, N.Y.: Anchor Books, Doubleday & Co., 1967.

Opie, Iona and Peter. *The Classic Fairy Tales.* London: Paladin Books, 1980.

Orwell, George. *1984.* London: Penguin Books, 1984.

Ovid. *Metamorphoses.* London: Penguin Books, 1955.

Oxford Universal Dictionary. 3rd rev. ed. Edited by C. T. Onions. New York: Oxford University Press, 1955.

Paul, B. D. "Symbolic Sibling Rivalry in a Guatemalan Indian Village." *American Anthropologist* 52 (1950).

Penn, Jean. "Everybody and His Brother." *Playboy* (January 1986).

Penny, Alexandra. *How to Make Love to a Man*. London: Papermac, 1981.

The Pentateuch. In *The Twenty-four Books of the Old Testament*. Vol. 1. Translated by Alexander Harkavy. New York: Hebrew Publishing Co., 1926.

Pepitone, Leslie. Review of *The Sibling Bond*. In *Am. J. Orthopsych.* 54, no. 2 (April 1984).

Pepys, Samuel. *The Diary of Samuel Pepys*. Vol. 2. London: J. M. Dent & Sons, 1906.

———. *The Diary of Samuel Pepys*. Vol 1. London: J. M. Dent & Sons, 1927.

Piers, Gerhart, and Milton Singer. *Shame and Guilt: A Psychoanalytical and Cultural Study*. Springfield, Ill.: Thomas Publishers, 1953.

Pindar. *The Odes of Pindar*. Translated by R. Lattimore. Chicago: University of Chicago Press, 1976.

Plath, Sylvia. *The Journals of Sylvia Plath*. New York: Ballantine Books, 1983.

Plato. *Symposium*. Translated by B. Jowett. New York: Bobbs Merrill & Co., 1956.

Plutarch. *Alcibiades*. In *The Rise and Fall of Athens: Nine Greek Lives*. Translated by Ian Scott-Kilvert. London: Penguin Books, 1987.

———. *Moralia*. Translated by P. Holland. London: Everyman's Library, 1906.

Potter, David. *People of Plenty: Economic Abundance and the American Character*. Chicago: 1954.

Prentice, Thomson. "Lennon: The Rebellious Voice of a Generation." *Now* (12 December 1980).

Pushkin, Alexander. *Mozart and Salieri: The Little Tragedies*. Translated by Anthony Wood. London: Angel Books, 1982.

Raddatz, Fritz. *Karl Marx: A Political Biography*. Translated by Richard Barry. London: Weidenfeld & Nicolson, 1978.

Radice, Betty. *Who's Who in the Ancient World*. London: Penguin Books, 1984.

Rae, John. "Success." *Punch* (11 March 1981).

Raiga, Eugène. *L'Envie*. Paris: Alcan, 1932.

Raphael-Leff, Joan. "Facilitators and Regulators: Participators and Renouncers: Mothers' and Fathers' Orientations Towards Pregnancy and Parenthood." *J. Psychosomatic Obstetrics & Gynecology* 4 (1985).

Restak, Richard M. "Newborn Knowledge." *Science/82* 3, no. 1 (1982).

Rheingold, Joseph. *The Fear of Being a Woman: A Theory of Maternal Destructiveness*. New York: Grune & Stratton, 1964.

———. *The Mother, Anxiety, and Death: The Catastrophic Death Complex*. Boston: 1967.

Riviere, Joan. "Jealousy As a Mechanism of Defense." *Int. J. Psycho-Anal.* 13 (1932).

———, and Melanie Klein. *Love, Hate and Reparation*. London: The Hogarth Press, 1967.

———. "Hate, Greed and Aggression." In *Love, Hate and Reparation*.

Roberts, J. M. *The Hutchinson History of the World*. London: Hutchinson & Co., 1976. *The Pelican History of the World*. Rev. ed. London: Pelican Books, 1987.

Róheim, Géza. *The Eternal Ones of the Dream*. New York: International Universities Press, 1945.

———. "Aphrodite or the Woman with a Penis." In *The Panic of the Gods and Other Essays*. New York: Harper Torchbooks, 1972.

———. *Psychoanalysis and Anthropology: Culture, Personality and the Unconscious*. New York: International Universities Press, 1973.

Rose, Kenneth. *King George V*. London: Weidenfeld & Nicolson, 1983.

Rosenfeld, Herbert. *Psychotic States: A Psycho-Analytical Approach*. London: The Hogarth Press, 1965.

———. "The Psychopathology of Hypochondriasis." In *Psychotic States.*

———. "A Clinical Approach to the Psychoanalytic Theory of the Life and Death Instincts: An Investigation into the Aggressive Aspects of Narcissism." *Int. J. Psycho-Anal.* 52, part 1 (1971).

———. "Negative Therapeutic Reaction." In *Tactics and Techniques in Psychoanalytic Therapy: Volume II, Countertransference.* Edited by Peter Giovacchini. New York: Jason Aronson, 1975.

Ross, Anne. "The Divine Hag of the Pagan Celts." In *The Witch Figure.* Edited by Venetia Newall.

Ross, John. "Oedipus Revisited: Laius and the 'Laius Complex.' " *Psychoanalytic Study of the Child* 37. New Haven, Conn.: Yale University Press, 1982.

Roszak, Theodore. *The Making of a Counter Culture: Reflections on the Technocratic Society and Its Youthful Opposition.* New York: Anchor Books, 1969.

Roth, Philip. *Goodbye Columbus.* London: Andre Deutsch, 1959.

———. *The Breast.* London: Jonathan Cape, 1973.

Roubin, Lucienne. *Chambrettes des Provencaux.* Paris: Plon, 1970.

Rubinstein, Hilary, ed. *The Good Hotel Guide, 1987.* London: Consumer's Association and Hodder & Stoughton, 1987.

Rudé, G. *The Crowd in the French Revolution.* London: Greenwood Press, 1986.

Ruitenbeek, Henrik, ed. *Psychoanalysis and Male Sexuality.* New Haven, Conn.: College and University Press, 1966.

Runciman, W. G. *Relative Deprivation and Social Justice: A Study of Attitudes to Social Inequality in Twentieth Century England.* London: Routledge & Kegan Paul, 1966.

Russell, Bertrand. *The Conquest of Happiness.* London: Unwin Paperbacks, 1978.

Ryan, Thomas. "The Roots of Masculinity." In *The Sexuality of Man.* Edited by A. Metcalf and M. Humphries. London: Pluto Press, 1985.

Rycroft, Charles. *A Critical Dictionary of Psychoanalysis.* London: Penguin Books, 1972.

Sabbadini, Andrea. "Possession Anxiety: The Other Side of the Castration Complex." *Brit. J. Psychoth.* 3, no. 1 (Fall 1986).

Sabri, Hussein Dhu'l-Figar. *Rose el-Youssef* (18 July 1975).

Sartre, Jean Paul. "My Political Will." *Strike* 2, no. 3 (October 1978). Translated and reprinted from *Mon Testament politique* (Edition "Gare L'explosion," 1977), courtesy of Edizioni della Rivisto "Anarchismo."

Schaffer, Rudolph. "*Mothering.* London: Fontana/Open Books, 1977.

Schatzman, Morton. *Soul Murder: Persecution in the Family.* New York: Random House, 1973.

Schoeck, Helmut. *Envy: A Theory of Social Behavior.* Translated by M. Glenny and B. Ross. New York: Harcourt, Brace & World, 1970. (Reprinted Indianapolis, Ind: The Liberty Press, 1987.)

———. "Individuality vs. Equality." In *Essays in Individuality.* Edited by Felix Morley. Philadelphia, Pa.: University of Pennsylvania Press, 1958.

———. "The Less Developed Countries As a Moral Issue: Risky Assignments of Guilt and Responsibility." *Humanitas: Journal of the Institute of Man* 9, no. 2 (May 1973).

Schreber, Daniel Gottlieb. *Kallipädie oder Erziehung zur Schönheit durch naturgetreue und gleichmässige Förderung normaler Körperbildung* (Education toward beauty by natural and balanced furtherance of normal body growth). Leipzig: Fleischer, 1858.

Schreber, Daniel Paul. *Denkwürdigkeiten eines Nervenkranken.* Leipzig: Oswald Mutze, 1903. *Memoirs of My Nervous Illness.* Edited and translated by Ida Macalpine and Richard Hunter. London: Dawson & Son, 1955.

Schüking, L. L. *The Puritan Family.* New York: 1970.

Schwenger, Peter. *Phallic Critiques: Masculinity and Twentieth-Century Literature.* London: Routledge & Kegan Paul, 1984.

Scott, W. Clifford M. "Self-Envy and Envy of Dreams and Dreaming." In *Remembering Sleep and Dreams, Int. Rev. Psycho-Anal.* 2, part 3 (1975).

Segal, Hanna. *Introduction to the Work of Melanie Klein.* London: The Hogarth Press, 1975.

———. *Klein.* London: Fontana Modern Masters, 1979.

———. "Notes on Symbol Formation." *Int. J. Psycho-Anal.* 38 (1957).

———. "Some Clinical Implications of Melanie Klein's Work: Emergence from Narcissism." *Int. J. Psycho-Anal.* 64, no. 3 (1983).

Segal, Julia. "Mother, Sex, and Envy in a Children's Story." *Int. Rev. Psycho-Anal.* 6 (1979).

Segaller, Stephen. *Invisible Armies: Terrorism into the 1990s.* London: Michael Joseph, 1986.

Shaffer, Peter. *Amadeus.* London: Andre Deutsch, 1980.

Shakespeare, William. *The Tragedy of Othello.* New York: Pocket Books, 1957.

———. *Merry Wives of Windsor.* In *The Complete Pelican Shakespeare: The Comedies and the Romances.* Edited by Alfred Harbage. London: Penguin Books, 1969.

———. *King Lear.* London: Penguin Books, 1972.

Shelley, Mary Wollstonecraft. *Frankenstein.* London: Gibbings & Co., 1897.

Shorter, Edward. *A History of Women's Bodies.* London: Penguin Books, 1982.

Shuttle, Penelope, and Peter Redgrove. *The Wise Wound: Menstruation and Everywoman.* London: Victor Gollancz, 1978.

Sichrovsky, Peter. *Schuldig Geboren* (Born Guilty). Cologne: Kiepenheurer & Witsch, 1987.

Simon, Julian L. "Resources, Population, Environment: An Oversupply of False Bad News." *Science* 208 (27 June 1980).

Skinner, Angela, and Raymond Castle. *78 Battered Children: A Retrospective Study.* London: NSPCC, 1969.

Slater, Philip. *The Glory of Hera: Greek Mythology and the Greek Family.* Boston: Beacon Press, 1968.

Smakowska, Christine. "Marital Problems and Family Violence." *NSPCC Information Briefing No. 7.* London: NSPCC, 1985.

Sophocles. *Oedipus Rex.* Translated by Albert Cook. In *Ten Greek Plays.* Edited by L. R. Lind. Cambridge, Mass.: Riverside Editions, Houghton Mifflin Co., 1957.

———. *Oedipus at Colonus.* Translated by Robert Fitzgerald. In *Greek Tragedies.* Edited by David Grene and Richmond Lattimore. Chicago, Ill.: Phoenix Books, University of Chicago Press, 1960.

Spanier, David. *Total Chess.* London: Secker & Warburg, 1984.

Spencer, B., and F. J. Gillen. *The Native Tribes of Central Australia.* London: Macmillan & Co., 1899.

Stärcke, August. "The Castration Complex." *Int. J. Psycho-Anal.* 2 (1921).

Starr, Kevin. *Americans and the California Dream 1850–1915.* Oxford: Oxford University Press, 1973.

Steinbeck, John. *East of Eden.* New York: Viking Press, 1952.

Steinberger, Peter. "John Sinclair Is Free." *Big Fat Magazine* (June 1970).

Steiner, John. "Turning a Blind Eye: The Cover Up for Oedipus." *Int. Rev. Psycho-Anal.* 12 (1985).

Stern, Karl. *The Flight from Women.* London: George Allen & Unwin, 1966.

Stoller, Robert. *The Transsexual Experiment.* London: The Hogarth Press, 1975.

———. *Sex and Gender: Volume 1, The Development of Masculinity and Femininity.* London: Maresfield Reprints, 1984.

Stone, Lawrence. *The Family, Sex and Marriage in England 1500–1800.* London: Weidenfeld & Nicolson, 1977.

Sullivan, Harry Stack. *Clinical Studies in Psychiatry*. New York: W. W. Norton, 1956.

Suttie, J. D. *The Origins of Love and Hate*. London: Paul, French Trubner & Co., 1935.

Taillevent, Guillaume Tirel *dit*. *La Viandier*. 1375.

Talese, Gay. *Thy Neighbor's Wife*, London: Collins, 1980.

Tannahill, Reay. *Sex in History*. London: Abacus, 1981.

The Tao of Power. Translated by R. L. Wing. Wellingborough, Northamptonshire, England: Aquarian Press, 1986.

Tart, Charles, ed. *Altered States of Consciousness*. New York: Anchor Books, 1972.

Tavris, Carol. *Anger: The Misunderstood Emotion*. New York: Simon & Schuster, 1983.

Tawney, R. H. *Equality*. London: George Allen & Unwin, 1931.

Taylor, John Russell. *Strangers in Paradise: The Hollywood Emigrés 1935–1950*. London: Faber & Faber, 1983.

Teresi, Dick, and Kathleen McAuliffe. "Male Pregnancy." *Omni* 8, no. 3 (December 1985).

Thomas, Hugh. *An Unfinished History of the World*. London: Hamish Hamilton, 1982.

Thompson, Clara. " 'Penis Envy' in Women." In *Psychoanalysis and Women*. Edited by Jean Baker Miller.

Thomson, David. "Sam Shepard: An American Original." *Playgirl* 12, no. 7 (December 1984).

Todd, John and Kenneth Dewhurst. "The Othello Syndrome: A Study in the Psychopathology of Sexual Jealousy." *The Journal of Nervous and Mental Disease* 122, no. 4 (October 1955).

Todd, John, J. R. M. Mackie, and Kenneth Dewhurst. "Real or Imaginary Hypophallism." *Brit J. Psychiat.* 119, no. 550 (September 1971).

The Torah: A Modern Commentary. New York: Union of Hebrew Congregations, 1981.

Torok, Maria. "The Significance of Penis Envy in Women." In *Female Sexuality*, Janine Chasseguet-Smirgel.

Tournier, Paul. *Guilt and Grace*. London: Hodder & Stoughton, 1962.

Trachtenberg, Joshua. *Jewish Magic and Superstition: A Study in Folk Religion*. New York: Atheneum, 1970.

von Treitschke, Heinrich. *Treitschke's History of Germany in the Nineteenth Century*. 7 vols. Translated by Eden and Cedar Paul. London: 1915.

Tresemer, David Ward. *Fear of Success*. New York: Plenum Press, 1977.

Tuchman, Barbara. *The March of Folly: From Troy to Vietnam*. London: Abacus Books, 1984.

The Twenty-four Books of the Old Testament. Vol. 1. Translated by Andrew Harkavy. New York: Hebrew Publishing Co., 1926.

Unamuno, Miguel de. *Abel Sanchez: The History of a Passion*. Translated by Anthony Kerrigan. Chicago: Gateway Editions, 1956.

Vanggaard, Thorkil. *Phallós: A Symbol and Its History in the Male World*. New York: International Universities Press, 1972.

van Leewen, Kato. "Pregnancy Envy in the Male." *Int. J. Psycho-Anal.* 47 (1966).

Vatikiotis, P. J. *Nasser and His Generation*. London: Croom Helm, 1978.

Veith, Ilza. *Hysteria: The History of a Disease*. Chicago: University of Chicago Press, 1965.

Vermaseren, Maarten. *Cybele and Attis: The Myth and the Cult*. London: Thames & Hudson, 1977.

Vickers, Hugo. *Cecil Beaton: The Authorized Biography.* London: Weidenfeld & Nicolson, 1985.
Vines, Gail. "Test-Tube Embryos." *New Scientist* (19 November 1987).

Waite, Robert. *The Psychopathic God: Adolf Hitler.* New York: Basic Books, 1977.
Walcot, Peter. *Envy and the Greeks.* Warminister, England: Aris & Phillips, 1978.
———. "Greek Attitudes Towards Women: The Mythological Evidence." *Greece and Rome* 31, no. 1 (April 1984).
Waley, Arthur. "Chinese Cinderella Story." *Folk-Lore* 58 (1947).
Webster's New World Dictionary. New York: William Collins & World Publishing Co., Inc. 1974.
Weidegar, Paula. *Menstruation and Menopause: The Physiology and Psychology, the Myth and the Reality.* New York: Alfred Knopf, 1976.
Weigart, Edith. "The Cult and Mythology of the Magna Mater from the Standpoint of Psychoanalysis." *Psychiatry I* (1938).
Wells, H. G. *H. G. Wells in Love.* London: Faber & Faber, 1984.
White, Rhoda. *From Infancy to Womanhood: A Book of Instructions for Young Mothers.* London: 1882.
White Panther Party, Abbey Wood Chapter. "Ten Point Programme." *Chapter?* 1 (London, 1971).
Whitmont, Edward. *Return of the Goddess: Femininity, Aggression and the Modern Grail Quest.* London: Routledge & Kegan Paul, 1983.
Widdowson, John. "The Witch As a Frightening and Threatening Figure." In *The Witch Figure.* Edited by Venetia Newall. London: Routledge & Kegan Paul, 1973.
Wideman, John. *Brothers and Keepers.* London: Allison & Busby, 1985.
Williams, Tennessee. *A Streetcar Named Desire.* New York: New Directions, 1947.
Willimott, Juliet. "Too Many Episiotomies." *Midwives Chronicle* (February 1970).
Wills, Garry. *The Kennedy Imprisonment: A Meditation on Power.* Boston: Little, Brown & Co., 1982.
Winnicott, D. W. *The Piggle: An Account of the Psychoanalytic Treatment of a Little Girl.* Edited by Ishak Ramzu. London: Penguin Books, 1980.
Woodcock, George. *Anarchy or Chaos.* London: Freedom Press, 1944.

Yeats, W. B. *Selected Poetry.* London: Pan Books, 1974.
Ye'or. "Aspects of the Arab-Israel Conflict." In *Weiner Library Bulletin* 32, 49/50 (1979).

Zilbergeld, Bernie. *Male Sexuality.* New York: Bantam Books, 1981.
Zilboorg, Gregory. "Masculine and Feminine: Some Biological and Cultural Aspects." *Psychiatry* 7 (1944).

This bibliography includes the books as well as journal and magazine articles that I have cited. It excludes newspaper and newspaper magazine articles. The following is a list of the newspapers to which I have referred in the text and notes:

BEIJING (P. REP. CHINA).
The People's Daily

CHICAGO (U.S.A.).
The *Chicago Tribune*

LONDON (G.B.).
The Daily Express
The Daily Telegraph
The Daily Telegraph magazine
ES (the Evening Standard magazine)
The Evening Standard.
The Guardian
The Hampstead and Highgate Express
The Independent
The Jewish Chronicle
The Jewish Chronicle magazine
The London Standard
The Mail on Sunday
The Observer
The Sun
The Sunday Times
The Sunday Times magazine
The Times
The Times Health Supplement

MOSCOW (U.S.S.R.)
Kurier

NEW YORK (U.S.A.)
The New York Times
The New York Times Book Review
The New York Post
USA Today (International Edition)

PARIS (FRANCE).
L'Observateur
The International Herald Tribune

WASHINGTON (U.S.A.).
The Washington Post

Index

Index